The Journal of Thomas Moore

Portrait of Thomas Moore by Gilbert S. Newton. In the collection of the Marquess of Lansdowne. *Reproduced by permission of the Earl of Shelburne.*

The Journal of Thomas Moore

VOLUME 2
1821–1825

Edited by
WILFRED S. DOWDEN

Associate Editors
BARBARA G. BARTHOLOMEW   JOY L. LINSLEY

Newark: University of Delaware Press
London and Toronto: Associated University Presses

Associated University Presses
440 Forsgate Drive
Cranbury, NJ 08512

Associated University Presses
25 Sicilian Avenue
London WC1A 2QH, England

Associated University Presses
2133 Royal Windsor Drive
Unit 1
Mississauga, Ontario
Canada L5J 1K5

Library of Congress Cataloging in Publication Data
(Revised for volume 2)

Moore, Thomas, 1779–1852.
  The journal of Thomas Moore.

  Vol. 2.: Published by University of Delaware Press.
  Includes bibliogaphies and indexes.
  1. Moore, Thomas, 1779–1852—Diaries. 2. Poets,
Irish—19th century—Biography. I. Dowden, Wilfred S.
II. Bartholomew, Barbara. III. Linsley, Joy L.
PR5056.A5 1983   828'.703 [B]   79-13541
ISBN 0-87413-245-2 (v.2)

Printed in the United States of America

Contents

Acknowledgments

My main debt of gratitude is to the firm of Longman, particularly the late M. F. K. Longman, J. F. G. Chapple, J. A. E. Higham, and Robert Welham, for permission to publish the Journal, and for their hospitality and assistance. I am especially grateful for the decision to make the manuscript of the Journal available by permitting me to bring it to the United States on a loan.

Had it not been for the invaluable work of the two associate editors, Barbara Bartholomew and Joy L. Linsley, the completion of the edition would have been considerably delayed and the text, annotation, and other matters of editorial practice much less polished than they are. Special thanks are due each of them.

Much more than common thanks are due those who have worked on the project from time to time as editorial assistants: Judy Craig, Ann Eutsler, Andrew Kappel, Kathryn Nall, Judy Nelson, Dale Priest, Kay Pope, Alan Rister, and Richard Schell.

I am also grateful for the assistance of O. C. Bartholomew and John Freeman.

The fine working facilities of the Fondren Library have made my task much easier, and I am grateful for the assistance of certain members of the staff: Samuel M. Carrington, Jr., Ralph Holibaugh, Ferne Hyman, Ola Moore, Richard O'Keefe, Nancy Parker, and Beth Wray.

For advice on the restoration of portions of the manuscript I owe thanks to Carolyn Horton, Win Phelan, and Peter Waters.

I am grateful to the Board and Administration of Rice University for financial support and released time from regular duties. Special thanks are due Frank E. Vandiver, Provost, and Virgil W. Topazio, Dean of Humanities.

For advice, assistance, and encouragement I am grateful to my colleagues Edward O. Doughtie, Helen Eaker, Alan Grob, Priscilla Jane Huston, Walter Isle, David Minter, Jane C. Nitzsche, the late John Parish, Robert Patten, William B. Piper, Ann Schnoebelen, J. D. Thomas, George Williams, Joseph B. Wilson, and Geoffrey Winningham.

Scholars in this and related fields have been most helpful. I wish to thank Leslie A. Marchand for answering questions concerning Byron and for supporting my efforts with advice and encouragement. Special thanks are due Hoover H. Jordan, whose knowledge of Moore saved me effort and time on more than one occasion. I am grateful to others who have given assistance of various kinds: Betty T. Bennett, Mary Dix, and Linda Crist (of the Jefferson Davis Association, Rice University), David V. Erdman, Paula Feldman, the late Howard Mumford Jones, Donald A. Low, Jerome J. McGann, the late Eoin MacWhite, Doris Langley Moore, Charles E. Robinson, Lord Russell, the Earl of Shelburne, Terence DeVere White, and Carl Woodring.

My gratitude is also extended to the National Endowment for the Humanities and the American Philosophical Society for grants that enabled me to carry on this extensive and expensive project.

Finally, I wish to thank my wife, Sumarie, and my daughter, Lorel, for understanding and encouragement during the preparation of this edition.

Note on Editorial Policy

Insofar as is possible, I have tried to reproduce Moore's Journal precisely as it was written. His own spelling, capitalization, and punctuation are transcribed exactly as they appear in the manuscript.

Moore was not always consistent in spelling. Sometimes, for example, he spelled his friend Lord John Russell's name with one *l*, and reversed the *i* and *e* in Fielding and other words. He used the dash as his all-purpose mark of punctuation at the end of sentences and even at times in the middle of the sentence where a semicolon would now appear. He was casual about capitalization, often beginning a sentence following a dash with a small letter. At other times words within a sentence were capitalized, apparently for emphasis. A bracketed *sic* is used only in the rare instances where ambiguity might result from a misspelling or syntactical lapse. Superior letters such as M.r or 3.rd have been lowered to Mr. and 3rd. Moore's practice of using & and &c (*et cetera*) has been followed throughout.

Boldface ornamental brackets { } have been used to enclose material omitted in the Lord John Russell edition. Square brackets [ ] enclose

1. words and phrases that could not be recovered from the manuscript and are supplied from the context.

2. fragments of sentences that seem significant but are deleted in the manuscript. These passages are always designated in the text as deleted. Example: 29–31 August 1818, [the "et incarnatus est" of].

3. afterthoughts that Moore placed at the end of the manuscript page with asterisks marking their locations in the text. A note is always added to explain why the passage is in square brackets.

Moore was careless about the spelling of, and the placing of diacritical marks on, foreign words. Insofar as is possible, his method of writing foreign languages has been followed verbatim.

Moore seldom broke for a paragraph and used "run-on" sentences at will. Russell supplied paragraphs and punctuation in order to make the text more coherent. I have chosen to reproduce Moore's text as accurately as possible in this respect, and often one finds that he ran two or more sentences together without any attempt to separate them for clarity by any punctuation other than the dash.

Annotation

Notes have been supplied as the text demanded them. Most, though not all, quotations have been identified, but only on rare occasions have the sources of foreign quotations been cited. Books, dramas, and operas that Moore read or saw have been identified by author, title, and date. For opera the date is that of the first performance; for drama, the date of publication or of the first performance.

Moore's penchant for naming *all* of the people he met at dinner parties or elsewhere has made comprehensive identification impossible. Hence identification is made, usually in a note, only when it is necessary to clarify the text. Otherwise, people whose names recur most persistently in the text are identified in a glossary of proper names at the end of the last volume.

Notes have been supplied to clarify political events mentioned by Moore, but no attempt has been made to explain fully the ramifications of these events.

The notes are numbered consecutively for each entry. There are a few cross-references, but, for the most part, the reader should consult the index for names of people or works identified in earlier notes.

Rice University
Houston, Texas

List of Scholarly Works Most Frequently Consulted

Byron, George Gordon, Lord. *Byron's Letters and Journals.* Edited by Leslie A. Marchand. 12 vols. Cambridge, Mass: Harvard University Press, Belknap Press, 1973–82.

———. *Lord Byron's Correspondence.* Edited by John Murray. 2 vols. London: John Murray, 1922.

———. *The Works of Lord Byron: A New, Revised and Enlarged Edition. Letters and Journals.* Edited by Rowland E. Prothero. 6 vols. London: John Murray, 1901–4.

———. *The Works of Lord Byron. A New, Revised and Enlarged Edition. Poetry.* Edited by Ernest Hartley Coleridge. 7 vols. London: John Murray, 1898–1905.

Gibbs, Lewis. *Sheridan.* London: J. M. Dent and Sons, 1947.

Greville, Charles C. F. *The Greville Memoirs.* Edited by Henry Reeve. 6 vols. London: Longmans, Green, and Co., 1875 and 1885.

Halévy, Élie. *A History of the English People in the Nineteenth Century.* Translated by E. I. Watkin and D. A. Barker. 2d ed., rev. 4 vols. London: Ernest Benn, 1949.

Hansard Parliamentary Debates, 1st series (1803–20); 2d series (1820–30); 3d series (1830–91).

Jones, Howard Mumford. *The Harp that Once—.* New York: Henry Holt and Company, 1937.

Jordan, Hoover H. *Bolt Upright: The Life of Thomas Moore.* 2 vols. Salzburg Studies in English Literature. Salzburg: Institut für Englische Sprache und Literatur, 1975.

Longford, Elizabeth Pakenham, Countess of. *Wellington.* 1st U.S. ed. 2 vols. New York: Harper and Row, 1969–72.

Marchand, Leslie A. *Byron, a Biography.* 3 vols. New York: Alfred A. Knopf, 1957.

Moore, Thomas. *The Letters of Thomas Moore.* Edited by Wilfred S. Dowden. 2 vols. Oxford: The Clarendon Press, 1964.

———. *Memoirs, Journal and Correspondence of Thomas Moore.* Edited by Lord John Russell. 8 vols. London: Longman, Brown, Green, and Longmans, 1853–56.

———. *The Poetical Works of Thomas Moore.* 10 vols. London: Longman, Brown, Green, and Longmans, 1853.

O'Connell, Daniel. *Correspondence of Daniel O'Connell.* Edited by W. J. Fitzpatrick. 2 vols. New York: Longman, Green, 1888.

———. *The Correspondence of Daniel O'Connell.* Edited by Maurice R. O'Connell. 2 vols. Dublin: Irish University Press, 1973.

Russell, Lord John. *Early Correspondence of Lord John Russell 1805–40.* Edited by Rollo Russell. 2 vols. London: T. Fisher Unwin, 1913.

Sheridan, Richard Brinsley. *The Plays and Poems of Richard Brinsley Sheridan.* Edited by R. Compton Rhodes. 3 vols. New York: Russell and Russell, 1962.

Sichel, Walter. *Sheridan.* 2 vols. Boston: Houghton Mifflin Company, 1909.

The Journal of Thomas Moore

1821

January 1st, 1821 [Monday]—Had rather an uncomfortable night, and fear that the tumour is suppurating—sent a note to Dupuytren by Mrs. Forster—read some of Jablonski & wrote two or three lines—Dupuytren did not come—

2nd [Tuesday]—A visit from Dr. Arthur, to offer his services—l'abondance de richesses in Doctors at all events—Gallois came and sat for some time—lamented that Lord John showed to so little advantage in society from his extreme taciturnity & still more from his apparent coldness & indifference to what is said by others—said that several here to whom he was introduced had been much disappointed in consequence of this manner. I can easily imagine that to Frenchmen such reserve & silence must appear something quite out of the course of nature—After Gallois came Y{oung} (another Doctor) & persisted in staying till Dupuytrens arrival, which quite put an end to my plan of keeping my *friends* out of the concern, and he was of course called into consultation—{a good fellow, but in every thing (except his brandy & water) rather weak—}It appeared that the tumour had already broken, and Dupuytren widened the aperture (roughly enough) with a lancet which Y{oung} said afterwards was unnecessary & would render it rather tedious in healing—Bessy who had walked out with Williams (*another* Doctor!) to make some purchases was a good deal alarmed on her return to find me bleeding—Williams dined below with her & came up to my room at night for supper,—during which I read out to them Irving's beautiful account of Christmas in his Sketches[1]—Looked this morning over the Curiosities of Literature—quotes from Bacon's will the following striking words "For my name & memory I leave it to men's charitable speeches, and to foreign nations & the next ages." {Sir Walter Raleigh used to say of his detractors "If any man accuseth me to my *face* I will answer him with my *mouth,* but my tail is good enough to return an answer to such who traduced me behind my back".}—a pretty quotation for small editions—"Quam brevis immensum cepit membrana Maronem!" Martl.—He says "though the fire-offices will insure books, they will not allow authors to value their own manuscripts"—a fair instance of Fairfax's admirable translation. Tasso [says] of Olindo "Brama assai, poco spera, nulla chiede" which Fairfax has done

> —he, full of bashfulnesses & truth,
> Lov'd much, hop'd little, and desired nought.[2]

3 [Wednesday]—Read & tried to write a little—{a good *erratum* mentioned in the Cur. of Literature—a writer applying to another the text "Quid vides festucam in oculo fratris tui et trabem in oculo tuo non vides" & the verse 5 of the same chapter of St. Mathew, the printer by leaving out the first O in the word oculus gave it sense which the author's adversary took advantage of to charge him with impurity obscenity &c. &c.—}[1] Nicolle of the Port-Royal Society said of a *show-off* man in society "He conquers me in the drawing-room, but he surrenders to me at discretion on the stair-case"—Noah (according to the Rabbins) when in the Ark, had no other light than jewels & pearls—Among the titles of the King of Ava is "absolute master of the ebb & flow of the sea, brother to the sun & king of the four & twenty umbrellas"[2]—Good *invalid* reading this kind of book is—I wish men oftener would give us what they *read* than what they *think*—Mr. Baring & Charles Sheridan have called upon me but I could not see them—Have been much easier since the lancing.

4 [Thursday]—Corrected the Revise of the advertisement to Sheridan and copied out with some difficulty the Duett of Blangini to send to Power—Williams in the evening—{He had succeeded with the French Baroness (rather a fine woman) whom we met in the Cuckoo the day we came from seeing four Venetians—that was the beginning of his acquaintance with her—she is a widow & her husband was the Captain who brought Bonaparte in his ship from Egypt—Told me that a short time since when he was with the baroness pressing impatiently she said with the true cold-blooded arrangement of a French Intrigue "not yet—not yet—wait a lit-tle—donnez–moi le tems de vous arrives".}

5 [Friday]—Have got a Sofa, which is less enfeebling—about 12 or 14 lines between to-day & yesterday—Saw Mrs. Story, who is just returned from England and has brought the shawl I commissioned her to bring for Bessy—came just in time for the dear girl's new-year's gift—Douglas called & said he had heard me highly praised yesterday by Mr. Irving—Williams in the evening—read me a passage from a letter of his wife's in which she calls down all the blessings of heaven upon him for my friendship & ser-

vices to him—poor fellow! I have done nothing for him—I wish I could
{have given him some advice about the Baroness—By the bye,} I see that
{Lord} Byron, in his Continuation, says that I advised him to go into the
detail of his loves more fully—but, if I recollect right, it was only his adventures in the East I alluded to, as in recounting these there could be but little
harm done to any one—He showed me once, I recollect, a letter of Lord
Sligo's relating the adventures by which the Giaour was suggested, and with
which he seemed to intimate that he himself was connected.[1]—

6 [Saturday]—Wrote 13 lines to-day—{Younge thinks I may dine in the
parlour tomorrow—}

7 [Sunday]—Came down to the *salon* & found myself much feebler than I
had the least idea of—Douglass called with Lady Susan & one of her
daughters—proposed to me to go out a little way in their carriage, and, the
day being so fine, went with them for half an hour—walked a little in the
garden afterwards—in the evening wrote a few lines, which I rejected
before I went to bed—{Younge dined with us to-day.}

8 [Monday]—Mrs. Story called to take me out in her carriage at half past
two—a gentle, kind-hearted little woman, worth hosts of your clever ones—
eat a very hearty dinner and wrote some lines in the evening—Have now
finished my 2nd letter within two lines.

9 [Tuesday]—Wrote the two continuing lines before I got up—this letter is
{now} 192 lines long, and I have been no less than five weeks about it! this
will never do—Walked about the garden for half an hour, and went for a
short drive with Mrs. Story at three—{Williams sat with me while I was at
dinner—has been reading the Citateur of Pigault le Brun against Christianity[1]—had some discussion on the subject—} read in the evening.

10 [Wednesday]—Drove out with Mrs. Story, and made calls—in the evening read over my Egyptian Notes for my Letter.

11 [Thursday]—Again drove out—all wet days—no walking—Miss Forster
dined with us & I sang to her & Bessy in the evening—{Lady Gwydir to call
upon Bessy—}

12 [Friday]—Drove out & walked a little—Bessy & I dined with the Forsters—music in the evening—an agreeable day—wrote words this morning to a Notturne of Blanginis—A letter from Lord John to-day, the second I have received from him since he went—A letter from Lord Byron yesterday, in which he tells me of his intention to visit England in Spring, and proposes (as a means of paying my debts) that he & I should set up a newspaper together on his arrival there[1]

13 [Saturday]—Drove into town rather late—not being able to return time enough for dinner, dined at Dupont's, the Restaurateur's (formerly Massinot, whom I have commemorated in the Fudges)[1] and got home to tea at seven—in the evening began copying at my Blangini Duett

14 [Sunday]—Began words to another Notturne of Blanginis, before I got up—Drove out with Mrs. S.—dined at home—and finished my copying of yesterday's Notturne in the evening.

15 [Monday]—Wrote letters to Lord John, Lady Donegall &c. & dispatched my Notturne to Power, besides finishing the words of the other—Had seen on Saturday (13) Lord B.'s verses to me ("My boat is on the shore") very incorrectly given in the Times—sent off a correct copy of them to-day to Perry, and added some verses of my own about Sir Richard Steele, the High Sheriff who has just dispersed a meeting in Dublin by the military, beginning

> Tho sprung from the *clever* Sir Richard this man be,
> He's as different a *sort* of Sir Richard as can be &c.[1]

dined at Story's—{company, Sir Godfrey & Lady Webster, and a whole host of gentlemen Black-legs—conversation all about the Turf & the Talon—} went to Villamil's music in the evening—the Sapios &c. &c.

16 [Tuesday]—Began my third letter—dined at home & read in the evening

17 [Wednesday]—Wrote a few lines went in with Bessy & the little ones to walk them about the Palais Royal—dined with the Storys & went to the Mille Colonnes in the evening for coffee & Ponch à la Romaine.

18 [Thursday]—Went out with Mrs. Story—called upon Douglas & asked him to meet Charles Sheridan at dinner with me to-day—Lord Granard the other guest—had asked Washington Irving too but he was engaged—C. Sheridan clever—but not a very negociable sort of cleverness—he will never turn it to much account in the world—mentioned a good story of a Robber who plundered the mail by means of four or five straw figures with muskets planted behind a hedge—told an anecdote of his father having induced a sentimental old maid to put a favourite Cock to death & then placing himself privately behind her bed at night & crowing faintly (as the Ghost of a Cock might be supposed to cry in order to frighten her, which he did effectually—I made Douglas dispatch a note to Lady Susan & her daughters to come in the evening—they arrived accordingly to tea & we had music—staid supper & did not leave us till near one.

19 [Friday]—Wrote some lines—Douglas Kinnaird called at two—walked with him in the Tuilleries Gardens for an hour—{met Lord Gwydir, who asked me to dine on Monday next—Sir H. Mildmay too invited me for Sunday—} Went to dine (Bessy & I) at the Two Swans—a sort of frisk set on foot by Douglas & Lord Miltown—Company Sir G. & Lady Webster, Baron & Baroness Roebeck, Lady Susan & her daughters, Douglas & Lord Miltown—rather a noisy & frivolous day—in the evening all adjourned to Douglas's, where we had music—Irving and Lord Sandon added to the party—

20 [Saturday]—Wrote some lines—walked by myself for a couple of hours on the solitary road that leads off from the Barrier of Neuilly, and brought back a few more lines—{dined at Lord Miltowns—Bessy too unwell to go—Company much the same as yesterday, with the addition of Mademoiselle d'Este & her mother—music}

21 [Sunday]—Went in, and left my excuse for dinner to-day at Sir H. Mildmay's—met Lord Granard, who took upon him to be sentimentally angry at my never dining with *him* & said I was cutting my old friends—dined at home—have done this week near fifty lines of my third letter.

22 [Monday]—Dispatched a fourth Duett of Blangini to Power—Vicomte Chabot (an old acquaintance of mine, who dined at Lord Miltowns on Saturday, and who is in the service of the Duke of Orleans) called & left a note for me to dine with the Duke tomorrow—I had had some conversa-

tion with Chabot on Saturday, in which I said how flattered I had been, to find, from the intimation I received through Mde. Montjoye, that the Duke had not forgot me & that only for the necessity of the dress coat, with which I was not provided, I should have gone to his levees—Chabot (as he tells me in his note) mentioned all this to his Highness, who has thus answered my confession of having no coat by asking me to dinner—Walked out with Charles Sheridan, for the purpose of leaving my answer at the Palais Royal—am engaged to Lord Rancliffe tomorrow, but, of course, cannot disobey the Royal Command—Sheridan told me that his father, being a good deal plagued by an old maiden relation of his always going out to walk with him, said one day that the weather was bad & rainy—to which the old Lady answered that, on the contrary it had cleared up—"Yes" says Sheridan—"it has cleared up enough for one, but not for two".—He mentioned too that Tom Stepney supposed Algebra to be a learned language & referred to his father to know whether it was not so—who said certainly "Latin, Greek & Algebra"—{and} "by what people was it spoken?"—"By the Algebrians, to be sure," said Sheridan—dined at Lord Gwydir's—company, the De Souzas, Rancliffe, {De} Montron, Alvanley, Kinnaird &c. &c.—the conversation chiefly in French—Made. De Souza said very truly that admiration is a feeling "qui ne désire qu'à finir"—I forgot quite the phrase, but it meant that admiration is always impatient to put an end to itself, and is glad to seize the first opportunity of doing so—went from thence with Bessy & the Storys to Sapio's concert, given at a Russian Nobleman's house—very crowded—heard but little—introduced Bessy to the Duchess of Sussex, who said she was very like what Lady Heathcote was in her day of beauty—and had "a very wild, poetic face"—Madlle. d'Este said to me too "what a very handsome person your wife is!"—had sandwiches at Story's afterwards.

23. [Tuesday]—Chabot called again to say that the Duke was obliged to go the Tuilleries this evening and as he wanted to have a little more of my company & "to talk over old times", he wished, if possible, I would dine with him on Tuesday next instead—Chabot offered to call at the Rancliffes on his way back, & tell them I was free now for an engagement to them—did so—The Company at Rancliffe's, Kinnaird, Cook, Alvanley {De} Montron, &c. &c.—six or seven English speaking broken French to each other, because there was one Frenchman (who could speak as good broken English) in company—this is too absurd—& the conversation was accordingly, as dull as it was ungrammatical—Even Alvanley is stupid in French—{Went with Kinnaird in the evening to show him a little of the humours of the Palais Royal, Cafe de le Paix, Cafe des Chinoinis &c. &c.}

24 [Wednesday]—Wrote a little—Bessy & I dined with the Douglas's—Company, Washington Irving, & his brother, Williams, & Lord Miltown—in the evening, Baroness Roebeck, a young bride of seventeen, with the most perfect Hebe eyes & cheeks I have seen for a long time—sang a good deal—supped & had a very pleasant evening—Called this morning before dinner on Mrs. Canning, and was most cordially received—Miss Canning & I to practise Blangini together.

25 [Thursday]—Wrote letters—& walked into Paris—saw the new Edinburgh announced & find that Madlle. de Tournon is in this number—dined at Boddington's—{dull dinner—Mrs. B. not at all attractive, though they say, very sensible & very grand—} went with the Forsters to a Ball at a Mr. Boode's, a Dutchman, very splendid & very raffish—{Lady Annesley there.} Came away immediately.

26 [Friday]—Called upon Chabot (whose rooms are over the Duke of Orleans's) at a quarter before six, in order to go under his escort to dinner—The Duke met me on my entering the room with "I wish you a very good night, Mr. Moore"—he however speaks English perfectly well—There was only their own family party, and though the thing was at first rather Royal & formidable, I soon found myself perfectly at my ease among as unaffected & domestic a circle as ever I witnessed in any station—The Duke drank wine with me at dinner à l'Anglaise & I was placed next the Duchess, who did all the civilities of the partridges, patés &c. before her in a very quiet & kind manner—after the dinner, which was over unusually soon, the Duchess sat down to work, and four or five fine children were admitted, with whom the Duke played most delightedly, making polichenelle caps for them—&c.—Mademoiselle showed me a Lithographical Work lately published—on the Antiquities of Normandy & the Duke & she at each side of me looked through the whole of the engravings—they then asked me to sing, and I have seldom had a more pleased audience—indeed the reiteration of "charmant"—"delicieux" &c. became at last almost oppressive—the Duke reminded me of the songs he had taught me at Donnington Park, "Cadet Rouselle" & "Polichenille est partout bien reçu" & I played them over, which amused him very much—he said he did not see the least alteration in my looks since we last met, which must now be near eighteen years ago—In talking of the fitness of the English language for music & the skill with which (they were pleased to say) I softened down its asperities, a Frenchman who was there said, in the true spirit of his nation, "Mais, la langue Anglaise n'est pas plus dure que l'Allemande", never seeming to

have the least suspicion that his own is the most detestable language for music of any—"The Evening Bells" seemed particularly to be the favourite, and the whole family understood English well enough to comprehend the meaning of the words—As I was engaged in the evening to the Forsters, I begged of Chabot to ask whether I might take an early leave, which was granted, with a thousand expressions of thanks for the pleasure I had given them &c. & I came away at a little after nine, very much pleased & flattered by the day—Music at Forster's. Madlle. Monck, Mrs. Dickens &c. &c.

27 [Saturday]—A free day—went into Paris, half intending to go to some spectacle in the evening, but returned home at six to an Irish stew, and read afterwards.

28 [Sunday]—{Was to have dined at Douglas's, but sent an apology yesterday—} Douglass Kinnaird called in the morning—had taken a box for the Variete's—agreed to join his party at the Trois Freres Provençaux—consisting of Sheridan, young Hibbert, Sir Charles Willoughby—Pieces at the Varietés, the Bonnes d'Enfans, Diable d'Argent, &c. &c.¹—called this morning at Canning's to answer their invitation for Friday—saw him & sat some time there.

29 [Monday]—Besieged by hosts of visitors now every morning, but contrived to do a little, and have this week written fifty lines of my Third Letter—{dined at Lord Granard's for a party to the Theatre—Bessy refused—went to the Vaudeville—the whole thing dull enough.}

30 [Tuesday]—Wrote ten lines—Sheridan called—asked him to dinner—the Forsters in the evening—

31 [Wednesday]—Wrote 14 lines—dined at the Villamils—some singing in the evening—Mercer, Sapio &c. a very pretty Trio just composed by Garcia—

Febr. 1 [Thursday]—Did nothing—dined with the Storys—a large party of Websters &c.—a most unprofitable day altogether—except that I went for about ten minutes in the evening to a Mrs. Fyler's, and saw a number of pretty English girls, as refreshing to the eyes in this country as a parterre would be in a desert—

2 [Friday]—Wrote a few lines—dined at Canning's—company Sheridan, Lord C. Churchill, Genl. Buchan & one or two more.—not much from Canning—in talking of letters being charged by {the} weight, he said that the Post-Office once refused to carry a letter of Sir J. Cox Hippesley's—"it was so dull"—{We had talked during dinner of the French custom of rising from the table with the ladies & two or three of us expressed some dislike of it, which made Canning very good naturedly whisper Mrs. Canning, when she was about to go, "we shall be after you in about ten minutes"—to which her answer was (with a look by no means placid) "I have no idea of that— certainly not", to which Canning very sensibly (but at the same time, looking rather sheepishly) submitted—*her* looks all the while showing what a scene might have ensued had he resisted. This corroborates what I have heard of her temper.} I sung for them in the evening—& Miss C. sang some Duetts of Blangini with me—Received an invitation this morning for the D. of Orleans's music on Sunday.

3 [Saturday]—Called at Chabot's, and left the First Number of my National Melodies (which I borrowed from Lady Webster) for Mademoiselle—had company at home—the Villamils, Washington Irving, Forster, & Story— Mrs. Story & the Miss Kingstons in the evening—Sapio came too, and we had a good deal of music—supped & did not break up till two—all seemed very happy

4 [Sunday]—Wrote some lines—{Bessy bled to-day for her head-ache, which has been very troublesome—fear she is about to add another little encumbrance to the family—} I dined at Douglas's—{Company, Col. Burton, Sheridan, &c—} went away between 8 & 9 to the Duke of Orleans's— the rooms looked very splendid—the music good—Cinti, Bordogni, Pelligrini &c. &c.—Lord Miltown took me back to Douglas's, where I sung & supped—This morning took Irving to introduce him to Mr. Canning.

5 [Monday]—Have now done fifty-three lines this week—went out rather early, and made some calls—dined at the Rancliffe's—took Irving with me to introduce him—Company Lord & Lady Charlemont, Lord Bristol, Kinnaird &c. &c.—an agreeable day enough—a letter from Lord Byron to-day, in which there is the following epigram upon the Braziers going up "in armour" with an address to the Queen—

> The braziers, it seems, are preparing to pass
> An Address & present it themselves all in Brass—
> A superfluous pageant—for, by the Lord Harry,
> They'll find where they're going much more than they carry.[1]

The Longmans tell me that in consequence of my article on Made. de Souza's Novel, they have had it translated.

6 [Tuesday]—Wrote some lines—dined with the Storys at Very's (Bessy of the party) and went to Feydeau to see the opera of Joseph by Mehul[1]—serious operas do not *do* at the Theatre—the French are as unfit for the Heroic in Music as in Poetry—the light, common style is their element in both—

7 [Wednesday]—Dined at Made. de Souza's—only Gallois & a Frenchwoman, whose name I could not make out—an Idolatress of Lord Byron, as almost all Frenchwomen are—Spoke of M. Mercier's prohibited play, La Demence de Charles 9.—his style bizarre & affected—M. Arnaud (the person, who has translated Lalla Rookh) has also written a play "Guillaume de Nassau", which, they think, will not be acted on account of its political allusions[1]—Talking of Authors reading their plays in Society, they asked if it was the practice in London—I said, no—that the English would not stand it—it would make them laugh—the Frenchwoman said "nous dissimulons mieux l'ennui"—The fact is the English have too quick a sense of the ridiculous to go decorously through such an operation—I remember when a party, many years ago, consisting of Monk Lewis, Miss Lydia White, Lady Charleville &c. got up a reading of Comus at Lady Corke's, I saw Lord Grey (who sat in the front of the audience) put his hat before his face, as soon as Lewis stood up to begin "The Star that bids the shepherd fold," and he was evidently concealing a laugh[2]—I had foreseen that this would be the case, and having at first undertaken to read Comus, contrived afterwards to smuggle myself out of it, and was merely concerned with the musical part of the business—returned home about ten & found Mrs. Story & her cousins, who supped with us—{I saw this morning the boy announced in the papers lately as an extraordinary instance of prematurity—he is certainly very wonderful—only 39 months old & besides the general Herculean cast of his frown, the sexual conformation is quite that of a man of twenty—the mother's ready account of the indications of prematurity, in this way, which he exhibits, rather startling—at least, it *would* be so from an English mother.}

8 [Thursday]—Wrote between to-day & yesterday 12 or 13 lines—to-day a

grand treat for the little ones—the Villamils, the Storys & ourselves had taken 4 boxes at Franconi's for our whole establishments, & mustered there, what with nurses, children & one or two adult friends, thirty in number—some of the very young ones fell asleep half-way in the evening, but all enjoyed themselves heartily & the whole flock was got home again without any sort of embarrassment—or accident—

9 [Friday]—Wrote about eight lines—dined at home and went in the evening for the purpose of seeing the new opera "La Mort du Tasse", but could not get in[1]—went from there to the "Gymnase", and saw two very amusing pieces "Le Colonel" & the "Cuisinier & Secrétaire"—the examination of the pretended Cook by the pretended Secretary in the latter excellent—"Comment entendez vous les ortolans à la Provençale?—quel est votre systême la-dessus?"—In one of his songs he calls himself "Le Cesar de la Béchamel & L'Alexandre de Rost-bif[2]—"

10 [Saturday]—About twelve lines—Received the Edinburgh Review with the article on Madlle. de Tournon—tremble a little about the way in which Made. de S. will take it—dined at Sir G. Webster's—company, his brother & Story & Lord Miltown—[the brother's story about "how do you feel yourself &c." not bad in its way—mentioned by somebody that Lord Bath signed the Treaty of Utrecht upon Lady B's _____—like the scene in the Liaisons Dangereuses[1]—The saying about Lord Anson that he "had been round the world but never in it" applied to him on another subject.]

11 [Sunday]—Walked out to look again at the Houses at Auteuil—Had some idea of taking an additional apartment there in, for the sake of a better kitchen, but upon my asking the woman whether I might "sous-louer" these extra rooms (which would be much more than I could make use of, she said that they had already suffered too much by the sub-letting of the apartments in separate chambers to individuals & added (as if she saw my radicalism in my face) "Je n'aime pas qu'on fasse une république ici"—dined at Villamil's—Music in the evening—the Sapios &c. &c.—left that with the Story's at twelve (Bessy & I) and went to sup at Lord Miltown's, where we found Lady Robert Fitzgerald, Lady Saltoun, &c. & did not get home till near three o'clock—

12 [Monday]—Fifty lines this {last} week—met Gallois—Made. de Souza, it appears, is much mortified at the article I have written—particularly at the extract I have made from her Adele de Senanges—This is unlucky—I

confess I hesitated about the passage myself, but it was coupled with a fling at the proceedings against the Queen & I could not bring myself to leave it out—Why did I break through the resolution I had formed never to review the work of a friend?[1]—dined at Lord Charlemont's—the Rancliffes, Kinnaird, Mrs. Henry Baring, Sir Sidney Smyth &c.—the last named person {is, I dare say, a bore, but one learns more from him than from other bores—at least, one hears amusing lies—He said that the young ladies in the East, from being ranged on sofas at each side of their mama, and continually leaning towards her in the attitude of deference & attention, become crooked or bent down like trees on the sea-coast—He} said that when he was at Jerusalem, there was no *Bible* to be had there for love or money—Mrs. Story called for me & I went with her to Lady Susan Douglass's—there was music there, but I came away immediately, notwithstanding a violent seizure upon me by Lady Susan, and by a much more irresistible person, Mademoiselle D'Esté.

13 [Tuesday]—Wrote to Lord Byron—called upon Kinnaird, who goes off to-day. dined at the Forsters—a family party—and took a lesson in quadrilles from the girls in the evening—Have determined to send Anastasia to Mrs. Forster, whose usual price for girls of her age is 100 guineas a year, but who has expressed a readiness to take her upon more moderate terms—found a note on my return home from Miss Drew to offer me a ticket of convoy to the funeral ceremony for the Duc de Berry at St. Denys tomorrow—

14 [Wednesday]—Went early to the Douglas's—but they, from not having heard from me, had given up the thought of going—breakfasted with them— & returned home—but was chased out again by visitors—the two Miss Forsters & Williams dined with us—

15 [Thursday]—Dined at the Storys—had written some lines in the morning—have received two or three kind notes from Made. de Souza, but fear there will never be the same cordial feeling between us again—{Company, the Websters, Lord Miltown, Villamils, Irving, &c—} some attempts at singing in the evening, but the card-tables got the better of us—

16 [Friday]—Dined at Mildmay's—{Sang with her in the evening and went afterwards to Dr. Ainslie's Ball—better this than letting him read his tragedy to me—}[1] Company Mildmay's, Lord Sandon, Lord Francis Leveson, the De Rooses &c.

17 [Saturday]—Dined with the Granard's, and was home early in the evening—

18 [Sunday]—Wrote near fourteen lines—dined at the Douglas's, and went to Lafitte's soirée dansante in the evening—prettier Frenchwomen there than it is often one's lot to see—

19 [Monday]—Have done, notwithstanding my abominable & frivolous dissipation this week, near fifty lines, & not bad—at least so I think *now*—what they will appear upon cooler revisal is another thing—{dined with Lord Miltown—Company, Lords Bristol & Charlemont, Chabot & Lady Isabella &c. &c.—more people in the evening—Wanted me to sing, but, having a bad cold, I fled—}

20 [Tuesday]—Worked at a second verse for one of the Irish Melodies ("oh the sight entrancing") which I had left unfinished[1]—Dined (Bessy & I) with Mrs. Story & her cousins, and went to the Variétes,—the Bonnes d'Enfans, L'Ennui, Ci-devant jeune homme, the Interieur d'une etude[2]—It is all settled with the Villamils, that we shall take the cottage of theirs that Col. King had last year—

21 [Wednesday]—Finished my verse—dined at the Rocher de Cancalle, with a party invited by Col. Cope, Lords Charlemont & Rancliffe, Fitzherbert, Fox, Lambton &c—a dinner at 20 francs a head & of course full of erudition—Bisque d'ecrevisses, Epigramme d'agneau and (still more literary) an *historical* salad—(salade d'homards historiée)—a Paté d'Angoulême one of the best things in it.—A good deal of laughing at very little expense of wit—{When we were at a stand-still for claret, I said that Cope ought to tap the Rocker, like Moses, and call wine instead of water from it[1]—but I was not understood—worse jokes did much better—} some of us afterwards adjourned to Mrs. Fitzherbert's, a pretty & rather gay little woman {whom Rancliffe affects to flirt with} —at home before twelve.—not a bad pun of Rancliffes to-day, that the *points* of the Epigrammes d'agneau were "pointes d'esperges" {Copes story of "I feel the strain" excellent.}

22 [Thursday]—Sent off my second verse to Power—Have received by Flahaut (who is arrived for a short time) a very kind letter from Lord Lansdowne—it is amusing to find that even he is becoming a Reformer & the same impulse of the times that makes him a Reformer will make others

Revolutionists[1]—dined at home—Williams of our party—Mrs. Story & her cousins & Kenny came in the evening & supped with us.—Kenny told a story of an outside passenger of a stage coach whom his fellow travellers called "the gentleman in black"—("won't the gentleman in black have some breakfast?" &c)—when the coach was overturned, and the coachman was collecting his passengers, he saw one of them sitting in a rut, powdered over with dust, and said "and pray who are you, Sir"—"I am the gentleman in black" was the answer.

23 [Friday]—Went out early to breakfast with Flahaut—showed me a letter from Italy, giving an account of the State of the Country, of the Carbonari & the opposite party, the Calderai—the former, though not regularly organized, are bound by an oath & their first principle is to forget all distinctions, and cooperate as Italians for the {one} great cause—they have contrived to get the lower clergy into their interest by connecting religion with the objects of the sect—Went & took a box at the Porte St. Martin—Bessy & I dined with the Storys and {thence} went all (joined by the Villamils) to the Theatre—the Vampire, Jeune Werther & the Dieux à la Courtille[1]—

24 [Saturday]—Walked into town with Irving—employed during the morning in finishing another Irish Melody "Yes—sad one of Sion—"[1] dined with Canning—company, Burgess & Lady Montgomery, Rancliffe, Lord Bristol & {his} daughters & Chenevix, whom I did not know at first, not having seen him for near twenty years—a good deal of conversation with him & Canning after dinner—Chenevix's *ultra-ism* (which was the motive of his writing those strong articles against France in the Edinburgh)[2] breaks out at every word—Talking of the sort of *enragé* that Ducis had made of Hamlet, he said that Talma, in acting it, was like Casimir Perrier in the Tribune[3]—remarked that for many years after the Revolution the French Artists never painted a picture without introducing *blood* into it—he spoke of the exceeding comicality of my translation of La Martine's verses in the last Edinburgh; but find he regretted the slight I had thrown upon this young author, as it had been his intention to introduce him to the notice of English readers, as the only, in short, the *earliest* French Poet[4]— From Canning's, Irving & I went to the opera, Henry de Roos having given me an order for two to his box—

25 [Sunday]—Went to the Chapel Royal with the Douglas's—a little girl and her mother in tears before me during the service—upon enquiring I found that it was the sight of the Duchesse d'Angoulême, who had had the

little girl educated & whom she had never seen so close before, that awakened *her* emotion & of course affected the mother also—Went afterwards with Villamil to see the collection of M. Portalis in the Place Vendome—he himself received us—some fine things—a good picture by Murillo—a head of a man full of expression by Spagnoletti—a beautiful small picture by Carlo Dolci of Christ surrounded by the Saints that preceded his coming—a portrait of an old man by the same author, and a female head surrounded by flowers, very pretty & delicate—some fine Vanhuysums—Portalis invited us to his house on Wednesday next—dined with Lord Rancliffe—company Lord Sandon, Lord Francis Leveson, Lord Granard & Lady Adelaide—rather agreeable—{Lady A. mentioned that the night of the scene at the opera, when the Duc de Berry was assasinated, Dupuytren, having examined the wound, retired to another room & dispatched a note off to Rotschild, saying "le coup est mortel—voyez ce que nous pouvons en faire," and that accordingly a considerable sum was made both by Rotschild & himself on the occasion—returned home early—}

26 [Monday]—Still correcting the 8th No. of my Irish Melodies—called on Lady Gwydir—dined with Kenny, by invitation, at the Boeuf a la mode—a stinking place, but not a bad dinner—Williams & a Mr. Emerson of the party—went afterwards to see the Mort du Tasse & the Carnavale de Venise.

27 [Tuesday]—Dined at the Palais Royal in consequence of an invitation through Chabot yesterday, who mentioned in his note that Mademoiselle had made arrangements for the music she promised me in the evening & that I should hear her play—All very kind—the Duchess told me soon after I came in rather a flattering piece of news—namely, that at a grande Fete at the Court of Berlin the other day, the Royal Family had represented, in character, the story of Lalla Rookh—{the Archdutchess herself playing Lalla Rookh}, and our own Duke of Cumberland Aurungzebe—Madame Dolomieu, one of the Dames d'honneur, promised to translate for me the Programme of the Fête, which is in German—the Duchess said that Chateaubriand had written home an account of it, and described it as the most spendid & tasteful thing he had ever seen[1]—Mademoiselle gave me her arm in going to dinner & I sat between her & the Duchess—After dinner had some conversation on politics with the Duke—seems to think there must be war, ere long, between England & Russia—spoke of the bad part France is acting with respect to Naples[2]—I sang a little, and they seemed to like it very much—at nine o'clock Paer arrived with his daughter & a flute-player—the girl sang & Madlle. played a sonata, accompanied by

Paer & the flute, very charmingly—At half past ten I came away with Chabot, who took me to Lady Rancliffe's ball—a very pretty assemblage of women, both French & English—among the former were two of the beauties of the day, Madame Barante & Made. Baufremont {neither worth much—} returned home early—

28 [Wednesday]—Still occupied in the disagreeable task of eking out verses for the eighth Number—dined (Bessy & I) at Villamil's and in the evening V. & I went to M. Portalis—those pretty rooms looking very well by candle-light & filled with very good company of both nations—Music by Pellegrin, Garcia, Made. Jidd &c—some Church singing, accompanied by an instrument called the Expressive organ, not very agreeable—had some conversation with the Duchesse de Broglie—Got home about one—Met Lord Charlemont on his way to me this morning for the purpose of consulting with respect to some opposition which he understands will be made among the red-hot Tories here to my taking the Chair on St. Patrick's-Day—{that fool, Wellesley Pole it seems, held forth about it at Lady Rancliffe's last night—} went with Lord C. to Colonel Cope's & after some consultation with them, decided upon the part I should take—both offered to stand by me, if I meant to persevere in being Chairman—but this would neither be good taste or good temper—

March 1 [Thursday]—Had some alarms this morning of a return of the tumour on my thigh—applied a plaster, and was rather downcast about it—{annoyed too by some disgusting conduct of Williams, with respect to money affairs, yet felt myself so far committed as to offer the loan of ten Napoleons to help him out of his difficulties,—} dined at Lady Montgomerie's—Company, Mr. & Mrs. Henry Baring {(by the bye, Baring's story of the Peddlar's Dog worth remembering—his not attacking the dog of a gentleman &c. &c.)} Lord Sandon, Dandy Montague, Warrender, Rotschild, the Rancliffes &c.—Montague mentioned that D'Este, when he first came to Paris, was persuaded that "belle comme le Pont Neuf" was a fashionable phrase when speaking of beauty, & applied it to some woman—{he also mentioned that upon its being proposed somewhere the other evening that Rotschild should be *baptized* before supper at the Ball he is about to give, a Lady said—"Yes & we must have as his *parrain*, Talleyrand, étant le moins Chrétien possible.} All going to Lady Elizabeth Stuart's Ball, except myself, who, in a fit of pride, stay away—have no idea of being asked merely with their *mob*.—Bessy too, asked to night—Mrs. Cadogan had invited me to go to her box at the opera, but I returned home early from Lady Montgomeries—

2nd [Friday]—Went to the meeting of the Committee about the Irish dinner at Cope's—was voted into the Chair—proposed Lord Charlemont to them as President of the Dinner—agreed to, of course—am a little sorry that I gave in so easily myself; for I now find that numbers are disappointed at my not being President, and I can trace the objections to no one but that "par nobile" of geese, W{ellesley} & F{inemore}—dined at Lord Granard's—company, Lords Sandon & Francis Leveson, Robinson & Lady Helena &c. &c.—a dull day—Rancliffe mentioned that Whitbread used to be called the "Chevalier de Malt," and that Lord Melville was said to be his "entire butt"[1]—Went afterwards with Bessy & the Storys to Sapio's Concert—a bad business—hear that the Fieldings are arrived—

3 [Saturday]—Williams called upon me—{anxious to get hold of the ten Napoleons} went with me to Lafitte's where I drew a bill upon Power for 40£ at 3 months, and lent Williams ten Napoleons out of it—went with the Villamils, and Storys to dine at Brizzi's, an Italian house—very dirty & disagreeable—the Duke of St. Carlos and all his family there—nurses, little children &c. all dined there almost every day—Villamil treated us to the dinner—adjourned to his house afterwards and had music till twelve, when we all went to the Bal Masqué at the Opera—Bessy much amused in teazing some of her acquaintances—left that at three, had sandwiches & hot wine at Story's, and did-not get home till near five—

4 [Sunday]—Received from the Marquise de Dolomieu a translation of the Berlin Programme, with a very civil note in which she says "Je ne saurais assez vous dire combien j'admire votre inimitable Pöesie"—Dined with Lord Charlemont at Véry's—happy to find Fielding of the party—not a very agreeable day—the dinner too French & the company too Irish—Galway politics and truffles *usque ad nauseam*—home early.

5 [Monday]—Dispatched at last the poetry of the 8th. Number, corrected, and filled up, to Power—Met again at Cope's about the St. Patrick's Dinner—forgot where I had been asked to dine & went to Grignon's, where I met Sir Henry Willoughby & we dined together—came home before ten & found poor Bessy very ill with cold—Willoughby mentioned that Talleyrand once, upon somebody who squinted asking him "comment vont les affaires" answered "comme vous voyez".—Received a letter within these few days from Florence from Lord Burghersh, directed "*Tom* Moore—Esq. Paris", inclosing an Italian Opera to which he has written music, and wishing me to translate it if it appeared to me good enough—

6 [Tuesday]—An idle morning—dined (Bessy & I) at the Villamils—Company, the Sapios, W. Irving & his brother—a party in the evening—Lord Granard & the two girls came—Mrs. Story &c.—singing and supper.

7 [Wednesday]—more idleness—called by appointment upon Made. de Dolomieu—another Frenchwoman with her—surprizing how well acquainted these women are with my poetry—on my mentioning that Lord Byron had said in one of his late letters to me that if honour came unlooked for upon him during this Neapolitan struggle, he hoped I would at least celebrate him by another "Oh breathe not his name",[1] they turned instantly to the pages of my book where the song is—left my card at the Duchesse de Broglie's—dined with Lord Rancliffe (one of the series of Restaurateur dinners) at Robert's—dinner very bad—

8 [Thursday]—Went into town early with Bessy in order to market for tomorrows dinner—dined at Cadogan's—Company, Fielding & Lady Elizabeth, Lord Miltown, Leveson & Mercer—rather agreeable—went from thence to Mrs. Hamilton's, where I met Denon & had some talk with him—he spoke of Bessy's beauty—from thence for ten minutes to a Doctor Laffian's, where there was music—Then to Lord Miltown's Ball—Bessy having refused to go, on account of the expense of a dress—a very brilliant Ball—in one quadrille set counted 8 pretty women, French & English—Madlle. d'Este, Lady A. Forbes, Miss Canning, Made. de Barante, Made. d'Oudenarde, Made. Shackerly &c.—left at two with Mrs. Story, who brought me home—

9 [Friday]—Mrs. S. drove me to the Cadran Bleu, in order to negotiate for our St. Patrick's dinner—Maurice asks the enormous sum of 65 franks a head, but I rather think the Cadran Bleu will do it for 40—there is a strong party still for my being {the} Chairman—Lord Miltown says he will put in his own claim against Ld. Charlemont, as being prior to him in rank, & will then yield in favour of me.—but I trust nothing will be done to offend Charlemont, who is a particularly manly and friendly person—our dinner at home consisted of Irving, Fielding, Villamil, and Colonel Corbet—an old college acquaintance of mine, who was obliged to leave Ireland in the "time of the troubles" and has been fighting in the French Service ever since—he was one of the 4 given up by Hamburgh {with Napper Tandy} to the English Govt[1]—Our dinner went off well—plenty of talk & wine—in the evening the Storys & Forsters—supped & left us at one—.

10 [Saturday]—Bessy & I dined with Mrs. S. and went to the Gymnase in the evening—a new Piece the "Gastronome sans argent"—Perlet excellent[1]

11 [Sunday]—Went to the Cadran Bleu and got their calculation of the wines that would be necessary—amusing to see how little they know of our mode of drinking—the great weight of the wine was, of course, thrown in the second service, and *after* dinner the allowance for fifty Irishmen was "2 bottles of Malaga, two of Lunele &c. &c."—I however explained the matter to them—dined at home & Bessy & I went to Villamil's in the evening—the Story party came & all supped there—Wrote a note to Lord Charlemont to beg he would decide as to the dinner.

12 [Monday]—Dined with the Douglas's,—Sapio came in the evening & we looked over some glees for Saturday—fixed to meet again at Douglas's on Wednesday—

13 [Tuesday]—Breakfasted with Henry Leeson, who drove me afterwards in his cabriolet to Lord Charlemont—Lord C. continues Chairman and I don't know but that it is all for the best—Drove thence to the Cadran Bleu, to give my final answer—took a box for the evening at the Porte St. Martin—dined (Bessy & I) with the Storys, and went to this Theatre in the evening—Potier in the "Ci-divant Jeune Homme" and pretty little Jenny Vert-pré in Riquet a la Houppe, both admirable[1]—Gave orders this morning for the printing of the tickets &c.

14 [Wednesday]—Dined with the Douglas's—Williams & Sapio there—had a good practice of glees in the evening.

15 [Thursday]—Met Lord Charlemont, Col. Burton &c at Cope's to make some arrangements about the dinner—dined with the Fieldings—Lady Payne, a Mr. Clay & Montgomery the party—Young Galignani (who has ever since his Father's death been anxious for me to give him such a cession of the right of publishing my works in France as may enable him to suppress the cheap editions now preparing here) called upon me this morning with the copy of a document, in which instead of the nominal sum of 4000 francs which was at first mentioned as the consideration for which I sold him the works, he has inserted, with the intention of making it *real,* the

sum of 2000 francs, of which he begged my acceptance—signed the paper & took the money.

16 [Friday]—This being our dear Anastasia's birth-day, Bessy has invited all the little Storys, Villamils, Forsters & Younges (amounting to near 20) to a dinner—on my return to dress found Bessy very ill with a head-ache, but endeavouring, notwithstanding, to do the honours to her little party—dined at Lord Charlemont's—company, Lord Bristol, Lady Montgomerie, Lady Saltoun &c—in the evening a large party—a very pretty French-woman Made. Chateaubriand—was introduced to the Duchesse de Cler-mont-Tonnerre, who asked me to a Concert on Sunday next—begged of Lord Bristol to propose Lord Charlemont's health tomorrow—on my re-turning home found that Bessy had been obliged to go to bed from sickness of stomach & head, but that at eleven o'clock, hearing from Villamil (who came to fetch his little ones) that my little god-daughter Mary had had two or three attacks of fits in the course of the day, she got up & set off to assist Mrs. V. in nursing & watching her—Waited up for her till half past one, but she did not return.

17 [Saturday]—Bessy came home at ten this morning, after having sat up the whole night with the child—Went out with Galignani to confirm the document I gave him on Thursday, by signature before a notary—have all along felt scruples at putting a false date to this paper, but felt these scruples still more strongly after confirming it thus formally by a second signature—begged of Galignani to suspend further proceedings in the business—went & consulted Le Roy (Villamil's notary) who thinks some mode might be adopted "plus conforme à la verité".—I begged of Galig-nani to let it be done in this way, & that I would most willingly refund the money rather than sign anything colourable or false even in form—called upon Douglas to make further arrangements about the dinner—at half past four went again with Galignani to his own Attorney, who seems to think the affair *may* be arranged so as to meet my scruples & yet secure the property to Galignani—went from thence to the Cadran Bleu to see how the Dinner was laid out, to look after the wine, & see the names written on the plates &c. &c.—Douglas there to assist me—About sixty sat down to dinner—the day very lively & interesting—never saw anything like the enthusiasm with which my health was drunk, and the speech with which I followed it, received—the manner in which I applied the circumstance of St. Patrick's name meaning originally the Devil had a particularly good effect—I spoke twice after—and in proposing the memory of the old Earl of Charlemont pronounced an eulogium on Grattan which was cheered

most rapturously—The glees we had got up told wonderfully. Altogether I have never seen a better public meeting, at twelve o'clock Lord C. left the chair, and we all separated—on my return found that Bessy was again gone for the night to nurse the little Villamil

18 [Sunday]—Williams called & I begged him to write some account of yesterday's meeting for Galignani's paper, which he did—{dined at Callaghan's the Irish Banker with the Villamils—met there my old acquaintance Lord Trimlestown—the dinner very dull—felt much inclined to exclaim with a little gourmande of nine years old, who sat next me & who, after stuffing himself with all sorts of comestibles, cried out "Maman; je m'ennuie et je m'endors"—after dinner Lord T. told one or two good things—one of them of a woman, in the Revolutionary times, who, speaking the new names of the months, said "La drolle [*unrecovered*] pour dire pour votre Brumaire, votre Pluviose &c. je ne sais que [*unrecovered*] porte toujours sur moi—voila mon Pluviose, et voila mon Ventose" accompanying the words at the same time, with appropriate action—Callaghan said that during the troubles on the Election Law, he heard an officer at the head of a party of Cavalry, use the following phrase in ordering them to clear away the crowd—"Lavez moi le derriere de cette Canaille-là"—did not go to Made. de Clermont-Tonnerre but got home early.}

19 [Monday]—Went out at ten o'clock to Galignani's, and attended him to his notary where a paper was drawn up, dated at the time when I actually did agree to transfer the right of publishing, which I, of course, very willingly signed—too happy to dine at home to-day—Bessy in low spirits at parting with our dear Anastasia, who goes to-day to Mrs. Forster's—Irving called near dinner-time—asked him to stay & share our roast chicken with us, which he did—He had been hard at work writing lately—In the course of ten days has written about 130 pages of the size of those in the Sketch Book—this is amazing rapidity—has followed up an idea which I suggested, and taken the characters in his Christmas Essay, Master Simon &c. &c. {as a sort of framework to fill up with sketches and remarks on life.} for the purpose of making a slight thread of a story on which to string his remarks & sketches of human manners & feelings[1]—left us at nine—Lady Gwydir had called in the morning to give me a coupon to her box at the opera, but I did not go—heard this morning to my great regret that about six or seven drunken fools {(Long Wellesley, at their head)} remained after the party broke up on Saturday, and disgraced it by a quarrel among themselves, which made it necessary to call in the Gens-d'armes.

20 [Tuesday]—Went to make some calls—dined at Lord Granard's— dullissimum dullorum—Irving came in the evening—went thence to Lady Montgomerie's Ball—full of pretty women—among whom Mrs. Shackerly the most concupiscible—Miss Canning the most loveable—paid one of these days (I forget which) 4 Napoleons to a man for copying out Lord B's. Memoirs—he had the conscience to ask 8 or 9.

21 [Wednesday]—Not very well—this company-going hurts & wearies me—dined at Doctor Laffan's—company, Chenevix, Sir. W. Peacocke, Bligh, &c.—Chenevix mentioned as an instance of the importance of Danc- ing-Masters, one who, the other day, when the person employing him wished to fix him to a particular hour, & said that the other artists were accommodating in that way, answered—"oh, oui, c'est bon pour ces autres artistes—mais un Maitre de Danse doit choisir ses heures—" he also men- tioned, "les Artistes Décorateurs" in the Palais Royal—went thence to Lady Gwydir's Box at the Opera—{Sir C. Stewart there, & rather agreeable.}

22 [Thursday]—Saw in the affiches that the Fille d'honneur was to be acted {in the evening,} & wrote off to Mrs. S. to take a Box—dined with her (Bessy & I) and went to the Francais.—Irving of our party—the Jeunesse de Henri 5 the entertainment[1]—in which Michot (who acts no more after this season) played Capitaine Copp admirably—Supped at Mrs. S's. afterwards.

23 [Friday]—Dined at home & read a little in the evening—rare occur- rences with me now—

24 [Saturday]—Went down to the Cadran Bleu with Douglas to see how our account lies there—find there is enough of wine left to settle all extras without calling upon the pockets of the stewards—took a box at Fran- coni's—Bessy and I dined with the Douglas's and all went to see "Attaque du Convoi"[1]—Military spectacles got up *con amore* at this Theatre.

25 [Sunday]—This *day ten years we* were married, and, though Time has made his usual changes in us both, we are still more like lovers than any married couple of the same standing I am acquainted with—asked to dine with Rancliffe, but dined at home alone with Bessy—This being Sunday, our dance in celebration of the day deferred till tomorrow—Received a

letter yesterday from my dear father, which, notwithstanding the increased tremor of his hands, is written with a clearness of head & warmth of heart that seem to promise many years of enjoyment still before him—God grant it!.

26 [Monday]—Bessy busy in preparations for the dance this evening—I went [and] Wrote to my dear mother, and told her, in proof of the unabated anxiety & affection I feel towards her, that a day or two ago, on my asking Bessy "whether she would be satisfied if little Tom loved her through life as well as I love my mother" she answered "yes—if he loves me but quarter as much".—Went into town too late to return to dinner, & dined at Very's alone—found on my return our little rooms laid out with great management, and decorated with quantities of flowers which Mrs. Story had sent—Our Company, Mrs. S. & her cousins, Mrs. Forster & her two daughters & Miss Bridgeman—the Villamils, Irving, Capt. Johnson, Wilder &c.—& the Douglas's—Began with Music—Mrs. V., Miss Drew & Emma Forster sung—our dance afterwards to the Piano-forte very gay, & not the less so for the floor giving way in sundry places—a circle of chalk was drawn round one hole—Dr. Yonge was placed sentry over another, and whenever there was a new crash, the general laugh at the heavy foot that produced it caused more merriment than the solidest floor in Paris could have given birth to—Sandwiches, negus & Champagne crowned the night & we did not separate till near four in the morning—Irving's humour began to break out as the floor broke in, and he was much more himself than ever I have seen him.—Read this morning, before I went out, Thérèse Aubert[1] & cried over it like a girl—

27 [Tuesday]—Two strings to our bow to-day—the Fieldings & the Francais, or the Douglas's and the Opera—Bessy too much knocked up for either, and I divided myself between both—Dined with the Fs. & went to the Opera with the Douglas's—the Barbiere—Heard of the surrender of the Neopolitans, without a blow, to the Austrians—*Can* this be true?—There is then no virtue in Macaroni.

28 [Wednesday]—The news but too true—curse on the Cowards!—dined at home—Lady Gwydir's Box at the Opera & Mrs. Arthur's Ball tempting in the evening—but went to neither—very kind note from Made. de Souza to-day.—Galignani told me the other day that every person setting up as bookseller in Paris is obliged to get four persons to testify solemnly for him that he understands Latin, Greek &c. &c.

29 [Thursday]—Dined at the Granards—was also asked to Lord Bristol, to meet Made. de Genlis—but could not get off the Granard's—(by the bye, met Made. de Genlis last Sunday at Denon's with Lady Charlemont—a lively little old woman—but by no means so fantastic a person as Lady Morgan makes her)—[Company at Lord G's, the Irvings Lady E. Fielding—& Warrender—more agreeable than usual—Went from thence (Irving and I) to Mrs. Forster's in order to accompany her to Lady E. Stuart's Ball—got through this operation of *escorting* better than I expected—home before two—}

30 [Friday]—Wrote a few lines about the rascally Neapolitans[1]—dined (Bessy & I) with the Fieldings, and went to the Gymnase in the evening.

31 [Saturday]—Went out (Storys, & Irving) to Sevres to show them the manufactory, and to make some arrangements in our Cottage for the summer—but old Colonel King would not give the key—the wheel of Mrs. Ss. carriage came off as we returned, our *chute*, however, very easy & innocent—dined with Chenevix—some agreeable conversation after dinner—talked of the rage for the Constitutions now—the singularity that it is no longer the English Constitution which is proposed as a model but the Spanish or French—said that I supposed it was because they knew the English C. took time to form it, and those they wanted must be like "Cotelettes à la minute"—the notion of being able to have a perfect Constitution at once, "per saltum" as it were, reminded me of a circumstance mentioned by Sir Gore Ousely—that once on his telling the King of Persia, to his great astonishment, that the revenue of the Post-Office alone in England amounted to more than that of his whole dominions, the King, after a few moments' thought exclaimed "Then I'll have a Post-Office"—forgetting the new necessary preliminaries of commerce &c. &c. and indeed the first necessary *sine-qua-non* of his people being able to write letters—[they mentioned Ali Pacha having some time ago sent a messenger to Corfu to look for a Constitution for him—and his once wearing his 3 tails of the 3 revolutionary colours.][1] A Frenchman there spoke of the Languedocian language—said it was the old Roman language & still exists—that the common people of the country all speak it, & that they say of any one who does *not* "il se donne des airs—il parle Francais"—he quoted a passage from one of their ancient songs in which the lover says "you ask me for your heart again—I would willingly return it if I could—but having placed it beside my own, I no longer know one from the other"—the idea it seems, inculcated & believed among the French is that the Duke of Orleans & English gold produced the Revolution—went from thence to Mercer's,

heard two or three things from Madlle. Munch & Sapio (not over well sung) & got home at 12

April 1 [Sunday]—Finished my lines about the Neapolitans—took a solitary walk (for the first time these many weeks) along the Boulevard du Roulé—dined at Lord Rancliffe's—company, the Duc de Guiche—Warrender, Lord Alvanley, and Lady Adelaide[1]—the talk at dinner all about horses & birds, {owing, I suspect, to the Duc's incapacity for any other—} but in the evening we had something better—Alvanley mentioned a book called "l'Histoire du Systême"[2] giving an account of Law's Money Plan, and full, he said, of curious anecdotes about that whole transaction—there was a hump-backed man, who made a good deal of money by lending his hump as a writing-desk on the street, the houses & shops being all occupied by people making their calculations—the story about the Irish chairman whispering to Sheridan on the night of the fire at Drury Lane—"don't make yourself uneasy, Mr. S.—in about ten minutes the devil a drop more of water there will be to be had"—Sir A. C{larke} once telling long rhodomontade stories about America at Lord Barrymore's table, B. (winking to the rest of the company) asked him "did you ever meet any of the Chick-chows, Sir Arthur?"—"Oh several—a very cruel race."—"the Cherry-Chows?"—"Oh very much among them—they were particularly kind to our men"—"and pray, did you know any thing of Totteroddy bow-wows?"—This was too much for the poor Sir A. who then first perceived that Barrymore had been quizzing him—came home early.—Lady {Rancliffe} said that Louis 18 called Tallyrand "une vielle lampe qui pue en s'éteignant"

2 [Monday]—Copied out my Neapolitan verses, and sent them to Perry—not bad—dined at home, and took Bessy in the evening to drink tea with Mrs. Villamil

3 [Tuesday]—Wrote to Lord Byron & went to the Post with the letter—called at Galignani's—a strange gentleman in the shop accosted me & said "Mr. Moore, I have not the honour of being acquainted with you but I was requested by the Princess of Prussia to tell you, if ever I met you, how beautifully the fete at Berlin, taken from your Lalla Rookh, went off—" he then told me several particulars—the Grand Duchess of Russia (daughter of the King of Prussia) who acted Lalla Rookh is, he said, very handsome, and the sister of Prince Radzivil, who played the Peri a most beautiful little girl—He expects some drawings that were made of the principal personages in their costumes and will show them to me[1]—took courage & called

upon Made. de Souza, for the first time since the article—was very kindly received & walked about her garden with her—dined (Bessy & I) at Storys—company, the Villamils, & Irving—sung a little in the evening—at ten Lady E. Fielding called to take me to the Duchesse de Broglie's—repeated my Neapn. verses to her & Fielding—she said they were {even} like sparks of fire running through her in all directions—saw there Made. de Barante, looking very pretty, the Duchesse de Raguse & the Marquise de Dolomieu, who called me "un monstre" for not having been to call upon her—Home at twelve—Have been reading a little miscellany these two or three days, from which the following things are worth preserving as illustrations—talking of "coral reefs & islands"—"There is every reason to believe that the islands which are occasionally raised by the tremendous agency of subterraneous volcanoes do not bear any proportion to those which are perpetually forming by the silent but persevering exertions of the sea-worms by which coral is produced"—"The transformation of insects is only the throwing off external & temporary coverings & not an alteration of the original form. Reaumur discovered that the crysalis or rather the butterfly itself was enclosed in the body of the caterpillar. The proboscis, the antennae, the limbs & the wings of the fly are so nicely folded up &c. &c."—In the diamond mines "when a negro is so fortunate as to find a diamond of the weight of 17 carats & a half, he is crowned with a wreath of flowers & carried in procession to the administrator, who gives him his freedom by paying his owner for it"—A pretty story might be made out of this—"When a negro is suspected of swallowing a diamond, he is confined in a solitary apartment, and means taken to bring the Gem to light".—

4 [Wednesday]—a desperately wet day—dined at Made. de Souza's, Company, the Gwydirs, & some unpronounceable Russians (Prince & Princess Sabatskoff, I believe), Count Funchall & Gabriel Delessert,—The Russians a very unaffected amiable mannered pair—Funchall just the same merry, hideous little fellow I remember 16 or 17 years ago at Tunbridge Wells, when he used to wear his hat in a particular way (as Wm. Spencer said) "to look like the Duchess of St. Alban's"—Delessert mentioned rather a comical trick of some English, who took an Ottoman Flag with them to the Ball of St. Peter's, and planted it over the Angel—the astonishment of the Cardinals next morning at seeing the Crescent floating over St. Peter's—went from thence with Funchal to Lady Gwydir's box at the French Opera—Sir C. Stewart & King there—afterwards to Lady Alborough's soirée—a good deal of conversation with Lady C. Stewart, who told me that Lalla Rookh, had been translated into German—It has now appeared in the French, Italian, German & *Persian* languages—Lady Saltoun told me that a gentleman had just said to her "If Mr. Moore wishes to be made much of—if Mr.

Moore wishes to have his head turned, he must go to Berlin—there is nothing else talked of there but Lalla Rookh."—Douglas took me home.

5 [Thursday]—Wrote to Rogers—went about the character of a new Cook we are hiring—and then out to Sevres (where Bessy & Mrs. Villamil had already gone) with the keys of the Cottage we are to take possession of for the summer—took measures for window curtains &c. &c.—dined at Lord Bristol's—Made. de Genlis could not come—Company, the Stewarts, Mrs. & Miss Canning, Lord & Lady Surrey, Funchal &c.—Dully placed at dinner—in the evening sung, and liked my audience much.

6 [Friday]—Dined at home—Miss Forster came to tea & the Kingstons—some singing—

7 [Saturday]—Bessy called away by the increasing illness of Mrs. V's. child—I dined alone at Very's—went afterwards to a book-auction & bought Rousseau's works, 37 small volumes {handsomely bound,} for 68 franks.[1] Brought Bessy home at night—had called in the morning on Lady Gwydir & repeated her my Neapolitan verses.

8 [Sunday]—Jane Power arrived from England on her long-meditated visit to us—brought the copy of the National Melodies, which I had ordered for Mademoiselle d'Orleans—most splendidly & tastefully bound—dined at Fielding's—Company, Lattin, Fazakerley (who has been the bearer of a copy of Roger's last edition of Human Life to Bessy "from an old friend") and Montgomery—Lattin very amusing—mentioned some Frenchman who said he had not read the History of France, "but had guessed it"—Talked of Forsyth's Book on Italy—its wonderful learning & ability—I mentioned some strange errors he had fallen into & Lattin noticed his assertion that Acton was the son of a barber[1]—{went to Story's for Bessy—}

9 [Monday]—Wrote to Lord Lansdowne—mentioned to him the Report of a Revolution at Constantinople & said "nothing now is wanting to bring "the Rights of Man" into proper disgrace but their being taken up by the Turks—the Spanish Constitution, translated into good Turkish would complete the Farce".—dined at Douglas's to meet Harry Bushe & his wife, just arrived. Bushe, a-propos of Lord Eldon's *larmoyant* propensity, quoted some verses about Provost Hutchinson from the Baratariana[1]—

who feels all his crimes, yet his feeling defies,
And each day stabs his country with tears in his eyes.

Douglas mentioned Hutchinson's having gone once to Lord Townshend to ask for some situation for his daughter Prudentia—and on Lord T's saying that he really had nothing just then left at his disposal but a Captaincy of Dragoons, the ready Place-hunter replied that he would be most happy to accept of it, & Miss Prudentia was accordingly made a Captain of Dragoons—Mrs. Bushe played in the evening & I sung—Bushe said that Grattan died possessed of an income of £9000 a year, owing fifty thousand, having borrowed to purchase. When I returned home found that Bessy had gone to sit up with Villamil's child—

10 [Tuesday]—Dined at home—had Irving, Doctor Williams, and Power's Man of business to dine with me—Poor Bess still at Villamil's—never was there a creature that devoted herself to others with so little reserve or selfishness.—In the evening went with the Kingstons & Jane Power to the Vaudeville—called at V's in my way home to try & persuade Bessy to return with me—but she would not—promised, however, to take off her clothes & go to bed there.

11 [Wednesday]—Dined at Lord Granard's to meet Lord Beauchamp {, a gentlemanlike & lovely young man but they say most prematurely debauched.—} went from there along to the Varietés—saw half the Marchande de Goujons and the Coin de Rue[1]—from thence to Villamil's—the baby better, but Bessy would not leave her.

12 [Thursday]—Power's man, Mr. Goodlad to settle the signing of the deeds of assignment he has brought—took him to Forster's, who was witness on the occasion—went thence to show him the Beaujon, & took Miss Forster with us—4 courses in the car with her—Walked Mr. Goodlad off then along the Boulevard to the Little Theatres, where I took a box for the evening at the Ambigu, and (as he wished much to dine at a Restaurateurs, but, not speaking French, did not know how to manage it) I gave him in charge to the Landlady of the Cadran Bleu and chose his dinner for him—dined at Story's & went to the Ambigu—the Famille Irlandaise, a piece found on the Rebellion of 98, General Lake[1] &c. &c.—called at Villamil's for Bessy & brought her home—The following extracts are from the Curiosities of Literature—"It is an odd observation of Clarendon in his own Life, that Mr. Chillingworth was of a stature little superior to Mr.

Hales; and it was an age in which there were many great & wonderful men of that size"—Lord Falkland was of low stature & smaller than most men; & of Sidney Godolphin "There was never so great a mind & spirit contained in so little room; so that Ld. Falkland used to say merrily, that he thought it was a great ingredient into his friendship for Mr. Godolphin, that he was pleased to be found in his company where he was the properer man."—{*An* Act *behind the scenes*—} "It is said that the frozen Norwegians on the first sight of roses dared not touch what they conceived were trees budding with fire"—an old writer calls coffee "this wakeful & civil drink".[2]

13 [Friday]—dined with Lord Trimlestown—company, Lord Granard, {Baron Roebach, Baron Dillon,} Lattin, Harry Bushe &c.—Lattin & I told Irish stories by the dozen—some of his very amusing—{The Irish Post—} A Posting Dialogue—"Why—this Chaise is very damp—" "And a very good right it has to be so, Sir—wasn't it all night in the Canal?"—{these verses on a certain subject—

> If it were not holy, churchmen would abuse it
> If it weren't lawful lawyers would not use it
> If it weren't dainty, rich men wouldn't crave it
> If it weren't plenty, poor men would not have it!

The servant saying his master must be very ill, as he had heard the physician say "they had driven a post chay (a bougie) into him[1] & that they were going to introduce a cathedral"—The fellow p——g after drinking very good wine, and saying "Ça ferait encore un joli petit vin à six sous."—} Lord Trimlestown mentioned a person saying upon seeing an upstart nobleman covered with stars & orders, "C'est de la noblesse plaquée".— Found on my return home at night Ld. Byron's letter about Bowles & Pope, which Fielding had sent me to look over—the whole thing unworthy of him—a Leviathan among small fry—He has had the bad taste to allude to an anecdote which I told him about Bowles's early life, which is even worse than Bowles, in his pamphlet quoting me as entirely agreeing with him in the system he is combating for.[2]

14 [Saturday]—Occupied all the morning in taking places in the diligence for Mr. Goodlad & Miss Forster, who avails herself of the opportunity of his return to go to England—Dined at Peters's—Lord Rancliffe took me in his Cabriolet—{Company, Lords Herbert & Beauchamp, Prince Paul of Würtemberg, King, Warrender, Col. Norton &c. &c. not forgetting Spy Derby, whom I saw for the first time—} a very handsome house & dinner— au reste, dull enough. {Called for Bessy at Story's & home before eleven.}

15 [Sunday]—Dined at Fielding's—George Dawson & Montgomery—Dawson told a good story about the Irish landlord counting out the change of a guinea—"Twelve, 13, 14—(a shot heard) Bob go see who's that that's killed—15—16—17—enter Bob—It's Captain Kelly Sir.—Poor Capt. Kelly—a very good customer of mine—18—19—20—there's your change, Sir"—the Storys called for me, at eight—came home with them, & they & Emma Forster supped with us—Bessy very much affected by my singing "I'm wearing awa'" and obliged to leave the room—

16 [Monday]—Days of idleness & waste—have done nothing for weeks past, except about a dozen lines to a Cavatina of Carafa's—walked into Paris with Bessy to provide for dinner—called afterwards to take leave of Emma Forster—a scene—had to dine with us Harry Bushe, Douglas & Irving—Bushe told of an Irish country-squire, who used with hardly any means to give entertainments to the militia &c. in his neighbourhood and when a friend expostulated with him on the extravagance of giving claret to these fellows when whisky punch would do just as well, he answered "you are very right, my dear friend—but I have the claret on tick—and where the devil would I get credit for the *lemons?*"—Douglas mentioned the son of some rich grazier in Ireland whose son went on a tour to Italy with express injunctions from the father to write to him whatever was worthy of notice—accordingly on his arrival in Italy had wrote a letter beginning as follows—"Dear Father—the Alps is a very high mountain, and bullocks bear no price"—Lady Susan & her daughters & the Kingstons came in the evening & all supped—a French writer mentions as a proof of Shakespeare's attention to particulars his allusion to the climate of Scotland in the word "Hail, hail, all hail—" Grele-grele-toute grele.

17 [Tuesday]—The Kingstons dined with us and all went to the Variétés in the evening—much amused with Vernet in the Marchande de Goujons—

18 [Wednesday]—Dined at home—Williams of the party—{walked into Paris after dinner, and read at the Reading-Room the Crim-Con Trial of Colonel Berkely & Mrs. Waterhouse—their mention of Lalla Rookh in the letters is good as an advertisement for the Longmans "Do you love poetry & music? Do you admire Lalla Rookh?" Which questions of the Lady's he answers that he thinks modern language has nothing to equal it—the tenderness of the heroine &c. &c.}[1]

19 [Thursday]—This being the great day of the Long-champ,[1] Mrs. Vil-

lamil lent Bessy her carriage on the occasion, and it was arranged that Anastasia should go with Mamma & that Tom & the two maids should be stationed on chairs in the Champs Elysées and bow to Mamma as she passed—Irving & I walked about there for hours, but saw nothing of any of them—grew alarmed about six o'clock & sent an apology to Rancliffe with whom I was to have dined to meet Czartorisky & Lady de Roos. I saw Bessy at last, who had been detained but not by any accident—dined by myself at the Trois Freres at 9 o'clock, & came home immediately

20 [Friday]—Walked in with Bessy to shop—saw the Examiner which quotes my Neapolitan verses from the Chronicle, and says "their fine spirit & flowing style sufficiently indicate the poet & patriot from whose pen they came"[1]—dined at Fielding's—Company, Lambton, Montgomery, Fazakerly, & young Talbot—the day very agreeable, as it is always at the Fielding's—

21 [Saturday]—Went to the Louvre with Mrs. Story, Bessy & the Kingstons—afterwards lounged about at bookstalls—read the newspapers at Galignani's—called on Charles Fox, who is just come from Constantinople, & is on his way to the Cape of Good Hope—says Lord & Lady Holland will be here in the course of the summer—dined at Storys.

22 [Sunday]—Went out to St. Cloud—to see the Chateau and Meudon with the Kingstons & Bessy—a lovely day, fit for laugh and idleness—dined at Storys—{S. a little savage—much annoyed by it.}

23 [Monday]—Have begun words to a Quadrille air—a young Frenchman called upon me with part of a translation of Lalla Rookh in verse—a professor of the Classics in Belgium—left his Ms. with me.—dined at Harry Bushe's—Company, Col. Cope, Lord Charlemont, Douglas, Lattin &c.—a noisy dinner.—Bushe told of B{eresford}, the Bishop of (I forget what) saying after his fourth bottle (striking his head in a fit of maudlin piety) "I have been a great sinner—but I love my Redeemer"—This Bishop is one of the opposers of the Catholic Claims—so is F{owler}!—godly Ecclesiastics! pity *their* Church should be in danger!—Went to Lady Elizabeth Stuart's in the evening—had some talk with William Banks, who is the bearer of an early copy of Lord B's tragedy—introduced Irving to Sir Charles Stuart—{Irving thinks him dull—but this is only his manner, than which nothing, to be sure, can be more common & ignoble.}

24 [Tuesday]—Dined at home & went with the S. & Bessy to the Francais—Madlle Duchesnois in Jeanne d'Arc[1]—attended watchfully to her recitative and find that in nine lines out of ten, "A cobbler there was & he lived in a stall" *is* the tune of the French Heroics—Took the Ss. this morning to see Gerard's Corinne.

25 [Wednesday]—dined at Ss.—Company, Cope, Irving, {Douglas, Henry Leeson &c. &c.—Dull enough.} Cope mentioned a good specimen of English-French, & the astonishment of the French people who heard it, not conceiving what it could mean—"Si je fais, je fais—mais, si je fais, je suis un Hollandais".

26 [Thursday]—Called upon Lady Charlemont, and walked some time in her garden with her—She has not yet seen Lord Byron's tribute to her beauty in his pamphlet[1]—dined at home & went in the evening with the Ss. and Bessy to the Odéon—a splendid Theatre, but wretched bad acting. The after-piece (the Voyage à Dieppe)[2] very amusing—copied out my Quadrille song this morning & sent it to Power—

27 [Friday]—The young French Professor called—showed me a Recueil of poems he had written—translations, some of them, from my Melodies—dined at Story's, to meet Caroline Kingston's lover, just arrived & a Captain Lane—The following little notices are from the Curiosities of Literature, which I have been reading occasionally during my idleness—"His notion (Dr. Campbell's in his Hermippus Redivivus) of the art of prolonging life by inhaling the breath of young women was eagerly credited. A physician, who, himself had composed a treatise on health was so influenced by it, that he actually took lodgings at a female boarding school, that he might never be without a constant supply of the breath of young ladies"—"They have the custom (the women in that long row of islands that divides the Adriatic from the Lagouns) when their husbands are fishing out at sea, to sit along the shore in the evenings & vociferate these songs (chaunts from Tasso), & continue to do so with great violence, till each of them can distinguish the responses of her own husband at a distance"—this is very poetical—"The laws of the Twelve Tables which the Romans chiefly copied from the Grecian code were, after they had been approved by the people, engraved on brass, they were melted by lightning, which struck the capitol & consumed other laws."—"A schoolmaster (in Rome) was killed by the *styles* of his own scholars".—"Virgil, when young, formed a design of a national poem, but was soon discouraged from proceeding, merely by the roughness & asper-

ity of the old Roman names, such as Decius Mus, Lucumo, Vibius Caudex".[1]—

28 [Saturday]—Dined at home—went with Bess & the Storys to the Panorama Dramatique—much pleased with the spectacle—

29 [Sunday]—Was to have gone to Malmaison—but the day not fine enough—took Lady Elisabeth Fielding & her daughter to see Gerard's Corinne, Made. Gerard having written me a very civil note to fix the time— walked with Irving to call upon Lady Saltoun—dined at Story's, intending to go to Lady Charlemont in the evening, but did not—

30 [Monday]—Went to the Louvre with the Kingstons, Mrs. S & Bessy— Villamil pointed out a female in one of Ruben's Luxembourg pictures whose face resembles Mrs. Story's—{dined at Lord Granard's—company, Sir C. Stuart, the Rancliffes, Feilding, Warrender &c.—Lady E. Feilding was to have called to take me to the Duchesse de Broglie's in the evening, but wrote to say she had a head-ache & could not—went to join Bessy at Story's & supped there.}

May 1st. [Tuesday] The commencement of the Fetes on the Duc de Bordeaux's christening—saw the procession in the morning; at least had a glimpse of it from the Quai Voltaire—dined at Ss. and in the evening walked out to see the illuminations & fireworks—were foolish to take Anastasia with us, & got into an immense crowd with her, to my very great alarm—the misty darkness of the night very favourable to the effect of the illuminations, which in the Tuilleries Gardens were most magnificent—the star by itself, in the middle of the dark sky over the "Legion d'Honneur" particularly striking, and the long arcade of light at the end of the gardens beautiful—saw the fireworks (but badly) from a Mr. Penleaz's windows on the Quai Voltaire—{Took Bessy & Jane Power in the evening—I returned alone with Mrs. Story.}

2nd. [Wednesday] Walked about the Champs Elysées to see the humours of the Mât de Cocagne, distribution of the sausages &c. &c.—{dined all together (Storys, Bessy, Irving, Mr. Cunliffe &c.) at Very's—} Had tickets for both Notre Dame yesterday & the Ball at the Hotel de Ville to-night, but not having a "habit habillé" made no use of them.

3rd. [Thursday]—Dined, the same party, at the Café Francais, and went to the French opera in the evening—saw a new allegorical opera got up in honour of the occasion called "Blanche de Provence"—the music (by Cherubini, Paer and two others) very pretty & dancing delightful[1]— Received this morning Lord Byron's Tragedy—Looked again over his Letter on Bowles—it is amusing to see through his design in thus depreciating all the present school of poetry—being quite sure of his own hold upon fame he contrives to loosen that of all his contemporaries, in order that they may fall away entirely from his side, and leave him unencumbered, even by their floundering—it is like that Methodist Preacher, who, after sending all his auditory to the devil, thus concluded—"You may think perhaps on the day of judgment to escape by laying hold of my skirts as I go to heaven—but it won't do—I'll trick you all—for I'll wear a spencer— I'll wear a spencer"[2]—so Lord B. willingly surrenders the skirts of his poetical glory rather than let any of us, poor devils, stick in them even for ever so *short* a flight,—The best of it is too that the wise Public all the while turns up its eyes & exclaims "How modest!"—

{4 [Friday]—Dined at the Ss. & went to the Ambigu Comique in the evening—dreadfully dull—}

5 [Saturday]—Went through the disagreeable inquisition of our furniture &c. by the Landlady & took leave of her & the Allée des Veuves for good & all.—Bessy & the servants set off for Sèvres about one, & I (after going to the Pere la Chaise with Mrs. S. at the Kingstons) got there at seven & dined with the Villamils—Kept awake at night by the nightingales—Finished today Lord B's. Tragedy—full of fine things, but wants that necessary ingredient, interest. Not one of the characters excites our sympathy, and the perpetual recurrence of our memory to Otway's fine management of the same sort of story is unfavourable even to Lord B's. great powers.

6 [Sunday]—The Storys (children & all) came out, and all (except Bessy, who was too tired with our déménagement) went to Versailles to see the Great Waters—dined at Made. Raimbault's (or rather her successors) with great difficulty, being obliged almost to battle for our dinners, and having called at La Butte on our way back proceeded to town with the expectation of a Fete at Beaujon, but there was none—Slept at Story's—{asked to dine with Lord Essex to-morrow.}

7 [Monday]—Went to the Beaujon—descended in the cars 3 times with

each of the Kingstons & 4 times with Mrs. S.—from thence for money to
the Banker's—met there old Montague, Burgess & Lord Sandon—had
previously called upon Lord Essex, who told me of the King's late civility to
the opposition at Brighton, & his having had Lord & Lady Lansdowne,
Lord & Lady Cowper &c. to dine with them—mentioned this to Lord
Sandon, who said he was himself at the dinner—that Lord Cowper was
very sulky, would hardly answer the King, and stayed outside in the passages as much as he could—Lord Lansdowne, on the contrary all courtesy{,
and particularly attentive to Lady Cunningham, who, in her turn, was
markedly civil to him & the rest, & seemed to imply in her manner (said
Lord Sandon) "we shall not always be enemies."} Burgess, who is setting off
for Scotland, repeated his invitation to me to visit him there on my return—{Montague mentioned that Lady Aldborough on receiving a letter
from some grand friends of hers in England, making enquiries, (with a
view to visiting Paris) as to the persons with whom she chiefly lived &c. &c.
answered "very pleasant society—there are the Blac-ases, the Duc-ases, the
Pudin-ases, and the Hard-ases *(Duras)*—and with the assistance of the
Comte de Pot-a-Pissy, we get on very well"—Her friends were delighted
with the account, & joined her immediately—Burgess} apropos of something,[1] quoted Lord Thurlowe's (?) two lines upon the Dutch

> Amphibious wretches, speedy be your fall,
> May man *un*dam you & G——d damn you all!

Montague spoke to me about my verses on his "dear friend" Perceval's
death[2]—dined by myself at Bombarde's and came out in the Celerifiere at
six—Received a note from Chabot announcing a present of a clock from
Madlle d'Orleans.

8 [Tuesday]—The first quiet morning I have had for a long, long time—
arranged my books &c—walked out—sketched two or three verses of a
song—dined well & comfortably—walked to shop with Bessy in the village—Received an invitation to dine with the Duke of Orleans at Neuilly
tomorrow—

9 [Wednesday]—Wrote to Chabot to make the best excuse in his power for
me to the Duke—walked, read & copied out my Song—dined with the
Villamils to meet the Princess Talleyrand, & a Comtesse & Marquis, whose
names I could not make out—It is said of Madame Talleyrand, that one
day her husband, having told her that Denon was coming to dinner, bid
her read a little of his Book upon Egypt just published in order that she
might be able to say something civil to him upon it, adding that he would

leave the volume for her upon his study-table. He forgot this, however, and Madame upon going into his study found a volume of Robinson Crusoe on the table instead, which having read very attentively, she was not long in opening upon Denon at dinner about the desert island, his manner of living &c. &c. to the great astonishment of poor Denon, who could not make out head or tail of what she meant—till upon her saying "Eh puis, ce cher Vendredi!" he perceived she took him for no less a person than Robinson Crusoe—There are various stories of her niaiserie—Upon being asked once what part of the world she came from she said "je suis d'Inde" (Dinde) meaning des Indes".—Sat next her at dinner—she talked much of Lalla Rookh, which she had read in the French prose—mentioned her having past three months with the King of Spain & his brother & uncle at Valencay—said it was all a story about Ferdinand's embroidering the petticoat & that it was the uncle who did it—seemed to remember nothing curious about them except her having eaten one day a dish of little fish caught expressly for her by the uncle, and that Ferdinand, who had been always accustomed to wear uniform, said to her upon his putting on a new suit of velvet "I think I look like a bourgeois to-day"—she seemed to think this very interesting—Praised Bessy's beauty to me—Some singing in the evening.

10 [Thursday]—Went into {the} town, partly to take in my letters & partly to bring out Mrs. Story for our party to Malmaison—left Paris with her & Miss Morris at ¼ past twelve & arrived at the Grille of Malmaison at two—were soon joined by the Villamils & Bessy—The Library here interesting, as having been Napoleon's Cabinet de travail, and still in the same state, they say, as when he left it—in one of the Salons the letters N. & J are alternately on the ceiling—went on afterwards to St. Germain—dined—saw the Chateau—the room into which Louis 14 used to descend by a trap to Made. la Valliere—the chambers of Jaques 2nd. &c. Returned to La Butte at nine—Received to-day Mademoiselle d-Orleans's letter, which, is highly kind & flattering—she signs herself "Votre affectionée"

11 [Friday]—Walked & read over what I have done of my Egyptian letters—must make great alterations—in the evening Mrs. S & Miss Morris surprized us with a visit—went to Villamil's & had some music.

12 [Saturday]—Resumed my Egyptian work & wrote seven or eight lines—it will require some thought & time to get back into the train of the story.

13 [Sunday]—Went into Paris early—called upon Mr. G. Moore (the author of the Lives of Ripperda & Alberoni &c.)[1] who has brought me a letter of introduction from Sir J. Macintosh—went to the Feilding's—{Lady E. read me a letter she had received from Lady Cowper, giving an account of the King's late civilities to the Opposition, which is supposed to be all Lady Cunningham's doing—the letter mentioned that Lady Cunningham was all brilliancy both in dress & looks—that her sash of diamonds was most magnificent and that the family pearls had lengthened considerably in the last year—"indeed they increased so fast (says Lady Cowper) that I believe they breed"—} called to return Greffulhe's visit—the first time I have {ever} seen his splendid house—twenty five acres of beautifully-arranged pleasure-grounds in the middle of Paris!—talked of Sheridan—he said that Sir A. Absolute was evidently taken from Old Mirabel in the Inconstant[2]— went from thence, according to appointment, to meet Lord Essex at Marshal Soult's, to see his pictures—a large assembly of English there, the Bessboroughs, the Ponsonbys, the Bristols, Canning &c. &c.—the collection remarkably fine—almost all Murillos, the most interesting among which appeared to me the Prodigal Son, Christ with the Man at the pool, and a Saint looking up at a burning heart—There is also a little sketch for a large picture very beautiful—I should like to see these pictures of Murillo's placed beside some of the best of the Italian school—There is a Christ of Titian here & a picture by Sebastian del Piombo, but the former does not strike me as very good, & the latter is not of a style to admit the comparison—as it is, I have never seen a collection that appeared to me more curious & valuable—Returned to Sevres with Mrs. Story & her children who dined with us—the rest of the party, Kenny, Story & Doctor Yonge— Music at Vs. in the evening.

14 [Monday]—Went into town with Bessy in a Cuckoo & called to see our dear Anastasia who looked very well & (selon nous) very pretty— {afterwards called upon Mr. G. Moore—(it was by mistake I mentioned this as happening yesterday)—} afterwards went with Villamil to see a copy of Michael Angelo's Last Judgment, which at least enabled me to see more of the detail than I was before acquainted with. What a strange jumble to be called sublime! {observed now for the first time the devil pulling the fellow down by his testicles & a serpent biting off the penis of another.—} From thence I went to Made. de Broglie's, who has written to me to fix a day to meet M. Lafayette at dinner; he having expressed a great wish to know me—saw Miss Randall & fixed next Monday—Miss R. said how much she had been struck by the resemblance between Lord Byron's smile & Bonaparte's—from thence to Chabot's to see my Clock—found Lady

Isabella at home—the Clock very handsome—a figure of Homer playing on his lyre—must have cost, perhaps, near 30 Napoleons—too splendid for any room *I* shall ever have to put it in—dined at Lord Essex's—company, Lord Thanet, Fazakerly, Vaughan, Denon & Cornwall, Lord E's daughter & her Governess—Lord Thanet spoke to me a good deal of Sheridan—Sheridan very unfeeling about Richardson's death—when Lord T. spoke to him about it a fortnight after, as a melancholy thing, he said "yes—very provoking indeed, and all owing to that curst brandy & water, which he would drink"—when I mentioned Ss. want of scruple about stealing other people's wit, Lord T. said he might have made use of Molière's apology for the same practice—"C'est mon bien—et je le prends partout où je le trouve".—he said that Sheridan at no part of his life liked any allusion to his being a dramatic writer, and that, if he could have spoken out when they were burying him, he would have protested loudly against the place where they laid him—as Poet's Corner was his aversion—would have liked to be placed near Fox &c.—said that Lord John Townsend & (I think) Hare went to Bath for the purpose of getting acquainted with Mathews & making enquiries about his affair with Sheridan—{On their saying what a pretty women Mrs. Sheridan was, Mathews answered "yes—& the prettiest creature stripped you ever saw"—} Mathews described the Duel as a mere hoax—in fact as no Duel at all—that Sheridan came drunk & that he (Mathews) could have killed him with the greatest ease, if he had chosen—a precious fellow this Mathews was!—Lord T. said he thought that Sheridan never was the same man after Richardson's death—R.'s argumentative turn was of great use to him in stirring up his mind & making him sift thoroughly any new subject he took up—this is not improbable—Cornwall mentioned rather a good story of Sheridan's taking Dowton's gig to come to town, while Dowton with all the patience & sturdiness of a dun was waiting in the parlour to see him—Denon remarked of Murillo's Prodigal Son that the traces of gold are seen on the rags he wears & that the remains of his shirt are of the finest texture—Vaughan said that there are 72 Titians in the Escurial—arrived at La Butte at ¼ past ten—

{15 [Tuesday]—Wrote eighteen lines—walked with Villamil in the evening—}

16 [Wednesday]—12 lines—went to drink tea at Kenny's in the evening—took Irving, who called, with us—Kenny told a story of one Jim Welsh, who said—"Rot me, if I don't take a trip to France & rot me, if I don't begin immediately to study the language"—He got a grammar, dictionary & master, and after about 3 months study, thought himself qualified to undertake the journey—Just a little before he set out Daraset came up to him one day

& said "Eh bien, Monsr. Welsh, comment vous portez-vous?"—Jim stared—looked bothered—turned his eyes to right & left & at last exclaimed "now, rot me, if I han't forgot what that is."—Mrs. V. & I sung— {Bessy not at all well this evening.}

17 [Thursday]—Wrote six or eight lines—the Storys came out early for the purpose of seeing Puteaux, the late Duke of Faltre's place—a very agreeable morning—all dined at Villamil's—a hearty evening & laugh & La Fitte went round merrily—but poor Bess confined at home by bad cold— {Fazakerly & Morier called to-day while I was out}

18 [Friday]—{Bessy very ill to-day—} wrote some lines—walked in the evening.

19 [Saturday]—{Bessy somewhat better—} Villamil & I went in to Paris to see the Palais Royal—took Mrs. Story & Miss Morris with us—the Duke's Pictures not very good—some of them in the very worst French taste—by Picot, Coudry &c. &c.—Horace Vernet's Battle of Jemappes a poor thing— Two portraits by Philippe de Champagne of the Cardinal Richelieu & Mazarin struck me more than any thing I saw there—{we dined at Story's— a party of dull ones as usual—returned home a little after twelve—}

20 [Sunday]—Have done 70 lines since last Saturday (12th)—Wrote a few to-day—Dr. Williams came out & dined with us—Mrs. S. & Miss Morris after dinner to see Bessy, who is still far from well.

21 [Monday]—Bessy much better—this is the day I fixed with Made. de Broglie to meet Made. la Fayette at dinner—went in at two—received two letters from Lord Byron—in one of them he says that the lines on the Neapolitans which I sent him "are sublime as well as beautiful & in my very best mood & manner"—Company at the Duc de Broglie's, Lord & Lady Bessborough, Duc & Duchesse d'Alberg, Schlegel (Wm.), Count Forbin, M. de la Fayette, Auguste de Staël, the Swedish Ambassador &, to my {agreeable} surprize, {Lord John's love} (Made. Durazzo) of whom I have been hearing so much in all directions—a fine woman—must have been beautiful, not at all like an Italian—Sat next Miss Randal & had much talk about Lord Byron—She said Lord B. was much wronged by the world— that he took up wickedness as a subject, just as Chateaubriand did religion, without either of them having much of the reality of either feeling in their

hearts.—{She told me that Lady Davy once actually said to her—"well—you really ought to like me for you know I am considered the English Corinne." "Indeed (answered Miss R.) I was not aware of that—but words suffer so much by translation, it is not wonderful I should not have discovered it."}[1] Had much talk with Schlegel in the evening who appeared to me full of literary coxcombry—spoke of Hazlitt, who he said "l'avoit depassé" in his critical opinion and was an Ultra Shakespearean—is evidently not well inclined towards Lord Byron—thinks he will out-live himself, & get out of date long before he dies—asked me if I thought a regular critique of all Lord Bs. works & the system on which they are written would succeed in England & seems inclined to undertake it—found fault with the Edinburgh & Quarterly, for not being sufficiently European—(in other words, for not taking notice enough of M. Schlegel & his works)—Auguste de Stael in praising these journals said if there came a being, fresh from another planet, to whom he wished to give a clear & noble idea of the Arts, Literature, Philosophy &c. of this earth, he would present to him the Edinburgh Review—M. Schlegel seemed to think that this planetary visitant had much better come to *him* for information—Sung in the evening—Madame Durazzo perfectly well acquainted with all my Melodies, Irish & National— all seemed much pleased with my singing—the Duchesse de Broglie exclaiming continually "Oh Dieu—que c'est joli!"—Mr. Schlegel said I made the English language sound as soft as Italian—{slept at Story's—}

22 [Tuesday]—Wrote to Lord Byron—Mrs. S. set me as far as the Bois de Boulogne on my way home—

23 [Wednesday]—The Villamils gave a child's party in honour of their little Philip's birth-day. Nineteen little ones & about 13 adults sat down to dinner—we danced in the evening—villainous weather—

24 [Thursday]—Went into town—wrote 12 lines before I started & six in the Cuckoo going in—went with Villamil to see a collection of pictures that are to be sold—a beautiful little Kuyp & some good Ruysdaels—Irving & I went out in a Cuckoo & dined at Kennys—Villamil of the party.

25 [Friday]—Wrote 16 lines—Bessy went into town—I dined at Villamil's with Kenny & walked in the evening.

26 [Saturday]—{Nothing but rain—Bessy has caught fresh cold & the pain in her face has returned—} wrote some lines—have now done 80 this week

27 [Sunday]—Went in at two about Lady Davy's lodgings, she having written to Bessy to procure some for her—could not get a place back in consequence of the Fete of Sêvres & dined alone at Rosset's—came out at six—Mrs. Story & her children to tea & supper.

28 [Monday]—My birth-day!—they come too quick—Went in & breakfasted with Mrs. S.—got some money & came out with Fielding, young Talbot & Montgomery, who dined with me—Villamil & Kenny of the party—a very nice dinner (as all seemed to think) and the whole day agreeable. Fielding told us that when Gouvion St. Cyr, at the beginning of the Revolution, happened to go to some Bureau (for a Pass-port I believe) and gave his name "Monsieur de Saint Cyr"—the clerk answered him "Il n'y a pas de De"—"Eh bien, M. Saint Cyr,"—"Il n'y a pas de *Saint*"—"Diable, M. Cyr, donc." "Il n'y a pas de *Sire*—nous avons décapité le tyran"—wrote 8 lines to-day.

29 [Tuesday]—Walked about—a beautiful day—the first we have had for a long time—wrote 18 lines—{Younge came out to see Bessy—ordered leeches to be applied behind her ear—dined with us, as did Mr. & Mrs. Villamil—} Kenny mentioned yesterday, as a specimen of translation from the French, "a room furnished with fifteen Shepherdesses". (bergères)[1]

30 [Wednesday]—{Wrote 6 or 8 lines—} Engaged to dine with the Fieldings to-day—went in with Mrs. Story—met Fazakerly on the way who told me that Lord & Lady Holland were arrived—called upon them—a very gracious reception from my Lady—showed me a letter she had just received from Lord John Russel in which he talks of going to Spa, but she said with an air of triumphant certainty "don't mind that, however—as soon as he knows *we* are here, he will change his plan." {Rather a good joke mentioned in his letter—some one said upon Drummond the banker's mistress being brought to bed, that they supposed he was going to set up a new firm of Drummond, Hoare & Child—} The Hollands have taken the fine house of Madame Crawford—no company at Fieldings—talked of strange etymologies—Poltron from "pollici tronci" Soldiers who cut off their thumbs to avoid going to the wars—Topsy-turvey, topside t'other way—Hocus Pocus, hoc est corpus &c.—Pantaloon from Pianta Leone—a good punning one, Méchant (wicked) from mêche (a *wick*) &c.—a letter from Lord Byron to-day, with some more sheets of his Memoranda—postage 10 fs. 12 s.—came home in the gondola at nine. Two lines {that} I met {to day} in Athalie—how else than according to the "Cobler there was" can they be repeated?—

N'a pour *servir* sa *cause*, et veng*er* ses inj*ures*,
Ni le *coeur* assez *droit*, ni les *mains* assez p*ures*.[1]

{31 [Thursday]—Wrote some lines—dined at home—Mrs. S. came out in the evening—}

June 1st [Friday]—Went into Paris at two—saw a copy of the Memoirs de l'Académie[1] in 74 volumes (duodecimo) which I am much tempted to buy—gave 20 francs to secure it till tomorrow, and in the mean time shall make enquiries about it—price asked for it 74 francs—dined at Story's—a large party, of which the only good ingredients were Feilding, Irving, Villamil, and a nice, newly-arrived girl, Miss Lee—sat between her & Mrs. S.—sung in the evening—took leave of Feilding, who starts tomorrow for a year or two's tour to Switzerland & Italy—wished me to go on with them to Fontainbleau & pass Sunday with them there, but cannot—returned to La Butte at twelve.

2nd. [Saturday] Have written 72 lines this week—went in to dine with Lord Essex—called at Galignani's to look at the Manuel des Libraires for the Editions of the Memoirs—find that the Duodecimo is in 102 Vols. so, of course, shall not buy this incomplete one—went to the bookseller, and got my 20 francs back again—Company at Lord Essex's, Young, the actor, Lord Thanet, Standish, & Denon—Sung for Miss Capel & Denon in the evening—the latter said it was the first time he ever heard English made to sound like Italian—came home in the Celerifere at 9—

3rd. [Sunday] Employed to-day in corrections of the 3rd No. of National Melodies—had company to dinner—the Storys, Villamil & the Sapios—went all to Kenny's in the evening—Little Mary Villamil again alarmingly ill—

4 [Monday]—Wrote two or three additional verses to "Hymen once, his love-Knots selling"[1]—wrote letters to Lord Byron, Power, &c—a desperate wet day—read some of Belzoni's Egypt[2] before I went to bed—Kenny said that Antony Pasquin (who was a very dirty fellow) "died of a cold caught by washing his face"—

5 [Tuesday]—A large party asked to dine at Villamil's to-day—begged of him to let the dinner take place at our Cottage instead, as the alarming state

of the child would make it uncomfortable for him to have company at his house—but he preferred letting it remain as it was—Company there, the Storys, the Sapios, Dr. Williams, Wilder, Irving, Mr. Hinchcliffe, & Kenny after dinner—neither Bessy nor Mrs. Villamil came down—Wilder said that an Italian who was with him while he was dressing, upon his mentioning that he was coming to me, wrote all' improvista an Acrostic upon me, which he had forgot to bring, but would give me another time—In seeing Mrs. S. down to the Grille at night, she & I & Irving lost our way in the wood, and had a good deal of laughing before we got out of it again—Bessy resolved to sit up with little Mary tonight, who was evidently dying.

6 [Wednesday]—At about ¼ after ten this morning the poor little thing died—Bessy & Dr. Williams sat up with it the whole night and Bessy had it for six hours on her lap where, at last, it died—Williams said he never saw any thing like the strength of mind and indeed of body which Bessy showed throughout the whole time—This day altogether very gloomy—we dined with Villamil, & he & I & Williams walked in the evening.

7 [Thursday]—This day still more miserable than yesterday—the weather wretched, and the house comfortless & deserted, from Bessy being away all day with Mrs. Villamil—wrote a few lines

8 [Friday]—Had fixed to-day to dine with Lord Bristol to meet Made. de Genlis—felt very ill inclined to it from my spirits & the barometer both being low—However went in without having quite made up my mind—at near six o'clock sent an apology to Lord Bristol, dated from La Butte, but the stupid servant said I was in Paris which brought a note back again from his Lordship entreating me, if possible, to come—I, however, persisted in my caprice & dined at Story's—not quite right, for he is a most amiable man & deserved the effort—but the necessity of returning home at night, and having to walk, in thin shoes, up the wet road from the Celerifere to my cottage, is too great an operation to expect from any one—Left Paris at eight—

9 [Saturday]—Have written some 50 lines this week, and come to the conclusion of my 3rd Egyptian letter, which now consists of about 520 lines—{went in to assist Story by being his interpreter about some mal-entendu, with his Banker—dined by myself at Dupont's, & came out with Mrs. S. in the evening—}

10 [Sunday]—Wrote a Dedication & short Preface for the Letter-press Edition of the Irish Melodies[1]—the weather still of the worst kind

11 [Monday]—Copied out the Dedication & Preface, and revised some things for the appendix of the same work—went in at one—received from Wilder the Acrostic of his Italian friend—well enough for an Improviso— Bessy & Jane Power in town—all dined with the Storys—Major Henley mentioned a play of Racine's (of which I now forget the name) the commencement of which is very applicable to the history of Buonaparte[1]—Met Luttrel to-day, who is just arrived—find that he took unkind my not acknowledging the receipt of his Julia—a sad trick of mine this laziness about writing, {and gets me into more scrapes than almost any crime I could be guilty of—}

12 [Tuesday]—Reading over my notes about the Pyramids previous to beginning my 4th letter—the weather & spirits still bad—Read Belzoni &c.

13 [Wednesday]—Went in for the purpose of dining with the Hollands— called on Lady Bessborough—told me that, when she was a child, she was *en pension* at Versailles & used to be a good deal taken notice of by Marie Antoinette—spoke of the very striking air of dignity her countenance could assume—On one occasion when she (Lady B.) had been playing with her in the morning, there was to be a reception of Ambassadors, whom it was the custom for the Queen to receive sitting at the bottom of the bed—The child, anxious to see this ceremony hid herself in the bed-curtains and was so astonished & even terrified by the change that took place in the Queen's Countenance on the entrance of the Ambassadors that the feeling has never been forgotten by her to this hour—went from thence to Lady Granard, who told me that Lord Forbes is appointed one of the Aids-de-camp to accompany the King to Ireland—called afterwards at Made. de Souza's & found Lady Holland there—met Luttrel on the Boulevards & walked with him—in remarking rather a pretty woman who passed he said "The French women are often in the suburbs of beauty, but never enter the town".—Company at Lord Holland's, Allen, Henry Fox, the *black* Fox (attached to Embassy) {Allen}, Denon, and to my great delight Lord John Russel who arrived this morning—Lord Holland told before dinner (apropos of something) of a man who professed to have studied Euclid all through & upon some one saying to him "Well, solve me that problem"— answered "Oh, I never looked at the cuts"—Allen told me of a Mr. Henry Scott being now in Paris, who was a great friend of Sheridan's & could, he thinks, give me some information about him[1]—The dinner rather *triste* &

gêné both from Lord Holland's absence (being laid up with the gout) and Denon's presence—*one* foreigner always playing the deuce with a dinner-party—Luttrel set me down at Story's—slept there.

14 [Thursday]—Went to breakfast with Lord John—has brought me a copy of his last book "on the English Government & Constitution",[1] which is already going into a second Edition—was bearer of a letter from the Long-mans which makes me even more down-hearted than I have been for some days, as it shows how dilatory & indifferent all parties have been in the Bermuda negotiation, and how little probability there is of a speedy, or indeed any end to my exile—mentioned Scott having shown a letter from him acknowledging a copy "from the Author of Kenilworth"[2]—I expressed my doubts as to the probability of one man finding time for the research (to say nothing of the writing) necessary for accuracy in costume &c. &c. of such works—but he says they are only superficially or apparently correct—that, if looked closely into by a person conversant in antiquities & the history of the respective periods they abound in errors—that, Charles Wynne detected some gross ones in Ivanhoe; besides others, very trivial which the orthodox Charles was as much horrified at as the more serious ones—for instance—"only think what an unpardonable mistake Scott has fallen into about the Earl of Leicester (this must have been in Kenil-worth)—he has made him a Knight of St. Andrew, when he was, in reality, a Knight of St. Michael!"—or vice versâ, for I forget which way it was—came home in the Gondola to dinner. Villamil in the gout—sat with him in the evening.

{15 [Friday]—Wrote a little—}

16 [Saturday]—Have been able to do but about 35 lines this week—Mrs. Story came out to-day with her two little ones to pass some time with us—had also Dalton, Irving and Kenny to dinner—went to Vs. in the evening & had music—

17 [Sunday]—Wrote 22 lines—dined, all of us, at Villamil's—had walked before dinner with the children, &c—to the Lantern in St. Cloud—a lovely day.

18 [Monday]—Went in at one—dined at Story's with Miss Morris (the gov-erness) at 3 o'clock—Champagne in ice, fine strawberries &c. &c.—called

afterwards on Lord John Russel, who was about dressing to dine with Lord Stafford—told him all I thought of the wisdom, moderation & usefulness of his last work—he is to dine with us Thursday—came home in the Gondola at 8—Kenny & his wife supped with us—he told some very amusing stories about Lanza,[1] the composer and Reynolds who was about to write an Opera for him—"Have you done some oder littel tings, Mr. Reynolds?" "Oh yes—several"—"vat is one, par example"—"Oh it was I, who wrote "Out of Place" last winter"—"God d{am}—I hope dis will be better than dat"—The scene too at the Rehearsal of the Music, when to Lanza's despair, they were cutting it by pages full in the orchestra, & when little Simons, imitating Lanza's voice out of a corner, said "you may cut dere"— "who de devil say dat? no—no—cut! cut! nothing but cut—you will cut my troat, at last". Wrote eleven lines to-day.

19 [Tuesday]—Took a cold dinner to the Park of Bellevue—had all the children with us, and passed a very delightful day—wrote some lines before I went out.

20 [Wednesday]—Wrote sixteen lines, chiefly in sauntering about the Park of St. Cloud.—{Bessy gone into town to provide for tomorrow's dinner— Mrs. S., Jane Power & I dined together.}

21 [Thursday]—Wrote a few lines in the morning—Irving, who was to dine with me, came about two & brought the MS. of the work he is writing to read to me—which he did, sitting on the grass in the walk up to the Rocher—It is amusing, but will, I fear much, disappoint the expectation his Sketches have raised[1]—between 3 & 4 Lord John & Luttrel arrived and all walked together to Meudon—{I was telling Luttrel that the last time Madlle Garnerin went up in the balloon, it was said a fortnight after that she had never come down again—"in short, that she stayed upstairs"—"Handed out, I suppose (says Luttrel) by Enoch & Elijah"—} We were speaking of the pedantic phrases of Physicians—the word "exhibit" for instance—and he said that "exhibit" was chiefly used for mercury—"you *exhibit* mercury, *throw in* the bark, *premise* a venaesectio {&c. *celebrate* a clyster}." Villamil, Mrs. S. & Jane Power were our other diners—The dinner (the physique of it) was not as good as usual; but I made up in the wines—Chambertin, Champagne, Madeira, White Hermitage, Claret & Muscat.—in speaking of my abuse of the Americans, Irving said it was unluckily some of my best verses that were upon that subject—"put them in his *strongest pickle*" said

Luttrel. Lord John, in going, asked me to fix a day to dine with him & Fazakerly—fixed Thursday next.

22 [Friday]—Wrote and walked—Lord Granard & Lord Rancliffe called before dinner—asked them to come dine on Wednesday next—Lady Augusta Leith & Miss Morris & the Villamils dined with us to-day, and Kenny came after dinner.

23 [Saturday]—Have done between 80 & 90 lines this week—went in with J. Power & Mrs. Story at one—got 30 pounds at Lafitte's—called upon Lambton & Lady Louisa—{he said Allen has got the room that is called "the Chapel" in the Hollands' new residence, and, that for spite against the name, he makes all sort of filth & mess in it—} dined at Story's & returned with her & Jane in the evening—

24 [Sunday]—Wrote 32 lines to-day in bed & sauntering about—dined at home—to Villamil's in the evening

25 [Monday]—A large *diner champetre* given by the Villamils in the Park of Bellevue—the Storys, Kennys, Williams, Irving, Poole (the author of Hamlet Travesti) &c. &c.—pleasant enough—after Williams & I had sung one of the Irish Melodies, somebody said "Every thing that's national is delightful"—"Except the National Debt, Ma'am" says Poole—took tea at Villamil's & danced to the Piano-Forte—Wrote 13 or 14 lines before I went out—in talking of the organs in Gall's craniological system,[1] Poole said he supposed a drunkard had a barrel organ.—

{26 [Tuesday]—Wrote some lines—dined at home.}

27 [Wednesday]—Lady Davy called—asked her to stay to dinner, which she did—our company Lords Grannard & Rancliffe, Kenny, Irving, Mrs. Story, & Jane Power—Kenny said of Luttrel's "Advice to Julia" that it was too long and not *broad* enough—{"His story about the young Irish Lieutenant's notion of the profligacy of theatrical people, very ludicrous—"I suppose the curtain is not sooner down than they are all . . . . .[1] smack"—} Rancliffe said that the Chancellor is of opinion the Queen must be ad-

mitted to the Coronation dinner, if she claims it, & that they are inventing all sorts of large tureens &c. &c. to hide her from the King—{The Archbishop of Canterbury's consternation about the first words of the Anthem which he has to give out "His horns shall be exalted".}

28 [Thursday]—Wrote some lines & went into town with the Storys—called on the Hollands—both very gracious—wanted me to stay dinner, as my engagement with Lord John & Fazakerley was put off—but I had promised the S. to go the Fête at Beaujon in the evening—Lord H. praised Lalla Rookh very warmly and my Lady declared that in spite of her objection to Eastern Things, she must, *some time or other*, read it herself—said she also hated *Northern* subjects, which Lord H. remarked was unluckily [*sic*] as the only long poem he had ever written was in that region—spoke of Canning—Lord H. said he was not ill-tempered, but wrong-headed, and had "la main malheureuse", always contriving to turn the worst view of his conduct towards the public—that this arose very much from over-refinement and from aiming at high delicacy of sentiment &c.—{I mentioned *Mrs.* Cs. evident want of temper, & Lady H. said she believed they were not on the best terms together—that they had at one time, from Canning's frequent infidelities & the impatience with which she bore them, lived in a state of separation from each other; but, on his being wounded she came up to town & nursed him—that the reconciliation, however, was but hollow & feverish—} On my saying that Authors now did not keep their poems nine years,[1] Lord H. said "No—no—who is to pay the *interest* all the while?"—Asked me to dine on Monday—dined at Story's, & went to the Beaujon—all dull, except 4 or 5 flights I took in the Cars with Mrs. S.—{slept in town.}

29 [Friday]—Bessy came into town at twelve to pay visits, having hired a job for the purpose—found Lady Davy & Lady Charlemont at home—went thence to Lady Rancliffe's & the Granards, where we were let in also—called to see our darling Statia, who looked very well & pretty—Bessy returned home & I dined at Storys—{a large dinner—dull as ever—} returned at night with the Villamils—

30 [Saturday]—Have written between 80 & 90 lines this week—must begin to transcribe, there being now, in all, about 1400 lines of my Egyptian work written—called at Kenny's in the morning, and found he had gone to bed, in a pet, because somebody had taken away his ink-bottle—dined with Villamil—Kenny came in the evening & all supped & drank tea with us. Have transcribed some to-day.

July 1. [Sunday]—Transcribed—dined at home—walked with Bessy &c. through St. Cloud in the evening, to look for a spot for our Diner Champetre next Wednesday.

2 [Monday]—Went into town early—called on the Lockes, who are arrived—took Irving to present him to the Hollands—my Lady very gracious to him—Lord John there—I had told him that Villamil meant to translate his last work into Spanish for the enlightenment of his countrymen, and find he is much pleased at the intention[1]—Lord Holland said there might be some useful notes added to the translation, containing hints to the Spaniards on the improvement of their present institutions &c. &c.—mentioned, as an instance of the foppery of the French about their language that an author some time since writing a play on the subject of Philipe le Bel, where the word *monnaie* must of necessity be introduced, found after consulting the chief literary men of his acquaintance, that it was impossible to introduce that word in the full dress of poetry, and accordingly found himself compelled to give up the plan altogether—quere—whether Cash is not subject to the same difficulty—Lord H. doubted that Cash was a legitimate English word, though, as Irving remarked, it is as old as Ben Jonson, there being a character called Cash in one of his comedies[2]—Lord H. said that Mr. Fox was of opinion that the word *mob* was not genuine English—{went from thence with Lord John to call on Fazakerley & Madame Durazzo—she, not looking so well as when I first saw her—} appointed to dine with Lord John at Riche's—went to Lady Mildmay for the MS. of Lord Byron I had lent her to read—sat some time with her—mentioned how much she felt afraid of Lord Byron, when she used to meet him in society in London, and that once, when he spoke to her in a door-way her heart beat so violently that she could hardly answer him—she said it was not only her awe of his great talents, but the peculiarity of a sort of *under* look he used to give that produced this effect upon her—separated from Lord John about eight, and returned in the Parisienne with Mrs. S. & Jane at nine—Lord John means to come & take a bed with us, at the Pavillion we had last summer.

3 [Tuesday]—Transcribed—& went in at three—dressed at Story's, where Luttrel called to take me to dinner to Lord Holland's—had met Morier, who offered to take me in the evening to Monsr. L'angles' Conversazione—Company at the Hollands', Lambton, Lady Louisa & her sister, Lord Alvanly, Lord John, Lattin, Lord Thanet, Lord Gower &c.—Talking of Delille,[1] Lord H. said that notwithstanding his pretty description of Kensington Gardens, he walked with him once there & he did not know then when he was in them—Madame de Stael never looked at any thing—

passed by scenery of every kind without a glance at it—which did not however prevent her describing it—I said that Lord Byron could not describe any thing which he had not had actually under his eyes, and that he did it either on the spot or immediately after—this, Lord Holland remarked, was the sign of a true Poet—to write only from *impressions*—but where then do all the imaginary worlds of Dante, Milton &c. go, if it is necessary to see what we describe, in order to be a true poet?—Lattin mentioned that Gail, the old Greek Professor here, who was a great friend of Delille's, embalmed him after his death and varnished him, and making a horrible figure of the poor poet put a wreath of laurel round his head. Lord Holland mentioned having once been betrayed into {paying him} a most exaggerated compliment, in saying that Virgil was lucky in meeting a poet a great as himself to translate him—to which Delille answered "Savez vous, milord, que ce que vous dites là, est joli—mais très joli"—Before dinner, on my remarking to Luttrel a fine effect of sunshine in the garden, which very soon passed away, he said "how often in life we should like to arrest our beaux momens—should be so obliged to the *five* minutes, if it would only stay ten {minutes}".—Allen, on our talking of persons, who described what they had not seen, said that Adam Smith never attended to any thing that was said in conversation and *yet* (or rather perhaps *because* he did not attend) used to give the most delightful & amusing accounts of all that had been said, filling up the few outlines his ear had caught from his own imagination—talked of the numerous editions of Voltaire now printed—(by the bye, Gallois mentioned the other day as an instance of the great increase of printing & publishing—that in Marmontel's life-time they did not venture to publish a complete edition of his works but printed the popular things separate from the rest, in order to facilitate the sale & that it took a long lapse of time even so to sell off the whole, whereas within some years past a collection of all his works (including the Theatre which nobody ever reads) has gone off not only successfully, but rapidly—he granted however that reading has not increased in proportion, but that books are become more an article of furniture & luxury than of study)—Lord Holland said that Lord Exeter burned his copy of Voltaire at the beginning of the French Revolution & that he had been told Lord Grenville had actually turned his copy out of his library at the same time—went with Fazakerly & Morier to Mr. Langles'—a dingy set of savans there—Mr. Langles very civil to me—talked of Lalla Rookh—offered {me} the use of his Library &c. &c.—introduced to Mr. Jullien, editor of the Revue Encyclopèdique,[2] who said he was about to write a detailed article upon my works, their character &c. &c.—was afterwards introduced to a Mr. B{achon (I think)} who addressed me in poetical prose, said he had *soupirè* after me for a long time—that he {had} last summer wandered through the country which I had immortalized by my Melodies—"Je n'y pensois qu'a vous—je vous demandois aux rochers &c. &c."—was rather bored by the whole thing & heartily glad to escape—Slept at Story's—

4 [Wednesday]—Came out early in the Gondola—Had asked a large party to a dinner in the woods to-day, but the weather so bad, that the cold meat must be eaten within doors—Lady Susan Douglas & the Drews came out early, in order to see the Sevres Manufactory—escorted them thither.—our company at dinner, they, the Forsters with our dear Anastasia, Dalton, the Storys, &c.—merry enough—sung & danced in the evening—

5 [Thursday]—Went in early with Villamil for the purpose of introducing him to Lord Holland—much talk about Spanish politics, on which subject Lord H. & Allen are very much interested—walked about the garden with them—dined at Morier's—Company, M. Langles, Denon, Pozzo di Borgo, Hamilton [(the secretary, author of the Egyptian) & his family, Fazaker-ley—Hamilton very much of the Jack in office—& Bankes, I am told, says his book is full of mistakes, which what I saw of the man makes me rather rejoice at—][1] Pozzo di Borgo very complimentary to me on my introduction to him—much talk about Egypt—a curious matter of speculation to trace the source from which she derived her knowledge & civilization—could not have been from the East by the Red Sea, because it is evident it proceeded immediately from *Upper* Egypt, a course it could not have got into upon this supposition—it must have been from Abyssinia, and the Interior of Africa, which bewilders the mind but to think of—the Interior of Africa! how little we really know of {the History of} this world! In talking of Soult's pictures, on my mentioning that I heard he wished to sell them, Pozzo di Borgo said that if so, he should be happy to treat with him for them for his master the Emperor—that he had made some very good purchases in Paris—among these the Gallery of Malmaison, which he had bought, I think for seventy thousand pounds—in this Collection was the Cupid & Psyche of Canova—In the evening a Frenchman came in who had dined with the Minister of Foreign Affairs, & brought the intelligence, that Bonaparte had died on the 5th of May—Pozzo di Borgo, in talking to me of the news said it was a "triste catastrophe", and that, in spite of every thing, he could not help feeling a "sentiment de tristesse" at it—{sensibility from Pozzo de B. is somewhat *too* good a joke—}He asked me if I was at work upon any subject & trusted I would not remain idle—Went from thence in Fazakerley's cabriolet to the Opera, to join the Forbes's, who had given me a ticket for their box—heard a few scenes of Don Juan & then joined Villamil, whose carriage took us home at twelve o'clock.

6 [Friday]—Busy preparing the Pavillon for Lord John—our company to dinner, Lord Granard, Lady Adelaide, Lady Caroline, Lord John, Luttrel, Fazakerley & Villamil—the day very agreeable—Luttrel in good spirits, & highly amusing—told of an Irishman who having jumped into the water, to save a man from drowning, upon receiving six-pence from the person as a

reward for the service, looked first at the six-pence, then at him; and at last exclaimed "by Jasus, I'm *over* paid for the job"—Lord John told us that, Bobus Smith one day in conversation with Talleyrand having brought in somehow the beauty of his mother, {& bored Talleyrand for a good while with his description & praising of her} T. {at last} said "C'étoit donc votre pere qui n'étoit pas bien." "It was your father, then that was not good-looking".—went up in the evening to Villamil's & had music—she sung some of her Boleros to the guittar, which delighted Fazakerley exceedingly—-By the bye, I yesterday gave Lady Holland Lord Byron's Memoirs to read, and on my telling her that I rather feared he had mentioned her name in an unfair manner, she said "such things give me no uneasiness—I know perfectly well my station in the world—and I know all that can be said of me—as long as the few friends that I really am sure of speak kindly of me (and I would not believe the contrary if I saw it in black & white) all that the rest of the world can say is a matter of complete indifference to me"—there are some fine points about Lady Holland—she is a warm & active friend, & I should think {even} capable of *high-mindedness* upon occasions—{Lord John stayed to sleep—}

7 [Saturday]—This week has been one of pure & unmixed idleness—have done absolutely nothing—so much at the beck of every one that chuses to have me—Had asked the Lockes to come out to-day to see the Sèvres Manufactory (of which I am now, I think, become the Concierge) and dine with us—accordingly they came with three children & a governess—Lord John wisely did not join our party, but sauntered about by himself till dinner at which time Kenny {also} joined us, making altogether 12—some agreeable conversation in the evening, after the company was gone—

8 [Sunday]—A proof that Lord John feels himself comfortable is that he has begun another book this morning—the subject, the French Revolution, or rather a Sketch of this long series of misrule & profligacy in the upper orders that led to it & made it necessary—It will, I have no doubt, be amusing because he means to found it upon anecdotes drawn from the French Memoirs, & it will be useful, as reminding those people who now talk of nothing but "the horrors of the French Revolution" that there were the horrors antecedent to it which must, in fairness, be taken into the account—dined at Lord Granard's, who had persuaded us to transfer our Restaurateur Dinner (fixed for to-day) to his house—Company, besides Fazakerley, Lord John, Luttrel and myself, Colonel Palmer, Mrs. Rawdon & one or two more—The usual clouds hung about the dinner, notwithstanding some of the materials—Lord John drove me to the Gondola office & I arrived at home at nine—

9 [Monday]—Irving came to breakfast, for the purpose of taking leave (being about to set off for England) and of reading to me some more of his new work—some of it much livelier than the first he read—he has given the description of a bookseller's dinner so exactly like what I told him {laughingly} of one of the Longman's (the carving partner, the partner to laugh at the popular author's jokes, the twelve-edition writers treated with claret &c.) that I very much fear my friends in Pater-noster Row will know themselves in the picture[1]—went with Villamil to dine with General Fuller at Versailles—a party of Ultras—high dispute about Spain with Villamil, in which two or three coxcomb Frenchmen exhibited their usual ill-breeding & mummery—sung a little in the evening—

10 [Tuesday]—Wrote about twenty lines—went in to dine at Lord Holland's, Villamil being unable to go, from the gout—Company, Lord John, Fazakerley, Irving & Allen—Left them at nine, & came out in Villamil's carriage alone at 11—Kenny & Irving set off together for England tomorrow—Lord John mentioned to me some verses written upon Lalla Rookh, he did not say (nor, I believe, know) by whom, but not amiss—{they are by Sneyd}

> Lalla Rookh
> Is a book
> By Thomas Moore
> Who has written four,
> Each warmer
> Than the former,
> So that the most recent
> Is the least decent.

11 [Wednesday]—Breakfasted at Villamil's to meet the Marquis Santa Cruz & his family—very amiable persons—am much inclined to think with Lord Holland that the Spaniards altogether are among the best people of Europe—A good deal of talk with the Marquis—he says Spain, whatever she may suffer or do, will not retrograde in Liberty—told me of the reception which the Comte d'Artois gave the other day to Torreno, the Spanish Minister to Berlin—he hardly looked at him when introduced by Santa Cruz but turning abruptly round to the Prussian Minister said "J'espere que vous serez content du ministre que nous venons d'envoyer chez vous—(meaning Chateau-briand)—au moins, il ne revolutionnera pas votre pays"—this is worse than foolish—wrote some lines and took a late dinner with Villamil—dear Statia passed this day with us—and returned with Mrs. Forster in the evening.

12 [Thursday]—Lost great part of the day in letter-writing &c.—dined at home—

13 [Friday]—Wrote something—went in at five to join the Villamils at Riche's, for the purpose of attending Mrs. Forster's musical party in the evening—the Storys went with us—Madlle Naldi sung very charmingly—Mrs. V. & I much teazed to sing, but both refused—too many foreigners & professors—home about twelve.

14 [Saturday]—Wrote a little—went into town at 4 to dine at Lord Holland's—company Lord Gower, Duc de Broglie, Dumont of Geneva, Lord John &c. Lord Holland said that Cheltenham waters are manufactured every morning for the drinkers & are *not* natural—some pleasant conversation with Lord Holland in the evening—he said that Apreece (the Cadwallader of Foote)[1] had a trick of sucking his wrist every now & then with a sort of supping noise, in which Foote exactly imitated him—upon this farce coming out, Apreece went to Garrick for the purpose of consulting him as to the propriety of challenging Foote for the insult but all Garrick said was was "my dear Sir, don't think of doing any such thing—why, he would shoot you through the guts before you had supped two oysters off your wrist"—spoke of Foote's Farces—"Witty, but wrong" in Smirke, which Foote used to say so well[2]—Lord H. said to-day that Mr. Fox was always an advocate for the mode of raising money by lotteries maintaining it was a just tax upon vanity & avarice—Lord H. however added laughing, that he believed the opinion rather arose from his uncle's strong passion for play in general—came out in a Cuckoo at ½ past nine—Villamil is getting on with his translation of Lord John's book—has bought, for the purpose, Father Conolly's Dictionary, which Lord Holland however says is a very bad one—heard to-day that Rogers is dangerously ill.

15 [Sunday]—Have written this week 70 lines—went in for the purpose of passing two or three days with the Storys—miserable wet day—S. & I went to Feydeau in the evening—Jean de Paris a very pleasant little piece.[1]

16 [Monday]—Went to the Chamber of Peers to hear sentence passed on the persons lately tried for a conspiracy[1]—sat with Dumont—dined altogether at Hardy's, with the addition of Dalton & Capt. Arbuthnot—chose them an excellent dinner—a Ball at Story's in the evening, in honour of her birth-day—a strange sort of evening, from various reasons—Bessy did not appear, not feeling well enough & fearing to bring on the Erysipelas again

by dancing—I danced quadrilles all night with Misses Drew, Pigot, Chichester, Arthur &c.—the supper very magnificent—did not get to bed till five o'clock.

17 [Tuesday]—Called upon the Granards &c. dined at Ss. & went to Tivoli in the evening—a true summer's night—bought a little set of books to-day, the Encyclopedie Poetique.

18 [Wednesday]—Called upon Gallois, who told me that he had just seen a pamphlet in prose professing to be "traduit de l'Anglais de Sr. Thomas Moore" on the death of Bonaparte, with an ode on the same subject annexed as written by Lord Byron[1]—an audacious catch-penny—but it is something that one's name can *furnish* a catch-penny in Paris—came out to Sevres at 3—a dinner-party at Villamil's—Lord John, Fazakerley, Luttrel, Lady Davy, Gallois & Ora, (a Spaniard)—the day very agreeable—Talking with Luttrel of religion before dinner, he mentioned somebody having said upon being asked what religion he was "Me! I am of the religion of all sensible men"—"and what is that?"—"Oh—sensible men never tell". He mentioned too, at dinner, a good sort of *sham* problem—"Given the tonnage of the ship, and the course she is upon—required, the name of the captain".—Singing in the evening—Ora sang to the guitar some thoroughly *Spanish* Songs—

19 [Thursday]—Gallois dined with Lord John & me—began this morning something for Power—words to an Air of my own which I mean to pass as National—

20 [Friday]—Villamil rode with Lord John in the morning—all dined with me.

21 [Saturday]—Went into town early in order to get Bessy's pass-ports, take her places &c.—dined (Lord John & I) at Villamil's—Dalton of the party—all I have done this week is a verse or two of a song for Power.

22 [Sunday]—Drove into town with Bessy at three—dined at Story's and came out at eight in the evening.

23 [Monday]—All in a bustle preparing for Bessy's departure—went in to provide money for the dear girl—dined at Story's—Dalton of the party—Bessy arrived with her trunks in the evening.

24 [Tuesday]—Could not sleep all night with anxiety about the morning's operations—{Bessy came into my bed about five—} all up & ready in time—saw her comfortably off at nine o'clock with Jane Power, Hannah & dear little Tom. Heaven guard her!—breakfasted at Very's and returned to Ss. to dress—made some visits to Made. Durazzo, Luttrel, the Bushes &c.—dined at Lord Holland's—Company, Ellis (Lord Cleveden's son) Mr. Sneyd (who, I find is the author of those verses on Lalla Rookh), Sir Charles Stuart, Lord John &c.—Ellis{, ridiculous in his imitation of Ward's manner—but} rather clever—{Mr. Sneyd in very bad t[*unrecovered*]t indeed—} had some very delightful conversation with Lord Holland after dinner—told me some highly amusing anecdotes about Doctor {Jebb}, a matter-of-fact Irish atheist, resident in France during the Revolution, who, Lord H. thinks, was mainly instrumental in heating Burke's imagination about that event, by writing letters to him in which he claimed for himself & brother atheists the whole credit of bringing it about. Burke believed him, & saw nothing thenceforth but atheism & all sorts of horrors at the bottom of it.—Lord H's memory of the man's manner—of his boast of proselytism among his patients "at those moments when the solemnity of their situation made their minds more open to the truth"—of his rising in a French coffeehouse, where some one had expressed doubts whether ever any man was really an atheist, and saying gravely "Monsieur, j'ai l-honneur de l'etre—non seulement je ne crois pas qu'il y ait un Dieu—mais je le sais et je le prouve" &c. &c. all was irresistibly comical & made me laugh as heartily as ever Liston did.—Sir C. Stewart afterwards joined us—talked of Foreign Ministers—their difficulty sometimes in making out their materials for dispatches—the Prussian government requires of its ministers to turn at least the first page—It appears that England manufactures at present a much greater quantity of silk than France.—Slept at Story's—

25 [Wednesday]—Called upon Lattin, who showed me the room which he destines for me in his house—a little dark, dirty bathing-room—I'll none of it—Went to the Granards, Lady Adelaide walked with me to Lord Rancliffe's, and ordered *his* bed-room to be prepared for me whenever I chose to come into town, Rancliffe himself having just gone to England—{great boot between this & Lattin's—} called at the Holland's—my Lady just going out to drive & offered to take me as far as the Bois de Boulogne on my way to Sèvres—Went thence to Galignani's to beg him to get a contradiction for the pamphlet imputed to me & Lord Byron into one of the French Jour-

nals—by the bye, forgot to mention that yesterday morning at the Louvre (whither I went for the purpose of seeing the fine statue discovered at Milo) I met Comte Forbin & Gerard the painter, who spoke of this *brochure* & advised me to contradict it in the French papers—came out in the Gondole at four with Williams & dined at Villamils—a party of foreigners, Spanish & German, rather amusing—slept at home.

26 [Thursday]—Wrote some letters, a verse or two of a Song &c. & went into town at two—called upon Benjamin Constant, to beg he would use his interest with some of the French papers to have the Brochure contradicted—he said no one believed it to be ours[1]—dined at Lattin's, Company Lords Holland, John Russel, Thanet & Trimlestown, Messrs. Maine de Biron & Denon, Luttrel, & Concannon—abundance of noise & Irish stories from Lattin—some of them very good—a man asked another to come & dine off boiled beef & potatoes with him—"That I will" says the other "and it's rather odd it should be exactly the same dinner I had at home for myself—*barring the beef*"—Some one using the old expression about some light wine he was giving, "There's not a head-ache in a hogshead of it" was answered "No—but there's a belly-ache in every glass of it."—In talking of the feeling of the Irish for Bonaparte, Lattin said that when he was last in Ireland, he has [*sic*] been taken to a secret part of the cabbin by one of his poor tenants, who whispered "I'll know *you'll* not betray me Sir—but just look there & tell me whether that's the *real thing*" pointing to a soi-disant portrait of Bonaparte, which was neither more nor less than a print of Marshal Saxe[2] or some such antient—[As an instance of ignorance of agriculture, he mentions some cockney farmer having said to a person who had purchased his turnips & asked whether he should send his sheep into the grounds to eat them—"No—No—I have no idea of letting your sheep go sh-tt--g about my lawn]". Denon told an anecdote of a man who, having been asked repeatedly to dinner by a person, whom he knew to be but a shabby Amphytrion, went at last & found the dinner so meager & bad that he did not get a bit to eat—when the dishes were removed, the Host said "Well—now the ice is broken {(la glace est rompue)} I suppose you will ask *me* to dine with you some day"—"most willingly"—"name your day then"—"aujourd'hui, par exemple" answered the dinner-less guest—Lord Holland told of a man, remarkable for absence, who dining once at the same sort of shabby repast, fancied himself in his own house & began to apologize for the wretchedness of the dinner— {Some of Ls. stories not recordable—The fragment of a Song Paddy [*unrecovered*], the priest, used to preach to the people, That a _____ like a church wants a _____ like a steeple. Green's answer to a person that asked "who was that young lady dancing down?" "That young lady, Sir, if she _____ _____ _____ would be my eldest son"—his speech, too at the Salon

about the two fives that turned up— "There they are, as black as the Pope's
_____." The story too about "Lift up that [*unrecovered*]"—"What am I to
lift?"—"Lift your _____that I may _____"[3]—Lord Trimleston mentioned
a man discussing gravely the consequences of different vices, and saying of
a certain one how hard it was that it is merely "zag-zag-zag-zag et l'âme est
donnée."—} Luttrel told of a good phrase of an attorney's in speaking of a
reconciliation that had taken place between two persons, whom he wished
to set by the ears—"I am sorry to tell you, Sir, that a compromise has
broken out between the parties"—Taking with Lord Holland about George
Lamb's translation of Catullus, I mentioned how beautifully Cowley had
done some parts of the Acme & Septimius—

> While on Septimius' panting breast,
> Meaning nothing less than rest.[4]

Upon which Lord H. said he would have sworn that this second line was my
own—{Remarked what an odd task, considering all things, the translating
of Atys was for poor George Lamb.—} Slept at Rancliffe's—

27 [Friday]—Breakfasted at Lord Granard's—called afterwards on the
Miss Berrys—Miss Berry employed about some work which will make it
necessary for her to come & live in France—Having a private opportunity
to Lord Byron sent him his (supposed) ode upon Napoleon's death, & a
ridiculous engraving of him {standing} upon a Rocher, in order "that he
might see what justice they do to his mind & body here"—came out to
Sevres at four—dined with Villamil—Williams of the party—slept at the
Pavillon—Got a letter in the evening from my darling Bessy, who had
arrived safe at Calais & gives the following laconic description of her fellow-travellers—"Little Tom on the way was delightful—Jane, very quiet—
poor Hannah very sick—the Gentleman very gentlemanly—& the Lady (*I*
think) a Lady's maid"—Received also a letter from Murray consenting to
give me Two thousand guineas for Lord Byron's memoir's, on condition
that in case of survivorship, I should consent to be the Editor.

28 [Saturday]—A day of incessant rain—home very, very dull—copied out
three songs to send to Power, and wrote a little of a fourth—dined with the
Villamil's—received a note from Miss Drew to join their party to Versailles
tomorrow—

29 [Sunday]—Went with the Douglas's to Versailles—a fine day, but a very
dull one—

30 [Monday]—Another letter from my darling Bessy, who has arrived safe at Dover—went into town saw dearest Anastasia in my way—called at the Hollands—asked me to dine, and though I went in with the determination of being free for the evening, I consented—Frere's brother, just arrived from Constantinople—told us something about the Turks but very muddily, and as if he had been himself dosed among them with opium—drove about a little with Mrs. S.—Somebody told at dinner of a little French boy from college saying, when his father remonstrated with him upon some insubordination or waywardness he had been guilty of—"Mais, Papa, il faut marcher avec son siecle"—Lady H. showed me some verses Lord Holland had written to her in English & Latin upon the subject of Napoleon's gift—some lines of Lord John's, too—she said *I* must do something of the same kind, and wished she could have a few lines from Lord Byron too to add to her triumph—Lord Holland's verses chiefly turn upon the circumstance of the box having been originally given to Napoleon by the Pope for his clemency in sparing Rome.—Frere objected to the last line of the Latin[1]—went about nine o'clock to Story's.

31 [Tuesday]—Made two sets of verses to Lady H. about the box, before I got out of bed, but did not write them down—called upon her, with the intention of breakfasting, but she looked so out of temper that though I sat down to the table, yet, as no one asked me to partake of what was going on, did not venture to say that I had not breakfasted—went, for that purpose, to Rosset's, the Restaurateur—idled about Paris—dined at Douglas's—Sir John Gifford & young Murray of the party.—Went to the Opera to join Lady Holland, who {had} asked me in the morning—pretended to think her box full & came away again—returned to Douglas's & took Lucy to Tortoni's to have ice.

August 1 [Wednesday]—Found Rogers was arrived—drove about a little with Mrs. S. & called upon Rogers at four—his sister & niece with him—received me most cordially, and I truly happy to see him again—Staid with him till it was time to dress for dinner at the Hollands—Company there, Lord Thanet, Lord John, Gallois, the two young Foxes &c. &c.—Somebody mentioned that Canning had said upon Ward's late tirade in the house against Austria "Then, I suppose, lodgings are very bad & dear at Vienna"—Lady H. read me a letter from Lord William Russel at Spa in which he mentions that the Grand Duchess of Russia is there & that she always carries about with her two copies of Lalla Rookh most splendidly bound & studded with precious stones—one of which he had seen—In the evening came Benj. Constant, Casimer Perrier (a very good looking man) Lord Alvanley &c.—Lady Holland proposed to Rogers & me to drive out with her on the Quays—a triste operation, in a shut-up carriage, at the rate of a mile an hour, {& my Lady not in the most *companionable* mood—} as soon I could escape, went to Tortonis & refreshed myself with an ice.

2 [Thursday]—Breakfasted at Lord Granard's—called upon Rogers—Luttrel with him—Luttrel said, {(in speaking of a sort of half matrimonial establishment of his which he has confided to me)} that he has all his life had a love for domestic comforts, though passing his time in such a different manner "like that King of Bohemia, who had so unluckily a taste for navigation though, condemned to live in an inland town"—walked about the Tuilleres gardens for an hour & half with Rogers—sarcastic & amusing, as usual. dined at the Storys—The company not worth enumerating, though amounting to about 15 dull souls in all—Went in the evening to Tivoli.

3 [Friday] Rogers having proposed to come out to the Pavillon to-day with his sister bustled away early with a pigeon-pye & some other provisions for the dinner—took up a pretty Dutch girl in my cuckoo, who deals in shawls & gave me her history—With the assistance of Mallard, the Traiteur, & Mrs. Villamil made out a very respectable Bill of Fare—the Rogerses arrived before two & went with me to Meudon & the Sevres Manufactory—our dinner very lively & agreeable—Villamil & Lord John of the party—Lord John slept in the little Pavillon—Rogers quite distressed at hearing from me that Lord Byron had just finished a Tragedy on the story of Foscari;[1] {as that story forms one of the chief gems in Rogers's long-meditated poem upon Italy.}

4 [Saturday]—{Lord John mentioned an Epigram written by Erskine in court on its being decided that a kick came under the meaning of the words "molliter manus imposuit—

A kick from the foot, direct in the anus,
The Court has just rul'd to be "molliter manus".}

Lord John went into Paris to prepare for his journey to Switzerland with Ward, a large dinner at Villamils—the Storys, McCleods, Dalton, a Mr. Wilks, a Dissenter who lives at Belle-Vue, author of a work on the Persecution of the French Protestants,[1] Capt. Arbuthnot &c. &c.—Mr. McCleod told Dalton that he had, himself, heard Walter Scott say that the Fire-Worshipers[2] is the best poem written by any of the living poets—*can* this be true?—music with Mercer & his sister in the evening.

5 [Sunday]—A sultry day—felt heavy & feverish, partly from taking too warm a bath—did but little—dined with Villamil, after a walk to St. Cloud to see the waters play—wrote a verse of a Song for Power.

6 [Monday]—Went into town with Villamil—called on the McCleods in order to fix a day for them to take me to Coulon's dancing school, to see the new Spanish dancer, of whose beauty & grace so much is said—dined at the Cadran Bleu with Rogers, his sister & niece & Lord John—Lord John has again given up his idea of leaving Paris, and means to come out to La Butte—rather inconvenient this, as the attendant Bessy has left me in the Cottage turns out to be a stupid, drunken, dawdler—This morning too our former Cook sent me a most earnest & well-written letter, telling me she had a good place offered, but that she preferred mine to any she ever lived in, that if I would take her back now, she would be most happy, or if I chose to wait till Bessy's return, she would come to us from the best place {in Paris at a minute's notice}—It is unlucky I have declined this as she would be most useful to me just now—all our party went in the evening to the Porte St. Martin to see the Solitaire[1]—Slept at Rancliffe's—a letter to-day from Bessy, who is safe in Wiltshire

7 [Tuesday]—Breakfasted at Story's—Had my little Anastasia in from Mrs. Forster's to show her to the Rogers's—walked her about a little afterwards, and met several of my acquaintances, who seemed to admire the dear girl a good deal—bought her a little French book—Mrs. Story took me in her carriage to pay a visit to Bowditch (the Ashantee man)[1] who has sent me a whole heap of his new publications—an immense journey off to the Quartier de Jardin des Plantes. One ought to be as great a voyager as himself to visit him—showed me the specimens of fossils which they are liberal enough to lend him from the Museum for the Lithographic drawings of his books on Natural History—dined with Rogers & his sister at Beauvilliers— {he said of a table prepared near us with the quantity of bread which they lay on the plates that "it looked like the Last Supper"—} they went to the Francais afterwards and I to Otello[2]—fine effects of harmony in this Opera and a few touches of feeling—such as Otello's "Si—dopo lei morrò" and the scene where Desdemona hears the Gondolier singing "nessun maggior dolore"—this whole scene very romantically imagined—

8 [Wednesday]—Asked to breakfast with the Hollands' this morning, (as I had been to dinner yesterday), but went to breakfast with Rogers, {whom it is necessary to keep in good-humor, if possible—find he is quite angry at the idea of my going out to Sevres with Lord John, while he stays—must

therefore return to him tomorrow]—Have been lucky enough to get my Cook back—Went to Chevet's to buy a pye towards my dinner at home to-day—Perdreaux aux truffles—gave 13 franks for it—Mrs. Villamil however, just came to town, says they expect Lord John & me to dine with them, which will be more convenient—called on the Hollands—Wrote out for Lady H. one of the sets of verses which I made upon Napoleon's gift to her, & which she seemed to like very well—Lord John drove me out to Sevres in his Cabriolet—dined with Villamil—[It is quite worrying to think how completely my time & thoughts are sacrificed to the unreasonable selfishness of others.—] By the bye, there have been lately some attacks upon me in the Courier, & a Defence in the Chronicle—the former, however, far more flattering than the latter, as bestowing warm praise in the midst of its censure—[I] suspect Croker of it.

9 [Thursday]—The Villamils were to have had a party to the Woods to-day, but the excessive rain made it impossible—Some of the invited however came—Capt. Arbuthnot & the McCleods—Lord John eat his boiled chicken alone in the little Pavillon—I dined with Villamil—went in at night to meet Rogers & his sister, by appointment, at Beaujon—but they were not there—went down the cars ten or twelve times with the young Scotch girl—Slept at Rancliffe's.

10 [Friday]—Breakfasted with Rogers—went afterwards to the Louvre with him—the nose of the new statue from Milo badly restored, which gives the face in some aspects an air of coarseness & vulgarity—but a very fine thing—would much rather have it than the lanky Diana—R. spoke depreciatingly of Chauntry & Canova—said Gerard's Henry 4th. was "like a tin-shop", which is true—a hard glitter about it—explained to me what is called breadth of light by Correggio's picture of the Nymph & Satyr—beautiful hands in one of the female portraits of Leonardo Da Vinci—Went to Denon's—his meeting with Rogers very comical—kissing him &c. &c.—the sweet character of his heads by Giambellino [(Q.E.E.)] on a gold ground—dined with Miss Rogers & the niece, R. being engaged to Lord Stafford's, and went to see Talma in Neron—the announcement of the catastrophe in long, dull speeches most tame & uninteresting—The touching exclamation "Oh ciel, sauvez Britannicus" given very coldly by Bourgoin[1]—supped at Mrs. Story's.

11 [Saturday]—Breakfasted with Rogers—a letter from my darling Bessy, who is about to leave Wiltshire for Derbyshire—dined with Rogers ([a] diner de commande) [& his sister, Luttrel of the party—the day not very

bright—Luttrel evidently constrained & out of sorts & Rogers as bad & disinterested—]—Went in the evening to Don Juan—

12 [Sunday]—Breakfasted at Tortoni's & went afterwards to see the new opera House—a rehearsal going on—Went at one o'clock, a large party of us, to see Soult's pictures—Lady Holland, Made. Durazzo & her husband, Lord Clare, Ellice (Lord Clifden's son) the Rogerses &c. &c.—was anxious to see whether this collection would conquer the prejudice R. has against Murillo—he confessed he never before had such a high idea of this master, but still saw all the faults of his manner, the want of strength & decision, the florid colouring, the undignified & ordinary nature of his figure & faces, &c. &c—dined at Lord Granard's—Company, Rogers, Lord Herbert, Mrs. Rawdon &c. the Miss Rogers called to take R. & I to the Beaujon—A military Fete—the storming of a Fort &c. Very beautiful—went down the cars 12 times—went to Lord Holland's afterwards—Rancliffe returned from England to-night. In talking to Rogers about my living in Paris I said "one would not enjoy even Paradise, if one was obliged to live in it"—"No (says he) I dare say, when Adam & Eve were turned out, they were {d____d} happy".

13 [Monday]—Breakfasted with Lord Rancliffe—drove about with Mrs. Story—a dinner given by Lord John at Robert's to the Rogerss, Luttrel & me—[a] gayer Day than Saturday—Rogers's story of his having called a Lady "une femme galante & genereuse" at Pere la Chaise to-day—her anger and the laughter of her companion, who seemed as if she said "it's all out—even strangers know it"—Went to the Varietes in the evening—Rogers joined us after a visit to Miss H. M{aria} Williams[1] and gave us an amusing account of it—the set of French Blues assembled to hear a reading of the "Memoires de Nelson"[2] which R. was obliged to endure also—the dialogue with Miss W. out on the stairs &c. &c.

14 [Tuesday]—Breakfasted at Mrs. Story's—dined at Lord Hollands—Company, Lord & Lady Sefton, Rogers, Humboldt &c.—Humboldt mentioned at dinner a theory of Volney's (I think) with respect to the influence upon language—that, in a cold, foggy atmosphere, people are afraid to open their mouths, and hence the indistinctness & want of richness & fullness in the sounds of their language, whereas in a soft, balsamic air, which the mouth willingly opens to exhale, the contrary effect takes place—{In the evening a conversation was revived which I had had with Rogers a night or two ago, when he mentioned an anecdote told in the Life of Racine by his Son[1] of a dinner which Boileau, Racine, Moliére & La Fontaine had

together, when they agreed that life was a melancholy burden & agreed to go down to the Seine for the purpose of drowning themselves, but afterward changed their minds—Rogers had got into one of his cross fits at my saying (inconsiderately enough, as is often the case in conversation) that there were two of the men (Moliére & Fontaine) with whom in point of genius, the others were not to be mentioned—This discussion was now brought on again, and all pretty much agreed that the remark was applicable as far as related to Moliere—our high idea of La Fontaine's genius is derived more, I think, from what one knows of the man—from the sort of natural, original fountain-head cleanness there appears to have been in his talent—than from any thing he has actually done in either his Tales or Fables—} Talked of the comic Dramatists of France, Regnard, Destouches &c. &c.—the Comedy of the Irresolu (by the latter, I believe)[2] and that amusing touch of character at the end "J'aurais mieux fait, je crois, d'épouser Céliméne."—Went, Rogers & I {(were to have had Luttrel & Henry Fox, but my Lady, as usual, decomposed our ingredients)} to the Italian opera—the Barbiere.

15 [Wednesday]—Breakfasted with R.—read me his story of Foscari,[1] which is told very strikingly—was to have seen the pretty Spanish dancer, Marie Mercandotti, this morning, but being a fête, no dancing at Coulon's—drove with the Rogerss to Bagatelle, but not admitted for the same reason—went thence with the two women to Notre-Dame & saw the Royal Family walk in procession—dined at Macleod's—party, Villamil, Mr. Gisdon & myself—a little Macleod (two years & half old) repeated to me quite correctly the lines from Lalla Rookh "Tell me not of joys above,"[2] taught by his young Aunt, who seems to have everything I ever wrote by heart—Sung in the evening—joined the Rogers's at Tivoli—went down the cars some half dozen times, & then to Lord Holland's—my Lady very anxious I should dine there tomorrow to meet Mercier (author of Louis 9th)[3] & Count Torreno—Rogers, speaking as we walked home of the sort of conscription of persons of all kinds that is put in force for the dinners of the Hollands, said "There are two parties before whom every body must appear—them & the Police". Took leave of him—he starts for Switzerland tomorrow

16 [Thursday]—Invited Anthony Strutt (who has brought a letter of introduction from his Uncle) to dine with me at Sevres to-day—met Fawcett the actor, & asked him out too—found when I arrived that Lord John was to dine with Villamil, who expected me also—had my party however to myself & joined them in the evening—Slept at Sevres—

17 [Friday]—Not very well nor in good spirits {to-day]—cried bitterly over the account of the Liverpool packet, lost the other day[1]—no letter from Bessy—endeavoured to write a song to a Sicilian Air, but in vain—worked all day at two lines, without success.—the Villamils & I pick-nicked our provender—had dinner chez moi—Lord John, they & Doctor H{aut-Bouf]—Mrs. S. came in the evening—a letter from Bessy too, which made a material alteration in my spirits—

18 [Saturday]—More successful with my Sicilian Air—wrote two verses. Sauntered about with Lord John—{told me of Lady Holland saying once of Rogers "How remarkably well he is to-day! he is in full venom"—as if speaking of a viper whose state of health was to be measured by its powers of mischief.}—Both dined with Villamil—Dalton of the party.

19 [Sunday] Began another melody to a Swedish Air—Lord John drove me in his cabriolet—both dined at the Hollands'—company, Villamil, Arnauld (the poet), Mrs. Rawdon, a Mr. Ponsonby &c.—It turns out to be quite an invention, what Made. Hamelin told me, at Montron's, of Arnaud [*sic*] having translated Lalla Rookh. What led to the mistake was his having mentioned to her that he was trying to put some of my {Irish} Melodies into French Verse—a good deal of talk with him before dinner—Said to be one of the authors of the Miroir—the Government persecute him incessantly—Lord H. told me that among the Thirty excepted from the Amnesty on the Restoration, Flahault's name was at first inserted, but through Talleyrand's interest, was afterwards removed and (as they thought it necessary to make up the exact number of Thirty) poor Arnauld's name, being the first that occurred, put in his place[1]—Went in the evening with Allen & Henry Fox to Beaujon—{Found there Lord John with Made. de Durazzo, her husband & another & joined them—} supped afterwards at Mrs. Story's

20 [Monday]—Breakfasted at the Café Hardy—{called at the Granards'—asked to dine there—said I would if I could—} made sick by the excessive heat—was too late for Ld. Jn. and went to Beauvillier's, where I found Harry Leeson sitting down to dinner alone and joined him—{told me that the other day Lord Beauchamp (Lady Hertford's grand-son) said to Lord Francis Conyngham, who was having him to meet the King at breakfast with his mother, "What! do you give him breakfasts? *in our time*, we didn't do that"—A note from Lord John, who is gone out to Sevres, to-day that Made. Durazzo & her sister Made. Borgnoli are to come to see the place tomorrow—went to the Palais Royal & bought a pye for luncheon at Chavet's}

{21 [Tuesday]—Went out at 12 & had luncheon prepared for the fair Italians, who, however (on account of the great heat of the weather) did not come—Lord John went in to dine with them, & I dined with the Villamils.—Wilder of the party—Lord J. returned at 10 & we sat together talking till twelve.}

22 [Wednesday]—Finished my Song to the Swedish Air and wrote it out—Lady Holland called to take Lord John & me in to dine with her—did not see her—he did, but refused—dined quietly together—Mrs. S. called in the evening to take me into a Fete at Marboeuf—but there was none—Slept at Rancliffes—

23 [Thursday]—Went with the Macleods to the Panorama of Athens, whose dreariness rather consoles one for not having been there—dined at Rancliffe's—Company, Villamil, Lord John, Long Wellesley, Daly, &c.—Wellesley mentioned an anecdote to show the insincerity of George 3rd.—that in giving the Ribbon to Lord Wellesley (after having done all he could, as Lord W. well knew, to avoid giving it to him) he said "I recollect, my Lord, having thought, when I saw you as a boy at Eton, that I should one day have to bestow this distinction upon you". Lord R. told a good thing about Sir E. Neagle's coming to {George 4th} our present King, when the news of Buonaparte's death had just arrived, and saying "I have the pleasure to tell your Majesty that your bitterest enemy is dead"—"No—is she, by Gad?" said the King—put this into verse afterwards—went & eat ice at Tortoni's in the evening.

24 [Friday]—Came out early for the purpose of looking after the arrangement of my dinner to-day—Company, Rancliffe, Lord John, Fitzherbert, Villamil & Wilder—rather a pleasant day—Had singing at Villamil's in the evening—

25 [Saturday]—Put another song on the stocks—went into Paris at two—a letter yesterday evening from my dearest Bessy, full of the most natural & touching phrases—just like herself in every word of it.—dined at the Hollands'—company, Lord Darlington, Made. Durazzo, Lord John, &c.—sat next Lord H. who was, as usual, most hearty & agreeable—talked of his early habits of mimicry—how difficult he had often found it to avoid mimicking people in re-stating what they had said—particularly Lord Loughborough—{had} heard his uncle mimic Pitt in the House—went in the evening to the Storys, & walked (a party of us, Col. Cooper, Wilder &

the women) to see the Fireworks (for the Fete of St. Louis) in the Champs
Élyseés—

26 [Sunday]—Breakfasted with Lord John at his new lodgings in the Rue
Chantereine—drove out with Mrs. S. to see my dear Statia—meant to have
dined with the Granards, but did not let them know till near six o'clock &
they had not room for me—dined by myself at Beauvillier's & went
afterwards to see the Fireworks in the Thuilleries, given by the Gardes de
Corps—very beautiful—just as if flights of luminous birds were shooting
about in profusion among the trees—lasted, too, near quarter of an hour.

27 [Monday]—Breakfasted with Lord John & read over some of what he
had lately been writing, which promises very well indeed—agreed to dine
with him at a Restaurateur's—read over some more of his Ms. before
dinner—dined at Riche's, and afterwards separated—he to go to the
Français & I to the Opera—La Vestale & the Carnival[1]—never tire of the
dancing.

28 [Tuesday]—Breakfasted with Lord John—and came out to Sevres at
one, anxious for a letter which I counted upon by yesterday's post from
Bessy—none arrived, which puzzles me with respect to my plan of meeting
her most awkwardly—dined with Villamil, and practised over some Duetts
with Mrs. V. in the evening.

29 [Wednesday]—Finished the Song I begun on Saturday to one of the
Mahratta Airs Lady Hastings gave me—Three verses.[1]—dined with Villamil to meet a Captain & Mrs. Fisher—went in the evening, for the purpose of sending off a letter by one of Meurice's coaches to Bessy at Calais—
found he has no coaches, but took charge of the letter—

30 [Thursday]—Called at Lord Holland's—Lord Darlington there—meant
to have gone & dined with the Granards, but Rancliffe wished me to go
with him to the Fitzherberts—did so—a partie quarrée—{She pretty but}
he drove me in his Cabriolet after dinner to the Hollands—then went to the
Granards—

31 [Friday]—Got up early and went to the Messageries Royales, for the
chance of seeing some one I knew going off in the Calais Coach, who might

bear a message to Bessy for me—gave a card to the Conducteur, on which I wrote with a pencil that I would wait her arrival at Paris.—breakfasted with Lord John—drove me afterwards to the Hollands—much talk with him about his intended political steps the next session—means to bring forward a plan of reform.—evidently displeased with the shilly-shally conduct of his party—found Lord Holland in high spirits, and reciting verses in all languages while he tore up his bills & letters—among other things the following of Cowper's—"Doctor Jortin Had the Good fortune To write these verses on tombs & hearses, Which I, being jinglish Have done into English"—this led us to talk of Jortin's "Quae te sub tenerâ" and Gruter's[1] including it among his collection of antient inscriptions which Lord H. said surprized him, there being some evident clues to its detection as modern—The word "oro," as it is here used, and the situation in the line of the word "crudelia" the one (I think) being of modern use & the latter only used in the early Latin authors—[Mimicked Rogers in two or three very characteristic sayings—of Lady Holland before he knew her very well—"They say she has a very pretty smile—she can even smile upon an ass"—of the nightingales in the grounds at Holland House "How sweet that is! sung [?just as] to Homer—Sidney Smith fabricated a saying for him about bees—"beautiful little busy things! I call them my [*two words unrecovered*]"—mentioned how Sidney Smith quizzed his lines in Human Life about the emmets coming "with curious urge" to look at him while he was asleep—"I can't imagine (said Sidney) what could induce an emmet,[2] however "curious," to come to look at Rogers, while he is asleep—a carrion crow might indeed"—In this vein Smith then went on in his way, to suppose the carrion crow eating him up & a servant being sent outside onto the lawn to look for him, finding nothing but his bones &c.&c.]—Lord H. repeated with much emphasis those fine verses of Dryden's about Transubstantiation ("Can I believe . . . that the great Maker of the World Could die)[3] which I have heard Mathew Montague say he has known Mr. Fox write about to amuse himself during an Election Committee—Lord H. showed me some verses he had written the day before—one upon a Clock with the design of "L'Amour fait passer le Tems" on it, beginning something this way

> Love, says the Poet, makes Time pass,
> But I'm inclined to doubt him—
> Dismiss the roving boy—alas!
> Time pushes on without him.

The other a string of similies on his son Charles, of which I remember the following—(N. B. Charles is a great person for recollecting dates)

> That he's like a palm-tree, it well may be said
> Having always a cluster of dates in his head.

Mrs. S. took me out to Villamil's with the hope (indeed the certainty) of finding a letter, by this post from Bessy—but no one arrived—to my no small wonder & uneasiness. Heaven send all may be right—came in at eight—dressed & went to Lord Hollands—a number of people there to take leave of them, as they go tomorrow—among others—Lavalette, who is a very gentle, interesting little man—slept at the Storys to-night, having lost my bed at Rancliffe's on account of the expected return of Lady R. tomorrow—

September 1st. [Saturday]—Have not been very well these some days past—{came out to La Butte—dined with Villamil, & took calomel at eight—}

2nd. [Sunday] Began a song to a Sicilian air—went into town at two—called upon Miss Capel, who played me a fine lesson of Beethoven's—Rancliffe called to take me to dinner at the Fitzherberts—company, {that fool,} Lord Fife, John King, Lady Augusta Leith & Dr. Gullefer—in the evening had some music—found two pretty airs among Mrs. Fitz's MSS.—

3rd. [Monday] A letter from Bessy, to my great delight—{a little alloyed by hearing that} her too hospitable spirit has induced her to invite two girls (the Miss Belchers) to pay us a visit here & that they are actually coming with her—went out with the Storys, after an early dinner, to the Fete at St. Germain's—dull enough, but the evening beautiful—

4 [Tuesday]—Came out to Sèvres to order every thing to be ready for Bessy's reception—dined with the Story's and drove in the evening to the Messageris Royales—at about eight the Diligence arrived & in it the dear girl & her little one, whom I was right happy to see—the Miss Belchers, too, with her—Mrs. Ss carriage brought us all out to Sèvres—

5 [Wednesday]—Passed the morning in talking over all that has happened since we parted—after dinner went in to fetch Anastasia.

6 [Thursday]—Sent off six National Melodies to Power—took Anastasia in—returned to dinner at Villamil's—a large party—the Macleods, Storys &c.—some singing in the evening—Lord John came out at nine for the purpose of seeing Bessy—is to dine with us tomorrow.

7 [Friday]—Lord John dined with us and slept.

8 [Saturday]—Took in Bessy & her young friends for the purpose of passing two or three days at the Story's, and showing them some of the Lions—I dined at Made. de Souza's—company, Count Funchal, Gallois, Lord John, and Binda—Talked of the clever men of Italy, Nicollini, Fabbroni &c.— Fontana was a strong materialist. Binda mentioned an Italian Epigram of Lord Holland's about "*Ratto,*" who was the paymaster of the witnesses against the Queen—the point of which was that in Italy the Rats paid, but in England "Ratti sono pagati".[1]—Gallois also alluded to some French Epigram, which Lord Holland had showed him, but which was radically faulty from a confusion in the meaning of the word on which the point turned— This must often happen in such school-boy attempts at foreign verse-making—Funchal mentioned Mathias as an instance of success in this way, but, Binda (I was glad to find) pronounced his verses to be very indifferent—Spoke of a Society or Academy at Rome (I forget the name) of which the Duchess of Hamilton was made a member under the title of "Polymnia Caledonia"—At a little after eight found Bessy &c. at the Porte St. Martin— saw the "Tailleur de J. Jaques" in which Potier was very amusing, and Riquet à la Houppe[2]—pretty little Jenny Vert-pré replaced in the character of Abricotine by a very inferior make-shift.—all supped & slept at Story's—

9 [Sunday] Breakfasted with Lord John—& afterwards went to look for Lord Lansdowne, who arrived last night—found him au Troisiéme in the Hotel du Mont Blanc—starts again for the Pyrenees, tomorrow—a good deal of talk about the Royal visit in Ireland—the good sense with which the King has acted, and the bad, servile style in which poor Paddy has received him—Mr. O Connel pre-eminent in Blarney & inconsistency—Many *good* results, however, likely to arrive from the whole affair, if the King but continues in the same state of temperature towards Ireland in which he is at present[1]—Drove about with Mrs. S. & Bessy—dined at the Story's— Colonel Cooper & Dalton of the party—went all in the evening to Beaujon & from thence to Tivoli, where I went down in the cars with the two girls, who are, by the bye, very pretty & much admired—slept at Ss.

10 [Monday]—Find that Lord Powerscourt (with whom the King dined the day he embarked from Ireland) was courageous enough to have a Song of mine—"The Prince's Day"[1] sung before him immediately after "God save the King", and that his Majesty was much delighted with it—The Song is laudatory, for I thought at the time he deserved such, but upon reading it rather anxiously over, I find nothing in it to be ashamed of.—What will

those cowardly Scholars of Dublin College, who took such pains at their dinner the other day to avoid mentioning my name, and who after a speech of some Sir Noodle boasting of the poetical talent of Ireland drank, as the utmost they could venture, "*Maturin* & the *rising* Poets of Erin"—what will those white-livered slaves say to the exhibition at Lord Powerscourt's?— The only excuse I can find for the worse than Eastern Prostration into which my countrymen have grovelled during these few last weeks is that they have so long been slaves, they know no better & that it is not their own faults if they are ignorant of any medium between brawling rebellion & foot-licking idolatry—as for the King, he has done his part well & sensibly, and his visit altogether may be productive of benefits, which the unmanly flatterers who have bedaubed him hardly deserve.—dined at Story's, and went to the French Opera {with Bessy &c.} in the evening—Iphigenie in Tauride & the Jugement de Paris.[2]

11 [Tuesday]—Took the women to the Louvre—dined at Storys, and went all to the Gymnase in the evening—little Leontini Fay & Perlet very amusing—a letter from Lord Byron, in answer to my communication about the sale of the MS.—very satisfactory[1]

12 [Wednesday]—Went to Denon's with the Belchers. He has put Grattan's Medal into hands—received a note from Lord John to say that he is for England & will take me—how lucky!—the 4th of this month two years since we started together from London—dined with him at Beauvilliers—he afterwards to the Gymnase & I to Sèvres.

13 [Thursday]—Made some arrangements for my journey, which is rather a perilous one, but I have made up my mind to it, ever since I found the Longmans had been so dilatory in their negotiation—besides, my poor Father & Mother are growing old & it is time I should see them again. Went in to dine at Beauvilliers with Hill & Horace Smith, one of the "Rejected" brothers[1]

14 [Friday]—Began words to a Neapolitan air—Mrs. Villamil brought to bed this morning—Lord John came out to take leave of Bessy—told him that as I knew he liked to change his mind, he must not be particular with me, as to his promise of going with me—he seemed however decided upon it—he made his luncheon while Bessy dined—I dined with Villamil & Doctor H{aut-bouf}, who described an organ in the *poitrine* of the new-born infant, which seems to have been placed there solely for the purpose of

nourishing it till the mother is capable of doing so—as it diminishes when the child begins to suck and at last disappears entirely—It is what is called the *fraise* (he said) in a calf—Mrs. S. came in the evening with Mr. Newton,[1] an American, who brought letters of introduction from his friend Irving to us

15 [Saturday]—Went in for the purpose of dining with Macleod—had a note from Lord John, to say [he] has changed his mind about going—this uncertainty rather a fault—My chief regret at it is the not having his assistance in my negotiation with the American agent, to whom I meant, through *him* to offer a thousand pounds immediately on my settling with Murray for the Memoirs—went to Lafitte's & drew upon Murray at 3 months for a hundred pounds—called upon Lord John, who seemed after a little conversation, to be half inclined to change again—bid me, at parting, not to give him up—Company at Macleod's, Villamil, Arbuthnot, & Girdon—sung in the evening—slept at Story's.

16 [Sunday]—Bought a pair of mustachios, by advice of the women, as a mode of disguising myself in England—came out at twelve—a party to dinner, the Storys, Doctor Lamb & Irving's friend—dined at four & went to the Fetes of St. Cloud in the evening—saw several shows, &c. &c.

17 [Monday]—wrote to Murray to say that I should start on Wednesday— inclosed also to Rogers's house-keeper the note he gave me for her, directing that I should have a bed at his house during my stay in London—went in with my letters—saw Lord John who says he is now determined to go, if I will stay for him till Saturday—promised to give him my answer tomorrow—dined alone at the Café Français, and came out to Sèvres at 8—

18 [Tuesday]—Resolved to wait for Lord John—wrote him a note to say so—went in with Villamil in his gig at 4, in order to dine at Story's and go with the Macleods to Made. Fodor's Benefit—the tickets, a Napoleon each—the entertainment a combination of the three best things in Paris, the Italian Singing, French dancing, & Madlle. Mar's acting—all excellent, but rather too much for one evening—not over till past twelve—eat ice with the ladies at Tortoni's afterwards, & slept at Story's—

19 [Wednesday]—Called upon Lord John, who is still in the mind for Saturday—went afterwards to the Louvre to meet Villamil, & Newton, who

is a painter—he is, at present, occupied at finishing a copy of Paul Veronese's Marriage of Cana, begun by another American artist, Leslie[1]—his
remarks upon some of the pictures interesting—the temptation the Vene-
tian painters had to gorgeousness in the rich & various costumes with
which Venice abounded—an approach to idiotcy (he said) in the faces of
Correggio—the angel in the picture at Parma an instance—the rough canvas of Titian favourable to rapidity of execution as it takes the colours more
quickly—the neatness & elegance of a little page in one of Rubens's Luxembourg pictures—the admirable portrait of Erasmus, which I have so often
stood before—saw Wilkie in the gallery, who thanked me with much
warmth for having called upon him—he was employed in taking a slight
copy of a picture of Kuyp's—told me the Royal Acads. had lately a private
dinner together at which my health was drunk with great enthusiasm—
called for my little Anastasia & brought her out to dinner—sung with girls
in the evening.—

20 [Thursday]—Read & sauntered about—a dinner at Villamil's—4
Spaniards (one of them the brother of Duke _____,[1] and a poet &
painter) Newton & ourselves—The Spanish Poet explained to me the nature of the rhyme called Asonante,[2] peculiar, I think, to Spanish Poetry,
and taken, he thinks, from the Arabs.—Moratin's Comedies are all written
in this kind of rhyme—Singing in the evening

21 [Friday]—Packed up to go and sleep in town to-night, preparatory to my
departure tomorrow—

22 [Saturday]—Left Paris with Lord John at a little after seven—slept that
night at Airaines—

23 [Sunday] Started at six—delayed for horses on account of the King of
England, who was expected at Boulogne—slept within two stages of
Calais—the evening most lovely.

24 [Monday]—Sailed from Calais at 20 minutes past eleven—a most sickening passage of 7 hours—The only persons aboard who knew me were Tyler
& Forster, the Duchess of Devonshire's son—Lord John recommended my
assuming some name, which I did, calling myself in the Packet and at the
Inn "Mr. Dyke"—Lord John & I searched at the Custom house—they took
from me a little locket with the hair of Anastasia & Tom, which I was

carrying to my sister, and a mother-of-pearl pocket-book I had for my mother—Lord John, however, (towards whom the change in the Comptroller's manner, upon finding who he was amused us exceedingly) got them back again—told me an anecdote of Fazakerly's books being stopped at a Dogana, and on his explaining that one of them was "Platone-filosofo antico" the Doganiere sagaciously answered "Si—si—filosofo antico—ma può contenere qualche cosa contra il governo"—{Slept at Wright's.}

25 [Tuesday]—Delayed by the Custom-House—Tierney, whose family are at Dover, called & sat some time with us—thinks the tide is setting now towards Royalty—When I said "the wind is fair for the King to-day" answered "Damn it—every thing's for him"—thinks the majority of the country are tired of the present ministry, but don't know where else {to look} to supply these places—a mournful avowal for the Whig leader. Started in a back-chaise at ½ past twelve—{talked of the profligate principles of the Devonshire-House school—one part of their tactics consisted in marrying a man off as soon as his connection with a woman already married became too conspicuous or dangerous—Singular enough that two such men as Byron and Brougham should have come within the sweep of this policy—the former of whom was led into his first proposal of marriage by Lady Melbourne in order to put an end to the affair with Lady C. Lamb, and the latter very much influenced to the same step by the situation in which he stood with Mrs. G. L.}—Lunched at Rochester—the King had gone through the day before & done the distance from Rochester to Sittingbourne (11 miles) in 42 minutes—set Lord J. down at his father's in St. James's Square & arrived at Rogers's about a quarter after eleven.

26 [Wednesday]—Wrote notes to summon Murray & Power—the latter came immediately—Lord John wants me to go to Woburn—no Murray—Lord J. dined with me on mutton-chops—supped at Power's.

27 [Thursday]—Power called—then Lord John—& at last Murray—there was a mistake in the delivery of my note to him yesterday, which caused the delay—agreed to all my arrangements about the payment of the sum for the Memoirs—took away the MS.—says that Lord Bs. two last Tragedies (Sardanapalus & Foscari) are worth nothing[1]—that nobody will read them—offered Lord B. £1000 for the continuation of Don Juan & the same for the 2 Tragedies, which he refused—advised Murray not to speak so freely of his transactions with Lord B. nor of the decrease which he says has taken place in the attraction of his works.—Don Juan to be discontinued at the request (as, according to him, Byron says) of the Contessa Guiccioli—

{talked of Lady H—says that she has forced Charles Fox into exile by her conduct to him—]a passage this morning in Marmontel's Memoirs² struck me—Talking of the choice of profession, his mother said to him—"Pour le barreau, si vous y entrez, je vous exige la parole la plus inviolable, que vous n'y affirmerez jamais que ce que vous croirez vrai, que vous n'y défendrez jamais que ce que vous croirez juste"—on these terms he never could have been a lawyer—but she was quite right—Lord J. repeated some verses by Home, author of Douglas.³

> Proud & erect the Caledonian stood,
> Old was his mutton & his claret good—
> "Let him drink Port" the English statesman cried—
> He drank the fatal potion & he died.⁴

The joke of the King giving a drawing-room (attributed to Rogers) that he was in himself a sequence "King, Queen & Knave".—dined with Power—looked over some of my songs in the evening.

28 [Friday] Lord J. would have dined with me—but is summoned off to Panshanger by Lady Holland—and made me promise to come to Woburn on Monday, if my affairs are in train—Longman called upon me—told him my intention of settling the Bermuda business with the money arising from the sale of the Memoirs—seemed rather disappointed—said I had better let matters go on as they were, & appeared labouring with some mystery—remarked that though I had with much delicacy declined the contribution of friends, yet that I could not surely feel the same objection to letting one friend settle the business for me—at length, after much hesitation acknowledged that a thousand pounds had been for some time placed at his disposal, for the purpose of arranging matters when the debt could be reduced to that sum, and that he had been under strictest injunctions of secrecy with regard to this deposit which nothing but the intention I had expressed of settling the business in another way could have induced him to infringe and that, finally, the person who had given this proof of warm & true friendship was (as I guessed in an instant) Lord Lansdowne. How one such action brightens the whole human race in our eyes!—entreated of me still to leave the settlement of the business in Lord L's hands—but, of course, will not.—supped at Power's.

29 [Saturday]—Sent to Tegart, who called & asked me to dinner tomorrow—Henry Rogers came & sat with me two hours & a half—dined at home—walked out in the evening, the only time when I venture abroad except in a hackney coach—the gas-lights very inconvenient for gentlemen incog.—called at Lady Donegall's & saw Philippa Godfrey—Lady D. comes

to town tomorrow—supped at Power's—found in Marmontel, that pretty thing said by Lord Albemarle to his mistress (Madlle. Guncher) who was looking earnestly at a star—"Ne la regardez pas tant je ne puis pas vous la donner"—saw Bessy's Mother this morning and gave her five pounds—

30 [Sunday]—Went to Newton's—dined at Tegart's—W{ebster} W{edderbourne} there—owes Lord Byron, he says, a thousand pounds and does not seem to have the slightest intention of paying him—a note from Lord John from Cashiobury (directed to Thomas Dyke Esqr.) inclosing one from the Duke, in which he says laconically "bring T. M{oore}"—read the proofs of Lord B's Sardanapalus, with which I was delighted—much originality in the character of Sardanapalus—but not a dramatic personage—his sly, insinuated sarcasms too delicate for the broad sign-painting of the stage—

October 1 [Monday]—A letter from Lord J.—dined at Lady Donegal's— she herself not able to sit at dinner but saw her in the evening—excellent warm-hearted women, in spite of their Toryism, which is, to be sure, most strong—{trying—}

2nd [Tuesday]—Preparations for departure—went to Power's—

3rd [Wednesday]—A quarter before seven started from Holbourn— arrived at the Duke's between two and three—Lord Tavistock there— invited me over to Oakley, but shall not be able to go—the Duchess full of farming & all its technicalities—disappointed in sale of pigs, price paid for driving bullocks &c. &c.—had music in the evening—the Duchess said she wished I could "transfer my genius to her for six weeks", and I answered "most willingly, if Woburn was placed at my disposal for the same time"— introduced to Mr. Wiffin, a quaker poet in the Library this morning—The Statue gallery of the Duke very interesting. Canova's graces exquisite—a cast of Somariva's Magdalen there—{music in the evening}

4th [Thursday]—A dreadful wet day, which deprived me of the first opportunity I had had of enjoying the air by daylight since I left France—Mr. Wiffin took my profile with a camera lucida—he had already had those of Campbell & Rogers—made him take Lord John's, also, to inclose to Bessy—{Lord Tavistock told of Tierney that some time ago when there was a prospect of the Whigs coming in, he said to him (Lord T.) "Lord Spencer & the Duke must really take situations, for if only such persons as

Brougham & I were to come into office, they would say we were going to rob the till"—} Singing again in the evening—{the Duchess herself strummed and croaked away for a considerable time.}

5 [Friday]—Walked with Lord J. to see Mrs. Seymour (sister of the Duke's first wife & of Lady Bath) after breakfast—Knew her very well in Ireland during the Duke's Lord Lieutenancy—when she was very intimate with my friend Mrs. H. Tighe—a person to be liked very much—they live in a pretty cottage of the Duke's adjoining the Park—the Duchess afterwards put me under the guidance of her niece, Miss Russell to see the grounds &c. &c. a pretty place, called the Tornery, where they sometimes drink tea in summer—the dairy, another pretty show-place—two milk-pails of Sèvres China there, made for Marie Antoinette & given by Lord Alvanley to the Duchess—went afterwards through the apartments of the house with Lord John—a whole room full of Canalettos—a good many Vandykes—Lord Russel's long gold-headed cane in one of the rooms, beside his picture—the Duchess told at dinner of Sir W. Farquhar's going into assembly & being bowed to by several girls, whom he did not know, upon which Lady Albrough said "go home & put on your night-caps, girls, if you wish him to know you—" Talked of the Duke of York who has lately been here—mentioned his having said (half jest, half earnest) speaking of the arrangements of the Coronation "By G——I'll have every thing exactly the same at mine"—the Duchess's mimicking of his R. H. very good—{Talked of the sauciness of servants—Duchess said they refused to eat hash, and that she had more than once exclaimed how happy her boy at sea would be to have what they refused—Lord T. said it was lately reported to him that the stable-boy's bed-curtains were torn out—} Talked of a picture of Rogers done for the Duke by Hayter[1]—[*several words unrecovered*]—asked me to put off my departure till Sunday & the Duchess proposed I should go tomorrow to see Ampthill—Sung again in the evening—the Duke's two favourite songs "The Boys of Kilkenny" and "Here's the Bower"—

6 [Saturday]—After breakfast went in the carriage with the Duke & Lord John (who were going to shoot) and Miss Russel—she & I walked to Ampthill Park—very old trees there—some of them declared superannuated in Cromwell's time—then to the church of Millbrook, a pretty village in the valley—a monument there of Georgiana Fox[1]—bust very like—figure of Christ in the basso relievo rather clumsy—an inscription in the church-yard struck me

> Praises on tombs are titles vainly spent,
> A man's good name is his best monument.

On another tomb is an apology from the defunct for not having left a P.P.C. card at his departure.

> "I had not time to bid my friends farewell."

Thence to Ampthill church—a column there erected by order of Lord Ossory to his memory; he being buried in Northamptonshire—some verses on it by Lord H.—one of the lines "His was the smile that spoke a mind at ease"—The last line, the Duke says is Rogers's, and that some one not knowing this, criticised it severely to him—the Seymours came to dinner—Lord J. told of a Mr. Hare upon being asked his quality in passing some barrier in Germany (having been long bored with such questions) saying that he was Grand Cabinet Trumpeter to the Prince of Tour and Taxis, and being taken out of his bed next morning by Gens 'd arms for the joke—Singing in the evening—Miss Russel promised to write out some pretty National Airs for me.

7 [Sunday]—The D. & Duchess made me promise to take Woburn in my way back, and she said, "if you are in ever such a hurry you must sleep somewhere—so make this your inn—" some conversation with Lord J. in the Library before I started—his new plan of a book of Sketches prefacing the story he showed me at Sevres to them & giving the sketches as the Remains of his Hero—much talk about the projected newspaper or Periodical work between Lord Byron, him and me[1]—received letters from dear Bess—started at twelve in the Duke's gig for Brickhill—missed the coach—posted on 29 miles to Daventry—slept there.

8 [Monday]—Up at three—off in Coach at 4—arrived in Birmingham at ten—somewhat tempted by Miss Wilson's name in the Bills for to-night, never having heard her—but took the mail—4 guineas to Holyhead & started at 11—a Cook, Tobacconist and a young man from Canterbury going as Preventive Officer to Ireland—let into some secrets about the smuggling trade by them—some good Bulls from the Tobacconist—such as "if the *absentees* would *stay* at home" &c. &c.

9 [Tuesday]—At Holyhead at 7—sailed in the Steam-Packet at 8—arrived at Howth at ½ past one—called by my fellow-travellers Mr. Dyke—found that the searching officer at the Custom-House was my old friend, Willy Leech—dined & slept at his house instead of the Hotel, where I intended to pass the night and get rid of my fatigued looks before I saw my father & mother—a good story of the fellow in the Marshalsea having heard his

companion brushing his teeth the last thing at night & then, upon waking, at the same work in the morning—"Ogh, a weary night you must have had of it, Mr. Fitzgerald—

10 [Wednesday]—Arrived at my Father's lodgings in Abbey St at ½ past twelve—felt very nervous in approaching the door—but, thank God, found them all as well as I could possibly expect—my mother still ailing but strong and my father looking aged, but in excellent health—dear Ellen, too, the meekest & kindest spirit that ever existed, if at all altered, rather for the better—dined at home—John Scully of the party—walked out with him at night on the way to the Dunleary Coach—In returning saw a fellow with a ridiculous travelling-cap that seemed too heavy for his head, and heard a girl say "Oh blood-a-nouns, there's a head-dress"—

11 [Thursday]—Corry called—right glad to see him—young Rawlins too— set off (Father, Mother, Ellen & I) for my sister Kate's cottage at Monks-town—a very happy day—the first time I have seen Kate for six years— looking much better than when we last met—her little girl very intelligent—when asked by Corry whether she could not play some tunes on the Piano-forte, she said "yes—I stagger over two or three".—Returned in Kate's jaunting-car—walked through the town home—heard a fellow say to another—"Well, I never *seed* the match of you, since the ould King died."

12 [Friday]—Drove out in a hackney-coach—called upon Mrs. Smith—told me that the poem of "the Universe" is not Maturin's, but a Mr. Wills's, who induced Maturin to lend his name to it by giving him the profits of the sale[1]—all dined at Corry's—Counsellor Casey[2] the only person besides our-selves—was in the Irish parliament—his account of the fracas between Grattan & Isaac Corry, which ended in a Duel[3]—Grattan's words were "To this charge (imputation of treason) what is to be said! my only answer to it *here* is that it is false—that it is false—any where else a blow—a blow!" at the same time extending his arm violently towards where Corry sat.—In another part of his speech he began his defense thus "There were but two camps in the country—the Minister & the Insurgent &c. &c."—Corry (our host) gave an account of Grattan's conduct on the day when he was wounded by the mob during his chairing—while under the hands of the Surgeon he said "The papers will of course, give an account of it—they will say he was unanimously elected—he was seated in the chair amidst accla-mations &c. &c. and on his return home was obliged to send for a surgeon to cure him of a black eye he had got on the way"[4]—He said also to some one who came in "you see me here, Like Actæon, devoured by my own

hounds"—Told a story of Grattan's taking some fine formal English visitors about his grounds & falling himself into a ditch by taking them a wrong way—Casey mentioned his extreme courtesy to Corry after he had wounded him—Corry wished to go back to the house—"no—no" said G. "let the curs fight it out—I'll be with you—not only now—but till you are able to attend." Grattan always annexed great importance to personal courage (readiness to *go out*)—Isaac Corry, in speaking of him to Casey, expressed himself in the most enthusiastic manner when Casey told him he had kept a minute of that memorable debate, seemed to regret it exceedingly as ashamed of his own intemperance on the occasion—on finding afterwards that the writing of this minute was effaced by lying in a damp place, rejoiced proportionably—

13 [Saturday]—Drove about in a hackney-coach with Corry—have had the precaution to secure the silence of the newspapers on my arrival—called on Mrs. P. Crampton—went to Mossop's, the modeller, he who did the fine head of Grattan from which Denon is having a model taken for me—is doing a series in this way of eminent Irishmen—begged me to sit to him—went thence to Kirk's, a sculptor of some talent—a bust there of my dear friend Dalton, painfully like—dined at home,—some friends of my father's (Mr. Abbot, his wife & her sister) formed the party together with young Curran—two or three more came in the evening & supped—sung to them—story of a man asking a servant "Is your master at home?" "no Sir—he's out"—"your mistress?"—"no, Sir, *she's* out" "Well—I'll just go in & take an air of the fire till they come"—"Faith, Sir, *that's* out too."—When Lord Castlereagh was at Belfast, a common fellow was asking him for money, & when some one remonstrated with him upon it, said, "why, bless your soul, for a tenpenny I'd engage to entertain all his friends in Belfast—" Have forgot to mention that on my way to Holyhead I wrote some lines for the little pocket-book I brought to my mother, with which she was, of course, much delighted[1]—

14 [Sunday]—Ventured to walk about the streets—it being my intention to start on Wednesday next (17th.) shall be able, I trust, to get through London before the echo of any noise I may make here reaches it—accosted oddly by a man in the street—"Pray, Sir, are you Mr. Thomas Moore?" and on my answering "yes, Sir" he turned to another that was with him & saying "There, now," both walked off without any further words or ceremony—there had evidently been a dispute or perhaps wager between them on the subject—met Frankland Lewis, who is one of the Parliament Commissioners, & spoken of for the new Secretary—walked some time with him—

very kind to me—all went out to dinner to Kate's—took Curran with us—
{this young man's likeness to his father in voice & manner very
disappointing—one expects every instant the flashes that used to follow this
manner & they never come. His book too promises more than one finds in
him¹—}the Abbots again—called on P. Crampton this morning—showed
me some lines of his to his daughter—

15 [Monday]—Sat to Mossop & to Kirk—space between the eyes indicates
memory of forms and Kirk has always observed that conformation in persons who were ready at knowing likenesses—the protuberance I have in the
forehead remarked in heroes, Napoleon, Duke of Wellington and the rest
of us—large ears a sign of eloquence—praised mine—so did Bartollini, by
the bye—Kirk said he had thought the ears in the busts of Demosthenes out
of nature till he saw the ears of Burton (an eminent Irish barrister)—sat to
Mossop again—all dined at Rawlins's, old friend of my father & mother's—
music in the evening—

16 [Tuesday]—Sat to Mossop & Kirk—Philip Crampton came while I was
sitting to the latter—forced me to let a mask be taken from my face—
disagreeable operation—dined (I only) at Mrs. Smith's—company Sir C. &
Lady Morgan, Shiel, Maturin, Wills &c—a large party in the evening—
Father, Mother & Nell among them—had music—then quadrilles—danced
with Lady Clarke's little daughter & a Miss Browne—after supper Lady
Clarke sung a song she had written on the occasion of my return—very
livelily done.

17 [Wednesday]—Gave my last sittings to Kirk & Mossop—went with Mrs.
Corry to chuse a Tabbinet for Bessy—Egan, the Harp-maker, most anxious
that I should judge of the power of his improved Irish Harps—sent his son
with one—the Chaise at the door at ½ past three, and some beautiful Irish
airs played to me during my last moments—Had wine in & all filled bump-
ers to the Irish Harp & our next happy meeting—the effect saddening—
Corry came part of the way with me—dined at Howth with Leech & slept
there.

18 [Thursday]—Sailed at ½ past eight in the filthy Talbot Steam Packet—
Lady Belmore & her sister & Lord Dunsaney aboard—the latter offered to
take me on in his carriage, which I accepted—dined at Holyhead & slept at
Gwyndu—

19 [Friday]—From Gwyndu at 10—had bread & cheese at Bangor & dined & slept at Carneyogie¹—Lord D. said that poor Lord Fingal had been obliged to borrow £2000 at 17 per cent to pay the expenses of his ribbon, which amounted (Lord D. saw the account) to £1350—the general insolvency in Ireland most deplorable—

20 [Saturday]—Started to 10—lunched at Llangollen, & slept at Shrewsbury—

21 [Sunday]—This slow travelling (occasioned by the severe asthma under which Lord Ds. son labours) would delay me too long—so took the Mail at nine—dined at Birmingham—took in a drummer there that amused me a good deal—one of my companions mentioned that an old woman said upon the regiment of the Enniskilleners lately entering that town "Well—Boys—you look mighty well—considering it's now a hundred & nine years since you were here before".

22 [Monday]—Arrived in London at 7—breakfasted at the Swan with Two Necks—Got to Rogers's before 10—wrote to Shee to say I would come & dine with him, if he had no company, I being incog.—was preparing, as usual, to sneak out in a hackney-coach when Rees arrived with the important & joyful intelligence that the agent has accepted the Thousand pounds & that I am now a free man again—walked boldly out into the sunshine & showed myself up St. James's St & Bond St.—Shee all wrong about the late servile pageant in Ireland—thinks that Paddy behaved exactly as he ought to do—Letters from Bess—in which alluding to what I had communicated to her of Lord Lansdowne's friendship and the probability of my being soon liberated from exile she says "God bless you, my own free, fortunate, happy *bird* (what she generally calls me)—but remember that your cage is in Paris & that your mate longs for you."

23 [Tuesday]—Called with Longman upon Sheddon to see whether he really meant to advance any thing towards the sum I am to pay—his conduct all along shabby & shuffling & now, when brought to the point, {in a sort of counting house agony almost ludicrous} his agony at the prospect of being made to *bleed* quite ludicrous—Upon my rising from my seat & saying with a sort of contemptuous air "Since Mr. Sheddon does not seem inclined to give any thing but advice, Mr. Longman, I think we may take our leave"—he, with much stammering, proposed to give two hundred pounds {towards the settlement}, and, upon Longman saying that really

this was not worth while talking about, he was at last with much pain & groaning delivered of three hundred, and having had a very difficult time of it indeed[1]—Resolved to let the remainder of the debt (£740) be discharged with Lord Lansdowne's money (in order that his generous purpose should not be wholly frustrated) and then to pay him immediately afterwards by a draft upon Murray—Called on Chauntry, who seemed heartily glad to see me—His atelier full of mind—never seen such a set of *thinking* heads as his busts—Walter Scott's very remarkable from the height of the head—the eyes, Chauntry says, are usually taken as a centre and the lower portion (or half) always much the greater—but in Scott's head the upper part is even longer than the lower—explained to me in what cases the eyes ought to be marked or picked out, and in what not—[*Two lines unrecovered*]—Dined with Power—in the evening to the Haymarket—Kenny's piece from the French (Le Présent du Prince) and the Beggar's Opera.[2]

24 [Wednesday]—Called upon Murray—Belzoni there—mentioned a Dutchman, who has just arrived from the Mountains of the Moon in Africa, & came through Timbuctoo—says Mungo Park was executed there[1]—met Luttrel, who asked me to dine with him on Friday—dined at Longman's—went to Covent Gardens in the evening—Exile & Poor Soldier[2]—Received a letter from Lord John this morning pressing me with a kind and almost jealous anxiety to take the £200 he had left in Longman's hands (the produce of his Life of Lord Russel) towards the settlement of the debt—says he had set it apart for sacred purposes, and did not mean to invest any part of it to the expenses of daily life, so hoped to hear no more of it—

25 [Thursday]—Made various calls—a bust of Lord Byron at Murray's by Thorwalsen[1]—does not do him justice—sad wet weather—met Sr. Robt. Wilson—told me he had seen my verses to Lady Holland on the Snuff-Box in the Chronicle—went to look at them—no great things in print[2]—Lord Holland's, however, not much better, which is a comfort—was to have dined with Beecher, but, instead dined alone at the George—met there a Captain Somebody, whom I had seen in Paris—proposed joining me to some Theatre, so went with him to the Adelphi—a piece from L'ours et le Pacha[3]—Wilkinson very comical—

26 [Friday]—Williams called upon me—has got in with Foscolo, & translates his articles for the Quarterly[1]—says he writes a Farrago of Italian, French & English—tells me he can live cheaper here than in Paris—dines for a shilling—a pint of porter included, & lives altogether for a guinea a

week, which Foscolo allows him—hopes to make something by adopting French pieces to the English stage, which is the great manufacture of the present day—met Luttrel & walked about with him—Lambton asked us to come to his box at Covent-Garden to-night—dined with Luttrel—Sandford & Mrs. Thompson {(La chere amie)} of the party—Sanford, in speaking of my good looks, said I seem to "feel less the change of Almanacks" than any one he knew—Told a story of a young fellow at a Chelsea Ball, who upon the Steward asking him "what are you?" (meaning what o'clock it was by him) was so consciously alive to the intrusion which he had been guilty of that he stammered out "Why Sir—I confess I am a barber, but, if you will have the goodness to say no more about it, I will instantly leave the room."—{Sandford repeated his lines about Rogers's Human Life.

> Quoth Sam "all Human Life is frail,
> And hence may not endure.
> So, lest it suddenly should fail,
> I'll hasten to insure."
> At Morgan's Office he arrives
> Reckoning without his host,
> "Avaunt" exclaims the judge of Lives
> "We can't insure a Ghost."
> "Zounds—tis my Poem—not my face—
> Listen, while I recite it—"
> Quoth Morgan "try another place,
> "We cannot *under*–write it"

This last joke about Human Life is Froeling's, but the Epigram altogether is well done—} Left them at 9 & went to Covent Garden—introduced to Miss Foote & conversed with her as I stood at the Prompter's door & she on the stage in the splendid scene of the Exile—went afterwards to the Duke of Bedford's box—he & Miss Russel there—thence to Lambton's—returned behind the scenes—a pretty after-piece from the Rendezvous Bourgeois[2]—those two nice girls Miss Foote & Miss Beaumont (with a third, not bad, Miss Love) making a racket behind the stage-door, being supposed to be locked up in a closet—helped them in their noise—

27 [Saturday]—Took Williams to introduce him to Murray—settled my business with the latter—amusing jealousy on the subject between the rival bibliopolists of Albemarle St. & Pater-noster Row—Murray claiming the credit of my liberation for himself & Lord Byron & the others for *themselves* & Lord Lansdowne—called in Clement's Lane on H. Rogers, but missed him—thence to Longman's—offered to discount the Bill upon Murray for 1000£ which I meant to pay into the hands of Lord Lansdowne's bankers—

said it would be handsomer to give him at once a draft for the £740 {(the sum drawn from him) but evidently *actuated* by the wish to keep Murray's name as much as possible out of the transaction}—called at Drury Lane— saw George Lamb & Elliston, who proposed to me to write a Drama on the story of Lalla Rookh—said that I should not like to risk this myself, but if any one else undertook it, I should be glad to assist—dined at the George at ½ past six—went to Drury Lane to see the Coronation & Mons. Tonson[1]— laughed heartily at the latter—drank spruce beer afterwards with Levius, who is bringing out a Piece, & bored me abundantly with the details of it[2]— received a letter this morning from dear Bessy—Fanny Belcher has been ill, & they have had, altogether, an hospital house of it—

28 [Sunday]—Sat to Newton, who arrived yesterday and has laid an embargo upon me for my picture—Campbell (Thomas) came while I sat, knowing from Williams that I was there—made the operation pleasanter— talked much about his Magazine[1] &c. &c.—walked in Hyde Park—joined by Lord Blessington & Frederick Byng—dined at Holland House—company, Colonel Anson, Tierney, D. of Bedford &c. &c.—Told them about Lord Byron's Cain—parallel with Milton—wrong for lovers of liberty to identify the principle of resistance to power with such an odious personage as the Devil—Abdiel's case often drawn in as a precedent for *ratting*—Allen said that Milton ought {not} to have let him escape without a knock in the battle—Sir J. Reynolds told Lord Holland that he had applied those verses about Abdiel ("faithful found among the faithless &c. &c") to Burke, as a compliment[2]—Long talk with Lord H. about poetry, Crabbe &c. &c.— repeated me some "vers libres" of Porson's {about the Duke of Gloucester on his going to the University & Mrs. Beadon, his tutor's wife}—he apologized for sending my verses on the Snuff-box to the Chronicle—but said it was done as a set-off against some savage lines Lord Carlisle had written on the same subject & which were published in John Bull[3]— Lord H. had produced the following Epigram on those verses of Lord Carlisle's—

> For this her snuff-box to resign!
> A pleasant thought enough.
> Alas, my Lord, for verse like thine,
> Who'd give a pinch of snuff?

Told Lady H. of Lord Lansdowne's kindness & how deeply I felt it, on which she said "From those who know you & have the means it is but what is due to you"—the D. of Bedford brought me home in his carriage—Made an arrangement this morning with a Mr. Stibbert to join him in the journey to Paris, he having a carriage at Boulogne—

29 [Monday]—Wrote letters to Lord Byron &c. &c.—called upon Douglas Kinnaird who showed me a good deal of Lord Bs. correspondence with him upon his pecuniary negotiations with Murray—got £1000 for Marino Faliero & Prophecy of Dante¹—£2000 offered by Murray for the 3 other plays & remaining Cantos of Don Juan, which Lord B. refuses—sat to Newton—Kinnaird took me to dinner to Chauntry's—Company, Mr. Hatchett (once a philosopher, now I know not what) & Jackson—Chauntrey's objections to subjects (in Sculpture) displaying muscular exertion—*mind,* the great material—difficulty of doing the mouth—said, laughing, that he "would do busts at ½ price if he had not to put in the mouth"—Lord Blessington called to take me to supper with him—mentioned some good jokes about the King—one a wicked toast, "may the King come home *in spirits"*—{The King called with Lady Conyngham on Lady Harcourt, and leaving, for message, "the King with his *best love"*—} Received a joint letter to-day from Hobhouse & Sir F. Burdett, congratulating me on the settlement of my business & full of the warmest expressions of friendship—

30 [Tuesday]—started at seven o'clock for Wiltshire—slept at Calne—wrote to the Phipps's to announce my arrival—

31 [Wednesday]—Answer from Phipps—breakfasted at Wans with him and Bennet (Member for the County.)—Mrs. Phipps at Benett's, near Salisbury—resolved to go there—Walked with Hughes to Sloperton & Bromham—the poor Cottage in a sad state of desolation—touched my Piano-forte (which is at Hughes's house) and found it sweeter than almost any I have met since I left it—set off in a chaise for Benett's—changed horses at Warminster—passed by Fonthill Abbey & arrived at four—a magnificent sunset—these two last days lovely—dined, sung & slept.

Nov. 1 [Thursday]—A walk before breakfast with Mrs. P.—she in my travelling-cap, which became her mightily—after breakfast through the grounds with her, Benett & Phipps—a beautiful place, but its master at his wit's end for money & haunted in this Paradise by duns—started at one in a chaise for Salisbury—dined there & left in the Coach for town at seven—

2nd [Friday]—Arrived in St. James's Place at eight—called upon Newton & Murray—Lord H. came to the latter's & took me away in his carriage—anxious to ask me about my Parody on the Regent's Letter¹—whether I had shown it to Lord Moira—heard that I had & that Lord Moira had advised the leaving out of some lines—told him that none of this was true—that no

one had seen it before it was circulated but himself, Rogers, Perry & Luttrel—he quoted something which he had been told Rogers had said about
his (Lord Hs.) having urged me to write this, and the likelihood of my
being left in the lurch after having suffered for doing so—Lord H. confessed that it was all very imprudent & that the whole conduct of the Party
(Whig) at that time was any thing but wise, so they must know the King
would never forgive the personalities they then beset him with—I should
like much to know the secret of his reviving this matter just now—dined at
Power's to meet Bishop upon musical matters—Said that Rossini chiefly
consisted of ornament—{that there} had but little staple of Air—praised
the genius shown in Paer's Agnese[2]—is employed, he & three others,
(Horsley, Wesley & some one else) on a Musical Dictionary—Koch, who has
been translated for them, their great resource—early to bed—Had called
upon the Longmans this morning & got my account from them—{a little
surprised to find that though they have got an unpublished work of mine
in their hands, which *would* be a more than ample set-off (in case of my
death) against the money I am arrears to them, they have, notwithstanding,
put me to the expense of two years inconvenience of my Life for the
amount—This is *rather* too keen.—} Called upon Croker one of these
mornings & had a long conversation with him about my Bermuda business,
Lord Lansdowne &c. &c.

3rd. [Saturday] Dreadfully wet day.—Received Lord Bs. tremendous
verses against the King & the Irish for their late exhibition in Dublin—
richly deserved by my servile {& hollow-hearted} countrymen, but not, on
this occasion, by the King, who, as far as *he* was concerned, acted well &
wisely[1]—Sat to Newton—Murray came, during my sitting, with the Anglo-
Saxon Attorney, Turner, to sign definitely the deed making over to him the
Memoirs of Lord Byron—went with Lord Blessington, Stibbert (both asked
at my request) and Chauntry to dine at {the} Longmans—dinner well
enough—to Lord Bs. to supper in the evening—a strange fellow, there.
Varley, the artist, full of all the nonsense of astrology—such a conjunction
producing revolutions & head-aches &c. &c.—but seems in earnest, which
makes him rather interesting—

4 [Sunday]—Sat to Newton—the Blessingtons drove me to Holland
House—& waited for me—read Byron's verses to Lord & Lady H. & Allen—much struck by them but advised me not to have any hand in printing
them—Lord H. expressed some scruples about my sale of Lord Bs.
Memoirs—said he wished I could have got the 2000 guineas in any other
way—seemed to think it was in cold blood depositing a sort of quiver of
poison arrows (this more the purport than the words of what he said) for a

future warfare upon private character—could not however remember, when I pressed him, any thing that came under this strong description, except the reported conversation with Made. de Stael, & the charge against Sir Samuel Romilly, which, if false, may be neutralized by furnishing me with the means of putting the refutation on record with the charge—dined at Lord Blessington's—Sir T. Lawrence in the evening—Lawrence's idea that murderers have thin lips—has always found it so—resolved to put off my departure from London—thrown into considerable anxiety & doubt by what Lord H. said this morning—determined, if on consideration it appears to me that I could be fairly charged with any thing wrong or unworthy in thus disposing of the Memoirs, to throw myself on the mercy of Murray & prevail on him to rescind the Deed—having it in my power, between the £500 I have left in his hands, Lord Ls. 740 & Lord John's 200 to pay him back near three fourths of his 2000—lay awake, thinking of it—

5 [Monday]—Decided upon leaving the whole transaction as it is at present—Wrote a long letter to Lord Holland, expressing all I had felt & thought since I saw him, the decision I had come to and the reasons which induced me to it[1]—found myself easier after this—Took Luttrel to Newton's—Lady B. came there & took me to see Lawrence's pictures—West, Scott, Duke of Bedford, Lady Jersey, admirable—dined with Luttrel—looked over his new edition with alterations of the "Advice to Julia"—by the bye, I received the other day a manuscript from the Longmans, requesting me (as they often do) to look it over & give my opinion whether it would be worth publishing anonymously—upon opening it found to my surprize, that it was Rogers's Italy,[2] which he had sent home thus privately to be published—went to Covent Gardens to the Bs. box & afterwards supped with them—Received this morning a letter from an unknown Poetess, intreating me to call upon her any day between three & nine in the evening—that I must not expect to find her a Blue-Stocking; for that she is "only a curly-headed little mortal &c. &c." & inclosing me the following (not bad) specimen of her talents—

Impromptu on their repealing the Act against Witch-craft in Ireland—

> So you think the days then of witch-craft are past
> That in Ireland you're safe from the magical art;
> Those who hold this belief may repent it at last,
> When the force of a spell is found deep in their heart.
> That the maidens of Erin in witchery deal
> By those who have seen them can ne'er be denied
> While the spell of their bards o'er the senses will steal,
> As by some hath been felt & by *Moore* hath been tried.
> Then think not to scape on such dangerous ground,
> Nor fancy that magic & witch-craft are o'er;

For in Ireland these powers will ever abound,
    While their witches are fair, and their Wizard is *Moore*.

6 [Tuesday]—Paid various bills—Wine-Merchant £66—Hodgkinson (for presents to Bessy's sister &c.) sixteen guineas—Hatter & Glover ten pounds &c. &c.—Breakfasted at H. Rogers's, Highbury Terrace—sent Miss R. the Proof Sheets of Cain—called upon the Poetess—{not very attractive—such creatures better *imagined* than *seen*}—wrote a letter to leave for Lord Landsdowne (whom I have been every day expecting from Paris) expressing as well as I could, my warm gratitude & inclosing him a draft for £740, referring him also to the two letters I had written to Lord Holland on the subject of the Memoirs[1]—In one of those, by the bye, were words to the following purport:—After saying that it should be perfectly in Brougham's power to read not only what was said about himself in these papers (which, however, I believe to be very trifling) but, what was of much more consequence, all that related to Lady Byron, in order that he might have an opportunity of correcting any thing that was misrepresented or misstated & so put the refutation on record with the charge, I added "Whatever may be thought of the propriety of publishing Private Memoirs at all, it certainly appears much more fair thus to proclaim & lay them open to the eyes of the world while all the persons interested or implicated are alive & capable of defending themselves, than (as is usually done) to keep them as a fire in reserve till those whom they have attacked have passed away & possess no longer the power of either retorting or justifying"—arranged with Stibbert for our departure tomorrow—dined at the George—called upon Power afterwards—packed &c—& got early to bed—

7 [Wednesday]—Off at seven in the Dover Coach—two Frenchmen our companions—talked of the niceties of the French language—"Parle par ma voix" in Racine wrong—Boileau full of faults in grammar (as I had already known from Saint Marc's notes)[1]—"je ne m'en rappelle pas" wrong—{mentioned a Calembourg[2] at the time of Nap's Coronation by the Pope—"Le Pape Pie sera (pissera) a Notre Dame demain"} arrived at Dover at 7—King's Head—wretched Inn—

8 [Thursday]—Sailed in the Rob Roy at ½ past seven—wind & sea against us—5 hours passage—arrived at ½ past two—obliged to stay till tomorrow on account of the Custom-house—met Brummel (the Exile of Calais) & had some conversation with him—

9 [Friday]—Set off in a hired Chaise at ½ past 11 for Boulogne—{sent for

Arthur Crookshort in order to perform the very ticklish commission Mary Godfrey entrusted to me which was no less than persuading him not to be so fond of his uncle's wife—he denied the whole charge altogether so that I had nothing to do but shake hands with him & leave him—not at all convinced however that he is not as improperly fond of his aunt as ever.]— dined at Boulogne & arrived in Stibbert's carriage, at Montreuil half past ten at night.

10 [Saturday]—Lunched at Abbeville—slept at Beauvais—

11 [Sunday]—Arrived in Paris at 4—Bessy out—but saw my darling little Tom quite well—dined at home—Bessy returned soon after—Thank God, all my dear ones are safe & well for me on my return.

12 [Monday]—Drove out with Mrs. Story & Miss Inglis—wet day—dined at home.

13 [Tuesday]—Paid visits—[to Made. Durazzo, to whom I gave the opera glasses which Lord John had entrusted to me—] Lady Jersey &c.—paid some bills—forgot, by the bye, to take notice of some verses of Luttrel's, which he gave me in town, and which he wrote as if from Rogers upon hearing, about the same time, that parts of Lalla Rookh were translated & sung in Persian & that Lord Lauderdale had all "Human Life" by heart.

A Set-off.

> I'm told, dear Moore, your lays are sung,
>   (Can it be true, you lucky man?)
> By moonlight, in the Persian tongue,
>   Along the street of Ispahan
> Tis hard—but one reflection cures,
>   At once, a jealous poet's smart—
> The Persians have translated yours,
>   But Lauderdale has mine by heart—

14—15, 16, &c. &c. [Wednesday–Thursday (22nd)] For this week I have not been able to journalize very accurately—Besides writing an additional verse to one of the National Melodies of the Third number, I began revising what is written of my Egyptian Work, and added a number of new lines— our lodgings (which are Rue d'Angou 17) seemed at first formidable to me from their noisy situation, but I find, that by lying in bed some hours in the morning, I may contrive to get on a little in my work during the winter—

Received a letter full of kindness from Lord Lansdowne, in which, however, he seems to agree with Lord Holland as to the sale of the Memoirs—at
least so far as to think that it *may* be a subject worthy my future consideration whether I should not redeem them out of the hands of Murray,
and saying that the £740 is at my disposal towards that purpose, if ever I
should decide upon it—This is enough—I am now *determined* to redeem
them—Received a letter from Croker to whom I had written, in consequence of a paragraph in the Courier¹ charging the Morn. Chronicle with
"importing Epigrams from Paris," begging him to set them right as to any
suspicion they may have of *me,* as I have not published any thing political,
except the verses about the Neapolitans for some years, & with respect to
the King, if I occupied myself about him at all, it would be to praise him
with all my heart for his wise & liberal conduct in Ireland, whatever I might
think of the hollow & heartless sycophants who were the object of it.—
Croker says in his answer that slight as this favourable mention of the King
is, he read it with pleasure, and should hail a "rapprochement" between us
on that point with real gratification &c. &c.—It is flattering enough to think
that I have now, within the last month, received letters full of the most
cordial attachment from three persons so widely sundered in the political
hemisphere as are Sir F. Burdett, Lord Lansdowne & Croker.—Dined the
19th. with Lord Granard—was to have joined Lord Dunsany & the Douglas's at a Restaurateur's—had the latter dinner on Thursday 22 at the
Rocher de Cancalle (Bessy of the party) & went in the evening to Franconi's—

23. [Friday] Dined at Lord Granard's to meet the Chabots, who, by the bye,
have sent me home the Clock (Mademoiselle's present) which is very handsome & now adorns my mantel-piece.

24 [Saturday]—Still occupied every morning in revising my Work—dined
at a Restaurateurs with the Villamils, Storys, Dalton & the Belchers, and
took our chances for places at the Italian opera afterwards—the Matrimonio Segreto¹—supped at Story's [afterwards]—

25 [Sunday]—Took a stall in the orchestra at the French opera for the
evening—dined with Story & both went—the Danaïdes¹—had called upon
Lady Jersey before dinner & read her Lord Bs. Irish verses—sat for near
an hour with her, Lord Jersey & Lord Thanet.

26 [Monday]—Bessy & I & the girls dined with Villamil & went to the

Gymnas—in the evening—L'Artiste, & L'Amant Bossu[1]—Perlet & Gontier the respective heroes—Forster came to tell me that poor Dr. Yonge was put in prison for debt, & that he was making a collection for him—gave 500 franks towards it.

27 [Tuesday]—Having finished the revisal of what I had written of the Egyptian Work, resumed my task & wrote 10 lines—dined, all, at the Douglas's—Lord Dunsany of the party—went in the evening to the Duchesse de Broglie, in consequence of a note I had had from her in the morning—a party there—Mades. Dolomieu, St. Aulaire, de Barante &c.—Lord Jersey & Lord Bristol—the Duchesse made me fix a day to dine there, Thursday week—

28 [Wednesday]—Dined at home & read & wrote in the evening—In the morning had gone to the Opera-House, and, saw Marie Mercandotti {(Lord Fife's élève)} dance[1]—a beautiful little girl—most perfectly shaped & promises to be a first-rate dancer.

{29 [Thursday]—Dined at Lord Jersey's—company Lord Thanet & Lord Kensington—from thence went & sat an hour with Mrs. Story & afterwards to Mrs. Gold Gents, where there were the Long Wellesleys &c. &c.}

30 [Friday]—Dined at Lord Bristol's, to meet Made. de Genlis—a large party, Charlemonts, Templetons, Granards &c.—Sat next Made. de Genlis—much conversation with her—some things she told of the "olden time" rather interesting—upon my mentioning Mickle's detection of Voltaire's criticisms on the Lusiad, she told a similar thing of some criticisms of Marmontel upon the same poem which she traced in the same manner to an old French translation[1]—spoke of his Tales, as in such *mauvais ton* of society—that he certainly met men of fashion at Madlle. Clairon's, but only knew them by the manners they put on there, (which were, of course different from what they would be in correct society) & painted from them accordingly. Mentioned some man of rank whom she had heard praising the manner in which Marmontel had sketched some characters saying that it was to the very life, and on her expressing her astonishment at this opinion, he added—"Yes life such as it is chez Madlle Clairon"—the same person, too, in praising any touch of nature in Marmontel, always subjoined "La Nature—comme elle est chez Madlle. Clairon"—told me that she once entrusted to Stone between 30 & 40 {MS} volumes of Extracts

which she had made during a most voluminous course of English reading; and which she never afterwards could recover—supposes that they are in the possession of Miss Helen Maria Williams—Sang in the evening—Translated "Keep your tears for me" into French for Made. de Genlis before I sang it—Went from thence to Made. de Flahaut's—heard some pretty good singing from the De {Lihues} & Flahault—some fine playing too on the French Horn by a M. Puzzi—

Dec. 1 [Saturday]—Dined with Stibbert—company, Lords Trimlestown, Kensington, Lisburne, &c. &c.—good dinner enough, but Lord Kensington too talkative—Went afterwards to Made. de Flahaut's box at the Italian's—found there the De Souzas & Gallois—L'Italiana in Algieri.

2nd. [Sunday]—Wrote in the morning, as I have done every morning—MaCleod dined with me *solus cum solo* & he & Lord Dunsany accompanied us to Made. Courtin's benefit at the Opera—Don Juan, from the Italians & Psyche—Bigottini beautiful in L'Amour.[1]

3rd. [Monday]—Have now done 72 lines in six days, which is not bad; considering my interruptions—Walked out with Mercer & made some calls—Had Lord Granard & Lord Dunsany to dine with us, and took them in the evening to the Villamils, where we had a swarm of Spaniards & music—Massimino accompanied us on the Piano-Forte.

4. [Tuesday] Wrote some lines—Went with Story to St. Pelagie to see poor Yonge, but were not admitted for want of a permission from the Prefecture de Police—dined at home—a note from Yonge in the evening to beg I would see Forster & try & prevent the sale of his furniture tomorrow morning—took a cabriolet & went off to Forster's, who promised to do what he could about it—My things laid out to dress for the Ambassador's, but changed my mind & did not go.

5 [Wednesday]—Finished my fourth Letter—{received a note from some Made. de Quincey begging me to call upon her soon after—"Give me [*several words unrecovered*]"—suspect the nature of this affair.} Dined at Story's with Dalton & MaCleod—all went (except Bessy, who is ill with a head-ache) to Forster's, where we had the old doubly-Dowager Lady Dysart, and some foreigners—sung & supped—

6 [Thursday]—Copied out some of my corrections & wrote letters—{called at Made. de Quincey's and found I was right in my suspicion}—dined at the Duc de Broglie's (had been asked to the Flahauts, too)—Company, the Jerseys, St. Aulaires, Comte Forbin &c.—very agreeable—A piece some time ago at one of the little Theatres called "La Mort d'Abel ou le Frere sans délicatesse"—talked of Grilparzer's tragedies (Sappho &c.)[1] with Made. de Broglie, who has read some of them but does not like them— sung in the evening & it did not seem lost upon them—Made. de Broglie sang with me "Go, where Glory waits thee" & pronounced the words (all, except "hearth" which she made rather a startling sound of) very prettily— Mad. St. Aulaire (who is married to the father of Mad. Decaze) a very pleasing person—{Gave this morning 20 franks to a distressed tradesman of the name of Griaturer.}

7 [Friday]—Went to call upon Mildmay at his own request—poor Yonge's situation the subject on which he wished to speak—Determined to try whether Lord Thanet (whom he once attended) will do anything—went to the Beaujon with Mrs. S. & the Macleods—went down 17 times with various partners—called at the Jerseys to ask Lord Thanet's address—he came in while I was there & I mentioned Yonge's case—have hopes it will produce something not only from him but Lord Jersey—received a ticket from Lord Fife for the Opera this evening—dined at home—went to the Opera for a short time—saw the Dance in Fernand Cortez[1]—Rose, Adelise, Roland, Buron rather pretty figurantes—{Houllain lives with the famous flute-player Trulen—Anatole was the great favourite of the King of Pompei & returned from Berlin loaded with presents by him—All this intelligence from Bramsen, my old travelling companion from Rome and now Lord Fife's chief Jack-all.—} Went afterwards to join Bessy & the girls at Mrs. Villamil's & practised over some Italian duetts.

8 [Saturday]—Read (as I have done for some days) Dupuis's Origine de tous les Cultes,[1] which I bought the other day for 40 francs—am reading it for my Letter of the High Priest[2]—dined (a large party, the Storys, MaCleods, Villamil & Dalton) at Beauvillier's, and went to Feydeau in the evening—Edmund & Caroline & Gulistan[3]—

9 [Sunday]—Began my 5th Letter—called with Bessy in the morning on Lady Rancliffe & Lady Granard—walked with her in the Thuileries afterwards—dined at home—Went to read in the news-Room—poor Perry's death![1]—{he has not left an honester or more genuine heart behind

him.} Lord Jersey brought me back this morning Lord Bs. Journal which I lent to Lady J.

10 [Monday]—A letter from Corry to say that Richard Power cannot live many weeks—what a dreary thing to see such noble hearts dying around one!—wrote three or four lines of my Priest's Letter, which I find difficult—Lord Granard dined with us to go & see Marie Mercandotti's debut at the French Opera—The Storys, Mc.Cleods & we have taken three boxes for it—Lord Dunsany of our party—The Caravane de Caire & Nina[1]—Marie succeded, but rather fell short of the expectations she gave us in rehearsing—Bigottini perfect in Nina—such dumb-show with sweet music beyond all the written tragedies in the world.

11. [Tuesday]—A few lines more of the letters—not good enough to stand—Have some thoughts of employing the few distracted moments allowed me in arranging the "Rhymes on the Road" for publication[1]—Went with Bessy to make calls, Lord Dunsany having lent her his carriage for the purpose—dined at home—after dinner a note from Lady Rancliffe, offering to take me to the Francais—accepted her offer—soon after arrived a note from Mad. de Flahaut, saying a seat in her box at the Italian was at my service—went to the Francais—Mars in La Jeune Femme Colère[2]—from thence accompanied Lady Rancliffe to the Ambassador's large assembly—conversed for some time with the Duke of Hamilton—saw Talleyrand for the first time—{Had another note to-day of the same sort as the former from a Made. [*unrecovered*]}

12 [Wednesday]—Called upon the Jerseys—Lady E. Stuart there—mentioned that it has long been the ton in France to press people to eat at dinner—instanced the Duchess of Orleans—that however some of the young French Women are beginning to get into the English fashion of leaving people to themselves—dined with the Storys, (Foster of the party) and went all to the Christening of McCleod's child in the evening—supped there, and went afterward to Mrs. Morier's Ball—home about one—

13 [Thursday]—Walked out earlier than usual to perform some commissions for the day's dinner—wrote letters—The Douglas's & Lord Dunsany to dine with us—more people in the evening—Storys, Villamils, McCleods &c.—were told that Made. Benjamin Constant (our neighbour au premier) had sent word that she would come down & take coffee with us—waited

upon her & found that it was Benjamin himself had sent this message—accordingly he came down & staid till eleven o'clock—had music & sandwiches & afterwards danced—left us between one & two.

14 [Friday]—Walked to the Bois de Boulogne—met Auguste de Staël, & had much talk with him about the change of Ministry—wrote about a dozen lines to-day—called on the Villamils at five & proposed to dine with them—did so, and returned home early.—De Stael to-day mentioned a joke about the new ministry—that (it being Monsieur's choosing) he had "escomptés son regne."

15 [Saturday]—Wrote a few lines & walked in the Champs Elysees for an hour & half—Made some calls—Bessy & I & the girls dined at Villamils—Kenny & Mercer of the party—had music in the evening—have written about forty lines of my Priest's letter.—

16 [Sunday]—Wrote & walked a little—received an invitation to the Duke of Orleans this evening—dined at Flahaut's—company, the Jerseys, a Mons. Labonne (I think) and young Lieven—dinner late on account of Flahaut's late return from la chasse—went between 8 & 9 to the Palais Royal—the Duchesse de Berri there & the Princess of Denmark—{some talk with Gerard, the painter—told me that the Prince of Orange shot sixteen hen pheasants—nobody daring to tell him how unsportsmanlike it was.—} Mademoiselle came & spoke to me & Gerard—asked him if he had heard me sing &c. &c.—he said, among other things, that I was the "flambeau de l'Angleterre"—few of the immense circle of women here worth a second look—the best among them Madame Sturmer & Lord Robt. Fitzgerald's fine colossal daughter—Boissy d'Anglas with his white hair spread out upon his shoulders a most extraordinary figure—introduced by Made. Durazzo to the Duchesse Litta, who is esteemed a beauty.

17 [Monday]—Wrote a few lines—went with Lord Dunsany & Douglas to dine with the Henrys, far away near the Chateau de Vincennes—was to have gone to Madame St. Aulaire's in the evening, but returned to Paris too late—

18 [Tuesday]—Wrote some lines—walked out with Bessy—dined at Gage Rockwood's—Company, Lord & Lady Kenmare, Douglas, &c. &c—the little Moscow girl acted a scene in the evening—from thence to the Ambassa-

dor's—some show of beauty—the Duchesse de Fiere-macon, {(who has however bad teeth, though only 21)} and a Miss Huxley an Irish girl—

19 [Wednesday]—6 or 8 lines—chiefly made out during a solitary walk beyond the Barrier—drove afterwards a little with Mrs. S. & the Macleods—dined at Robinson's—Lady Helena very agreeable—in the evening to Mad. de Flahaut's, & from thence to the Duchesse de Broglie's—a great beauty at the former place, Made. de Vicence, and Benjamin Constant, who said he had come to pay a visit to me this evening & had sat some time with Mrs. Moore—got into a scrape about dinner to-day, having promised also to dine with the Grahams & forgot—

20 [Thursday]—Wrote letters—dined at home—Mrs. Story dined with us—Received a parcel from Sir Robt. Wilson from Calais, where he is detained with Lambton, Lady L. her sister and Lady Ossulston, they having sailed in an open fishing-boat from Dover, and left carriages, baggage &c. behind them—the parcel consisted of two copies of Lord Byron's new Tragedies (sent off some days before publication) now one of which Murray wishes me to found a bargain with Galignani for the right of publishing here—took a cabriolet & went off to Galignani's after dinner.

21 [Friday]—Galignani called & agreed to give a hundred pounds—wrote a few lines—dined at C. Hutchinsons—company, Mackenzie, Mills, Greathead &c. &c.—sang a little & went from thence to Lady Charlemont's Ball. Home early.—Sent a copy of the Tragedies to Lady E. Stewart this morning

22 [Saturday]—Have done now in all 100 lines of my fifth Letter—have read also two or three volumes of Dupuis—he has abridged this book & well he might—never was any work so full of repetitions & redundancies— Walked in an unfrequented road beyond the Barrier, from which the view of Mont Calvaire & the Aqueduct in the setting sun is very fine—felt one of those fits of faintness, in returning, which always come over me when I do not eat enough.—Dined by myself at the Café Francais (in consequence of Bessy's early dinner with the little ones) and sauntered off alone to the Ambigu Comique afterwards—L'Homme à trois visages[1]—our dear Anastasia came home for the Holidays—Called upon Lady de Ros this morning who showed me some of her very clever Lithograph drawings—one subject of the child & ruffian in "Paradise & the Peri",[2] charmingly imagined— promised to give me copies of them—

23. [Sunday]—Revised some of what I had written—walked to call upon Kenny—thought I was invited to Villamil's to dinner, but found it was not the case—dined with Dalton at the Café Francais—from thence for an hour to Lord Fife's Box to see the Dance in Fernand Cortez & then to Villamil's, where we had music & supped—

24 [Monday]—Wrote some lines—dined at home—went to Made. St. Aulaire's in the evening—some conversation with the Duchesse de Broglie—told her of Power's having supposed (from my telling him that I saw her some years ago dance the Cossack Air, which Knyvet claims as his) that she was an Opera dancer and begged me to enquire of her in what Ballet she danced it—went from thence to the McCleods to join a party for the Messe de Minuit at St. Roch—Mrs. Story, Miss Moore, the McCleods &c.—a dull & cold operation—got home at one.

25 [Tuesday]—Wrote & walked—dined at home—took Anastasia & Tom to a children's ball at Douglas's—Bessy too ill to go—danced & played at blind-man's buff with the children—little Tom much admired—the adults danced afterwards—supped & sang.—Douglas is making a table to surprize Bessy with on New-Year's Day—adorned with poetical emblems, the Irish Harp &c. & scrolls containing the words "Lalla Rookh" and "Irish Melodies".

26. [Wednesday]—A few lines—dined early for the purpose of taking the children to Franconi's—the Bataille de Bovines,[1] the Elephant &c. &c.—little Tom, notwithstanding his raking last night full of animation.

27 [Thursday]—Wrote letters—walked in the Thuilleries—first with Genl. Cheron & Wilder—then with Capt. Waldegrave & Cadogan—{the latter talked of the Memoirs of the Duc de Lauzun just published[1]—promised to send them to me—Flahaut said the other night that this man of gallantry was supposed to have been impotent or nearly so—} dined at Lord Granard's—Mercer, Burrel, the Robinsons &c. &c.—much curious talk with Lady Adelaide about Lord Hastings—went in the evening with Lady Helena to Lady De Roos to thank her for the beautiful Lithograph drawings she sent me.

28 [Friday]—Dined at Villamil's—Story, Dalton, Capt. Popham, Mercer &c.—Music in the evening—Massimino accompanied & very ill—Lady

Popham & daughter joined the party in the evening—After the departure of a few, became more merry & supped—forgot Lady Charlemont's Ball.

29 [Saturday]—Meant to go see the Paria[1] to-night, but met the Macleods who said they had got Lord Fife's box for the Italian—dined with the Stories & went—the Barbiere—Fodor in her very best voice[2]—Did not go to the Duchesse de Broglies—Have done near sixty lines this week—

30 [Sunday]—Wrote ten lines—Walked on the road beyond the Barrier—a glorious day. A bright sun on one side and a misty shower & double rainbow on the other—dined at Brummel's, having nearly fainted beforehand with the pain of blow I got on my knee while dressing—Company, Mr. & Mrs. White & William Dawson—{an excellent thing mentioned by Mr. White of the Firm of "Rogers & Greavis" Gloves in the Strand, being a translation of the "Omne Animal post &c. &c."—} sung in the evening, and two or three pair of bright eyes weeping around me—did not go to Made. de Flahaut's from whom I had a note this morning entreating me not to fail being at her supper tomorrow night—

31 [Monday]—Went with the Douglass to dine at Henry's, under a promise that I should be back in town time enough for Made. de Flahaut's New Year's Eve Supper—left that at nine, and was in the Grand Rue Vert a little after ten—a very select party—the Jerseys, Lady Ossulston, the Lambtons, Lady E. Grey, (a most charming person) the Elliss, Prince Beauveau, Mrs. G. Lamb, Sir R. Wilson, & one or two more—A Jeu de loterie occupied the time before supper, in which some of the prettiest things from the Petit Dunkerque were won—wished much that Lady E. Gray should win a beautiful paper-presser in the form of a butter-fly with the wings for handles, but she did not—{Lord Jersey, who did, to my still further disappointment gave it to Lady Ossulston—After supper singing by Flahaut & the Miss De [?Lihus]—did not ask me—very glad to be off, but none but a Frenchman (and one "qui aime s'écouter") would have allowed me to escape so—}

Notes to 1821 Entries

2 January

1. Irving's accounts of Christmas comprise No. 5 of *The Sketch Book*.
2. Isaac Disraeli, *Curiosities of Literature*, 4 vols. (Boston, 1859). The quotation from Bacon is found in 4: 227: "My name and memory I leave to foreign nations, and to mine own country-men, *after sometime be past over.*" The quotation from Martial is in 1: 94, bk. 14, Epigram 186. Disraeli's comment about insuring books is in 1: 109. The allusion to Olindo is found in Tasso's *Gerusalemme Liberata,* bk. 2, st. 16, 1. 4. See Tasso, *Jerusalem Delivered,* trans. Edward Fairfax (Carbondale, Ill., 1962).

3 January

1. Matthew 7:3: "Why do you see the speck that is in your brother's eye, but do not notice the log that is in your own eye?" By omitting the "o" from "oculus" (eye), the word becomes "culus" (buttock).
2. See Disraeli, *Curiosities of Literature,* 1: 252.

5 January

1. *The Giaour* (1813).

9 January

1. Charles Antoine Guillaume Pigault Lebrun, *Le Citateur,* 2 vols. (1803).

12 January

1. Marchand, *LJ*, 7: 253–55.

13 January

1. *Fudge Family in Paris, Works,* 7: 163.

15 January

1. Coleridge, *Byron's Poetry,* 7: 46. Byron's lines to Moore were published, with numerous alterations, in the *Times* for 9 January 1821. Moore's lines did not appear in the *Times.*

28 January

1. Théophile Marion Dumersan and Nicolas Brazier, *Les Bonnes d'Enfans, ou une soirée aux boulevards neufs* (1820). Armand d'Artois de Bournonville, (Edmond?) Rochefort, and Emmanuel Théaulon de Lambert, *Le Diable d'Argent* (1820).

5 February

1. See Marchand, *LJ*, 8: 67–69, and Coleridge, *Byron's Poetry*, 7: 72–73. E. H. Coleridge explains the allusion by referring to Rivington's *Annual Register* 62 (1820): 114, 115, which mentions that a splendid procession of brass-founders and braziers presented to the Queen an address enclosed in a brass case.

6 February

1. Étienne Nicolas Mehul, *Joseph* (1807).

7 February

1. Louis Jean Népomucène Lemercier, *La Démence de Charles VI,* tragedy in five acts. It was to have been performed at the second Théâtre-Français on 25 September 1820; published 1820. Antoine Vincent Arnault, *Guillaume de Nassau,* tragedy in five acts, was also scheduled to be performed at the Théâtre-Français. Published 1826.
2. Milton, *Comus* (1634), 1. 93.

9 February

1. Cuvelier and Hélitas de Meun, *La Mort du Tasse* (1821).
2. Eugène Scribe and Germaine Delavigne, *Le Colonel* (1821). Eugène Scribe and Anne Honoré Joseph Duveyrier, *Le Secrétaire et le Cuisinier* (1821).

10 February

1. Pierre de La Clos, *Les Liaisons dangereuses* (1782). The scene comparable to Lord Bath's signing the Treaty of Utrecht occurs in Letter 47 from the Vicomte de Valmont to the Marquise de Merleuil, in which the Vicomte mentions "une lettre écrite du lit et presque d'entre les bras d'une fille." See *Les Liaisons dangereuses* (Paris, 1926), p. 134.

12 February

1. The review of "The French Novels," *Edinburgh Review* 34 (1820): 372–83. See entries for 25 January and 10 February 1821.

16 February

1. Dr. Whitelaw Ainslie, *Clemenzai; or, the Tuscan Orphan,* produced at Bath 1 May 1822.

20 February

1. *Works,* 4: 51–52.

2. For *Bonnes d'Enfans* see entry for 28 January 1821. Henri Dupin, Eugène Scribe, and Anne Honoré Joseph Duveyrier, *L'Ennui, ou le Comte Derfort* (1821). Jean Merle and Nicolas Brazier, *Le Ci-devant Jeune Homme* (1812). Eugène Scribe and Henri Dupin, *L'Intérieur d'une étude, ou le Procureur et l'Avoué* (1821).

21 February

1. Exodus 17:1–7. The Lord commanded Moses to strike the rock, from which water flowed.

22 February

1. Lord Lansdowne consistently adopted liberal causes and opposed illiberal measures, such as the bill for the prevention of "blasphemous and seditious libels" in December 1819. He championed free trade in a speech made in May 1820 and advocated abolition of the slave trade and the granting of Catholic claims in Ireland.

23 February

1. Eugène Scribe and Anne Honoré Joseph Duveyrier, *Le Vampire* (1820). Michel Charagnac, *Le Jeune Werther, ou les Grandes Passions* (1819). Nicolas Brazier and Anne Honoré Joseph Duveyrier, *Les Dieux à la Courtille* (1820).

24 February

1. *Works*, 4: 32–34.
2. Richard Chenevix's articles are "The Comparative Skill and Industry of France and England," and "The State of Science in England and France," *Edinburgh Review* 32 (1819): 340–89 and 34 (1820): 383–422.
3. Jean François Ducis, *Hamlet, tragedy imitated from the English* (1769). Casimir Périer (1777–1832) was Minister of State. Talma's acting in the play resembled the behavior of Périer when at the rostrum making a speech.
4. Moore's translation of Lamartine's verses and his "slight" of the author occur in the review of French Novels, *Edinburgh Review* 68 (1820): 372. Moore remarks that Lamartine's "Méditations Poétiques" was well received, but that the work "appears to us a very unsuccessful attempt to break through the *ancien régime* of the French Parnassus, and transplant the wild and irregular graces of English poetry into the triumparterre of the Gallic muse."

27 February

1. The presentation of *Lalla Rookh* was made on 27 January 1821 and was later published by Wilhelm Hensel as *Die Leben den Bilder und pantomimischen Darstellungen bei dem Festspiel Lalla Rukh aufgeführt auf dem Königlichen Schlosse in Berlin* (1823). Ernest, Duke of Cumberland, a son of George III, later became king of Hanover (1837–51).
2. The government in England feared that Russia's support of Greek independence meant that Russia hoped to expand her empire by the defeat of Turkey. Hence Canning placed obstacles in the way of Greek independence, though he declared England's neutrality.
The reference to France concerns that country's policy of maintaining neutrality in the face of Austria's invasion of Naples in March 1821. See Halévy, *History*, 2, 137; 186–87; and passim.

2 March

1. The following note (not in Moore's hand) written on a sheet of notepaper was inserted in the MS at this point: "A joke of the Duchess of Gordon—She said to Mr. Whitbread in 1805, 'Do you know what I call Lord Melville now Mr. Whitbread? I call him your entire butt'—"

7 March

1. *Works*, 3: 227. The poem was written upon the death of Robert Emmet. See Marchand, *LJ*, 7: 218–20, for Byron's letter to Moore.

9 March

1. After William Corbet was expelled from Trinity College, Dublin, in 1798 for treasonable politics, he made his way to France, where he received a commission in the French army. In November 1798, while at Hamburg planning a military descent upon Ireland, he was arrested, contrary to the law of nations, together with Napper Tandy, Blackwell, and Morres. In 1793 Corbet and Blackwell escaped from Kilmainham prison, where they were being held without trial, and returned to France, where Corbet resumed his military career.

10 March

1. Eugène Scribe and Brulay, *Le Gastronome sans argent* (1821).

13 March

1. Charles Augustin Sewrin and Nicolas Brazier, *Riquet à la houppe* (1821).

19 March

1. *Bracebridge Hall, or the Humourists*, 2 vols. (1822). The passage in ornamental brackets was apparently deleted by Moore himself.

22 March

1. Armand d'Artois and Marie Émmanuel Théaulon de Lambert, *La Fille d'honneur, ou l'Hôpital dramatique* (1819); Alexandre Vincent Pineu Duval, *La Jeunesse de Henri V* (1806).

24 March

1. Jean-Guillaume-A. Cuvelier de Trie, *L'Attaque du Convoi* (1821).

26 March

1. Jean Charles Emmanuel Nodier, *Thérèse Aubert* (1819).

30 March

1. "Lines on the Entry of the Austrians into Naples," *Works,* 7: 392–95. Russell cites this poem and quotes the first line: "Aye—down to the dust with them, slaves as they are. . . ."

31 March

1. Moore placed the passage in square brackets at the end of the MS page, with an asterisk indicating its proper location in the text.

1 April

1. Lady Adelaide Forbes.
2. B. Marmant du Hautchamp, *Histoire du système des finances sous la minorité de Louis XV pendant les années 1719 et 1720. Précéde d'un abregé de la vie du Duc Régent, et du Sr. Lau,* 6 vols. (1739).

3 April

1. For a more detailed account of the Berlin performance see the letter to Andrew Doyle of 15 June 1846 in Dowden, *Letters,* 2: 885–86.

7 April

1. Jean-Jacques Rousseau, *Œuvres complètes,* 37 vols. (1788–93).

8 April

1. Sir John Francis Edward Acton (1736–1811). English officer; commander-in-chief of the Neapolitan navy, prime minister under Ferdinand I, King of the Two Sicilies. See Forsyth, *Italy,* 2: 265.

9 April

1. *Baratariana. A Select Collection of Fugitive Political Pieces, Published during the Administration of Lord John Townshend in Ireland,* by Henry Grattan, Henry Flood, Sir Hercules Langrishe, H. M. Boyd, and the Rev. _____ Simpson (1773).

11 April

1. Marie François, Denis Thérèsa Le Roi, Baron d'Allarde, and Armand d'Artois, *La Marchande de goujons, ou les Trois bossus* (1821). Nicolas Brazier and Théophile Marion Dumersan, *Le Coin de Rue, ou le Rempailler des chaises* (1820).

12 April

1. Théodore Nézel and E. F. Varez, *La Famille Irlandaise* (1821).
Moore refers to the insurrection of 1798, caused largely by the brutal policies of General

Lake, who succeeded Sir Ralph Abercrombie, Irish Commander in Chief, when the latter was forced to resign after issuing an order declaring the army to be "in such a state of licentiousness as must render it formidable to every one but the enemy." See Edmund Curtis, *A History of Ireland* (London, 1964), p. 341. For a complete account of the 1798 rebellion see Thomas Pakenham, *The Year of Liberty* (Englewood Cliffs, N.J., 1969).

2. See Disraeli, *The Curiosities of Literature*, 4 vols. (Boston, 1859). For the quotation from Clarendon, see *Curiosities*, 3: 36; the reference to the Norwegians and roses as well as that to coffee is in ibid., 3: 53 and 61.

13 April

1. A "bougie," according to the *OED*, is a thin, flexible surgical instrument for introduction into the passages of the body for purposes of exploration, dilation, or medication.

2. Lord Byron, *A Letter to John Murray on the Rev. W. L. Bowles' Strictures on the Life and Writings of Pope* (1821). For the passage in which Byron says that Moore approves of Bowles's "invariable principles of poetry" see Prothero, *LJ*, 5: 558.

18 April

1. See Prothero, *LJ*, 5: 310 n: "The case of Waterhouse v. Berkeley was tried at Gloucester Assizes in April, 1821. It was an action for damages brought by John Waterhouse for the seduction of his wife by Colonel Berkeley. The jury returned a verdict for the plaintiff to whom they awarded £1000 damages."

19 April

1. See entry and n. 1 for 31 March 1820.

20 April

1. "Lines Written on Hearing that the Austrians Had Entered Naples" appeared in the *Examiner*, no. 693, 15 April 1821.

24 April

1. Marie Émmanuel Théaulon de Lambert and Armand d'Artois, *Jeanne d'Arc*, (1821).

26 April

1. "Bowles's Strictures on Pope," Prothero, *LJ*, 5: 549: "for the head of Lady Charlemont . . . seemed to possess all that sculpture could require for its ideal."

2. Jacques Vafflard and Joseph Fulgence de Bury, *Le Voyage à Dieppe* (1821).

27 April

1. Disraeli, *Curiosities of Literature* (1859). The references are cited in the order given in Moore's text: "Literary Blunders," 2: 416; "Ariosto and Tasso," 2: 59; "Origin of the Materials of Writing," 2: 181–82: *ibid.*, p. 183; "Influence of a Name," 2: 232.

3 May

1. Marie Émmanuel Théaulon de Lambert and de Roncé, *Blanche de Provence*. Mus. de Cherubini, Breton, Boïeldieu et Paër, ballets de Gardel et Milau (1821).
2. A short, double-breasted overcoat without tails.

7 May

1. Russell substitutes "He" for Burgess.
2. "Lines on the Death of Mr. P--RC--V--L," *Works*, 7: 73–74.

13 May

1. George Moore, *Lives of Cardinal Alberoni and the Duke of Ripperda*, 2 vols. (1806).
2. Sir Anthony Absolute in Sheridan's *The Rivals*. Old Mirabel is a character in George Farquhar's *The Inconstant, or the Way to Win Him* (1702). He is described as "an aged gentleman, of an odd compound, between the peevishness incident to his years, and his fatherly fondness towards his son."

21 May

1. Lady Davy was considered the "English Corinne" after *Corinne, ou l'Italie*, by Mme de Staël (1807). The heroine is a beautiful poetess and mysterious genius.

29 May

1. *Bergère* means both "shepherdess" and "easy-chair."

30 May

1. From Racine's *Athalie* (1691), 3. iii, 1091–1092.

1 June

1. There were a number of *Memoirs* of various academies in France published at this time, and the number of volumes varied widely.

4 June

1. "How Shall I Woo?" *Works*, 4: 244–45.
2. Giovanni Battista Belzoni, *Narrative of the Operations and Recent Discoveries within the Pyramids, Temples, Tombs, and Excavations in Egypt and Nubia . . .* (1820).

10 June

1. *Irish Meoldies . . . With an appendix, containing the original advertisements, and a prefatory letter on music* (1821).

11 June

1. See F. Loliée, *La Comédie Française 1658–1907* (Paris, 1907). Loliée raises the question of Napoleon's irritation at the production of two plays in the répertoire: *Athalie* and *Mérope*. In a note to *Athalie,* he says that the library of the Comédie-Française has a copy of the play that contains two passages in Act 1, sc. i that were deleted by the *censure napoléonienne*. The first is of four lines, in which Joad says to Abner, *au nom du Dieu des Juifs:*

> Quel fruit me revient-il de tous vos sacrifices?
> Ai-je besoin du sang des boucs et des génisses?
> Le sang de nos rois crie et n'est point écouté
> Rompez, rompez tout pact avec l'impiété.

The second censored passage is a dialogue between Abner and Joad in which Abner begins by saying, "Athalie étouffa l'enfant même au berceau."

13 June

1. In 1798 Scott married Anne Ogle, sister of Sheridan's second wife, Hester.

14 June

1. Lord John Russell, *History of the English Government from the Reign of Henry VII* (1821).
2. Scott, *Kenilworth* (1821).

18 June

1. Either Francesco Gieuseppe Lanza (b. ca. 1750), or his son Gesualdo Lanza (1779–1859), both of whom lived in London during part of their musical careers.

21 June

1. Irving's *Sketch Book* appeared in 1820. Moore here refers to *Tales of a Traveller* (1824). See entry for July 9 and its n. 1.

25 June

1. Franz Joseph Gall (1758–1828), physician and founder of phrenology. His chief work, with Johann Caspar Spurzheim, was *Anatomie et physiologie du système nerveux en général* (1810–19).

27 June

1. Moore's ellipsis.

28 June

1. *Ars Poetica,* ll. 386–90; Horace advises the young poet to put his poem away for nine years after showing it to "some Maecius . . . your father and me."

2 July

1. Villamil did not publish a Spanish translation of Russell's *History of the English Government*.
2. Thomas Cash in Jonson's *Every Man in His Humour* (1598).

3 July

1. Jacques Delille, *Les Jardins* (1780). A series of descriptive poems.
2. Marc-Antoine Jullien de Paris founded the *Revue Encyclopédique* in 1818.

5 July

1. William Richard Hamilton, *Aegyptiaca, or Some Account of the Ancient and Modern State of Egypt* (1809). Hamilton was an antiquarian and diplomat and an aide to Lord Elgin, whom he assisted in collecting the Elgin Marbles; at one time he frustrated an attempt by the French to steal the Rosetta Stone from Egypt.

9 July

1. Washington Irving, "A Literary Dinner," *Tales of a Traveller*, ed. William Lyon Phelps (New York, 1897), pp. 147–51.

14 July

1. Cadwallader, a character in Samuel Foote's *The Author* (1757).
2. Foote, *The Minor* (1760). In the play Samuel Swift assumes the character of Smirk, an auctioneer.

15 July

1. Either Godard d'Aucourt de Saint-Just's opera *Jean de Paris* (1812) or Marsollier's melodrama by that name (1807).

16 July

1. The trials of conspirators were held in 1821 and 1822. Moore mentions them in a letter to Lord Lansdowne in 1822. See Dowden, *Letters*, 2: 506 and note.

18 July

1. *La Morte de Napoléon, dythrambe traduit de l'anglais de Lord Byron (par Alfred de La F***; précédé d'une notice sur sa vie et la mort de Napoléon Bonaparte par Sir Thomas Moore* (1821).

26 July

1. "Mine" written in pencil above "ours." Russell transcribes the word "mine."
2. Comte Hermann Maurice de Saxe (1696–1750), known as "Maréchal de Saxe." French marshal.
3. Moore himself rendered this passage meaningless by using long dashes (as indicated in the text) instead of obscenities.

4. Abraham Cowley, "Ode: Acme and Septimius Out of Catullus," *Occasional Verses* (1668), ll. 1–2. George Lamb's translation of Catullus appeared in 1821.

30 July

1. Moore's lines are entitled "To Lady Holland. On Napoleon's Legacy of a Snuff-Box," *Works*, 9: 398. For a detailed account of Napoleon's gift, see Lloyd Sanders, *The Holland House Circle* (London, 1908), pp. 42–43.

3 August

1. Byron, *The Two Foscari: An Historical Tragedy* (1821).

4 August

1. Mark Wilks, *History of the Persecutions Endured by the Protestants of the South of France*, 2 vols. (1821).
2. The third tale in *Lalla Rookh, Works*, 6: 203–322.

6 August

1. E. Crosnier and A. V. de Saint-Hilaire, *Le Solitaire, ou l'Exile du Mont-Sauvage* (1821).

7 August

1. Thomas Edward Bowdich accompanied the party that visited the King of Ashantee in 1816. In 1819 he published *A Mission to Ashantee*.
2. i.e., the Théâtre Français, Rossini, *Otello ossia il Moro di Venezia* (1821).

10 August

1. Racine's *Britanicus* (1669). Moore saw Joseph Talma (1763–1826), a popular dramatic actor, as Nero, and Marie Thérèse Étiennette Bourgoin (1785–1833) as Junie. Moore quotes the closing lines of 5, iii.

13 August

1. Helen Maria Williams (1769–1827), one of the "French Blues." A poetess born in England who moved to Paris in 1790.
2. Though several *Memoirs* of Viscount Nelson are listed in the *British Museum Catalogue of Printed Books*, the catalogue of the *Bibliothèque Nationale* does not list a French translation.

14 August

1. Louis Racine, *Mémoires sur la vie de J. Racine* (1747), 2 vols.
2. Philippe Destouches (surname Néricault), *L'Irresolu* (1713). Moore quotes the last line of the drama.

15 August

1. "Foscari," *Poetical Works of Samuel Rogers,* ed. Edward Bell (London, 1892), pp. 243–50. The poem first appeared in November 1821, one month before Byron's drama.
2. *Works,* 6: 196.
3. Louis Jean Lemercier, *Louis IX en Égypte* (1821).

17 August

1. On August 8th the packet *Earl Moira* went down on its voyage from Liverpool to Dublin. Survivors reported that rough weather forced the ship aground twice, but that the captain and most of the crew were so drunk that they refused to return to port. There were over one hundred people on board when the ship finally sank, and only sixteen were rescued.

19 August

1. Antoine Vincent Arnault (1766–1834) was a friend and a supporter of Napoleon. Upon the restoration he was exiled to Brussels, where he remained until 1819. He did not publish a translation of the *Irish Melodies.*

27 August

1. M. Spontini, *La Vestale* (1807); and probably Saint-Germain de Panard, *Le Carnaval* (1728).

29 August

1. The only *National Air* identified as Mahratta has two stanzas: "Ne'er Talk of Wisdom's Gloomy Schools," *Works,* 4: 218.

31 August

1. Cowper's lines on the English divine and critic John Jortin (1698–1770) were enclosed along with Jortin's poem, "In Brevitatem Vitae . . . Spatii Hominibus Concessi," in a letter to Newton. See *The Poetical Works of William Cowper,* ed. H. S. Milford (London, 1926), pp. 562–63 and note. The other work to which Moore refers is Jan Gruter's *Inscriptiones Antiquae Totius Orbis Romani* (1602–3).
2. "Emmet," an ant.
3. "The Hind and the Panther," *The Poetical Works of John Dryden,* ed. H. T. Swedenberg, Jr., et al (Berkeley, 1969), 3: 125:

> Can I believe eternal God could lye
> Disguis'd in mortal mould and infancy
> That the great maker of the world could dye?

8 September

1. Halévy, *History,* 2: 9, refers to the "rabble of bought spies" who testified against Queen Caroline in her trial before the House of Lords in August 1820.
2. Antoine Jean Baptiste Simonnin, Balisson de Rougement and Jean Toussaint, *Le Tailleur de Jean-Jacques, ou les Deux Rousseau* (1819) and Charles Augustin Sewrin and Nicolas Brazier, *Riquet à la houppe* (1821).

9 September

1. The King's good-will visit to Ireland in August 1821, was received with applause. See Halévy, *History*, 2: 104.

10 September

1. *Works*, 2: 285–7.
2. M. Guillard and Christophe Gluck, *Iphigénie en Tauride* (1778); Marie-Anne Barbier and Jean-Louis Bertin, *Jugement de Paris* (1718).

11 September

1. Byron's letter to Moore dated 24 August 1821, Marchand, *LJ*, 8: 89.

13 September

1. Horatio (Horace) and James Smith first published *Rejected Addresses* in 1812.

14 September

1. Gilbert Stuart Newton (1795–1835), American painter.

19 September

1. "The Marriage of Cana" by Paulo Caliari, called Paulo Veronese, was commissioned in 1562. The American artist is Charles Robert Leslie (1794–1859).

20 September

1. Moore's omission.
2. Asonante: rhyming in the stressed vowel but not in the following consonant, as in casa, mata, pala; used in the versification of Old French, Spanish, Celtic, and other languages, but not defined in English until 1823 (see *OED*).

27 September

1. Byron's two tragedies were published with *Cain, a Mystery* in December 1821.
2. Moore may have read the *Mémoires* in any one of several editions of Marmontel. The first separate edition of the *Mémoires* was published in 1827.
3. John Home (1722–1808), Scottish clergyman and playwright. His play *Douglas, a Tragedy* was written in 1756.
4. "his spirit died" in Russell.

5 October

1. Sir George Hayter (1792–1871), portrait and historical painter.

6 October

1. Georgiana Caroline Lennox Fox (1723–74), created Lady Holland, Baroness of Holland in her own right in 1762; mother of Charles James Fox; grandmother of Moore's friend Lord Holland.

7 October

1. For Byron's proposal that he and Moore edit a weekly newspaper see Marchand, *LJ*, 7: 253–55, and entry for 12 January 1821.

12 October

1. *The Universe, a Poem* (1821) bears Maturin's name, but was written by James Wills (1790–1868), Irish poet and journalist.
2. Probably Thomas Casey, member of Ireland's Parliament 1798–1800.
3. The conflict between Grattan and Isaac Corry was caused by the former's strenuous efforts to thwart the union between Ireland and England in 1800. Although Grattan's speeches against the Union were for the most part unavailing in the House, he did succeed in arousing a good deal of public opinion against the proposal. To counteract the influence of Grattan with the people, Corry, then Chancellor of the Exchequer, rose in open debate on 14 February and accused Grattan of treason, of conspiring with the United Irishmen, and of trying to instigate another revolution. Grattan replied with a defense of his character and his conduct and a devastating attack on Corry's mediocre political achievements. On the following day the two men fought a duel, in which Corry was wounded in the arm.
4. See note 2 for 8 September 1818.

13 October

1. "To My Mother. Written in a Pocket Book, 1822," *Works*, 7: 390.

14 October

1. *The Life of the Right Honourable John Philpot Curran*, 2 vols. (1819).

19 October

1. "Keninge" in Russell.

23 October

1. Three lines are deleted in the MS at this point, which say, in only slightly different wording, exactly what is said in the sentence that follows.
2. James Kenney, *Match-breaking; or the Prince's Present* (1821); John Gay, *The Beggar's Opera* (1728).

24 October

1. On his second expedition to the Niger (1805), Mungo Park reached Bamako but died in the rapids during an attack by the natives.

2. Frederic Reynolds, *The Exile: or the Deserts of Siberia* (1808); John O'Keefe, *The Poor Soldier* (1783).

25 October

1. Thorwaldsen's bust of Byron was done in 1817. See Marchand, *Byron: A Biography*, 2: 844.

2. The lines appeared in the *Morning Chronicle* for 24 October. See n. 1 for 30 July.

3. Eugène Scribe and Xavier Boniface, *L'Ours et le pacha* (1820).

26 October

1. Moore refers to Dr. William Williams' unsigned review of "Italian Tragedy," *The Quarterly Review* 24 (1820): 71–102. The article contains a discussion and translation of several passages of Ugo Foscolo's *Ricciarda: Tragedia* (1820). For Williams's quarrel with Foscolo, see entry for 23 February and note.

2. B. F. Hoffman, *Les Rendez-Vous Bourgeois* (1807).

27 October

1. *The Coronation,* a reproduction of the coronation of George IV (1821); William Thomas Moncrieff, *Monsieur Tonson* (1821).

2. Barham Levius, *Maid or Wife; or, the Deceiver Deceived* (1821).

28 October

1. Thomas Campbell edited the *New Monthly Magazine* from 1821–27.

2. Abdiel is the angel who denounces Satan and deserts him to disclose the revolt. *Paradise Lost,* 5. 803–6. 28. Moore refers to the following passage:

> So spake the seraph Abdiel faithful found
> Among the faithless, faithful only he. . . .
>
> (5. 896–97).

3. The first stanza of Lord Carlisle's verses is:

> Lady, reject the gift! 'tis tinged with gore!
> Those crimson spots a dreadful tale relate;
> It has been grasp'd by an infernal Power;
> And by that hand which seal'd young Enghien's fate.

These lines prompted the following parody by Byron:

> Lady, accept the box a hero wore
> In spite of all this elegiac stuff:
> Let not seven stanzas written by a bore,
> Prevent your Ladyship from taking snuff!
> (Coleridge, *Byron's Poetry*, 7: 77 and note)

29 October

1. *Marino Faliero, Doge of Venice* and the *Prophecy of Dante* were published together in April 1821.

2 November

1. "Parody of a Celebrated Letter," *Works*, 3: 160–68. The letter parodied is that written by the Prince Regent to the Duke of York, 13 February 1812, informing him that the Regent planned to retain the Tory ministry.
2. Ferdinando Paer, *L'Agnese* (1811).

3 November

1. "The Irish Avatar," Coleridge, *Byron's Poetry*, 4:555–62. The poem was first published in Paris on 19 September 1821. For Byron's letters to Moore on the subject see Marchand, *LJ*, 8: 213–16, 219.

5 November

1. See Dowden, *Letters*, 2: 497–99.
2. Samuel Rogers, *Works*, 188–360. The first part of the poem was published in 1822 and 1823; the second in 1828. Editions of the complete poem were issued in 1830 and 1838.

6 November

1. See Dowden, *Letters*, 2: 500.

7 November

1. *Œuvres de M. Boileau-Despréaux . . . avec des rémarques et des dissertations critiques, par M. de Saint-Marc*, 5 vols. (1747).
2. i.e., "calembour," a pun.

14–22 November

1. For the reference to the *Courier* see entry for 8 August 1821.

24 November

1. Domenico Cimarosa, *Matrimonio Segreto* (1792).

25 November

1. Antonio Saliéri, *Les Danaïdes* (1794).

26 November

1. Adrien Perlet and Eugène Scribe, *L'Artiste* (1821); Eugène Scribe, Anne Honoré Joseph Duveyrier, and Raoul Chapais, *L'Amant Bossu* (1821).

28 November

1. Marie Mercandotti, born in Spain in 1801, danced at the Paris Opera in 1821 and 1822.

30 November

1. William Julius Mickle published his translation of *The Lusiad* in 1775. Mickle precedes his work with several long introductory essays, one of which, the "Dissertation on the Lusiad, And Observations Upon Epic Poetry," discusses Voltaire's criticism of *The Lusiad* in his "Essay Upon Epic Poetry," published in English in 1727. Mickle maintains that many of Voltaire's remarks are based not upon readings of the original poem, but rather upon the grossly inferior translation of Sir Richard Fanshaw (1655). A text of Mickle's *Lusiad* is in *English Translations, From Ancient And Modern Poems* (1810), vol. 3; his comments on Voltaire begin on p. 606. Marmontel probably used *La Lusiade de Camoëns*, by Louis Adrien du Perron de Castera, 3 vols. (1735).

2 December

1. Probably Mozart's *Don Giovanni;* L. J. Saint-Amans, *Psyché et l'amour* (1778).

6 December

1. Gabriel Marie Jean Baptiste Legouvé, *La Mort d'Abel* (1792); Franz Grillparzer, *Sappho* (1819).

7 December

1. Spontini, *Fernand Corlez, ou La Conquête de Mexique* (1809).

8 December

1. Charles François Dupuis, *L'Origine de tous les cultes, ou religion universelle*, 4 vols. (1795).
2. Letter 4 in Moore's *Alciphron*, *Works*, 10: 342.
3. Charles Frédéric Kreubé, *Edmond et Caroline, ou la Lettre et la Réponse* (1819); Charles Guillaume Étienne and Nicolas Dalayrac, *Gulistan, ou le Hulla de Samarcande* (1805).

9 December

1. James Perry, editor of the *European Magazine* and the *Morning Chronicle*.

10 December

1. André Ernest Grétry, *La Caravane du Caire* (1784). For *Nina* see n. 1 for 20 December 1820.

11 December

1. Published 1823. *Works*, 7: 267–350.
2. Charles Guillaume Étienne, *La Jeune Femme Colère* (1804).

22 December

1. René-Charles Guilbert de Pixérécourt, *L'Homme à trois visages* (1801).
2. In Moore's *Lalla Rookh*, *Works*, 6: 156–85.

26 December

1. René Périn and Ferdinand Laloue, *La Bataille de Bouvines* (1821).

27 December

1. Armand-Louis de Gontaut, Duc de Lauzun, later Duc de Biron (1747–93). His *Mémoires* appeared in 1822.

29 December

1. Casimir Delavigne, *Le Paria* (1821).
2. *The Barber of Seville*. Moore refers to Josephine Fodor, a Dutch soprano.

1822

Jany. 1, 1822 [Tuesday]—Walked out with Bessy in the morning to chuse an Etrenne for Mrs. Story—Had Villamil, Dalton, Douglas & Dr. Yonge to dine with me—In the evening came Mrs. Story & at supper arrived the Macleods, {who had been dining with Lady Jane—Dined—} —drank champagne & brandy punch—took to games of forfeits afterwards—then to dancing, and did not separate till near three o'clock—

2 [Wednesday]—Dined at Macleod's—Mrs. Story of the party—went from thence to the Opera (Lord Fife having sent me a ticket)—too late for the divertissement in the opera—Miss Drew was to have called to take me to Mrs. Roche's ball, but instead of her came Mrs. Story & Mrs. Macleod & her sister—drove with them about the Champs Elysées—a fine moonlight night and a merry one—they left me at Mrs. Roche's—found that Miss D. had called for me at the opera—staid only a short time at the Ball—on my return home found our two maids still engaged with their company, we having treated them with an entertainment for their friends to-day.

3 [Thursday]—Kept in a bustle all the morning—so much so as to forget (for I believe the first time since I have been in France) my letter to my dear Mother, to whom I write twice a week, and have done so with but few failures, for more than 20 years past—dined with the Robinsons—no one but Cadogan—a good dinner & agreeable day—sung to them in the evening, & saw in Lady Helena's eyes those *beads* (to use the language of distillers) which show that the spirit is *proof*—{or rather *not* proof, perhaps—} Went from thence to Lady Pigott's Ball—Bessy going to the Italian Opera, where Dalton procured her a box—

4 [Friday]—A Mr. Rose called upon me with a letter from Murray & a miniature of Lord Byron's little girl which he wishes me to forward to him—dined at Villamil's—two Spaniards of the party—Mrs. S. called to

take me to the opera to see Marcia's last appearance before her departure for England—nothing could be more beautiful than her face, dress & figure in dancing the Guaraccia[1]—

5 [Saturday]—A children's ball at the Story's—Macleod, Story, Dalton & myself dined together at the Café Anglais, and adjourned to the Ball at 10 o'clock—danced, supped & sung till near three—wrote ten lines to-day.

6 [Sunday]—Wrote a little in walking beyond the barrier—dined at Story's—Macleod of the party—in the evening all went to Douglas's, very sleepy after last night. Ombark Boubi, the Moor, there—expects to be made Chargé d'Affaires from Constantinople to England—requested to me to write to Lord Strangford in his favour.

7 [Monday]—Walked, wrote letters &c.—dined by myself at the Trois Freres, and found great pleasure in the few moments of silent repose it gave me—never did I lead such an unquiet life—Bessy ill—my home uncomfortable—anxious to employ myself in the midst of distractions, and full of remorse in the utmost of my gaiety—Came home early & read— Have this week done but about 40 lines.

8 [Tuesday]—Dined, by Kenney's desire & instrumentality, at Pictet's, a Swiss banker—Villamil of the party—the Newtes &c.—found that I was to be shown off in the evening to his customers and took flight—called on the Macleods & went from thence to Lady E. Stuart's assembly—some talk with Sir Charles—Lady Rancliffe brought me home—Have got Lord Byron's Irish verses printed on a single sheet by Galignani.[1]

9 [Wednesday]—Dined quietly at home for a wonder—In the evening went to Mrs. Armstrong's ball, as chaperon to the two Belchers—the prettiest Ball I have seen in Paris.—the music delicious—Colinet's best. The ease with which all Rossini's lively songs & choruses may be turned into quadrilles & waltzes shows the character of his music.—Did not get to bed till five o'clock.—Fanny Belcher very much admired, and supposed to be Bessy by most of the company.

10 [Thursday]—Was to have dined with Stibbert, but preferred Lambtons—Company only his brother, Lady Louise, Lady Elizabeth, & Mrs.

Ellis—all went to the Francais afterwards to see the new tragedy of M. Jouy, Sylla.[1]—full of allusions to Napoleon, which were loudly applauded—Talma very fine in the last scene.—Home early—Lambton quoted to-day a Persian proverb, "The words of Kings never fall to the ground."

11 [Friday]—Lambton called & left me a coupon for the Varietés this evening—Looked over my Rhymes on the Road for the purpose of seeing what sort of a Rifacimento I can make of them—how lucky I did not publish so slight a trifle!—Dined at Lord Henry Fitzgerald's {(N. B. Mrs. S. & Miss I. setting me down there)—} Company the Jerseys, Sir C. & Lady E. Stuart & Lord Thanet.—Sat next to the latter & found him agreeable. Lady E. Stuart said that the Memoirs of the Duc de Lauzun (which, of course, she did not own to have read) were supposed to be "genuine, but not true". Lord T. said nothing improbable in them & found them even dull from this probability—his women were all such easy triumphs.—Lady Jersey asked me for a copy of my verses on Naples, and the words of "I love but thee"[1] which I had promised her—a good deal of conversation with Sir Charles S. about cruelties, suggested by a portrait of Brinvilliers the poisoning woman in the reign of Louis 14,[2] which Lady de Roos had got from the Louvre to copy—This woman was punished by the torture of water—being made to drink it till she burst—Mentioned the old book with engravings about the cruelties of the Dutch at Amboyna.[3] {The nailing a man's gut to a pole, and making him go round it till the gut was all spun out upon it.—Sir C. mentioned that our own soldiers in Spain used almost always when the bullocks were wearied out & unable to go any further, tie a cord tightly round the root of their tongues & force them out of their mouths, while they were yet alive in order to make a meal of the fresh tongues.—} Went away at 9 to the Varietés—found only Lambton & Lady Louisa in the box.—laughed almost to pain at "Je fais mes farces".[4]—went afterwards to the Macleods, and from thence at 12 o'clock to Lady Charlemont's Ball.—a good deal of talk with Lady C.—Home between 1 & 2.

12 [Saturday] Dined at Douglas's—in the evening to Mercer's (where I was to have dined)—the Villamils there—sung a little—was called for by the Douglas's and went with them to Lafitte's Ball—was introduced, at her own request, to the wife of one of Bonaparte's generals (I could not make out her name) to whom Napoleon has left a large sum in his will—told me he had also left money to Arnaud & to Labédoyère's children[1]—{Left at 12 o'clock with [*several words unrecovered*] to the Storys' (where there was to be [*several words unrecovered*] at the opera) but found them in bed—from there to the [*unrecovered*] but was told they were in bed also [*several words unrecovered*]—& home.}

13 [Sunday] Walked beyond the barrier, and wrote an Epigram or two for the Rhymes—dined at Colonel Ellice's—Company, the Robinsons Lady Hunloke, Lord Marcus Hill, and Cornwall—very agreeable—in the evening Mrs. Ellice played some of the Choruses of the Gazza Ladra & I sung—thence went to Made. de Flahaut's, where I found Lady E. Grey suffering in the midst of Crapauds[1]—all French but herself—did not stay long, but meaning to go to Mrs. Gent's assembly, went to a wrong place, & found myself in splendid rooms, where there was not a single English face to be seen.—on enquiring of the servant found it was Maréchal Suchet's & made my escape.—Dirtied my shoes in seeking for the carriage & gave up Mrs. Gent—went to the Macleods, and took Miss I. off with me in the carriage to fetch Mrs. Story, who had set off on foot, & we found her on our return. {(N. B.)—supped at the Macleods & brought home by Mrs. S.}

14 [Monday] Walked in the Champs Elysées—and wrote a couple more trifles—dined at the Douglas's to meet the Henrys—A party in the evening—went for half an hour to Mrs. Newte's Ball & returned—did not stay late.

15 [Tuesday]—Dined with Macleod & Major Handley at a Traiteur's near the Odéon in order to go see the Paria[1]—some fine situations—in the Paria's discovery of himself to his mistress I suspect the Author was thinking of my Fire-Worshipper[2]—altogether dull—went & supped at Mrs. Story's afterwards—found a coupon for the Francais from Lambton on my return.

16 [Wednesday]—Wrote a little—Had a letter from Lady Jersey thanking me for the words of "I love but thee" which I sent her, & asking me to dine with her tomorrow but am engaged to Lord Grannard's—dined at Lambton's—Cottu, the author of the Work on English Jurisprudence[1] & Sr. Robert Wilson—Wilson's slap-dash politics & slap-dash French in his disputes with Cottu, very amusing—his pronunciation of La Pologne as if it was L'apollon & Cottu taking for granted {that} he meant the latter & saying "non—non—on ne ferait pas la guerre pour L'Apollon"—Cottu's supposition of a case (in ridiculing the present minute subdivision of property) of a man planting a large cabbage, which would overshadow his neighbour's grounds &c. Sir Robert's pun "vous aimez les choux—moi—je n'aime pas les *Chouans*"—did not go to Made. de Flahaut's in the evening.

17 [Thursday]—{Have at last heard of an opportunity by which we may be rid of our young ladies—not sorry for it—} dined at the Granards—received while I was dressing a coupon for the Francais, which I thought came from the Lambton's—company, the Chabots, Rotschild, Lord Marcus Hill, &c. &c.—introduced to Rotschild in the evening—offered to send any things to Italy for me by his courrier, but did *not* ask me to his Ball, which is what I want—Went off between 8 & 9—found no one but Darby in the box, which was the Ambassador's—looked again at the Coupon, and found it was a ticket for the whole box which Lady Elizabeth had sent me—an unlucky mistake, as I wanted to take the Belchers & might have saved the hire of a box tomorrow night by it—The play Sylla—Went after it was over behind the scenes to Talma's dressing-room—was introduced there to Jouy, the author of the play—Talma mentioned a portrait of Shakespeare on a bellows which has fallen by accident into his hands, & which he considers authentic—several inscriptions on it from Shakespeare in the orthography of his time.—Went from thence to the Arthurs' Ball—a particularly nice girl, either daughter or niece of Prince Pignatelli {[*several words unrecovered*]—Was waked at 4 by Bessy's ringing for Hannah, being in violent pain with her face—Went into her bed & remained with her till morning—}

18 [Friday] Up early to go look after the person that is to take charge of the Belchers—went afterwards to {the} Lambtons, and thence with them to Somariva's, who showed us some beautiful cameos in oriental stones from his pictures & statues—took a box for the Francais—dined at home & went with the Belchers & Mrs. Story—Play, the Tartuffe—Entertainment, the Ménage de Moliere[1]—Moliere represented as jealous of his wife—

19 [Saturday]—Dined with the Storys, who had made a party to go to the Bal Masqué at night—some *embarras* about the Belchers wishing to go—Had procured their pass-ports & taken their places in the morning for Tuesday next—{Staid at Story's till one o'clock when I saw the party (Storys, McCleods &c.) off to the Bal Masqué, not liking to go myself, and came home—}

20 [Sunday]—Walked to the Bois de Boulogne—Have done nothing but some 40 or 50 lines of trifling doggrel this week—called upon Darby to know whether his dinner stands good for Tuesday, as Lambton has asked me to meet the Portalis's on that day—saw with him a M. le Garde, who asked me whether I could speak French, & on my replying "a little" said—

"ah—oui—on ne pourrait pas avoir escrit de si beaux vers sans savoir le Francais"—this is excellent {beyond any thing I have yet met with of French mind—} Darby's dinner stands good—Called in at Villamil's at five & stopped to dine, having sent an excuse to Colonel Huxley's, where I was invited—returned home early.

21 [Monday]—Got up early & went to Darby's he having invited me to breakfast for the purpose of attending the Chamber to-day—Darby had gone out, there being no Chamber in consequence of the anniversary of Louis Seize's death—went & breakfasted at Tortoni's—walked afterwards in the Champs Elysées.—dined at home—went in the evening to the Palais Royal, to purchase bon-bons & Music for the Belchers.

22 [Tuesday]—Up early to see the Belchers off to the Coach—when we arrived there, found they had forgot their pass-ports, and had to drive back furiously for them—just came as the coach was driving off—Told me that they had not money enough & that I must send them some to Calais—Went off to Lafitte's & dispatched to them an order upon a Banker at Calais for eight Napoleons having already advanced them £25—This, with the five hundred francs I gave to Yonge's subscription & four hundred I lent the other day to Dalton, leaves a melancholy vacuum in my already shallow purse—dined at Darby's—Company, Etienne (the famous journalist & deputy, who made on Saturday last the best speech that has been focused on the Law for restraining the Press)[1] Thiard, another Deputy, Dupin, the Advocate, Prince Paul of Wirtemberg, Sir H. Mildmay, King, Mackenzie &c. &c.—a good deal of savage cleverness about Dupin—His story of P[erronnet] (a Chief Judge & now Minister)[2] asking of a girl, whose pardon some one solicited, "est elle jolie, la petite?"—Etienne said it was "De Sade en robes"—The day altogether curious & amusing—went afterwards to Lambtons—found there the Portalis (both brothers & their wives) Lady Jersey, Made. de Broglie & the Duke & Sir R. Wilson—the Duc de Broglie said that Fanaticism no longer exists in France, & that Religion is only used as a political instrument—from thence went to the Macleods & had a merry supper with them & the Storys—

23 [Wednesday]—Dined at home—received a *coupon* from Lambton for the Gymnase—went & laughed very heartily at Clausel in M. Beaufils—from thence Lambton & I went first to his house & then to the Duke de Broglies'—a very good party—did not stay long—saw Lord Auckland there—

24 [Thursday]—Wrote a little & walked—dined at Mercer's—Company, Made. d'Ameland & Miss d'Este, Lady Glenlion, Warrender &c. &c.—some music in the evening—from thence to Lady Rancliffe's Ball—home pretty early.

25 [Friday]—Dined at home & took Bessy to the Variétés in the evening— Sans Tambour ni Trompette—Les Comediens de Paris &c.[1]—supped at home

26 [Saturday]—Dined at Villamil's—Company, Dawson, Mercer, the Macleods—Music in the evening—went neither to Made. de Broglie's nor Lafitte's Ball—Have done some few trifing lines every day.

27 [Sunday]—Wrote words to a Neapolitan Air—dined at Lambton's— Company, Duc & Duchesse de Guiche, Lady Ossulston, Sir R. Wilson &c.— the Pourtalises & Ellices in the evening—

28 [Monday]—Sent off the Air to Power—dined at Sir H. Mildmay's— Company, Warrender, Gerffulhe, Denon, &c.—sung in the evening— Denon told me that the Medal of Grattan was nearly finished, which I am not very glad to hear, as nobody has yet paid me & I shall have to give the 1000 francs it costs out of my own pocket—went afterwards to sup at Story's—Bessy who had been at the Francais with Villamil (Made. de Flahaut having sent us coupons for her box before dinner) came there too.

29 [Tuesday]—Dined at Douglas's—a party in the evening—singing & dancing—Went away for an hour to Lady E. Stuart's—returned to Douglas's for Bessy—

30 [Wednesday]—Went out early to order wine, ice &c. having a dinner party at home to-day—Company, Douglas, Kenny, Stibbert, Story & Millingen—The dinner (thanks to my dear girl's management & superintendence) most comfortable and Villamil's excellent Lafitte (of which he sent me a dozen—the other day) not the worst part of the feast—drank of this; six bottles, two of Madeira, & one of Champagne—. A party in the evening— sung, danced, drank 3 bottles more of champagne, besides lots of negus, & did not part till two—one or two of my dinner-guests rather *lively*.—

31 [Thursday]—Dined with my fellow traveller, M. Mariton—Stibbert too of the party. The remainder (about 8 or 10) all French—very curious, as giving a perfect idea of the genuine French mode of living—abundance & variety of the dishes, handed round by the guests themselves & never-ceasing—nothing but ordinary wine during dinner, except towards the end, two small decanters of red wine one *de* Grenache, the other, I think L'amalque, (both southern, strong & good) of which no one tasted but Stibbert & I, then with the dessert, a bottle of a white mousseux wine called Clairette de Di, made of the sweet grape, & for the conclusion, a liqueur glass round of vin de Samos, sucré & hardly to be known from other sweet wines—violent party politics talked—an old hot Liberal, who was Ministre de la Marine under Napoleon, foremost in violence—The ultra Champion a shrewd little Doctor, who was all astonishment at the absurdity of the Minority in still speaking, when they so well knew all measures would be carried against them—leaving entirely out of sight the effect their speaking had upon the country—a good deal of talk about Etienne, and his cele-brated plagiary of the Deux Gendres from a Ms. by the Jesuit Conaxa, found (during the Revolution when they were burning the works of the Jesuits) by M. Maltebrun, and given by him to Etienne who founded on it his Deux Gendres & got both money & reputation by it—still having re-fused to share *either* with his friend Maltebrun, the latter took revenge by revealing the whole transaction to the Public, and the thing has never been forgotten to Etienne since[1]—The Doctor also mentioned the famous De-jeuners de Rovigo during Napoleon's time, where Etienne (then the virtual Censor of the Press) used to denounce the publications that were to be suppressed—After dinner two ladies played on the Piano-Forte—said they saw I liked music & asked whether I played myself—said "a little"—was pressed to sit down to the Piano-forte—sung, "When midst the gay I meet"[2]—Went from thence to the Princesse Talleyrand's to hear Vieni (author of a successful play, Clovis) read a new tragedy he has written called "Achille"[3]—heard two acts declaimed by him with true French ges-ticulation—the ludicrous effect of his missing one of the *feuillets* in the middle of a fine speech and exclaiming in the same tragic tone "Grand Dieu! qu'est ce que c'est que ça?"—was introduced to him—said he should like to have had Talma to act Priame, but that there was no getting him to play with Lafond—by the bye, how convenient as a rhyme "Madame" is!—for Priame, Pergame, &c. toujours prête.—Though pressed by the {cast-off} Princess to stay, bolted & went to an assembly at the Conte Jules de Polignac's—introduced to him by Lady Ossulston—saw there Made. de Broglie, Lady Rancliffe &c—and a number of high-flying Royalists, Décars, Chateaubriands &c.—from thence went to their very Antipodes in politics at Clermont's Ball—saw some Bad Waltzers dancing to a beautiful thing from the Gazza Ladra, and left for Mrs. Story's to supper at a quarter before twelve—home a little after one.

Febr. 1 [Friday]—Had determined (from the difficulty I find in writing here)—that Bessy should set off for England in ten days & prepare the Cottage—but received by the Post of to-day a letter to say that old Hall, my rival in Sloperton, had wheedled farmer Hutton out of the Key & got possession of the house so that this is all at an end—dined at home & went to the Porte St Martin in the evening.

2nd. [Saturday] Dined at home—Went to Mrs. Story's (a children's party chiefly)—supped there.—Mean to make an effectual struggle against engagements henceforth—if I can.

3rd. [Sunday] Have written some straggling trifles for the Rhymes this week—altogether have done more than 200 lines in this way—dined at Lord Grannard's—had promised to go to Made. de Broglie's in the evening, but went to Villamil's, to hear Weiss, a flute-player—a party of Spaniards there—Duc & Duchesse of San Lorenzo—Duchess of Rivas, Marchioness of Santa Cruz &c. &c.—

4th. [Monday] Wrote a letter to Lord John—dined at home & read in the evening. Mrs. Story & Miss Norris to supper.

5th. [Tuesday] Walked & wrote a little—dinner & evening at home—d[itt]o to supper.

6th [Wednesday]—Dined at Douglas's—a large party in the evening, to which Bessy came—Went away for an hour to Made. Pourtalises's Ball, which was a very good one—

7th [Thursday] Received an anonymous note, written evidently by a Frenchwoman, inviting me to meet her at the Bal Masqué on Saturday next—"une rose a la main me fera connaitre"—evidently a hoax, & I have no doubt, originated with Mrs. S. & Miss Inglis.—dined at home—worked a little in the evening & went at ten to sup at Mrs. Story's—the Macleods there—did not go to Mrs. Drummond's Ball.

8th. [Friday]—Have begun my prose part of the Work these two days past[1]—walked beyond the Barrier—offered myself to dinner at the Villamil's—left them between 8 & 9 & came home to dress—a soirée upstairs at Benjamin Constant's, to which I went—plenty of Libéraux—Lafayette, Excelmans, Abbé de Pradt &c.—a good deal of talk with M. Buchon, and another Littérateur, who reminded me he had sent me a translation of Alexander's Feast[2] some time ago—introduced to the celebrated French Bleu, Made. Sophia Gay, who is herself overwhelming—but has pretty daughters—from thence went to Lady Charlemont's Ball—home before one—Have been negotiating with Galignani for Lord Byron, who has given up publishing with Murray, and has some things ready, which he wishes to have printed at Paris—

9 [Saturday]—Dined at home—Had received a note from Made. de Broglie in the morning asking me to come to her—engaged also to a great Ball at Made. de Chabanais, & promised to meet Denon at Lafitte's in order that he might introduce me to Marchal Soult—went for a short time to Made. de Broglie's,—In talking of Peyronnet {(the Minister's) profligacy}, and wondering how he would look in going to receive the sacrament in public, it was said that he & all the rest of the Ministers ought to be confessed *en gros,* as they do a regiment—"Let every one who has committed this sin, hold up his hand—"The priests of the Greek Church read out a long list of crimes (such as only Greeks would think of) to the penitent, who nods his head at every item of which he has been guilty, and the priest puts a mark of his thumb-nail before it accordingly—at the conclusion the whole is summed up, and a receipt in full given for the Total by absolution—In some places people *abonner* themselves for some one favourite vice for six or eight months to come—Went from thence to Villamil's, where there were Spaniards & music—did not go to my other places, but supped there—

10 [Sunday]—Took a long walk to the Bois de Boulogne—Have done but little of my prose—dined at Colonel Ellice's—Company, Made. de Menon, a young Monsieur something (coxcomb, of course) Warrender, & Lambton's brother—Left them early & went to Villamil's—

11 [Monday]—Dined at the Café Francais—received a letter from the Longman's to-day to say that another Bermuda claim has been brought forward—an after-clap of that thunder-storm!—the amount twelve hundred pounds, but think it may be reduced to three and offering, if a letter which they advise my writing to old Sheddon (the father of that Jew, Robert) should fail to advance me the money—shall not take it—came home early—did not go to Made. St Aulaire's or Mrs. Gold Gents.

12 [Tuesday]—Bessy and I went with the Miss Drews to dine at Lady Emily Henry's—{an operation for both of us—} Some beautiful playing on the violin in the evening by a young man, Obrecht (I think) an elève of Viotti's & possessing much of the sensibility of his touch—brought the Drews home to sup with us—Received Lord Byron's MS. of "Werner"¹ this morning— paid 5 Napoleons for the postage

13 [Wednesday]—Dined at the Rancliffe's—Company, Lady Jersey, the Ellices, Fox, & Mrs. George Lamb—the dinner very agreeable—asked Rancliffe to dine with me on Friday, which he promised—from thence to Made. de Flahaut's, & afterwards to sup at the Macleods—{Lady Jersey to-day, asked me about Rogers's "Italy" said she heard it was the worst thing ever written.}

14 [Thursday]—Power has sent me 3rd. number of the National Melodies, and wishes me to secure the copy-right of the words for him in France— dined at home and went to the Gaieté in the evening La Forêt Enchantée¹

15 [Friday]—Went to the Marais to Smith's to have the words of the National Melodies printed—Dinner at home—Rancliffe has remembered another engagement & Benjamin Constant will be detained at the Chamber—Company, Villamil, Brummel, Daveson and Mercer—Mrs. & the Miss Brummels in the evening, the Constants & some friends they brought with them, the Macleods, Mrs. Story, Mrs. Villamil &c.—a good deal of music— supper, dancing, blind-man-buff &c. till four o'clock in the morning—

16 [Saturday]—Rather knocked up with my last night's achievements— walked to see Kenny—he & Macleod dined with us off the scraps—Went together to Feydeau—dull work—supper at Mrs. Story's—persuaded Bessy to give up the Bal Masqué & brought her quietly home—

17 [Sunday]—Dined at home—went by Bessy's wish to the Douglas's in the evening—introduced to a Madame Thayer, an American married to a Frenchman who owns the hotel in which they live & the whole of the Passage du Panorama—she "Sir Thomas-ed" me all the time we spoke together—home at one.

18 [Monday]—Up early—wrote letters & a little of my Job-work—Bessy

very ill with her late hours—takes no care of herself when she is the least well—dined at home—uncomfortably—went to the French Opera & forgot my annoyances a little in the beauty of the Ballet.

19 [Tuesday]—Got some books on St. Domingo I wished to consult—walked about to see the Boeuf Gras & the other fooleries of the Carnival—Dined with Villamil—a Frenchman of the party, who, when Villamil introduced him to me as a distant relation of Bonaparte's, said "ce n'est pas le plus beau de mon histoire"—It was mentioned of Talleyrand {that} one day, when Davoust excused himself for being too late because he had met with a "Pekin" who delayed him, Talleyrand begged to know what he meant by that word—"nous appellons Pekin (says Davoust) tout ce qui n'est pas militaire"—"Ah, oui, c'est comme chez nous (replied Talleyrand) nous appelons militaire tout ce qui n'est pas *civil*".

{20. [Wednesday] Taken in for a dinner at Gravilli's by Dawson—Company, the Villamils, Morier (the traveller) Mr. Kneller (a Wiltshire man) &c. &c.—the dinner bad & dull—music in the evening—trios of flutes and all sorts of charivaris—ran away as soon as I could & got home early.}

21 [Thursday]—Dined with Villamil's & went to the Italian Opera—La Gazza Ladra—Music in the trial-scene & after the Condemnation misplaced & frivolous—shows a want of feeling—"sends the girl's soul upon a jig to heaven"—

22 [Friday]—Have taken to translating some passages of Catullus for my Letters[1]—am not at all well—a bad cold in addition to my other ills—dined at home—bathed my feet & went through the operation of gruel &c. at night.

23 [Saturday]—Wrote 36 lines of translation from Catullus—dined at Lord Grannard's (to whom after having fought off invitations from Chenevix & Peters, I struck)—company, the Chabots, Lord Marcus Hill, Lord Harvey &c. &c.—left early in the evening intending to go to Made. de Broglie's, but contented myself with accompanying Bessy to the Macleods—a most dull evening—I too ill to sing {and they too stupid to do any thing else}—by the bye, called upon Stewart Rose {this morning}, who has brought me a letter of introduction from Lord Lansdowne—talking of Scott (with whom he is

intimate) says he has no doubt of his being the author of all the novels—Scott's life in Edinburgh favourable to working—dines always at home & writes {all} the evening—writing quite necessary to him—so much so that when he was very ill some time ago he used to dictate for 3 or 4 hours at a time—from combining circumstances Rose thinks it was the Bride of Lammermoor[1] he dictated in this way—Told me of sad conduct of Williams to Foscolo[2]—

24 [Sunday]—Walked & wrote a little—am continuing my translations from Catullus—dined by myself at Riche's and came home & worked a little in the evening—read a long article about myself to-day from Blackwood—the tone insolent but flattering in the main.[1]

25. [Monday] Took a Stall in the orchestra to see the Lampe Merveilleuse[1]—asked Dalton to dine with me, and both went to the Opera together—bad music & dialogue—but the scenery & spectacle altogether like magic—

26 [Tuesday]—Wrote one or two trifles—dined at Bushe's—company Lord Charlemont, Ellices, Mr. Ricketts[1] (quondam Secretary of Lord Hastings in India) Sir Sidney Smyth &c—bad dinner & dull day—Sir Sidney never stirred out of Jean d-Acre for hours—kept strict possession of it, like a gallant Commander {and bore} as he is—Read the newspapers in my way home & got to bed early—Rickett's account of Lord Moira giving into his hands all the letters & applications for appointments after his arrival &c. &c. all characteristic of his Lordship—

27 [Wednesday]—Wrote some more of my prose—dined at Lord Charlemont's—Company, the {Wellesleys} Kenmares, Bushes &c. &c. another bore in the shape of W{illiston} who fought over the Wiltshire Election as pertinaciously as Sir Sidney did Acre—Mrs. Cadogan saying she would show me some verses written to her by an amateur Poet. "a *gentleman* Poet".—Meant to have gone to Made. de Broglie's in the evening, but too late—Went to Made. de Sapenay's Concert, (through the intervention of my Literary friend, M. Dorion, who has written Epics, Lyrics, & God knows what & sent them *all* to me to read) and heard some music—the best of which was M. Obricht's violin—a Made. Molinos (formerly Madlle. Lafitte) Galli, and a Garde du Corps were the vocals—went from thence & supped at the Macleods.

28 [Thursday]—More of the prose—walked about with Bessy—dined at Daly the banker's—a very good set-out—excellent wines—Company, Sir T. Webbe, Wellesly, Ricketts, King, Peters &c. &c.—[Peters told me of Lady Albourough's saying to Sir T. Webbe on a report of his being about to be married to Lady Boyne "you'll find the passage easier than King William did."—] called for Bessy at ten & took her to a party at Davisons—cold & meagre—Heard a Frenchman sing Spanish songs to the guitar—from thence went both of us with the Villamil's to Lady S. Douglas's, where there was dancing—home ½ after one—by the bye, Wellesly mentioned that Lord Castlereagh, in speaking of the females who were common in the Manchester Riots said "as for those wretched women, I shall leave them to *purge themselves.*"—Dorion told me that to print 1000 copies of such an octavo Volume as his, in Didot's best manner, cost but about 70 pounds English—

March. 1 [Friday]—Dined with Villamils & they & I & Bessy went to Miss Corri's concert—bad enough—except a few very touching bars in Benazet's violoncello, & Made. Fodor's song from the Barbiere—Amor possente is the name of the beautiful Duett from Armida[1] in which there are such affecting passages—

2nd. [Saturday] A meat breakfast at Villamil's at two for the purpose of practising some music, but neither practiced nor dined—Went all to the Varietés, and made up by a most hearty hot supper at Vs. afterwards.

3rd [Sunday]—Dined at Cadogan's—company, the Charlemonts, Lady Warrender, Sir Sydny Smith, the Robinsons &c. &c. sat next to Sir Sidney!—told me some curious things—the distillation of salt water a most useful discovery for the Navy—the water fade[1] & insipid but quite pure & fresh—Some navigator he mentioned is going to take out casks of *coal* with those of water—if it succeeds, there will be so much stowage saved as the calculation is that one cask of coal will make 3 of water—Sea-scurvy arises from the want of fresh air—the knowledge of this has led to the almost total extirpation of it.—Mrs. Cadogan told me that Sir Sidney *amused* her for a whole evening by explaining how she might see the ball coming out a cannon's mouth in time to avoid it—[went afterwards to Mrs. Storys where there was Lochitt, his son & another Derby man, just arrived with Story—supped there.]

4th [Monday]—A party proposed for the Gymanase to-night with the Storys—received a letter from Lord Byron who signs himself now Noel Byron—He has called out Southey, as I expected he would and he has done right—no man should suffer such a letter as Southey's, signed with his name, to pass without this sort of notice—Lord B. *ought* not to have brought it upon himself, but, having done so, there was but this left for him. Neither will there any harm result from it, as Southey, I am sure, will not meet him[1]—wrote a little now every day but very little—dined with Story's men (their first appearance) at a Restaurateur's, & afterwards went with them & the ladies to the Gymnase—three very pretty pieces—the Artiste, Memoires d'un Colonel & Michel & Christine[2]—Bessy quite uncomfortable about the fate of poor Stanislas in the last—said it would haunt her for a week—

5th [Tuesday]—Wrote—walked with Bessy—dined at home—Afterwards to Made. de Broglie's—some amusing conversation among the Frenchmen there—Talked of National Songs—"Vive Henri Quatre", almost the only *Royal* one—except "Fils d'un Béarnois" written when Louis 16 was in prison—disclaimed "Charmante Gabrielle" as a National Song—praised the words of the first verse—seemed to think it written by Henry himself—mentioned some verses upon a Pun by the present King, but I could not collect them—"Les chaleurs extrêmes" one of the phrases & the Duke seemed to doubt if the plural "chaleurs" was admissible—one of the talkers, an old fellow, spoke (with a license of language we should not well tolerate in England) about the illegitimacy of the Duc de Berri {from the Comtesse d'Artois's public intrigues with a Garde, a handsome strong fellow she had selected—there was a consultation held, he said, whether both the children (for the Duke was one of twins by this Garde) should not be put out of the way, but she succeeded in preserving the Duke—she was not pretty—Made. de Broglie mentioned an important speech made about Anne d'Autriche (upon whom the legitimacy of the Orleans depends—Q.E.E.)[1] at the Palais Royal}—from there went to the ambassador's where I found Talleyrand coming out, and (a much better thing) that pretty girl, Miss Huxley, going in—talked a little to her & came away early—

6 [Wednesday]—Have been reading Saint Foix on Paris, and a wretched thing "les Amours de Cabelle"[1]—dined at Villamils—a large party—the Marquis of Yruco (who was in America) & his wife, the Drummonds, &c.{—sat next Miss Drummond at dinner, & was rather amuséd with her

pretty coquettish eyes—} some singing in the evening—Bessy came—supped afterwards.

7 [Thursday]—Had fixed to-day for a restaurateur dinner with Kenny & Elliston—Villamil Macleod, Hunter (the King's messenger) & his son formed the party—dined at a bad traiteur's, Peyton, on the Boulevards—bad & dear—went, five of us, in the evening to see Madlle. Begrand in Suzanne at the Porte St. Martin[1]—much changed in figure from what she was four years ago—an extraordinary exhibition—brought them home to supper—had also the Storys, Mrs. Villamil, & the Douglas's—left us at two.

{8 [Friday]—Wrote & read a little—dined at Lady Susan Douglas's—went afterwards to Massimino's Concert—from there to Madame Thayer's (a dance), and from that to Lady Charlemont's Ball.

9 [Saturday]—Dined at Peters's—Company, Lords Herbert, Rancliffe & Stair—Sir Sidney Smithe, Berkely Craven, Campbell, Irvine &c. &c.—a good dinner—from thence to Lady Pigot's dance—Wellesley brought me home.}

10 [Sunday]—Can do but little—ruinous work—had Elliston & Villamil to dine with us (Kenny was to have been of the dinner) in order to go to Madame Fodor's Benefit in the evening—tickets 20 francs each—Bessy went—Opera, the Elizabeth of Rossini[1]—some fine things, but seemed heavy as a whole—went & supped at Mrs. Storys afterwards—

11 [Monday]—Walked to look at some of the remarkable streets mentioned by St. Foix—dined at Lord Stairs—Company, Rancliffe, Lord Paulet, Col. Milman (brother to the Poet) Dalton, &c. &c.—Magnificent style of living—{the master himself the worst part of the establishment—}went to his box at the French Opera afterwards—Aladin[1]—did not go to Mrs. Gent's Ball. {Conversation upon a very delicate subject to-night with Rancliffe—enjoined me strict secrecy}

12 [Tuesday]—Walked & wrote a little—my course either to-day or yester-day (I forget which) by the Rue du Temple & the Rue St. Avoye which took me out on the Quay by the Place de Greve—was looking for the Rue des

trois Pavillons but could not find it—The Rue du Petit Bourbon (from a house in which[,] that had belonged to the Constable de Bourbon[,] Charles 9th. fired on his Huguenot subjects as they crossed the water to the Fe. St. Germain) is, as far as I can discover, demolished[1]—dined at Villamils—Company, Captn. Light, Princesse Talleyrand &c. &c. music in the evening—at 12 o'clock went with Bessy to the Macleods & staid till near two—

13 [Wednesday]—Weather very hot—dined with the Locketts & Storys at Riche's—sent an excuse to the Drummonds.

14 [Thursday]—Dined at De Flahaut's—company, Made. de Souza, Monsr. Le Serre, Count Pahlin, & a Frenchman, whose name I don't know—very agreeable—De Flahaut, made me a present of Courrier's Pamphlets & Made de Flahaut of Beranger's Songs[1]—Had before dinner received tickets for the Duke of Orleans's Box at the Italian—sent the Villamils & Bessy—joined them there afterwards—Count Pahlin took me—some conversation with him about Rossini—Rossini at Venice being employed to write an opera for the Carnival passed off an old one upon them, but was, I believe, imprisoned three days for the deceit. In comparing him to Cimarosa, critics say Cimarosa never repeated himself—but there is but one of his pieces that keeps the stage—the Matrimonio.—The opera to-night L'Italiana[2]—returned home to dress again & went to Lady E. Stuart's Ball—very splendid—a blaze of English beauty—

15 [Friday]—Went to show the Lockett's Sommariva's collection & lost my day by it—dined with the Storys—they & Bessy went to the Varietes taking also our dear Anastasia—I returned home & played over the whole of L'Italiana, which Made. de Flahaut lent me—

16 [Saturday]—my dear Anastasia's birth-day—preparations for a young party on the occasion—Weather as warm as summer—walked to the Rue des Fossés de St. Germain Auxerrois—saw the Cul de Sac de Sourdis, where was one of the residences of Gabrille d'Estrees—saw also the Rue Bailleul (a very narrow street), where (according to St. Foix) she also lived "a l'Hotel de Schomberg qui subsiste encore, derrière l'Hotel d'Aligra." This latter Hotel is still there with the same name—saw also in the Rue Bethisy, which is a continuation of the Rue St. Germain Auxerrois the site of the house (the second on the left "en entrant par la Rue de la Monnaie")

where Admiral Coligni was assassinated the night of St. Bartholomew—
The Church of St. Germain &c. from which the signal was given is opposite
the facade of the Louvre[1]—

17 [Sunday]—dined at Colonel Huxley's, the father of the beautiful
Blonde—Company, General Ramsey, Sir C. Green &c. &c.—sung in the
evening—went from thence to Villamils—Kenny, Davison & Miss Holcroft—some music & supper.

18 [Monday]—Went with Flahaut & Le Serre to see a match at the Tennis
Court—great activity exhibited by two boys—Flahaut bet on the "Vieux" (as
they were called, about 29 years of age) and won—Dined at Fitzherbert's—
Lord Rancliffe, Daly & Dr. Gullifer—a little music in the evening—
Returned home early—

19 [Tuesday]—Dined at the Cafe Francais with Bessy, the Story's & Major
Handley, & went to the Varietes in the evening—Potier in the Freres
Feroces[1] excellent—took ice at Tortoni's afterwards—

20 [Wednesday]—Dined at Robert's with Campbell of Saddel—Company,
Lord Beauchamp, Berkeley Craven, Irvine, Henry Baring, McCleod, &c.—
Beauchamp & Craven {most amusingly profligate—} both clever in their
way—the story of Montron falling into the saw-pit at Newmarket—
{Alvanley's trick upon the Parson in the place behind the Canals &c. &c.—}
meant to go to Frascati afterwards, but changed my mind & came home
early.

21 [Thursday]—Walked all the way to the Place de la Bastille, and round by
the Boulevard St. Antoine—dined with Handley at Robert's, a dinner given
chiefly for Bessy, but she was too tired with her shopping in the morning to
come—The Storys, Miss Maurice, Lady Augusta Leith, & the two Macken-
zies—had received a note from Lady Rancliffe in the morning to ask me to
join her at the Francais—went—just in time to see Mars in the Suite d'un
Bal Masqué.[1]

22 [Friday]—Went with Bessy, Mrs. Story & Miss Drew to see Soult's pictures—Denon took us—Denon said to me "if ever you describe Jesus
Christ, take that for your model (the figure of him in the Healing of the

Sick)—it is the only true idea ever given of him—c'est la morale de Jésus Christ."—Soult very civil to me—spoke about Lady Holland &c. &c.— walked to look at the Rue Git-la-cour, where Francis 1st built a {small} palace to be near the Hotel of the Duchesse d'Etampes—dined at Chenevix's—company, the Payne Galways, the Howards, the Montalemberts, Fox, &c. &c.—went to the opera to join Bessy and Mrs. Story, and supped afterwards.

23 [Saturday]—Dined by myself at Very's—joined Bessy at Mrs. S. in the evening & supped there—

24 [Sunday]—Write every day a few lines of some trifle or other for my Omnium Gatherum—dined at Villamil's—a large party, the Storys, Douglas's, Dawson, Kenny &c. &c.—went away in the evening for a short time to Made. La Briche's (where I had been asked to dine) and saw there some high-flying Royalists, Duc de Duras &c. returned to Villamils & supped— {The subject of Rancliffe's confidence to me the other night has eclaté with a most dreadful explosion—It was out of a house in the Rue Refincero (a reception-house) she was coming with her lover Morton, when caught— Rancliffe seems to have done it rather harshly—employed police &c. It might have been the very morning of the night I was with her at the Français, & perhaps, the morning after—every body full of it to-night at Made. la Briche's—} Story last night won two thousand six hundred pounds at Ecarté!—began with 33 Napoleons—offered to-day to lend me as much of it as I chose, but declined with many thanks—a kind-hearted fellow as can be—

25 [Monday]—Anniversary of my Wedding-Day—the Storys all start for England—the Villamils, Dawson &c. Kenny dined with us—went in the evening to Feydeau to see the Paradis du Mahomet[1]—dull enough.

26 [Tuesday]—Weather like mid-summer—the Dandies all mounting their white trousers & straw hats—am reading Lacretelle's "History of the Wars of Religion in France"[1]—strange style sometimes—he says under Henry 4 Love "redevenait une passion digne des Francais"—This is like Franconi's—"Pendant que le roi de Navarre (ah! je me sens impatient de le nommer Henri 4) &c. &c."—"A travers tant de scènes confuses, l'histoire n'a qu'une resource, c'est de s'attacher au panche blanc de Henri 4". On coming in to dress found that Tom had had a fall, which alarmed me a good deal—had him stripped & examined, but it was only a bruise on his

shoulder—dined at Sir H. Mildmay's—Henry Leeson, Fox, King, & Latouche—agreeable enough—Two of Fox's stories good—The Prince de Poix stopped by a sentry, announced his name—"Prince de Poix! (answered the sentry) quand vous seriez le Roi des Haricots, vous ne passay[2] pas par ici".—the wife of a Colonel at a Review in Dublin, stopped by a sentry in the same manner, & telling him she was "the Colonel's Lady"—"no matter for that ma'am—if you were even his wife, you couldn't pass"—came home early (being anxious about Tom) instead of going either to Made. Talleyrand's or Made. Sassenay's—[Have had a note from Rancliffe to dine with him on Friday, but do not like the appearance of giving my vote on either side & shall accordingly refuse]

27 [Wednesday]—Dined with the Ellices—Cornwall, the Standishs, Lambton, Ellices brother—went in the evening to Made. de Broglie's—some conversation with Count Torreno & the Duc, who promised me a copy of his late speech—from there went to Mrs. Gent's *infant* Ball—

28 [Thursday]—Was to have dined with Sir T. Webbe but sent an apology & agreed to go with the Villamils (Bessy & I) to see Made. Georges in Merope—dined with them—the play very affecting—a good farce afterwards "Les Deux Ménages".[1]—remarked the odd effect of the word "autel", occurring so often in the tragedy & sounding like "hotel"—

29 [Friday]—Was asked to four dinners to-day—dined with Stibbert at Robert's—a large party—Lords Thanet, Kensington, Stair, and Beauchamp—Henry Baring, Sir Granville Temple, King &c. about sixteen in all—very splendid dinner, & very dull—returned home at ten to see how Bessy (who has been very ill these two days past) was going on—found her in bed asleep & went out again—eat ice at Tortonis—

30 [Saturday]—Went at twelve with young Thayer to the College in the Rue St. Jacques (College de France?) to hear a lecture by Monsr. Guizot, who has given a course on the History of the Representative Government in England. This lecture embraced the period of the 14th, 15th & 16th centuries—The parallel with which he concluded between those times & the present very striking—our superiority to them in intellectual acquirement & our inferiority in moral energy—happiness & rights were then so rare & so difficult of attainment that it was necessary to exert the whole force of men's nature to gain ever so small a portion of them out of the struggle—now comforts are so diffused & "la vie est si facile" that men

grow indifferent and are contented with knowing the rights they are entitled to without taking any extraordinary pains to possess themselves of
them—hence their theories are bold, but their practice timorous & com-
promising—it is, in short, the age of what he well described "les esprits
exigeans et les caracteres complaisans"—Went from thence to the Sor-
bonne, where a new Lecture-Room has been fitted up and heard M. Biot
on Physical Science—His Lecture was upon Sound—not very interesting.—
an exceedingly crowded auditory, & many young men here (as at M.
Guizot's) taking notes[1]—dined at Villamil's, with Dawson & went to join the
Macleods at the Variétés in the evening—supped with them afterwards—

31 [Sunday]—Dined at home—was to have gone to Made. la Briche's in the
evening to hear Made. Orfila sing, but got occupied with Bessy in examining & tearing up letters & papers & did not go—

April 1st [Monday]—No letter to decide me about my going—dined at
home—Villamil joined me over a leg of lamb & sausages, and enjoyed his
little dinner exceedingly—

2 [Tuesday]—The Macleods called—wanted Bessy & me to join them at the
Café Francais or rather to be their guest. Bessy not liking to do so, I went—
{but Macleod taking fright at their being no ladies in the room sent to bid
his wife & her sister stay at home, and I had the happiness of dining tete-à-
tete with Mc*Clod,* myself and, paying into the bargain 15 francs for the
treat—all I got out of him was the interesting information that he had read
Adam Smith seven times through & Hume's History[1] nine times—Left him
as soon as possible, & came home}

3 [Wednesday]—A note from Mrs. Macleod to beg that, as they are off to-
morrow, I should join them, Campbell &c. at the Café Francais to dinner—
half promised—preferred however going with Bessy & Mrs. Villamil to the
Cadran Bleu—Bessy ill with a pain in her face which prevented her going
to one of the little Theatres (as was intended) in the evening—I went alone
to the Ambigu & saw the Forêt d'Herminstadt[1]—

4 [Thursday]—Dined with Rancliffe—company, Mildmay, King, Lumley,
Lord Charlemont &c.—heard that the party I was to have joined yesterday
at the Cafe Francais had a row with some Frenchmen, who abused them—
called them poltroons &c.—the men, Macleod, Gordon, Campbell & Irvine

took no notice till the ladies had retired but then found that this fellow was gone & could not make out who he was—

5 [Friday]—Saw Campbell at Long-champs—who told me the particulars—{it} all arose from Miss Inglis shutting the door of the Cabinet they were in & (it is supposed) hitting the Frenchman's arm in doing so—The party, after they had got rid of the ladies, cast lots to decide who should call him out—it fell upon Irvine—Macleod & the ladies are off this morning—They have not yet discovered who is the man, but have put up affiches in the Coffee-House, & advertised to day in Galignani—my lucky stars, not to have been of this party!—dined at Greffulhe's—company Sir Sidney & his ladies, and some Frenchmen—sung in the evening—had a letter from the Longmans to-day to say that the new claim is £1400, that instead of 300 which it was expected they would take, they actually demand £600—so that I must not think of leaving France—shall take a run over however for Power's sake—

6 [Saturday]—Walked to Montmartre where I had heard there was a nice house to be let but saw nothing—sauntered about the Cemetery and lost myself for a while in very sad thoughts—Came home for Bessy & walked her about a little—dined by myself at St. Lambert's, and came home early—Smith, the banker, (Lord Carrington's brother) who has taken La Butte for the summer months offers me, I am told, in the kindest manner the Pavillon I have already occupied, rent-free—worth consideration—met Campbell to-day—they have got into a further scrape by the affiches they stuck up, which were resented by some young French officers, as reflecting on the army in general—General Gourgaud, too, tore down the affiche at the Café Francais—these matters, however, have been explained away by the interference of Henry Baring—they have found that the original offender is at Bordeaux & mean to set off there immediately (the whole three, as the lot is *again* to be cast) for the purpose of calling him out—What a pleasant business I should have had of it! {It is too too bad that these fine young fellows should go thus deliberately to be shot through the head by Cowards—for I fear that *one* duel will not settle the matter.}

7 [Sunday]—Hired a carriage to take us all out (children &c.) to a cold dinner at La Butte, previous to its being given up to the Smiths for the summer—Dawson of the party—sauntered about—looked at a pretty house in the avenue—very tempting, but too dear—home early.

8 [Monday]—Dined with Bessy & Villamils & Dawson at the Rocher de Cancalle, & went to see the Chateau de Kenilworth[1] at the Porte St. Martin afterwards—a shocking story—Have nearly made up my mind to accept of Mr. Smith's offer—Gordon came into our box to-night to take leave on his departure for Bordeaux to-morrow—seemed in a state of much excitement—Handley goes with them as friend, & was asking my advice this morning about some points he was a little doubtful in—told him he must positively confine the quarrel to *one*.

9 [Tuesday]—Walked about with Bessy—was to have dined with Mildmay, but preferred Bushe, having been asked so often by him without being able to go—Company, Lord & Lady Charlemont, Lady Sligo, Sir G. Warrender &c.—sat next to Lady Charlemont—a good deal of talk with her about Made. de Genlis &c. &c.—asked to Mrs. Armstrong's in the evening, but came home.

10 [Wednesday]—Had a note yesterday from the Peters offering me their box for to-night's Opera—sent for Statia to take her there—dined at home & went with Bessy & Anastasia—the Danaides[1]

11 [Thursday]—Went & took my place in the diligence for Saturday, and got a pass-port—dined with Rancliffe—Lords Thanet & Herbert, King, Fitzgerald,Flahaut &c.—story of Alvanley writing to a friend—"I have no credit with either butcher or poulterer, but if you can put up with turtle & turbot, I shall be happy to see you"—came home early—

12 [Friday]—Have been transcribing these two days some of the trifles I have written lately, and marking on the proofs of "Rhymes on the Road" the poems which I wish to have omitted in case any accident might prevent me from superintending their publication myself—Met Mr. Smith this morning who invited me to join him in his carriage tomorrow morning, instead of going by the Diligence—accepted his offer & am to be off at six o'clock.

13 [Saturday]—Started between six and seven, and slept at Amiens—our party, Smith, Abercrombie & *young* Smith—

14 [Sunday]—Smith told some anecdotes of the Revolutionary time in France—two brothers, one of whom was so shaken in his nerves by the scenes around him, that the other was in perpetual anxiety lest he should be surprized with some act of cowardice & disgrace himself—they lived concealed—ventured out together to see the execution of Charlotte Corday[1]—the horror of the nervous man &c. &c.—bribed a soldier to aid in their escape from Paris, who told his wife, & she, in her fears for the husband, gave information—both executed—Another of a man, who, in making his escape in disguise, in coming to one of the frontier towns, asked a party, whom he did not know but with whom he had been singing revolutionary songs through the streets to dine with him—drank republican toasts &c.—the same party saw him out of town in the evening, singing as in the morning—His escape from them & breathless run when he got beyond the frontier—heard afterwards that the whole of the party had been seized as his accomplices & most of them (a young girl among the number) executed—Met Lord Lansdowne on the road to-day—got out & shook hands with him—Arrived at Boulogne at 8 in the evening, and decided for going in the Steam Packet from thence—

15 [Monday]—The scene of our departure (at about ½ past four) very amusing—All the fashionables of Boulogne in gigs, carriages, curricles &c. on the pier—Resurrection of many Irish friends, whom I had thought no longer *above the world*—Tom Grady—who told me that there was some other region (unknown) to which those, who exploded at Boulogne, were blown—told of some half-pay English officers, who having exhausted all other means of raising the wind, at last levied Subscriptions for a Private Theatre, and having announced the Forty Thieves for the first representation, absconded on the morning of the day with the money—Our passage only four hours but very disagreeable—{Heard a fellow during my sickness, recommend brandy to some one because it was "as good coming up as going down";—Like the Irishman, who, after drinking lots of Claret at dinner and of Whiskey Punch at supper and being as might be expected, dog-sick, exclaimed any way while disgorging, "oh Christ! when will I come to the Claret?"}

16 [Tuesday]—Separated from the rest of the party, and started in the Coach at ½ past ten—Cunningham & Colonel Meyrick my companions— C. mentioned that Prince Paul of Wirtemberg, one day at Rotschild's, upon being frequently addressed as plain "Paul" by the Jew said at last casting his eyes towards the servant at his back, "Monsieur le Baron Rotschild, mon domestique se nomme Pierre".—{mentioned a French caricature, representing Cherabim—all head & wings, in the presence of the Deity, who

addressed them "asseyez-vous, nos enfans" to which they answer "Il n'y a pas de quoi, mon Seignieur!"—} Meyrick mentioned several puns against Napoleon at the Variétés (it must have been during the Cent Jours) one of which was something of this kind "le Garde mérite la croix de la Legion d'honneur—L'empereur l'accorde" (la corde.)—Went on my arrival to Power's & slept there—

17 [Wednesday]—Took Lodgings at Blackie's, the Baker, in Bury St, from whom I learned that my good old friend & landlady Mrs. Pineaud died near a year since at Edinburgh—Went to the Longmans—dined there & Rees & I went to Covent-Garden afterwards to see Cherry & Fair Star[1]—

18 [Thursday]—Found my lodgings so uncomfortable that I paid part of the week & took others at 24, Bury St—dined at the George, and went to Drury Lane—Elliston (whom I had called upon in the morning, but who was ill in bed) had a private box prepared for me—saw Made. Vestris in Don Juan & was delighted with her[1]—{Rogers said to me once, in describing her to me, "She'd make you wretched—she made me so"—poor Sam!}

19 [Friday]—Dined with Lord Essex—Company Brougham, Lord A Hamilton &, Bob Smith,—Brougham mentioned having heard some one describe the execution of a *Crétin,* as particularly horrible—the creature's unconsciousness of what was to be done—his pride at being the object of so much crowd & bustle &c—went in the evening to Lord Blessington's—found a party there, among whom was Galt, the writer—met Henry de Roos to-day, who gave me a ticket for the Opera—Lady Blesinton has given me another—

20 [Saturday]—Dined with Lady Donegall, and went to the Opera in the evening—part of the evening in the Blesinton's Box, where I met the Speaker, who very civilly volunteered his permission for my entrance under the Gallery the night of Canning's Catholic motion[1]—went afterwards to Lady Grey's Box—

21 [Sunday]—Went out to dine at Holland House—Company, Lord & Lady Cowper, Lord & Lady Morpeth, Lord Jn. Russel, Lord Gower, Lord Clanwilliam, &c. &c.—{Allen told me an anecdote before dinner mentioned by Talleyrand—When the latter was with Colonne, an old lady came in one day, who described most pathetically the situation of a young or-

phan girl, the anxiety she felt about her fate in the world &c. &c. Colonne, after hearing her quietly out, without raising his eyes from the paper he was writing, at last, to Talleyrand's astonishment, said at the end of the old lady's harangue—" tu [*unrecovered*] ca bien tournée?"—he knew well the real object of this old Mother Cole's visit—} Some conversation with Lord Holland at dinner—I said if Burke & Bacon were not poets (measured lines not being necessary to constitute one) I did not know what poesy meant— Lord H. said that Macintosh did not consider Burke poetical—talked of the Duke of Orleans (Egalité)—was not such as he will be represented in History—that is, weak & wicked—but very clever, and only shabby— {Mirabeau said of him [*French unrecovered*]—mentioned some man saying of the Ruins of Rome "very much out of repair"—} Lord H. mentioned a curious fancy of Lord Wycombe (late Lord Lansdowne) attaching himself to a Colonel Neale of the 9th. Regmt. of Foot, merely on account of his extraordinary ignorance—"a phenomenon of a man, having lived so long, without learning any thing"—used to delight in persuading him that he was clever &c. &c. &c.—{Told of a dispute that just had happened between Lady O & Lord Woodhouslie about a rookery which the latter had established close to her windows in Brook St.—her method of getting rid of them &c. &c.—Lady Cowper told me of some one praising *cider* at Paris that it was "du cidre à faire chanter".—} slept there in a beautiful little bedroom.

22 [Monday]—Irving, with whom I arranged the matter yesterday, came out at eleven o'clock to pay his homage—Lady H. said "what an uncouth hour to come at!" which alarmed me a little but she was very civil to him— Showed me her Napoleon treasure and the extracts from the will—Wanted me right or wrong to stay to-day to meet Lord Grey & Jeffrey, but could not, being engaged to Lord Blesinton—by the bye, met Jeffrey on Saturday—did not know me, I being as he said so full of bloom & youth, whereas the last time he saw me I looked pale & careful—Walked in with Irving— called at Kingston House (Lord Listowel's) in our way—Want me to dine there on Thursday, but Lord John's motion for Reform will prevent me[1]— Met the Sergeant at Arms to-day, who told me that the Speaker had mentioned me to him as to be let in under the Gallery on Canning's Motion— Called upon Lady Grey & sat with her some time—dined at Ld. Blesinton's—Company, Lord Erskine, Doctor Parr, Captain Morris, Lord Auckland, Galt, &c.—none of the veterans very bright, though the old American sung some of his songs—What a venerable Triumvirate of Learning, Law & Lilting!—{Was to have gone to Lady Grey this evening, but did not—} ought to have mentioned that, soon after my arrival I spoke to Murray upon the subject of Lord B's Memoirs—of my wish to redeem them and cancel the deed of sale which Murray acceded to with the best

grace imaginable—Accordingly there is now an agreement making out, by which I become his debtor for two thousand guineas, leaving the MS. in his hands as security, till I am able to pay it—This is, I feel, an over-delicate deference to the opinions of others, but it is better than allowing a shadow of suspicion to approach within a mile of one in *any* transaction—and I know I shall feel the happier when rid of the bargain—Got an Opera Ticket from Lady Grey and sent it and another to the Forsters

23 [Tuesday]—Dined with Shee—showed me a poem he had written upon Scott, Lord Byron & me—"Three poets in three different regions born"— left him early for the Opera—The house splendid—most of the women in their drawing-room dresses, and the general rising to God Save the King most striking—What a contrast to the Canaille-looking audiences of Paris!—Some time in the Grey's Box—went behind the scenes, my old haunt at this House—many years since I was there before—Went to the British Museum this morning with the Forsters—

24 [Wednesday]—Dined with Chauntrey—went with him in the evening to Sir Humphrey Davy's scientific soirée, where I met Sotheby &c. and from thence to Almack's—a very pretty show of women, though not quite what it *used* to be—N. B. Chauntrey's remark about sculpture having taken the lead of painting in ancient time & vice-versâ among the modern—the consequences of this

25 [Thursday]—Sat to Newton—took an early dinner at the George & went off to the House of Commons to hear Lord John's speech on the Reform— got a very good place under the Gallery—Lord J. sat with me till the time for his motion came on—His speech excellent, full of good sense and talent, and though occupying nearly 3 hours in the delivery, listened to throughout with the profoundest attention. Towards the end of the debate Canning spoke, and far surpassed every thing I had expected from him— It was all that can be imagined *agreeable* in oratory—nothing certainly profound, or generalizing, or grand, or electric—but for good taste, for beauty of language, for grace, playfulness, and all that regards manner & display, it was perfect—Eat cold meat at Bellamy's (introduced by Lambton) and did not leave the house till near two—

26 [Friday]—Called upon Lord J. — sat with him some time—upon Canning, whom I congratulated on his speech of last night—"What you were there? (he said) I was little aware I had such a critical auditor"—was asked

to dine to-day at Lord Burghersh's but dined at Kingston's—Company—
Mrs. Story, Twiss, Hallam, Sotheby & Irving—Went in the evening to Lady
Burghersh, and afterwards to Mrs. Thomas Hope, where I saw Miss
Edgeworth—

27 [Saturday]—Walked about with Lord John—dined at Holland House—
Jeffrey, Wishaw, Irving, Knight &c. &c. Talked of a worm that destroys
books in India, and the difficulty of getting rid of it—{"Send him Sir J.
Sinclair's works"[1] says Jeffrey—} Irving & I went to the Opera.

28 [Sunday]—Sat to Newton—went & worked at the National Melodies
with Bishop, for about two or three hours—dined at Abercrombie's—met
Lady Morgan this morning who begged me to join her, Lady C. Lamb, and
General Pepe (a glorious "triumvirate" as she herself calls a man & his cow
& something else in the Wild Irish Girl)[1] to a soirée at Lydia White's tomorrow night—

29 [Monday]—Called upon Luttrel after breakfast—Found there Beresford, author of the Miseries—a grotesque-minded person very amusing—
{Luttrel quoted some one saying of Rogers "How shy he must be of the
Coroner"—"yes"—said Beresford, "Having been so often sat upon"—then
proceeded to tell us that, when a boy, he really believed that the Coroners
sat actually on the body, and imagined them complimenting each other
with the offer of the softest seat—the belly.—} Dined at Kinnaird's—
Company, the Duke of Sussex, Sir F. Burdett, Jeffrey, Hobhouse &c. &c.—
sat next to Jeffrey—talking of the trouble of the Ed. Review he said "Come
down to Edinburgh and I'll give you half of it"—I told him I thought the
Public would find in that case, one half of the disc obscured—Duke of
Sussex asked me to dine with him tomorrow, but excused myself on account of Canning's motion—A long conversation with Hobhouse about
Lord B's. Memoirs, which confirmed me more & more in my satisfaction at
having rescinded the bargain—Hobhouse an honest & upright man, {I
believe, but a coarse one—}in speaking of Lord B. he said—"I know more
of B. than any one else & much more than I should wish any body else to
know."—Gave up Lady Grey's again & walked down to the House of Commons with Jeffrey—talked about Lord Byron—Expressed his fear that
Lord Byron {was totally devoid} had but few of the social sympathies in his
heart—Went in for a short time, and heard Brougham on Finance.

30—[Tuesday]—Breakfasted with Luttrel & walked out with him—

alluding to my restlessness he said I was "like a little bright ever-moving ball of quicksilver— It still eludes you, and it glitters still"—We did nothing but repeat our respective verses to each other—some of his admirable—called upon Irvine with him—Met Hat Vaughan, who said in answer to my enquiries about the £200 sent by the Prince to Sheridan, that it was understood to be merely for the moment, & that more was to come, when wanted—This alters the complexion of the thing materially[1]—L. mentioned a poetical Midshipman who described the weather in the Log-book thus "Light airs, languishing into calms."—Laid in some cold meat, & went to the House of Commons—Avenues all blocked up with unsuccessful candidates for admission—after several repulses & at last giving it up in despair, was taken in by Jerningham, as one of the Catholics on his List, Mr. Blunt.—Sat next Lord Limerick, and Randolph,[2] the famous American orator—a singular looking man—with a young-old face, and a short small body mounted upon a pair of high crane legs & thighs, so that when he stood up, you did not know where he was to end, and a squeaking voice like a boy's just before breaking into manhood—His manner too, strange & pedantic—but his powers of eloquence (Irving tells me) wonderful— Canning's speech very able & statesman-like, but far less beautiful as a display, than that of the other night—*that* was indeed the bouquet of his *feux* d'artifice—Supped at Steven's—The last time I supped there was with Lord Byron at 3 in the morning—

May 1st [Wednesday]—Took Irving to dine at Lady Donegall's—Lord Clifden & Charles Moore of the party—Irving & I went afterwards to the ancient Music, where "I'd mourn the hopes that leave me"[1] was performed (the first time that any thing of mine has presumed to breathe in this venerable atmosphere) and encored—from thence I went to Catalani's concert, where also (proud triumphs for Irish Music!) the thing that produced most sensation was "The Last Rose of Summer"[2] on Nicholson's flute—& finished the night at Almack's, having been obliged to go home & dress again, & being nearly excluded for my lateness—Some conversation here with Canning & Lord Grey

2nd. [Thursday]—Went with Irving to breakfast at Holland House—Duke of Bedford came in after breakfast, fresh from his duel with the D. of Buckingham.[1] Introduced Irving to the Longmans, and dined with him there, in order to go to see Mathews in the evening—Rees went with us— very clever & amusing, but too much of it—Too tired to go to Devonshire House (which I have now missed 3 Thursdays) & went with Irving to sup at the Burton-ale House.

3rd [Friday]—Called & sat with Lady Lansdowne, who was full of kindness—Went to the Private view of the Exhibition with Mrs. Chauntrey & Lady Dacre—Two fine things of Westmacott's among the Sculpture, a Psyche & a beggar-woman—the latter full of sentiment, carrying the art, too, into a new region—Lawrence's *Adonized* George 4th. disgraceful both to the King & the painter—a lie upon canvas—was to have dined to-day with the Artists Benevolent Society, but preferred a dinner alone at Richardson's Coffee-House & went to Covent-Garden in the evening— Miss Stevens delightful—Received on my return home a letter from Jeffrey, saying that he had "heard of my misfortunes & of the noble way I bore them" & adding "would it be very impertinent to say that I have £500 entirely at your disposal, to be paid when you like, and as much more that I could advance upon any reasonable security, payable in 7 years."—The letter concludes with the most anxious & delicate apologies for having taken the liberty, & assuring me that he would not have made the offer if he did not feel that he would most readily accept the same assistance from me—This is deeply gratifying.

4 [Saturday]—Breakfasted with Lord Lansdowne—told him of my last arrangement with Murray—he said that his chief objection to the disposal of the Memoirs was removed by Lord Byron's having given me full powers (as to correction & alteration) over the whole of the MS. —Signed by Bond &c. &c to Murray—dined with Power—sent to Rees to come to me in the evening, & told him what I had done with Murray—Staid at Power's & looked over some of my music, having given my Opera Ticket for to-night to Irving—

5 [Sunday]—Sat to Philipps, the painter, for the finishing of the picture he began two or three years ago—went to Stothard to give him my ideas of the Designs he is about for the 4th. No. of National Mels.—Irving walked about with me—called together at Lady Blesinton's, who is growing very absurd—"I have felt very melancholy & ill all this day," she said—"Why is that?" I asked—"Don't you know?"—No—"It is the anniversary of my poor Napoleon's death"—four invitations to dinner on my list to-day, but, owing to some puzzlement about Holland House, lost all & dined alone at a Coffee-House in Covent-Garden. Met Lord & Lady Tavistock, who were to dine with the Hollands, & begged them to explain why I did not go out— Went to Powers in the evening and wrote out a National Melody—

6 [Monday]—Sat to Newton & to Phillips—went with Mrs. Story, Irving, & Newton to the Exhibition—dined at Lord Lansdowne's—company, the

Abercrombies, Oakden, young Mc.Donald & Wishaw—Went with Ld. &
Lady Lansdowne at ten o'clock to St. Paul's to see it lighted up with gas, for,
I believe, the first time—afterwards to Lady Grey's, where I sung, and the
girls played—

7 [Tuesday]—Occupied in calls & packing—desperate rain—Irving went
with me to the Inn in St. Clement's from which the Dover Mail starts, where
we dined, & at ½ past seven I was off.

8 [Wednesday]—A stiff breeze—had some thoughts of not venturing
across, but at last decided for it—a most stormy & sickening passage—
found Macdonald (Mrs. Armstrong's brother) among the passengers, and
joined him on landing to the Hotel du Bourbon, where we were very
comfortable—Went to the Theatre, where some English actors performed
in the evening—

9 [Thursday]—Started in the Diligence (Armstrong & I) at ½ past nine—

10 [Friday]—Arrived in Paris at 6—found Bessy not at all well, & looking
wretchedly—dined at home—Villamils called in the evening, and soon
after, Denon—told me the Medal of Grattan was nearly finished—By the
bye, when Lord Holland was in Paris, I mentioned to him the plan I had
for ten persons subscribing £5 each to have a medal executed, and he bid
put down his name for two subscriptions—{When I told this to Rogers, he
said, "You had better have his money for one than his name for two"—& he
was right, for when he was later in London Lord John told me that on his
applying to Lord Holland for his five pounds towards the medal he got for
an answer that he knew nothing whatever about the matter,—} Informed
by Denon that Rogers is arrived in Paris from Italy—

11 [Saturday]—Called to look for Rogers at the Hotel de Breteuil, but not
there—told by Lord Grannard (who wants R. & me to dine with him on
Sunday or Monday) that he was at the Hotel de Londres—Went to dine at
Very's with the Villamils & Bessy—saw Rogers there dining with Milligen—
seemed very good-natured & glad to see us—

12 [Sunday]—R. agreed to dine with me at Lord G's—went out to La Butte
to Mrs. Smith, who is about to give up the place, thinking that it does not

agree with her, and thereby upsets all my plans for the summer—never was quiet & study more necessary to me & never did I seem much farther from them—[She proposed that Bessy & I should go to the large house immediately—"so much more comfortable for us," but evidently that she may herself get rid of the responsibility of the plate and linen—] no one at Ld. Granard's but ourselves Rogers & I and Lady Rancliffe—Went together in the evening to the Duchess of Hamilton's, where we found the Duke & her, and one or two foreigners—[What would I take to be doomed to live with the Duke of Hamilton? aye—or even with the Duchess?]

13 [Monday]—Walked about with Rogers for 2 or 3 hours—asked me to dine with him tomorrow at Robert's—

14 [Tuesday]—[In much doubt whether I should not occupy the Pavillon at La Butte, till the place is re-let, my books &c having been all moved there—] joined R. at Robert's at 5—Had asked Gallois & Stewart Rose, but they were engaged—sat down (he & I) to a splendid dinner at 15 francs a head—exclusive of wine—Poets did not feed so in the "olden time"—Went to the Italian Opera afterwards—Camille (by Paer)[1]—Made. Pasta very fine—R. told me a good deal about Ld. Byron, whom he saw both going & coming back—expressed to R the same contempt for Shakespeare which he has often expressed to me—Treats his companion Shelly, very cavalierly.— By the bye, I find (by a letter received within these few days from Horace Smith) that Lord B. showed Shelly the letters I wrote on the subject of his "Cain", warning him against the influence Shelly's admiration might have over his mind, and deprecating that wretched display of attention which Shelly had given into and in which Lord B himself seemed but too much inclined to follow him—Shelly has written anxiously to Smith to {beg he would} say how sorry he should be to stand ill in my opinion, making some explanation of his opinions which Smith is to show me—Rogers starts for England tomorrow morning—[Flew into a passion to-day on finding that the subscription for the Grattan medal was only set as five pounds and determined that he shall have nothing to do with it.]

15. [Wednesday]—Went out to look at the House near Bellevue which Mrs. Cunningham occupied last year, but it was let—Joined the V.s & Bessy at Very's to dinner—Called yesterday on Mrs. Smith at Auteuil where she has taken a house—[Pressed me very much to go to La Butte, but at the same time intimated that her people of business thought my residing there might embarrass the letting of it—This decides me, of course, to give up all thoughts of it—wrote to her to say so.}

16 [Thursday]—Drove out with Bessy & Villamil to call upon Mrs. Smith—
{a pedantic person, full of verbiage & professions but not imposing at [*word unrecovered*] the least—Have had rather a happy escape of her Society for the summer—}Looked at the Apartment in Auteuil, which I have so often looked at—but it won't do.—In coming past Passy got out of the Carriage, and walked through it house-hunting—Found one that I think will just do.—Dined at Very's with the V. and went to the Italian to see Romeo & Juliet—Made. Pasta in Romeo delightful[1]—

17 [Friday]—Drove out with Bessy & Mrs. V. to see the Pavillon at Passy—all liked it exceedingly—agreed for it—1500 francs for six months, & power to keep it on a year for 500 more—Dined at Very's with the V.'s and went afterwards to some shows in the Palais Royal, & the Café des Nymphes de Calypso—Evidently not a very virtuous place—

18 [Saturday]—Bessy went out with one of the Maids to Sèvres to bring away our things, and the other went to Passy to air beds &c.—dined with the V. at Very's—Bessy did not return till eleven at night—much fatigued with her operations.

19 [Sunday]—Went over the Etat of our Rue d'Anjou lodgings with the old Porter, &c. came off to Passy—have now some prospect of quiet—

20 [Monday]—Walked in for the purpose of ordering wine & other little arrangements—wet day—returned to dinner—

21 [Tuesday]—My first task completing the unfinished verses of 4th. No. of National Melodies—

{22 [Wednesday]—The same.}

23 [Thursday]—Wrote out what I had done & walked with my packet into Paris—Bessy had gone in the morning—both dined with the V.s at the Café Francais—

24 [Friday]—Began writing for my little Work (the Letters from

Abroad)[1]—finished the poem on Country Dance & Quadrille[2]—wrote 32 lines of it—walked at ½ past 3 to meet Villamil at the Tir le Page in the Champs Elyseés—tried my hand at firing & after some trials hit a poupée—the V.s dined with us—

25 [Saturday]—Some lines of the Quadrille thing—

26 [Sunday]—Finished this poem, having written more than 100 lines of it since I came—Miss Drew to dinner—All walked for Anastasia in the evening—With some people the heart is the spoiled child of the imagination.

27 [Monday]—Wrote my letters & began a Poem called "the Three Angels"—a subject on which I long ago wrote a prose story & have ever since meditated a verse one—Lord B. has now anticipated me in his "Deluge"—but n'importe—I'll try my hand[1]—went into town with my letters & dined with the Villamils at Very's.

28 [Tuesday]—More of the Poem—Horace Smith, Kenny & Villamil to dinner—Smith {talking of Berguer as a *bore* & a sitter, said "he is quite a fixture—& one I would not take at any valuation"—}mentioned a conundrum upon Falstaff—My first is a dropper, my second a propper, & my third a whapper—{(N. B. young lady's method of enouncing it)—} promised to dine with Smith on Monday next—My birth-day, but forgot to have my health drunk—which wouldn't have been the case if Bessy had dined with us.

29 [Wednesday]—Roasting weather—worked at the Poem—Bessy & I walked to take Anastasia to Mrs. Forster's in the evening—I turned in to the Tir le Page & tried some shots—but fired wide of my mark.

{30 [Thursday]—Wrote more lines & some letters—dined early & went into town in the evening—}

31 [Friday]—Bessy & I started at ten o'clock in order to go with the Villamils to see Raincy, which now belongs to the D. of Orleans—Day scorching hot—had luncheon there under the trees—& then walked about—The Riviere Anglaise (which we were told the old D. of Orleans had "depensé

une somme enorme" to make "sur la crête de la montagne") a poor little gutter about as wide as the River down the Prince Regent's table at his memorable Fête—in going went by Pantin, the great reservoir & laboratory of the "Poudrette" & therefore insufferable for stench[1]—but thanks to the quarter of the wind, not very offensive to-day—Returned by Montreuil (les Peches)—the sight of the country here covered with walls & espaliers very curious—but a dreary place—no shade in summer, nothing but bare walls in winter—arrived at Very's between six & seven & dined—The whole day very agreeable.

June 1st [Saturday]—At work—expect to have written 100 lines by tomorrow evening, which with yesterday's idleness is doing wonders within the week—no walking beyond the garden to-day—a violent storm of rain thunder & lightning came on between 3 & 4 which lasted all the evening & night.

2nd [Sunday]—{I set a verse and a half to the little air I composed the other day and sent it off to [*sentence incomplete*]}—Turned my 100 lines in the course of this day—Walked to the Bois de Boulogne with Bessy &c. after dinner & looked at the dancing—

3rd [Monday]—Set off at two in the Parisienne to dine with Smith at Versailles—the weather, insufferably hot—Company, Greathead, Berguer, Kenny & Grattan—some amusing stories told—Harry Erskine saying to a man who found him digging potatoes in his garden "This is what you call otium cum diggin a taty"—{A young lady asking Swift to translate a motto on a ring given by a girl to the man she was going to be married to—"Qui dedit se dedit"—"That may mean (says Swift) when *he* did it, *she* did it"—The joke about old Coutts complaining after his massage of a stiffness in his back—"I hope it will soon come round"—} It appears that Dante Cary is the author of those pretty translations from the old French Poets in the London Magazine[1]—

4th [Tuesday]—A letter, most kind & affectionate, from Lord Strangford—says that the game is up with the poor Greeks, and that they will be now in a worse situation than they have been in since the taking of Constantinople—dined at home & worked.—walked with Bessy & Tom to the Bois de Bologne after dinner—on our return found the Forsters, who drank tea—{told them I could dine with them on Thursday}

5th [Wednesday]—Wrote & walked—weather tremendously hot—the thermometer some days at 90 in the shade—Feel that it does not agree with me—

6th. [Thursday] Villamil called—went into Paris with him—heard of the arrival of my good friend G. Bryan & his family—had not time to call—dined at the Forsters. Bessy came in the evening—all went to Beaujon—several turns down in the cars with Emma & the rest of the girls—my Anastasia among the number—no hackney coach to be got at night & obliged to walk Bessy home after 12 o'clock by that dreary Boulevard—

7 [Friday]—Wrote a note to Bryan—and sent for Otello[1] to Calais where I have subscribed for 3 months music—after dinner played over some of it—nothing any good except the Duett in which "Si dopo lei morro" occurs & Desdemona's Scene in the last Act—went to walk in the B. de B. & on my return found the Bryans—agreed to dine with them tomorrow.

8 [Saturday]—Went {in} at Two—Bessy & I—eat ice in the Palais Royal with Bryan—they had at dinner Mrs. B's brother & his wife & George & *his*—a pretty woman, {but most gothically gauche}—left them pretty early & called at the Drews—thence home—

9 [Sunday]—Finished to-day (within 1 or 2) my 100 lines for the Week—{dined at home—Lucy Drew came in the evening—walked with her (Bessy & I) beyond the barrier on her return—}

10 [Monday]—Went into Paris to attend a meeting for the purpose of relieving those unfortunate Irish, who are always in some scrape or other, either rebelling or blarneying or starving, which is, perhaps, the worst of all—Sir C. Stuart took the chair—found myself named on the Committee—Sir S. Smith made a speech, and contrived to bring some of his whims & theories to bear even upon the subject of Irish starvation—proposed sending them Wine from Bordeaux, and portable soup from Paris—Walked about the Palais Royal with Bryan for an hour—a thundering storm came on—Went to Very's to write my letters, which I sent off by a Commissionaire & dined there—When half done, the Villamils came & joined me—Called for Anastasia on my way home in the evening—Have done nothing to-day.

11 [Tuesday]—Wrote some lines—Bryan & his son George came out to dine with us—

12 [Wednesday]—Had put down my name at Lafitte's for 100 francs to the Irish Subscription, but have removed it till I see what are the arrangements under this new plan—Wrote & walked.

13 [Thursday]—Walked into town to attend the Irish Committee— Returned to dinner at 5—

14 [Friday]—Wrote & walked.

15 [Saturday]—Went into Paris to attend the Committee—am appointed one of the Collectors at the door for the Charity Sermon tomorrow— subscribed 200 francs—dined with Bessy, Bryan & the Villamils at Very's—

16 [Sunday] In at half past two to attend the Sermon—very little on my plate—but near 200 pounds altogether collected—Bessy & I dined at Lady Susan Douglas's & drank tea at the Bryans—

17 [Monday]—Wrote out an Air for the Blindfolding of Love and sent it off to Power—Have done my 100 lines this week—{walked in the evening to ask Emma Foster to dinner tomorrow—}

18 [Tuesday]—Wrote about 20 lines—Emma to dinner—Bois de Boulogne in the evening—

{19 [Wednesday]—Working & walking—}

20 [Thursday]—Went in with my letters, intending to dine with the Bryans but found they were engaged—called on Dr. Sigmond, who brought me a letter from Lady Burdett & her nice daughter Susanna, who inclosed some music—called afterwards on Kirk, the Sculptor, who told me he had (under the idea that I was in London) brought a cast of me as far as Liverpool, in

order that I might sit to him for some little details—& that Croker, upon hearing it was there, insisted upon having it & made him write to Liverpool for it—Appointed to take Kirk tomorrow to see Somariva's Magdalen—dined by myself at Riches, and called in my way home for Anastasia, the Bryans wishing {that} she should accompany us to dine with them there tomorrow—

21 [Friday]—Went in at two with Bessy & Anastasia, after writing my usual number of lines—Waited at Somariva's for Kirk three quarters of an hour, but he never came—dined all at Bryan's—their carriage brought us home in the evening—a long letter from Lord Byron to-day—he has lost his little natural daughter, Allegra, & seems to feel it a good deal—When I was at Venice, he said in showing me this child "I suppose you have some notion of what they call the parental feeling—but I confess I have not. {I don't know what it means}—this little thing amuses me, but that's all"[1]—This, however, was evidently all affected—he feels much more naturally than he will allow—

22 [Saturday]—Lounged about & wrote—Have just finished the first Angel's Tale—By the bye, a brother of Mrs. Goold, who is in the navy, called upon me some evening since—said with what delight he & his brother-officers had read my Bermuda Poem on the spot—how they had looked for the little bay &c.[1]—told me that my pretty little friend Mrs. W. Tucker was dead, and that they showed her tomb at St. George's as being that of "Nea".[2]

23 [Sunday]—Working & walking—began a Song to send to Power tomorrow—

{24 [Monday]—Finished two verses of the Song, & copied it—went into Paris with my letters—dined at Very's, where I found the Villamils—called on Bryan in the evening & found him ill in bed.

25 [Tuesday]—Wrote some lines of the Poem, but not my usual quantity—walked before dinner to return the visit of Mr. Denne Baron, one of the French poetasters that pesters me—Walked with Bessy in the evening to Forsters.

26 [Wednesday]—Wrote some lines—went into town to see Bryan—sat with him an hour & half—called upon Lady Charlemont, & sat with her some time—home to dinner at half past five—walked by myself in the Bois de Boulogne in the evening—

27 [Thursday]—Was to have gone with Kirk to the Louvre but did not— Bessy & I went in the evening—called to see Bryan, who brought us home to Passy in the evening—

28 [Friday]—Wrote as usual—had the Forsters & Kirk in the evening to tea & supper—seeing a good deal of them—}

29 [Saturday]—Went with Bessy into town to see her off to Montmorenci with the Villamils—she & I dined at Riches (they being engaged to the Duc de San Lorenzo's)—saw her off at seven—went to Bryan's—a saying at Paris "Il faut etre *Riche* pour diner chez Hardy, et {il faut etre}*hardi* pour diner chez Riche"

30 [Sunday]—Worked very well—have finished my 100 lines—went into town to dine with Bryan—took him to the Cafe de la Paix in the evening— came home by the Gondole—an amazing reciter of verses among the passengers—set him right about some lines of Malesherbes—seemed rather astonished at my exclaiming from my dark corner at the end of each of his recitations—"C'est de [Malesherbes], ça"—"oui, Monsieur"—"C'est de Scarron"—"oui, Monsieur"—

July 1 [Monday]—Have now done 500 lines of the Poem—dined at Very's & went to Bryan's in the evening—called at Forster's on my way home & offered myself to dinner there tomorrow—went to the Louvre this morning with Kirk to look at the modern sculpture—some of it very good—the son of Niobe by Pradier very clever—a sleeping nymph with a Faun stealing fruit from her by Lemoyne some parts of it charming—Innocence weeping the death of a snake by Ramy full of beauty & simplicity—took him to Denon's afterwards—Denon told me of a picture at the Louvre this year the subject of which is a set of pigs, with underneath the inscription (seen on several) "Sociétés des Amis des Arts"—

2 [Tuesday]—Wrote about 20 lines—dined at Forster's, & passed the evening in the garden with the girls—

{3 [Wednesday]—Went in at five to dine with the Bryans—have not heard from Bessy—went in the evening to one of the little Theatres in the Boulevard with the B's.—found a cuckoo & came home at eleven—}

4 [Thursday]—Met Kirk at Forster's at three, that he might see our dear Anastasia & give an account of her to my mother—She was in high beauty & he seemed much struck with her countenance—walked in with him— dined at Very's & went to the Beaujon with the Bryans in the evening— luckily found a cuckoo at 11 to bring me out—

5 [Friday]—Not very well—went in late—dined at Riches & thence walked to the Ambigu Comique—staid but a short time, and, not finding a carriage at the Place Louis 15, had the whole way to Passy to walk back again.

6 [Saturday]—Went out with the Douglas's to Montmorenci—had completed within a few lines my 100 during 5 days, which is good going— found Bessy and her dear little fellow very well—walked before dinner in a very pretty Park, & after went on the water—the effect of the coming storm on one side of the heavens & the remains of sunset on the other very fine— had half intended to stay till Monday, but thought I should lose less time by returning to Paris—slept at Lady Susan's—Lucy & I sung duetts in the midst of all the lightning coming home—tremendous flashes & the carriage open—

7 [Sunday]—Got home to Passy about one—dined at home—sauntered into Paris in the evening.

8 [Monday]—Surprized by a visit from Bessy—went into Paris & dined with her & the Villamils at Very's—saw her off again in the evening, and went to see an act of Fernand Cortez at the Opera—found a note on my return from Lady Mildmay, saying that the Tancredi[1] is to be tomorrow, and reminding me that I was to dine & go with them—

9 [Tuesday]—Not the Tancredi, but resolved to go—dined with the Mild-mays—Opera, Romeo—They may talk of the profanation of turning Shakespeare's stories into operas, but Pasta's Romeo & Desdemona are to me as touching as the Poet's[1]—got home about 11—

{10 [Wednesday]—Wrote, as I do now everday—dined with the Bryans—called in going in on the Granards, who wanted me to stop dinner, but promised for tomorrow—met Rancliffe, who also wanted me to dine with him—is off tomorrow—went with the B's. to the French Opera—The Danaides—induced to sleep at Bryan's Hotel—disagreeable bed.

11 [Thursday]—Not well—started early—took a bath at Bains Chinois & coffee at Tortoni's—arrived at home at 1—did not do much—dined at Lord Granard's—no company but Lord Henry Cholmondeley—left there at 8—& went to saunter about Beaujon for an hour—thence home}

12 [Friday]—Did not go in till very late—took four or five turns about the Palais Royal (the weather being very wet) before I dined—alone at Verys. called on Bryan afterwards—mentioned some one {(Johnson)} saying that second marriages were "the triumph of hope over experience"[1]—home early—had another message yesterday from the Prince Royal of Prussia about Lalla Rookh—he told the writer of the letter he always sleeps with a copy of the Poem under his pillow

13 [Saturday]—Bessy & her dear little fellow came home from Mont-morenci—found them so much better for their trip that I am resolved they shall go back again—Went in to dine with the Bryans—Bessy too tired to accompany me—came home early.

14 [Sunday]—A troublesome gentlemen who has called several times in-sisted upon seeing me—said his business was of a romantic nature, and the romance was his asking me to lend him money enough to keep him for a month—told me he was the author of the Hermit in London, but begged me to keep his secret[1]—Told him I had no money myself, but would try what a friend I was going to dine with would do for him—this, merely to get rid of "the Hermit"—Bessy & I went in to dine with the Bryans—

tremendous storm in the evening—Bryan's coachman wanting to put us out in the midst of it—

15—[Monday]—Have done pretty well this week—near 120 lines—Bessy went in to meet Mrs. Villamil—joined her at five—thought Mrs. V. would join us at a Restaurateur's (Villamil being away on a visit to the Princess Talleyrand) but she feared returning so late—Dined Bessy & I at Riche's— went to Forsters in the evening—

16 [Tuesday]—Worked pretty well—dined at home—walked in the evening on my return found that Bessy upon sending for Anastasia to come home (in order to meet the Bryans tomorrow) was informed that she was ill & had [walked] off to see her—followed & overtook her—both a good deal alarmed, but found the dear child but little the worse for the attack, which was a giddiness in the head from deranged stomach—

17 [Wednesday]—Bessy went in early to provide for today's dinner—saw Anastasia in her way & found her much better—the Bryans to dinner— Received to-day a letter from Brougham, inclosing one from Barnes (the Editor of the Times) proposing, as he is ill, I should take his place for some time in writing the leading article of that Paper—the pay to be a hundred pounds a month—This is flattering—to be thought capable of wielding so powerful a political machine as the Times newspaper is a tribute, the more flattering, (as is usually the case) from my feeling conscious that I do not deserve it.

18 [Thursday]—Wrote to decline the proposal of the Times[1]—

{19 [Friday]—Dined with Peters—Company, Forster, Stibbert, Browne &c. &c.—Had taken the Bryans in the morning to Somariva's & Denon's. B. bought a memento of Napoleon from the latter for which he gave him 240 francs.

20 [Saturday]—Went in with Bessy, who returned to Montmorenci to-day & takes Anastasia too with her—dined alone at Very's[1]—

21 [Sunday]—Dined at the Douglas's—Have worked pretty well this week.

22 [Monday]—Dined with the Bryans—Byrne dined there

23 [Tuesday]—Dined wtith the Peters—to go to their box with them at the Italian—the Cenerentola[1]—very bad singer Bonini—

24 [Wednesday]—Bessy came in with the Villamils, & all dined together at Verys—Poor Bessy not looking at all well—Went by myself to the French Opera & saw Aristippe & the Rossignol—Met there my old acquaintance, Richard Thamor, who rebels violently against Rossini.}

25 [Thursday]—Dined with the Mildmays, & accompanied her to the Opera to see Pasta in Tancredi—nothing could be more perfect than the pathos of both her acting & singing—Greffulhe said that Talma declares she is as much superior to Duchesnois in acting as Duchesnois is to V{alnais}—Got home rather late. Called this morning & sat some time with Emma Forster.

{26 [Friday]—Dined with the Bryan's.

27. [Saturday] Dined with Latin—dressed at the Douglas's—Company, Mrs. Hutchinson, Genl. & Mrs. F. Dillon, Leeson, &c. &c.

28 [Sunday]—Went down to Montmorenci with the Douglas's & dined there—Bessy not looking better, but the little ones quite well—went to the Montmorenci fête in the evening—rather pretty—slept at Lady Susan's—

29 [Monday]—Wet morning—my day lost—Went about looking for lodgings with the Bryans, who mean to stay here the winter, & dined with them—have done near 150 lines within these 8 or 9 days, & if it had not been for to-day & yesterday could have brought the Poem all together to a 1000 before the 1st. of August.—Sent off to-day to Power the slight sketch of a Song to a little air of Beethoven's—

30 [Tuesday].—Did very well this morning—went into town expecting the Villamils & Bessy to arrive for the Opera, which they half intended but the plan given up—dined at the Forsters—home early}

31 [Wednesday]—Have done 50 lines within these two days which, contrary to my expectation completes my 1000 to-day—dined at Bryan's—

August 1st [Thursday]—Worked away—dined with the Douglas's, under the idea of going to Beaujon but the weather too wet.

{2nd [Friday]—Dined at Bryan's—find, by a letter from Power, that Bishop is arrived—called at Miss Stephens—to enquire his residence, but did not see her.

3rd. [Saturday] Bessy arrived from Montmorenci at eleven—she & I dined with the Bryans who left us at home in the evening—the Son & his wife went off this morning—}

4th [Sunday]—Called upon by the Douglas's at three to go & dine at Mr. Thayer's (an American, to whom their Hotel (de Montmorency) and the Passage du Panoramos belongs). his Country-House at Sceaux—a large & strange party there—among others the famous M. Say whom I found agreeable—In speaking of La Martine he said that his school which was that of Chateaubriand met with strong opposition from the critics—M. Chenier particularly had attacked it—praised Chenier—said his Epistles were some of them equal to Voltaire's[1]—no truth whatever in the story of his having been accessory to his brother's death in the Revolution—said that the school of Chateaubriand consisted in producing effects more by words than ideas—that it added to the stock of phrases without increasing that of thoughts—for instance, he said, Chateaubriand in calling God "Le grand célibataire du Monde" (what wretched affectation!) conveyed no more than if he had called him "Le Pere Eternel" or any other common name—Madame Thayer (a very hearty, good-natured person) told me at dinner of a friend of hers M. Labourdonnaye, who is enthusiastic about Lalla Rookh—carries it about with him every where &c. &c.—Among the company too was Garat, brother to the old singer of that name, who sings himself with much spirit and gave an Anacreontic after dinner with great effect—In the evening went to the Dance in the Park, which was very pretty—returned & had Music—a French girl, Madlle. Picheraut, sung some things of Rossini's accompanied by Consul, of the Opera—I sung too.—Home at 12—Lucy & I chanting duetts in the moonlight all the way.

5th. [Monday] Rather interrupted this morning—Mrs. V. to breakfast—she and Bessy took me in at three—called on Bryan—thence to Lafitte's, where in talking of the disgraceful outrage on the English Actors last week somebody said that in Bonaparte's time, when there was a violent opposition to a play called Christophe Colombe[1] (merely because it was written in violation of the critics) Napoleon sent down to the Theatre not only some troops of Gendarmerie but a piece of artillery, and carried the Tragedy off smoothly—what a powerful support at an author's back!—dined alone at Very's & home early in the evening—

6 [Tuesday]—Have finished to-day 1100, making at the rate of 20 lines a day since last Thursday—Took Bessy at four to dine with the Bryans, who had a box at the Opera for the night—the Barbiere—remark on the pathos of the accompaniment to a Basso Duett

{[*Word unrecovered*]
yet much sweetness would be lost if forbidden]—home before 12—

7 [Wednesday]—At home—wrote to the Bryans in the evening to say that I meant to take Bessy to Tancredi tomorrow & asking them to join us.— walked in

8 [Thursday]—Note from Bryan to say he had taken a Box—went in & dined with them—Pasta charming—the way she sings "Traditore" [in the Duett of "M'abboncine"]—her actions with the finger in the girdle—her dignity in pronouncing "saprai, quando cadrai"—all delightful.

{9 [Friday]—Walked in after dinner to order wine, ice for my dinner tomorrow—found the Bryans on my return

10 [Saturday]—Had Bishop & the Forsters to dinner—the girls in the evening singing &c.}

11 [Sunday]—Dined at home & went with Lucy afterwards to Lady Virginia's at the Observatoire to see the Jardin Suisse—very pretty—went down in the cars—a dreadful rainstorm came to dissolve the vision— supped afterwards with Lady Virginia, who gave Bessy a pretty bronze kettle—left at home by Lucy

12 [Monday]—Have done since the 6th. (Tuesday) 100 lines more—walked in to make visits—to Mr. Brodie (introduced to me by Godwin) to Miss Stephens who, I delight to find, is as wild about Pasta as myself—says her heart never was thoroughly touched by a singer before—Bessy & I dined at Douglas's—John Bushe and an Algerine, one of Douglas' monsters from the East—Mrs. Armstrong & singing in the evening

13 [Tuesday]—Bryan rode out in the morning with a present of a pretty watch set in pearls & a gold chain for Anastasia to wear at the Children's Ball given by the Douglas's to-night—but Bessy too ill to take her—dined at home & called upon the Bryans in the evening to go to the Ball—a large party—Ladies Isabella Chabot, Emily Henry, Lucy Foley, Sligo, Clanrickarde, Kensington &c. &c. with their respective little ones—very sorry that little Stasy did not make one of the number—came home early—

14 [Wednesday]—Bessy & I dined with the Bryans—am not writing much to my satisfaction this week.

15 [Thursday]—Nervous & uncomfortable—dined at Forster's to meet Bishop—Some talk about Music—B. said that Handel was the first to study general effect & brought his voices & instruments into *masses,* as a painter would call it—Mozart carried this to perfection—Haydn had not so much of it—too fond of finishing up bits to the injury of the whole—Does not think Rossini's music will live—Had some singing in the evening—tried over "mi manca la voce" which he owns to be perfectly beautiful—Had a hackney coach home for Bessy, who came after dinner

{16 [Friday]—Dined (Bessy & I) at Bryan's—Company, Sir W. & Lady Sheridan, Lattin, Dalton & little Byrne—an abundance of talk & claret—Lattin the only person worth listening to—very ill in coming home from having drunk so much sour claret.

17 [Saturday]—Stomach wretchedly sick—nothing would stay on it, till Bessy gave me some rhubarb in pepper-mint—dined at home—walked in the Bois du Bologne afterwards.

18 [Sunday]—Quite well again—wrote a good many lines—dined at home—weather tremendously hot—took a solitary walk in the evening—

19 [Monday]—Have now done *1300*—dined at home, but wrote only a very few lines.

20 [Tuesday]—Bessy went off to Montmorency with little Tom to stay till Saturday next—I went in to dine with Douglas's, and to the Opera with them in the evening—they having taken the Mildmay's Box for this month at 200 francs—Gazza Ladra—Bonini the heroine, very bad—drove me home at night—

21 [Wednesday]—wrote near 24 lines—went in late—called on Bryan & Bishop—dined alone at Very's—smotheringly hot.[1]

22. [Thursday] Same number of lines—dined at Douglas's—a Mr. Boyd of the party—Opera in the evening—Tancredi—left at 10 for the Fête Monarchique at Tivoli—arrived too late for the fire-works—went down in the car 4 or 5 times with Lucy—they drove me home afterwards—Miss Rogers called this evening, & left word for me to come breakfast tomorrow—

23. [Friday] Walked in pretty early—called on Miss Roger's—her brother Henry with her—dined with the Bryans—drove about in the Champs Elysées afterwards—

24 [Saturday] Went in to meet Bessy, but missed her, by the mistake of the Porter of the Rue Duphot, & she came out to Passy—saw her at five in Paris—she returned with Mrs. V. till Monday—dined with the Douglas's— Daly of the party—walked in the Thuilleries afterwards to hear the music— drove me home—Bessy to-day fixed Anastasia's little party to be on Wednesday next.}

25 [Sunday]—Walked in through the mummeries of the Champs Elysées, at 3 o-clock—Received a very kind letter last night from Lord Lansdowne, chiefly relative to the Cottage at Sloperton, which, by the death of Hale, there is now another chance of my having, if I chuse—one paragraph of his letter as follows—"I can only say that if an address from all the neighbours of Sloperton could recall you, you would speedily receive one as cordial & affectionate, & perhaps rather more sincere than those which his Majesty is now collecting from the loyalty of his Scottish subjects, and in which the

inhabitants of Bowood would certainly not be behind hand"—dined at Bryan's & went at seven to join the Douglas's for the purpose of seeing the Fireworks &c.—walked & drove about till past ten, & then the Ds. took me home—have done now 1400 & some odd lines.

{26 [Monday]—Bessy arrived pretty early—poor Tom with a very bad cough—dined at home & walked in after dinner.

27 [Tuesday]—A wet day—had a remise & drove in for Bessy's prepara-tions against tomorrow—dined at Bryan's to meet a Mr. & Mrs. Askew—went in the evening to the Opera with the Douglas's—The Cenerentola some of the Music very brilliant—the Duett of Zitto Zitto[1] &c.—By the bye, I went one day last week to subscribe for a new Edition of Mozart—up two pair of Stairs in the Rue du Richelieu—The Editor an intelligent looking young man, on my writing down my name, stared with all his eyes at me and said, "Mais Monsieur, est-ce donc au celebre Thomas Moore que j'ai l'honneur de parler?"—Dear Anastasia home this evening for tomorrow's party.}

28 [Wednesday]—Very much interrupted these two or three days—obliged by having fixed the day myself, to go in & dine with Darby—Company, Lattin, Sir Robt. Wilson, Beckett (Under Secy.) Lord Sligo &c. &c.—did not dine till near seven & left them at eight, being called for by the Bryans to attend the little dance at home—found the young ones all at tea—a very merry evening—played blind-man's Buff with them, sung &c.—our new neighbour, Mrs. Clifton & her children of the party—separated a little after 12—our dear Stasy the flower of the flock—dances very gracefully & altogether a thing to be proud of.

29 [Thursday]—Not a line to-day, but letters—Tom's cough a confirmed hooping-cough—God send the sweet fellow well over it! my anxiety about these children almost embitters all my enjoyment of them—Bessy is more sensible on the subject "doats" without "doubting"—Both went in the eve-ning to join the Villamils to the Opera (the same Box) Romeo & Juliett—Pasta something more touching than ever I yet saw on the stage, except Miss ONeil—Bessy cried through the whole last act.

30 [Friday]—Dined at Davison's to meet my old friend Carlo Doyle, who has returned from India some months & within these few days arrived at

Paris—much talk about old times—All of us who were such early & close companions still alive—Lord Forbes, Rancliffe, Strangford &c.—but some breaches, alas, of the friendship have taken place—Forbes & Strangford being now decided enemies—{Could collect from Carlo that Lady Londour's *absence* from India was of great use to her Lord's popularity there—as soon as she & her ceremonials were got rid of, he, of course, came more into social contact with the people—Home early.}

31st. [Saturday]—Dined at home & walked in the evening—Called upon Bryan—Have not got on very vigorously these some days past—
   This Book now contains Three Years of my Life "quam *nihil* in medio invenies!"

[*There is a hiatus in the MS of the Journal extending from 1 September 1822 through 19 October 1825. The entries for these inclusive dates have been transcribed from Lord John Russell's edition.*]

September 1st [Sunday], 1822. The Bryans called for Bessy in the morning, to go see the Rosiere, at Suresne. Dined with them: a Frenchman of the party, a Royalist, who told of a girl he walked with last year, at the *bal masqué*, being arrested while with him, for having a tri-colour ribbon on her gown; and (as he since found out) imprisoned six months; no other offence, and it was by chance the poor girl put on the ribbon. Home early.

3rd. [Tuesday] Walked in. Dined at the Douglases'. Before dinner, Bessy and I went to order some of Rossini's operas, she having hoarded (by little occasional thefts from me) six Napoleons, which, with three more from the same source, which she lent me some time ago, are to be devoted to this purpose. Ordered four, and some ballets. All went to the opera in the evening; "Otello." Papers thrown from the Quatrième into the parterre, which proved to be a list of the jury at present sitting on the affair of the conspirators at La Rochelle.[1] The Douglases drove us home.

5th. [Thursday] Went in at two. Accompanied Bessy and Mrs. Bryan to the Diorama: a beautiful invention; the artists, Daguerre and Bouton. Dined at the Bryans, and went all to the Opera Comique in the evening; "Ninon chez Made. de Sèvignè," and "Le Solitaire;"[1] the latter new, and no great things. Madame Prudher very charming.

7th. [Saturday] A German called upon me, to ask my opinion with respect to some alterations he was about to make in an opera brought out by Spontini last year, at Berlin, on the subject of the "Feast of Roses," in "Lalla Rookh," but which Spontini thinks requires enlargement and an addition of incident to secure its further success.[1] Being engaged to be in town at twelve, I took him to walk in with me, during which he explained his plan. An intelligent man; spoke of Schultz (I think), a German composer, who has great reputation for ballads. Expressed great anxiety to hear some of the Irish Melodies, and promised me some of his country airs. Begged him to order for me from Berlin a set of the engravings the king has had made from the costumes worn at the Court Fête founded on "Lalla Rookh," as well as the translation of the poem by Baron Fouquet, author of "Ondine," &c. &c.[2] Said that the style of this translation was so elaborate, so full of *recherché* words and compound epithets, that it was almost impossible, upon hearing it read, to understand it. Talked with much rapture of Pasta. Was with Lucy at twelve, in order to go with her to Massamino's singing school for girls, which she attends. Very few there; there being in general between twenty and thirty. One very pretty little girl, full of wicked looks and coquetry, called Zoé, only fourteen years of age, sung very nicely, particularly the duet of Desdemona and Emilia, in "Otello." Lucy called for me at nine, with her mama, and drove me home; a delicious night.

8th. [Sunday] Have done only between sixty and seventy lines this week. Went in to dine with the Bryans: Bessy not well enough to go. A son of—— at dinner; a very rough-grained sort of gentleman, but came out with one or two things that smacked of the Irish *esprit*. Said that the Irish administrations of late (consisting of a liberal Lord-Lieutenant and a bigot Secretary, or *vice versâ,*) wore sometimes an orange coat with green facings, sometimes a green coat with orange facings. In talking of——, too, he said (what is, I think, perfectly true) that his patriotism is and always has been humbug; and that the difference of the currency between English and Irish money would at all times be sufficient to decide him between Toryism and Whiggism.

10th. [Tuesday] Dined with the Douglases, in order to go and see Pasta in "Elisabetta." Had called in the morning at the Denons, to meet the artist, and give him instructions about the inscription for the medal. No one at Douglas's but the Murrays. Rather a *triste* dinner. The suspension of Lady Susan's annuity has thrown them into much embarrassment. Most sincerely sorry for Lucy, who is a fine creature. The opera a complete failure. Pasta could not reach the pitch of her part through the whole first act; and the only thing worthy of herself was the cavatina at the end of the second.

Quite mortifying to see her fail thus. Lucy and her mama drove me home; near twelve when I arrived.

11th. [Wednesday] Have now completed 1600 lines. Do not mean to attempt any more till my return from Rouen. Have seen Bishop, who promises to have the "National Melodies" finished this week. Mr. Abbot called upon me, of whose coming I had notice from my father and mother, with a request that I would be very kind to him. Brought me a letter from Rees, who says that there is nothing wanting towards the arrangement of the last Bermuda claim but the consent of an insurance company in Edinburgh, which meets but five times a-year; that there is no doubt of its being given, and that I may count upon my liberation in a few weeks. Mr. Abbot is empowered by Harris (whose agent he is) to engage Catalani for Dublin. Offered to accompany him to her country house to-morrow. Dawson afterwards called with a friend of his, whose MS. translation of the "Pucelle"[1] he had sent me to decide upon, and which I pronounced unpublishable. The author very gentlemanly and good-humoured about the matter. Mrs. Bryan took Bessy in. Called at the Burghershes; saw Lady B. but for a short time, as she had begun her toilette for dinner at the Duke of Orleans'. Dined at Bryan's; drove us home in the evening.

12th. [Thursday] Went to Abbot's to breakfast. Arrived at St. Brice (the château where *Vallabrique* lives) at twelve. Found that Catalani had gone to Paris the day before. Walked about the pretty grounds of the place for an hour and a half, while the horses rested, and then returned to Paris. Abbot mentioned two or three legal anecdotes. Judge Fletcher once interrupted Tom Gold in an argument he was entering into about the jury's deciding on the fact, &c., when Gold, vexed at being stopped in his career, said, "My Lord, Lord Mansfield was remarkable for the patience with which he heard the Counsel that addressed him." "He never heard you, Mr. Gold," was Fletcher's reply, given with a weight of brogue which added to the effect of the sarcasm. The same judge, who, it seems, is a very surly person, once said to an advocate, "Sir, I'll not sit here to be baited like a bear tied to the stake." "No, *not* tied to the stake, my Lord," interrupted the Counsel. He mentioned the excellent joke of Curran's upon a case, where the Theatre Royal in Dublin brought an action against Astley for acting the "Lock and Key." "My Lords, the whole question turns upon this, whether the said 'Lock and Key' is to be a *patent* one, or of the *spring* and *tumbler* kind."[1] Talking of jokes, there is a good story of Lattin's which I doubt if I have recorded. During the time of the emigrants in England, an old French lady came to him in some country town, begging, for God's sake, he would interfere, as the mob was about to tar and feather a French nobleman. On

Lattin's proceeding with much surprise to inquire into the matter, he found they were only going to *pitch* a *marquee*. Called at Catalani's on our arrival in Paris; found her; asked us to dine at five, which we did. Her *naïveté* and cheerfulness very delightful. Spoke of Pasta with enthusiasm, as the singer that had most touched her heart, next to her own master, Marchesa. I mentioned the defects of Pasta's voice: "Yes, but she can do beautiful things with it." Praised Mrs. Salmon for her church-singing. Very amusing in her imitation of the mincing-pincing style of talking among the French women. All went to the Feydeau except me. Showed me a splendid box given her by the King of Prussia, containing the Medal of Merit. Went from thence to the Douglases. Some conversation with Lucy, whose rapid change of looks within these few days is quite melancholy.

14th. [Saturday] Walked in with Bessy. Called at the Forsters' to see our dear Anastasia, who has a bad cough; have no doubt it will turn to a hooping-cough. Got my passport at the Ambassador's, and having left Bessy at Bryan's, went to the Ministre de l'Interieur and the Préfecture to be visé. Was with Bishop at three o'clock, and went over all he has done (nine) of the fourth number. Succeeded very well with them. Seemed to think "Heaven knows what" a little too free for this work. Agree with him, and shall substitute another. At dinner had Duruset and Poole, besides Bishop's lady, who is rather a fine woman. Poole told of a man, who said "I can only offer you for dinner what the French call a *lever* (liévre) and a *pulley* (poulet)." I said to Bishop that "this sort of dinner would do for our men of business, the mechanic *Powers*." Went thence to the Douglases, where Bessy dined. Curran, too, had dined there.

16th. [Monday] Was at Bryan's, in the Rue d'Artois, before half-past six, though stopped at the barrier to have my trunk opened and examined. We started in his carriage at a little after seven. A most heavenly day. The first sight of Rouen, on descending the hill, very beautiful; the long, richly planted island in the river, the faubourg and villages over the plain opposite to the city, and the black, lofty towers of the cathedral, one of which (as our post-boy first told us in descending the hill) had been struck by a thunder storm the day before and very much injured, produced altogether a most striking effect in the bright, but indistinct, sort of light which sunset threw over them. Did the journey in eleven hours, six minutes. Drove to the Hotel de France, where —'s unfortunate daughter (to see whom was the sole object of the journey) met us with as much easy self-possession as if she had been the best-conducted person in the world. The inn a wretched one; my bed seemed to me to be damp.

17th. [Tuesday] All walked out for the purpose of seeing the cathedral, but, on account of the workmen being employed in repairing the late damages, were not admitted. Went from thence to the Museum in the Hotel de Ville; a wretched set of pictures. M. L—, a Rouen artist, the perpetrator of a great many of them, and of the best, perhaps. The catalogue has the audacity to give a bad copy of Raphael's glorious Dresden Madonna as an original. Dined wretchedly at our inn, where the only comfort was a very good pianoforte in our sitting room, with some music books, oddly enough consisting for the most part of Stevenson's songs and mine. Went all to the theatre in the evening. The pieces were the "Coquette Corrigée" and the "Rivaux d'Eux Mêmes."[1] A Mademoiselle Le Grand the coquette.

18th. [Wednesday] Not at all well. The filth of our inn very disgusting; the cookery poisonous. Went to the library; vacation time, and no permission to read, which is rather a disappointment, as I had some references to make, on the subject of angels, which I had hoped to have employed myself in here. The town allows 3000 francs a-year for additions to the library, whose *fond* seems chiefly theological. Another wretched dinner; to the play in the evening. "La belle Fermière" and "Un Moment d'Imprudence;"[1] the latter very good. Bryan mentioned a ridicule he once saw on "Otello," where the harlequin says to his lamp, "*Si j'éteins ta flamme, j'ai mon briquet, mais on n'allume pas une femme comme une guinguette.*" To-day before dinner walked by myself to a height above the road, by which we first came in sight of Rouen, and had a magnificent view, not only of the city, but of the river to the left, studded with islands to a great extent.

20th. [Friday] Up before six, and off a little after seven. Arrived in town at seven, and found Bessy and Mrs. B. waiting dinner for us. Called in our way home for Anastasia, whose cough is now decidedly a hooping one. A letter from Rees to say that we may safely return to England as soon as we like.

21st. [Saturday] Went into town pretty early to make some calls; one of them on the bookseller, who some time ago sent me an English poem, called "Cleon," and has now written to say that as I was pleased to express approbation of it, he trusts I shall not be less interested in its success for knowing that it was written by a young lady of seventeen, now his wife. A thorough take in; the first symptoms of which were his saying *Elle est actuellement plus agée;* and the lady's own appearance in a few minutes quite dispelled any hope I might have had of seeing the youthful muse he led me to expect; the lady being a *rather* elderly Jewess. Joined the Murrays afterwards at Marechal Soult's.

22nd. [Sunday] The artist employed by Denon to engrave Grattan's medal for me, called with the die. Abbot called and sat some time. Spoke with much warmth about my mother; her warm-heartedness, her animation, the continual freshness and energy of her thoughts and affections. All very true, and, of course, delightful to hear. Dined at home. Have not yet resumed my work.

23rd. [Monday] Called on Abbot, and thence to Denon's. Upon my proffering a thousand francs to the medallist (which according to my impression was the *prix convenu*), he exclaimed, *Ce n'est pas ça diable, ce n'est past ça; c'est cinquante louis,* making the difference of ten napoleons, which I was obliged to pay. Denon seemed a little ashamed of the price, and suggested that I should *porter ces deux cent francs sur le tirage,* the *striking* being three francs cheaper for each medal than I had expected; but this, though very French, was not my mode of doing things. Denon, to console me, read us a *notice* on the life of Puget, the sculptor, which he has written for some forthcoming work. Very neatly done. Puget, it seems, upon remarking the resemblance a mountain at Marseilles bears to a sitting figure, proposed to make out the form, and so realise the Mount Athos project, but met with no encouragement for his sublime undertaking.

The statue of Milon at Versailles is by Puget, and one of his finest works. In talking of Claude Lorraine, Denon having said that his talent broke out at a late period of life, without any instruction whatever, I remarked that this rather lessened one's respect for the art, as in other subjects a certain degree of intellectual preparation and instruction was necessary; he answered very livelily, *Ah, oui, il faut de l'instruction pour faire de manuvaises copies de ce qu'il a fait, mais*—for original genius it requires no such thing; it is like your Shakespeare, &c., &c." Went from thence with M. Galli to the mint. Ordered sixty medals to be struck at two francs each. The mint keeps six (not included in the sixty). Two must be given to the artist, one to Denon, and one to Mossop (the Irish artist from whose wax model the portrait was taken); so that I shall have six over to pay the expenses of the *tirage.* Dined at the Douglases'. Company in the evening. Had some conversation with Gallatin, the American ambassador. Told me the Duke of Wellington mentioned to him a day or two since, that Lord Londonderry had a similar attack of madness at the time of the Union in Ireland.

27th. [Friday] Called upon the Miss Dalys at Passy. Walked in the Bois de Boulogne. Dined at home. Have been reading Manon l'Escaut;[1] rather disappointed; as yet there is no variety in the scrapes she and her lover get into.

28th. [Saturday[Have written since Tuesday (24th) near sixty lines. Bessy very ill to-day. Emma Foster called; saw her home on my way into town. Went to the mint; received my sixty medals, and had the die *biffé*, or broke, which excited a great senation in the mint; it being, I take for granted, a rare occurrence. Told me the last time they had any such task was in destroying the *timbre* of Napoleon, and that there was a guard of soldiers both inside and outside the Bureau during the three days it took. Carried my medals and the broken die to Douglas's, and begged of Lucy to set about wrapping up each medal in separate papers for me. Went to call upon Wishaw, who was all kindness. Returned to Douglas's, and found the medals all neatly papered, as I wished. Dined there, and went to the coach-office in the Rue du Bouloi, where I found Mrs. Branigan just arrived. Brought her to Passy in a hackney coach.

29th. [Sunday] Lady Susan called for me in the morning to go and hear Douglas preach at the Ambassador's Chapel; was not ready. Wrote some lines. Went in at three to atone for my morning's failure, and heard D. at the Oratoire. The close of his sermon very spirited. Dined at home.

30th. [Monday] Left Abbot's five medals, with one for Mossop (who mod-elled the head from which I had the medal engraved), at Cumming's, in the Faubourg St. Honoré, to be taken over to Ireland to him. Bessy and Mrs. B. all day shopping in town. Called upon the Granards. Lady G. told me of her giving a note of mine to Count Orloff, who was in search of my hand-writing. Dined at home. Wrote a note to-day to M. Langlés, head of the King's Library (which is now in *vacance*), to beg he would, if possible, show it to the Murrays before their departure.

Oct. 1st. [Tuesday] A very civil note from Mons. Langlés, beginning, *Je suis si heureux de vous donner une faible preuve de ma haute estime pour votre personne et pour votre talent, &c. &c.* Went in at twelve, and took the Murrays and Lucy to the Bibliothèque. Showed us the autographs. Told M. Langlés I wanted to consult some books on the subject of Angels. Mentioned to me a translation by Laurence of the "Book of Enoch," and lent it me, together with the second volume of his own "Norden,"[1] which I asked him for. Particularly kind and obliging. When I spoke of the liberality of the French about books, he said, *C'est pour cela que nous les avons.*

2nd. [Wednesday] Walked a good while in the Bois de Boulogne. Met with rather an adventure; girl singing the air from the "Solitaire," *Il voit tout, il sçait tout, &c.* A lovely soft day.

3rd. [Thursday] Have at last completed the 1700th line of the poem. Narrowly escaped M. ——, one of those wretched French literati who pester me. Had a large copy of Propertius (which he is translating) under his arm. Went to the Ambassador's, Lafitte's, &c., and was at Bryan's at four, having bought two of the pieces to be given at the Variétés to-night, where we have a box. Feared that Bessy would not be well enough to come in; but at five, she and Mrs. B. arrived. Pieces at the Variétés, "Le Paris de Surenne," "Les Petits Acteurs," and "L'Actrice en Voyage;"[1] the last a *premiere representation* to show off little Jenny Vertpré, who was charming in it.

5th. [Saturday] Am in much doubt and perplexity about my return to England, on account of the expense and of the difficulty I shall have in mustering the supplies. Bessy, however, making preparations to go with Mrs. Branigan the week after next. Dined at home.

8th. [Tuesday] Doing a few lines every day. Wrote to Lord Strangford by a courier going off to the Duke of Wellington at Vienna. All went in to dine at Bryan's. The Douglases, Lord Trimlestown, and little Byrne of the party. Byrne's story of the priest, saying to a fellow who always shirked his dues at Easter and Christmas, and who gave as an excuse for his last failure, that he had been very ill, and so near dying that Father Brennan had anointed him: "Anointed you, did he? faith, it showed he did not know you as well as I do, or he would have known you were slippery enough without it." The Irishman's defence of the palavering reception given to the King in Ireland: "Well, faith, after all, you know the only way to deal with a humbugger is to humbug him." The King of France,[1] who asked one of his courtiers, why he had gone to England? and on his answering, *Pour apprendre à penser,*" said quickly, "*Les chevaux?*" *(panser).* Curran's old story of the piper cutting off the legs of the hanged man for the sake of the stockings, then leaving the legs behind him in a cow-house where he was allowed to sleep, and the woman supposing, on finding them there (he having gone off early), that the cow had eaten him up all but the legs; then driving the cow to the fair, bidding a piper stand out of the way, because this was a cow that eat pipers, &c. &c.

9th. [Wednesday] Went in at two to sit to a French minature-painter [*sic*] for Galignani. Dined at Bryan's. Mrs. B., Lucy, and little Byrne of the party. Went to the Français afterwards to see Talma in "Regulus," a three-act tragedy: Talma very fine. The "Grondeur" followed it, a wretchedly dull farce.[1]

10th to 18th. [Thursday-Friday] Must here take several days *en gros*, having been too much occupied to minute down the details. Received letters from the Longmans and Powers that at last decided me to go to England. Wrote to Goddard about the cottage, and recieved an answer offering it to me at 25*l.* a year for whatever term I chose. Wrote to say I agreed. Preparations for Bessy's departure. Completed 1800 lines of my poem, which I see is announced for the 1st of December.

23rd. [Wednesday] Up at six, and at nine my darlings started. Heaven bless them! If ever creatures deserved that God should particularly watch over them, it is they. The day beautiful. Dined at Bryan's. The night stormy, and kept me thinking with much anxiety of the dear travellers. Home to Passy a little after eleven; the house looking very dreary.

24th. [Thursday] Still very stormy. Dispatched off a letter to Calais by the post to beg of Bessy for the hundredth time not to venture across in bad weather.

26th. [Saturday] Got a letter in the evening from my darling girl, announcing their safe arrival at Calais. Dined at Douglas's.

28th. [Monday] Packed up, and left the operation of surrendering the house &c. to my cook, Mary. Have taken lodgings at the Hotel de York on the Boulevard, and at 32 francs and half a week. Got a letter announcing Bessy's arrival at Dover.

29th. [Tuesday] Began the revision of my poem, and read "Suarez de

Angelis," which M. Langlés has lent me from the King's Library. Told me they have not got "Bonaventura de Alix Seraphim,"[1] which I also asked for.

November 1st to 5th. [Friday–Tuesday] Have not had time to keep any accurate diary of the next few days. Passed my evenings chiefly at Douglas's, and was in the morning occupied with the revision of my poem, one half of which I sent off on Monday 4th, and the remainder on Thursday 7th. Not able, from want of time, to correct or fill up the blanks for epithets in the latter half; must do it in the press. Idea of a farewell dinner to me resumed; promises very well. Hopes of Lord Granard, Vaughan (secretary to the Embassy), and some other Tories coming: Douglas most active and good-natured about it, and Lucy most anxious. Dined with Bryan twice. Stories of Lattin's. Lord Muskerry saying on his death-bed "that he had nothing to reproach himself with, having never through life denied himself anything." Dined with Lattin on the 4th: company, Douglas, Mr. and Mrs. Sartorius, Princesse Beauveau, and Nugent. Heard from Bessy of her arrival at the cottage, and her being welcomed by peals from the village bells.

6th. [Wednesday] Accompanied Lucy in the morning to the *marché aux fleurs;* bought her a white japonica; and breakfasted afterwards with Lady Virginia. Went out to Versailles to dine with Greathead: company, H. Smith, Grattan (with whom I went out), and Kenny. Smith told, after dinner, the dreadful ghost story of the woman with the black collar, &c.; also about the Englishman at Calais, *Pourquoi vous dites* hem *quand moi passe,* &c. &c.

7th. [Thursday] Dined with Douglas: Richard Power of the party: never was there anything like my surprise and delight at seeing him the other day, just arrived, and looking almost as well and strong as ever; such a resurrection from the grave as I never expected to see.

9th. [Saturday] Went to the Bibliothèque du Roi in the morning: introduced by M. Langlés to M. Vonpradt, and took a hasty look at the Tarquin of Onkelos.[1] Dined at Douglas's; Dawson there too. Practised in the evening one or two things to sing at the dinner on Monday: civil notes from several people about said dinner, which honest Douglas files: Sir C. Stuart has sent Nugent to say that if he is asked, he must certainly (rather than show any slight to me) *come;* but that, for many reasons, he would rather that the invitation was not sent. This is quite as civil as could be expected from him in his situation. Supped at Douglas's; and stayed, as usual, late: Lord Trimlestown and Lattin came in in the evening.

11th. [Monday] The dinner took place at Robert's; about fifty sat down: Lord Trimlestown in the chair: among the company were Lord Granard, Sir G. Webster, Robert Adair, &c. Collinet's band attended; the dinner one of Robert's best; and all went off remarkably well. In returning thanks for my health, I gave "Prosperity to England," with an eulogium on the moral worth of that country, which was felt more, both by myself and the company, from its being delivered in France, and produced much effect. Douglas, in proposing Bessy's health, after praising her numerous virtues, &c. &c., concluded thus:—"We need not, therefore, gentlemen, be surprised that Mr. Moore is about to communicate to the world 'The Loves of the Angels,' having been so long familiar with one at home." In returning thanks for this, I mentioned the circumstance of the village bells welcoming her arrival, as being *her* triumph in England, while I had mine this day in France, and concluded thus:—"These, gentlemen, are rewards and atonements for everything. No matter how poor I may steal through life—no matter how many calamities (even heavier than that from which I have now been relieved) may fall upon me—as long as such friends as you hold out the hand of fellowship to me at parting, and the sound of honest English bells shall welcome me and mine at meeting, I shall consider myself a Crœsus in that best wealth, happiness, and shall lay down my head, grateful for the gifts God has given." In introducing the subject of the village bells, I said, "This is a day of vanity for me; and you, who set the fountain running, ought not to complain of its overflowing." Lattin proposed the health of my father and mother, and mentioned the delight he had felt in witnessing my father's triumph at the dinner in Dublin. In returning thanks for this, I alluded to Southey's making his Kehama[1] enter triumphantly in through seven gates at the same moment, and said: "This miraculous multiplication of one gentleman into seven has been, to a great degree, effected by the toasts into which your kindness has subdivided me this day;" concluding thus:—"I have often, gentlemen, heard of sympathetic ink, but here is a liquid which has much better claims to that epithet; and if there is a glass of such at this moment before my good old father, it must, I think, sparkle in sympathetic reply to those which you have done him the honour of filling to him." In proposing the health of Richard Power (who was present), I spoke of him "as combining all that is manliest in man, with all that is gentlest in woman; that consistency of opinion and conduct which commands respect, with that smooth facility of intercourse which wins affection; a union, as it were, of the stem and flower of life—of the sweetness which we love, and the solidity on which we repose." In alluding to the charitable object of the Kilkenny Theatre, I called it "that happy expedient for enlisting gaiety in the cause of benevolence, and extracting from the smiles of *one* part of the community a warmth with which to dry up the tears of the *other;*" the happiness we had enjoyed together at that time, "days passed in studying Shakspeare, and nights in acting or discussing him; the happy freedom of those suppers (*Tamquam sera libertas*—late enough, God knows) where, as in the suppers described by Voltaire—

> La liberté, convive aimable
> Mit les deux coudes sur la table,
> Entre le plaisir et l'amour.

In proposing the health of Lord Trimlestown, spoke of his being particularly fit to take the chair at such a meeting, not only from our old acquaintance, &c. &c., but his love of literature, and "the success with which he had practised it; his intimate knowledge of French and English, which placed him as a sort of Janus between the two languages, with a double-fronted insight into the beauties of each, and enabled him not only to make the wild tale of Atala resound, in language worthy of its sweetness, on the banks of the Thames, but to occupy himself (as I was proud to say he was doing at present) in teaching the story of 'Lalla Rookh' to the lighter echoes of the Seine." A song was sung by Grattan during the night, which he had written for the occasion. Left them between one and two, and went to Douglas's, where I supped.

13th. [Wednesday] Went to the Library in the morning, and worked very hard for two or three hours. Dined at Villamil's; Dawson and Douglas of the party. Mrs V. sung some of her *boleros* to the guitar in the evening; the last time of my hearing them God knows how long. Went to D.'s in the evening, and looked over some papers and music with L. Villamil said, very prettily, that Bessy was quite a female Bayard, *sans peur et sans réproche*.[1]

14th. [Thursday] Went to Smith's, the printer, for the purpose of destroying the printed copies of my "Rhymes on the Road," but he was not at home. Made arrangements for its being done on Saturday. An account of my speech about England has appeared in Galignani. Grattan was preparing to give details of the whole dinner, the persons there, the speeches, &c. &c.; but I put a stop to it, as, however honourable to me, such publicity might give pain to many who were there (Tories, &c.), whose courage in going at all was very praiseworthy, and ought not to be put to any further test.

15th. [Friday] Breakfasted at D.'s, and went to the Library. What a shame I should not till now have availed myself of the facilities of this treasury! Went at nine o'clock to Grattan, in order to sing to his wife (according to promise), and found some men assembled, which was contrary to compact.

Among others, a Capt. Medwin, a friend of Lord Byron's, who passed a great part of last year at Pisa, and has written a volume of poems.¹ Tells me Hunt's whole family is living in the same house with B., and he believes Mrs. Shelley also and her children.

16th. [Saturday] Went to Smith's, and set about tearing the sheets of the "Rhymes," with the assistance of two journeymen and Grattan, whom I found there; but finding that it would take me all the rest of the day (there being 500 copies), entrusted the task of destruction to Smith's chief man, and came away. Grattan, very much amused with the operation, said, while we were about it, "How useful Doll Tearsheet would be here!"

18th. [Monday] Started in the diligence at nine. Leicester Stanhope, one of my companions inside, and Lord Mountcashel in the *galeria* behind. Travelled all night. Took up some Frenchmen half-way, who went as far as Boulogne. A good deal of conversation with them; complimented me much on the accuracy of my French; but said I pronounced it something like a German, and that, indeed, I looked much more like a German than an Englishman. According to their imitation of the Gascon pronunciation, it consists very much in pronouncing (?) the final *es*.

19th. [Tuesday] Arrived between six and seven. Went to the Hotel de Bourbon, where, there being but the one bed to spare, I got rid of my fellow-travellers. Dined alone in my bedroom. Bad prospect for to-morrow. No steam-boat at this side; nothing can get in or out of Dover. Dreadfully feverish at night, and haunted by tumultuous dreams.

20th. [Wednesday] No steam-packet arrived. A French sail-boat to start for Ramsgate, but preferred waiting till to-morrow. Called upon Brummel. Saw his fine toilette (which the King gave him in the days of his favour) set out in a little bedroom, 8 feet by 9. Walked outside the town for some hours, translating a passage from St. Basil for my notes. Dined alone, and to bed early, having to be up at four for the steam-boat.

21st. [Thursday] Sailed about seven. Arrived at Dover in about four hours. Had to get out into boats. The Captain had made some work about receiving my luggage on board, thinking it merchandise (three or four large packing-cases with my books &c. having come to Calais before me), and was beginning to be very uncivil about it, till some gentleman aboard told him who I was. Found I could not get my things through the custom-house time enough to be off to-day. A long operation, but the people very civil. Kept the pieces of china which Young gave Bessy: but told me, if I sent a memorial to the Lords of the Treasury they would let me pay duty for them. Dined alone.

22nd. [Friday] Started at near eleven for town, having waited an hour for a little French milliner, who was going through the operation of the custom-house; went without her after all. Reached town about nine. Went to the George Coffee House, where I had begged the Longmans to get me a bed. Despatched a porter off to Mrs. Power for letters, which I expected to find from Bessy. Sent me word there were some, but I could not have them till the morning. Too tantalising this, as I had not heard from my dear things at home for more than a week.

23rd. [Saturday] The letters from Bessy did not come till past ten, but all, thank God, well. Called at Rogers's; found he was at Holland House. Left a note for him to say I would go out and dine there to-morrow, if they would have me. Went to dine at Longman's. Found them in high spirits about the poem. Agree to my taking it down with me to Sloperton for revision. Left them rather early, and went to Drury Lane; behind the scenes.

24th. [Sunday] Had a note from Lady Holland, to say that they will be glad to have me, but that I shall meet no one but themselves, as Rogers is obliged to dine in town. Called upon Shee, &c. Went to dinner at six. None but Lord and Lady H., and Allen. Conversation chiefly about the state of France.

25th. [Monday] Dined with Rogers, and went to Lady Holland's box in the evening to see Miss Kelly in Juliet. Very bad; but (as it seems) good enough for the public, who are delighted with her. Lord John Russell (who is just arrived from Hastings) came into the box. Received his tragedy ("Don Carlos")[1] yesterday, and mean to keep the reading of it for Sloperton. Went behind the scenes. Told Miss Foote how much I had heard of her Desdemona; her answer very modest and sensible. Fixed to meet Lord J. next day at two. By the bye, the Longmans have made use of the 200*l.* he has left so long in their hands (the receipts of his "Life of Lord Russell")[2] towards paying this last Bermuda claim. I expected they would have advanced the money themselves; but it cannot be helped. Besides, he seems to have set his heart on my appropriating it in this way, and it is but owing to him instead of to them.

26th. [Tuesday] Went to the Foreign Office to get my two packets of medals. Gave Lord John ten for himself and the Duke, and, in spite of my resolutions to the contrary, allowed Rogers, too, to have five. Wished Lord J. to dine with me at Rogers's, but he had already engaged himself to Lord Bradford at Brookes's. Persuaded him however to get off this, which he did. Nobody at dinner but Rogers, he, and I. In the evening all went to the Duke's box at Covent Garden to see the "Two Gentlemen of Verona." Miss Tree charming in Julia. By the bye, Shee told me a *bon-mot* of Rogers's the other day. On somebody remarking that Payne Knight had got very deaf, " 'Tis from want of practice," says R.; Knight being a very bad listener.

27th. [Wednesday] Have been in expectation of the Donegals from Brighton, and their nephew has been entreating me to act as mediator. They were to have arrived to-day, but are not. Had promised Lord J. to dine with the Hollands to-day, to meet him; but offered myself to Murray instead, wishing to have some conversation with him. Found, however, it was a regular dinner party; Mr., Mrs., and Miss D'Israeli, Mr. Hamilton, Newton, &c. Came away early in order to pack up. The Longmans have received an anonymous letter about my poem, beginning, "I conjure the respectable house of L. R. H. O. and Browne to pause ere they, &c. &c.;" and ending, "Beware of the fate of Murray and of Cain!"

28th. [Thursday] Set off at seven in the coach for Calne. Arrived at home between seven and eight, and found all well, except poor Bess, who looks wretchedly. Lost my great coat in leaving town. The dear girl has worked hard to get the cottage into order, and it is most neat and comfortable. The change made in my study, by throwing the two rooms into one, a wonderful improvement. Most happy to be at home again. *Oh quid salutis est, &c. &c.*

29th. [Friday] Set busily about correcting and revising my "Angels," which the Longmans have had printed all upon slips for that purpose. Walked with Bessy to see the Phippses, and got a wetting.

Dec. 1st. [Sunday] Sent off the first sheet through Croker, who had offered me the use of his franks in town. This was the day announced originally for the publication; and some people asked the Longmans (who of course were not aware that the 1st fell on a Sunday), whether the poem was so *very* sacred, that nothing less than a Sunday would do for its publication.

2nd. [Monday] Walked to Bowood, and met Lord Lansdowne, who had rode to call upon me. Walked on to Bowood with me. A good deal of talk about France. His high opinion of the Duc de Broglie. Saw Lady L.; both all kindness; expressed the same alarm as others with respect to the title of my poem. Promised, if I could, to dine with them on Saturday.

3rd. [Tuesday] A letter from the Longmans to say they must have the whole of the poem and notes by the middle of next week, or they cannot get it out in time to supply the Christmas customers; there are about 3000 copies already ordered.

5th. [Thursday] Had a letter from Lord L., expressing his surprise at not having been called upon for the sum he held at my disposal; and saying that if I had been able to arrange everything "through the help of the Muse alone," he would rejoice at it, as he knew it was the mode most satisfactory to my own feelings; but that if I had applied to any other person than him, he could not help feeling a little jealous, &c. Can anything be more thoroughly and sterlingly kind? Wrote him a short note to say I should inform him of all the particulars on Saturday.

7th. [Saturday] Dined at Bowood; company, Lord Malmesbury, the Barings, and Bowles. Lord L. mentioned Pitt's dislike to Erskine, and his frequent attacks upon him. On one occasion, when E. followed Mr. Fox in a long speech, Pitt said, "The learned gentleman has followed his Right Hon. Leader, running along the line of his argument, and, as usual, attenuating it as he went." Baring, a sensible, good kind of man. Sung in the evening. Am afraid I shall be obliged to go to town, to expedite the flight of my Angels. Lady L. begged me to dine again on Thursday next, to meet Charles Grant, whom they expect.

9th. [Monday] A note from Lady Lansdowne to Bessy, to invite her to dinner to-morrow. Prevailed on her to say yes.

10th. [Tuesday] Went (in a hack chaise) to Bowood; company, the Barings, Mr. and Mrs. A'Court, and some other people, whom I knew nothing about. Lady L. all kindness to Bessy. I sung in the evening, and so did one of the unknown ladies to the Spanish guitar. Baring, at dinner, applied the French phrase, *un homme qui avait oublié de se faire enterrer.*

11th. [Wednesday] Sketched out my preface and one or two notes.

12th. [Thursday] Set off in the Regulator for town, where I arrived between nine and ten. Had written to bespeak a lodging at Mrs. Soanes', where I found myself very comfortably received.

15th. [Sunday] Wrote to Lady Donegal, to tell her I was in town, and that if she could put off dinner for me till between six and seven, I might, perhaps, manage to come to her. Answer in the affirmative. Went at half-past six; found her pretty well, and all as kind as ever. Took Barbara a present of one of the Cupids sent me last New Year's Day, with which she was much delighted. Left them at half-past eight and returned home to work, at which I continued till past one, when I sealed up the last notes (written in far too great a hurry), and ordered the servant to take them in the morning to Paternoster Row.

16. [Monday] Went after breakfast to call on Rogers. Thence to the Hollands; asked me to dine. Walked out with Lord Holland to the Park. A wretched cold day, and even the sunshine of his conversation did not atone for the total want of it in the heavens; besides, he walked so slow, and I had no great coat. He mentioned what his uncle one night said in a reply to Mr. Pitt: "The Right Honourable Gentleman seems to have a very high notion of his own abilities, and I must say it is the only one of his opinions in which I most perfectly coincide with him." Dined at the Hollands. In the evening went with Lord H. and Henry to the play.

17th. [Tuesday] Dined with Murray, to meet Wm. Spencer. The rest of the company, Harry Drury, the D'Israelis, a Mr. Coleridge, &c. &c. A long time since Spencer and I met before, and he is but little altered, either in looks, spirits, or good nature. Told some good anecdotes about French translations from the English. In some work where it was said "the air was so clear, that we could distinctly see a *bell-wether* on the opposite hill," the translator made bell-wether, *le beau temps*. Price, on the Picturesque, says, that a bald head is the only smooth thing possessing that quality, but that if we were to cover it over with flour, it would lose its picturesqueness immediately; in translating which, some Frenchman makes it, *une belle tête chauve couronnée de fleurs*. Scroope Davies called some person, who had a habit of puffing out his cheeks when he spoke, and was not remarkable for veracity, "The Æolian Lyre." Left them at eleven, almost suffocated with a severe cold, and more wine than was good for it. Found proofs waiting for me at home, and sat up till two o'clock correcting them.

18th. [Wednesday] Passed the whole morning between Paternoster Row and Shoe Lane, correcting the last of the revises. Dined at Lady Donegal's. Came home early and went to bed, which I much wanted.

19th. [Thursday] took my place for Sunday in the York House coach. Made an agreement for a hackney coach, and went out to Hornsey to visit the grave of our poor child Barbara, Bessy having heard it was much neglected. Found this not to be the case. Sought out the sexton, and bid him have it new sodded, giving him at the same time five shillings, and promising him more when I should come again. Went to Rogers's on my return, to say I would dine with him if he had room for me, and proposing to him, by Lady Holland's desire, to accompany me to her box in the evening to see a new opera. Three of his nephews at dinner. Left him early and went to Drury Lane. The opera very bad; Lady H.'s box full; the Tierneys, &c.

20th. [Friday] Went to Chantrey's, but did not find him at home. Croker called upon me in his carriage at half-past five, to take me out to his apartments at Kensington Palace to dinner. The company, Sir George Cockburn, Mr. and Mrs. Barrow, and Admiral Moorsom. Cockburn's *noli me tangere* manner with me the few times I have met him since his advancement to office, highly amusing; somewhat less to-day however. Ridiculously enough, in looking round Croker's room before dinner, I saw a bust, which I took to be the King's; on looking nearer, however, I found it to be myself, a cast from the bust in Dublin by Kirk. Mrs. Croker said several persons took it to be the King. Returned at night with Admiral Moorsom.

21st. [Saturday] Called upon Bishop. Thence to the Longmans, where I found some copies of my book ready, and sealed up seven or eight of them for Paris; for Lucy, for Villamil, &c. &c. Called to take leave of the Donegals. Dined between seven and eight at the George Coffee House, and went home early. By the by, I have within this day or two (in order to enable me to get on for a little while) drawn upon Corry for £100 at three months, meaning to take up the bill myself when it becomes due. Out of this, I gave £40 to Mrs. Power, as a set-off against the sum Power paid for my life insurance.

22nd. [Sunday] Up before six, and off at seven. Arrived at home a little after seven, and found my darling girl pretty well, and her little ones bravely.

23rd. [Monday] Walked over to Bowood, and took Lord L. a copy of my book. To-day it is published.

24th. [Tuesday] Arranging my books.

25th. [Wednesday] Went with the two little ones to church; Bessy not well enough to go.

26th. [Thursday] Rather fidgetty about the fate of my book. Bessy had a note yesterday from Lady L. with a present of some toys for the children, but not a word about the "Angels." Rather ominous this. Wrote to Lady Donegal yesterday about some silver tissue for Mrs. Phipps's dress for the fancy ball, and said, "Don't say a word about the 'Angels' in your answer; stick to the silver tissue."

27th. [Friday] An answer from Lady Donegal, with the following sentence in it, which, from the state of nervousness I had got into about my book, came upon me like a thunderbolt. "You bid me not say anything about the 'Angels,' but I must so far disobey you as to say that I am both vexed and disappointed, and I think that you will feel I am right in not allowing Barbara to read it." I never remember anything that gave me much more pain than this. It seemed at once to ring the death-knell of my poem. This at once accounted for the dead silence of the Longmans since the publication, for the non-appearance of the second edition, which I was taught to expect would be announced the third day, for Lord Lansdowne's reserve on the subject, for everything. My book, then, was considered (why or wherefore it was in vain to inquire) improper, and what I thought the best, as well as the most moral thing I had ever written, was to be doomed to rank with the rubbish of Carlisle and Co.[1] for ever. Bowles, who was with me at the time, endeavoured most good-humouredly to soothe me, and, though he had not read the poem, gallantly made himself responsible that I could not have written anything to bring upon me such a censure. It was all in vain. I wrote off to the Longmans to beg they would tell me the worst at once, and to my mother, to prepare her for the failure which I now considered as certain. In this mood Bowles left me, and in about an hour after, luckily for my peace of mind, Lord Lansdowne and Byng arrived. Their coming was like an avatar to me. Lord L. declared, in the warmest manner, that he thought the poem not only beautiful, but perfectly unexceptionable and pure, and that he had no hesitation in preferring it to anything I had ever written. Byng too (who two or three weeks since had expressed himself with some degree of alarm about the title), told me that, on reading the poem, he had instantly written off to some friends who felt the same apprehensions as himself, that "it might be safely trusted in the nursery." It is inconceivable the relief all this was to me, and not less so to my darling Bessy, who had seen the wretched state I was thrown into by Lady D.'s letter, and had in vain employed her good sense and sweetness to counteract its effect. Walked part of the way back with Lord L. and B.

28th. [Saturday] Dined at Bowood; company, Jekyll (just arrived with his two sons), Mr. and Mrs. Abercromby, Byng, Macdonald (the member), Miss Fox, and Miss Vernon. Lady L. spoke in raptures about the poem; said they were all enchanted with it, and could not conceive how any imagination could contrive to extract an idea of impropriety from it. Lady L.'s favourite, the first story; Miss Fox, and others, preferred the second. Jekyll more silent than he used to be, but still very agreeable. In talking of cheap living, he mentioned a man who told him his eating cost him almost nothing, for "on Sunday," said he, "I always dine with my old friend——, and then eat so much that it lasts until Wednesday, when I buy some tripe, which I hate like the very devil, and which accordingly makes me so sick that I cannot eat any more till Sunday again." Said that when the great waterworks were established at Chelsea there was a proposal for having there also a great organ, from which families might be supplied with sacred music, according as they wished, by turning the cock on or off; but one objection he said was, that upon a thaw occurring after a long frost, you might have "Judas Maccabeus" bursting out at Charing Cross, and there would be no getting him under. He said that it was an undoubted fact that Lord (?), the proprietor of Lansdowne House before the old Lord Lansdowne, had a project of placing seven and twenty fiddlers, hermetically sealed, in an apartment underground, from which music might be communicated by tubes to any apartment where it was wanted. Lord L. bore witness to the truth of this (with the exception of its being an organ instead of Jekyll's hermetically sealed fiddlers), and said that the pipes which had been already laid for this plan were found during some repairs that took place at Lansdowne House. Walked home.

29th. [Sunday] Received the "Literary Gazette," "Literary Chronicle," and "Museum," all containing reviews of my work, and all favourable enough.[1] The last the least so, but (from its being connected with clergymen) the most useful, as giving me credit for a moral design in the poem. Wrote a letter to Lady Donegal, telling her the opinions of Lord Lansdowne, &c. &c., and of this journal, as a set-off against her own.

Notes to 1822 Entries

4 January

1. Moore probably means "guaracha," a rapid Spanish dance to guitar accompaniment. The *OED* lists *guaracia* as an erroneous form of the word.

8 January

1. "The Irish Avatar," Coleridge, *Byron's Poetry*, 4: 555–62. The poem was sent in a letter to Moore on 17 September 1821 (Marchand, *LJ*, 8:213), with the following comment by Byron: "The enclosed lines, as you will directly perceive, are written by the Rev. W. L. B. ** [Bowles]. Of course it is for *him* to deny them if they are not."

10 January

1. Victor Joseph Étienne (called de Jouy), *Sylla* (1821).

11 January

1. *Works*, 5: 190–91.
2. Marie Madeleine, Marquise de Brinvilliers, née d'Aubray, who successively poisoned her father and her two brothers, as well as patients at hospitals. She was executed in 1676.
3. Ambon (or Amboyna), a small island in Eastern Indonesia, an important port first of the Portuguese then of the Dutch colonial empire.
4. Marc-Antoine Desaugiers, Gentil de Chavagnac, and Nicolas Brazier, *Je fais mes farces* (1815).

12 January

1. The Comte de la Bédoyère, aide-de-camp to Napoleon, was arrested for treason after the battle of Waterloo.

13 January

1. i.e., "brats" or "urchins."

15 January

1. Casimir Delavigne, *Le Paria* (1821).
2. In *Lalla Rookh, Works,* 6:203–322.

16 January

1. Charles Cottu, *De l'Administration de la justice criminelle en Angleterre . . .* (1820).

18 January

1. Molière, *Le Tartuffe* (1669); J. A. N. Naudet and Justin Glensoul, *Le Ménage de Molière* (1822).

22 January

1. Étienne's speech dealt with the attempt by the Ultra-Royalist party to make even more repressive the censorship powers of the Press Law of 1820. The original provisions of the law allowed for prior censorship of all newspapers and periodicals in France, and prosecution for anything deemed slanderous or seditious. The new measure called for suppression of any publication that showed a "general tendency" to be unfavorable to the government. The revised Press Law was passed in 1822 and remained substantially the same until 1828, when it was somewhat relaxed.
2. Comte Charles Ignace de Peyronnet.

23 January

1. Victor-Joseph de Jouy, *Monsieur Beaufils ou La Conversation Faite d'Avance* (1806).

25 January

1. Jean Toussaint Merle, Niciolas Brazier, and Pierre-Frédéric-Adolphe Carmouche, *Sans Tambour ni Trompette* (1822). Armand et Eugène (pseudonyms for François Armand d'Artois and Hugues Marie Humbert Bason de la Merlière), *Le Comédien de Paris, ou Assaut de Travestissemens* (1822).

31 January

1. Étienne's *Les Deux Gendres* was produced in 1810 and published in 1811. Almost immediately there arose charges that the material for the play had been plagiarized from several different sources. The work most frequently cited was a play by an unknown Jesuit entitled *Canaxa, ou les Gendres duppés* (ca. 1710). The accusations of plagiarism became so widespread that Étienne was moved to include in the fourth edition of his play (December 1811) a preface defending himself and the originality of his work.
There followed a long series of pamphlets on both sides of the controversy. The one to which Moore refers is *Mes Révélations sur M. Étienne, les Deux Gendres et Conaxa* (1812) by Jean-Antoine Lebrun-Tossa (not M. Maltebrun as Moore states). Lebrun-Tossa explains that about ten years earlier he had found the manuscript of an old play among papers he was burning, and that he had suggested to his friend Étienne that they collaborate on a comedy based upon

it. A few years later Lebrun-Tossa renounced the proposed collaboration and advised Étienne to make public his use of the old play, which he refused.

For a more detailed discussion of this controversy see Charles Beaumont Wicks, *Charles-Guillaume Étienne, Johns Hopkins Studies in Romance Literatures and Languages* (1949).

2. *Works*, 5: 183–84.

3. Jean Guillaume Viennet, *Clovis* (1820). According to Larousse's *Grand Dictionnaire*, "Achille" was never performed.

8 February

1. Moore probably refers to *The Epicurean.*
2. John Dryden, *Alexander's Feast* (1697).

12 February

1. Byron's *Werner* was published by Murray in November 1822.

14 February

1. Louis Charles Caigniez, *La Forêt enchantée, ou La Belle au bois dormant* (1799).

22 February

1. Moore's translations from Catullus are contained in "Miscellaneous Poems," *Works*, 7: 372–76.

23 February

1. Scott's *Bride of Lammermoor* was written in 1818 and published in 1819.
2. In the autumn of 1821 Moore's protégé Dr. William Williams began working as a translator and secretary for Foscolo. In November Williams was sent to prison for debt, and upon his release he broke with his employer over money he claimed was owed him. He wrote to Foscolo, calling him a cheat and a coward, and challenging him to a duel. The quarrel was settled by an arbiter in February 1822. See E. R. Vincent, *Ugo Foscolo* (Cambridge, 1953), p. 175.

24 February

1. "Irish Melodies, No. I," *Blackwood's Edinburgh Magazine* 10 (1821): pt. 2, 613–22.

25 February

1. Jean Toussaint Merle, Pierre Carmouche, and Xavier Boniface, *La Lampe Merveilleuse* (1822).

26 February

1. Probably Sir Henry Ricketts.

1 March

1. Haydn's opera *Armida* (1784).

3 March

1. i.e., tasteless, flat.

4 March

1. For detailed discussions of the Byron-Southey controversy see Coleridge, *Byron's Poetry*, 4:475–79, and Marchand, *Byron: a Biography*, 3:967–68.
2. *L'Artiste:* see entry for 26 November 1821. Eugène Scribe and Joseph Duveyrier, *Les Mémoires d'un colonel de hussards* (1822); Eugène Scribe and Henri Dupin, *Michael et Christine* (1821).

5 March

1. Anne d'Autriche, daughter of Philip III of Spain and wife of Louis XIII of France. Their son Philippe, duc d'Orleans (1640–1701), was born during the period in which the king and queen were estranged and virtually separated (1620–43). Moore wrote "Query all this" in pencil at the end of the MS page.

6 March

1. Germain de Saint-Foix, *Essais historique sur Paris* (1754–55). The word *Cabelle* is rendered "Camille" by Russell.

7 March

1. Jean Baptiste Blache, *Suzanne et les vieillards, ou l'innocence reconnue, a pantomime, en deux actes*, which opened at the Porte St. Martin theater in 1817.

10 March

1. Rossini, *Elisabetta, Regina d'Inghilterra* (1815).

11 March

1. Nicole and Benincori, *Aladin, ou la lampe merveilleuse*, libretto by Étienne (1822).

12 March

1. The incident to which Moore alludes is the St. Bartholomew's Day Massacre (24 August 1572), in which thousands of Huguenots were slaughtered in Paris.

14 March

1. Paul-Louis Courier de Méré, *Collection complète des pamphlets politiques et opuscules litéraires* (1826); Pierre Jean de Béranger, *Chansons morales et autres* (1816) and *Chansons* (1821).
  2. Rossini, *L'Italiana in Algeri* (1808).

16 March

1. Gaspard de Coligni, a French admiral and leader of the Huguenots, was murdered in the St. Bartholomew's Day Massacre (see entry for 12 March 1822). The tolling of the bell of St. Germain l'Auxerrois was the signal to begin the slaughter.

19 March

1. Balisson de Rougement, Jouslin de La Salle, and Pierre Carmouche, *Les Frères féroces, ou Monsieur Bonardin à la répétition* (1819).

21 March

1. Mme de Bawr, *La Suite d'un bal masqué* (1813).

25 March

1. Rodolphe Kreutzer and Charles Frédéric Kreubé, *Le Paradis de Mohamet, ou la pluralité des femmes*, libretto by Eugène Scribe and A. H. J. Duveyrier (1822).

26 March

1. Charles Jean Dominique de Lacretelle, *Histoire de France pendant les guerres de religion*, 4 vols. (1814–16).
  2. "Passeriez" in Russell.

28 March

1. Voltaire, *Mérope* (1743); Louis Benoit Picard, Alexia Vafflard, and Joseph Desire Fulgence de Bury, *Les Deux Ménages* (1822).

30 March

1. François Guizot (1787–1874): statesman and historian, author of works on European history; Jean-Baptiste Biot (1774–1862): mathematician, physicist, and astronomer.

2 April

1. Hume's *History of England from the Invasion of Julius Caesar to the Revolution of 1688*, 8 vols. (1763), and Adam Smith's *Inquiry into the Nature and Causes of the Wealth of Nations*, 2 vols. (1776).

3 April

1. Louis Charles Caigniez, *La Forêt d'Hermanstadt, ou la fausse épouse* (1806).

8 April

1. Eugène Cantiran de Boirie and Henri Lemaire, *Le Château de Kenilworth, tiré du roman de Sir Walter Scott* (1822).

10 April

1. Antonio Saliéri, *Les Danaïdes* (1784).

14 April

1. Charlotte Corday was guillotined on 17 July 1793 for the murder of the terrorist Jean-Paul Marat.

17 April

1. Anonymous, *Cherry and Fair Star; or, The Children of Cyprus* (1822).

18 April

1. Anonymous, *Giovanni in Ireland,* first performed at Drury Lane on 22 December 1821. Mme Vestris (the stage name of Lucia Elizabeth Mathews) sang in this opera as well as in W. T. Moncrieff, *Giovanni in London* (1817).

20 April

1. On 30 April 1822 Henry Canning moved that the House approve the Roman Catholic Peers Bill, which would restore to Catholics the right to sit in the House of Lords. The motion was seconded by George Agar Ellis, and after a long debate the House voted 249 for, 244 against the bill.

22 April

1. On 25 April 1822 Lord John Russell delivered a long speech in which he outlined the various inequities in the present system of representation in Parliament. He then moved that the House of Commons give "serious consideration" to this matter; the motion was defeated 164 to 269.

27 April

1. Sir John Sinclair wrote *A General View of the Agriculture State and Political Circumstances of Scotland* (1814) and other works on agriculture.

28 April

1. Sydney Owenson (afterwards Lady Morgan), *The Wild Irish Girl: A National Tale*, 3 vols. (1806).

30 April

1. The version of this incident given in Moore's *Life of Sheridan* (2:456–58) was disputed in the *Quarterly Review*'s article on the *Life*. See Dowden, *Letters*, 2:254–56 and notes.
2. John Randolph of Roanoke (1773–1833).

1 May

1. One of the *Irish Melodies, Works*, 3:330–31.
2. *Works*, 3:314–15.

2 May

1. Moore first entered this item under date 22 April, later deleting it in favor of its present location, thus indicating that he was writing after a lapse of several days. The duellists met in Hyde Park. Buckingham fired first and missed; Bedford discharged his pistol in the air. See Ben C. Truman, *The Field of Honor* (New York, 1884), p. 213.

14 May

1. Ferdinando Paer, *Camilla, ossia il Sotteraneo* (1799).

16 May

1. Probably Niccolo Zingarelli's opera *Romeo e Giulietta* (1796), although Mme Pasta's greatest triumph came later in Bellini's *I Capuleti ed i Montecchi* (1830).

24 May

1. Probably part of "The Fudge Family in Italy," which was never published.
2. In "Miscellaneous Poems," *Works*, 8:119–26.

27 May

1. Moore's poem was published as *The Loves of the Angels* on 23 December 1822 (*Works*, 8:3–104). Byron's work on the same subject is *Heaven and Earth; A Mystery*, which Byron himself called "The Deluge." Upon Murray's refusal to publish the work, Byron sent it to John Hunt, who published it in the second number of the *Liberal* on 1 January 1823. For a discussion of the two works see Coleridge, *Byron's Poetry*, 5: 279–82.

31 May

1. Pantin was a village near Paris, one of whose industries was the treatment of human sewage for use as dry fertilizer (poudrette).

3 June

1. Henry Francis Carey's translations of French Poetry were printed in the *London Magazine* from November 1821 through April 1824 and were collected in *The Early French Poets. Notices and Translations* (1846). He also translated *The Divine Comedy;* hence the "Dante Cary."

7 June

1. Rossini's *Otello, ossio il Moro di Venezia* (1816).

21 June

1. Letter dated 8 June 1822, Marchand, *LJ*, 9:170.

22 June

1. "To the Marchioness Dowager of Donegall. From Bermuda, January, 1804," *Works*, 2:226–32. This poem contains a description of St. George Harbor in Bermuda.
2. Hester Louise Tucker, the wife of William Tucker, was one of the models for Moore's "Odes to Nea," *Works*, 2:243–73, written in Bermuda. See entry and n. 8 for 31 December 1840, and Jones, *The Harp that Once—*, pp. 73–74.

8 July

1. Spontini, *Fernand Cortez, ou la conquête du Mexique* (1809), libretto by Esmérand and Étienne, based on a tragedy by Alexis Piron; Rossini, *Tancredi* (1813), libretto by Gaetano Rossi, based on Tasso's *Gerusalemme Liberata* and Voltaire's *Tancrède*.

9 July

1. See n. 1 to entry for 16 May 1822.

12 July

1. "A gentleman who had been very unhappy in marriage, married immediately after his wife died: Johnson said, it was a triumph of hope over experience," Boswell, *Life of Johnson*, ed. Edmond Malone, intro. Chauncey Tinker (London, 1946), 1: 421.

14 July

1. Felix MacDonough, *The Hermit in London, or, Sketches of English Manners . . .* (1819).

18 July

1. See Dowden, *Letters*, 2:507–8. The statement in the introduction to the *Letters* (p. xx) that Moore was offered the editorship of the *Times* is in error; he was offered the principal editorial task of writing lead articles (see entry for 17 July 1822).

20 July

1. Except for the words "& takes Anastasia with her," this entry was made on 19 July, then deleted.

23 July

1. Rossini, *La Cenerentola, ossia La Bonta in Trionfo* (1817).

4 August

1. Jean Baptiste Say (1767–1832), French economist. Marie Joseph de Chénier (1764–1811) published several "epistles," including *Épître à Voltaire* (1806).

5 August

1. Népomucène Lemercier, *Christophe Colomb* (1809).

21 August

1. This entry was made on 20 August and deleted.

27 August

1. *La Cenerentola*, 1. i.

3 September

1. See entry for 16 July 1821 and Dowden, *Letters*, 2: 506 and note.

5 September

1. Henri Mouton Verton, *Ninon chez Madame Sévigné* (1808); Michèle de Carafa, *Le Solitaire* (1822).

7 September

1. Spontini's *Nurmahal, oder das Rosenfest von Cashmir* was presented in Berlin on 27 May 1822. It is based on Spicker's German translation of Moore's *Lalla Rookh*.
2. For an account of the Fête in Berlin see Dowden, *Letters*, 2: 886 and note and entry for 3 April 1821. Friedrich Heinrich Karl de la Motte Fouqué translated the poem as *Lalla Rukh, oder die mongolische Prinzessin* (1822).

11 September

1. Voltaire, *La Pucelle* (1762), a burlesque epic based on Joan of Arc.

12 September

1. Prince Hoare, *Lock and Key* (1796). The joke is that Astley was an equestrian performer.

17 September

1. Jean-Baptiste de Lanoue, *La Coquette corrigée* (1756); Charles Antoine Pigault-Lebrun, *Les Rivaux d'eux-mêmes* (1798).

18 September

1. Alexis Joseph Vafflard and Fulgence de Bury, *Un Moment d'imprudence* (1819). *La Belle Fermière* may refer to Nicolas Brazier and Emile Vanderburch, *La Fermière ou mauvaise tête et bon coeur* (1822).

27 September

1. Abbé Prévost, *Manon Lescaut* (1731).

1 October

1. *The Book of Enoch the Prophet*, trans. Richard Laurence (1821). Langlés translated Friderek Norden, *Voyage d'Égypte et de Nubie* (1795).

3 October

1. Francis, Brazier, and Dumersan, *Les Petits Acteurs, ou les merveilles à la mode* (1822); Gabriel and Philibert, *Le Paris de Surêne, ou la clause du testament* (1821); anonymous, *L'Actrice en voyage* (1822).

8 October

1. "Louis the XVth." (Russell's note.)

9 October

1. Nicolas Pradon, *Regulus* (1688); David Augustin Brueys and Jean Palapral, *Le Grondeur* (1691).

29 October

1. Saint Bonaventura, Cardinal Bishop of Albano, *De Sex Alis Seraphim*. See *Sancte Bonaventurae*, ed. Cardinal C. Boccaferoco and F. Lanatu, 7 vols. (1588–96).

9 November

1. The Aramaic paraphrase of the Pentateuch known as the *Targum* by the 1st or 2nd century A.D. was written by Onkelos.

11 November

1. Robert Southey, *The Curse of Kehama* (1810), chap. 24, st. 2.

13 November

1. Pierre Terrail, Seigneur de Bayard (?1473–1524), "Chevalier sans peur et sans reproche."

15 November

1. Thomas Medwin, *Sketches of Hindostan with Other Poems* (1821).

25 November

1. Lord John Russell, *Don Carlos, or Persecution,* a tragedy (1822), a translation of Schiller's drama.
2. *The Life of William Lord Russell,* 2 vols. (1819).

27 December

1. Probably a reference to Richard Carlile (1790–1843), who was imprisoned from 1819–25 for publishing free-thought papers.

29 December

1. Moore refers to reviews in the *Literary Gazette,* 28 December 1822, pp. 817–19; the *Literary Chronicle,* 28 December 1822, pp. 815 ff; and the *London Museum,* 28 December 1822, pp. 561–62.

1823

January 1st. [Wednesday] The coat (a Kilkenny uniform) which I sent to town to be new-lined for the fancy ball tomorrow night, not yet arrived. Walked to Bowood. Found Lady Lansdowne and Jekyll, Lady L. again expressing her strong admiration of the poem. Said she had proposed to the Bowleses to dine at Bowood on Saturday, and hoping that Bessy would have no objection to be of the party.

2nd. [Thursday] Obliged to make shift for to-night, by transferring the cut-steel buttons from my dress-coat to a black one, and having it lined with white silk. Dined with the Phippses. Went in the same way as before; Mrs. P. dressed as a Sultana, and looking very well. The ball at a Mr. Hardman's (a German), beyond Devizes: odd enough, and amusing, though in a small ill-lighted room. Two fine girls there, the Miss Holtons, the eldest beautiful. Not home till between four and five.

4th. [Saturday] The day very wet. Had promised the Bowleses to meet them at dinner at Bowood to-day (Bessy having given up the whole plan), and go on with them to Bremhill to stay till Monday, but sent an excuse, and offered myself to the Lansdownes for to-morrow instead. An answer from Lady Lansdowne, begging me to stay till Tuesday, and as much longer as Mrs. Moore could spare me.

5th. [Sunday] Have received several newspapers with reviews of the poem; all very favourable. Dined at Bowood; taken by the Phippses. Company, besides them and the Bennets, Mrs. Abercrombie, Misses Fox and Vernon, the Jekylls, Stanley (Lord Derby's son), Lord Auckland, and Macdonald, a young Irishman. Got nothing out of Jekyll, who was talking all the while to Phipps, except that when I offered my arm to him to help him down to dinner, he said, "This is making a mistress of Chancery of me." Sung in the

[611]

evening several of the "Irish melodies," which seemed to produce considerable effect. Slept there.

6th. [Monday] After breakfast had a good deal of conversation with Jekyll. Quoted those lines written upon John Allen Parke, by a man who never wrote any verses before or since:—

> "John Allen Parke
> Came naked stark
>   From Scotland;
> But now has clothes,
> And lives with beaus
>   In England."

Mentioned Lord Cranley having been caught up, curricle and all, by a crane, in Thames Street, and the verses to him which he (Jekyll) wrote on the occasion. A joke about the "Pigmies warring with the Cranes."[1] Told of the actor saying by mistake,—

> "How sharper than a serpent's *thanks* it is,
> To have a *toothless* child;"[2]

and old Parker who used always to say the "coison'd pup" instead of the "poison'd cup;" and one night, when he spoke it right, the audience said, "No, no!" and called for the other reading.[3] A good deal of talk about Sheridan. Said that Mrs. S. had sung once after her marriage, at the installation of Lord North at Oxford;[4] and as there were degrees then conferring *honoris causâ*, Lord N. said to Sheridan that he ought to have one *uxoris causâ*. Spoke of Tickell's discontent with Sheridan; his idea that S. might have brought him forward, but would not. Described Tickell's anxiety on the first night of Parliament's meeting after the publication of his pamphlet "Anticipation." The laughable effect on the House of Col. Barré's speech; he being the only one (having just arrived from the country) ignorant of the pamphlet, and falling exactly into the same peculiarities which the pamphlet quizzed, particularly that of quoting French words and then translating them. At every new instance of this kind in his speech there was a roar of laughter from the House, which Barré, of course, could not understand.[5] A friend went off to Tickell (who in his fidget had gone to bed in a coffee-house in Covent Garden) to tell him the successful effect of the pamphlet. His next pamphlet, "The Cassette Verte, &c." (?) was a failure.[6] Said, from his own observation, Sheridan was a most painstaking writer. Knew it in the instance of his Prologue to the "Miniature Picture" (a piece written by Lady Craven, and first acted at Benham, but not successful on the public stage), which Sheridan corrected and altered over and over again.[7] Jekyll wrote the Epilogue; and it was said, "that the *frame* was much better than the *picture*." Mentioned some lines which he (Jekyll) had written upon the Emperor of China's hint to Lord Macartney, that he had better hasten his departure, as the rainy season was coming on:—

> "The sage Chian-ki-ti
>   Has look'd in the sky,
> And he says we shall soon have wet weather;
>   So I think, my good fellows,
>   As you've no umbrellas,
> You'd better get home, dry, together!"

Canning and some one else translated these lines into Latin verse, and the word they chose to express the want of umbrellas was very happy—*vos inumbrelles video.* They sent across the House to Jekyll one night to beg for the rest of the verses, and his answer was "Tell them, if they want papers they must move for them. We find it very hard to get them even so." Set out to walk home and see Bessy, but, the rain coming on, turned back. Found Jekyll and Macdonald in the library on my return, and had some conversation, during which they laughed heartily at some stories I told them. After dinner sung a good deal, and talked; and had altogether a very pleasant evening. Lord L. mentioned the conclusion of a letter from a Dutch commercial house, as follows:—"Sugars are falling more and more every day; not so the respect and esteem with which we are, &c. &c." Slept at Bowood.

7th. [Tuesday] At breakfast Jekyll told of some one remarking on the inaccuracy of the inscription on Lord Kenyon's tomb, *Mors janua vita;* upon which Lord Ellenborough said, "Don't you know that *that* was by Kenyon's express desire, as he left it in his will, that they should not go to the expense of a diphthong?" He mentioned Rogers's story of an old gentleman, when sleeping at the fire, being awakened by the clatter of the fire-irons all tumbling down, and saying, "What! going to bed without one kiss," taking it for the children. Talked of Gen. Smith, a celebrated Nabob, who said, as an excuse for his bad shooting, that he had "spoilt his hand by shooting peacocks with the Great Mogul." Lord L. told of the same having written to put off some friends whom he had invited to his country seat, saying, "I find my damned fellow of a steward has in the meantime sold the estate." This Gen. Smith was the original of Foote's "Sir Matthew Mite" (his father having been a cheesemonger); and Jekyll told of some one having taken Foote to Smith's country-house on their way to town; his sleeping there, and being treated with every civility by Smith; and saying, before they were a hundred yards from his house, "I think I can't possibly miss him now, having had such a good sitting."[1] Came away at one, after having been much pressed to stay another day. Found my darling Bess not very well on my return. Confessed to me she had not been able to sleep ever since, from the idea that I was offended with her about something in going away. Far from it; I do nothing but bless her whenever I think of her.

8th. [Wednesday] Have now done another sacred song to an air of Crescentinis, and have begun a third to an air of Kozeluch. Have begun reading books on Greece for the new plan I have relative to the Miscellany.[1] Raffenel's "Account of the Revolution" seems a very fair one.[2] In Lady Jersey's last note, she says, "I am very much in love with one of your Angels, but won't tell you which. Your poem is charming; so like the Italian; full of beautiful similes." Have had a letter also from Lord John, in which he says, "I am delighted with your poem. Fairly speaking, I think the second story the best, and the *third a falling off.* The verses are beautiful and full of imagination." He adds afterwards, "I am happy to find that all here agree with me in opinion. Lady Jersey, Luttrel, Agar Ellis, all like the 'Angels' exceedingly."[3] It is curious to see the difference of tastes. Lord J. here says, "The third story is a falling off," and just before I received his letter, I had been reading a Review, in which the wise critic says, "The third story, which is unquestionably the best of the three." Lord John, of course, is right; it is a falling off after the second.

9th. [Thursday] Read and wrote. Received a copy of last Sunday's John Bull, in which (as was to be expected) the "Angels" are grossly abused, and strong efforts made (which I rather fear may be but too successful in some quarters) to brand it with a character of impiety and blasphemy.[1] This is too hard. Received a letter also from Rees, in which he mentions a criticism of Miss Aikin's, somewhat of the same tendency. The old proverb, "Give a dog a bad name, &c. &c." Should not wonder now if the tide were to set decidedly against it.

11th. [Saturday] Mrs. Phipps came. Said the "Angels" were torn to pieces yesterday at Locke's. Hardly any of the party had read it, but all abused it. Was just going out to call on the Lockes. Found Mrs. L. at home. Said (Mrs. Phipps having given me leave) that I heard how actively I had been dissected yesterday. She made some awkward explanations, and I turned the whole matter carelessly into a jest.

12th. [Sunday] Went to Church with Bessy and the little ones. Called on Mr. Awdrey afterwards, who told me how his house had been haunted by my "Angels," that his daughters could do nothing else but repeat verses out of it. The Phippses and their nephew came to us in the evening, and supped. Have read Muller's "Account of the Ionian Isles," and Charles Sheridan's pamphlet;[1] written a verse of the Third Sacred Song, and begun words for a fourth on the sixtieth chapter of Isaiah.[2] Macdonald called, according to promise, upon me this morning, and lunched. Walked back with him on his way to Bowood.

13th. [Monday] Brought up some arrears of this Journal. Read Hughes's pamphlet on the Greeks.[1] Have resolved now to adopt as a nucleus for my Miscellany the plan of "Letter from a young Irishman on his way to join the Greeks."

14th. [Tuesday] Read and wrote a little. Walked over to Bowood, where I have promised to stay till Thursday. Was to have taken Anastasia with me but the weather too bad. Company at dinner, Miss Emily Napier, and her two nieces, the Miss Bennetts, natural daughters of the Duke of Richmond (the reforming Duke), and Stanley. Dinner very agreeable. Miss N. mentioned a French lady, of whom she inquired, by way of compliment, "in what manner she had contrived to speak English so well?" and the answer was, "I begun by <i>traducing</i>." Lord L. in the evening, quoted a ridiculous passage from the preface to Mrs. Piozzi's "Retrospections,"[1] in which, anticipating the ultimate perfection of the human race, she says she does not despair of the time arriving "when Vice will take refuge in the arms of Impossibility." Mentioned also an Ode of hers to Posterity, beginning, "Posterity, gregarious Dame;" the only meaning of which must be, a Lady <i>chez qui</i> numbers assemble,—a Lady <i>at home</i>. I repeated what Jekyll told the other day of Bearcroft, saying to Mrs. Piozzi, when Thrale, after she had called him frequently Mr. Beercraft, "Beercraft is not my name, Madam; it may be <i>your</i> trade, but it is not <i>my name</i>." Dr. Currie once, upon being bored by a foolish Blue, to tell her the precise meaning of the word idea (which she said she had been reading about in some metaphysical work, but could not understand it), answered, at last, angrily, "Idea, Madam, is the feminine of Idiot, and means a female fool." Sung a good deal in the evening.

15th. [Wednesday] A very bleak, snowy day. The whole party played shuttlecock in the conservatory. I played with the Miss Bennetts. Lord L. and Stanley kept it up 2050 times. Wrote some letters. Walked a little with Lord L. before dinner. Mentioned the old Lord Liverpool (when Mr. Jenkinson) saying, in answer to some one who had called him, "That evil genius, who lurks behind the Throne," "Mr. Speaker, I am <i>not</i> an evil genius; I am not lurking behind the Throne. I again repeat, I am not an evil genius, but the member for Rye *in every respect whatsoever*" (this last a familiar phrase of his). Stanley mentioned, at dinner, that on Lord Harrowby's going down to Brighton last year, the King (who was out of temper with his Minister)[1] received him with a coldness almost rude, saying, "You are come down my Lord, to see your son, I suppose." "Yes, your Majesty," answered Lord H., "and for that solely." In talking of Geneva, and the sort of miniature scale everything is upon there, Lord L. said, that one time when he was passing there, they had contrived to get up a little Catholic Question, a cession having been made to them from Savoy, of a village (Colonge, I believe), which made it necessary to discuss the privileges of these new Catholic subjects, &c. &c. Talleyrand's quizzing the Genevese, by saying that geographers had quite forgot in enumerating the parts of the world, Europe, Asia, &c. &c., to add a fifth part, Geneva. Mentioned the trial of Lord Capel in the State Trials, and the sympathy attached to his fate, as resembling very much that of Ney (?)[2] Sung again; went through quantities of the Irish Melodies.

16th. [Thursday] Lord L. pressed me to stay over to-day. Made some excuses; but he brought Lady L. to his assistance, who offered to drive me over to Sloperton, that I might get my letters, and tell Mrs. Moore of my intention to remain another night. Went with her and Miss Napier. Lady L. proposed to bring Anastasia too, and she would send the carriage back with her before it was dark. Bessy did not much like my leaving her for another night; but at last she consented. 'Statia could not be ready in time to go. Walked over to Bowood about four. Bessy went with me as far as Mrs. Phipps's, who is not very well. An additional guest at dinner to-day—a Mrs. Fuller, who has travelled a good deal in Greece. Sung a good deal in the evening. Read, when I went to bed, a little of "Cellini's Life;"[1] his father giving him a box on the ear to remind him of the salamander, &c.

17th. [Friday] In talking of Ricardo, at breakfast, some one mentioned that he had been buried,—which is the ceremony among the Jews towards any one who quits their faith. The friends of the convert, too, go into mourning for him. Some talk with Mrs. Fuller, after breakfast, about Greece. Has been at Scio. The people there were highly civilised; had two or three universities. The women pretty and coquettish, but ignorant, as the Greek women are. Lord L. sent me word from his room, that if I waited till after luncheon, he would walk home with me. Did so; and he, Stanley, and Mrs. Fuller, left me nearly at home. Found Mrs. P., who slept at the Cottage last night, Phipps having gone to Bath.

18th. [Saturday] Had written to the Longmans (who have apprised me that I must revise for a fifth edition, as they are almost half through the fourth), that if they thought it would not be too late, I could make the "Angels" completely *eastern,* and thus get rid of that connection with the Scriptures, which they fear will, in the long run, be a drag on the popularity of the poem. Received a letter to-day, in which they say, "your idea is the very thing," and encouraging me to follow it up by all means.[1] Took a long walk. Mrs. P. remained to dinner and sleep.

19th. [Sunday] Turned over my "D'Herbelot," &c., for the project of turning the poor "Angels" into "Turks."[1] Walked to Melksham. Phipps and his nephew came and dined in their way from Bath. Received, to my most agreeable surprise, a portrait of my dearest father, in wax, which some artist of the name of Moore has executed lately in Dublin, and sent to me from London.

20th. [Monday] Reading "D'Herbelot." Have finished also Santa Rosa's account of the "Revolution of Piedmont,"[1] which I brought away from Bowood. A sad story, and told sensibly and interestingly. What an immortality of contempt such fellows as Prince Carignan[2] secure to themselves!

21st. [Tuesday] Received a note from Lord L. with last night's "Courier," which contains the noble answer of the Spaniards to the Allies.[1]

22nd. [Wednesday] Walked to Bowood. Saw Lord and Lady L. Asked him if his library contained Prideaux's "Life of Mahomet," and Beausobre's "Manicheism."[1] Has only the latter. Disapproves of my idea of orientalising the "Angels," as it would be a sort of avowal that I was wrong in my first plan, which does not strike *him* in the least. Shall think a little more about it. Lord L. walked with me on my way home. Talked of going to Bath some day next week, and will take me if I like to go.

23rd. [Thursday] Received "Beausobre" from Lord L. and some gingerbread nuts for Bessy from Lady L. By the by, I have forgot to mention that in the course of last week, having written to Murray to have what was preparing *for* (or *against*) me in the "Quarterly," and saying that, from something which dropped from Croker, I had half a hope *he* might undertake me, I received a letter from Croker reminding me that we had both agreed no friend should ever review the work of a friend; but that still, if he had time (which he had not), nothing would give him more pleasure than attempting to do justice to my poem, &c. &c.[1]

25th. [Saturday] Received a letter from Lady Donegal (to whom I have not written since my reply to her criticism), expressing great anxiety lest I should be angry with her, and asking forgiveness most amiably.

26th. [Sunday] Received a letter from the Longmans (to whom I had communicated Lord L.'s dissent from the plan of orientalising the poem), saying that they had again given it their best consideration, and that they continued to think such an alteration would materially serve me and my future works with the public. Wrote to Lady D. to say that I never had the slightest idea of being angry with her, &c. &c.

27th. [Monday] A deluging thaw and rain. Wrote up to the Longmans for Hyde's "Religio Persarum," "Philo-Judæus," "Martin's Travels," &c., for my notes.[1] No stirring out of the house.

29th. [Wednesday] Lady Lansdowne called to take leave of Bessy, as their horses go up to town to-morrow. Full of kindness: offered her a chair-bed from the park for her confinement, &c. &c.

30th. [Thursday] A letter from Lady D., expressing great pleasure at my having taken her frankness so good-humouredly, and saying that my last letter had "raised me, if possible, higher in their opinion than ever;" that she could not help showing it to Rogers, who seemed to think the same of it. Copied out and sent off three sacred songs to Power.

31th. [Friday] Lord L. came to bid us good-by: sat some time with me talking of the Spaniards, the approaching war, &c. Mean to write a few such poems as my "Dream" about the Holy Alliance.[1]

February 1st. [Saturday] Received from the Longmans the "Monthly Review," containing an article on the "Angels:" very twaddling; and, though meant to be kind, will do the poem mischief, as it takes up the Puritan tone about it.[1]

3rd. [Monday] Nothing particular.

4th. [Tuesday] Walked over to Bowood to look at the "Mémoires de l'Académie" for the notes.¹ Sat near an hour and a half in the library, reading and transcribing; and brought a volume away with me. Dined at Phipps's. A Mr. Legge of the party. Asked me to come again to-morrow to meet a Captain Amyot. Received to-day four more reviews of my poem in the "New Monthly," "London," "Gentleman's," and "Old Monthly" Magazines; all favourable enough except the "London," whose violence luckily defeats its own purpose.²

5th. [Wednesday] Sent up two sheets of the corrected "Angels."

7th to 9th. [Friday–Sunday] All passed at home, and almost entirely in the house, from the badness of the weather. Our dear Tom not at all well; took it for the measles at first, but it turned out to be an inflammatory cold, very common just now. Sent up more sheets of the "Angels." Have heard nothing of the Longmans for a long time, and fear my faithful correspondent, Rees, must be very ill. Received a letter from Miss Lefanu, with some very pretty verses in praise of my "Angels."

10th. [Monday] Answered Miss Lefanu, and said, if she had no objection, I would have her verses inserted in the "Morning Chronicle." The uneasy sensations still continue, and alarm me a little.

11th. [Tuesday] Bowles called, on his way to Bath. Is about to publish a poem anonymously, and wishes me to have it announced for him.¹ Advises we should send our Anastasia to the Moravian Establishment near him.

12th, to March 15th. [Wednesday, 12 Feb.–Saturday, 15 March] Have now been more than a month *sine lineâ,* and during that time have not stirred beyond the gates of my cottage, not being able to take the least exercise on account of these very disagreeable pains, &c. My chief occupation has been writing the new notes for the "Angels," and my "Fables for the Holy Alliance," which have been frequently advertised and puffed since the commencement of this month. Received several more reviews of the "Angels," and the long-expected broadside from "Blackwood" among the number, which is a tolerably murderous discharge, and (I must say for it) very ably served: another very abusive one in the "Monthly Museum," but ill done, and, therefore, not so mischievous. A memoir of me and a portrait in a new periodical called the "British Magazine;"[1] very flattering; at least the memoir. Received a letter from Murray about my bond to him for the Byron Memoirs; far from civil: returned an answer in kind, and have received no reply.[2] Wrote to Lord John, with Bessy's request that he would stand godfather for *her* forthcoming production: answered in the affirmative. Sent me some verses of his about the French armament against Spain,[3] in which he says,

"And the part of the Eagle's performed by the Goose."

A long letter from Croker on the intended metamorphosis of my "Angels" into Turks: very kind and sensible. Wrote two Irish Melodies for Power. Received an application (an attorney's letter in fact, but very civilly disguised) from the solicitor of the Middle Temple, on the subject of my long-owing fees: shall pay them when I go to town. Two letters from Lord Byron, not at all as lively as formerly: indeed Douglas Kinnaird told me when I was in town that the vivacity of his correspondence is very much dimmed. Bessy went one day to Bath, attended by Hughes (as I was not able to go myself), and settled upon a school for our dearest Anastasia; a Miss Furness's, where there are but five girls at present, and twelve the limited number. Bessy much pleased with the lady herself, and the general air of the establishment. A sad thing that the sweet child cannot be educated at home; but there are no masters to be got; and though I would willingly myself give up all the accomplishments in the world for the great object of keeping her heart and manners as they are now—pure, kind and simple,—yet Bessy is naturally anxious about the cultivation of her mind; and having done all she can for her herself, wishes to give her the advantages that every other child possesses: so we must send her. The 17th of this month (the day after her birthday) fixed for her going. A call or two from my neighbour, Mr. Awdrey, and occasional visits from Mrs. Phipps, are the only interruptions the quiet of this interval has received. Nor should I ask anything happier or gayer if these pains did not hang about me obstinately. Shall consult Astley Cooper when I go up to town. Had a letter from my sister Nell, in which she mentioned (and as a matter of course) my dear old father "going out to a party" somewhere with her: long may he be able to do so! Received a letter from Murray, explaining away most anxiously any appearance of offence there might have been in his former one, and concluding "with the most unfeigned admiration and esteem," &c. On the 16th we kept my dear 'Stasia's birthday, and on the 18th Bessy took her to school. Wrote to Woolriche to know whether he was likely to be in London the latter end of the month, as I was anxious to consult him. Received an answer to say that the Duke of Bedford had got the gout, and seemed unwilling to leave Woburn; but that, notwithstanding, if I would let him know my movements, he would manage to run up to town for a couple of days to me. Lingered on in this way, without taking any exercise, but still getting gradually better, till the

27th. [Thursday] Left home in a chaise for town at 2 o'clock. Took Bessy and Tom with me as far as the corner of the road to Wans. Arrived at Newbury a little after six, where I slept.

28th. [Friday] Started in the Marlborough coach at half-past ten: alone all the way, and suffered much less inconvenience from the journey than I expected. Arrived at Hatchett's at six, and dined there. Found my lodgings in Duke Street comfortably ready for me.

29th. [Saturday] Called at Sir A. Cooper's at ten. Out of town, and will not return till Monday. Breakfasted at the George. Called upon Power, and returned home (all in a hackney coach) before one. Saw in the newspapers a work announced, called "Angelographia," by a clergyman, "On the Nature and Offices of the Holy Angels, partly occasioned by two poems, lately published, the name of one of which, and the subject of both, is the 'Loves of the Angels.'"[1] Had a letter from Lucy Drew, announcing her intention of being in London about this time. Dined at the George; and home early.

30th. [Sunday] At home and alone all day. Delicious weather for the Easter Sunday folks. Dined at the George, and home early. Employed in transcribing my Fables.

31st. [Monday] Called at Sir A. Cooper's in the morning, but such crowds waiting for him that there seemed no chance. Breakfasted at the George, and returned, but still crowds. Determined to write and request an appointment. Power and Orme called upon me. Orme very smiling, particularly when I read him some of the Fables, which he seemed to think would do. Made arrangements for money with him, taking up Corry's bill, &c. &c. Dined at the George, and home early. A civil note from Sir A. Cooper, fixing to-morrow at twelve.

April 1st. [Tuesday] Saw Sir A. Cooper, who apologised for "giving *such a man* the trouble" of coming to him. Said there was no cause for uneasiness in the symptoms I felt. Recommended me, among other things, the use of the shower-bath. Begged me to let him see me again, "as a friend, if I would do him that honour." Altogether very courteous. Walked afterwards (for the first time since I came to town) to Rogers's. Very agreeable. In talking of the "Angels," said the subject was an unlucky one. When I mentioned Lord Lansdowne's opinion that it was better than "Lalla Rookh," said he would not rank it so high as the "Veiled Prophet" for execution, nor the "Fireworshippers" for story and interest, but would place it rather on the level of "Paradise and the Peri." Asked me to dine with him, which I did; company, Wordsworth and his wife and sister-in-law, Cary (the translator of Dante), Hallam, and Sharpe. Some discussion about Racine and Voltaire, in which I startled, and rather shocked them, by saying that, though there could be no doubt of the superior taste and workmanship of Racine, yet that Voltaire's tragedies *interested* me the most of the two. Another electrifying assertion of mine was, that I would much rather see "Othello" and "Romeo and Juliet" as Italian operas, and played by *Pasta,* than the original of Shakspeare, as acted on the London stage. Wordsworth told of some acquaintance of his, who being told, among other things, to go and see the "Chapeau de Paille" at Antwerp, said, on his return, "I saw all the other things you mentioned, but as for the straw-hat manufactory I could not make it out."[1] Sharpe mentioned a curious instance of Walter Scott's indifference to pictures: when he met him at the Louvre, not willing to spare two or three minutes for a walk to the bottom of the gallery, when it was the first and last opportunity he was likely to have of seeing the "Transfiguration," &c. &c. In speaking of music, and the difference there is between the poetical and musical ear, Wordsworth said that he was totally devoid of the latter, and for a long time could not distinguish one tune from another. Rogers thus described Lord Holland's feeling for the Arts: "Painting gives him no pleasure, and music absolute pain." Wordsworth's excessive praise of "Christabel,"[2] joined in by Cary, far beyond my comprehension. The whole day dull enough. Went away to call on Lady Donegal, whom I found pretty well, and very glad to see me. Mary Godfrey has been ill. Walked home, and had a restless night, as if I had exerted myself too much. Received from the Longmans a copy of the new "Edinburgh Review," in which Lord Byron and I are reviewed together, and very favourably.[3]

2nd. [Wednesday] Lucy arrived with Mrs. H. Ogle. Called upon her. Called upon Lord Lansdowne; admired a pretty picture of a child by Sir J. Reynolds, of which he told me that, at the sale where he bought it, the day had been so dark and misty that people could hardly see the pictures, till just at one moment a sunbeam burst suddenly in and fell upon this, lighting it up so beautifully that the whole company broke, by one common consent, into a loud peal of clapping. This sunbeam, he added, cost him at least fifty pounds in the purchase of the picture. Saw Lady L. too, who was particularly friendly; just going out of town; and asked me to dine with them next Tuesday. Dined at Lady Donegal's; and went nowhere else afterwards.

3rd. [Thursday] Wet weather. Driving about in a hackney coach; Lucy's; the Temple, in order to ascertain the amount of the fees I owe. Begged of the solicitor to inquire for me how many terms I have got to serve for the English bar: think of being called, for the form of the thing. Dined at Longman's; Power of the party. They mentioned, as a proof of Walter Scott's industry, that when he was editor of the "Edinburgh Annual Register," being allowed books, as is the custom, to cut up for extracts, &c., he would often, in order to save a book worth 15s. for his library, pass the greater part of the day transcribing the necessary passages. Home afterwards.

4th. [Friday] Called upon Lucy to go to Chantrey's, with some specimens of Douglas's casts from medals (a valuable discovery, as he thinks), in order to know Chantrey's opinion of the invention. Poor Chantrey, but just recovering from a long illness; and his wife now dangerously ill. Seemed to think nothing whatever of Douglas's discovery, as a means of emolument. Went afterwards, in a hackney coach, with Lucy to Murray's, to show her his room and his pictures; thence to the Foreign Office. Dined at Mr. Monkhouse's (a gentleman I had never seen before), on Wordsworth's invitation, who lives there whenever he comes to town. A singular party: Coleridge, Rogers, Wordsworth and wife, Charles Lamb (the hero, at present, of the "London Magazine")[1] and his sister (the poor woman who went mad with him in the diligence on the way to Paris),[2] and a Mr. Robinson, one of the *minora sidera* of this constellation of the Lakes, the host himself, a Mecænas of the school, contributing nothing but good dinners and silence. Charles Lamb, a clever fellow certainly; but full of villanous and abortive puns, which he miscarries of every minute. Some excellent things, however, have come from him; and his friend Robinson mentioned to me not a bad one. On Robinson's receiving his first brief, he called upon Lamb to tell him of it. "I suppose," said Lamb, "you addressed that line of Milton's to it, 'Thou *first* best *cause*, least understood.'"[3] Coleridge told some tolerable things. One of a poor author, who, on receiving from his publisher an account of the proceeds (as he expected it to be) of a work he had published, saw among the items, "Cellerage, 3l. 10s. 6d.," and thought it was a charge for the trouble of *selling* the 700 copies, which he did not consider unreasonable; but on inquiry he found it was for the *cellar*-room occupied by his work, not a copy of which had stirred from thence. He told, too, of the servant-maid where he himself had lodged at Ramsgate, coming in to say that he was wanted, there being a person at the door inquiring for a poet; and on his going out, he found it was a pot-boy from the public-house, whose cry, of "any *pots* for the Angel," the girl had mistaken for a demand for a *poet*. Improbable enough. In talking of Klopstock, he mentioned his description of the Deity's "head spreading through space," which, he said, gave one the idea of a hydrocephalous affection. Lamb quoted an epitaph by Clio Rickman, in which, after several lines, in the usual jog-trot style of epitaph, he continued thus:—

> "He well performed the husband's, father's part,
> And knew immortal Hudibras by heart."[4]

A good deal of talk with Lamb about De Foe's works, which he praised warmly, particularly "Colonel Jack," of which he mentioned some striking passages.[5] Is collecting the works of the Dunciad heroes. Coleridge said that Spenser is the poet most remarkable for contrivances of versification: his spelling words differently, to suit the music of the line, putting sometimes "spake," sometimes "spoke," as it fell best on the ear, &c. &c. To show the difference in the facility of reciting verses, according as they were skilfully or unskilfully constructed, he said he had made the experiment upon Beppo and Whistlecraft (Frere's poem),[6] and found that he could read three stanzas of the latter in the same time as two of the former. This is absurd. Talked much of Jeremy Taylor; his work upon "Prophesying," &c.[7] C. Lamb told me he had got £170 for his two years' contributions to the "London Magazine" (Letters of Elia). Should have thought it more.

6th. [Sunday] Breakfasted at Rogers's, to meet C. Lamb. Repeated some of my "Fables," which they seemed to like. Called on Mrs. Story. Went out to Holland House, having had a kind note from Lady Holland, asking me to pass some days; but answered that I would only stay over to-night. Found Lord and Lady H. with Lord Granville. When he went away, repeated to them "Church and State," from my "Fables," which they seemed to like very much. Lady Holland went to dress; and I repeated to Lord H. the "Looking Glasses," which he said was excellent, "very *radical*, but very good." The "Dissolution of the Holy Alliance" did not seem to strike him much; but he seemed pleased with the "Fly and the Bullock:" said they were like Swift.[1] Company at dinner, Vernon and Lady Elizabeth, Lord Grey, Lord Howard de Walden, and Sidney Smith. Smith told some stories of Judge Park; his addressing the young woman in the court, "Young woman, don't stand so close to Mr. Donellan; it is'nt to the credit of any young woman to be so close to Mr. Donellan:" Mr. Donellan's demand for an explanation, &c. &c. In the evening, Lord Holland assisted me to consult some books of Heraldry, in the library, for the exact number of the pearls on the different coronets, which I wanted to ascertain for my "Epitaph on a Tuft-hunter."[2] My Lady catechised me very kindly about my health; wondered I could go to such a savage fellow as Astley Cooper; cautioned me against the shower-bath; said that Willis had declared he owed to it more patients than to any other cause. Sidney Smith very comical about the remedy that Lady H. is going to use for the bookworm, which is making great ravages in the library. She is about to have them washed with some mercurial preparation; and Smith says it is Davy's opinion that the air will become charged with the mercury and that the whole family will be salivated. "I shall see Allen," says Smith, "some day, with his tongue hanging out, speechless, and shall take the opportunity to stock a few principles into him." Slept there.

7th. [Monday] Ordered a hackney coach to take me away; but my Lady countermanded it, and said she would send me in the carriage. Made me repeat the "Looking Glasses," of which Lord Holland had told her; said it was very witty. Gave me the engraving of her Napoleon's snuff-box. Her pretty daughter, Mary, and the Governess, came in with me in the carriage.

8th. [Tuesday] Wrote to Lady Holland for her box, to-morrow night, at the theatre, for Mrs. Ogle and Lucy. Dined at Lord Lansdowne's: company, Misses Fox and Vernon, Sidney Smith, Jekyll, Hallam, &c. &c. Smith gave me a very cordial invitation to his house in Yorkshire.

9th. [Wednesday] Dined at Power's, to meet Bishop. Jackson, the boxer, had called upon me in the morning, to know where that well-known line, "Men are but children of a larger growth," is to be found,[1] said there was a bet depending on it, and he thought I would be most likely to tell. Not, he said, in "Young's Night Thoughts."[2] Promised to make out, if I could. Received a note from Lady Holland, enclosing the order for her box. Called upon by Lucy and Mrs. Ogle at eight, and went with them; Ogle himself and C. Sheridan of the party. "Count Julian," and a melodrama, in which Miss Foote looked very pretty.[3]

10th. [Thursday] Dined at Rogers's. A distinguished party: S. Smith, Ward, Luttrel, Payne Knight, Lord Aberdeen, Abercrombie, Lord Clifden, &c. Smith particularly amusing. Have rather held out against him hitherto; but this day he conquered me; and I now am his victim, in the laughing way, for life. His imagination of a duel between two doctors, with oil of croton on the tips of their fingers, trying to touch each other's lips highly ludicrous. What Rogers says of Smith, very true, that whenever the conversation is getting dull, he throws in some touch which makes it rebound, and rise again as light as ever. Ward's artificial efforts, which to me are always painful, made still more so by their contrast to Smith's natural and overflowing exuberance. Luttrel too, considerably extinguished to-day; but there is this difference between Luttrel and Smith—that after the former, you remember what good things he said, and after the latter, you merely remember how much you laughed. Ward's delight at the report of bad news from Portugal (defeats of the Constitutionalists, &c.),[1] very disgusting. Went at ten, to join the Storys at Drury Lane, and saw a melodrama. Supped with them afterwards.

11th. [Friday] Dined early with Rogers and his sister, in order to go see "Simpson and Co."[1] (of which successful piece, by the by, I brought the MS. from Paris). On our way to the theatre received a note from Lucy, fixing for me to come to Mrs. Ogle's in the evening. Rogers took me to Lady Spencer's box, to which he is a subscriber, and not a little proud thereof.

12th. [Saturday] Was to have breakfasted with Lord Lansdowne, but sent him an excuse, Rogers having fixed for me to meet Barry Cornwall (Mr. Proctor) at his house; a gentle, amiable-mannered person in very ill health, which has delayed his marriage with a person he has long been in love with; she, too, an invalid; and somebody, the other day, described the two lovers supping together at nine o'clock on water gruel. Returned home at twelve, to copy out for the printer. Called on by Lucy and her maid to go to Davison (the printer, who has married the little governess that lived with Lady Virginia). He wishes me to interest myself with Murray for him. Thence to Valpy, about my "Thesaurus," which I thought of exchanging for his "Classics;" but find the latter would amount (what is already published) to £41: requires consideration. After this to Longmans', where I gave my copy, and made them show Lucy the premises. Went, as Lord Lansdowne's guest, to dine at the King of Clubs; Wishaw took me. Company—Sharpe, Lord Lansdowne, Lord King, William Smith, Luttrel, Payne Knight, Phillips, and Wishaw; agreeable enough. Lord King amusing about the Church, which is now the standing butt for all irreverent jokes. Lord Bexley's motto, *Grata quies,* is by Canning translated, Great Quiz. Payne Knight's operations on the turbot; thought of the preface to his new poem,[1] where he says his senses are *blunted* by age. Went afterwards to the opera with Lord Lansdowne; Mercadanti's "Claudio è Elisa;"[2] saw the last act in Lady L.'s box; rather pretty, but not very striking. Went afterwards to join Mrs. Ogle and Lucy in the pit; saw them to their carriage at the end, and then home.

13th. [Sunday] Went to the Lansdownes' at half-past six, to be taken to Holland House to dinner. Company—the Duke and Duchess of San Lorenzo, Sir F. Burdett, Hobhouse, Lord Arthur Hill, &c. Dinner too large to be very agreeable. Lady H.'s mystery in the evening; making me sit by her in the *privileged* chair, saying that I would be of use to her there, as she had got into a scrape; then pointing vaguely to where a pretty girl (a ward, I believe, of Lord Holland's) sat, and muttering something about "the little god," &c.; all of which was so much Hebrew to me. Returned with the Lansdownes, whose carriage took me home. Was asked to the Harringtons' (to meet the Duke and Duchess of Leinster, who are arrived), but too late to go.

14th. [Monday] Received an impatient letter from Bess, which rather disturbed me, both on her account and my own. Perceive she is getting quite uncomfortable without me, and yet have quantities of things to do in town. Must manage as well as I can. Woolriche called while I was dressing, having just arrived; thinks a shower-bath will do me service, though, as I told him, Lady Holland last night rather alarmed me about this remedy, by mentioning that Willis said it has sent him more patients than any other cause. W. told me that Lord John is just arrived. Went to dinner at Lansdowne House at half-past seven, Lord L. having asked me to dine quietly with themselves in his room before their assembly. He did not come from the House of Lords till about eight. Dined without dressing; young Macdonald of the party. A good deal of talk about Ireland and the Irish parliament. I said that, notwithstanding the corruption of that parliament, its existence was serviceable in keeping alive (by the principles continually and eloquently broached in it) an active political feeling, a circulation of public spirit, which is the only antiseptic that can keep a country from decay and degradation, and which is now, in Ireland, totally gone; that this is evident from the fact of there not being, in the convulsions which agitate her, one political motive to give the slightest degree of dignity to her tumultuousness; that if there had not existed that parliament (bad as it had always been), there never would have been enough of public spirit generated to produce the grand spectacle which Ireland exhibited in '82.[1] Lord L., who seemed to question all this, and to consider the getting rid of so profligate a parliament, at all events, a benefit, remarked that if the events of '82 were to be attributed to the influence of a parliament, there was no reason why that influence should not be progressive; whereas, on the contrary, public spirit had so retrograded from that period, that the profligacy developed by the measure of the Union was such as never had before disgraced any assembly or nation. To this I answered, That the interval between (occupied as it was by the agitation produced everywhere by the French Revolution, and which in Ireland ended in a bloody rebellion) was not a fair trial of the influence of such principles as triumphed in '82; that England herself was "frighted from her propriety," and put in a position unnatural to her during that interval; and that therefore we cannot possibly judge how far the dawn of independence which rose upon Ireland in '82 might have brightened if it had not been overcast by this general convulsion of the whole civilised world. Sat talking a long time, though the assembly was commencing, and Lady L. came in two or three times to urge Lord L. to go and dress. Assembly not very large: saw numbers I knew. Talked a good deal with Lady Jersey, who was full of praise of the "Angels." Home pretty early.

15th. [Tuesday] Went down to Longmans' with more copy. Had reserved myself to-day for a dinner at the Ogles', and play after; but no tidings of it. Left word for Woolriche, that if he was disengaged to-day, we might dine together. Called upon Lord John, but he had gone to the House. Called upon W. Spencer, to fix to-morrow to dine with him.

16th. [Wednesday] Woolriche called on his way to return to Woburn. To Longmans' with more copy. Called on Mrs. Story and the Donegals. Dined with W. Spencer. Spencer not in very high feather. Mentioned those two good lines, written, he said, on Madame de Genlis, though in general supposed to be on Madame de Stael:—

> "Elise se consume en efforts superflus;
> La Vertu n'en veut pas, le Vice n'en veut plus."

What Madame de Stael said of Paris, *C'est la ville du monde où on peut le mieux se passer du bonheur.* Her reply to a man who, upon finding himself placed between her and a very pretty woman, said how lucky he was *de se trouver placé entre le Génie et la Beauté. C'est la première fois* (said Madame de Stael) *qu'on m'ait loué pour ma beauté.* A long discussion upon French heroics: had in volumes of Racine, &c. Went afterwards to Miss Drummond's, where I sung a little with Lucy; and from thence to Almack's: rather thin. Saw Mrs. Bennet and Miss Russell,[1] and an old London acquaintance of mine, a pretty woman, whose name I forget. Talked some time with the Lady Greys; stayed but half an hour; home before one. Have not been able to make out the source of the line for Jackson. Stewart Rose said some one had asserted it was in Roscommon; but it is not.[2]

17th. [Thursday] Went to Power's with Lucy to choose some music; thence to the Bazaar. Had gone in the morning to see Barbara Godfrey take her lesson of dancing, with my old acquaintance, Billy Jenkins. His poetical language very amusing; begging her, in the Minuet de la Cour, to imagine him and herself as sylphs that had not met for some time; the surprise, the recognition, &c. &c.; the under part of the body alone to move, the upper to remain quiet; to avoid looking like a quadruped, &c. &c. Received, on my return home, a note from the Longmans, full of panic at an opinion they have just had from their legal adviser, Turner, that the "Fables" are indictable, as "tending to bring monarchy into contempt." Dined at Lord King's (was asked also to Lord Essex's): company, Mr. Thos. Grenville, Payne Knight, Sharpe, Sir G. Robinson (who came from the House at the end of dinner, and brought us an account of Canning's foolish interruption of Brougham, "That is false," &c.),[1] and a scientific gentleman whose name I could not make out. Conversation chiefly about grammar: Prior's "than her" and "than me" pronounced, with Lowth, to be wrong.[2] Milton's "than whom" discussed. Knight said that the test of soundness or propriety in phrases was translating them into Latin, that language being, beyond all others, the language of good sense. I quoted those lines of Lord Byron in the "Giaour" as defying all grammar, and yet impossible (for dramatic effect) of being altered for the better—

> "Faithless to him, he shrunk the blow,
> But true to me, I laid him low."[3]

Robinson quoted, as another instance, the celebrated

> "Je t'aimais inconstant, qu'aurais-je fait fidèle?"[4]

Told Sharpe of the Longmans' panic; thought it very absurd. Lady King offered to take me to Mrs. T. Hope's, where I had promised to go; but went, instead, to Miss Drummond, where I found Mrs. Humphrey Butler and her daughters, &c.; quadrilles going on.

18th. [Friday] Lady H.'s last note leaving me an excuse for considering myself as let off for to-day, resolved not to go. Went to the Longmans, and had a discussion with Turner on the subject of his opinion about the "Fables." The Longmans expected I should make alterations, but told them that was impossible. Asked Turner whether he thought the Constitutional Association (which is what he dreads) would be content with having the author delivered up to them. Said it was most probable they would. "This then," said I, "might settle perhaps all alarms, as I was perfectly ready to meet the consequences myself in every way; though of there being any such consequences from the publication I had not the slightest apprehension."

Left them to consider the matter. Bought the Bishop of Winchester's "Life of Pitt"[1] for four or five and twenty shillings in Holborn.

19th. [Saturday] Dined at Phillips's. Drove first, by mistake, to his son's in Hill Street, where the servant who opened the door said, "Perhaps, sir, it is to Mr. Phillips's of Mount Street you meant to go, for *we* are going to dine there too." Company, Sidney Smith, the George Phillipses, the Ordes, the Macdonalds, &c. Sidney Smith had that day gone through the ceremony at Lambeth, which it appears all persons must do upon receiving a second living: they are shut up by themselves, with pen and ink, and the choice of four subjects given them, on one of which they must write a Latin prose Thesis. This is really a greater tax upon pluralists than I had supposed to exist; for nine out of ten reverends must be sadly posed by the task. Not that their examiner is likely to be very strict. He says doubtless of these pluralists, *Ubi* plura *nitent non ego paucis offendar maculis.* Found in Mrs. G. Phillips, whom I sat next, an old Derbyshire acquaintance, one of Lord Waterpark's daughters. Smith and I walked home together. Had a letter from Lady H. to-day, to say I was expected yesterday; my cover vacant, and a bed ready for me.

20th. [Sunday] Called upon Rogers, and consulted with him about this hitch that has taken place in the publication of the "Fables." Advised me to require a decisive answer. Called at Lansdowne House; saw Lady L., who was all amiability. Has offered me, by the by, the use of her shower-bath from the Park, till they go down themselves. It is delightful to see how that cold uncertainty which at first hung upon her manner towards me is clearing away, and giving place to a friendly, frank familiarity, which is both more becoming to her and far more comfortable to me. Home at two to receive Lord John, who has called two or three times without finding me. Walked out with him. Called afterwards on Shee, the painter; glad to find that he has been pleased with the "Angels." Says he thought it the most beautiful thing I had ever written, or that ever had been written in that style; but that I had given the world so much in the same strain they naturally must relax in their eagerness about it; and that it was necessary for me now to change my hand. He is right. Dined at Sir G. Warrender's; company, Lady Saltoun and her daughters, Lord Lovaine, Lord Lynedoch, Sir P. Doyle, &c.; splendid dinner, both in cookery and service. Doyle's account of the Spaniards (corroborated by Lord Lovaine), that there is no answering for what they will do or will not do; they may all suddenly join the French, or start up as suddenly in universal array against them. In the evening, Countess San Antonio, Lady Farquhar, and a rather pretty girl, Miss Bennet, Lord Ashley (very like Lord Byron), my old friend Beecher,

&c. &c. There was a young man (Captain Somebody) who sang very sweetly. I sang several songs, besides an unhappy duet with the Countess San Antonio. Warrender most cordially and earnestly entreated me to make his house my home when I should come to London; that I should be free after breakfast for the day, except upon some particular days, when he would lay an embargo upon me for a home dinner; all very kind. Was home before one, Lord Ashley walking with me the greater part of the way.

21st. [Monday] A sort of half promise to go to Holland House to-day; having refused Lord Darnley on that plea, also one of the Vice-Presidents of the Covent Garden Fund dinner; and ought to go there; but determined for young Perry's, where I shall meet Kenny. Went down to Paternoster Row to learn the final resolve of the Co. Told me they had, to satisfy themselves, submitted the sheets to Denman, and would let me know his opinion as soon as they received it. Walked about St. James's to see the crowds the levee brought together. Company at Perry's, poor old doubled-up Skeffington, Beazley the architect, Hill, Kenny, and a gentleman whose name I forget, who sung in the evening to the pianoforte. Sung a couple of songs for them myself, though hating such an operation with *he* hearers; and got home early. Found a note from the Row, inclosing one from Denman to the attorney; very clearly written, and saying (just as I expected) that, though he could not guarantee against the folly of people in prosecuting, he would venture to guarantee the result of such a prosecution, which had been anticipated by Horace and Pope—

> "The plaintiff will be hiss'd,
> My Lords the Judges laugh, and you're dismiss'd."[1]

22nd. [Tuesday] Met Lord John when I went out; walked together some time; promised to breakfast with him in the morning. Took my place in the coach for Thursday morning. Must, after all, leave my printing unfinished; and the work, which was announced in all the papers for yesterday, will not be out now for a fortnight. Went down to the Longmans; had 60*l.* To Power's, on my way back, and looked over some music. To Mrs. Story's; promised to dine with her to-day. Left them at eight to go to the opera. Went to Lady Lansdowne's box, and found there Lady Davy, Mrs. Orde, and the Duc de Dalberg; Lord L. himself afterwards came in. Sat some time in Lord Essex's box; thence to Lady Farquhar's, to make my excuse for not calling this morning.

23rd. [Wednesday] Breakfasted with Lord John; showed me a letter he received, a day or two ago, from the Duke, on the politics of the day, very clearly written, and full of quite a youthful ardour on the subject.

24th. [Thursday] Started at seven in the White Lion coach; companions, an elderly military gentleman, and a poor sickly girl, brought up in France. Arrived at home at seven, and found my dear Bessy looking wonderfully well, but little Tom ill with a feverish cold. Had brought away a wrong portmanteau, and mine was gone on to Bath.

25th. [Friday] Got my own portmanteau; and sent off some corrected proofs to town.

26th. [Saturday] Have determined to set up a little four-wheeled gig and pony, as I doubt whether I shall ever be able to take such long walks as I used. Consulted Phipps about it, who has promised to set inquiries on foot for me.

27th [Sunday] Sauntering about the garden with Bess.

28th. [Monday] Sent off my preface and title.

29th, 30th. [Tuesday, Wednesday] Little or nothing. Received a letter from the Longmans, suggesting the omission of the epitaphs, to which I readily acceded; except that upon a Lawyer, which I wished to have retained.

May 1st. [Thursday] Walked over to Phipps's. They proposed going to Buckhill to show me Hughes's cottage. Mrs. P. drove me, and he rode. Dined with them on our return; and they came home and played cards, and supped with Bessy afterwards.

2nd. [Friday] Borrowed a donkey chaise from our neighbour, Farmer Gaby, and drove Bessy over to Buckhill to see her friend, Mrs. Hughes, who returned yesterday evening. Met Dr. Hindley on the way (who has been all kindness to my dear Bessy, both during the accident to her nose, and lately), and he seemed to think her expedition so far rather adventurous in her present situation. Went on, however, and did not get back till eight o'clock.

4th, 5th. [Sunday, Monday] Employed myself in bringing up this Journal.

Have read since I came home Madame Campan's "Memoirs of Marie Antoinette;"[1] a sad story.

6th. [Tuesday] Received from the Longmans two copies of the "Fables,"
which are to be published to-morrow. Found, to my great mortification,
that I had by mistake sent up the uncorrected slips instead of the corrected
ones (they having sent me down two sets); in consequence of which the two
last sheets are published exactly as the printer's devils left them, *comme il a
plû aux diables,* with all those errors of my own, too, which I had corrected in
the unsent proofs. This is too provoking. Wrote off to the Longmans
immediately, to bid them put a list of errata in the newspapers; but too late
for the post.

7th. [Wednesday] Corrected one of the copies of the "Fables," and despatched it to the Longmans, who seem to think another edition will be
wanting instantly.

8th. [Thursday] A notice of the "Fables" in the "Chronicle;" favourable, of
course, but ill done.[1] Dined at Phipps's. The General very gentlemanly.

9th. [Friday] A notice of the "Fables" in the "Times;" done (as everything in
that Paper is) with the utmost skill and good taste.[1] Mrs. P. and the General
called in their ride, and entreated me to join them again to-day; which
Bessy thought it would be but kind to do. Did so. Read them the "Looking
Glasses" out of the "Times;" but it did not tell upon them. This is what I
feared;—those allegories are too abstract for common readers. Wretched,
uncomfortable walks home these two nights from the badness of the
weather.

11th. [Sunday] Wrote a song for the new musical work I mean to do for
Power,[1] founded upon Sappho's beautiful lines, Γλυκεια ματερ, ου τοι.
Read "Clarke's Travels," "Dodwell," &c.[2] Mrs. P. called in the evening. Tom
and I walked part of the way home with her. Received to-day three reviews
of my book; two of them (though I bid the Longmans send me nothing
abusive this time) full of contemptuous (but at the same time contemptible)
attacks upon it. These were the "Literary Gazette," and the "Museum;"[3] in
the latter, too, a heavy, canting (but rather respectful) essay upon the
character of my poetry in general, repeating the old charge of its danger-

ous effects upon female minds, &c. The third review was that of which little Jessy the governess's husband is the proprietor, and kind of course.

12th. [Monday] Reading the Bishop of Winchester's "Life of Pitt," and some of the speeches of Fox and Burke.

13th. [Tuesday] A kind letter from Lord Lansdowne, enclosing one from Rogers, both speaking favourably of the "Fables." R. says that none of those who had read them (and he knew some who had read them twice) seemed to have been aware of the errors I mentioned to him. An article full of praise in the "British Press."

14th [Wednesday] Wrote, between to-day and yesterday, another song for the musical work, the scene of which I mean to lay in Greece.[1]

15th. [Thursday] Begun another song to an air of my own, which Lucy used to like very much; "Oh, Maids of Zion."[1] Do not see any announcement of the second edition in the papers; another flash in the pan. Application from an upholsterer in Devizes to pay his bill, as he is distressed for money. Wrote to announce to the Longmans that I must draw upon them. A "John Bull" newspaper today (of course filled with abuse of the "Fables") sent from the same kind hand that forwarded me this paper's attack upon the "Angels."[2] Disappointed, however, the kind soul's intentions (whoever he or she may be) by putting it in the fire, without looking at more than my name.

16th. [Friday] Finished "Oh, Maids of Zion." Received the French translation of my "Loves of the Angels" with a most encomiastic notice of me and my works prefixed to it.[1]

17th. [Saturday] An account in the papers of the public meeting for the Greeks on Thursday. Sir James Mackintosh concluded a splendid speech by quoting (with most flattering mention of me) three stanzas from the "Torch of Liberty," in the "Fables." My name received with "loud cheering." This is gratifying. How I lament not having been able to attend this meeting! Such an opportunity for me to speak in public may hardly ever again occur; the subject, the audience,—all would have been what I am most ambitious of.[1] The Phippses came in the evening; played cards, and supped.

18th. [Sunday] Copied out my three songs, and a fragment of a fourth, and dispatched them to Power. Received from the Longmans the "Scotsman" paper, in which there is most enthusiastic praise of me and the "Fables;" says in one part, "If everybody felt as we do on the subject, the whole country would decree to him a crown of laurel." See in the "Times" report of the great meeting that when Mackintosh mentioned my name there was "much cheering." Lady Lansdowne arrived at Bowood.

20th. [Tuesday] In returning from a saunter to Chitto Valley, met Lady L. and Lord Kerry, who had walked to call at the cottage; but were not let in, Bessy being, they said, fast asleep. Turned about with her, and walked some way; promised to come to Bowood before she goes.

22nd. [Thursday] Began another song for the Greek work. Employed at intervals, for some days past, reading the speeches of Burke, &c., on the Hastings business, Bisset's "History of George III.,"[1] Bishop of Winchester's "Life of Pitt," &c.

23rd. [Friday] Received a very kind note from Lady L., in which she says she had been charged by Lords Lansdowne, Holland, and Lord John (as well as various others), to tell me how much my "Fables" were admired; that it was impossible to say in a note half of what she was charged with, but that the admiration of them was so cordial, it could not but give me pleasure; and that when she was at Holland House, the two copies they had there were fought for. This is all very gratifying. I only wish the public would catch a little more of the same enthusiasm, and buy me up more rapidly. Sent to Lady L. a letter for Rogers, in which I begged of him to put down my name to the Greek subscription for £5.[1]

24th. [Saturday] My darling girl's symptoms became decisive after breakfast; a message was dispatched for the midwife; and, in little more than half an hour after she arrived, a little boy was born.[1] My anxiety rendered still more painful by the absence of the physician, who did not arrive till an hour after all was over, to Bessy's great delight, who has a horror of his being even in the house on these occasions. However all, thank God, was as well as possible. Added a few lines announcing the event to several letters of Bessy's, which she had left open for the purpose, and wrote two or three myself.

25th. [Sunday] Bessy doing marvellously well, and the little fright (as all such young things are) prospering also. Wrote several letters.

26th. [Monday] Began another song. Mrs. Hughes came over to see Bess; and dined with me.

27th. [Tuesday] Still no second edition of the "Fables," nor any letter to report progress, from the Longmans. Dined with the Phippses to meet Captain Amyot. Home at ten.

28th. [Wednesday] Being my birthday, dined in my dear Bessy's bed-room, who still keeps wonderfully well. Received a letter from Jeffrey in answer to mine about the "Edinburgh Review."

30th. [Friday] Set off in Phipps's gig for Melksham; found there that I had left all my money at home; borrowed a pound of P.'s coachman, and set a note by him to Bessy, to forward me the money by the evening coach to Bath. Arrived, by the Devizes coach, at Bath at eleven o'clock. Called immediately on my darling Anastasia, at Miss Furness's; took her out to walk. Showed me a pretty way through the fields. Sweet child! I could not help stopping every instant to look at her and kiss her. Weather very hot. Left her at home, and walked about Bath; saw my name placarded on the walls everywhere. In one book-shop's windows saw a work entitled "A Miscellany from the works of Moore, *Little*, Byron, &c." William, our servant, arrived with my money at two, Bessy having dispatched him on horseback immediately. Had to stand a very intense stare from the Bath fashionables in Milsom Street. Walked with Lady Burdett's little doctor to Sydney Gardens. Dined at the White Lion inn alone. Went afterwards to the theatre; "Lover's Vows;" Amelia played very naturally and prettily by a nice girl, Miss Carr.[1]

31st. [Saturday] Off at six in the White Lion coach. Amused by the fine dress, and plain, humble manners of a Mrs. Clarke (wife to a coach-owner in Bond Street), who, with her little child, was my only company. Her details of her father-in-law's farm, &c. &c. Passed through Hyde Park Corner at twenty minutes past six, and arrived at Story's (with whom I had arranged to dine) at seven. Have only the garret in Duke Street, all the rest of the house being occupied.

June 1st. [Sunday] Called at Rogers's: not in town. On to Burdett, who is confined by the gout; sat with him some time. Thence to Lord Lansdowne's, whom I saw also. To Lady Donegal's, with whom I promised to dine to-day; told me of the different opinions about my "Fables;" their admiration of some parts, and their lamentations over others, &c. &c. Thence to Lord Essex, whom I found descanting, over his luncheon, on the beauties of Baring's new house; took me out in his cabriolet, after tempting me much to a desertion of Lady Donegal, by asking me to meet Brougham and Lady Jersey. Made several calls with him; at Lady Jersey's (where we saw Lord J.); at Lord W. Bentinck's, at Grey's, &c. Had some conversation with Lord Grey on the subject of Spain, about which he desponds. Always pleased to meet Lord Grey. Walked through the Park. Called at Baring's; showed me his house, which is not yet furnished; his chimney pieces, by Bartollini, spoiled from over-polish; hopes to be able to un-polish them again. The bas-relief over the door, a cast from Thorwaldsen's "Triumphal Procession of Alexander." Thorwaldsen had hardly ever looked at a horse before he undertook to represent them here. Met Lady Davy, who asked me to dinner for the 15th; also Lady Farquhar, who told me Sir. G. Warrender had music to-night, and begged me to go. Had a note from Sir G. to the same effect while at dinner at Lady Donegal's, and reminding me, too, of my promise to take up my abode at his house, which he now meant to claim the performance of. Went from Lady D.'s to Lord Essex's; found Lady Jersey, and Brougham, and (what I did not expect) Lord John Russell; also a Miss Thellusson, with whom I sung two or three Italian duets. Walked away with Lord John—he to Lady Jersey's, who was at home, and I to Warrender's, where I found Miss Stephens, her niece, Mrs. Blackshaw, Captain Ratcliffe, &c. Supper and singing; Miss Stephens seemed to like my singing exceedingly. Amused her by mentioning an "Essay on Music," which I had seen in some periodical publication in which the writer, after discussing the various styles of music, declares himself at the end for "Nature, Tom Moore, and Kitty Stephens;" she expressed great delight at the alliance. Warrender again importunate on the subject of my domesticating myself *chez lui;* promised I would answer for certainty in a day or two. Did not reach home till three; and, on entering my garret (though small, and not very odorous), resolved to stick to it in preference to the baronet's fine chambers; such charms has independence! Lady Jersey told me that, in going to see her sister in the country to-day, she took my "Angels" with her to read the third or fourth time.

2nd. [Monday] Paid visits. Called upon Croker. Met Bowles, who wanted to take me off to dine with Linley in Furnival's Inn, where there was to be music; but too far for my existing engagements. Dined at Richardson's in Covent Garden; weather become dreadfully wet and chilly. Home and dressed. Went first to Lady Farquhar's; a girl there with pretty features, but all awry, of whom some one said she was *La Beauté Chiffonnée*. A beautiful little girl, too, Miss Mathison, with that foreign cast of countenance which is such an improvement on continental beauty, having good English flesh and blood for its substratum; as the cookery of France in England is always better than in its native element, having the superior English materials to show off its art and piquancy upon. Caradori and Curioni sung, but not very agreeably. Went from thence to Lady Jersey's, and heard (for the first time in my life) an Italian *improvisatore*, of the name of Pistrucci. He had already done three or four subjects, of which one, "Don Quixote and the Windmills," must have been a puzzler to him. The subject on which I heard him was "Hero and Leander," which must have been part of his stock in hand; but still the facility surprised me. He sung it through, and was accompanied by Mad. Renaudin on the pianoforte. Went afterwards to a dance at Mrs. Bennet's (our M. P.'s wife); some pretty people there, among whom was Miss Houlton.

3rd. [Tuesday] Breakfasted with Rogers; Constable, of Edinburgh, the great publisher, and Bowles, of the party. In talking of the craft of bookselling, Constable said, "Mr. Moore, if you will let me have a poem from your pen, I will engage to sell thrice as many copies as the Longmans ever did, even of 'Lalla Rookh.'" Very encouraging this, and comes seasonably to put me in better conceit with myself. In conversing with me afterwards, he intimated his strong wish that I should connect myself with the "Edinburgh Review." In talking of Walter Scott, and the author of "Waverley," he continually forgot himself, and made them the same person. Has had the original MS. of the novels presented to him by the author, in forty-nine volumes, written with his own hand; very few corrections. Says the author to his knowledge has already received more than a hundred thousand pounds for his novels alone. Walter Scott apparently very idle: the only time he is known to begin to study is about three hours in the morning before breakfast; the rest of the day he is at the disposal of everybody, and rarely retires at night till others do. Went with Constable and Bowles to Sir George Beaumont's. A curious picture by Paul Panini of the Picture Gallery of the Colonna Palace; fine bas-relief of the Virgin and two children by Michael Angelo. Raphael has borrowed this composition in one of his pictures. In talking of this, and saying that Raphael was not very scrupulous about plagiary, bringing for instance, his "Paul preaching at

Athens," which was borrowed from Masaccio, &c. &c., Sir George mentioned, that some great craniologist (Spurzheim it was) on examining Raphael's skull, had found nothing remarkable but the organ of *theft* very strongly developed. Received an opera ticket from Lady Lansdowne. Went early to the opera, "Donna del Lago;"[1] visited about through the boxes, Lord Lansdowne's, Lord Essex's, &c. &c. Lord L. told me that Mad. Renaudin sang very beautifully after I left Lady Jersey's last night; Miss Stephens, too, sang at Lady Farquhar's. This is what one loses by running about.

4th. [Wednesday] Breakfasted with Luttrel; Sandford came in; asked him (being of the Treasury) to get Bessy's china out of the custom-house of Dover for me; said he would if I wrote an application to him in *verse*, not otherwise; hardly worth this. Quoted from "Tristram Shandy" an amusing passage: "'Brother, will you go with me to see some dead bodies?' 'I am ready, brother, to go see any body?' 'But these bodies have been dead three thousand years.' 'Then, I suppose, brother, we need not *shave.*'"[1] Must see this passage. Luttrel read me part of a journal (a large volume) which he kept on his tour to Italy; seemed very clever. Thence to Longmans, and saw a rough memorandum of my account on the "Angels" and the "Fables;" much more satisfactory than I could have expected. They have very handsomely declined taking any thing to themselves beyond the mere commission, and accordingly have put to my credit 1000*l.* for the "Angels," and £500 for the "Fables," being exactly the sums I would have originally asked for the copyright of the respective works. This is doing very well in so few months; it, however, merely clears away my debt to them without giving me any supply in hand. Went to Drury Lane, and had some conversation with Dunn, the treasurer. Dined at Sir J. Farquhar's. Went to Almack's at night; full of beauty; sat awhile with the Barings, whom I like; Lady Jersey and Lady Tankerville sending various messengers after me through the room. Found it was for a dinner on the 15th, which Lady Tankerville wished to secure me for; but engaged. Some talk with Mrs. and Miss Canning. Lord John and I, reminding each other of our engagement to breakfast together in the morning, came away arm in arm, in order to be time enough, to the no small amusement of Mrs. Canning.

5th. [Thursday] With Lord John before eleven. Met Brougham and the Duke of Leinster on my way to him; Brougham going to Court, with his hair and beard fresh cut, "all shaven and shorn." Much talk with Lord John about my Sheridan work; how far I should venture in passing judgment on the political events of the time; better merely to draw my conclusions from the general and obvious features of every transaction, such as they appear on the surface of history, than, by attempting to trace negotiations or develop secret motives, run the risk of being falsified hereafter, when memoirs written by the actors themselves may appear, and prove that I was completely on the wrong scent in my conjectures. An instance of this in Mr. Fox's "History," where he attributes to Argyle at one period during his invasion of Scotland, what the publication of Sir P. Hume's "Memoirs" proves to have been completely unfounded. It is with respect to the attempt to release their friends who were prisoners, which Fox represents Argyle as anxious to undertake.[1] It is supposed that Adam has actually written memoirs of those political events in which Sheridan and himself were engaged, and they will appear after his death.[2] Lord John is about a work on the "Political History of Europe;"[3] showed me some verses he had written about "Love and the Marriage Act;" very good; suggested some alterations. Called upon Burdett; driven home to my garret. Sir G. Warrender called to say that he dined to-day exactly at six, on account of the opera. Afraid he should find out I was a *garretteer,* and return to his importunities; but they showed him into the parlour, the proprietor of which was not at home. Dinner, consisting of Mrs. Blackshaw and Lady Farquhar. Opera (for Camporese's benefit), "Ricciardo," by Rossini,[4] first time: several pretty things in it, but ill-performed; the *finale* of first act very good; the famous *cruda sorte* overrated.

6th. [Friday] Breakfasted at the George. Called upon Mrs. Story; upon Murray, to beg him to make out my account and arrange with him about discounting my bills on Power. Went to see the picture of the Queen's Trial, and happened to seat myself next Mr. Sheddon (my Bermuda friend), who looked a little awkward on finding me at his elbow; affected, however, to be very civil, and said that he had received from Bermuda *some* of the money he had advanced towards my release of the claims, adding, that he was trying to get more from the same quarter for *me: credat Judæus.* Called upon Dr. Williams; glad to see signs of more prosperity about him. Dined at Lord Lansdowne's: company, Lord and Lady Cawdor, Sir J. Mackintosh, &c. &c. Hume, lately, at some meeting, in referring to allegations made by some one who preceded him, called him the "honourable allegator." A notable receipt for *raising* Newtons in France, suggested by Beyle (the author of "Histoire de la Peinture en Italie," &c. &c.); *Pour avoir des Newtons, il faut sémer des Benjamin Constants.* Conversation about French words expressing meanings which we cannot supply from our own language, *verve* given as an instance. Whether the vagueness may not (instead of their definiteness) be the great convenience we find in them; just as Northcote, in looking at a picture, said "Yes, very good, very clever; but it wants, it wants (at last, snapping his fingers), damme, it wants *that.*" May not our use of *verve,* and such other words, be from the same despair of finding anything to express exactly what we mean? Suggested this, which amused them; but they stood up for *verve,* as more significant than the snap of the fingers. Mackintosh's test of what is more excellent in art, "That which pleases the greatest number of people," produced some discussion; differed with him; may be true, to a certain degree, of such a sensual art as music, but not of those for the enjoyment of which knowledge is necessary—painting, for instance, and poetry. In the latter, he adduced as examples, Homer and Shakspeare, which certainly for *universality* of pleasing are the best, and perhaps the only ones he could mention. Mackintosh quoted in praise what Canning said some nights before, in referring to Windham, "whose *illustrations* often survived the subjects to which they were applied." If he had said *stories* instead of illustrations, it would be more correct, though not so imposing: illustrations can no more survive their subjects than a shadow can the substance or a reflection the image; and as Windham's chief merit was *applying* old stories well, to remember the story without reference to its application, might be a tribute to Joe Miller, but certainly not to Windham. Instanced Sheridan's application of the story of the drummer to the subject of Ireland, when remarks were made upon the tendency of the Irish to complain. The drummer said to an unfortunate man, upon whom he was inflicting the cat-o'-nine-tails (and who exclaimed occasionally, "a little higher," "a little lower"), "Why, do what I will, there is no such thing as pleasing you." Would any one think that he paid a compliment either to Sheridan's wit or his own, by saying that the mere caricatures of this old story had survived in his memory the admirable application of them? Thus it is that the world is humbugged by phrases. Mackintosh said that Pitt's speeches are miserably reported. He was himself present at the speech on the Slave Trade in '92 (which Mr. Fox declared was the finest he had ever heard), and the report, he says, gives no idea whatever of its merits.[1] Burke's and Windham's the only speeches well reported; being given by themselves. Went from thence to Devonshire House, where there was very bad music; two new women, Castelli and Maranoni, execrable. The Duke, in coming to the door to meet the Duke of Wellington, near whom I stood, turned aside first to shake hands with me (though the great Captain's hand was waiting, ready stretched out), and said, "I am glad to see you here at last." A good deal of talk with Lady Normanton and Lady Cowper. The Duchess of Sussex, bantering me upon the two fine ladies she saw so anxious to get hold of me the other night at Almack's (Ladies Jersey and Tankerville), said that some one near her remarked, "See them now, it is all on account of his reputation, for they do not care one pin about him." While she spoke, Lord Jersey stood close beside her, and she was (or at least affected to be) much annoyed at finding that he had heard her. Sir Thomas Lawrence introduced me to Lady Waterford, who said we used to be acquainted, and asked me to her house on Monday night.

7th. [Saturday] Breakfasted at Stephens's. Met, on turning a corner, my old, excellent friend Douglas (the admiral). Promised to run down and see him at his country seat before I returned to Wiltshire. Called upon Mrs. Story; on Murray, to settle my accounts and talk over my Sheridan task. Tried to see Creevey on the same subject, as I hear he knew a good deal of S., but could not. Dined at Longmans', to meet Constable and Kenny. Thence to Drury Lane, and had some conversation with Wenston, the stage-manager, who is collecting materials for a "History of the Stage,"[1] and is likely to have something relating to Sheridan's connection with it. Promised me that I should look over his stores. Thence to the opera: Lady Lansdowne's box. In talking of a children's ball, lately given by Lady Jersey, she said, "How little Tom would have shown off there!" Must communicate this to Bess. To Mrs. Baring's box, where I found Prince Leopold, and was introduced to him: very gracious. Stayed in the Barings' box, after they left it, to see the ballet, till Lord Bective came, sent by my Lady, to take me across the house to her. Saw her out, and promised to go breakfast some morning.

8th. [Sunday] Breakfasted with Lord John. Well said by Bobus Smith, to those who were inclined to take part against Plunkett, in his late contest with the Orangemen, "Would you pull down the house to destroy a single rat?"[1] Lord John said that he had heard of Sheridan's having walked about for several hours with Fox, trying to dissuade him from the coalition with Lord North, and that the conversation ended with Fox's saying, "It is as fixed as the Hanover succession."[2] Called at Lady Donegal's. Drove out with Edward Moore, in his tilbury, to Lady Bective's. Her little Edward so reminds me of poor Dalton![3] Went thence to call on the Cannings at Glouces- ter Lodge (Moore driving about while I paid my visit). Canning himself engaged, but saw the ladies: Lord Kensington there. Told of his being with the King of Naples shooting larks; said he was in expectation that Lord Spencer (who was of the party, and is famous for bringing down either keepers or dogs, or some part of the company, whenever he shoots) would have *bagged the king*.[4] Took Moore to Chantrey's, who seems much broken by the illness of his wife. Some talk about the monument to Grattan, for which he is to be employed. Dined at Lord Lansdowne's: company, the Cowpers, the Tankervilles, Lords Essex, Caernarvon, J. Russell, Roslyn, Lauderdale, Bob Adair, Lambton, and myself. Went in the evening with

Lambton to see Lord Grey. No one there but Lord Fitzwilliam. A good deal of talk about the peculiarities of the late Duke of Norfolk.

9th. [Monday] Breakfasted with Newton, to meet Kenny. Sat a little for my picture. Took them to see Rogers's house; R. himself at home. A note from Lucy, to announce her arrival. Called upon her about two, and went with Mrs. Ogle and her to the Exhibition. Dined at Lord Essex's: company, Lord and Lady Jersey, Lord Auckland, and a whole family of Hibberts. Went to Lady Davy's: found them talking of Irving, the preacher; Tierney the only one who seemed not *quite* pleased with him.[1] Thence to Lady Waterford's, where I heard some good music: Ronzi, notwithstanding her thin reedy voice, very charming. The beautiful duet "Amor possente," well sung. Met several old Irish acquaintances; Sir Edward and Lady E. Baker, Sir J. Beresford, &c.

10th. [Tuesday] Breakfasted at Rogers's, to meet Luttrel, Lady Davy, Miss Rogers, and William Bankes, who gave, as an apology for his being late, a visit he had had before he was out of bed from the Dean of Winchester, in most pious alarm about Lord Nugent's bill for the relief of the Roman Catholics.[1] Rogers showed us "Gray's Poems" in his original handwriting, with a letter to the printer; also the original MS. of one of Sterne's sermons. Remarkable, in comparing this with the printed one, to see how he had spoiled a passage in correcting it; calling the Jews (instead of the "thoughtless and thankless people," as he had it at first), this "ungrateful and peculiarly obstinate people" (or "peculiarly perverse," I do not exactly recollect the printed words).[2] Went thence to the private view of Watson Taylor's pictures. Most remarkable, the "St. John" of Parmigiano (the price of which Holwell Carr traced to me from £120 to £7000), the brilliant landscape of Rubens, with the rainbow, two beautiful Hobbemas, a portrait by Murillo, Sir Joshua's "Mrs. Siddons as Tragic Muse." Thence with L. to Fetter Lane, &c. &c. Went to Murray's for my account. Not very correctly drawn out; left it to be revised; has not given me credit for the £200 I left in his hands on the "Memoir" account. Dined at Sir C. Douglas's: company, Sir P. Codrington, Lord Strathmore, &c. Taken in for an evening party, and obliged to sing. Miss Doyle, a very pretty girl (who was not in existence in those days when Doyle and I were cronies), sang some Spanish things very pleasingly. Ran away as soon as I could, to the opera. Reminded by Miss Canning of my promise to give her some songs of mine.

11th. [Wednesday] Breakfasted with Rogers; Kenny and Luttrel of the party. Witticisms of Foote. His saying to a canting sort of lady that asked him, "Pray, Mr. Foote, do you ever go to church?" "No, madam; not that I see any harm in it." Called on Bishop. Dined at Luttrel's: Lord Cowper, Sandford, and a Mr. Vincent. Went to Almack's.

12th. [Thursday] Breakfasted at Lady Donegal's. Went to W. Taylor's pictures. Phillips (the R. A.) going over the faults of some of the pictures: the light in the portrait by Murillo not falling as it would in nature; Rubens's rainbow not like a rainbow; no country ever half so blue, &c. &c. Agreed with him perfectly; but connoisseurship in painting is to me a "sealed fountain;" there seems to be no standard of merit in it but the *price*. Thought I was engaged to Agar Ellis for to-day, and refused every other invitation in consequence. Met him going into the picture-room, and he said, "Don't forget me this day week," which dispelled the illusion. Suddenly freed for the day; felt as if chains had fallen off me. This "pre-established harmony" of dinners, in which one is carried along so inevitably, day after day, becomes servitude at last. Thought of offering myself to the Lansdownes, but decided for Richardson's Coffee-house in Covent Garden. Previously went to the British Institution, to meet Henry Grattan, with whom I had appointed, for the purpose of talking over the "Life" of his Father, which he has been engaged about, but which he seems half inclined to transfer to me. There is no task I should feel greater pride in. Found I could not fix him to any thing.[1] Had a note from Hobhouse, saying it was the wish of the committee for the Spanish meeting to-morrow, that I should move or second one of the resolutions to be proposed. Went to Burdett's, where I found Hobhouse, and talked the matter over. The time too short now to prepare myself as I ought. It is not so much what one is to say, as what one is *not* to say, that requires consideration. Told them I would let them know in the morning.[2] After dining, dressed and went to Mrs. Ogle's. Thence, very late, to Lady Lansdowne's assembly. The gallery opened, and the effect of it very fine. Lady Cowper, who had asked me to dine for Thursday (when I am engaged), proposed Friday—Saturday; but bound for all. Lady Jersey, who stood by, said, "I have contrived to squeeze in a day." Some talk with Lord John about to-morrow. Mentioned to him my doubts whether it was quite in good taste for a person like me, neither a parliamentary man, nor a monied man, nor even a city man, to take any leading part in such a meeting. Did not quite agree with me, and I rather think the scruple *is* over-fastidious.

13th. [Friday] Breakfasted at home. Drove about with Lucy, and left my name at Peter Moore's, preparatory to my application to him for materials towards Sheridan's Life. In consequence of which found a note upon my table in coming home at night, beginning, "Mr. and the Miss Moores are happy to renew their acquaintance with Mr. Thomas Moore, and will be happy to see him and Mrs. Moore," &c. &c.; asking me for dinner to-morrow, or, if engaged, "to tea and supper" in the evening. Lucy said that at Miss Johnes's, in Portman Square, where I had called to inquire about her, the servant told her afterwards that a "young gentleman" had been there to ask for her. What a *take in* upon the servant! Went, at a quarter before one, to Mrs. T. Hope's ball. Insufferably hot, and every one panting for Vauxhall. Lord John told me the success of to-day's meeting. Regret now that I lost the opportunity. The resolutions were moved by Lord J., Mackintosh, Brougham, and Lynedoch, &c. &c. Away at two.

14th. [Saturday] Breakfasted with Rogers. Nobody but Kenny and Miss R. Story of a fellow who, upon being requested by a gentleman to carry his portmanteau from the boat, inquired his name, place of residence, &c. (as if for the purpose of performing the task), and then sent him a challenge for the insult.

15th. [Sunday] Breakfasted at home. Made some calls. Found Burdett limping about his garden. Expressed his regret at my not going to the meeting, and lamented the backwardness of the great Whigs, Lords Grey, Lansdowne, &c. on this occasion. Spoke highly of the honesty and straightforwardness of Lord John and the rest of the Russells. Lady Davy had offered me a seat in her pew to-day, to hear the great preacher, Irving. Called upon Edward Moore, whom I had asked to drive me out to Hornsey to-day. Drove to the Hornsey church-yard, and saw my dear Barbara's grave. Nothing amiss but the looseness of the headstone, from the dryness of the earth. Spoke to the gravedigger to look to it, and said I would send him something by Edward Moore in a few weeks. Drove on to the foot of Muswell Hill, to look at the cottage I inhabited there, the only one I do not again see with pleasure. Thence to Kensington Gardens, where we walked to see the gay crowd. Dined at Sir Humphrey Davy's: company, Mackintosh, Lord Archibald Hamilton, the Barings, &c. Mackintosh's ideas of the separation there exists (or should exist) between poetry and eloquence. Granted to me what I said (in talking of Bacon) that poetry is naturally connected with philosophy, but adding, "and eloquence with logic." Find, to my no small alarm, that Mackintosh did not get the note I sent to him at the Crown and Anchor, informing him of my intention not to assist, and enclosing five pounds as my subscription. Rather a serious loss, this. Had promised Lady Tankerville to go in the evening (not having been able to dine with her), but did not.

16th. [Monday] Breakfasted at Lord Bective's. Affected a good deal by little Edward's singing to me (before Lord and Lady B. made their appearance) a little tune which he had himself composed, to words written for him by his poor father, part of which were as follows:—

> "When I rise in the morning, I fervently pray
> To that God who protects me by night and by day,
> To bless my papa, *who's* in *heaven above*,
> And my dearest mama, whom I equally love."

Something particularly melancholy in this line, written as it was by poor Dalton, in anticipation of his approaching death—and such a death! Dined by myself at Richardson's, having set apart this day to pay a visit to my friend Douglas in Buckinghamshire, but not having been able to effect it. Went out before ten to the Storys', to join their party to Vauxhall: night very chilly, and the whole thing dull. Met Keene there, who gave me most enthusiastic greeting.

17th. [Tuesday] Breakfasted with Power, and went with him to call on Bishop: not at home. From thence to Moore's, the artist who sent me the portrait of my father: found that he had made a sketch of my mother, which he gave up on finding that my sister Kate did not like it: it, however, has a considerable degree of resemblance; and I requested him to finish it for me. Called at Charles Kemble's; found only her: fell down stairs in coming away, and strained my wrist. Dined at Lambton's, though scarcely able to dress, from the pain of my wrist, and totally without the power of cutting my meat at dinner. A strong political dinner: Lord Grey, Brougham, Hobhouse, Denman, S. Williams, Creevey, D. Kinnaird, &c.: some talk upon the Queen's business, which would have been interesting from such authorities (her three defenders),[1] but something turned it into another channel. Brougham seemed to think that she was not quite right in her head, and that the chief pivot her insanity turned upon was children. By this he accounted for the circumstance which Lady Douglas deposed to;[2] and most of which he believed to be. She was on the *point* of committing a folly upon this very same subject when she died, which would have exposed her to much obloquy. From a violent fancy she took to a child of young Wood's (the son of the Alderman), she was going to dismiss her valuable and most attached friends, Lord and Lady Hood, and put Wood and his wife in their places.[3] Asked Creevey to meet me at Rogers's on Saturday morning to breakfast: promised he would. Found a card, on my return home, from Canning, inviting me to dinner on Sunday next: had called this morning on Lord Essex to apologise for not going to Cashiobury on Saturday next (as I half promised) to stay till Monday; so shall accept Canning's invitation. Did not go to the opera.

18th. [Wednesday] To Bishop's, and gave him the things I had done for our great work. Went to Miss Linwood's exhibition. Dined at Lord Jersey's: company, Prince Esterhazy, the Morpeths, Granvilles, William Russells, and Morleys. Sat next Lady Wm. Russell. When I mentioned the story of the new opera (the "Freischütz"), which is making such a sensation in Germany, her look of enthusiasm, on remembering having read the story when she was young, became her prodigiously.[1] Am sorry, however, to perceive that the continent has weaned her a good deal from England: her indifference about the House of Commons, and ignorance of what is going on there, drew from Lady Jersey a very well applied story of Luttrel's, about a man from India, who, on hearing the House of Commons mentioned, said, "Oh, is that going on still?" Called, on my way from dinner, to inquire about Lady Donegal, who has had another nervous attack: found them just going to bed. Made Barbara sing two or three songs, for me to hear what sort of voice she has: very promising.

19th. [Thursday] Breakfasted with Rogers: only Kenny; Creevey did not come. Went with Kenny to hear him read his new piece to the actors at the Haymarket; rehearsal of "Figaro" going on: very amusing altogether.[1] Two lines in one of Kenny's songs for Liston rather amused me: talking of his hard-hearted mistress—

> "And when I kneel to sue for mercy,
> I meet with none—but wice-wersa."

My five-pound note has at last reached Mackintosh's hands, and is acknowledged among the list of Spanish subscriptions. Dreamt last night that I saw Bessy falling out of a gig; and find, from her letter, that she and Mrs. Phipps were to drive in our new pony carriage to-day to Buckhill: wrote to her (as indeed I had done before) to beg she would not drive out any more till my return. Dined at William Ponsonby's: company, the Bouveries, Lord Besborough, Payne Knight, Sir T. Lawrence, Dibdin (the bibliographer), Heber, Wm. Spencer, &c. &c. Sat next to Lady Davy, and told her of her friend Lord Dudley, that (though I was not very apt to suspect such things) it struck me that when I met him walking with the Duke of Wellington yesterday his bow to me was more shy and evasive than usual. She said this was not like him, and could not be the case; so probably I was mistaken. Told me that when my "Angels" appeared, she had a letter from him, saying that he was happy at last to see something of mine exhibiting higher powers of writing than he had been in general inclined to allow me. This confirmation of a suspicion which I have always had, that Lord Dudley holds but a mean opinion of my talents, is, of course, not calculated to lessen much the distaste which I own I have (notwithstanding many efforts to the contrary) invariably felt towards him. I am not given to dislike people, and therefore tried hard to be pleased with him; but it would not do. Wm. Spencer, as usual, amusing. Knight mentioned what old Lady Townshend used to say about her son's anxiety to trace the antiquity of his family; that he ought to be prouder to have sprung from the loins of old Roger Townshend than from Chilperic, King of the Franks. Had received a note from Lady Dacre two or three days ago, asking me this evening; and at the same time begging me to fix a day to dine with them; adding, with very skilful flattery, "you must excuse my worrying you in this way; I do not so much run after the *poet* for my own self as the *patriot* for Lord Dacre."

20th. [Friday] Breakfasted with Lord John, who seems to have nearly made up his mind to go to Ireland with me. The party promises most agreeably: we are to join the Lansdownes at Killarney; Lord Kenmare has invited us to make his house our quarters; and the Cunliffes, who are also going, expect us to pay them a visit in our way through Wales. Went to Power's; to Longmans'. Called at Charles Kemble's, and saw the Miss Siddonses; himself at the theatre; went there, having heard that he is anxious to show me a piece from the Spanish, which he thinks might be made something of. It is called "Figlia dell' Aria," which sounds romantic; but turns out to be the story of Semiramis; and the machinery, Venus and Diana, &c. &c.; what poor Lewis used to call "the tag, rag, and bobtail of the classics;" won't do. Went with E. Moore to look after a house in a little passage of Pall Mall, whose top windows look into the Park, and which may be had, he says, for forty guineas a year; begged him to inquire further about it. Dined at Alex. Baring's: company, Brougham, Lord Dudley, Adair, Lord John Russell, &c. Struck with the difference between Brougham and Lord D.; the former so natural, the latter so painfully artificial: the one, a vast Niagara of intellect, overflowing for ever, in spite of itself, from a thousand reservoirs; the other, like the cascades in his own neighbourhood at Hagley, got up ostentatiously for the occasion, artificial in his liveliest flow, and making up by preparation and dexterity for the shallowness and penury of his supply. These latter terms, I, of course, use as comparing his powers with those of Brougham; for that Lord D. is no ordinary man, with all my distaste to him, I must allow. A good deal of talk about law; its contradictions and unintelligibleness; how far it would be practicable to get rid of these absurdities; the danger that would arise to property from any change in its forms; various suggestions for this purpose. Remarks upon the system of *registering* the conveyance of property, which exists in Scotland, and in Yorkshire, and Middlesex; preference people have for estates in *register* counties. Yet Blackstone is against the extension of this plan, as he thinks more disputes arise from the inattention of parties, &c. &c., than are produced by the want of registers. Went from thence to Lady Cowper's, where were the Lansdownes, Jerseys, Morpeths, &c.; some talk with Lord Cowper. Left with the Agar-Ellises, who set me down at Lady Cork's. Had not been two minutes in the room before Lady Cork came to me with the (junior) Duchess of Rutland, entreating me to sing. Begged a little respite, under the pretence of having run and put myself out of breath; and the moment they left me, actually *did* run; making altogether about three minutes and a half that I was in the house. A letter from Bessy to-day, to say, that in spite of my dream, she had got very safely and pleasantly over her drive.

21st. [Saturday] Have drawn from Murray £120 of the £300 bill upon Power at six months, which he has discounted for me. Went to the Greek Committee; Hume in the chair; hardly any answers to the 2000 letters they have sent about to solicit subscriptions; no feeling in the country on the subject. Hume begged me to put some papers about Napoli di Romania, &c., which he gave me, into a proper form for publication. Called, by appointment, on Constable; long conversation with him; most anxious that I should come to Edinburgh; and promises that I shall prosper there. The "Review" (he told me in confidence) is sinking; Jeffrey has not time enough to devote to it; would be most happy to have me in his place; but the resignation must come from himself, as the proprietors could not propose it to him. Jeffrey has £700 a year for being editor, and the power of drawing £2800 for contributors. Told him that I could not think of undertaking the editorship under £1000 a year, as I should, if I undertook it, devote myself almost entirely to it, and less than £1000 would not pay me for this. He seemed to think that if Jeffrey was once out of the way, there would be no difficulty about terms; read me a letter he had just received from his partner on the subject, in which he says, "Moore is out of all sight the best man we could have; his name would revive the reputation of the 'Review;' he would continue to us our connection with the old contributors, and the work would become more literary and more regular; but we must get him gradually into it; and the first step is to persuade him to come to Edinburgh." All this (evidently not intended to be seen by me) is very flattering.

22nd. [Sunday] Called upon Edward Moore to ask him for the use of his tilbury in dispatching two or three calls. Before driving out, had gone with Moore to Warwick Chapel, where we heard the latter part of the service, and most solemn and touching it was. It seemed to come with more effect over me, after the restless and feverish life I have been leading; and brought tears instantly from the very depths of my heart. Music is the true interpreter of the religious feelings; nothing written or spoken is equal to it. Took my place in the Regulator coach for Tuesday morning. Had a note yesterday from Lady Holland (they having just returned from Paris) to ask me to sleep there to-night and stay over to-morrow. Sent out my clothes, with a note to say I would sleep, and would breakfast there in the morning, but could not stay to-morrow. Made an arrangement with a hackney coach to take me out to Gloucester Lodge, and from thence to Holland House at night. Took Chinnery with me. Arrived first, and found Mrs. and Miss Canning, with whom (and Canning himself, who joined us soon) I had some agreeable conversation. In talking with Miss Canning about girls reputed clever, mentioned the Miss Copley I met the other day; "You will see her at dinner," she said. Company, Lord Melville, Sir Joseph Copley and his two daughters, Lord Hervey, Lord Kensington, Lady Caroline Wortley, and Stuart Wortley himself, who (among other disagreeable things about him) took the seat next Miss Canning, which was intended by her for me. Sat next Lord Melville, who did not condescend to say a word to me, until he heard my name mentioned, then became very civil and communicative. Dinner altogether rather flat; though I now and then caught a sly thing said by Canning, who was at a distance from me. When we went up to coffee, took an opportunity of asking C. whether what Dennis O'Brien had told me of his sending £100 to Sheridan (in consequence of an application from the latter, a short time before his death) was true. Said it was; that soon after his return to England, S. sent him (I believe to the House of Commons) a draft upon him for £100 to be accepted, which, upon learning the state Sheridan was in, he did.[1] Sat down together on the sofa, and had a good deal of talk about S.; said he had always thought that S. was the author of the Prince's famous letter about the Regency; and even remembers, though a boy at the time, hearing some passages of it from Sheridan before it appeared; though this might have happened without its being actually written by him. Agreed with me that it was in a chaster style of composition than he usually adopted; though in the passage, "that an experiment should be made in my person," &c. &c. seemed to think there were traces of Sheridan's finery; never understood it was by Sir Gilbert Elliot.[2] S. did nothing good for many, many years before his death; the passage in his speech about Bonaparte, "Kings were his sentinels," &c., wretched stuff;[3] said he seemed to have been spoiled by "Pizarro." Was sure that he might have come in advantageously with Lord Sidmouth, and believes that an offer was made him to that effect. What makes his resistance to this more meritorious was, that he totally differed with the Whigs on the subject of Lord S., and thought that they ought to have joined him, as the only means of keeping out Pitt.[4] Altogether found Canning very communicative and amiable. Showed, as a specimen of the progress of the arts in Sierra Leone, an attempt at a female figure, a sort of parody on the Venus de Medici, with a long neck like a corkscrew, and every thing else most grotesque and comical. Said that Wilberforce gazed on it with delight. On my taking leave, he begged I would ascertain whether he was at home whenever I came to London. Arrived at Holland

House a little after eleven, and found only my Lord and Lady, and Allen. Lady H. told me she had found the sister of the late Duc de Richelieu (Madame de Jumillac, I think) busily employed in translating my "Loves of the Angels." Lord John arrived soon after me, and after him Lord and Lady William, who had been at the Duchess of Kent's, where they met all the princesses. Some conversation, and to bed.

23rd. [Monday] Conversation at breakfast upon the peculiarity of Frere's humour. Lord W. Russell directed my attention to an order from the Horse Guards in to-day's newspaper, beginning thus: "His Majesty has been graciously pleased to approve of the discontinuance of breeches," &c. Came away between twelve and one; called at Lord Listowel's in my way; anxious that I should dine there to-day to meet the Bectives, but could not. Went about various commissions. Forgot to mention that two or three days ago Dr. Williams called upon me, and insisted on repaying the ten Napoleons I lent him in Paris, which tells well for the state both of his morals and his purse. Dined at Story's at seven; Newton of the party. Left with him; doubting whether I should go home, pack up, and to bed for two or three hours; or give up sleep for the night entirely, as I must be up so early. Determined on the latter, and agreed to meet him at Richardson's to supper at twelve. In the interval he went to the British Gallery and I to the Haymarket. Home at half-past one, chilly and sleepy; continued packing till three, when I lay down for an hour.

24th. [Tuesday] Off in the coach at six; a very pretty person of the party. Arrived at Calne a little after five, and expected to find our new carriage (as Bessy promised) in waiting for me. Set off to walk home; met our man William on the way, who told me that the carriage could not come on account of something that was the matter with the harness. Sent him on to Calne, and walked home, which I found rather fatiguing after my sleepless night. Met by Bessy at the·door, looking very ill, and her face and nose much disfigured; upon inquiry the secret came out, that on Sunday evening (the evening before last), she and Mrs. Phipps and Tom drove out in the little carriage (which Bessy herself had driven two or three times before), and in going down by Sandridge Lodge the pony, from being bitten, they think, by a forest-fly, set off galloping and kicking, without any possibility of being reined in, threw them all into a ditch, ran off with the carriage to Bromham, and knocked both it and himself almost to pieces. Much shocked and mortified, though grateful to God that it had not been worse. Bessy, in protecting little Tom in her arms, came with her unlucky nose to the ground, which is much swollen, though (as Dr. Headly says, who has seen it) not broken. The rest of the party escaped with some bruises. What a strange coincidence with my dream! It was a great effort for me to compass the expense of this little luxury; and such is the end of it.

25th, 26th, &c. to July 5th. [Wednesday, Thursday; 5 July: Saturday] It is needless to note each particular day, as all are alike. The horse-doctor gives hopes of the pony's recovery, and the carriage is to be made as good as new for two guineas. Took to reading over the Sheridan papers, and preparing myself to resume my task; shall take it up at the trial of Hastings. Read Mill's History over again; Burke's speeches, &c. &c.; and, after dinner and supper, got through a very pretty novel with Bessy, called the "Favourite of Nature." There is another (called "Osmond") by the same author, which she has read during my absence, and was much affected by it.[1] Wrote one or two songs for Power; "Slumber, oh slumber," "There is a bleak desert;" and sent him up what I had written before, "The halcyon hangs o'er ocean."[2]

July 6th and 7th. [Sunday–Monday] Received a letter from Lord John to say that he must give up his intention of going with me to Ireland, on account of Lord Tavistock's precarious state of health; but begging me not to mention this as his reason. A sad disappointment, and changes the aspect of my journey considerably.[1]

8th. [Tuesday] Bowles called; made him stay dinner. Quoted this odd passage from an article of Sidney Smith's in the "Edinburgh Review:" "The same passion which peoples the parsonage with chubby children animates the Arminian, and burns in the breast of the Baptist." Recommended Mosheim's account of the first age of Christianity as a more interesting work than his "Ecclesiastical History."[1] Much talk about the Establishment, after dinner, and the attacks now made upon it. Said that the Calvinism of one of the Articles is considerably neutralised by another that followed it (the 16th I believe); accounts for the introduction of the Athanasian Creed by the necessity under which the Reformers found themselves of answering the objection made to them by the Catholics, that they were about to get rid of Christ and the Trinity altogether; the same motive influenced Calvin in burning Servetus; denied that the Church had shown itself hostile to liberty, and instanced the spirited conduct of Magdalen College and Dr. Hough in their contest with James II., which Mr. Fox, he said, had not done justice to.[2] A thorough Churchman. Bowles, and his efforts at liberality both on politics and religion, quite diverting from their abortiveness. Asked me to meet the Ricardos at dinner on Friday.

9th. [Wednesday] Promised to dine with the Phippses on Saturday, to meet a large party whom they have invited.

10th. [Thursday] Bowles arrived while we were at breakfast, to say the Ricardos have fixed Saturday instead of Friday; very amusing in his agonies and exclamations, when he found I was already tied to the Phippses. Promised, however, if he could not put off the Ricardos, to come to him on Saturday.

11th. [Friday] Reading and scribbling. Have begun to *write* about Sheridan; take him up at the trial of Hastings, for which I have prepared myself by reading all the books I have on the subject over again. A note from Bowles to say the dinner is to be to-morrow.

12th. [Saturday] Went to Phipps's at one, and found the Miss Walkers and their mama and brother; sung a good deal, and so did the girl; some of my duets she did very prettily with me. Left them at four in tremendous rain (the Walkers having lent me their carriage) to go to Bowles's. Company at dinner,—Mr. and Mrs. Clutterbuck, and Mr. and Mrs. Ricardo; the women very pretty and amiable. Mrs. R. is more than pretty, and may be called lovely; her manners, too, very agreeable. Bore chiefly the *frais* of the conversation at dinner. After dinner sung, and was joined by Mrs. R. in a duet or two. Slept at Bowles's.

13th. [Sunday] A letter which Hughes produced from his son at breakfast mentioned a work of Dr. Routh's upon the "Fathers of the Middle Ages," which puzzled Bowles and me a good deal.[1] Looked over the "Chronological Catalogue" at the end of Mosheim's History; was surprised to find that I knew somewhat more of many of these ecclesiastical Worthies than my reverend friend. Bowles showed me some verses written upon Bells in Nares's "Dictionary"[2] (article, Clamour) which, he said, first made him in love with poetry when he was a child. Begged him to come and christen our young one, which he promised to do on Monday. Said he would choose for his text to-day my words, "Fallen is thy throne, O Israel,"[3] which I sung last night, and which is one of his greatest favourites. Told him I believed these words were not in Scripture, and that he had better not venture to make them his text. He, however, introduced them thus (for he preaches always extempore):—After quoting "By the waters of Babylon,"[4] he said, "Such was the pathetic song of the Jews when they mourned over their lost country; but a still more pathetic song might be founded on that period, when they saw their temple itself destroyed, &c., and when they might say, 'Fallen is thy throne, O Israel.'" He introduced this line more than once. Left him in a chaise at two, and called at Bowood to see Lady Lansdowne, who is some days arrived; found her at dinner with the children. By the by, Mr. Bowles copied out those pretty lines of his for me from Miss Bailey's "Miscellany," "When last I saw thee, thou wert young and fair," which he wrote to the lady whom he was so violently in love with when he composed his first sonnets, and went abroad in despair of not being able to marry her from the narrowness of their circumstances.[5] I was with him at Bath when he saw her for the first time after an interval of thirty years, and when the lines in Miss Bailey's book were written. Went over to Awdrey in the evening to ask him to stand as proxy for Lord John to-morrow. A very pretty letter from Lady Donegal, giving me instructions as to what I am to see at Killarney.

14th. [Monday] Awdrey breakfasted with us; and Bowles arrived soon after. The little fellow baptized "John Russell."

15th. [Tuesday] Writing some of the "Sheridan;" and reading. Received another translation of the "Loves of the Angels" by a Madame Belloc, with a most flattering letter from herself, and a most laudatory preface to the translation;[1] also a letter from Mrs. Hutchinson in the same packet, informing me that Madame Belloc, besides being so clever, is young and pretty. Madame Belloc says that there are two other persons employed in translating the "Angels" into verse.

16th. [Wednesday] Walked over to Bowood, and saw Lord L., who arrived last night, and means to be off to Ireland on Friday; said that he had not yet arranged his plan of operations, but would let me know them before he went away.

17th. [Thursday] Received after dinner a most kind letter from Lord L., telling me that if I would join him at Killarney or Kenmare any time between the 1st and the 10th, he would ensure me at the latter place such accommodation as the *locale* afforded, and I should find him in a good inn at the former; that from thence he could manage to bring me as far as Limerick, where we should part till he reached Dublin, from which place he would bring me back home into Wiltshire. A splendid present of fruit came with the note, for Bessy. Sent me also Baron Fain's book about Napoleon.[1]

18th. [Friday] Tried over the Spanish music sent me by Mr. Quin; the "Canciones Patrioticas" (which he pronounces to be the best) very common stuff. Found, however, three pretty *tirannas*. Read and wrote.

20th. [Sunday] Employed in copying out what I have written about Sheridan this week past, and what I wrote before I went abroad about his speeches in Parliament.

21st. [Monday] Writing letters and making preparations for my departure to-morrow. Bessy much saddened and out of sorts at my leaving her for so long a time; but still most thoughtfully and sweetly preparing every thing comfortable for me.

22nd. [Tuesday] Dined at two; and at half-past three set off in a chaise for Bath, taking my dear Anastasia with me, to leave her again at her school: arrived between six and seven; and having deposited her at Miss Furniss's, went to the White Hart. Saw, in walking through Bath, the new cantos of "Don Juan;"[1] bought a copy of the shilling edition; also a number of "Cobbett," and two numbers of the "Literary Examiner."[2] Supped at nine, and read, with my brandy-and-water, two of the cantos: some pretty things in the first; but altogether there is a falling off, both poetically and ethically.

23rd. [Wednesday] Off at a quarter-past seven, in the coach, for Birmingham: an old gentleman my only companion for the greater part of the way. Read my "Cobbett," which was very amusing; then my "Examiner;" then began "Read's Tour through Ireland." Arrived at Birmingham about eight; went to the Hen and Chickens; thence to the play, where I saw "Simpson and Co." Supped: a very bad inn; wretched bed: hate Birmingham altogether.

24th. [Thursday] Disappointed of a place in the mail, by which means I lose a day; obliged to go by the coach. Met Moore of Birmingham (my old music-meeting acquaintance), who invited me most earnestly and kindly to their approaching festival. Set off in the coach at eleven; lucky enough to find in it Casey, the Irish barrister, whom I found very agreeable the whole way. Arrived at Shrewsbury at five; thought it better to go on in a chaise to Oswestry, and let the coach take us up there in the morning. Dined at Oswestry at nine, and finished a bottle of strong port between us.

25th. [Friday] On the arrival of the coach, found that, from some mistake with respect both to Casey's place and mine, we were to be forwarded together in a chaise. A *third* person was attempted to be put in with us; but upon Casey's making serious lawyer-like speeches on the subject, they were forced to give in, and we set off comfortably together in the chaise: a good deal of conversation all the way. Curran, in speaking of Baron Smith's temper, and the restraint he always found himself under in his company, said, "I always feel myself, when with Smith, in the situation of poor Friday when he went on his knees to Robinson Crusoe's gun, and prayed it not to go off suddenly and shoot him." Story of an Irish fellow refusing to prosecute a man who had beaten him almost to death on St. Patrick's night, and saying that he let him off "in honour of the night." Of his overhearing two fellows talking about Lord Cornwallis when he was going in state to the theatre of Dublin; and accounting for his not going early by the fear of being pelted. "True enough," says one of them, "a two-year old paving-stone would come very nately to *compose* his other eye" (Lord C. having a defect in one of his eyes).[1] Assistant barrister keeping an old woman in jail, and having her up now and then (always sending her back again upon some excuse or other), in order to prolong the commission, and continue his pay. Examination of a witness:—"What's your name?" &c. &c. "Did you vote at the election?" "I did, sir.—" "Are you a freeholder?" "I'm not, sir."—"Did you take the freeholder's oath?" "I did, sir."—"Who did you vote for?" "Mr. Bowes Daly, sir."—"Were you bribed?" "I was, sir."—"How much did you get?" "Five guineas, sir."—"What did you do with it?" "I spint it, sir."—"You may go down." "I will, sir." Bowes Daly, upon being told this, said it was all true except the fellow's having got the money. Of an aid-de-camp, during an expedition of the lawyers' corps into the county Wicklow, riding up to ask the reason of a halt; they made answer by some one, "It is the law's delay;" and upon the corps being ordered to take ground to the right, one of them saying, "Here now, after having aired my mud, I am obliged to go into damp wet." Story of Keller answering some one who came into court to look for Gould, having searched him everywhere without being able to find him, *Aurum irrepertum et sic melius positum.* Dined at Bangor; and slept at that most disagreeable of all inns, Spencer's, at Holyhead.

26th. [Saturday] Sailed in the Ivanhoe; took to my berth and peppermint lozenges, but felt deadly sick all the way. Came in a chaise (Casey and I), from Howth, and broke down when near Dublin; got into a jaunting-car, and arrived at Casey's, where I dined. Never shall forget the welcomeness of his good mutton broth, to which was added some very old port, and an excellent bottle of claret. Went afterwards in a hackney-coach to Abbey Street. Found my dearest father and mother watching for me at the window; my mother not looking so well as when I last saw her, but my father (though, of course, enfeebled by his great age) in excellent health and spirits. Sweet little Nell, too, quite well. Called at Bilton's Hotel, to inquire after the Lansdownes; and found that Lady L. had been very ill and in her bed for two or three days past.

27th. [Sunday] Called upon Lord L. Asked me to dine with him at Franks's (his agent's) to-morrow, but am engaged to Casey; promised to dine with him on Tuesday. Dined at home, and walked about a little in the evening.

28th. [Monday] My mother expressing a strong wish to see Lord Lansdowne, without the fuss of a visit from him, I engaged to manage it for her. Told him that he must let me show him to two people who considered *me* as the greatest man in the world, and him as the next, for being my friend. Very good-naturedly allowed me to walk him past the windows, and wished to call upon them; but I thought it better thus. Dr. Percival having declared Lady L. fit to travel, they intend to start on Wednesday, and will give me a seat in the carriage with them. Went and bought a travelling cloak, as Jupiter Pluvius still continues his operations. Called upon Lady Morgan, who is about to publish a Life of Salvator Rosa;[1] has heard that Lord L. has some Salvators, and wishes to know the particulars of them. Walked about with Corry. Dined at Casey's: company, Tickell, Hare, the Fellow, Corry, and some others. Forget to mention that Casey, during my journey, mentioned to me a parody of his on those two lines in the "Veiled Prophet"—

> "He knew no more of fear than one, who dwells
> Beneath the tropics, knows of icicles."[2]

The following is his parody, which I bless my stars that none of my critics were lively enough to hit upon, for it would have stuck by me:—

> "He knew no more of fear than one, who dwells
> On Scotia's mountains, knows of knee-buckles."

On my mentioning this to Corry, he told me of a remark made upon the "Angels," by Kyle, the Provost, which I should have been equally sorry any of my critics had got hold of:—"I could not help figuring to myself," says

Kyle, "all the while I was reading it, Tom, Jerry, and Logic *on a lark from the sky.*" Few such lively shots from our University. Dinner not very agreeable, owing chiefly to the Fellow, who mentioned the great increase that has taken place since my time in the number of the students; and seems to think that the outpouring of such a portion of cultivated intellect upon society will produce rather a dangerous swell in the public mind (not his words). Corry and I went afterwards to the theatre, to join my father and mother and Nell, whom Harris has made free of the house, to their very great pleasure and delight, particularly my dear father's, who told me, in his playful way, that he was so fond of it, he had some idea of going on the stage himself. Went behind the scenes with Abbot. He and Corry came home and supped with us. Saw this morning a poor fruit-woman on the steps of a door, eating her own currants; while another who was passing by and observed her said, "That's *one* way of carrying on trade."

29th. [Tuesday] Paid visits to Mrs. Smith, &c. &c. Saw Henry Webster, who told me Lord Wellesley would like to see something of me before I left Ireland, and bade me leave my name at the Castle; which I did. Dined at Lord Lansdowne's: company, Corry, Charles Fox, Henry Webster, and Franks. Lord L. mentioned an epigram, comparing some woman, who was in the habit of stealing plants, with Darwin; the two last lines were—

> "Decide the case, Judge Botany I pray;
> And his the laurel be, and hers the *Bay.*"

30th. [Wednesday] Off at half-past seven; we in the open carriage, with four horses, and the valet and Lady L.'s maid in the chariot with a pair after us. The pretty cottages in the neighbourhood of Lord Mayor's Place, near Johnstown, very creditable to him. Fine Gothic window at Castle Dermott-Geraldine. The river Barrow, from Carlow, rather pretty; remembered the Irish poet's lines to it:—"Wheel, Barrow, wheel thy winding course." Dined and slept at Kilkenny, at our old club-house, now turned into an inn. Went with Lord and Lady L. to see the Castle, whose thick walls, and deep windows, and tapestry, delighted her exceedingly. The man, in showing us the country from the top of the tower, said, "That house belongs to rich Maguire, who is very poor and distressed." Walked with Lord L. about the town, and recollected the days of my courtship, when I used to walk with Bessy on the banks of the river; looked into Cavenagh's, where she and her mother and sister lived, and where we used to have so many snug dinners from the club-house. Happy times! but not more happy than those which I owe to the same dear girl still. Fine round tower annexed to the Cathedral.

31st. [Thursday] Ran to the post-office before starting, to know if there were any letters for Lord L. or me; post-master answered, "I am sure there are not, sir; being two such great public characters, if there had been any I should have remarked them." Saw at Collan, for the first time in my life, some real specimens of Irish misery and filth; three or four cottages together exhibiting such a naked swarm of wretchedness as never met my eyes before. The ruined house of Killcash, on the road, that once belonged to a Mr. Buller, struck me both from the appropriateness of its name (Killcash), and the dreary, shaven look of the country round it: not a bush left standing. These recent ruins tell the history of Ireland even more than her ancient ones. A line of mountains all along the way. Knocklofty a very gentlemanlike-looking place, and its vicinity comfortable and creditable. Read in the Road-Book the following euphonious designation: "Mr. Clutterbuck, of Killgroggy." Arrived at Lismore Castle to dinner; received by the duke's agent, Col. Currie, who, with his family, lives in the Castle. My old acquaintances, Dean and Mrs. Scott, came to dinner. The Lansdownes being strangers to all these people, the evening passed rather tamely. Mrs. S. told some Irish stories. One, of a conversation she overheard between two fellows about Donelly, the Irish champion: how a Miss Kelly, a young lady of fine behaviour, had followed him to the Curragh, to his great battle, and laid her gold watch and her coach and six that he would win; and that when Donelly, at one time, was getting the worst of it, she exclaimed, "Oh, Donelly, would you leave me to go back on foot, and not know the hour?" on which he rallied, and won. How the Duke of Wellington said to Donelly, "I am told you are called the hero of Ireland;" "Not the hero, my Lord, but only the champion." Walked with Col. Currie before dinner to the school, and heard the boys examined. He has succeeded in removing the objections of the Catholic priest to the introduction of the Bible, which is one of the great obstacles to schools in other places. Part of this Castle supposed to be the rooms which Sir W. Raleigh inhabited when commissioner for the government of Munster. Some talk next morning with Currie about the country. Is surmounting a good deal the objections to the Scotch plough; the potatoes about here planted in the English way; 40s. freeholders the great curse of the country; no getting rid of them; nobody would incur the unpopularity of a proposal to disfranchise so large a portion of the population; such a change would remove one of the chief objections to Catholic emancipation.[1]

August 1st. [Friday] Intended to have gone down the Blackwater, from Cappoquin to Youghal, but could not, on account of the violent rain. Took to the close carriage. Found luncheon prepared for us at the College at

Youghal, another house of the Duke's. Got into the open carriage again at Middleton. Youghal an interesting-looking place: saw some pretty faces out of the windows there, which were a rarity. The approach to Cork by Glanmire magnificent; a sort of sea avenue up to the town, with beautiful banks on each side, studded over with tasteful villas; gives a "note of preparation," however, which Cork itself by no means comes up to. Drove to Conway's, and dined and slept.

2nd. [Saturday] O'Driscoll, author of the "Views of Ireland,"[1] came to breakfast; left him and Lord L. together, and walked out. Went to the booksellers', Edwards and Savage; bought a travelling map of Ireland; told me there was not much demand for books, and that their chief gain was by other articles, stationery, &c., &c. One of them went with me to the Commercial Rooms, where I read the papers. There is another institution called the Chamber of Commerce, a sort of secession, on political grounds, from this; the Chamber of Commerce the liberal one. Purchased a book of Orange, or "Williamite," songs, at a little shop, where the man told me that the Williamites had much increased; confirmed to me by Edwards, who said that some Orange Lodges, dormant since the year '98, had lately been revived. Find since, that Edwards and Savage were Orangemen themselves. The Tithes Leasing Bill not acted upon, as no landlords will venture to be responsible for the tithes of their tenantry.[2] A specimen of the good to be effected by the linen manufacture evident at Dingle, where, on one side of the bay, all is comfort in consequence of it, and on the other side, all is misery without it. Have heard since, however, that the manufacture there is on the decline. Walked about with Hickson, the brother of Lord Lansdowne's agent. On my mentioning to him what has been dinned into my ears all along about Lord L.'s being a bad landlord, he said, "If there be the least ground for that assertion, believe me, it must be the agent's fault alone; as never was there a representation made by my brother, with respect to the propriety of reductions or allowances, that Lord Lansdowne did not promptly assent to them." Was rejoiced to hear this, as it has all along vexed and puzzled me to hear such imputations cast upon one whom I know to be so just and humane. Went to the Dyke Walk, which is one of the best ornaments of the town. Afterwards with Lord L. to Beamish and Crauford's brewery; had the whole explained; thence to the Institution, where a relative of Davy and of the same name is the acting person. A poor display of Cork science: among the curiosities is the jack-boot of a French postilion! O'Driscoll and Hickson dined with us. In talking of the state of the country, O'Driscoll asserted that there was a regular organisation among the lower orders all over the south; that their oath was only "to obey orders," and that instructions came from Dublin; that their objects were chiefly to get rid of their landlords and establish the Catholic religion. This, though coming from such authority, appeared to me exaggerated and incredible. Took leave of Lord and Lady L. who start for Kenmare in the morning, where, if I can, I shall join them about the end of the week.

3rd. [Sunday] The Lansdownes set off before I was up. Received a petition, in prose and verse, from a drunken scribbler of Cork, who signs himself "Roderick O'Conner, the last of all the Bards," and in one sense of the phrase, truly so. The following are some of his lines:—

> "Which has more renown,
> Moore or Lansdowne,
> One a coronet—t'other a laurel crown?
> Needy and poor, I come to Moore;
> Romantic author of 'Lalla Rookh,'
> On thy bard with pity look."

Sent the "last of all the bards" five shillings. Set off in the steamboat for Cove (to see my sister Kate Scully) between ten and eleven. Saw the view to more advantage there than before, as the Glanmire side, which is the most beautiful, was now brought into the picture, with its fine seats, Demkittle, Lotabeg, Lotamore, Lota, &c. &c.; Amethyst Rock on the opposite bank. Shown a house held on the King's life, the proprietor of which cannot insure the royal life; such insurance being forbid by the law, as coming, I suppose, under the charge of compassing and imagining "the King's death." Saw Smith Barry's flag flying on his tower, and was told his fortune is rated at £40,000 a year; this Orange gentleman left his card for me at Cork. Some gentleman aboard the boat inquired with anxiety how long I meant to remain at Cork on my return, as it was the intention of the inhabitants, they said, to pay me some public tribute, if I would allow them the opportunity. Arrived at Cove about half-past twelve. Walked with Mr. Mark (a gentleman who introduced himself to me in the boat) to see Mrs. Conner's cottage, which is very high, and commands a fine view of the Harbour. Spike Island (in fortifying which, £1,100,000 having been laid out, it was found at last this expenditure was all useless, as the island is commanded by another point); Magazine Rock (in whose excavations below the sea powder is kept), &c. &c. Kate and her husband received me with much delight; she quite well and grown fat; John not so well. About two, we all embarked aboard the steamboat to take a cruise up the Carrigaline river, whose windings are very pretty; went up as far as Mr. Newnham's fishing cottages. John Scully disbelieves O'Driscoll's account of the organisation of the people; says it is merely a war of the poor against rich; condemns the new Tithe Bill, as tending, if it was enforced, to the clergy a greater burden than ever; the omission, however, of the compulsory clause, has fortunately rendered it a nullity. Is contented with the laws about tithe as they are, if the poor people could only enforce them by obliging the parson to take his tithe in kind; means of course, that they might be embarrassed in this process, so as to leave them but little gain or comfort. The cotters, however, are too poor to enter into conflict with the parson; besides, the latter always has them in his power by holding over their heads those notes which they pass to him for their tithes from year to year. The valuators never will let the people know their demand upon them till the corn is actually in. A ship, called the "Barrosa," now in the harbour, to take out 300 settlers to the Cape of Good Hope; the only one, besides the Admiral's, now at Cove. John remarked upon the misnomer of *settlers* applied to the Irish, who are always un-settling both at home and abroad. Walked with John and Kate in the evening; all the *fashionables* abroad; had to stand such broadsides of staring, as disconcerted even me, used as I am. 'Twas the same yesterday in Cork; and amusing enough to see, when I walked with Lord Lansdowne, how distracted the good people's attention was between the peer and the poet; the former, however, as usual, had the best of it. Slept at a very comfortable little inn kept by a widow woman.

4th. [Monday] After breakfasting with Kate and John, set off in the steam-boat for Cork; the day tolerably fine, and the view magnificent. A great pity there is not some fine architecture to meet the eye at the bottom of this approach; if they had turned the new custom-house, with a handsome façade, towards the water, it would have enriched the scene incalculably. Forgot to mention that, before I started this morning, a deputation of eight or ten gentlemen of Cove waited upon me to request I would name a day, either now or before I left the south, to dine with the inhabitants; answered that I hoped to return this way, and would, in that case, have great pleasure in accepting their invitation. John told me there were two or three Orange-men in this deputation, which I was glad to hear. An intelligent young man aboard the steamboat, who went also up the Carriagaline river with us yesterday, on my mentioning my intention of setting off for Beecher's to-day, said he was going to Mallow too, and would, if I chose, secure a place for me in the coach when he took his own. Walked a little about Cork; visit from the French Consul. Off in a sort of diligence to Mallow at half-past two; went outside with my boat friend, whose name I find to be Sullivan. Country barren and dreary till within some miles of Mallow: the first thing at all pretty, a house of Mr. Williamson's[1], on the Clydagh, a beautiful stream. Near it are the ruins of a preceptory of the knights of St. John of Jerusalem, called Ballynamona. A good deal of conversation with my companion upon the state of the country; says there is a strong feeling among the lower orders, that if they persevere in their present harassing and violent system, the Church must give in; that Deism is spreading very much among the common people. Beecher's gig met me about a mile from Mallow; and I arrived at Ballygiblin to a late dinner; found Lyne, an old college acquaintance, just arrived too. He mentioned old Rose having once asked Sheridan what he thought of the name he had just given his little son, "George Pitt Rose," and Sheridan replying, "Why, I think a Rose by any other name would smell as sweet."[2] Mrs. Beecher's sister sung in the evening; and so did I a little.

5th. [Tuesday] Nick Beecher drove me in the curricle to Mallow. Pretty view from the lodge; the glen on one side, through which the Blackwater runs, under the high wooded grounds of Ballyellis; Mr. Jephson's old tower covered with ivy, but spoiled by the fine gilt clock. Asked Beecher whether he thought it true that Deism has got among the lower orders; says it is not impossible; such phrases are continually in their mouths as the "Religion of the heart," "God is the only judge, &c. &c." Explained to me (being himself a clergyman) the different modes of getting the tithes. The most peaceable way is by lettings, where the parson (either himself or his agent) bargains with them for a certain sum to be paid in lieu of the tithe; frequently he summons them before the Ecclesiastical Court, which is the most vexatious and expensive mode to the poor people; or he may have them before any two magistrates,—whose jurisdiction, however, does not extend beyond cases of ten pounds. The story about the fight at Skibbeeren true; Morrit, the clergyman, who is in continual warfare with his parishioners, is an Englishman. The average of the seven years, in the new Composition Bill, unfair, because it comprehends the years of highest value.[1] One good in this Act is, that by the applotments being made on the whole parish, including the agistment[2] tenants or graziers, the proportion that the poorer tenants have hitherto paid will be considerably reduced. Thinks he will himself be able, by taking a fairer average, to make some such composition, to be regulated every three years by the price of wheat, and rise or fall with it. In reply to my inquiries as to the secret organisation of the people, is of opinion that they are, to a certain degree, organised; the oath they take is, "to be secret and to be ready." Very little regard to truth among the lower orders; are tolerably educated; at least most of those under forty. Went to Ballyellis, and to another pretty place; and in returning called at a pretty cottage where Beecher's sister lives. Mrs. Beecher not able, from rheumatism, to dine with us to-day. In the evening read the new Tithe Act, and find that the oath which Dean Scott objected to so much the other day is that which the commissioner is empowered to put to the parson (as well as to the parishioner) for the purpose of coming at the truth with respect to the average value of the tithes, &c.&c.

6th. [Wednesday] A letter from my dearest Bess. Some more talk about the spread of Deism among the people; instances known in which fellows have given up going to mass, and, upon being addressed by the Methodists (as loose fish likely to come into their net), answering that their intention was not to belong to any church. Walked with Lyne to see Lohort Castle; high and narrow, the outworks gone; belongs to Lord Arden; lunched there, and was introduced to Mr. Cotter, the clergyman of the place, who has invented a new musical instrument, which he calls the Basso Hibernicon, of the *serpent* family. Walked over to his house with him to hear it; a dreary spot called Castlemagner, from a ruin (named after one of Cromwell's generals) which stands on a bank above the stream. The property immediately here Lord Limerick's, who within twenty years has shorn down every tree around; and left no signs of life but a few wretched cottages. The parson's own house, a waste and ruinous concern; and the embrasure in the hall door, to fire through, speaking volumes for the comfort of his neighbourhood. Had his wife down to accompany the display of his Basso upon a wretched little old pianoforte. The instrument very sweet and powerful, and will be, I have no doubt, an acquisition to bands and orchestras; it is seventeen feet long. Told me he took it over to London, and played on it before the officers of the First Life Guards, taking the precaution of covering it with cambric muslin lest the invention should be borrowed. What a treat for Francis Conyngham, &c.! A parson from the county Cork with his huge Hibernicon wrapped up in cambric muslin! Lyne quoted to me Lord Bellamont's description of Kerry, "All acclivity and declivity, without the intervention of a single horizontal plane; the mountains all rocks, and the men all savages." Story of the hunted stag of Killarney coming near where Lord Avonmore (then Attorney-General) and Dr. O'Leary were standing, and O'Leary saying, "How naturally instinct leads him to come to you to deliver him by a *nolle prosequi*." The name of Captain Rock is said to be the initials *Roger O'Connor, King*.[1] A vast deal about me in the Cork newspapers. Amongst other things, a letter from my own "Zaraph,"[2] describing the way in which he watched over me through Cork, his amusement, at the Commercial Rooms, in "seeing the matter-of-fact merchants staring at the Poet." Another paragraph says, after stating that Lord and Lady Lansdowne had walked about the streets of Cork, "We observed Mr. T. Moore (of poetical celebrity) leaning on the Marquiss's arm. We shall only remind him of his own lines, how—

> Sooner or later, all have to grieve
> Who waste their morn's dew in the beams of the great,
> And expect 'twill return to refresh them at eve."[3]

7th. [Thursday] Started in the gig with Nick Beecher at eleven, in order to be time enough to catch the Killarney coach at Mill Street. Passed the Castle of Kanturk, which is a much more considerable edifice than that of Lohort. Met Mr. Leader, who has a property in this neighbourhood. Made me a speech which was rather unseasonable, I being in a hurry. "This is the region, Mr. Moore, of which Sir James Mackintosh said, that religious persecution has completed in it what confiscation had begun. From the Shannon to the Blackwater all the ancient proprietors swept away, &c. &c." The coach just setting off when we reached Mill Street, and, to my horror, full. On Beecher, however, speaking to the company inside, and mentioning who I was, they consented to take me in. Found 'twas a party that had taken the coach to themselves, servants and all, eleven in number. The ladies very civil. One of them, a Mrs. Barton, whose husband, a guardsman (I think), was outside. The other her sister, with a brother, two young Cavendishes (Lord Waterpark's sons), and a Mr. Hort, a friend of Lord Lansdowne's. What luck! Found that my "Fables" was one of the books they had made provision of for rainy weather at Killarney. Arrived at Lord Kenmare's at four. Lord L. out on the lake with Mr. Sullivan (Lady Harriet's son), who has been here two or three days, and goes to-morrow. The dinner very good, and Lady Kenmare very pleasing.

8th. [Friday] The weather rather favourable. Drove down to Ross Island, and embarked on the Lake at eleven. Lady Kenmare's first time of being on her own lakes, having been but ten days here, and reserving her *debût* (as she says) for my coming. Landed on Inisfallen, and enjoyed thoroughly its loveliness. Never was anything more beautiful. Went afterwards to Sullivan's Cascade, which was in high beauty. Curious effect of a child on high, crossing the glen; seemed as if it was flitting across the waterfall. The peasants that live on the opposite bank come over with fruit when strangers appear, and their appearance, with their infants, stepping from rock to rock, across the cascade, highly picturesque. Mr. Galway (Lord Kenmare's agent) and his wife at dinner. Instance of the hospitality of the poor cotters, that it is the practice with many of their families to lay by, each individual, every day, one potatoe and a sup of milk for the stranger that may come. Intended riots at fairs (from the spirit of sept-ship) have been frequently put a stop to by orders from Captain Rock. Sung a little in the evening.

9th. [Saturday] Wretched weather. Made an attempt, however, with Lord and Lady K., to see the Upper Lake, and, in spite of the weather, was enchanted with the echo at the Eagle's Nest, and the view from Dinis of the old Weir Bridge on one side, and the plank bridge over the entrance into Turk Lake on the other. This river, between the lakes, delicious. On reaching the Upper Lake could see nothing, from the shroud of mist and rain that was over everything. Lunched at Hyde's cottage, and returned by Turk Lake. Found the weather in this region much better, and paid another visit to Inisfallen.

10th. [Sunday] Read Smith's "Kerry."[1] Was waited upon by a deputation of the gentlemen of Killarney, to request I would name a day to dine with them; but my stay is too short to do so. At three, drove out with Lady Kenmare. Called at Mr. Herbert's of Carinane, who showed us a large and most satisfactory map of the lakes, not published. Thence to Mucross. Saw the abbey, with its sculls, and the tomb of the O'Donoghue, who died lately. A sort of hermit lived some few years since in the abbey, planking up the recess which formed his lodging with coffin boards. Used to dine about with the gentlemen of the neighbourhood. Drove through those beautiful grounds, where the *ars celandi artem* has been exerted with wonderful effect; as I understand all this lovely and natural-looking disposition of the grounds has been the product of much toil and enormous expense, not less than £30,000 having been laid out upon them. Visited the pretty cottage on Turk Lake, which is to be let, and anywhere else, but in wretched Ireland, would be an Elysium. The new road from Kenmare is to pass close behind it. Drove through the grounds to the copper-mines, and quite enchanted with their endless variety of beauty. Dined at eight; only Lord and Lady K. A note for her from the Lough Lane Club, proposing to give her a stag-hunt whenever she might desire. Persuaded her to fix Wednesday, in the hope that the Lansdownes, who come on Tuesday, may stay for it. O'Connell's brother was one of the deputation that came to me this morning.

11th. [Monday] A letter from Lord Lansdowne, to say that he cannot stay longer than Tuesday. Much inclined to give him up for the stag-hunt. To-day too stormy for the lakes. Took a walk through the town of Killarney, joined by Galway, with whom I had some conversation about the state of the country. Thinks the great object of the people is to get rid of the profit that is made upon them by sub-letting. The *gentlemen* are the most troublesome tenants, and the worst pay. ——, the swaggering patriot, who holds considerable property from Lord K., cannot be made pay by love or law. Says it is most ungentleman-like of Lord Kenmare to expect it. This reminds me of an epigram I heard the other day made upon him and O'Connell, when the one hesitated about fighting Sir C. Saxton on account of his sick daughter, and the other boggled at the same operation through the interference of his wife.[1]

> "These heroes of Erin, abhorrent of slaughter,
>   Improve on the Jewish command;

One honours his wife, and the other his daughter,
That their days may be long in the land."

The rental of Lord Kenmare's property, £23,000 a year; but so encum-
bered in various ways, that he has but £7000, rather precariously paid, to
spend. Drove with Lord and Lady K. to their park, and walked about. A
very pretty glen, with the river Devenagh running through it. O'Connell
and his brother came to dinner. Says the facilities given to landlords, since
1815, for enforcing their rents, have increased the misery of the people;
particularly the power of distraining upon the crop. Mentioned a case,
which occurs often, of a man, or his wife, stealing a few potatoes from their
own crop when it is under distress, being put in prison for the theft as
being felony, when at the worst it is but *rescue,* and kept there till the judge
arrives, who dismisses him as improperly committed, and he is then turned
out upon society, hardened by his wrong, and demoralised by the society
he has lived with in prison. The facility of ejectment, too, increased since
1815. On my inquiring into the state of intellect and education among the
lower orders, said they were full of intelligence. Mentioned, as an instance
Hickey, who was hanged at a late Cork assizes, a common gardener. He
had fired at a boy, who he thought knew and might betray him, and his gun
burst, and carried away three of his fingers, which were found on the place.
A man, in seeing them, said, "I swear to those being Hickey's fingers," on
which Hickey was taken up, and his guilt discovered by the state of his
hand. This fellow was a sort of Captain Rock, and always wore feathers to
distinguish him. During his trial, he frequently wrote notes from the dock
to O'Connell (who was his counsel), exhibiting great quickness and intelligence; and when O'Connell was attempting to shake the credibility of the
boy, who was witness against him, requested him not to persevere, as it was
useless, and his mind was made up to suffer. Said that a system of organisation had spread some short time since through Leinster, which was now
considerably checked, and never, he thought, had extended to the south.
He knew of an offer made by the chiefs of this Leinster organisation,
through some of the bishops (I believe), to him (O'C.), and by him to the
Government, that they would turn out for the Lord Lieutenant, against the
Orangemen, if necessary. Says that Lord Wellesley forwarded the
notification to the English Government, but no answer was of course returned. Thinks the population of Ireland under-rated, and that it is near
8,000,000. Difference between the two archbishops that died lately; him of
Armagh, whose income was £20,000 a year, and who left £130,000 behind
him, and Troy, the R. C. archbishop of Dublin, whose income was £800 a
year, and who died worth about a tenpenny. Shows how cheap archbishops
may be had. On my remarking the numbers of informers now coming in as
inconsistent with that fidelity which he attributes to the lower orders, says it
is always the case when an organisation is breaking up, as the late one is;

never, while it is going on. Even now the *depôts* of useful arms are preserved, it is only the broken, used-up ones, that are informed on or delivered up (as it is with the old stills). The Church possesses 2,000,000 of green acres. His conversation with Judge Day: "What remedy is there for Ireland's miseries?"—*O'C.* "I could tell you some, but you would not adopt them."—*J. D.* "Name them."—*O'C.* "A law that no one should possess an estate in Ireland who has one anywhere else."—*J. D.* "I agree to that."—*O'C.* "That tithes should be abolished."—*J. D.* "I agree to that."—*O'C.* "That the Catholics should be completely emancipated."—*J. D.* "I agree to that."—*O'C.* "That the Union should be repealed."—*J. D.* "I agree to that too."—*O'C.* "Very well, since that is the case, take a pike and turn out, for there is nothing else wanting to qualify you." Mentioned a joke of Norbury's to Judge Baily lately, when they were comparing ages, "You certainly have as little of the *Old* Bailey about you as any judge I know."

12th. [Tuesday] A beautiful day at last. Went with Lord Kenmare to see the Upper Lake. The whole scene exquisite. *Loveliness* is the word that suits it best. The grand is less grand than what may be found among the Alps, but the softness, the luxuriance, the variety of colouring, the little gardens that every small rock exhibits, the romantic disposition of the islands, and graceful sweep of the shores;—all this is unequalled anywhere else. The water-lilies in the river, both white and yellow, such worthy inhabitants of such a region! Pulled some heath on Ronan's Island to send to my dear Bessy. Lunched at Hyde's cottage, and met there the party I joined in the coach, and who were going on to Dunloe Gap. Sorry not to go with them, as I shall lose that feature of the Lakes. The echoes much clearer, and more like enchantment, than the last day, and (as Lady Donegal expressed it in her letter of instructions to me) "quite take one out of this world." Just home in time to receive the Lansdownes, who give a most delightful account of the prosperity of the town of Kenmare. Cannot stay for the stag-hunt to-morrow. Lord L. gave me a letter he received for me, poetry from Tipperary. In much doubt whether I shall give up the stag-hunt to-morrow; on one side there is the pleasure of travelling with the Lansdownes, and the difficulty of getting on by the Limerick road without them; on the other, there is the stag-hunt, and my promise to Lady Kenmare. To-morrow morning must decide.

13th. [Wednesday] A fine day for the hunt, but preferred the Lansdownes. Started after breakfast. Lady L.'s resolution in climbing to the top of the abbey at Ardfert, though in evident fear of giddiness. The windows of the abbey very perfect; the narrow lancet windows of the cathedral. At Lixnaw visited the ruins which the Kerry family inhabited; a spacious and formal dwelling. Lady L. wished to sketch it, but could make nothing of such a wilderness of chimneys. A pretty summer-house, however, which she took, is the monument of the Earl of Kerry, to preserve which Lord L. has been left the farm around it, about forty acres, being all that he inherited with the title; the Earl of Kerry having sold all his estates for a life-annuity. The family lived here in feudal state; the old Earl and Countess dining by themselves, and when in company being the only persons sitting on chairs, the rest having tabourets. Had their Board of Green Cloth like royal personages; the shutters of the windows inlaid with silver. Beyond Listowel got out to walk through the wood by the river to the Knight of Kerry's house, where we were to dine and sleep. The name of his place Ballinruddery. The walk most beautiful, being high over the river (Feale) and wooded. Hickson (Lord L.'s agent) and his brother came along with us from Killarney, and it is another brother, a clergyman, who lives in Fitzgerald's house during the absence of the family, and who, with his wife, received us at dinner. The house a mere cottage, but gentlemanlike and comfortable, and the place altogether beautiful, worthy of its excellent and high-spirited owner, from whom, by the by, I received a letter enclosed to Lord L. today, expressing his regret that he is not in Ireland to assist his constituents in doing due honours to me on my arrival among them. Excellent salmon at dinner. The evening most silent and sleepy. Forgot to mention that on my arriving at Tralee this morning, a poetess, a Miss ——, who was evidently lying in wait for me, had a book popped into my hand at the inn, with a note full of the usual praises of my talent and diffidence in her own. The binding very pretty, and will, at least, look well in my library. Had some conversation with Lord L.'s agent, who tells me that considerable reductions and allowances have just been made to the tenants; that three gales are due, and that Lord L. has done more altogether than any landlord in Kerry, except Judge Day. The latter has, not long since, remitted a whole gale to his tenants.

14th. [Thursday] Off between nine and ten. The bridge of Listowel, which had been broken down, was within a few days propped up for the Judges. Thought, as it had been *sub judice,* we might venture. The view of the Shannon, as we came upon it from Tarbert, very striking. The place of Sir R. Leslie here, on an island, beautifully situated. Had been invited to lunch at Mr. Rice's, of Mount Trenchard (the father of Spring Rice), and arrived there about two. A fine old gentleman. Told us of the magnificence of the last Earl of Kerry; of his being attended always out of Dublin by his tradesmen as far as Naas, where their bills were paid, and then met on his return at the same place by the same *cortège.* Fine sweep of the river before Rice's house, and a pretty place, belonging to a Mr. Scott, in a wooded bay on the opposite side. Passed through Adare. Quantities of ruins, no less than five or six, which, from the Limerick side, have a most romantic effect through the trees. Arrived at Limerick (coming this last stage very quick) at seven: Swinburne's hotel. Lord L.'s account of his Kerry tenantry. His chief difficulty is to keep them from underletting. Some, who pay him but £8 or £10, will let their small portion out in corners to poor wretches, who marry upon the strength of this *pied-à-terre,* and swarm the little spot they occupy with children. These are they who put the key in the thatch in summer, and go begging about the country, and, under the name of "Lord Lansdowne's tenants," bring disgrace upon *him* and his property.

15th. [Friday] Walked with Lord L. to see the spot where the bridge is to be, connecting Limerick with the county Clare, and with his property, which will be, of course, a great advantage to him. Received a note from another authoress, a Miss ——, saying she wished me to call upon her. Did so. A very handsome, showy person; has published a novel, "Isabel St. Albe," dedicated to Scott, and is about to publish another, which she proposes to dedicate to me.[1] Walked with her to see Mr. Roche's curious gardens, made on the roof of the great corn-stores, which he lets to government. Was already discovered to be in Limerick, and saw the staring and running begin. Had taken my place in the Dublin mail for three o'clock, and was not a little gratified to find, on passing the Commerical Rooms in it, a number of gentlemen drawn up on the flag-way, who all took off their hats to me as I went by. A priest in the coffee-room, before I started, introduced himself to me; told me how much he admired everything I had written; had all my books in his possession, &c. &c. Is the priest of Castlebar; and said how comfortably the people in the west get on by means of the linen trade, in which they have been greatly helped by the money received from the English charitable subscriptions. An intelligent young man in the mail, who came as far as Nenagh, and (as I found on his leaving me) had put himself on the coach upon knowing that I was to be a passenger by it, and had come thus far with no other motive. Found him very useful in pointing out the different gentlemen's seats. Mentioned the very high character Lord Clare had held in this neighbourhood as a humane landlord and kind master. Arrived at Roscrea about eight, where I dined and slept, having secured a place in the coach to take me on to-morrow morning. The Lansdownes, after a short stay at Limerick and Mount Shannon, will proceed to Mr. Cosby's, in the Queen's County (where I was invited to meet them), and thence, in the course of about eight days, to Dublin.

16th. [Saturday] A small round tower at Roscrea, and a very fine ancient portal, which serves as a gate to the church; the ruins of a castle in the town. Started about ten o'clock. The curious rock, with ruins on it, in the neighbourhood of Maryborough, called Dunamase. Sorry not to be able to stop and see it. Dined at Naas, and arrived in Abbey Street before ten. Found a letter from Lord John, directed to Sloperton, dated the 6th, saying that he had changed his mind about the journey to Killarney, and would now be very happy to accompany me; proposing we should set out the 16th, this very day! Letters also from dear Bess; all well at home, thank God!

17th. [Sunday] Walked about a good deal. Called on P. Crampton, and found him laid up on the sofa. His story of the boy wishing for a place under government; his powers of "screeching free-stone." "Sure, its me you hear in Dublin every Wednesday and Friday. Did you ever hear me?" &c. Told him how perfectly all my suspicions of Bushe were cleared away by his conduct since he became a judge, by his last charge in particular. Answered that Bushe had always been kept down till now by Saurin, and was unable to show himself.¹ Lord Farnham saying, during the Queen's trial, that he would not make up his mind till he had heard one Italian witness, who had often been mentioned, and who might be expected to throw much light on the matter, "one *Polacca*."² Dined at home, and had Abbot to dinner. Said the great grievance of the law in Ireland lay in civil process; the delay of the sub-sheriffs; their being bribed to hold the writ suspended; ought to be forced to file it immediately, as in England. Lord Landaff used to pay regularly £1500 a year to the sub-sheriffs of his county, to keep off executions, but has lately discontinued this, and mounts guard upon his house instead.

18th. [Monday] Made a number of calls. Stared and run after at every step. Dined at home: the Abbots to dinner. Went (all of us) to the theatre in the evening to hear Catalani. Went to her dressing-room, and met there Stevenson, who most unfortunately goes out of town tomorrow, not to return for some time. Had brought over some sacred songs for him to arrange, which this will, I fear, put out of the question. Abbot brought Mrs. A. and my sister Ellen to introduce to Catalani. Her kindness to Nell, calling her *la sœur d'Anacréon*. A good trait in Catalani, the veneration she always felt for Grattan, and when told of his death she burst into tears. On Abbot making her a present the other day of one of the medals of him, she kissed him. Grattan was always an ardent admirer of hers, and Catalani showed Abbot a letter of his in French to her, which she keeps treasured in a splendid box, and had either the policy or good taste to say she preferred it to all the tributes she has from kings and emperors. The letter expresses a hope that, after having enchanted the world with her song, she may be called late to add to the melody of heaven. The Abbots supped with us; and my dearest father and mother seemed perfectly happy. Had a MS. book and note this morning from another poetess, Miss ——; and a letter from a Mr. Clarke, of Limerick, enclosing a poem of his to me (which has appeared in the Limerick paper), rather good.

19th. [Tuesday] Called upon Miss——, and found her (for a poetess) pretty well. Said "she was afraid I should think her a very bold girl for writing to me." Called this morning upon Lover, the artist, who is anxious to take my picture; but have not time. Went also with Abbot to see the machinery of the Bank, which is most curious and beautiful, and does great credit to Oldham, who presides over it, and has invented some of its most interesting contrivances. Had a letter from Lord Lansdowne to say he will be in town on Friday or Saturday.

20th. [Wednesday] Called upon Lover, with Curry and Jerry Bushe. Took us to see some pictures in Dawson Street, which were collected with a view to an Institution, but without success. A very delightful picture by Northcote of a girl riding on an ass; also Sir Joshua's portrait of Primate Robinson, very striking. Dined at Abbot's; a large party—Vallebraque and Catalani, Harry Harris, Sir Charles Geisicke of the Dublin Society, Magee of the Evening Post, Dr. Letton librarian of the D. Society, my father, mother, and Ellen, &c. Catalani took a violent fancy for my dear mother; overheard her saying to Vallebraque, *cette chère Madame Moore.* Gave me a long account, in the evening, of her quarrel and reconciliation with the King of Bavaria.

21st. [Thursday] Paid a visit to Mason, who has sent me, with a very flattering letter, a copy of his three-guinea book on St. Patrick's Cathedral.[1] Went to see the Rev. Mr. Pomeroy's pictures; some of them very good indeed. Dined at Lady Morgan's: company, Lords Cloncurry and Dunsany, Caulfield (Lord Charlemont's brother), old Hamilton Rowan, and Burne the barrister. The style of the dinner quite *comme il faut.* Lord Cloncurry mentioned his having interceded with Lord Wellesley for the pardon of a man who had been, with several others, found guilty of a murder at Athy, but who, there was every reason to think, was completely innocent. A priest, riding up to Dublin, for the same purpose of intercession, died on his arrival from the over-haste with which he had travelled. Lady Morgan mentioned, that Owen had brought her one day a pattern of the sort of short tunic or shift which he meant the people of his parallelograms to wear, hinting, as a secret, that this was only a preparatory step to their not wearing any clothing at all: she hung it up, she said, in her drawing-room, to exhibit it. In the evening a most crowded soirée—Ladies Cloncurry,

Cecilia Latouche, &c. Lady Clark's little girls sung with an Italian, and I also sung two or three songs. Introduced to Mr. Hughes, the American Minister to Sweden, who has been here a few days. Catalani came late; and I took flight on her appearance, seeing strong symptoms of being asked to sing for her. Took leave of Corry this morning, who starts for Wales to-morrow.

22nd. [Friday] Called upon Joe Atkinson, &c. &c. Saw Henry Webster, who has been down to the county Wicklow to communicate to Lord Wellesley the time of Lord Lansdowne's arrival. Thinks Lord L. ought to go down to him before his departure, and wished that I should go with him, as Lord Wellesley has expressed a regret at his not being in town to see me. Was anxious I should translate some Greek ode he had, &c. &c. Dined at home with my dear family. Went to walk in the Rotunda Gardens in the evening, but being alone could not stand the staring I had to encounter; one man, whom I did not at all know, seized my hand, and held it while he made me a speech. Was off in a few minutes: should like to have sauntered there a little longer, listening to the music, as the scene altogether brought back young days of courtship and carelessness to my mind. Heard, in passing their hotel, that the Lansdownes had arrived.

23rd. [Saturday] Called upon the Lansdownes. He goes down to Lord Wellesley to-morrow, and will sail certainly on Monday. Begged him, if Lord W. mentioned me, to say how flattered I had been by his kind messages. Went to the theatre, but did not arrive till the curtain was falling; saw Catalani in her dressing-room, and handed her to her carriage; a crowd outside waiting to see her, who said "God bless you!" as she passed.

24th [Sunday] Breakfasted with Abbot, who gave me the "Anti-Union," Scully's "Penal Laws," &c.[1] Took my old portmanteau to Milliken's, that he may pack in it the books I have bought and send it after me; found Rees there, who kindly asked me did I want any money. A note from Lady Lansdowne, to say that they mean to set off for Howth this evening at eight, and will take me if I choose; otherwise, I may join them there in the morning. Determined on having the last evening with my friends at home, and ordered a bed at Morrisons, in order to be nearer the Howth coach in the morning. Dined at home; packed up after dinner, took my farewell supper with them, and off for Morrison's.

25th. [Monday] Coach called for me at a quarter after seven. Skinner, in whose packet we sail, the only passenger in it. Told me of the havoc these

English commissioners are making in the Post Office. So much the better; it is the great seat of Orangeism; and Lord Wellesley says he *knows* that all the libels against him, during the late row, were circulated *gratuitously* through the medium of the Post Office.[1] Found Lord and Lady L. aboard. Took immediately to my berth, and was in Holyhead in about seven hours, where we dined, and set off immediately afterwards for the first stage, Mona House.

26th. [Tuesday] Stopped at Bangor Ferry, Lord L. having a letter to Mr. Wilson, the director of the works of the bridge, to show and explain the operations to us. Enormous undertaking, and never, I think, to be completed, though there seems, as yet, no doubt entertained of its success! It is a little extraordinary, however, that, according to Mr. Wilson's account, they have not yet made up their minds as to the mode of carrying the chains across, the great, and, in my mind, insurmountable difficulty. Went down into the rock, where the pins or bars, by which the chains hold, are fixed. Arrived to dinner at Llangollen, in the beautiful inn overhanging the water; my bedroom commanded the same view. Much amused with the folly of those who have scribbled in the book kept here. Among the late transits was one which called up rather melancholy thoughts; "Earl and Countess of Bective, Lord Taylor (the infant), and Master G. Dalton," in her hand-writing.

27th. [Wednesday] Off early, and arrived in the evening to dinner at Worcester. Sauntered by myself through the town a little afterwards. Lord L. mentioned an amusing blunder of Madame de Staël's, when in England, in mistaking Charles Long for Sergeant Lens (who had just refused some situation from the Government), and complimented Long (who is the most determined placeman in England) on his disinterestedness.

28th. [Thursday] Walked with Lady Lansdowne after breakfast to a china-shop, where Lord L. afterwards joined us. On Lady L.'s buying a pretty pastile-burner for herself (price, a guinea), Lord L. bought the fellow of it for Bessy, and bid me give it to her from him. Went out of our way a little for the purpose of seeing the beautiful view from Froster, which is of the finest kind of English prospects, extensive, rich, cultivated, animated, with a noble river wafting numerous sails through its hedge-rows and cornfields. By some mistake at Gloucester we were sent wrong, and lost about ten miles of our road. Met at Malmesbury by Lord L.'s horses, and near Chippenham by Lord Kerry, riding. At Chippenham I parted with them, and took a chaise for Sloperton, where I arrived between seven and eight, and found Bessy and her little ones, thank Heaven, quite well. Thus ended one of the pleasantest journeys altogether I have ever taken. It is in travelling with people that one comes to know them most thoroughly, and I must say, that for every good quality both of temper and mind, for the power of enjoying what was enjoyable, and smoothing all that was disagreeable (though this latter quality, it is true, was rarely put to the trial), for ready attention to whatever was said or proposed, and for those *piacevoli e bei ragionamenti,* which make (as Ariosto says) the roughest way seem short, I have never met any two persons more remarkably distinguished than those I have just travelled with.

29th, 30th, &c. &c. [Friday, Saturday] Set about reading for the little work upon Ireland, which I mean to despatch;[1] must work for Power too. Borrowed "Wakefield upon Ireland" from Lord Lansdowne, who, in sending it to me, begged I would look over it as speedily as I could, because, with all its faults, it was his dictionary of reference on many subjects which he had to correspond about with his agents, &c.[2]

9th. [September, Tuesday] Lord L. called just as we were preparing to set off to Devizes to dine with the Hugheses. Said he had read my translation from Catullus of the "Pæninsularum Sirmio"[1] (which I had mentioned to him as, in my own opinion, pretty well done), and expressed himself highly pleased with it. Company at Hugheses, Col. Hull, and Mr. Mayo, the chaplain of the jail. Col. H. said that the missionaries were laughed at in the East Indies, and the few wretched creatures of whom they made converts nicknamed "Company's Christians." Came overland from India. In crossing the Desert he and his two friends brought a good supply of Sneyd's claret, and used to finish a magnum or two every evening. Sneyd's claret in the Desert! times are altered.

10th. [Wednesday] Sent an Irish Melody to Power yesterday, beginning "When vanquish'd Erin," to the tune of the "Boyne Water," which I have long wished to give a different *colour* to; this is *green* enough.[1]

11th. [Thursday] Reading hard and fast upon Irish subjects. Just finished "Newenham,"[1] which I borrowed from Lord L. on sending him back "Wakefield."

12th. [Friday] Dined at the Lansdownes. The Phippses took, as company, besides them and ourselves, the Bowleses, the Joys, and the Duncans. Bowles's comical description of "Young *Angel* riding after a red herring" very amusing at dinner. Mr. Duncan mentioned, that Blackstone has preserved the name of the judge to whom Shakspeare alludes in the gravedigger's argument, "If the water comes to the man, &c.;"[1] must see this. Sung in the evening. On Bessy telling Bowles that Mrs. Phipps and she meant to go hear him preach some Sunday, he asked us all over to breakfast and dinner to-morrow. Agreed to go.

13th. [Saturday] Set off at nine in Phipps's carriage. Bowles took for his text (as he promised yesterday he would) the "impotent man" at the Pool of Bethesda; sermon very interesting. Showed us about his place afterwards. I took a volume of Johnson's "Poets"[1] with me, and walked through the fields to Calne till dinner-time. Lord Lansdowne came to dinner. In looking over the library, I mentioned that it was singular enough that Sir J. [*sic*] Browne, the exposer of vulgar errors, should himself have been a witness on a trial for witchcraft, and given testimony to the existence of witches in Germany.[2] Bowles said he had discovered in the names that occur throughout the "Tales of the Genii" the anagrams of those of some of the author's (Ridley's) friends.[3] I cannot, however, perceive any of them.

17th. [Wednesday] Received my books after dinner, and amused both Bessy and myself by reading over in the "Anthologia Hibernica"[1] poems I sent to it when I was but twelve and thirteen years of age. "Our esteemed correspondent, T. M.," diverted Bessy exceedingly. Received a note from Lord L., sending me the last volumes of "Las Casas,"[2] and asking me to fix a day to dine.

18th. [Thursday] Read four of the Irish pamphlets since last night. Walked into Devizes in order to draw for £100 at three months, on the Longmans. Got an order for £42 of it to send to Bath to pay the half-year of Anastasia's schooling. Found Mr. and Mrs. Hughes come to dinner with us on my return home. Walked to Phipps's with Bessy in the evening, making about twelve or thirteen miles to-day.

19th. [Friday] Sent off an Irish Melody to Power, beginning "Quick! we have but a second!"[1] Reading pamphlets on Irish affairs; M'Nevin's "Pieces of History," Curry's Reviews, &c. &c.[2]

20th to 23rd. [Saturday–Tuesday] Have begun writing my "Irish Tour,"[1] but get on very slowly, though I was in hopes I should be able to dispatch it in a few weeks, and get back to "Sheridan."

24th. [Wednesday] Walked to Bowood; found them at home, and took a long walk with them and Oakden across the park to the Calne road. Lord L. mentioned a book called "A Journey to the Moon,"[1] which he had given a commission for at the Fonthill sale. The man's method of flying to the moon was by means of little phials filled with dew, which he hung about him, and which were exhaled up by the morning sun, and carried him with them. Lord L. said it had given the idea of Swift's "Gulliver;" but I mentioned Lucinus's "True History"[2] as the original of all this class of fictions. Talked of "The Journey Underground," &c.[3]

25th. [Thursday] Sent an Irish Melody to Power, beginning "Sweet Innisfall."[1]

27th. [Saturday] Started for Melksham on foot at seven, in order to catch the Bath coach. Bessy to join Mrs. P's carriage. Arrived at Bath between eleven and twelve; breakfasted at the York House, and went thence to my dear Anastasia, whom I found in trouble. Great complaints against her from the schoolmistress for inattention to her lessons. Perceived the schoolmistress had mistaken her disposition, and supposes that it is obstinacy prevents the child from answering what she knows; when, in fact, it is the confusion arising from a strong feeling of reproof or disgrace that puts all her ideas to flight, and makes her incapable of any thing while she is in that state. Lectured my dear little girl very gravely as I walked with her to meet her mama, who also was as serious as she could be about it, though feeling all the while, with me, that the schoolmistress had (as she herself used to do) mistaken the child's disposition. Home at seven.

28th. [Sunday] Wrote away as fast as my slow *prose* pen would let me. The Awdreys came to take leave, and Miss Awdrey gave me a pretty sketch she has made of the cottage. In the evening took Tom a long walk with me.

October 1st. [Wednesday] Dined at Bowood. Fellowes called to take me. Rev. — Ashe and his pretty daughter, and two other parsons. Talked of the sepulchres of the Hungerfords at Farley (Colonel Houlton's place). The bodies preserved in pickle. The shoulder of a Lady Margaret of the family uncovered, and found firm and white. An antiquarian introduced a quill into it, in order to extract some of the pickle, and taste it, which he did; and his only remark was, that it was "very stimulant." Talked of Beckford; the passion he and some other men have had for the mere spending of money. Johnes of Hafôd in Wales delighted when he heard his magnificent house was burnt down, because the sum for which he insured it (£30,000) would be forthcoming, and he could begin to spend again. Lord L.'s new statue (by Westmacott) of the beggar woman and child just arrived; gave 500 guineas for it.

2nd. [Thursday] Wrote three verses of an Irish Melody for Power, begin-ning "'Twas one of those dreams,"[1] and sent it up to him; also a page or two of my Irish work.[2] Walked about all day, and enjoying the fresh sunny weather.

3rd. [Friday] Walked over with Bessy and Mrs. Phipps to call upon our new neighbours, the Starkeys.

4th. [Saturday] Left home at three to walk to Buckhill, before my dinner at Bowood. An Irishman, who called upon me some days ago to beg I would get some "ginteel situation" for him, has just written to me from Bristol to say that he came from Ireland expressly with the sole hope of my assisting him, and that he now has not money enough to pay his passage back again. Begged of Hughes to let his agent at Bristol pay the man's passage, and see him on board. Met Lady Lansdowne and Lady Cawdor in the lane to the school, returning from their drive. Lady L. gave me the key of the grounds to walk through on my way back. A glorious evening: walked backwards and forwards in the lane for half an hour, observing the effect of the setting sun upon the foliage. Company at dinner, Lord and Lady Cawdor, Mr. Grenville, and the Bowleses. Felt rather a restraint at dinner from the little *hitch* there has been between me and Mr. Grenville about Sheridan's letters. In talking of ghost stories, Lord L. told of a party who were oc-cupied in the same sort of conversation; and there was one tall pale-looking woman of the party, who listened and said nothing; but upon one of the company turning to her and asking whether *she* did not believe there was such a thing as a ghost, she answered, *Si j'y crois? oui, et même je le suis;* and instantly vanished. Bowles very amusing; his manner of pronouncing Catalani's speech about Sheridan at Oxford, that he had *beaucoup de talent, et très peu de beauté,* convulsed us all with laughter. Mr. Grenville mentioned that the last Mrs. Sheridan used to say, "As to my husband's talents, I will not say anything about them, but I *will* say that he is the handsomest and honestest man in all England." Bowles told the ghost story from Giraldus Cambrensis. An archdeacon of extraordinary learning and talents, and who was a neighbour of Giraldus, and with whom he lived a good deal, when they were one day talking about the disappearance of the demons on the birth of Christ, said, "It is very true and I remember on that occasion I *hid myself* in a well."[1]

5th. [Sunday] Meant to have walked home to see Bess, but the morning too wet. After breakfast, being alone with Mr. Grenville, broached the delicate subject of Sheridan, by saying that I had some letters of his (Mr. G.'s) which I should long since have sent to him but for the hurry in which I was obliged to leave England. This brought on a conversation about S., in which I found him very kind and communicative. S. after his marriage lived at a cottage at Burnham (East or West, I don't know which); and at a later period of his life, when he and Mrs. S. were not on the most peaceable terms, Mr. Grenville has heard him saying half to himself, "Sad, that former feelings should have so completely gone by. Would anything bring them back? Yes, perhaps the gardens at Bath and the cottage at East Burnham might." Was very agreeable when a young man, full of spirits and good-humoured; always disguising his necessities and boasting of the prosperity of his views. His jealousy of Mrs. S. more from vanity than affection. Fox took a strong fancy to her, which he did not at all disguise; and Mr. G. said it was amusing to see the struggle between Sheridan's great admiration of, and deference to, Fox, and the sensitive alarm he felt at his attentions to her. At the time that Mr. G. and his brother left Bath to go to Dublin, old Sheridan was acting there; and Lord Townsend (the Lord Lieutenant), wishing that they should see him in "King John," ordered that play; but on the morning of the representation, wrote them a note to say he had just had a letter from Mr. Sheridan, informing him that he had been thrown out of his carriage the day before, and had strained his shoulder so violently, that it was *impossible* for him to act King John,—but rather than the young gentleman should be disappointed, he would appear in a comedy, and play, as well as he could, "Sir Charles Easy." This is a joke of Lord Townsend's. Great Queen Street was where S. lived when he became connected with the theatre. Story of the "Manufacturer of Shows" from Stafford, who was witness on a petition against Lord Auckland's Commercial Treaty with Ireland.[1] Story of the elector asking S. for a frank, and another doing the same immediately, saying, "I don't see why I'm not to have a frank as well as John Thompson." "What direction shall I put upon it?" said Sheridan. "The same as John Thompson's, to be sure." Thinks S. used, when a young fellow, to pick up a guinea or two by writing for newspapers, which is confirmed by the fragments of letters of this kind among his papers. Lived at a coffee-house in Maiden Lane. Is this "the Bedford" to which I find Grenville's and other letters directed? Mr. Grenville heard Erskine ask Fox, the day before his (E.'s) first speech in the House of Commons, what kind of coat he thought he had best wear on the occasion, and whether a black one would be best. Fox answered him with perfect gravity, and said, "As he was oftenest seen in black, that would be perhaps the best colour," but laughed heartily when he went away. I showed him and Lord L. an item in the Index to Wakefield's "Ireland,"[2] where it is quietly said, "Catholics will in a few years exterminate the Protestants." At dinner it was mentioned that Lord Alvanly said Sir William Scott was like a conceited Muscovy duck, which is excellent; better than Canning's comparison, who said he was like a turtle in a martingale. Mr. G. described Lord North's method of looking through his notes when he had lost the thread of his discourse, talking in his oratorical voice all the while, "It is not on this side of the paper, Mr. Speaker, neither is it on the other side." In talking of Mirabeau, Lord L. said he had been told by Maury, that one time when Mirabeau was answering a speech of his, he put himself in a reasoning attitude, and said, *Je m'en vais renfermer M. Maury dans un cercle vicieux;* upon which Maury started up, and exclaimed, *Comment! veux-tu m'embrasser?* which had the effect of utterly disconcerting Mirabeau. In the evening wrote out some verses in Lady L.'s album, and sung with Lady Cawdor. Slept there. Upon my expressing my intention of going before breakfast in the morning, Lady L. insisted I should not.

6th. [Monday] Stayed breakfast, and set out soon after; Lord L. having asked me to come over again the end of the week, to meet Lord John, who is coming, and the Knight of Kerry. Mr. Grenville and I parted most amiably. Visits from the Starkeys and Henry Joy on my return; the latter to ask me to dine with him on Wednesday.

7th. [Tuesday] Wrote letters, and sauntered about in the sweet sunshine all the rest of the day, stringing together a few (*very* few) sentences of my Irish work.

9th. [Thursday] Phipps drove me to Bath to see my dear Anastasia. A dreadful thunder-storm on our way: took shelter in a public-house. My dear little girl quite well, and everything cleared up between her and her schoolmistress; stayed some time with her. Lunched at Phipps's mother's. Went to different shops to look after a lamp which I wish to purchase for my study, and left Bath at past three.

10th. [Friday] Bessy and Mrs. P. drove to Devizes in our little carriage with a pony hired of a carpenter in our neighbourhood. Have determined to change the plan of my Irish work, and make it a "History of Captain Rock and his Ancestors," which may be more livelily and certainly more easily done. But all I have already written, by this change, goes for nothing.

11th. [Saturday] Read O'Hallaran's "History of Ireland"[1] for my new plan, and wrote a little.

12th. [Sunday] While dressing to walk to Bowood, Lord John came. Sent away his horses and we walked there by Chitway; delighted with the country round me, the day being most favourable for it. Much talk about Ireland; told him my plans for a work on the subject. Company at dinner, Lord Aberdeen and Rogers (who came together from Lord Bathurst's), Abercromby and his son, Lady Harriet Frampton (sister to Lady L.) and her daughter, Mr. Strangways, brother to Lady L., and Lord John. Dinner rather noisy; very little conversation. The evening somewhat better. Told Lady L. of an extract I saw from a work on the genealogy of the Earls of Kerry, mentioning the fondness which Thomas, the first Earl, had for Kerrystone buttons, and giving some poetry commemorative of said buttons. Lord John mentioned that, when in Spain, an ecclesiastic he met told him of a poor Irishman who had lately been travelling there, to whom he had an opportunity of showing some kindness; but from the Irishman not knowing Spanish they were obliged to converse in Latin. On taking his leave, the grateful Hibernian knelt down and said to the Churchman, *Da mihi* beneficium *tuum*. "No, no," replied the other, "I have done as much as I could for you, but *that* is rather too much." Talked of McDiarmid's "Lives of Statesmen;"[1] R. praised his account of Lord Strafford. Of Gilpin's writings; his "Life of Cranmer."[2] The unfitness of Cranmer for the scenes he was thrown into; his elegant habits; wearing gloves at supper whenever he did not mean to eat anything. Spoke of Lingard's "History of England;" reign of Philip and Mary very curious. Allen has detected him (it seems) in falsifying, or rather giving a false colour to, his authorities; particularly about the vices of the clergy, which he contrives to suppress or soften off. This is, I suppose, in the Reports of the state of the monasteries made in the time of Henry VIII.[3] Allen's hatred to the Swiss for their late conduct to the *exiles*. Wishes he could get musicians to play the "Ranz des Vaches" all through London to see if it would have the effect imputed to it of sending them all home. I looked over Murphy's "Arabian Antiquities of Spain."[4] The apartments of the Alhamra or Alhambra (for he spells it both ways), though they look so imposing in engravings, are all very small. One of the fine buildings of Granada given is a coal-house, *Casa de Carbon*, House of

Charcoal. Asked Lord John as to his progress in the work he has been employed in.[5] Promised to let me read what he has done. Slept there.

13th. [Monday] Read some of McDiarmid's "Life of Lord Strafford" before breakfast. Some talk with Abercromby about it; agreed with me, that though one could not help admiring the vigour and talent with which Lord S. carried on his government in Ireland, it was the duty of an historian to reprobate the violent principles upon which it was all founded, and that to speak of it in the softened tone McD. did, was more culpable than even the original commission of the wrongs, as the latter had at least the excuse of passions, ambition, &c. &c. A good deal of conversation after breakfast arising from Southey's remark in his "History of the War in Spain and Portugal," that Pitt and Fox were both overrated men.[1] I said Lord Chatham's was a fame much more independent of party and circumstance than theirs; that there were several men in their time nearly equal to them in debate, and superior to them in general talents; but, that Lord Chatham stood out from the canvass of his age alone. Nor was he indebted, as each of them was, to the adoption of his name by a party for that kind of corporate celebrity which such an association always gives. Lord Aberdeen rather contested all these points with me. Rogers produced some English verses of Lord Grenville's, to the surprise of all the party, who seemed to agree that he was one of the least poetical men they could point out. The verses were a paraphrastic translation of the lines at the beginning of the "Inferno," *O degli altri poeti onore e lume,* and very spiritedly done. After luncheon, went with Lord John to his room to look over the MS. of his French work. Walked out with him and Rogers. R. complained of the disposition of the walk along the water, without any trees between to break the view of it into glimpses; said he had been talking to Lord L. about it, but in vain. Sung a little for Lady Harriet Frampton and her daughter before dinner. Sung in the evening. Lord Aberdeen produced a fac-simile (which Mr. Bankes has sent him) of two or three lines from a papyrus MS. of Homer, found lately wrapped round a mummy. Must be older than any of those we have, though they have accents, which are looked upon by some to be a modern invention.

14th. [Tuesday] Got up early and walked home before breakfast. Morning delicious. Brought away Lord John's MS. with me, and read some of it. Rather too heavy and prolix in some parts, particularly his account of the Jansenists and Jesuits; but the anecdotes of the court of Louis XIV., and his character of the nobility of that time, very striking and interesting. Put pencil-marks where I thought the style wanted mending. Wrote some of my "Captain Rock." After dinner walked with Bessy to the village, and left her to drink tea with the Falkeners. A kind letter from Croker to-day, sending me a large Paris *affiche* of my publications, which he thought might amuse me.

15th. [Wednesday] Various disturbances. Could do but little. Took Bessy to Bowood to dinner, she looking uncommonly well. Company the same, with the addition of the Barings and the Knight of Kerry. Was glad to see Lord John took Bessy out to dinner, as I knew she would feel more comfortable with him. Day very agreeable. Have seldom seen my dear girl in better looks, and her plain barège gown particularly becoming. Told me in coming home that all the women admired it exceedingly, and were very kind to her. Lord L. asked me to come to breakfast in the morning, as the Knight of Kerry is obliged to leave them.

16th. [Thursday] Set off for Bowood at nine. Rogers came halfway to meet me; very agreeable and in high good humour. After breakfast heard the various criticisms on Cockerell's door to the new chapel. Baring agreed with Mr. Grenville's remark, that the door would look neater if the *small* knots were removed. Rogers thought they ought to be of the same colour as the wood, which the ancients would have made them by having the whole in brass, as the door of the Pantheon is. The door-case is copied exactly from a temple in Athens. Conversation about the architects, Cockerell, Smirke, and Wilkins; the first and last too little acquainted with the common part of their art, the conveniences, &c., of a house; and Smirke, on the contrary, too much hacked and vulgarised by the common part to succeed as he ought in the ornamental; a combination of the two would be perfection. The Knight of Kerry, after breakfast, told me of a curious dialogue which Lord Wellesley mentioned to him as having passed between Archbishop Magee and himself. Magee, in protesting against the Tithe Bill,[1] and other innovations on the Church of Ireland, said that the fate of the English Church was involved in that of the Irish one. "Pardon me," says Lord Wellesley, "the two Churches differ materially; for instance, the English bishops wear wigs, and you don't wear any. I'll *wig* you, if you don't take care." The knight seemed to think he did right in employing this *persiflage*, as the best method of getting rid of Magee's remark. Lord L. wanted me to stay dinner, but I promised to come to-morrow. Saw Rogers and Lord Aberdeen off to Longleat, and returned home to dinner, having, before I came away, pointed out to Lord John the alterations both in the plan and particular passages in his work which seemed to me necessary. Very sleepy in the evening, and could do nothing but read over Leland's "History of Ireland," which Lady L. lent me.[2] My Irish harp arrived from Ireland, and a little one of two octaves with it for Anastasia.

17th. [Friday] Finished a verse of an Irish Melody and dispatched it to Power; did nothing else. Dined at Bowood; the Barings, Abercrombies, and Lord John, with the addition of George Fortescue. Said that Canning and Lord Sidmouth had been at Cirencester (Lord Bathurst's), before he left it; Canning very absent and silent. In talking of the way in which any criticism or ridicule spoils one's enjoyment ever after of even one's most favourite passages, I mentioned a ludicrous association suggested to me about a passage in Haydn's "Creation," which always recurs to me to disturb my delight at it. In that fine *morceau,* "God said, Let there be light," there is between these words and the full major swell, into which the modulation bursts upon "and there was light," a single note of the violin, which somebody said was to express the "striking of the flint." After dinner Lady Lansdowne said to me, in remarking upon the good looks Bessy is in now, "How *very* pretty she is! it's quite refreshing to see any thing so pretty." Was escaping about ten o'clock, but George Fortescue came after me with a deputation, as he said, from the ladies, to beg I would sing one song before I went. Returned and sung a good deal. Walked home. Quite an Italian moonlight.

19th. [Sunday] Set off at about eleven in my little pony carriage, with the carpenter's pony, and the carpenter himself to drive me. Arrived, by dint of hard beating, in three hours at Warminster. Took a chaise there, and got to Bennet's before six. Company at dinner, Heber, Sir Alexander Mallet, a Miss Partridge, and the Phippses. Heber said he had heard from Dr. Henley (who wrote the notes upon "Vathek"), that the foundation of this romance was certainly some Persian manuscripts, which came into Beckford's possession, and which he translated into French as an exercise. Do not believe this; the design, as well as style, is all western.[1] In talking of false quantities, mentioned an instance of Sir J. Mackintosh pronouncing *ludicra* with the *i* short, in a quotation from Virgil, *neque enim levia aut ludicra petuntur præmia.*[2] Canning's horror when Heber mentioned it to him. Mackintosh's defence was that he had "decomposed" it; *i.e.,* made prose of it. In talking of Lord Grenville's verses, said that he had seen a good many of his Latin verses; mentioned particularly his verses on the death of his dog Tippoo; also some verses of Pitt's, made in conjunction with Canning, on Sir F. Eden.

20th. [Monday] Set off to walk to Fonthill between eleven and twelve o'clock. No sale going on to-day, being Monday. Very much struck by the singularity and fancifulness of the Abbey. The ascent up the stairs at the grand entrance particularly striking, and the effect of the *coup d'œil* above and around, as you stand under the lantern, quite new and beautiful. Went up to the top of the tower, and sat on the chimney to look at the extensive prospect. Took luncheon in the servants' hall, which is converted into a coffee-room by the *restaurant* from Bath, who has established himself here. Several parties at different tables in this dark vaulted place gave quite the idea of banditti. Walked about the grounds, and caught several beautiful views of the Abbey, combined with the woods, and the small lake in a little valley under it. Met Hallam, and Mr. Addington (Lord Sidmouth's nephew), who had come express from London to see it. Benet asked them to dinner, which rejoiced me, as it gave the rational talkers a majority. Heard an imitation of a storm on the organ; very wonderful; done in the manner of the Abbé Vogler. Walked home in time to dress for dinner. Talked of Latin verses; those of Jortin's, *Quæ te sub tenerâ.* Whether the couplet beginning, *Tu cave Lethæo,* or *Te sequar,* should be the concluding one. The former certainly is better for an ending, from its point and workmanship, but the natural flow of feeling is in favour of *Te sequar* being the conclusion. Mentioned some Latin verses quoted by Taylor in his "Holy Living,"[1] which he never could find out the source of, addressed to Pancharilla. Said I believed they were Bonifonius's, that being, if I recollect right, the name of his poetical mistress. Hallam mentioned some pretty verses by Markham, in the "Adventurer," which I must look for.[2] H. told of a quotation of Pitt's, one day at dinner, when Canning, and, I believe, Frere, were trying *par méchanceté* to get G. Ellis to speak of the "Rolliad;" he having, in his time of Whiggery, written in it, and the severe character of Pitt being from his pen. Pitt, from the upper part of the table, overhearing their efforts to introduce the subject, leaned across, and said to G. Ellis, *Immo, age, et a primâ dic, hospes, origine nobis.* The *hospes* here very happy, as addressed to a new convert. He might, too, have gone on to *erroresque tuos.* Talking of Sheridan's habit of borrowing other people's jokes, H. mentioned some one having said, "I don't know how it is, a thing that falls flat from me seems quite an excellent joke when given at second-hand by Sheridan. I never like my own *bon mots* till he adopts them." Endeavoured to sing in the evening to a wretched pianoforte, four notes of which were (as Sir A. Mallet said) "in Chancery."

21st. [Tuesday] Rose early, and breakfasted with Phipps before the rest of the company, in order to drive over and see Wardour, Lord Arundel's place. Day delicious. Fine ruin of the castle which Lady Blanche defended.[1] Her picture in the house; very feminine-looking. A portrait of Hugo Grotius, too, very different from what I had conceived him, fat and rubicund: the chest must have been of no common size in which he effected his escape from prison.[2] The chapel at Wardour very handsome. Home in time to attend the ladies to the sale at Fonthill. Stayed there till five. In coming away the setting sun lighted up the windows of the Abbey most beautifully. Immediately after dinner set off for the Abbey to see it illuminated; went in the carriage with the five ladies. The effect of the octagon and the lantern very striking, and with a sufficiency of light, the whole would be magnificent. Introduced to Lady Arundel, as I was to-day at the sale, by his own wish, to Lord Arundel. Told ghost stories to the ladies all the way home. Got Mrs. Benet to let me have a cup and saucer out of a broken set she bought, in order to take home some little memorial of Fonthill to Bessy. Regret so much she could not come here with me.

22nd. [Wednesday] Up at seven, and set off in a chaise for Warminster, taking with me several volumes on tithes, which Benet has lent me, besides his own Controversy on the same subject with Archdeacon Coxe.[1] By the by, Heber repeated to me, in going up to bed last night, some pretty verses of Cyril Jackson's, in which he talks of *Curtatis Decimis.*

24th. [Friday] Tom's birth-day. He was to have had a party on the occasion, and to have celebrated in due form his inauguration into breeches, which takes place this day; but the illness of Hannah prevents all but the assumption of the *toga virilis,* in which he is at this moment strutting about, as proud as any five-year old gentleman in the kingdom. Mr. Britton to breakfast. Showed me a sketch-book of Thomas Hope's, full of beautiful bits of architecture from Italy. Wrote some of my Irish work. A letter from Anastasia, who is much better and (like a true little Irish girl) thanks mama "for *putting* off Tom's *birth-day* for her." Sauntered about in the sweet valley of Chitway, enjoying all the sunniness and leafiness that still lingers around us so deliciously. Wrote in the evening.

28th. [Tuesday] Bessy went to Báth for Anastasia. Walked to pay a visit to the Starkeys. The Dr. asked me to dine, and I did; amused with his odd stories of himself after dinner. Home early, and found Bessy and her little ones fast asleep in bed. Looking at them, and blessed them. Saw that 'Statia was looking as well as ever.

29th. [Wednesday] Insisted upon having the nurse into the house for Russell to sleep with, as Bessy had brought on, by her restless nights with him, the erysipelas she suffered so much with in Paris, from the same cause with Tom.

30th. [Thursday] Tremendous weather. Sent off to Power, either yesterday or to-day, words to a Spanish air, beginning "Oh, the joys of our evening Posada."[1] Walked through the storm to Phipps's, and got completely wet. Wanted me to stay and sleep, but refused, and ventured out through such a night as has seldom been witnessed. To add to the horrors, lost my way, and was obliged to retrace my steps for a considerable distance in the very teeth of the tempest, fearing every moment that my lantern would be blown out, in which event I should have to wander about till morning.

31st. [Friday] The havoc of last night visible every where. Trees blown down in all directions. Bath coaches endeavouring to come this way, instead of their customary road, but obliged to return. Read and wrote. Saw a tree which had fallen over the path I came last night. An Horatian escape this!

November 1st. [Saturday] Read and wrote.

2nd. [Sunday] Walked with Bessy in the evening, and called upon the Starkeys.

3rd. [Monday] Had a pony from Calne to try; and Bessy and Mrs. Phipps drove to Buckhill. Walked on before them, and as far as the Park; and took 'Statia to call upon Lady Lansdowne, who showed me a good epigram Lord L. had sent her from London; the two last lines of which are,—

> "D'Angoulême se donne à Dieu
> Et Donnadieu se donne au Diable."

Walked from thence with 'Stasia to leave her with mama at Buckhill, and returned myself home on foot. The pony does very well: think of exchanging my other for her, if I can manage it.

4th. [Tuesday] The celebration of Tom's birth-day, which was deferred till to-day, again frustrated by the bad weather; none of the children came, nor any body but the Phippses, who dined and supped. Played with our little ones in the evening.

5th. [Wednesday] Had promised Bowles to go and dine with him to-day, but the weather so bad, that it was impossible to venture in my gig; so gave up all thoughts of it, and dined with Bess at two. A little after four, however, arrived a chaise ordered by Bowles; so was obliged to go. Company at dinner, Mr. and Mrs. Lysons and their two daughters (from Gloucestershire), Mr. Clarke (the Winchester man, who wrote a pamphlet against Brougham on the Education question)[1] and his wife, and Mr. Hume, the Vicar of Calne. Day very pleasant; music in the evening. Mr. L. and one of his daughters sung duets. "God save the King," it seems, has been at last ascertained to have been composed by a man of the name of John Bull in the time of James I. The pretty melody sung in churches to the "Evening Hymn" was composed, Bowles says, by Tallis, the famous musician in the reigns of Henry VIII., Edward, and Mary, whose responses to the Litany are still performed in cathedral service. Talked of the beautiful words there are to some of Purcell's things; the four following lines charming:—

> "We heard the nightingale, the lark,—
>   And all around seemed blithe and gay;
> We ne'er grew sad till it grew dark,
>   And nothing mourned but parting day."

Mrs. L. and her daughters sung "Verdi prati" to the English words. Slept there, as did the Lysonses.

6th. [Thursday] The L.'s started after breakfast. Tried over some of Purcell's songs for Bowles; one that I sung at first sight rather surprised him; and with "Mad Bess" he was enchanted. Said my performance of these things (he being all for the old school) had elevated his opinion of my musical powers exceedingly. Proposed to him to undertake with me a set of biographical notices of these old composers; said he would. Looked over Hooker for the splendid passage about Law; found it near the beginning. Looked over J. Taylor's "Living and Dying"[1] for a fine passage about the setting sun, which Mrs. Bowles says Irving had borrowed in one of his sermons. Could not find it; but discovered in Irving the extraordinary description of Paradise, in which he introduces an allusion to me; "Angels, not like those Three, sung by no holy mouth." His own Paradise, however, almost as naughty a one as either I or Mahomet could invent. Set off for home between two and three, and arrived to dinner. Find that the man with whom I wished to swap ponies requires five pounds with mine.

7th. [Friday] Sent to the man to offer *four* pounds; says that my servant mistook him, and that it is *six* pounds he requires, allowing but six guineas for mine, which cost me thirteen; the poor man's luck always. Sent off to Power a song, words and music by myself; "Let thy joys alone."[1]

8th. [Saturday] Read and wrote. Made up my mind to give the six pounds, and sent William with it; so that my new pony now stands me in about twenty pounds.

10th. [Monday] Working away; find my Irish work more troublesome than I expected from the historical detail I have undertaken at the beginning of it.

14th. [Friday] Bessy drove over to Buckhill to ask them to the reliques of yesterday. Hughes and his daughter came, and Mrs. P. Sent a song to Power, beginning, "Being weary of love."[1]

15th. [Saturday] Dined at Phipps's; though Bessy at first refused, this being her birth-day, and it having a long been a fancy of hers that she was to die at the age of thirty, which she completed to-day. Company, the Bowleses, Lockes, Dr. Starkey, Mrs. Fisher, Edmonston, &c.

16th. [Sunday] My dear girl, who acknowledged that the fancy about her dying at thirty had haunted her a good deal, gave me a letter which she had written to me in contemplation of this event; full of such things as, in spite of my efforts to laugh at her for her nonsense, made me cry. Went to church. Dr. Starkey offered us the pew the Hugheses used to occupy.

23rd. [Sunday] Read and wrote. Have received a portrait of my dear mother to match that of my father; and though it does not do her justice, there is, in particular lights, enough of resemblance to make it very precious to me.

28th. [Friday] Bessy drove me to Buckhill, where the Bowleses met me in their carriage. Arrived with them in Bath at about half-past two. Raining all day. Walked to see my dearest Anastasia, and found her quite well. The Knight of Kerry had come the day before, to ask her to dine with his children, and accompany them to the opera. Called upon the Knight, and thanked Mrs. F. for her kindness to my little girl. Dined with the Bowleses at the White Hart, and B. would give me a bottle of claret. To the opera in the evening, where my greatest pleasure was looking at Anastasia, in the front of a box opposite to us. Opera, "Il Turco;" Ronzi de Begnis charming.[1]

29th. [Saturday] Breakfasted with the Knight of Kerry. Thence to Anastasia. Performed some commissions, and started with the Bowleses at one. A good deal of conversation about the religion of the Church of England. James's introduction of the words "verily and indeed" into the Catechism, respecting the Eucharist, unlucky, as amounting very much to the same thing as the Popish belief. The scholastic word Trinity introduced late into Christianity, and productive of much mischief. In the contest with the Unitarians, Athanasius's Creed is one of the weapons which the Church wields as authentic, though considering it all the time a forgery. Owned that these inconsistencies were unlucky. Does not think Locke was inclined to Arianism; praised his preface to the Epistles.[1] Arrived at Buckhill about four, and found my little gig in waiting. Hughes, who had been asked to meet me at Dr. Starkey's to-day, came with us, and (as there was no time for me to go home to dress) we proceeded straight to Bromham. Company, the Phippses, Hughes, and ourselves. The P.'s left us at home at night.

December 4th. [Thursday] Power arrived after breakfast. Brought me some of the things Bishop has done for the Greek work, besides copies of the "Irish Melodies" and "Sacred Songs," the latter of which he wishes to have first out. My own little glee, in the Greek work, "Here, while the moonlight dim," goes very prettily.[1] Asked the Phippses to dinner, as Power had brought fish and oysters with him.

5th. [Friday] Bessy drove Power through Bowood to Buckhill, while I finished some verses of the incomplete songs for him. The Phippses again dined with us, to finish the fish; also Hughes.

6th. [Saturday] Looked over the different works with Power. Happy to find that his zeal for the continuance of our engagement together has not the least relaxed. Made some arrangement with him to facilitate the payment of my Christmas bills. After dinner a chaise arrived, to take him to Devizes, to catch the mail. Left us at half-past five.

7th. [Sunday] Reading "Selden on Tithes," &c.[1]

10th. [Wednesday] Walked over to Bowood, to call upon Lord Lansdowne. Wrote, during my walk, a new verse to one of my "Sacred Songs." Miss Fox and Miss Vernon at Bowood. Lord L. walked the greater part of the way back with me. Showed him Croker's letter to me, begging I would ask him, in case there should exist among his papers any letters of Col. Barré's, that he would have the goodness to give me one of them, for Croker to bind up with a portrait of Barré in Cadell and Davis's Collection. Said he would look when in town, and will give one, if he has it. Says the reputation of England on the Continent has sunk considerably, with one party, for having shown an inclination to oppose them without being (as they think) able to venture; and with the other, for having given them hopes of assistance, and then left them in the lurch. The famous Gentz spoke to Wishaw in an affected tone of concern for the embarrassments that England is surrounded by, particularly in respect to the state of Ireland; and said it was rather strange that a country which took such mighty interest in the way *other* powers governed their dominions, should not have learned better how to manage her own.

11th. [Thursday] Sent off to Power three of the "Sacred Songs," fit for the press. Went with Phipps to dine at Walker's, at Melksham, to meet my old Moorish acquaintance, Ombark. A good deal of talk at dinner about the Mahometan religion, and religion in general. In the evening looked over some sermons with Walker. Compared the strutting and labouring style of the fashionable Irving with that of Hall, the famous Leicester preacher. Read over some of the very pleasing passages in Horne's preface to his work on the Psalms: that where he compares the Psalms to the Garden of Paradise, and another, where he speaks of the delight the task had afforded him.[1] A little affectation in such sentences as, "very pleasantly has it," &c. &c., but altogether full of sweetness and elegance.

13th. [Saturday] Beautiful day. Employed about my chapter of "Tithes,"[1] but walking about the fields all the while.

14th. [Sunday] Received a note from Croker, proposing that I should belong to a new club for literary and scientific persons, to be formed on the model of the United Service, &c. Wishes me to propose it to Lord Lansdowne also, and says, "We should not feel that we did our duty to the proposed institution if we did not express to Lord Lansdowne and to you the wish of all the present members of the committee that his Lordship and you should belong to us."[1] Wrote my long-threatened letter to my deputy at Bermuda.

15th. [Monday] Wrote a letter to Lord Byron, on his long silence to me; saying that I could not account for it unless it arose from "one of those sudden whims against the absent which I have often dreaded from him; one of those meteor-stones which generate themselves so unaccountably in the high atmosphere of his fancy, and come down upon one, some fine day, when one least expects to be so lapidated; begging, however, if I am to be in the list of the *cut dead,* he will tell me so, that I may make my funeral arrangements accordingly."[1] Lord Lansdowne called; walked part of the way home with him. Promised to dine at Bowood on Friday.

19th. [Friday] Drove over to Bowood to dinner: company, Lords Malmesbury and Arundel, Bailey, a Scotch lawyer whose name I forget, Miss Fox, and Miss Vernon. In the evening Lord M. produced an original letter of Locke's to a Mrs. Springer; very prosy indeed. A curious statement also of the husband of this lady (a solicitor) having fallen down ill in the street, and a rough copy of the Exclusion Act found upon him, which, with the rest of his papers, was laid before the council. Sir Robert Sawyer, who had assisted in drawing up this Act, caught a glimpse of his own hand-writing (having interlined this very copy), and accordingly, huddling up the papers, proposed that each of the Law Officers should carry a certain portion of them home with him, in order to examine their contents more carefully, taking care that this unlucky copy should be among his own share.[1] Talked of the correspondence between Newton and Locke, given by Stewart in his Preliminary Dissertation to the Encyclopedia.[2] Lord L. read them out. The *abandon* of Newton's contrition, for having once said, upon hearing that Locke was ill, "it were better he were dead," very interesting even in its weakness. He signs himself "Your unfortunate friend." Locke's answer thought by some of our party cold and stiff, but it has, perhaps, quite sufficient kindness, with certainly a considerable portion of dignity.[3] Verboseness is its great fault, as it is of most of Locke's writings, except (as Lord L. remarked) in a sort of a report of a debate at which he was present, inserted in his works, where he has given one of the concisest and clearest specimens of reporting that perhaps exist.[4] The feeling of Newton against Locke was in consequence of the injury he thought Locke's theory of innate ideas inflicted on the cause of morality. Looked at the little casts by Hemming, a Scotch artist, of the Phigaleian, and Elgin bas-reliefs. Was expected to sleep to-night, but the weather being very clear, drove home. Lord L. will belong to this new club, but bid me impress upon Croker strongly the necessity of keeping it select, as we shall otherwise be overrun with all the pretenders to literature and the arts, than whom there is not anywhere a more odious race.

21st. [Sunday] Went at two to assist at the opening of the new domestic chapel that Lord Lansdowne has built. Bessy most anxious to go, but prevented by the want of a new bonnet; Bowles's sermon much too long and desultory. The organ a very good one. Wanted me to dine, but returned home, Lord and Lady L. walking some part of the way with me.

22nd. [Monday] Read and wrote. Our dear Anastasia came home for the holidays. Made my first appearance on horseback for these nine or ten years. Rode to meet Bessy, who was at Devizes. Met the Phippses half way and rode back with them, the little pony going very well in company.

25th. [Thursday] This being Christmas Day, allowed our servants to have their friends to dinner. A large party, and most uproariously jolly in the evening. The Phippses supped with us.

26th. [Friday] All dined at Dr. Starkey's. Danced and sung in the evening.

27th. [Saturday] Abercromby (M.P. for Calne) and young Macdonnel called upon me from Bowood. Walked part of the way back with them. A good deal of conversation about Ireland. Told them my plan of Captain Rock's Memoirs, which Abercromby said was a very "clever thought;" urged upon me the importance of setting the Rebellion of '98 in its true points of view, as an event purposely brought about by the Government. Macdonnel mentioned some curious proofs of the increase of the Catholic population in the north. Dined all at Phipps's. The same sort of Christmas party as yesterday.

28th. [Sunday] Drove over to Bowood to dinner: company, Lord Auckland and sister, the Abercrombys, Macdonald (member), the Vernon Smiths, Knight of Kerry and son, &c. Dinner very agreeable; sung in the evening; slept there. Forgot to mention that I received a letter from Charles Sheridan a day or two since, which seems to throw a new difficulty in the way of my "Life of Sheridan." He still considers himself as having a claim on Murray for a share of the profits (to be given to the family), in consideration of having allowed the use of the papers, a claim which Murray is not disposed to admit.[1]

29th. [Monday] Walked home after breakfast, for the purpose of getting C. Sheridan's letter, to consult Lord L. upon it. Dinner again most agreeable. Sung a good deal in the evening; Rossini, Purcell, my own, &c. &c. Had some more talk with Abercromby about Ireland. Was happy to hear him say that his father, if bid to select from his whole life the portion he was most proud of, would have named the time of his command in Ireland.[1] Slept there.

30th. [Tuesday] After breakfast had some conversation with Lord L. upon the subject of C. S.'s letter. His advice pretty much what I had anticipated: evidently of opinion that I shall have no reason to be sorry even if obliged to sacrifice all the trouble I have taken, and give up the task entirely. Much pressed to stay over to-day, but returned home to dinner. Lord Auckland, Smith, and Macdonnel walked the greater part of the way with me.

31st. [Wednesday] Wrote to Sheridan. Had a kind letter from Jeffrey, expressing some fears lest his last to me should have contained something I did not like, as I had not answered it, and entreating me to help him out with an article or two for the next number of the "Review." This I cannot do.

Notes to 1823 Entries

6 January

1. The warfare between pygmies and cranes was a common motif in classical mythology. Cf. *Iliad*, 3. 3–6.

2. Cf. *King Lear*, 1. iv.

3. Cf. *Hamlet*, 5. ii: "It is the poisoned cup! it is too late!"

4. See *The Letters of R. B. Sheridan*, ed. Cecil Price (Oxford, 1966), 1: 80–81 and notes.

5. Richard Tickell's *Anticipation* . . . (1778) was, as its subtitle stated, an imagined version of the King's address to Parliament and of the subsequent debate on the message in the House of Commons. See *The Parliamentary History of England . . . to 1803*, 19 (1777–78): 1363–65, for an account of Col. Isaac Barré's speech during the debate.

6. *La Cassette verte de M. de Sartine* (1779).

7. Elizabeth, Baroness Craven, *The Miniature Picture* (1780). For Sheridan's prologue see Rhodes, *Plays and Poems of Sheridan*, 3: 278–80.

7 January

1. Sir Matthew Mite is the main character in Foote's *The Nabob*, first performed in 1772 and published in 1778. The man who served in part as the basis for Foote's character was a Gen. Richard Smith. See Simon Trefinan, *Sam. Foote, Comedian, 1720–1777* (New York, 1971), pp. 204, 206–7.

8 January

1. See entry for 13 January 1823.

2. C. D. Raffenel, *Histoire des événements de la Grèce, depuis les premiers troubles jusqu'à ce jour* . . . (1822).

3. See *The Early Correspondence of Lord John Russell 1805–1840*, ed. Rollo Russell (London, 1913), 1: 233–34.

9 January

1. The review of Moore's *Loves of the Angels* in *John Bull*, 6 January 1823, p. 5, and 13 January 1823, p. 13, labeled Moore a shallow dilettante and declared that many of the poem's details were unfit for the public.

12 January

1. Christian Müller, "Journey through Greece and the Ionian Islands, 1821" in vol. 8 of Sir

Richard Phillips's *New Voyages and Travels, consisting of originals and translations and abridgements,* 9 vols. (1819–25). Charles Sheridan, *Thoughts on the Greek Revolution* (1822).

2. "Awake, Arise, Thy Light Is Come," *Works,* 4:292.

13 January

1. Thomas Smart Hughes, *An Address to the People of England in the cause of the Greeks* . . . (1822).

14 January

1. Hester Lynch Thrale, afterwards Piozzi, *Retrospection; or a review of the most striking events, characters, situations, and their consequences which the last eighteen hundred years have presented to the view of mankind* (1801).

15 January

1. Dudley Ryder, Earl of Harrowby, was Lord President in Liverpool's cabinet.

2. Arthur, Lord Capel of Hadham (1610?–49), was among a group of peers who in 1642 signed a declaration disavowing any intentions of making war on parliament. In 1648 however he led a royalist force against the parliamentary army and was arrested and charged with high treason. He escaped from the Tower but was soon recaptured and executed.

Marshal Michel Ney (1769–1815) had sworn allegiance to Louis XVIII, but he joined Napoleon on his return to France and fought in the battle of Waterloo. When Paris capitulated after the battle, Ney attempted to escape to Switzerland, but was captured and shot for treason.

16 January

1. There were two translations of Cellini's autobiographical writings available to Moore at this time: *The Life of Benvenuto Cellini: A Florentine artist . . . Written by himself . . . and translated . . . by Thomas Nugent,* 2 vols. (1771); and *Memoirs of Benvenuto Cellini . . . written by himself . . . with the notes and observations of G. P. Carpani, now first translated by Thomas Roscoe,* 2 vols. (1822).

18 January

1. In the fifth edition of *The Loves of the Angels,* Moore changed the angels into "Turks" (i.e., Moslem angels) and God into Allah in response to the hostile reception of his poem.

19 January

1. Barthélemy D'Herbelot, *Bibliothèque Orientale* (1697).

20 January

1. Count Santorre Annibale Derossi Di Santa Rosa, *De la révolution piémontaise* (1821).

2. At this point Russell added the following note: "Prince Carignan was afterwards the rash and unfortunate, but not contemptible, Charles Albert!" Moore's opinion of Charles Albert, Prince of Carignan (1798–1849), no doubt derived from the prince's involvement in the 1821 revolution in the Piedmont, in which he failed to support the liberal leaders in their constitutional fight as he had promised he would do.

21 January

1. The Holy Alliance issued letters of protest to the Spanish government concerning the restoration of Ferdinand VII to the throne in January 1823. Spain's response to these notes is the "noble answer" to which Moore refers. See Halévy, *History,* 2: 166–67.

22 January

1. Humphrey Prideaux, *The True Nature of Imposture fully displayed in the life of Mahomet . . .* (1976); Isaac de Beausobre, *Histoire critique de Manichée et du Manïcheisme. . . ,* 2 vols. (1734, 1739).

23 January

1. See Dowden, *Letters,* 2: 511–12.

27 January

1. Thomas Hyde, *Historia religionis veterum Persarum . . .* (1700). Moore also refers to the works of Philo (often called Philo Judaeus). There were several collections available to him, including, according to the *British Museum Catalogue,* "Philonis . . . opera . . . textum cum MSS . . . illustravit Th. Mangey, Gr. & Lat. MS Notes [by J. Markland] 2 vols. London, 1742." Mangey also brought out a 5 volume edition of the *Opera Omnia,* 1785–1792. "Martin's *Travels*" probably refers to P. Martin, *Histoire de l'expédition Française en Égypte* 2 vols. Paris, 1815.

31 January

1. Moore's *Fables for the Holy Alliance . . .* by Thomas Brown the Younger was published in 1823. See *Works,* 7: 207–68.

1 February

1. *Monthly Review* 100 (1823): 79–95.

4 February

1. *Mémoires de l'académie des inscriptions et belles-lettres, 50 vols.* (1717–1809).
2. *New Monthly Magazine,* n.s. 9 (1823): 74–75; *London Magazine* 7 (1823): 212–215; *Gentleman's Magazine,* 123 (1823): 41–44; *Monthly Magazine* 55 (1823): 35–39.

11 February

1. Bowles published his poem *Ellen Gray; or the dead maiden's curse* (1823) under the pseudonym "Dr. Archibald Macleod."

12 February–15 March

1. *Blackwood's Edinburgh Magazine* 13 (1823): 63–71; *Ladies' Monthly Museum,* improved ser: 17 (1823): 99–101; *British Magazine, or Miscellany of Polite Literature* 1 (1823).

2. See Dowden, *Letters,* 2, 513–14 and notes.
3. See entry for 21 January 1823 and its note. After delivering their notes of protest, the Holy Alliance powers continued their preparations for an invasion of Spain and on 7 April 1823 the duc d'Angoulême led a powerful army across the border of France into Spain. The rebels, taking Ferdinand prisoner, fled to Cadiz but were soon captured.

29 March

1. Charles Spencer, *A Scriptural Account of the nature and employment of the Holy Angels,* etc. (1823).

1 April

1. "Le Chapeau de Paille" is a painting by Rubens, ca. 1620.
2. Coleridge's *Christabel* was published in 1816.
3. "Loves of the Angels—Moore and Byron," *Edinburgh Review* 38 (1823): 27–48. James A. Greig, *Francis Jeffrey of the Edinburgh Review* (Edinburgh, 1948), p. 150, identifies Jeffrey as the author of this review.

4 April

1. The *London Magazine* published Lamb's "Essays of Elia" from 1820 to 1823.
2. Moore refers to Mary Lamb (1764–1847). See E. V. Lucas, *The Life of Charles Lamb* (London, 1906), 1: 93–94, and 2: 89, for further accounts of her insanity.
3. "Thou great first cause, least understood." Alexander Pope, "Universal Prayer," l. 5.
4. Samuel Butler, *Hudibras* (1663–78).
5. Daniel Defoe, *The History and Remarkable Life of the truly Honorable Col. Jacque, commonly Call'd Col. Jack* (1723).
6. "Whistlecraft" is the pseudonym used by John Hookham Frere, author of *Prospectus and specimen of an Intended National Work . . . relating to King Arthur . . .* (1817–18), later changed to *The Monks and the Giants . . .* (1818). Byron's *Beppo* appeared in 1818.
7. Jeremy Taylor, *A Discourse of the Liberty of Prophesying* (1647).

6 April

1. "Church and State," "The Looking-glasses," "The Dissolution of the Holy Alliance," and "The Fly and the Bullock" are *Fables* 5, 2, 1, and 4 respectively of *Fables for the Holy Alliance, Works,* 7: 216–58.
2. *Works,* 8: 185–86.

9 April

1. Dryden, *All for Love,* 4. i.
2. Edward Young, *The Complaint: or, Night-thoughts on Life, Death, and Immortality* (1742–45, 1747).
3. Mary Russell Mitford, *Julian* (1823).

10 April

1. Moore alludes to the defeat of the constitutionalists by the monarchists at Chaves on 13 March 1823.

11 April

1. John Poole, *Simpson and Co.* (1827).

12 April

1. Richard Payne Knight, *Alfred, a romance in rhyme* (1823).
2. Saverio Mercadante, *Elisa è Claudio ossia L'amore protetto dall'Amicizia* (1821).

14 April

1. In 1782 the Irish Parliament declared its independence from the English Parliament and also passed a bill removing many of the disabilities placed on Irish Catholics.

16 April

1. Russell notes here that these ladies are daughters of Lord William Russell.
2. See entry for 9 April 1823 and its n. 1. Wentworth Dillon, fourth Earl of Roscommon (1633?–85), was an English poet and translator of Horace and Ovid.

17 April

1. On 17 April 1823 Brougham referred to Canning's "monstrous truckling" on the Catholic relief issue. Canning rose and shouted that Brougham's charge was false. See *Parlia.Debates*, ser. 2, 8 (1823): 1070–1123.
2. See entry for 21 November 1818 and its n. 1.
3. Byron, *The Giaour*, 11. 1064–65. The first line, which Moore quotes, should read, "he gave the blow." See Coleridge, *Byron's Poetry*, 3: 133.
4. Racine, *Andromaque* (1667), 4. v.

18 April

1. Sir George Pretyman Tomline, successively Bishop of Lincoln and Winchester, *Memoirs of the life of the Right Hon. William Pitt* (1821).

21 April

1. Pope, "The First Satire of the Second Book of Horace," 11. 155–156.

4, 5 May

1. Jean Louis Henriette Campan, *Mémoires sur la vie privée de Marie-Antoinette*, etc., 3 vols. (1822).

8 May

1. The *Morning Chronicle* for 7 May 1823 gave the *Fables* a favorable review. The reviewer noted particularly the section on the "Destruction of the Holy Alliance," saying "We . . . cannot

. . . love the Holy Alliance; for from its off-setting, we foresaw that it boded no good to the trade in journals." "Kings and journalists are as natural enemies as cats and mice. . . . It would be unnatural in Kings not to love bayonets better than printing presses, but it would be as unnatural in us to share their affection."

9 May

1. The London *Times* 7 May 1823 published a short and very favorable notice of Moore's *Fables* along with all of Fable 2, "The Looking Glasses."

11 May

1. The first edition of Moore's *Evenings in Greece* was published by Power in 1826. *Works*, 5: 5–83.
2. Dr. Edward Daniel Clarke, *Travels in Various Countries in Europe, Asia, and Africa*, 6 vols. (1810–23). Edward Dodwell, *A Classical and Topographical Tour through Greece, during the years 1801, 1805, and 1806*, 2 vols. (1819).
3. *The Literary Gazette*, May 10, 23, pp. 289 ff. The "Museum" refers to the *Ladies' Monthly Museum* 18 (1823): 101–2.

14 May

1. See entry for 11 May 1823 and its n. 1.

15 May

1. The opening song in *Evenings in Greece, Works*, 5: 5.
2. The review of *Loves of the Angels* appeared in *John Bull* for 5 and 12 January 1823.

16 May

1. *Les Amours des anges, poème en trois chants, traduit* . . . [par Davésiès de Pontès] (1823). See entry for 15 July 1823 and its note for another French translation of Moore's poem.

17 May

1. This meeting to raise a subscription for the Greek revolutionists was held on 15 May 1823. An account of the speeches and the reading of Moore's verses appeared in the London *Times*, 16 May 1823.

22 May

1. Robert Bisset, *The History of the Reign of George III*, 6 vols. (1803).

23 May

1. See Dowden, *Letters*, 2: 517.

24 May

1. John Russell Moore (1823–42), Thomas Moore's youngest son.

30 May

1. Mrs. Elizabeth Inchbald, *Lovers' Vows . . . From the German of Kotzebue* (1798).

3 June

1. Rossini, *La donna del lago* (1819), libretto adapted from Scott's "The Lady of the Lake."

4 June

1. See Laurence Sterne, *Tristram Shandy,* ed. J. A. Work (New York, 1940), p. 513.

5 June

1. Sir Patrick Hume (1641–1724) accompanied Archibald Campbell, ninth Earl of Argyll, in the expedition to restore James, Duke of Monmouth, to the throne in 1685. The account of the affair that Charles James Fox gave in his *History . . . of James II* (1808) was challenged by George Rose in his *Observations on the Historical work of the late . . . C. J. Fox . . . with a narrative of the events which occurred in the enterprise of the Earl of Argyll in 1685, by Sir Patrick Hume* (1809).
2. The Memoirs of William Adam (1751–1839) were never published.
3. Lord John Russell, *Memoirs of the Affairs of Europe from the Peace of Utrecht* (1824–29), vols. 1 and 2, reprinted as *History of the Principal States of Europe*, 2 vols. (1826).
4. Rossini, *Ricciardo e Zoraide* (1818).

6 June

1. Pitt spoke in support of Wilberforce's motion for the abolition of the Slave Trade on 2 April 1792. See *Parlia. Hist.* 29 (1791–1792): 1055–1158.

7 June

1. James Winston's work was published as *A Collection of Memoranda . . . etc. relating to Drury Lane Theatre from the earliest period, 1616, to 1830. . . ,* 23 vols. (1830).

8 June

1. William Conyngham Plunket (1764–1854), attorney-general for Ireland, brought charges of riot and conspiracy to commit assault against the Orangemen who had participated on 14 December 1822 in demonstrations at the Theatre Royal in Dublin. The charges were dismissed by a grand jury obviously packed with Orangemen; Plunket was so outraged that he issued his own *ex officio* charges against the protesters. The men were never prosecuted, and Plunket was called before the House of Commons to explain his actions. See Hereward Senior, *Orangeism in Ireland and Britain* (London, 1966), pp. 199–204.
2. "This story, which I had heard, does not appear to be true," (Russell's note.) Moore is referring to the Coalition government formed in 1783 with Lord North as Home Secretary and Sheridan as Secretary to the Treasury. See Sichel, *Sheridan,* 2: 28–9 for Sheridan's feelings on this alliance of North and Fox.
3. Olivia, Lady Bective, was the widow of Edward Tuite Dalton when she married Thomas Taylour (son of the Marquess of Headfort and the Earl of Bective) in 1822.
4. "Lord Spencer was a very good shot, and not likely to have 'bagged the king.'" (Russell's note.)

9 June

1. Edward Irving (1792–1834), a Scottish divine, who became extremely popular when he began preaching in London in 1822. One of his early works was *For Judgment to come, an argument in nine parts* (1823), an attack on the profanity of both Southey's and Byron's respective works entitled "Vision of Judgment."

10 June

1. On 23 June 1823 George Grenville, Baron Nugent (1789–1850), introduced a bill to grant the franchise to English Catholics and to make them eligible for certain elective offices. Ultimately the bill was defeated in the House of Lords. See *Parlia. Debates,* ser. 2, 9 (1823): 573–92, 1127–39, and 1476–89.

2. Laurence Sterne, *The Sermons of Mr. Yorick,* 7 (1769): Sermon 18, "The Ingratitude of Israel." Moore has apparently confused the MS passage with that in the printed text, which reads, "[God] foresaw they would certainly prove a thankless and unthinking people. . . ."

12 June

1. Henry Grattan the younger published the biography of his father as *Memoirs of the life and times of the Rt. Hon. Henry Grattan,* 5 vols. (1839–46).

2. On 13 June 1823 a public meeting was held in support of Spain in its struggle against the French invasion. Several resolutions were passed, including one affirming Spain's right to self-determination. The London *Times,* 14 June 1823, gives an account of the meeting. See also entry for 21 January 1823 and its n. 1, and entry for 12 February to 15 March 1823 and its n. 3.

17 June

1. Brougham and Thomas Denman were Queen Caroline's defense attorneys in her trial before the House of Lords in 1820. Moore lists Lord Grey among the Queen's defenders because he opposed the Bill of Pains and Penalties brought against her.

2. Queen Caroline confided in Lady Charlotte Douglas that Austin Warren (born 1802) was her son; Lady Charlotte and her husband, Sir John, spread the story, but in 1806 an inquiry conducted by the Prince of Wales determined that Warren was the son of Sophia Austin. See Joanna Richardson, *George IV: A Portrait* (London, 1966), pp. 66–71.

3. Sir Matthew Wood (1768–1843), alderman and M. P., was a friend and adviser to the Queen. John Page Wood (1796–1866), his oldest son, was her chaplain and private secretary. William Page Wood (1801–81), his second son, was a protégé of the Queen. Henry, Viscount Hood (1753–1836), and his wife Jane (d. 1847) were gentleman and lady-in-waiting on the Queen.

18 June

1. Carl Maria Von Weber, *Der Freischütz* (1821). The libretto is based on a tale by J. A. Apel (1810) and a tragedy of the same title by Franz Xavier Von Caspar (1812).

19 June

1. Kenney's new play was *Sweethearts and Wives,* first performed at the Haymarket Theatre 7 July 1823. The piece being rehearsed was Mozart's *The Marriage of Figaro* (1786), performed at the Haymarket that evening, 19 June 1823.

22 June

1. See Moore's *Sheridan,* 2: 446–47.
2. In 1788 Pitt introduced the Regency Bill, designed to limit drastically the power of the Regent. While Parliament debated the bill, the Prince of Wales sent Pitt a letter written by Burke and Sheridan protesting his actions. See Richardson, *George IV,* pp. 42–44. For the complete text of the letter see Sichel, *Sheridan,* 2: 393–96 (appendix 2). Sichel (2:194n.) accepts Elliot's denial of having written the letter.
3. See entry for 18 October 1818 and its n. 4.
4. In 1801 Henry Addington, later Viscount Sidmouth, formed a new administration in which he himself served as First Lord of the Treasury and Chancellor of the Exchequer. Unlike several of his political associates, Sheridan supported many of Addington's policies. See Sichel, *Sheridan,* 2: 306, 309.

25 June to 5 July

1. Mary Ann Kelty, *The Favourite of Nature. A tale,* 3 vols. (1821), and *Osmond* (1822), both published anonymously.
2. *Works,* 4: 227, 296–97, and 5: 241.

6, 7 July

1. See Russell, *Correspondence of Lord John Russell,* 2: 235.

8 July

1. Johann Lorenz von Mosheim, *J. L. Moshemii . . . de rebus Christianorum ante Constantinum magnum commentarii* (1753), translated into English by R. S. Vidal as *Commentaries on the affairs of the Christians before the time of Constantine. . . ,* 3 vols. (1813–35). Mosheim wrote several works on Church history, the most important of which was translated into English by A. Maclaine as *An Ecclesiastical History, ancient and modern . . .* 2 vols. (1765).
2. In April 1687 James II ordered the fellows of Magdalen College to elect Anthony Farmer as their president, which they refused to do, electing one of their fellows and graduates, Dr. John Hough (1651–1743), instead. In September 1688 the King was finally forced to accept their choice.

13 July

1. Probably a reference to the contributions of Martin Joseph Routh (1755–1854) to the *Patrologiae Cursus Completus,* ed. Jacques Paul Migne, 221 vols. (1844–64).
2. Robert Nares, *A Glossary: or collection of words, phrases, names and allusions . . .* (1822).
3. *Works,* 4: 257–59.
4. Psalm 137:1. See Coleridge, *Byron's Poetry,* 3: 402.
5. Joanna Baillie, *A Collection of Poems, Chiefly Manuscript, and From Living Authors* (1823). Bowles's sonnet is printed anonymously (p. 77): it is also included in Bowles's *Poetical Works,* ed. George Gilfillan (Edinburgh, 1855), 1: 24–25. The first line of the poem reads, "When last we parted. . . ."

15 July

1. *Les Amours des anges et les melodies irlandaises, de Thomas Moore, traduction de l'anglais par Mme Louise Sw. Belloc* (1823).

17 July

1. Agathon Jean François, Baron Fain, *Manuscrit de mil huit cent quatorze, . . . contenant l'histoire des dix derniers mois du règne de Napoléon* (1823), trans. anonymously as *The Manuscript of 1814. A history of events which led to the abdication of Napoleon . . .* (1823).

22 July

1. Cantos 6–8, 9–11, and 12–14 of *Don Juan* all appeared in 1823.
2. *Cobbett's Annual Register,* also called *Cobbett's Political Register* and *Cobbett's Weekly Political Register,* ed. William Cobbett (1802). *The Literary Examiner: consisting of the Indicator, a review of books and miscellaneous pieces in prose and verse,* ed. Leigh Hunt, no. 1–26 (1823).

25 July

1. Charles Cornwallis, first Marquis and second Earl Cornwallis (1738–1805), was lord-lieutenant of Ireland and commander-in-chief of the British forces during the rebellion of 1798.

28 July

1. Sydney Owenson, afterwards Lady Morgan, *The Life and Times of Salvator Rosa,* 2 vols. (1824).
2. *Works,* 6: 49.

31 July

1. See entry for 18 September 1830 and its n. 1.

2 August

1. John O'Driscol, *Views of Ireland, moral, political, and religious,* 2 vols. (1823).
2. The Tithes Leasing Bill, introduced in the House of Commons in 1822 and passed with the Irish Tithes Composition and Commutation Bills of 1823, allowed the Irish clergy to lease for a fixed sum the rights to the tithes owed to the church by Irish tenant farmers.

4 August

1. "This was a lodge of Lord Muskerry's. The whole valley from Ballynamona (or Mourne Abbey, the ruin nearly opposite to Mr. Williamson's) to Mallow, is very beautiful." (Russell's note.) Since Russell enclosed the note in quotation marks, it was probably originally Moore's own note to this passage.
2. See Sichel, *Sheridan,* 1, 87. The sons of George Rose (1744–1818) were named George Henry and William Stewart Rose.

5 August

1. See the entry for 2 August 1823 and its n. 2. A provision of the new Irish Tithes Bill required that settlements on new tithes be at least as high as the average sum for the seven years preceding 1821. The objection was that this period included several years in which the prices of grains were unusually high, thus raising the average.

2. "Applotment": division into plots; "agistment": the taking in of line stock to feed at a rate of so much per head.

6 August

1. "Captain Rock" was an imaginary leader of Irish Catholics in whose name a number of inflammatory proclamations were issued. He was also the basis of Moore's *Memoirs of Captain Rock, the Celebrated Irish Chieftain, with some Account of his Ancestors* (1824). Roger O'Connor (1762–1834) was an Irish Nationalist and member of the United Irishmen. The anagram *Rock*, however, is more likely based on the name Roderick O'Connor (1116?–98), high king of Ireland (1155–98).
2. "Zaraph" is one of the characters in *Loves of the Angels*. See *Works*, 8: 91 ff.
3. "Lines on the Death of Sheridan," *Works*, 7: 82.

10 August

1. Charles Smith, *The Antient and present state of the county of Kerry* (1756).

11 August

1. A reference to a challenge to a duel issued in 1815 by O'Connell to Sir Robert Peel, who sent Sir Charles Saxton as his second. The duel never occurred because Mrs. O'Connell alerted the police. O'Connell's second, a man named Lidwell, and Saxton did fight an inconsequential duel. See Norman Gash, *Mr. Secretary Peel* (Cambridge, Mass., 1961), pp. 163–67.

15 August

1. Miss Crumpe, *Isabel St. Albe: or Vice and Virtue*, 3 vols. (1823). *Geraldine of Desmond*, 3 vols., appeared in 1829.

17 August

1. Charles Bushe (1767–1843) was appointed Lord Chief Justice of the King's Bench of Ireland in 1822. William Saurin (1767–1840) was an Irish jurist and later attorney-general of Ireland.
2. "Polacca" is the name of the type of ship in which Queen Caroline and Bartolomeo Bergami sailed from Augusta to Tunis in 1815. Several of the witnesses against the Queen were members of the crew of this ship, and they and their testimony were often referred to as the "polacca." See Joanna Richardson, *The Disastrous Marriage* (London, 1960), pp. 163 ff. and 184.

21 August

1. William Monck Mason, *The History and Antiquities of the Collegiate and Cathedral Church of St. Patrick . . .* (1820).

24 August

1. Denis Scully, *A Refutation of the Statement of the Penal Laws which aggrieve the Catholics of Ireland* (1812). *The Anti-union* was a periodical published in Dublin in 1798–9 and 1799.

25 August

1. See entry for 8 June 1823 and its n. 1.

29, 30 August

1. *Memoirs of Captain Rock.* See entry for 6 August 1823 and its n. 1.
2. Edward Wakefield, *An Account of Ireland, statistical and political,* 2 vols. (1812).

9 September

1. *Works,* 7: 374–75.

10 September

1. *Works,* 4: 67–68, where it is entitled "As Vanish'd Erin."

11 September

1. Thomas Newenham, *A View of the natural, political and commercial circumstances of Ireland* (1809).

12 September

1. *Hamlet,* 5. i.

13 September

1. Samuel Johnson, *Prefaces, Biographical and Critical, to the Works of the English Poets,* 10 vols. (1779–81).
2. Sir Thomas Browne, *Pseudodoxia Epidemica: or Enquiries into very many received Tenets, and commonly presumed Truths* (1646, 1650). For Browne's testimony on witchcraft see Joan Bennett, *Sir Thomas Browne* (Cambridge, 1962), pp. 11–16.
3. James Ridley, *The Tales of the Genii, or the Delightful Lessons of Horam, the son of Asmar,* etc. (1764).

17 September

1. A monthly magazine founded by Richard Edward Mercier in Dublin in January 1793. Moore's first published poems appeared in the October 1793 issue. See Jones, *The Harp that Once—,* pp. 20–21.
2. Bartolome de las Casas wrote several works on America, one of which is *Brevissima Relación de la destruycíon de las Indias* (Sevilla, 1552).

19 September

1. *Works,* 4: 60–61.
2. William James MacNeven, *Pieces of Irish History* (New York, 1807); John Curry, *An Historical and Critical Review of the Civil Wars in Ireland . . .* (1775).

20–23 September

1. Moore later published the work as the *Memoirs of Captain Rock* (1824).

24 September

1. See Cyrano de Bergerac, *Histoire comique des états et empires de la lune et du soleil,* ed. P. L. Jacob (Paris, 1858), pp. 31–32.
2. Lucian of Samosata (ca. A.D. 120–80) wrote an imaginary travelogue entitled *Vera Historia.*
3. Holberg, Ludwig, Baron, *A Journey to the World Under-ground* by Nicholas Klim (1742). Moore probably saw the edition of 1812.

25 September

1. "Sweet Innisfallen," *Works,* 4: 53–54.

2 October

1. *Works,* 4:55–56.
2. *Memoirs of Captain Rock* (1824).

4 October

1. See "The Itinerary through Wales. . . ," *The Historical Works of Giraldus Cambrensis,* ed. Thomas Wright (1863), p. 411.

5 October

1. A reference to a treaty of 1780 by which the Irish were permitted to export goods of their manufacture, a privilege denied them since the reign of Charles II. See W. E. H. Lecky, *A History of Ireland in the Eighteenth Century,* abr. L. P. Curtis, Jr. (Chicago, 1972), p. 174.
2. Edward Wakefield, *An Account of Ireland, Statistical and Political,* 2 vols. (1812).

11 October

1. Sylvester O'Hallaran, *An Introduction to the Study of the History and Antiquities of Ireland* (1772).

12 October

1. John McDiarmid, *Lives of the British Statesman* (1807).
2. William Gilpin, *The Life of Thomas Cranmer, Archbishop of Canterbury* (1784).
3. John Lingard, *A History of England from the First Invasion by the Romans to the Accession of Henry VIII,* 8 vols. (1819–30). For John Allen's attack on this work, see *Edinburgh Review* 42 (1825): 1–31; 44 (1826): 94–155.
4. James Cavanah Murphy, *The Arabian Antiquities of Spain* (1815).
5. Russell's *Memoirs of the Affairs of Europe* (see entry for 5 June 1823 and its n. 3). Moore subsequently refers to this as the "French work" since volume one begins with an account of France at the end of Louis XIV's reign.

13 October

1. Robert Southey, *History of the Peninsular War*, 3 vols. (1823–32).

16 October

1. See entries for 2 and 5 August 1823 and nn. 2 and 1, respectively.
2. Thomas Leland, *The History of Ireland, from the Invasion of Henry II, with a preliminary Discourse on the antient state of that kingdom*, 3 vols. (1773).

19 October

1. In 1786 Samuel Henley (1740–1815) published without permission the translation and notes for *Vathek*, which Beckford had commissioned him to prepare. In his preface Henley stated that the work was a translation of an Arabic manuscript, and to correct this misconception, Beckford published in 1787 his original French version of the tale. See Lewis Melville, *The Life and Letters of William Beckford* (London, 1910), pp. 136–44.
2. *Aeneid*, 12.764–65.

20 October

1. Jeremy Taylor, *The Rule and Exercises of Holy Living* (1650).
2. Though William Markham (1719–1807) published Latin verse in such works as *Musae Anglicanae* and *Carmina Quadragesimalia*, none of the 140 numbers of John Hawkesworth's and Samuel Johnson's *The Adventurer* (1752–54) contain any of Markham's verse.

21 October

1. In 1643 Lady Blanche Arundell (1583–1649), wife of Thomas, second Lord Arundell, successfully defended Wardour Castle for eight days against the attacks of a parliamentary army led by Sir Edward Hungerford and Col. Strode. Lady Arundell surrendered on 10 May 1643, when two mines were exploded under the fortress, but only after gaining honorable terms from her captors.
2. Hugo Grotius (1583–1643), elected in 1615 to represent Rotterdam in the States of Holland, became involved in a theological and political dispute between Holland and Utrecht on the one hand, and, on the other, the more orthodox Calvinist majority in the states-general. In 1618 he was arrested for treason and in 1619 was sentenced to life imprisonment. He escaped, however, hidden in a chest, and fled to France.

22 October

1. In 1814 John Benett published *An Essay on the Commutation of Tithes*. . . . William Coxe (1747–1828), the Archdeacon of Wiltshire, responded to this work with his *Letter to John Benett . . . on his Essay relative to the Commutation of Tythes . . .* (1814). Benett countered with his *Reply to the Letter of the Revd. William Coxe . . .* (1815), and Coxe apparently answered this work as well, for in 1816 Benett published *Replies to the Three additional Letters of the Rev. William Coxe*.

30 October

1. "The Young Muleteers of Grenada," *Works*, 5: 153–54.

5 November

1. Liscombe Clarke, *A Letter to H. Brougham . . . in reply to the strictures on Winchester College, contained in his letter to Sir Samuel Romily* (1818). Brougham's open letter to Romilly had attacked, among other things, the abuses of charity at Westminister College. See Chester New, *Life of Henry Brougham to 1830* (Oxford, 1961), pp. 218–22.

6 November

1. Jeremy Taylor's *The Rule and Exercises of Holy Living* (see entry for 20 October 1823, n. 1) was often reprinted with *The Rule and Exercises of Holy Dying* (1651). The combined work was commonly referred to as "Holy Living and Dying."

7 November

1. *Works*, 5: 192–93.

14 November

1. "The Pretty Rose Tree," *Works*, 5: 150–51.

28 November

1. Rossini, *Il Turco in Italia* (1814).

29 November

1. John Locke, *A Paraphrase and Notes on the Epistles of St. Paul . . . To which is prefix'd, an Essay for the understanding of St. Paul's Epistles, by consulting St. Paul himself* (1705–9).

4 December

1. *Works*, 5: 36–38.

7 December

1. John Selden, *History of Tythes . . .* (1618).

11 December

1. George Horne, *A Commentary on the book of Psalms . . .* (1776).

13 December

1. Bk. 2, chap. 4 of Moore's *Captain Rock* is entitled "The Captain's opinions on Tithe matters."

14 December

1. See Louis J. Jennings, *The Croker Papers* (London, 1884), 1: 253–57. The club was soon named "The Athenaeum" and began meeting formally in 1824.

15 December

1. This letter is not among Moore's letters to Byron in the John Murray collection. Moore mentioned being "cut" by Byron in a letter to Murray dated 6 December 1823; see Dowden, *Letters,* 2: 520.

19 December

1. The Exclusion Act was designed to prevent James, then Duke of York, from becoming king at the death of his brother Charles II. The bill passed the House of Commons in 1680 but failed in the House of Lords. Sir Robert Sawyer (1633–92), who helped draft the measure, later served as attorney-general under James II.

2. Dugald Stewart, *Dissertation, exhibiting a general view of the progress of metaphysical, ethical, and political philosophy* . . . , 6 vols. (1824).

3. For Newton's letter of apology and Locke's reply see *The Correspondence of Isaac Newton* (Cambridge, 1961), 3: 280 and 283–84.

4. "A Letter From a Person of Quality . . . Giving an Account of the Debates and Resolutions of the House of Lords, in April and May, 1675 . . . ," *The Works of John Locke* (London, 1823; reprint ed. 1963 by Scientia Verlag Aalen), 10: 200–246.

28 December

1. See Dowden, *Letters,* 2: 520–21.

29 December

1. Sir Ralph Abercromby (1734–1801) was commander of the English army in Ireland from December 1797 to April 1798.

1824

January 1st. [Thursday] Edward Moore comes to-morrow.

2nd. [Friday] Moore arrived early. Walked with him to Bowood, to give him a glimpse of the house; to Bromham Church, too. The Phippses dined to meet him, and young Starkey, the Doctor being ill with gout.

3rd. [Saturday] Went into Devizes (E. Moore and all) to see the gaol. Practised at the treadmill, and did not find it so very bad; to light men, with pliant limbs, it is not one tenth of the punishment it must be to those who are heavy and stiff. Moore went on to Bath. Walked home.

6th. [Tuesday] Had a little dance in the evening for the Starkeys, Phippses, and Hugheses. Our annual present from Power of a twelfth-cake gave rise to much fun; and the whole party, children and all, remained till late.

9th. [Friday] Walked over to Bowood to dinner. Had been asked for yesterday to meet Lord Suffolk, "whom," says Lord L. in his note, "you will find a Whig to your heart's content, if not something more," and Lord Duncan. The latter went to-day. Company, the Suffolks, and Byng, just arrived. Sung in the evening. Slept there.

10th. [Saturday] Meant to have returned home, but they made a point of my dining again to-day. Walked to Phipps's, where Bessy met me with the gig to take me to Devizes, it being necessary I should draw for money to-day. Left me at the foot of Devizes Hill. Drew upon Power for £150 at two months. Went to some of the tradesmen to ask for their bills. Walked back to Bowood, which is about seven miles, making in all about ten or eleven, through dirty and slippery roads. The Suffolks gone, only Byng, and Lord Fitzharris, who, with his tutor, arrived to-day. Sung a little. Slept there.

11th. [Sunday] Returned home after breakfast, and worked a little.

15th. [Thursday] Dined at Hughes's at Devizes, Bessy and I, and the Phippses: company, Mr. Bingham (a nephew of Bowles's), young Awdrey, and Mr. Powell. Bingham clever and talkative. Much conversation about tithes; amount generally to near a third of the rent. Sung in the evening; so did Mr. Bingham, some of Burns's and of mine, with a good deal of spirit. Suspect the article Miss Hughes gave me the other night, which is on vocal music and very cleverly done, to be by Bingham. It is for Bentham's new Review (the "Westminster"), and has abundance about me in it, all very flattering.[1] Received a long letter from Abercromby about my Irish work, in which he seems to take a good deal of interest.

17th. [Saturday] Lady Lansdowne called to see little Russell. Asked us to dine at Bowood this day week, and insisted on sending the carriage to take us there and back.

20th. [Tuesday] Bess had a chaise to take our dear Anastasia to Bath. In walking met Lord L. riding; he sent back his horses, and we had a long walk together. Mentioned an article in the "New Monthly," which he thought might be Luttrel's, about Voltaire and Rousseau, following up my opinion of the latter in my "Rhymes on the Road," and speaking of me with praise.[1] This led to conversation about Voltaire; his *bonhomie,* his benevolence, and the interest he took to the last in every improvement of the condition of mankind. In talking of his religious opinions, I said that line might be applied to him, *à force d'esprit tout lui parut matière;* for he was himself the best argument against materialism that could be furnished, from the unimpaired vivacity which his mind continued to possess when his body had become merely a shadow.

24th. [Saturday] Dinner at Bowood: company, the Phippses, Bowleses, young Talbot, and ourselves. Day agreeable. Bowles's story about the two Catholic girls that had been Protestants, and were inclined to be converted back again. His bidding them read Chillingworth, and one of them marrying an Irish labourer, who beat Chillingworth out of the field, and kept her Catholic still, &c. &c. Talk about Chillingworth. His saying that if any one could answer his book against the Catholic Church, he should not be ashamed to show the world the example of a "second conversion," he having been originally a Papist.[1] Neale, in his "History of the Puritans" (Bowles said), has given a false account of Laud's conduct on the condemnation of Prynne, and has suppressed what both Whitelock and Rushworth have stated of his kindness to Prynne on that occasion, and Prynne's thanking him for it.[2] Praised Whitelock's book. Lord L. said his father had told him that one day in calling on Lord Chatham he found he had been setting his son, Pitt, to make an abstract of Whitelock's memorial as a task. How much more sensible than to set a boy to make dull Greek or Latin verses, as Lord Grenville or Lord Wellesley would probably have done! Lord L. mentioned Whitelock's Embassy to Sweden as interesting, though little read. He gives a minute account of the proposal of the embassy to him, of his conversation with Mrs. Whitelock abed about it, &c. &c.[3] Sang a little in the evening.

28th. [Wednesday] Received a letter from Lord Lansdowne, written just as he was starting for town, and sending me the charge of the Archbishop of Cashel, which contains some statements with regard to the reputed wealth of the Irish Church, which, Lord L. says, I ought to look to, so as not to fall into the errors on this subject which Hume, &c. have committed.[1]

29th, 30th. [Thursday, Friday] Bowles called upon me. Walked part of his way home with him. Long conversation about the Church, which he defends through thick and thin. Received a letter from Mr. Bingham, sending me the first number of the "Westminster Review," acknowledging rather a severe article in it upon me, to be written by him, and making a very candid and manly explanation on the subject.[1]

February 1st. [Sunday] Dined at Dr. Starkey's with his son John and Phipps. Answered Mr. B., and sent him a paragraph to put into "The Times," &c., in order to counteract the impression of what his article states with respect to my feelings towards the Americans.[1]

2nd, 3rd. [Monday, Tuesday] Working hard.

11th to 26th. [11 Feb: Wednesday; 26 Feb: Thursday] From this to the 27th had no time to attend to my Journal, being so closely occupied with the "Captain," which I had promised the MS. of to the Longmans much sooner. Sent up the copy of the First Book about the 19th or 20th, and told them I should be up myself with the rest by the end of the following week. Found myself very hard run towards the conclusion, and obliged to leave the transcribing till I should go to town. Our dear little Russell, who becomes prettier every day, has at length cut two teeth, which mama insists upon my recording in this Journal. Wrote to Sir J. Newport to say I was coming, and meant to ask his assistance in furnishing me materials for my work.

27th. [Friday] Set off from Calne in the York House coach. Two gentlemen and a lady my companions. One of the gentlemen, I found as we approached town, was a Lord, evidently a naval one: knew intimately my old friend Admiral Douglas. The young lady (who was with my Lord) was met by a gay chariot at Kew Bridge, to take her home. What a change has taken place in coach company within these few years! Arrived a little before seven; and after depositing my things at my lodgings in Duke Street, went to Edward Moore's, who had dinner prepared for me. He has fitted his house up very elegantly, and had it lighted from top to bottom to display it to advantage. Brownlow (Lady Darnley's brother) was the only other guest. Wrote to Sir J. Newport (from whom I had, before I left home, received a very kind answer, expressing his readiness to assist me in every possible way), announcing my arrival, and saying I should be with him next morning.

28th. [Saturday] Immediately after breakfast called upon Sir J. Newport, and had a good deal of conversation with him. Sent me various House of Commons papers, Reports of the Board of Education, accounts of schools, &c. &c. Called upon Lord Lansdowne. Saw a pretty picture he had just purchased, by a young Scotch artist, Graham; the subject, Scott's "Rebecca."[1] A Mr. Toole came in. Talked of Shee's tragedy, rejected by the new licenser (G. Colman), and the Duke of Montrose's most un-ducal letter, which is now the reigning topic.[2] Lord L. asked me to dinner to-day, to meet Spring Rice, Macdonald, &c. but had long engaged myself to the Longmans. Called upon the Donegals. Dined at Longmans; company, Shee, Abbot (the actor), &c. Rather amusing. Shee told us he had got five hundred guineas for the copyright of his rejected play. Abbot, in coming away with me in a hackney coach, remarked how lucky Shee was, as the sort of success that his play was calculated to obtain would not have been half so profitable as the grievance had turned out. "The fact is," said he, "all that about liberty is gone by. It won't do any longer." This, though spoken *professionally,* is but too true also politically. It *is* gone by; thanks to the

Spaniards, the poltroon Neapolitans, &c. &c. Went to the opera (Lord L. having given me a ticket in the morning), but was refused admittance, having gaiters on. They were French gaiters, and I flattered myself were, like French curl-papers, invisible, but it was not the case. Went home.

29th. [Sunday] Set to work at transcribing. Have an immensity of work before me. The new materials from the papers given me by Sir J. Newport to be got in. Rogers called, and asked me to dine with him to-day to meet Luttrel and Lord John, but had promised Power. Macdonald called. Power, too, who is full of impatience for the finishing of the "Sacred Songs" and "Irish Melodies," so that I shall have this also to perplex me. At home all day till dinner, when I had a hackney coach and went to Power's. Corrected and looked over some songs in the evening. Then to Rogers's; found Luttrel, Lord John, Mrs. Graham, Miss Rogers, and Lady Davy. Talked of Lord Byron marching with the Greeks. By the by, I forgot to mention that, before I left home, I had a letter from Lord B., written just as he was starting for Missolonghi, in which he says that he means to take the field with the Greeks, and adds, "If famine, pestilence, or a bullet, should carry off a fellow-warbler, mind that you remember him in your smiles and wine."[1] It is said that the Greek Committee have written to him requesting him *not* to fight!

March 1st. [Monday] Hard at work. Lord John called, and sat with me some time. Remarked that it would be a very apt quotation for the Orangemen, in case of the accession of the Duke of York to the throne, "Now is the winter of our discontent made glorious summer by the sun of York."[1] Talked of the high character Lord Lansdowne bears, even among people one would least expect it from: for instance, —— and ——, both so much more violent, and yet both expressing to Lord John their strong confidence in Lord L. and their warm admiration of his conduct. Dined at Lady D.'s, and home early. Jekyll says that people who inflict long speeches upon the country gentlemen in the House might be prosecuted under Martin's bill for "tormenting dumb animals."[2]

2nd. [Tuesday] Find that my close confinement for these two days does not agree with me, and walked in the Park a little after breakfast. Luttrel called, and sat a good while with me, which, though very agreeable, interrupted my work a good deal. Dined with Moore *tête-à-tête* to go to the opera. Went to Lady Lansdowne's box, after having seen the Divertisement from the front of the pit.

4th. [Thursday] Went out with Rogers, and paid numerous visits. Called at Lord Essex's, and sat some time; at Lady Jersey's, who asked us to go there to-night, it being her birth-day. Brougham has bargained for a broiled bone for supper. Intended to dine at a coffee-house, for the purpose of being home early, but, Rogers being off at seven for his "Antient Music," did still better. So dined with him, and worked in the evening.

5th. [Friday] At work all day. Lord John came. Showed him some of the proof-sheets of the "Captain," with which he seemed much amused. By the by, was pleased to hear from Rogers that Luttrel said, "If any body can make such a subject lively, Moore will." Wrote to tell the Donegals I would dine with them to-day. Played and sung with Barbara after dinner, and thence to Lady Lansdowne's assembly. Was introduced to Falk, the Dutch ambassador, a frank, sensible man. A good deal of talk with the Duchess of Somerset, who introduced me to her pretty daughter. Told the Countess San Antonio how disappointed I was she had not asked me to hear Rossini the evening before. Said she had no idea I was in town, and to make up, invited me to come on Sunday morning, and hear him try over his opera "Semiramide."[1] Was to have dined with Lord Auckland to-morrow, but gave it up, on finding his sister was not to be at home, and promised Lord Essex to dine with *him.* Luttrel and I walked home together. Have been inquiring, since I came to town, about Charles Sheridan, in order to know what is to be done as to the "Life," but cannot find him out.

6th. [Saturday] The proprietor of the "European Magazine" came, with a letter of introduction from Shee, requesting that I would enable him to give a portrait and memoir of me in the next number of his magazine. Also Moore, the sculptor, called, begging me to sit to him before I leave town. Walked a little in the Park, and again before dinner with Byng. Dined at Lord Essex's; company, Hayter, the painter, De Roos, &c. To the opera in the evening.

7th. [Sunday] Breakfasted at Power's, in order to look over and correct proofs, &c. &c. Thence to call on Luttrel, to go to the Countess San Antonio's, where we arrived (according to appointment) at one. Lady Caroline Worsley and her son came soon afterwards. I sung a little to them. Rossini did not come till near three. Brought with him Placci, Curioni, and Cocchi; Mercer came afterwards; and we joined in the choruses of the "Semiramide." Rossini, a fat, natural, jolly-looking person, with a sort of vague archness in his eye, but nothing further. His mastery over the pianoforte miraculous. A good scene ensued upon the entrance (without leave) of Count Vandramin (?), bringing in, of all people, Sir Thomas Farquhar. The Countess's burst of anger and bad Italian at the Count, and her perseverance till she got both the intruders fairly out again, was all very diverting, and seemed to amuse Rossini a good deal. Her volley of Italian admirable. Said "Sir Thomas Farquhar, indeed!" who was only *eccellente par contare i denari.* Rossini remarked, after they were gone, on the unfitness of persons who were not connoisseurs as audience at *prova* or rehearsal, because they "did not know enough to make allowance for the blunders and slovenliness that always necessarily occurred on such occasions." Dined at Holland House, taken by Abercromby and Wishaw. Tierney, at dinner, breaking out about "Lalla Rookh." "Upon my soul, I must say (though Moore is present) that's the prettiest thing I ever read in my life." Lord Holland amused at Tierney's manner of saying it, "as if he was afraid Moore wouldn't agree with him." Some talk with Lord Holland after dinner about Carte's "Ormonde," which he has just been reading.[1] Seems to fear that I will lean too much to the Catholics in my Irish work. Mentioned (what I was not aware of) that Cromwell had, at first, on going to Ireland, hesitated between the two very opposite plans of either attacking the Catholics with fire and sword (as he eventually did), or of giving a certain sanction and establishment to their religion.[2] This, I think he said, is mentioned in Carte.

8th. [Monday] Called upon Murray to ask him to cash a bill upon Power for me, as he did last year. Had told me at that time it was no favour whatever; but now refused, saying he should have occasion for all the money he could muster up for some time. Went to Longmans; asked them whether, if Charles Sheridan should take away the Sheridan papers from Murray, they would have any objection to undertake the work. Said not, if it did not appear to be interfering improperly with Murray. Dined at Lord Lansdowne's; company, Lord Essex, the Cawdors, Luttrels, &c. &c. Talked of the Duke of Montrose being called the "Goose," when Lord Graham (in the Rolliad).[1] Lord North, one night, when, as usual, asleep, was waked to be told that Lord Graham was going to speak. "No, no," says Lord North, "he'll not speak till Michaelmas!"

9th. [Tuesday] Went out to look after some Scotch songs for poor Lucy Drew, who has been long suffering with severe illness; packed them off to her through the Foreign Office. Called upon Croker; had some talk with him about his new club. Dined at Lord Auckland's; no one but his sisters, Luttrel, and Mr. Baring Wall. In talking about Stephen Kemble, whose sole qualification for acting Falstaff was his being able to do it without stuffing, Luttrel said, "The most difficult character I know to act without stuffing is a fillet of veal! I have seen it attempted, but it failed."

10th. [Wednesday] Walked about for two hours; met Hallam. Dined at Mrs. Tighe's; company, Jekyll, Lord and Lady Belhaven, Lord James Stuart, William Spencer, &c. &c. Talked of the manner of concluding letters. William Spencer quoted a French letter, in which the writer, complaining of a hurt he had received in his *jambe,* goes on *avec luquelle j'ai l'honneur, &c. &c.* Jekyll told of a letter from the Duke of ———, when abroad, complaining how much the whole party had been bitten by bugs: "Lady Mary is also much bitten. The only person that has escaped is he who has the honour," &c. &c. Stopped for half an hour to Mrs. Tighe's assembly in the evening; some very pretty people there. Home early, as I am obliged to be every night, for the purpose of rising early to my work.

13th. [Saturday] Have four invitations to dinner to-day. Among others to Abercromby, whom I am sorry to lose. Company at Longman's, Mr. Jerdan (the editor of the "Literary Gazette"), Mr. Mill (who has written about Hindostan), &c.[1] Had a letter from Tom Campbell this morning, expressing his great regret at not being able to join the party; says in it, that he dreamt the other night I told him I was occupied about a great poem, and hopes it is not merely ουλος ονειρος. Went to the opera; found the Duchess of Hamilton, and Souza, in Lady Lansdowne's box; had it all to myself when they went away, and prepared to enjoy the ballet alone; but Souza returned, and spoilt my treat. Charles Sheridan called when I was dressing for dinner to-day, and fixed to come up again from Hampton Court on Wednesday, for the purpose of settling definitely about the "Life."

14th. [Sunday] Had but a short walk in the Park. Dined at Sir H. Davy's; company, the Lansdownes, Lord and Lady Colchester, Sir John Nicholl, and Stratford Canning. Story of Lord Coleraine taking off the hat of the person walking with him, instead of his own, when bowing to some one in a shower of rain. Had a long discussion about divining rods. Mentioned a magnetiser in Paris who professes to correspond by means of the magnetic fluid (which he sends in a parabola over the tops of the houses) with a young lady in the Rue de Richelieu, himself living in the Place Louis Quinze. Sometimes the fluid is intercepted by other people in its way. The same professor of magnetism also produces a sympathetic feeling in his patients, by means of a lurid atmosphere, which surrounds him and them. Performed this experiment with a man's wife in the dark, the husband himself being of the party, but not able to perceive the atmosphere, which was only visible to the wife and the magnetiser. Some company in the evening, among whom was Tom Campbell. Talked to him about "Capt. Rock," and hoped he would give it a lift in his Magazine, as I felt more than an author's anxiety about its circulation and success. Promised to do so.[1] Spoke of the dinner intended to be given to the Greek deputies; anxious that I should be in town for it, as he wished I should undertake the giving of Lord Byron's health. Went from thence with Lord Lovaine to Sir G. Warrender's, where there was music; Begrez, Mad. Vestris, Caradori, &c. &c. Among the company was the Duke of Wellington, Princes Polignac and Lieven.

15th. [Monday] Walked out a little. Dined at Orme's. It turned out very agreeable; particularly in the evening, when there was a very gay assemblage of faces, quite new to me, and some of them very pretty. Sung a good deal, and danced a quadrille afterwards with a beautiful little girl, the daughter of a Circassian; there were two of them (Miss Bruces), and both quite worthy of a mother from Circassia. Had been asked to Lord Alvanley's to hear Rossini, but thought it wisest to stay where I was; and accordingly remained to supper.

16th. [Tuesday] Dined with Lord Darnley, "to talk," as he said, "over the woes of Ireland." Is very anxious for my book before his motion on the state of Ireland;[1] and it ought to have been out long since; but it takes an immense time transcribing, and I am interrupted every moment; besides, it swells out, in copying, to a much greater extent than I had anticipated. Found, on going up stairs, Madame Biagoli at the pianoforte, and symptoms of music; at which I took fright, and ran away to the opera with Lady Davy.

17th. [Wednesday] Charles Sheridan came according to appointment; expressed himself anxious that, at all events (whether he could secure better terms for his brother's family or not), the work should be taken out of the hands of Murray. Advised him, however, to sound Murray as to what he would be willing to give before he finally decided. Left me to do so; and returned in an hour with the intelligence that Murray would offer nothing; that he considered the thousand pounds to me cleared everything; and that, accordingly, Charles Sheridan had signified to him that the papers would be transferred into other hands. Agreed to try the Longmans, and to let Sheridan know the result on Saturday, S. saying many flattering things about his luck in being in such honourable hands as mine, &c. &c. Luttrel said, in the course of conversation, "What a prodigality of invention there is in mankind! only think, to invent such a language as Greek, and then let it die!"

18th. [Thursday] Hard at work. Called for by Lady Davy to go to dinner at Hallam's; sat next to a pretty girl at dinner, Miss Morse; Rogers and Spencer of the party. In the evening went to Mrs. Stewart Nicholson's to hear Rossini (who receives fifty guineas a night for these parties). Sung his song in the "Barbiere," "Figaro quà," admirably; sung also "Assisa al pie d'un salice," and "Mi manca la voce," with Colbra, &c.

19th. [Friday] Breakfasted with Power, to look over proofs. Mrs. Spottiswoode's carriage came for me at five to take me to dinner at her father's (Longman's) at Hampstead. Told Longman and Rees what had occurred about the "Life;" and Rees appointed to meet C. Sheridan on the subject at my lodgings to-morrow. Sung in the evening, and home.

20th. [Saturday] Sheridan and Rees met, and had their consultation; and Rees's proposal was, that besides making up my thousand pounds to me, they would agree, after the sale of 1000 copies quarto and 1500 octavo, to give Mrs. T. Sheridan's family half the profits of all further editions that might be printed. C. Sheridan asked a little time to consider, and said he would let us know his determination in a day or two. Dined at Holland House; taken out by Lord John Russell in his cabriolet. Company, Lord Jersey, Luttrel, Byng, young Wortley, &c. Brought back by Byng; went to the opera. Adair told to-day of Sheridan's saying, "By the silence that prevails, I conclude Lauderdale has been cutting a joke." Some talk with Lord Holland about Junius and Churchill, in which I said I would much rather, for my pleasure, read the latter than the former. "Aye, that's the jingle?" (think he said).

21st. [Sunday] Obliged to leave my writing, and walk out in the rain, to try and get rid of a headache. Have called several mornings upon Sir J. Newport, who has lent me several other House of Commons papers. Dined at Orde's; company, Hobhouse, W. Spencer, &c. &c. Went from thence (taken by the Ordes) to Miss White's; Captain and Mrs. Cater and Mrs. William Baring there, singing duets and glees without accompaniment, there being no pianoforte. Wanted me to sing, but only took a part in one or two glees. Promised to dine with Miss White on Sunday next, if I should stay so long in town; fixed with Newton (who was here) to breakfast with him in the morning.

22nd. [Monday] Breakfasted with Newton; and sat to him afterwards. Told me Lord Lansdowne had been to see his pictures, and thought mine very like. Returned home to write. Woolriche came, having arrived in town with the Duke of Bedford yesterday. Dined at Sir H. Davy's; the Ordes, Sir —— Willoughby, Capt. Spencer, &c. In the evening, the Belhavens, Mrs. Tierney, &c. Sung a good deal; Lady Davy sobbing violently at "Poor broken heart!" The Lansdownes came late; sung my new song, "Sing, sing," for the third time, to them.[1]

23rd. [Tuesday] Lord John called upon me; walked out. Dinner at Rogers's to meet Barnes, the editor of "The Times;" company, Lords Lansdowne and Holland, Luttrel, Tierney, and myself. Barnes very quiet and unproductive; neither in his look nor manner giving any idea of the strong powers which he unquestionably possesses. Dinner very agreeable; Lord Holland, though suffering with the gout, all gaiety and anecdote. A number of stories told of Lord North. Of the night he anticipated the motion for his removal, by announcing the resignation of the Ministry; his having his carriage, when none of the rest had, and saying, laughingly, "You see what it is to be in the *secret;*" invincible good humour. Fox's speech on the Scrutiny, one of his best, and reported so well, that Lord Holland said, "In reading it I think I hear my uncle's voice."[1] Lord H.'s story of the man stealing Mr. Fox's watch, and Gen. Fox laughing at him about it,[2] &c. &c. Lord H., too, told of a gentleman missing his watch in the pit one night, and charging Barrington, who was near him, with having stolen it. Barrington, in a fright, gave up a watch to him instantly; and the gentleman, on returning home, found his own watch on his table, not having taken it out with him; so that, in fact, *he* had robbed Barrington of some other person's watch. Went to the opera with Lord Lansdowne; Mrs. Baring (whose box I sat in some time) renewed very kindly her invitation to me and Mrs. Moore for the summer, and begged we should bring the two little ones with us. Barnes, this evening, asked me to dine with him on Sunday next, and Rogers advises me to get off my engagement with Miss White, and go with him, as he is a person well worth cultivating; have refused Lord Lansdowne also for Sunday, but rather think I shall take Rogers's advice.

24th. [Wednesday] Dined with Watson Taylor: company, C. Ellis, Planta, Wilmot (the Under Secretary), Jekyll, Lord Ancrum, Lady Sandwich, the

Davys, &c. &c. Got near Jekyll and Wilmot, and found it agreeable enough. Story of Lord Ellenborough's saying to a witness, "Why you are an industrious fellow; you must have taken pains with yourself; no man was ever *naturally* so stupid." Conversation about the negroes; Davy's opinion that they are decidedly an inferior race, and that it would take many generations of high culture to bring them to a level with whites. It required, he said, forty generations to make a wild duck a tame one; and to bring the negroes to the perfection of civilised whites, would take nearly the same lapse of time. Sir Humphry talks wildly sometimes, and *de omni scibili.* Went from thence to Mrs. Hope's; had promised her I would sing, and got hastily through two songs, but refused any more, as there were too many people assembling. Found there the Hollands. Lord H. asked me whether I could get him the particulars relative to the attainders of Harvey and Colclough in Ireland; as, now they are revising the Scotch attainders, he thinks something might be done with respect to these Irish ones; said I would inquire.[1] Was to have gone to Mrs. Mitchell's ball, but did not.

25th. [Thursday] Lord Belhaven called upon me between four and five to take me to the House of Lords to hear Lord Kingston's motion about tithes; walked down with him. Much fun expected from Lord Kingston's account of the terrible tithe-proctor "Cruel Delany;" but Lord Harrowby produced more laughter by his seriousness about it, than any of the others did by their jokes.[1] Asked to dinner in the House both by Lord Essex and Lord Auckland; but was engaged to Lord Cawdor. Company at Lord C.'s, Seymour Bathurst, Lady Georgina Bathurst, Lord J. Thynne, Greville, &c. Sat next Lady Georgina, and found her very agreeable; talked of a prologue written by Canning last summer, for a charade acted while he was at Saltram; during which time, they said, he seemed to have resumed all his former vivacity. Greville repeated the prologue, which turns chiefly on allusions to craniology, and is pleasant enough; but might have been written by any other lively member of society as well. Introduced to Lord Bath, in the evening, who expressed a wish to see me at Longleat.

26th. [Friday] Woolriche called; walked out. Dined at William Maddocks's: an immense dinner, chiefly of Welsh people; knew none of the company, but Lord Limerick and Lord Kinnoul. Singing in the evening; Linley and Mr. and Mrs. Gattie (formerly Miss Hughes); I sung a good deal and was much lauded. Went from thence to Mrs. G. Phillipps's assembly. Quite ridiculous the swarms of invitations that beset me; entreated that "I would fix a day, however distant," &c. &c. Met my old friend Admiral Douglas, who wants me to meet Lord Exmouth at his house, some twenty miles from town, to-morrow; but it is impossible.

27th. [Saturday] Was to have dined at Holland House to-day to meet General Mina; but found myself so hard run with my printing and transcribing that I could not spare the time. C. Sheridan (who wrote to me a day or two since, communicating his assent to the proposal of the Longmans, and enclosing a copy of an agreement for them to sign) called this morning, and received from me the paper signed by them; so that I have now only to give Murray a draft upon the Longmans for the money I have had of him (about £350), and transfer the MS. at present in his hands (containing the early part of the "Life") from him to them. Dined alone at Richardson's; and returned home to work in the evening.

28th [Sunday] Walked a little in the Park after breakfast. Dined with Barnes in Great Surrey Street, beyond Blackfriars Bridge, having written the day before yesterday to explain to Miss White, and promised to come to her in the evening. Company at Barnes's, a Secretary of the French Embassy, Haydon the painter, and a Scotch gentleman whose name I could not make out, but who is also a chief writer for "The Times." Barnes more forthcoming a good deal than he was at Rogers's. Spoke of that day, and said how much he was delighted with Lord Lansdowne, whose unaffected modesty struck him as particularly remarkable in a person of such high talent and rank; was also very much charmed with Lord Holland, as far as regarded the liveliness and variety of his conversation; but considered his manners so evidently aristocratic and high, as to alarm the pride of persons in his (Barnes's) situation, and keep them on the alert lest this tone should be carried too far with them. Told him that this latter apprehension was altogether groundless, as Lord Holland's good nature and good breeding would be always a sufficient guarantee against any such encroachment; but, at the same time, could not help agreeing with him (though rather surprised at his perceiving it so soon through all the cheerfulness and hilarity of Lord Holland's manner) that there is actually a strong sense of rank and station about him; while, notwithstanding the greater reserve and discretion of Lord Lansdowne's conversation and address, there is not anything like the same aristocratic feeling in him as in Lord Holland; indeed, few noblemen, I think, have less of this feeling than Lord Lansdowne. A good many stories about Lord Ellenborough. Went to Miss White's; found Rogers, Tierney, Wordsworth, Jekyll, &c. who had dined there; told Rogers what Barnes had said about Lord Holland; made me repeat it to Tierney, who seemed to think it very extraordinary, and to have quite a different opinion himself; looking upon Lord Lansdowne, as, if anything, the more aristocratic man of the two.

29th. [Monday] Had half promised to dine with the Davys to-day, but gave

724 / *The Journal of Thomas Moore*

it up, in order to work in the evening. Told Moore I would come and eat a cutlet *tête-à-tête* with him; found, however, that, in the interim, he had asked two men to meet me, Prendergast, M.P., and Bonham.

30th. [Tuesday] Dined with Bingham at Gray's Inn; company, Mrs. Austen, a Mr. Gattie, and another gentleman; all Benthamites, and quite different from other people. The lady talked political economy; told me she had taken a young Frenchman in hand; had tried to get Mill and Bentham into his head, but that he said they were "too *clear* for him." How far he must carry his *beau ideal* of the unintelligible!

April 1st. [Thursday] Have been finishing the preface to "Captain Rock" these two mornings in bed, and hurried over some of it clumsily enough; took down the last copy to the Longmans myself. Forgot to mention that yesterday I received Murray's account, and that, between the money he advanced me and the books he has supplied me with, it amounts to £350. Has written me also a note, begging that I would apply to Douglas Kinnaird for the assignment of Lord Byron's "Memoirs," which he continues, he says, to withhold from him, leaving him no security for his property in them. In consequence of this, called upon Kinnaird; read over the assignment with him and Hobhouse; and they being of opinion that there was no objection to letting Murray have this instrument in his possession, till such time as I should be able (according to my intention) to redeem the "Memoirs" altogether, I brought it away with me.[1] Called upon Murray, but did not find him at home. Asked to Lord Belhaven's and several other places to-day, but could not go in consequence of an early and odd engagement I had made to accompany Lord Dillon to a *coterie* of blue stockings at Paddington. Dined with the Lansdownes, who were going to the Matthewses, and from whom I could therefore get away in time. Called upon by Lord Dillon at eight, and went to Paddington.

2nd. [Friday] Breakfasted with Newton. Went from thence to Murray, and gave him the assignment.

3rd. [Saturday] Breakfasted again with Newton, in order to meet Russell the actor, who had promised me a dress to take down with me to Bath, Bessy having expressed a wish to go to a masquerade there on Monday, and I having agreed to meet her in Bath for the purpose. Excellent this; having an appointment with my wife at a masquerade! Promised me a Figaro's dress.

4th. [Sunday] Up at half-past five and off in the White Lion Coach at a quarter before seven; two shrewd solicitors my companions: much talk about public characters; and evidently puzzled to make out who I was; seemed for some time to think I was Hobhouse. Arrived in Bath at the White Lion between seven and eight; supped, and to bed, a good deal fatigued; my last two days in town having been full of worry and bustle.

5th. [Monday] Bessy and Tom arrived between eleven and twelve. The dear girl has not been at all well for some weeks, but as brisk and alive as usual, notwithstanding. Went to see dear Anastasia, and took her and Julia Starkey to see the panorama of the Coronation; ordered our dominoes for the night, *my* Figaro dress being given up. Dined at Mr. T. Phipps's; home and dressed. The masquerade, as a spectacle, beautiful, and when we were allowed to cast off our masks very agreeable; the room, with the booths for refreshments on each side, better imagined and managed than any thing of the kind I ever saw, and no expense spared to make all perfect. Bessy delighted; and danced towards the end of the night with Tom Bayly. Not home till between six and seven in the morning.

6th. [Tuesday] Walked about Bath with Bayly. Had visits from the Holtons, Mrs. Elwin, &c. &c., and left Bath for home at three. Met Dr. Crawford, by the by, and made demonstrations of feeing him for his visits to 'Statia; but he took me aside, and said he hoped I would not rob him of this opportunity of showing what he felt towards me, and that he was most cheerfully ready to attend her in the same way whenever she might require him. Very kind this. Glad to be at home after my five weeks of anxiety and bustle.

9th. [Friday] Received copies of "Captain Rock," which is published to-day. Rees tells me in his letter that Lord Liverpool sent for a copy yesterday morning; this was on account of Lord Darnley's motion on the state of Ireland last night.[1] Notices of the work to-day in "The Times" and "Morning Chronicle;" the former of which devotes one of the leading articles to me. Very flattering.[2] The "Chronicle" gives near two columns of extracts.

10th. [Saturday] Had people in the evening. John Starkey just arrived, and joined them.

11th. [Sunday] A letter from Lady Holland, full of the warmest praise of "Captain Rock," which she says abounds with "wit and sprightliness:" the historical part she calls "a *chef-d'œuvre* of perspicuity and pleasantry." Had John Starkey and his sister to dinner; sung to them in the evening.

12th. [Monday] Working at my "Sacred Songs." Received a letter from the Longmans, which I ought to have had yesterday, saying that at their sale on Saturday there were so many "Captain Rocks" ordered they should find it necessary to print off a second edition of a thousand on Monday (to-day); and that if I had any corrections to make they would be in sufficient time by being sent off immediately. This, of course, out of the question now; but proceeded to make some corrections upon the chance of being time enough.

13th. [Tuesday] Finished my hasty correction of the work, and sent it off. Started at three o'clock for Farley Abbey (Colonel Houlton's place), in consequence of a promise made at the masquerade that Bessy and I would pay them a visit of a few days this week; Bessy, however, not well enough to go. Went in my little gig as far as Trowbridge, and took a chaise from thence; did the four miles in less than twenty minutes. Company at dinner (besides their three fine girls and John Houlton), Colonel Davy, Mr. Elwyn of Bath, and a Mr. Langford. Mr. Elwyn mentioned (what I have heard Lord Lansdowne tell) of a French *exposition,* in which some *coiffeur* exhibited an image of a bald head, with a Cupid hovering over it, and about to let a new-invented wig fall on it; the motto underneath, *Le génie répare les torts du tems.* Young Houlton and the third girl sung, in the evening, Cimarosa's duet of "Se non credi" very well; and Isabella played some airs on a two-stringed guitar beautifully. I tried to sing, but the pianoforte so loud and harsh that I could not manage it.

14th. [Wednesday] Walked about the grounds with Mrs. Houlton and the girls; and was much delighted. Saw the ruins of the old castle and chapel, and the mummies of the Hungerfords. One of these broached some time since by an antiquarian, who introduced a quill into Lady Margaret's shoulder, and tasted some of the liquid from it, which was strongly aromatic. The first Speaker of the House of Commons is lying there, perfect still. A fine monument of the time of Charles I. in high preservation in the chapel. The Phippses arrived to dinner; the day very agreeable, and could hardly be otherwise. A pretty house, beautiful girls, hospitable host and hostess, excellent cook, good champagne and moselle, charming music; what more could a man want? The nursery pianoforte was brought up in the evening, and I sang to it with somewhat more success; Isabella, too, had recovered her voice, and sung as well as played, forming a picture like one of Stothard's, as she hung over her guitar.

15th. [Thursday] Had some music after breakfast. I sung a good deal; one of the songs, "Could'st thou look as dear,"[1] sent poor Mrs. P. out of the room. Again visited the ruins; and set off with the Phippses, to return home, at a little after two. Stopped at Trowbridge to call on Crabbe, but he was not at home. On my return found letters from Lords Holland, Lansdowne, John Russell, and Dillon, about my book. Lord Holland says, "It has far surpassed my expectations; and my expectations were very high. It is so full of wit and argument, learning, and feeling." He then proceeds to some details with respect to First Fruits, which I wish I had known before I published.[2] Lord Lansdowne says, "Every one that I have seen is delighted with your book;" and Lord John begins his letter, "Success! success! The 'Captain' is bought by every body; extravagantly praised by Lady Holland; deeply studied by my Lord," &c. &c. Dillon says it is the finest thing since Swift, &c. &c. All this very encouraging.

16th. [Friday] Answered Lords Holland, &c.; and sent off some things to Power.

18th. [Sunday] Had a letter from Rees, telling me that the second edition was published, and 550 of it ordered. The corrections had not arrived in time, but would appear in the third edition, which they were soon about to put to press.

20th. [Tuesday] Odd enough, no attack yet upon me in "John Bull!" My task now writing additional verses for the new number of "Irish Melodies;" have also to find airs for two more, there being as yet but ten that I shall retain: pretty airs deplorably scarce.

23rd. [Friday] A letter from Rees, inclosing one from Milliken, the Dublin bookseller, in which he speaks of the great sensation produced by the "Captain" in Ireland. "The people," he says, "through the country are subscribing their sixpences and shillings to buy a copy; and he should not wonder if the work was pirated." Milliken's letter also contains an order for a further supply of copies, which, when executed, Rees says, will leave but 100 on hand; so that he expects the third edition will be called for on Saturday (to-morrow).

24th. [Saturday] Have written two new Irish Melodies, "She sung of love," and "Oh bear me to that gloomy lake," which completes the number.[1]

25th. [Sunday] Drove to Bowles's to dinner. Left my gig at Hughes's, and walked with H. to Bremhill; found Bowles suffering, more from nervousness and apprehension, than from real illness; is horrified by some extracts he has seen from "Captain Rock."

29th. [Thursday] Dined at Dr. Starkey's. Had a letter from Lord Lansdowne, in which he says he has not heard a single dissentient voice as to the merits of "Captain Rock."

May 1st. [Saturday] Mrs. Bowles called, with a General Peachey; asked me to go back with her to dinner, which I did. Walked from Money's through Bowood to Bremhill; found Bowles in the same nervous state as before, but laughed him out of it; and he was as hearty and lively at dinner as ever. Would insist that he was a Whig; a Whig of Burke's school. I said, "Yes, such a Whig as Burke was after he turned." Took my book to leave with him, but he refused to read it. His paper, the "St. James's Chronicle," abuses it, he tells me, most violently; and he will read the abuse readily enough, though he won't the book. General Peachey, who is a neighbour of Southey's, mentioned some amiable traits of him.

3rd. [Monday] Went to Bath, Bessy and I and Mrs. Phipps; the post-horses took us there in somewhat less than an hour and three quarters. Went with Bayly to the rehearsal of a play which the amateurs of Bath give to-night for some benefit; all very anxious that I should stay for it. Our darling Anastasia walking about with us. Went to Upham's to look over the newspapers; find that "John Bull" has at last taken notice of me; but shabbily enough; expected he would have shown better fight. The "Westminster Review," too, has an article about me, written, I rather think, by ——; *quantum suff.* of praise, but so managed on the whole as to be disparaging.[1] Had a cold dinner at the inn; and left Bath at six o'clock. A letter from Lord Byron at Missolonghi; has had an attack of epilepsy or apoplexy; "the physicians," he says, "do not know which; but the alternative is agreeable."[2]

4th. [Tuesday] Still writing verses for the new number of "Irish Melodies." Received the "Irish Observer" (O'Driscoll's new paper), with an article about "Rock" in it, highly laudatory. Received, too, under Lord Lansdowne's frank, a letter from the Secretary of the Catholics of Drogheda, thanking me in their name for my "able and spirited exposition of their wrongs," &c. &c. This is gratifying and satisfactory, as I rather feared the Catholics would not take very cordially to the work on account of some infidelities to their religion which break out now and then in it.

10th. [Monday] Called upon Lord Lansdowne: told me he had the other day (in consequence of the passages quoted in "Captain Rock" from the Report of the Hibernian Society)[1] refused to take the chair at the meeting of that society, unless a pledge was given that no more such attempts at proselytism should be made. Talked of Stanley's speech, the other night, in defence of the Church of Ireland; I said he had misrepresented me with respect to my estimate of Church livings, and that I had some thoughts of putting a paragraph in the paper to correct him.[2] Saw Lady L.; congratulated me on what she calls "the complete success" of "Captain Rock." Met Newton, who spoke of Lockhart (Sir W. Scott's son-in-law), now in town; said he met him and some other "Blackwood's Magazine" men lately, and was surprised to find (notwithstanding their tone in print) with what liberal praise they spoke of me; asked me to meet Lockhart at breakfast to-morrow. Bursts of congratulation from every one I meet on the success of "Rock:" Lord Essex, Lord Cowper, all loud in praise of it. Dined at Longman's to meet Murray (Bessy's brother-in-law), an agreeable, sensible man.

11th. [Tuesday] Breakfasted at Newton's with Lockhart; found him agreeable. Told of Sir W. Scott once finding Crabbe and some Scotch chieftain (in his full costume) trying to converse together in French, Crabbe having taken the tartan hero for a foreigner, and the other, on being addressed in French by Crabbe, supposing him to be an Italian abbé. Called upon at Newton's by Murray, with whom I walked for some time, talking of our respective wives, and praising them *à l'envi.* Dined at the Wiltshire Anniversary. Sir F. Burdett was to have been in the chair, but detained at the House. Gordon, M.P. for Cricklade, took it. My health given and drunk with great cordiality: indeed it was almost the only toast that seemed to rouse the party to anything like enthusiasm. Made them a speech; said that the possession of a thatched cottage and half an acre of garden was the only claim I had to being accounted a Wiltshire gentleman. Irishmen, however, could take many disguises. An Irish Colonel, once, upon meeting a man whom he thought he recognised in the uniform of the 42nd Regiment, said, "How's this? you are an Irishman, aren't you?" "Faith I am, your Honour." "And in the uniform of a Scotch regiment?" "Yes, your Honour,

I am what they call a lamb in wolf's clothing." I should have said that Gordon, in proposing my health, alluded to "Captain Rock," saying that I had lately appeared in a new character, that of a writer of statistics.

12th. [Wednesday] Breakfasted at Rogers's. Told me it had been remarked invidiously, that the only persons I had praised in "Captain Rock" were Peel and Canning, and that some had *defended* me (most probably himself) by saying, "It is a hard case that Moore, who has been abusing people all his life, should not be allowed to praise a little now." Carpenter (who has been costive enough in his praises since I ceased to publish with him) said to me, speaking of "Rock," "Sir, there is but one opinion as to its cleverness among men of all parties; it has placed you high too upon a ground which many were not inclined to think you could ever occupy." Lunched with Bennet, while he was dining. Overtook Mrs. T. Sheridan alone on her way to Almack's for her ticket; gave her my arm, being on the same pursuit. Went to the Literary Fund Dinner, of which I was a steward. Surprised on finding so large a portion of its directors and visitors to be persons whose names I had never heard before; in short, the only downright literati among them were myself and old George Dyer, the poet, who used to take advantage of the people being earthed up to the chin by Dr. Graham, to go and read his verses to them. Lord Lansdowne in the chair, and Lord John Russell next him; I sat opposite to them. Lord L. gave my health in a most flattering manner, and nothing could be more warm than the reception it met with from the company; made them a long speech, which was interrupted at almost every sentence by applauses. It had been proposed to me before dinner to take the chair after Lord Lansdowne, who was obliged to go away early, but I declined it.[1] Left with him and Lord John, who went to the French play, while I went home to refresh and dress myself again for Almack's. Everybody there, and all overflowing to me with praise of "Rock." A good deal of conversation with Lord Downshire, who said he thought it would do considerable good; that Englishmen, in general, knew nothing of the history of Ireland; that he, himself, brought up as a boy in England, was for a long time ignorant of everything relating to Ireland, except that it was the place where his estates lay; that this book will turn the attention of Englishmen to the subject. Stanley came to me, and, with much earnestness, said that Lord Lansdowne had mentioned to him my idea of his having quoted and misrepresented me, but assured me that all he quoted from me was the assertion with respect to the incorrectness of the pamphlet on the wealth of the clergy. Praised Lady Grantham's beauty to Miss D'Esté, who lost no time in mentioning it to her, and I was, in consequence, by Lord G.'s desire, introduced to her; asked me for Friday. A note from Lord Jersey to tell me that Lady J. and her little child were doing very well, and adding, that both he and Lady J. thought "Captain Rock" one of the cleverest books ever published.

13th. [Thursday] Drove to Hampstead to see Miss Robinson; strange scene. Dined early with Rees in order to go to a party at Longman's in the evening. Rees asked me had I called upon Murray yet to complete the arrangement entered into when I was last in town for the redemption of Lord Byron's "Memoirs;" said I had not. Told me the money was ready, and advised me not to lose any further time about it.

14th. [Friday] A letter in the "Morning Herald" to-day about my speech at the Literary Fund, accusing me of having represented Napoleon as a friend to the liberty of the press. What absurdities malice will, in its blindness, rush into! Calling at Colbourn's library to inquire the address of the editor of the "Literary Gazette," was told by the shopman that Lord Byron was dead.[1] Could not believe it, but feared the worst, as his last letter to me about a fortnight since mentioned the severe attack of apoplexy or epilepsy which he had just suffered. Hurried to inquire. Met Lord Lansdowne, who said he feared it was but too true. Recollected then the unfinished state in which my agreement for the redemption of the "Memoirs" lay. Lord L. said, "You have nothing but Murray's fairness to depend upon." Went off to the "Morning Chronicle" office, and saw the "Courier," which confirmed this most disastrous news. Hastened to Murray's, who was denied to me, but left a note for him, to say that "in consequence of this melancholy event, I had called to know when it would be convenient to him to complete the arrangements with respect to the 'Memoirs,' which we had agreed upon between us when I was last in town."[2] Sent an apology to Lord King, with whom I was to have dined. A note from Hobhouse (which had been lying some time for me) announcing the event. Called upon Rogers, who had not heard the news. Remember his having, in the same manner, found me unacquainted with Lord Nelson's death, late on the day when the intelligence arrived. Advised me not to stir at all on the subject of the "Memoirs," but to wait and see what Murray would do; and in the meantime to ask Brougham's opinion. Dined alone at the George, and in the evening left a note for Brougham. Found a note on my return home from Douglas Kinnaird, anxiously inquiring in whose possession the "Memoirs" were, and saying that he was ready, on the part of Lord Byron's family, to advance the two thousand pounds for the MS., in order to give Lady Byron and the rest of the family an opportunity of deciding whether they wished them to be published or no.

15th. [Saturday] A gloomy wet day. Went to D. Kinnaird's. Told him how matters stood between me and Murray, and of my claims on the MS. He repeated his proposal that Lady Byron should advance the 2000 guineas for its redemption; but this I would not hear of; it was I alone who ought to pay the money upon it, and the money was ready for the purpose. I would then submit it (not to Lady Byron), but to a chosen number of persons, and if they, upon examination, pronounced it altogether unfit for publication, I would burn it. He again urged the propriety of my being indemnified in the sum, but without in the least degree convincing me. Went in search of Brougham; found him with Lord Lansdowne; told them both all the particulars of my transaction with Murray. B. saw that in fairness I had a claim on the property of the MS., but doubted whether the delivery of the assignment (signed by Lord Byron) after the passing of the bond, might not, in a legal point of view, endanger it. Advised me, at all events, to apply for an injunction, if Murray showed any symptoms of appropriating the MS. to himself. No answer yet from Murray. Called upon Hobhouse, from whom I learned that Murray had already been to Mr. Wilmot Horton, offering to place the "Memoirs" at the disposal of Lord Byron's family (without mentioning either to him or to Hobhouse any claim of mine on the work), and that Wilmot Horton was about to negotiate with him for the redemption of the MS. I then reminded Hobbhouse of all that had passed between Murray and me on the subject before I left town (which I had already mentioned to Hobhouse), and said that whatever was done with the MS. must be done by *me*, as I alone had the right over it, and if Murray attempted to dispose of it without my consent, I would apply for an injunction. At the same time, I assured Hobhouse that I was most ready to place the work at the disposal, *not* of Lady Byron (for this we both agreed would be treachery to Lord Byron's intentions and wishes), but at the disposal of Mrs. Leigh, his sister, to be done with by her exactly as she thought proper. After this, we went together to Kinnaird's, and discussed the matter over again, the opinion both of Hobhouse and Kinnaird being that Mrs. Leigh would and ought to burn the MS. altogether, without any previous perusal or deliberation. I endeavoured to convince them that this would be throwing a stigma upon the work, which it did not deserve; and stated, that though the second part of the "Memoirs" was full of very coarse things, yet that (with the exception of about three or four lines) the first part contained nothing which, on the score of decency, might not be most safely published. I added, however, that as my whole wish was to consult the feelings of Lord Byron's dearest friend, his sister, the manuscript, when in my power, should be placed in her hands, to be disposed of as she should think proper. They asked me then whether I would consent to meet Murray at Mrs. Leigh's rooms on Monday, and there, paying him the 2000 guineas, take the MS. from him, and hand it over to Mrs. Leigh to be burnt. I said that, as to the burning, that was her affair, but all the rest I would willingly do. Kinnaird wrote down this proposal on a piece of paper, and Hobhouse set off instantly to Murray with it. In the course of to-day I recollected a circumstance (and mentioned it both to H. and K.) which, independent of any reliance on Murray's fairness, set my mind at rest as to the validity of my claim on the manuscript. At the time (April 1822) when I converted the *sale* of the "Memoirs" into a *debt,* and gave Murray my bond for the 2000 guineas, leaving the MS. in his hands as a collateral security, I, by Luttrel's advice, directed a clause to be inserted in the agreement, giving me, in the event of Lord Byron's death, a period of three months after such event for the purpose of raising the money and redeeming my pledge. This clause I dictated as clearly as possible both to Murray and his solicitor, Mr. Turner, and saw the solicitor interline it in a rough draft of the agreement. Accordingly, on recollecting it now, and finding that Luttrel had a perfect recollection of the circumstance also (*i.e.* of having suggested the clause to me), I felt, of course, confident in my claim. Went to the Longmans, who promised to bring the 2000 guineas for me on Monday morning. Paid eleven shillings coach-hire to-day, and got wet through after all. Dined with Edward Moore, finished a bottle of champagne, and home. Was to have dined to-day with Watson Taylor to meet the Phippses.

16th [Sunday] Called on Hobhouse. Murray, he said, seemed a little startled at first on hearing of my claim, and, when the clause was mentioned, said, "Is there such a clause?" but immediately, however, professed his readiness to comply with the arrangement proposed, only altering the sum, which Kinnaird had written, "two thousand *pounds,*" into "two thousand *guineas,*" and adding "with interest, expense of stamps," &c. &c. Kinnaird joined us, being about to start to-day for Scotland. After this I called upon Luttrel, and told him all that had passed, adding that it was my intention, in giving the manuscript to Mrs. Leigh, to protest against its being wholly destroyed. Luttrel strongly urged my doing so, and proposed that we should call upon Wilmot Horton (who was to be the representative of Mrs. Leigh at to-morrow's meeting), and talk to him on the subject. The utmost, he thought, that could be required of me, was to submit the MS. to the examination of the friends of the family, and destroy all that should be found objectionable, but retain what was *not* so, for my own benefit and that of the public. Went off to Wilmot Horton's, whom we luckily found. Told him the whole history of the MS. since I put it into Murray's hands, and mentioned the ideas that had occurred to myself and Luttrel with respect to its destruction; the injustice we thought it would be to Byron's memory to condemn the work wholly, and without even opening it, as if it were a pest bag; that every object might be gained by our perusing and examining it together (he on the part of Mrs. Leigh, Frank Doyle on the part of Lady Byron, and any one else whom the family might think proper to select), and, rejecting all that could wound the feelings of a single individual, but preserving what was innoxious and creditable to Lord Byron, of which I assured him there was a considerable proportion. Was glad to find that Mr. Wilmot Horton completely agreed with these views; it was even, he said, what he meant to propose himself. He undertook also to see Mrs. Leigh on the subject, proposing that we should meet at Murray's (instead of Mrs. Leigh's) to-morrow, at eleven o'clock, and that then, after the payment of the money by me to Murray, the MS. should be placed in some banker's hands till it was decided among us what should be done with it.

[*The following passage is Russell's summary of the meeting at Murray's, 17 May 1824.*]

[I have omitted in this place a long account of the destruction of Lord Byron's MS. Memoir of his Life. The reason for my doing so may be easily stated. Mr. Moore had consented, with too much ease and want of reflection, to become the depository of Lord Byron's Memoir, and had obtained from Mr. Murray 2000 guineas on the credit of this work. He speaks of this act of his, a few pages onward, as "the greatest error I had committed, in putting such a document out of my power." He afterwards endeavoured to repair this error by repaying the money to Mr. Murray, and securing the manuscript to be dealt with, as should be thought most advisable by himself in concert with the representatives of Lord Byron. He believed this purpose was secured by a clause which Mr. Luttrel had advised should be inserted in a new agreement with Mr. Murray, by which Mr. Moore was to have the power of redeeming the MS. for three months after Lord Byron's death. But neither Mr. Murray nor Mr. Turner, his solicitor, seem to have understood Mr. Moore's wish and intention in this respect. Mr. Murray, on his side, had confided the manuscript to Mr. Gifford, who, on perusal, declared it too gross for publication. This opinion had become known to Lord Byron's friends and relations.

Hence, when the news of Lord Byron's unexpected death arrived, all parties, with the most honourable wishes and consistent views, were thrown into perplexity and apparent discord. Mr. Moore wished to redeem the manuscript, and submit it to Mrs. Leigh, Lord Byron's sister, to be destroyed or published with erasures and omissions. Sir John Hobhouse wished it to be immediately destroyed, and the representatives of Mrs. Leigh, expressed the same wish. Mr. Murray was willing at once to give up the manuscript on repayment of his 2000 guineas with interest.

The result was, that after a very unpleasant scene at Mr. Murray's, the manuscript was destroyed by Mr. Wilmot Horton and Col. Doyle as the representatives of Mrs. Leigh, with the full consent of Mr. Moore, who repaid to Mr. Murray the sum he had advanced, with the interest then due. After the whole had been burnt the agreement was found, and it appeared that Mr. Moore's interest in the MS. had entirely ceased on the death of Lord Byron, by which event the property became absolutely vested in Mr. Murray.

The details of this scene have been recorded both by Mr. Moore and Lord Broughton, and perhaps by others. Lord Broughton having kindly permitted me to read his narrative, I can say, that the leading facts related by him and Mr. Moore agree. Both narratives retain marks of the irritation which the circumstances of the moment produced; but as they both (Mr. Moore and Sir John Hobhouse) desired to do what was most honourable to Lord Byron's memory, and as they lived in terms of friendship afterwards, I have omitted details which recall a painful scene, and would excite painful feelings.

As to the manuscript itself, having read the greater part, if not the whole, I should say that three or four pages of it were too gross and indelicate for publication; that the rest, with few exceptions, contained little traces of Lord Byron's genius, and no interesting details of his life. His early youth in Greece, and his sensibility to the scenes around him, when resting on a rock in the swimming excursions he took from the Piræus, were strikingly described. But, on the whole, the world is no loser by sacrifice made of the Memoirs of this great poet.]—J.R.

18th. [Tuesday] Dressed in a hurry, having been invited this week past to meet the Princesses at Lady Donegal's at two o'clock. Found there Col. Dalton, the attendant of the Princess Augusta; and soon after their Royal Highnesses came, viz., Augusta, Mary (the Duchess of Gloucester), and Sophia of Gloucester. The rest of the party were Jekyl, and Lady Poulteney and her daughter. Sung for them, and then the Princess Augusta sung and played for me; among other things, new airs which she had composed to two songs of mine, "The wreath you wove" (rather pretty) and "The Legacy!"[1] She played also a march, which she told me she had "composed for Frederick" (Duke of York), and a waltz or two, with some German airs. I then sung to her my rebel song, "Oh, where's the slave!" and it was no small triumph to be *chorused* in it by the favourite sister of his Majesty George IV.[2] We then sat down to luncheon; and it was quite amusing to find how much at my ease I felt myself; having consorted with princes in my time, but not knowing much of the female gender of royalty. A good deal of talk about Lord Kenyon. Jekyl said that Kenyon died of eating apple pie crust at breakfast, to save the expense of muffins; and that Lord Ellenborough, who succeeded to the Chief Justiceship in consequence, always bowed with great reverence to apple pie; "which," said Jekyl, "we used to call apple pie-ty." The Princesses also told of how, "the King" used to play tricks on Kenyon, sending the Despatch Box to him at a quarter past seven, when he knew Kenyon was snug in bed; being accustomed to go to bed at that hour to save candle-light. Altogether the repast went off very agreeably. Gave up my other engagements and dined with Woolriche, at Richardson's. I ought to have mentioned that in the course of my conversations these two days past with Hobhouse, he frequently stated that, having remonstrated with Lord Byron the last time he saw him on the impropriety of putting a document of the nature of these memoirs out of his own power, Lord B. had expressed regret at having done so, and alleged considerations of delicacy towards me as his only reason for not recalling them. This, if I wanted any justification to myself for what I have done, would abundantly satisfy me as to the propriety of the sacrifice.

19th. [Wednesday] A statement in "The Times" to-day; true as to the leading facts of the destruction of the MS. and my repayment of the money to Murray, but incorrect as to other particulars.[1] Occupied about the insurance of my life. Dined with the Bryans, and went to Mrs. Story's in the evening. Not well.

20th. [Thursday] Went to breakfast at Holland House. Lord John and Sydney Smith there. Smith told me, in speaking of "Captain Rock" (which he had not yet read), that he once drew up a little manual of Irish History, much, as he conceived, in the same spirit and intention. Went from thence to pay a visit to Canning; driven part of the way by Lord John; not at home; left card. Met Stanhope (Lord Mansfield's son-in-law), who asked me whether the statement in "The Times" was true. Told him the two chief facts were; on which he said, "You have done the finest thing that ever man did—you have saved the country from a pollution." Here I stopped him, and assured him that this was a mistake; that there was but very little of an objectionable nature in the first or principal part of the memoirs, and that my chief objection to the total destruction of the MS., was the sanction such a step would give to this unjust character of the work. A clever letter to day from Corry about "Rock;" thinks me too Catholic. Dined at Lord Charlemont's: company, Lord and Lady Wicklow, Lord Ellenborough, Caulfield, &c. Went to Lansdowne House; a large assembly. Duke of Gloucester said to me, nearly in the words of Stanhope, "You have done the handsomest and finest thing that ever man did;" spoke also of "Rock," and said he feared there was but too much truth in it. The Duke of Sussex, too, very civil: said he had a quarrel with me, because I never came to see him. Walked about a good deal with the Phippses, to point out to them the lions of the party. Long conversation with Luttrel, who has had a letter from Wilmot Horton, urging my acceptance of the money back again from Murray: Luttrel strongly of opinion that I ought to take it. Repeated my determination not to do so; but promised to talk with him on the subject in the morning. The most ridiculous statements going about these two days; one, that the parties broke by force into my lodgings, and carried off the MS.; another, that Hobhouse had held me down with all his might while they were burning it. By the by, met the Misses Law this evening at Lord Charlemont's, and found them all kindness to me, notwithstanding my sad offences against their father.[1]

21st. [Friday] Breakfasted with Luttrel. Discussed the offer of W. Horton over, but he could not convince me. My views of the matter simply these: from the moment I was lucky enough (by converting the *sale* of the MS.

into a *debt*) to repair the great error I had committed, in putting such a document out of my power, I considered it but as a *trust*, subject to such contingencies as had just happened, and ready to be placed at the disposal of Lord Byron, if he should think proper to recall it; or of his representatives, if, after his death, it should be found advisable to suppress it. To secure this object it was that, at Luttrel's suggestion, I directed a clause to be inserted in the agreement with Murray, giving me a lapse of three months after the death of Lord Byron to raise the money and redeem my deposit. That the clause was not inserted, as I intended, was a strange accident, and would have been to me (had the omission been discovered in time to take the disposal of the MS. out of my hands) a most provoking one. But, luckily, by the delay in producing the agreement, I was enabled to proceed exactly as if all had been as I intended; and to restore, of my own free will, and without any view to self-interest, the trust into those hands that had the most natural claims to the disposal of it. Were I now to take the money, I should voluntarily surrender all this ground, which I had taken so much pains to secure to myself; should acknowledge that I *had* put the MS. out of my power, and surrendering all the satisfaction of having disinterestedly concurred in a measure considered essential to the reputation of my friend, should exhibit myself as either so helplessly needy, or so over-attentive to my own interests, as to require to be paid for a sacrifice which honourable feeling alone should have dictated. Luttrel proposed our calling upon Hobhouse, assuring me, at the same time, that no one could be more kindly disposed towards me than Hobhouse was. I felt glad of the opportunity, and we went; the meeting very cordial. Talked again over the offer of the family, and Hobhouse (to whom Wilmot Horton had also appealed on the subject) concurred with Luttrel in urging it on me. I went over, as strongly as I could, my reasons against it; and at last Luttrel, with a candour that did him much honour, said, "Shall I confess to you, my dear Moore, that what you have said has a good deal shaken me; and if you should find (but not till *after* you have found) that Lord J. Russell and Lord Lansdowne agree with these views of yours, pray mention the effect which I freely confess they have produced on me." This avowal was evidently not without its influence upon Hobhouse, who, after a little more conversation, looked earnestly at me and said, "Shall I tell you, Moore, fairly what I would do if I were in your situation?" "Out with it," I answered eagerly, well knowing what was coming. "I would *not* take the money," he replied; and then added, "The fact is, if I wished to injure your character, my advice would be to accept it." This was an honest and manly triumph of good nature, over the indifference (to say the least of it) to my reputation, which must have dictated his former advice. He then talked of Murray's dissatisfaction at the statement in the "Times;" on which I offered to draw up a paragraph correcting its errors, and giving Murray full credit for having at first declined receiving the money, when proffered to him. Did so, to the satisfaction of both L. and H. and took it to the "Times" office.[1] Went to Longmans' to finish my insurance transaction, and brought them round, without much difficulty, to approve of my refusal of the money; this was a great point gained, and more easily (considering their commercial views of matters) than I expected. Dined at Lansdowne House. Went early for the purpose of consulting Lord L. with respect to my refusal of the money, or rather *to tell him what I meant to do;* for, having made up my mind, it would have been mockery to affect to ask advice. Told him therefore, at starting, that though I should be most delighted to have the sanction of his opinion, yet that nothing could change my own views of the matter. Had but little time, however, for my statement to him and Lady Lansdowne before the company arrived. The party were the Hollands, the Gwydirs, the William Russells, the Cowpers, the Duke of Argyle, and Sydney Smith. Saw in my short conversation with them, that both Lord and Lady L. were strongly for my taking the money. Went off at ten o'clock to Paddington; a rather strange scene. Forgot to mention that one of the days I called upon D. Kinnaird, he read me a letter he had just received from a girl, entreating of him (in consideration of her family, who would be all made unhappy by the disclosure), to procure for her her letters, and a miniature of her, which had been in the possession of Lord Byron. Told Kinnaird I could guess the name of the lady, and did so. Forgot to mention that Hobhouse told me W. Horton had said, that "if there was any power in law to make me take the money, he would enforce it."

22nd. [Saturday] Was early with the Lansdownes. Went over all my reasons for the refusal, but did not make much impression on them; begged me to consult Abercrombie, and hear what Lord John had to say on the subject. Met Murray in St. James's Street, who said, taking me by the hand, "I hope there is no objection to me shaking hands;" received this coldly, and said, I hoped he was satisfied with the statement in the "Times" to-day? "Pretty well," he answered; but added there were dreadful statements against him going about, and that Lord Lansdowne (who of all men, he should be most sorry to have think ill of him) had said such things of him the other day at the Literary Club, that he had thought it due to himself to write a letter to his Lordship on the subject. I answered, "Mr. Murray, you need not fear any injustice from Lord Lansdowne, who is well acquainted with every particular of the transaction between you and me from beginning to end. As to this last affair, I am ready to bear testimony that your conduct in it has been very fair." So saying, we parted. Went home. Lord John called upon me, full of Wilmot Horton, who had been working at him too on the subject; was of opinion that there existed no objection whatever to my taking the money. A long conversation; said he would think over what I had said against our next meeting. Went to Rogers's, and found him and his sister equally inclined with the rest to consider my refusal of the money as too romantic a sacrifice. Recapitulated my reasons, much more strongly and eloquently than I could ever put them to paper. Saw they were both touched by them, though Rogers would not allow it; owned that *he* would not receive the money in such a case, but said that my having a wife and children made all the difference possible in the views he ought to take of it. This avowal, however, was enough for me. More mean things have been done in this world (as I told him) under the shelter of "wife and children," than under any other pretext that worldly-mindedness can resort to. He said, at last, smiling at me, "Well, your life may be a good *poem,* but it is a damned bad matter-of-fact." Dined at Lord Belhaven's; company, Lady Uxbridge, Lords Duncan and Maitland, &c. &c. Sung a little before I went to the Opera. That beautiful person, Lady Tullamore (who came in the evening), so affected at "Poor broken heart,"[1] that she was obliged to leave the room, sobbing violently. Lady Belhaven took me to her: told her how little reason she had to be ashamed of feeling music so much, &c. &c. Too late for "Tancredi." A long statement of the whole transaction of the burning, &c. in the "Courier" this evening, affecting to be very minute, but full of falsehoods, suppressing, too, the material fact of my having paid the money, and leaving it to be implied that the whole merit of the sacrifice lay with Murray. Evidently the manufacture of one of Murray's clerks. Lady Mansfield at the Opera. Asked me to dine with her early next Tuesday to see the whole of "Tancredi." Promised to get off from Lord Auckland's, if I could.

23rd. [Sunday] A bouncing lie in "John Bull" to-day; says that it was Mrs. Leigh's friends redeemed the MS., and that "in the meantime little Moore pockets the money."[1] In writing a note to Hobhouse I said, "for God's sake don't let any one contradict that lie in 'John Bull' to-day; its worth any money." Had reserved this day and to-morrow to go and pay a visit to Admiral Douglas, but gave it up. Walked about, and made calls. Dined by myself at the George, and having one hour before Countess St. Antonio's party, went to the Houltons. Found them at home, and sat listening to Isabella's guitar, and singing to them till it was too late for the Countess'. Home early. This morning Bryan delighted me with a piece of intelligence, which showed the kindness of *his heart,* as much as it made mine happy. He means to put out a thousand pounds to interest for my dear Anastasia, to whom he considers his duty of godfather transferred, since the death of poor Barbara. Said that he would not have mentioned this to me, but that he thought it might be some relief to my mind now in the sacrifice I was making: presented me also with a gold repeater; evidently much pleased with my conduct in this transaction, though he, at first, thought with the rest that I ought to take the money.

24th. [Monday] Called upon Lord Lansdowne. Found him strongly of opinion that I ought to give some public contradiction to the statement in Saturday's "Courier," and the "Observer" of yesterday.[1] However I might despise it myself, and however little impression it might produce upon him and those who knew the circumstances, "yet to others it conveyed the idea that Murray had the whole merit of the sacrifice, and that the money was not paid by me." Went to consult Luttrel and Hobhouse, who thought a short statement from myself was the best mode of setting all right. Drew up one, and took it to Barnes; who undertook to send a copy of it to the "Chronicle." Called at Longmans'. Went home, and sent copies of the statement to Hobhouse, Luttrel, Frank Doyle, and Wilmot. Lord John, who came in while I was thus occupied, took charge of the inclosure to Wilmot Horton, as he was going to the House of Commons. Informed them all that there would be time enough before ten that night to make any alterations they might suggest in the statement. Drove, with Edward Moore to the Regent's Park, with which I was enchanted, never having seen it before. Dined with him in order to keep myself open for the evening. Received, while at dinner, notes from Doyle and W. Horton, both entreating me to defer my statement, and reconsider my resolution against receiving the money. "You are, I think," says Doyle, "(though from motives of high honour) mistaken in your view of the matter." W. Horton requested that I would at least wait for a narration of the whole proceedings, which he would draw up against twelve o'clock next day, and transmit to me for the purpose of being shown to Lord Lansdowne, and my other friends, before my final decision should be taken.[2] Drove off with E. Moore to the "Times" and "Chronicle" offices, to countermand the statement. Found Barnes on his Panopticon of Europe: and were a good deal interested by seeing the great machine of the political world at work. Wrote a slight paragraph, *ad interim,* to counteract the lies that are afloat; thence to the "Chronicle," and did the same; struck by the more scatter-brained appearance of the "Chronicle" establishment. Called on the Aucklands this morning, who promised to dine early enough for the Opera to-morrow.

25th. [Tuesday] W. Horton's narrative not having arrived at one o'clock, went out. Called upon Lady Mansfield, to say that Lord Auckland held me to my engagement, and promised to dine early enough. Lady Caroline sang *Ombra Adorata* for me; much improved since I heard her in Italy. On my return home found W. Horton's narrative (as he calls it), detailing the circumstances of Murray's having called upon him on the Saturday after the news of Byron's death arrived: his offers to place the MS. at the disposal of the family, upon receiving the sum he had given for it: W. Horton's taking time to consult the family on the subject: my interview with him on Saturday; and so on through the whole of the circumstances that ensued. All very fairly and truly stated. The point, however, on which he founded his argument for my accepting the money was, that as the property was now proved to have been in Murray, and a negotiation, or rather a parole agreement for the purchase of it had taken place between him and Murray on Saturday, he had thus a *prior* claim to me, and Murray had no right to part with the MS. to me, or any one else under such circumstances. That, therefore, the obvious and natural way of settling the matter was for Murray to give me back my money, and for the family to be allowed to proceed in the arrangement they had begun with Murray. I inclosed the narrative, according to his desire, to Lord Lansdowne; at the same time telling Lord L——that it had made no difference whatever in my views of the transaction. Dined at Lord Auckland's: company, Miss Villiers, Macdonald, &c. Went pretty early to the Opera. Countess St. Antonio, in reproaching me for not having come to her the Sunday before, desired that whenever I heard that she was at home I should consider myself invited, whether I received cards or not.

26th. [Wednesday] Had written part of my answer to W. Horton yesterday. Breakfasted with Lord John, and took it with me to finish it there. Found Lord John converted to my opinion with respect to the refusal of the money. Went from thence to Lord Lansdowne, who also (under the new view which the narrative gave him of the transaction) approved of my not taking the money. He had thought before it was from the family I was to receive the remuneration, and in that case he still said he saw no objection to my receiving it; but in the manner it was now proposed to repay me, namely, by having the money given back to me by Murray, he certainly agreed that I was right in declining it. Was rejoiced at the sanction of his concurrence, though not perfectly understanding the distinction he drew; for, after all, it was the family that would actually pay the money in both cases. Went to Moore's, where I finished my answer to Wilmot Horton. His argument of a "prior claim to the purchase" was easily despatched. I then went over much of what I have already stated: my views in converting the sale of the MS. into a debt: my precaution in ordering a clause to be inserted in the agreement, giving me a power of redeeming it after Lord B.'s death, all for the purpose of keeping the trust in my own hands, and enabling me either to restore it to Lord Byron, if he should change his mind with respect to its destination, or, in the event of his death, placing it at the disposal of those most naturally interested in all that concerned him.

Had the omission of the intended clause been sooner discovered, I might have found some difficulty in acting up to these intentions, but luckily the ignorance in which we were left with respect to the terms of the agreement, left me free to pursue the course which I had always resolved upon, and to put self-interest completely out of the question in concurring with the other friends of Lord Byron in a step thought so necessary to his own fame and the feelings of those he left behind him. With respect to the argument used by some of those who advised my acceptance of the money, that Lord Byron, having given me these memoirs for my benefit, the family were but *making good* to me the intentions of their relative: I said that if Lord Byron were himself alive, and should say to me, "Here, Moore, was a gift which I meant for your advantage; circumstances have frustrated my intention, but I insist on your receiving from me an equivalent," I would, without hesitation, have accepted such an equivalent from the hands of my friend; but I acknowledged no such right to make me a present in persons with whom I had not even the honour of being acquainted; nor could I, by deriving profit from a work which they had pronounced unfit for publication, lend my sanction to the old satirical proverb, *bonus odor nummi*, let it come from whatever source it may. This (with a few acknowledgments, of the delicate manner in which Mr. Horton had conducted himself through the negotiation), was the substance of the answer which I despatched to him, and the chief of the reasons which I alleged for declining to receive the money in any shape, or through any channel whatever. Drove with Moore in his cabriolet, and left the letter at W. Horton's myself. Thence to the "Times" and "Chronicle" offices with my statement, which I now felt myself at full liberty to publish. Dined with Rogers at six, to meet a party who were going to the Ancient Music: Lord Essex, and Miss Capell, Miss Stephens, Sir P. Codrington, Dr. Woolaston, &c. &c. Left them at half-past seven, and went to dine at Lord Wicklow's, where I met the Aberdeens and Charlemonts. Sung a little in the evening.

27th. [Thursday] My letter in the "Morning Chronicle," "Herald," "Post," and "Times."[1] Called upon W. Maddocks, found Peter Moore with him, who promised me materials about Sheridan. Met Lord Lansdowne; said my letter was quite right, but that he still grudged the money. Called upon Admiral Douglas, and fixed to come to him on Sunday. Went at one o'clock to the Comte de la Garde's, who has translated my "Melodies" into French with French airs, and fixed this morning for me to hear them. A large party, chiefly English, assembled. Madame Castelli and her husband sung the Melodies, and Ciarchottini accompanied; also a French girl on the harp, and a flute player from the French opera. At the conclusion a Cantata was sung with full accompaniments, written and composed for the occasion in honour of me; words by M. la Garde, the music by Signor Castelli. Rather an embarrassing honour; did not know how to look while they were shouting out *C'est nommer Moore à la postérité!* Adair was among the audience. Dined at Lord Belhaven's; company, Lord and Lady Cathcart, &c. &c. Lord Caernarvon said to me, while they were singing a quintet, "Really I don't see any difference between this and any other kind of noise." Talked with Frankland Lewis about my affair with W. Horton; he said, my conduct in it was perhaps rather "chivalrous;" but that I was, of course, the best judge of what my own feelings required.

28th. [Friday] Was to have dined at Lord Cowper's, but went to Sir H. Davy's; company, Lord and Lady Darnley, Andrew Knight, &c. &c. Had called in the morning on Devereux, the busy Catholic, and found Eneas Macdonnel with him, who thanked me for the way in which I had mentioned his pamphlet in Rock. Sir H. Parnell, by the by, made the same sort of acknowledgment the other day for my mention of his speech.[1] Went to Mrs. Turner's in the evening; heard the "wonderful boy" Liszt.

29th. [Saturday] Dined at Lord Fortescue's; sat next Lord Ebrington, who talked to me abundantly about "Captain Rock," as did also Sir J. Newport, who never ceases praising it. Went to the Opera, and sat in Lady Lansdowne's box.

30th. [Sunday] Off at eight to Douglas's, near Uxbridge; a most cordial reception from him and his wife, but a wretched cold spoiled my enjoyment of the evening.

31st. [Monday] Returned to town at half past twelve. Dined at Moore's to meet the Phippses; company, Washington Irving (just arrived from Paris), Lattin, and Beecher. Lattin amusing after dinner.

June 1st. [Tuesday] Dined with Wilbraham, joined Mrs. Story and Irving at the play afterwards.

6th. [Sunday] Started between seven and eight, and arrived at Bath between nine and ten, having gone out of our way to take a son of Major Armstrong's from school. Bessy met us at the York House.

8th. [Tuesday] Called upon Edward Moore's mother and sister, and promised to go again to-morrow to be introduced to a Catholic Bishop, Dr. Baynes.

9th. [Wednesday] Was presented to the Bishop, who is a violent admirer of "Captain Rock." Showed me a letter from the famous Dr. Doyle, in which he "My Lords" and "Lordships," his brother Baynes, in every line.

10th. [Thursday] Bessy and I set off for the cottage before the Bryans, who were to dine with us, but who did not arrive, from an accident happening to their wheels, till between five and six. Seemed really delighted with our little establishment. Left us for Chippenham, on their way to Holyhead between eight and nine.

12th to 14th. [Saturday–Monday] Nothing remarkable. Nervous and languid from the agitation in which I was kept in town. Ordered some tonic draughts from the apothecary, which were of service to me.

15th. [Tuesday] Went to Bath, Bessy, Mrs. B. and I to the Music Meeting. Met Irving, who had come there to join us. He and I dined together (the ladies having dined before we left home), and all went to the evening concert, which was not very good.

16th. [Wednesday] All went to the Music at the Cathedral; the Mount of Olives very dramatic. Some of the Bowles's "Ark," composed for the occasion and performed; wretched.[1] Bessy and Mrs. B. returned home afterwards, taking Anastasia with them; and Irving and I dined with Mr. Elwyn. Company, Mr., Mrs., and Miss Houlton, and Dr. Crawford. Went to the concert in the evening.

17th. [Thursday] Called upon Vallebraque; Catalani not visible; gave me an order for the Messiah to-morrow; not likely to make use of it. Irving and I set out for the Cottage between ten and eleven. Took Irving after dinner to show him to the Starkeys, but he was sleepy and did not open his mouth; the same at Elywn's dinner. Not strong as a lion, but delightful as a domestic animal. Walked him over this morning to call on Lord Lansdowne (come down in consequence of Lord King's illness), who walked part of the way back with us. Read me some parts of his new work "Tales of a Traveller."

Rather tremble for its fate. Murray has given him £1500 for it; might have had, I think, £2000. Told him the story which I heard from Horace Smith about the woman with the black collar, and the head falling off; thought it would do well for his ghost stories,[1] but mentioned H. Smith having told me he meant to make use of it himself; probably *has* done so in the "New Monthly Magazine."

18th. [Friday] Irving full of the woman with the black collar; intends to try his hand at it. Resolved to leave us this evening, though evidently much pleased with our little quiet establishment; owned he did not expect to find us in such perfect comfort. After dinner walked with him to Buckhill to meet the coach, having sent his baggage there before us. Missed the coach and took a chaise to Bath, intending to proceed to his sister at Birmingham to-morrow. Forgot to mention that, during the last week of my stay in town, I heard from Moore, the artist (to whom I was sitting for a model), of an old friend of mine being in London; one whom I knew at Bermuda, when she was about eighteen or nineteen, and I three and twenty, and never had seen, or even heard of her since. Moore said she had expressed a strong wish that I should call upon her, which I did, and the meeting was, from a variety of considerations, interesting to me. She had been married some time to a Major Moore, brother to General Moore, with whose wife I found her. Time has made considerable alteration in her, but still the soft black eyes remain.

19th to 30th. [19 June: Saturday; 30 June: Wednesday] The two or three ensuing weeks may be taken *en gros,* as they were diversified by little that calls for detail. I resumed my Sheridan task and worked at it with tolerable industry, writing with more facility and quickness than usual. Forgot to mention that before I went to town, Charles Sheridan had written to say that he had been requested by Lord Fitzwilliam to allow the Bishop of Rochester to have the Westminster Hall speech for his forthcoming "Life of Burke."[1] Told him when in town the objections I saw to his complying with such a request; the injury it would do to our work by taking away the novelty or rather authority which this authentic report would give us, the voluminousness of it, &c. &c. C. Sheridan, however, said, that having promised it, he could not be off his word; and, besides, he thought it would be creditable to his father's fame to have this speech placed beside those of Burke's upon *equal terms;* those of the latter upon this occasion not having been dressed up for publication, like his other great speeches. Upon my mentioning, however, his intention to the Longmans, they said they should consider it as a breach of his agreement with them, if he gave any papers furnished for our work, into other hands till we had first published them.

Wrote also some songs for Power, "Go and forget what now," and "Thou lovest no more;"[2] besides correcting the proofs of a new editon of the "Irish Melodies." Received several letters from Rees, partly concerning inquiries connected with "Sheridan's Life" in which I employed him, and partly to urge my immediate application to Lord Byron's family, and to all other sources likely to furnish them, for materials towards my intended "Memoirs of Byron." Answered that I would do so, as soon as the funeral was over, but that it would be indecorous till then. Looked over the Journals, &c. I have of Byron's, and find much in them that may be made use of. Received an application (through Mrs. Hutchinson) from Madame Belloc, the translator of the "Loves of the Angels," requesting that I would allow her to have the translation of my "Life of Byron," whenever it appears; her letter most enthusiastic.[3] Answered most graciously, and told her I had heard of her beauty; said also to Mrs. Hutchinson in my note, "your fair friend is too faithful a translator to deserve more than half of the title, *La belle Infidelle*, which somebody gave to one of the versions of old Amyot."[4] Went one Sunday to Bowles's church (Mrs. B. with us), and dined with him. Bowles still wild against "Captain Rock;" has begun an answer to it, part of which he read to me, "all in good humour," as he pathetically says, when he is most bitter. Received a copy of "Captain Rock detected;" suspect it to be by a friend of my Sister Kate's, O'Sullivan; tolerably abusive of me; but worse of Lord Lansdowne, which I regret for many reasons.[5] Have now seen the following comments, reviews, &c. of Captain Rock:— "Blackwood's Magazine," intended to be very fatal, but overcharged and inefficient; calls the work "dull," "weak," &c. &c. "The London Magazine," laudatory. "Westminster Review," half and half.[6] "Universal Review," have *not* seen, but hear from Bowles that it is powerful against me. Baron Smith's "Prefatory Notice," very flattering to the talent, but thinks the work likely to be mischievous. To these and the newspapers, may add Stanley's notice of me in the House of Commons; and the Bishop of Limerick's in the House of Lords. The latter quoted my words, "It has been called an omnivorous church (hear, hear); a preposterously rich church (hear, hear). The noble lords, who cheer these expressions, if they knew," &c. &c.[7] At a Baptist Meeting, also, the other day, some reverend gentleman did me the honour to quote it thus: "In that most pestilent and detestable book the 'Memoirs of Captain Rock;'" this is charming. Have received two copies of verses from women about it; one anonymous, and the other from the little Paddington Sappho. The fourth edition reduced to two or three hundred, and the Longmans about to print a fifth. Answered a letter I had received from a Miss Sophia —— in France, expressing the most passionate feelings about Byron's death, and entreating me to inform her of the particulars; whether he suffered much pain; whether he had any friends with him, &c. &c. Gave her all the information I could. Received a letter in English from some German (whether female or male, don't know) near Dresden, beginning "As you are not only the first poet in the world, but also the best man," and inclosing me a letter to transmit to Lady Byron, signed with a most unpronounceable name, Graff Whackerback, or some such horror. Sent the letter to Lady Byron through Frank Doyle.

July 1st to 9th. [1 July: Thursday; 9 July: Friday] Began to think whether it would be necessary for me to go up to Lord Byron's funeral. Wrote to Hobhouse, who told me his own wish had been to have him buried in Westminster Abbey; but that Mrs. Leigh had decided for Newstead, and that therefore the only mark of respect would be sending carriages.

9th. [Friday] Saw in the papers that the friends of Lord B. would accompany the funeral out of London, and determined to go up; wrote to Rogers to-day, to know what his intentions are; cannot, however, wait his answer, which would not arrive till Sunday (the day after to-morrow), and the funeral is to be on Monday. Resolved to start to-morrow morning.

10th. [Saturday] Mrs. B. went with me in the gig to Buckhill, where I took the coach and arrived in town five minutes after six; no rooms at 15 in Duke Street; was obliged to go to a glazier's opposite. Dined at Richardson's. Called at Power's, who showed me a thing called the "John Bull Magazine," in which there is a long rigmarole, professing to be an extract from Lord B.'s "Memoirs." Rees told him that people believe this to be genuine; people will believe anything.[1] Called and left my name at Hobhouse's.

11th. [Sunday] Called on Rogers after breakfast; said he had written in answer to my letter, that I need not disturb myself to come up, as there was no occasion. Hobhouse had asked him to go in one of the mourning coaches, but he did not intend it; seemed inclined, however, to change his mind: and at last I persuaded him to accompany me to the funeral. Called upon Lord Lansdowne, who was surprised to see me. Walked with Edward Moore. Was with Rogers again at four, to go with him to dine at Highbury (his brother's). A good deal of talk in the hackney coach about Burke, Pitt, and Fox; seemed to think Fox's opinion was right as to Burke's changing his style after the Westminster Hall Speech of Sheridan; fired out impatiently at my hinting that I thought Burke and Sheridan men of more real talent than Fox and Pitt; politics and party alone having given the latter a station above them. He said that William Pitt in speaking of Fox had called him "the greatest of us all." Forgot, by the by, to tell him (what I think I heard from Tierney), that Pitt thought Sheridan a man much superior to Mr. Fox. Company at dinner, Offley and his daughter, and Mrs. Rogers and her son. Conversation about the arts; the history of which (R. says), Offley knows more than any one. Returned at night in the stage; found a letter from the undertaker requesting me to go as mourner, and fixed nine to-morrow morning as the hour. Agreed to breakfast with Rogers at eight.

12th. [Monday] Was with Rogers at half-past eight. Set off for George Street, Westminster, at half-past nine. When I approached the house, and saw the crowd assembled, felt a nervous trembling come over me, which lasted till the whole ceremony was over; thought I should be ill. Never was at a funeral before, but poor Curran's. The riotous curiosity of the mob, the bustle of the undertakers, &c., and all the other vulgar accompaniments of the ceremony, mixing with my recollections of him who was gone, produced a combination of disgust and sadness that was deeply painful to me. Hobhouse, in the active part he had to sustain, showed a manly, unaffected feeling. Our coachful consisted of Rogers, Campbell, Colonel Stanhope, Orlando (the Greek deputy), and myself. Saw a lady crying in a barouche as we turned out of George Street, and said to myself, "Bless her heart, whoever she is!" There were, however, few respectable persons among the crowd; and the whole ceremony was anything but what it ought to have been. Left the hearse as soon as it was off the stones, and returned home to get rid of my black clothes, and try to forget, as much as possible, the wretched feelings I had experienced in them. Stanhope said in the coach, in speaking of the strange mixture of avarice and profusion which Byron exhibited, that he had heard himself say, "He was sure he should die a miser and a bigot." Hobhouse, to-day, mentioned as remarkable, the change in Byron's character when he went to Greece. Finding that there was ardour enough among them, but that steadiness was what they wanted, he instantly took a quiet and passive tone, listening to the different representations made to him, and letting his judgment be properly informed, before he either urged or took any decided course of action. Campbell's conversation in very bad taste; among other subjects talked of poor Bowles, calling him "rascal," &c., upon which Rogers took him up very properly. Fixed with Stanhope to come to breakfast with Rogers on Wednesday. Walked with R. into the park, and met a soldier's funeral, which, in the full state my heart was in, affected me strongly. The air the bugles played was, "I'm wearing awa, like snow-wreaths in the thaw." Walked down to Paternoster Row, and dined with Rees. Told him I had consulted Rogers with respect to my applying to the family for materials, and that his decided opinion was, that I should make no such movement at present; and that he thought I would rather injure my chance by doing so than otherwise. Rogers, by the by, in expressing this opinion to me, spoke as if there was something more in his mind than he chose to communicate. He said, "I entreat of you to take no step of this kind till *I* release you. I have particular reasons for it." Have little doubt, though I did not say so to him, that this mystery relates to some plan of the family for settling the £2000 on little Tom. *A la bonne heure;* so I am not consulted on the subject, it is not for *me* to interfere. Went from Paternoster Row to call upon the Morgans. Found Lady Morgan half-dressed, and had the felicity of seeing the completion of her toilette; looking, however, much more at her handmaid (Morgan's pretty daughter) than at herself. From thence went to Mrs. Story's, and supped with her. I and the girls went to Vauxhall: a most delicious night. Rogers told me of Burke taking a tour on foot with his brother, and when they came to two branching roads Burke held up his stick to decide which they should take. The stick said Bath. Burke went there and was married.

13th. [Tuesday] Breakfasted at our new club, the Athenaeum. Called on Mrs. Montgomerie, who had written to the Cottage to say she had a parcel from Lucy for me. Her account of poor Lucy very disheartening: told me, and cried while she said so, that there was little hope of her getting through the autumn. Lucy's own account, however, is much more cheering, and this I will try to believe. Gave me a little memorandum book, which L. sent by her for me. Walked about with Woolriche. Asked by Bennet to dine with him; but dined with Rogers and his sister. Thence to the Opera, Lord Lansdowne having given me a ticket. Sat quietly, for a wonder, at the front of the pit, and heard almost the whole of the "Donna del Lago;" Ronzi charming. In looking over Rogers's "Common-place Book" with him this evening, found some highly curious records of his conversations with eminent men, particularly Fox, Grattan, and the Duke of Wellington. Grattan thought that Mr. Fox's best speeches were during the American war; his best time about 1779. Quoted several fine passages from Lord Chatham. "I care not from whence the wind comes," &c.&c. (which I must procure from R.), and the passage about the intention of the Americans to resist, "I am pleased to hear," which Grattan thought surpassed anything in Demosthenes, "Mr. Pitt," said Grattan, "is a discreet man; he is right nine times for once that Mr. Fox is right, but that once of Mr. Fox is worth all the other nine times of Mr. Pitt."

14th. [Wednesday] Breakfasted with Rogers to meet Leicester Stanhope. Much talk about Lord Byron, of whom Stanhope saw a good deal at Missolonghi. Byron entirely guided in his views by Mavrocordato; "a mere puppet in his hands;" Mavrocordato always teazing him for money, till Byron hated the very sight of him. The story of Byron's giving four thousand pounds to raise the siege of Missolonghi not true. A little money goes an immense way in Greece. A hundred pounds might sometimes be the means of keeping a fleet or army together. Mavrocordato appointed B. to command the army of western Greece. Stanhope thought this appointment of a stranger injurious to the dignity of the Greek nation, and told B. so, which annoyed him. S. expressed the same to some members of the Greek government, who said it was done by Mavrocordato, without consulting them. In the passage from Cephalonia, the ship, aboard which were Count Gamba, Byron's servants, packages, &c. &c., was taken the carried into a Turkish port; but, by some management, got off again. Byron himself, next morning, at break of day, got close in with a Turkish frigate, which, however, took his small vessel for a fire-ship and sheered off. B. gave but little money. After his severe attack, when he was lying nervous and reduced in bed, insurrection took place among the Suliots, who would frequently rush into his bedroom to make their remonstrances. Byron would not have them shut out, but always listened to them with much good nature; very gallant this. Asked Stanhope as to his courage, which I have sometimes heard the depreciating gossips of society throw a doubt upon; and not long ago, indeed, was told of Lord Bathurst's saying, when somebody expressed an apprehension for Lord Byron's safety in Greece, "Oh, never fear, he will not expose himself to much danger." Stanhope said, on the contrary, he was always for rushing into danger; would propose one day to go in a fire-ship; another time, to storm Lepanto; would however, laugh at all this himself afterwards, and say he wished that——(some one, I don't know whom, that was expected to take a command) would come and supersede him. Stanhope had several stormy conversations with him on business. In one of them Byron threatened to write a pasquinade against him; and Stanhope begged him to do so, and he would give him a hundred pounds for the copyright. Said it was an extraordinary scene when the leeches had bit the temporal artery in his first attack; the two physicians squabbling over him, and he, weak as he was, joking at their expense. Capt. Parry was his favourite *butt* at Missolonghi. Went from Rogers to call on Charles Sheridan; mentioned to him the objections of the Longmans to the speech being given out of my hands;[1] said he had promised Lord Fitzwilliam, and would rather break the agreement with the Longmans than fail in his word to him; told me, however, I might delay giving the MS. a little longer, as Lord F. was told it could not be had, till I was quite done with it. Went off at two o'clock to the Chapter Coffee House, where Rees had got me a private room for the purpose of looking through the old pamphlets in search of something about Sheridan. Stayed there till five, but got very little. Dined at Longmans': company, Archer (bookseller from Dublin), Abbot (the actor), Oldham (from the Bank of Ireland), &c. &c. Oldham told some good Irish stories. Had fixed to go with Mrs. Story to Vauxhall, but a tremendous storm of rain, thunder, and lightning put it out of the question.

15th. [Thursday] Breakfasted with Newton, and sat to him. Called upon Lady Lansdowne, who asked me to dine quietly with them, but was engaged to Rogers. Called, and sat some time with Lady Jersey, who also wished me to dine with her to meet Lord Grey; found Agar Ellis there, who offered me a ticket for Garcia's benefit in the evening, if I would call for it at his house. Dined at Rogers's; company, Newton, Kenny, and Leslie, the painter. Expected that Irving, who arrived to-day, would be of the party, but he dined with W. Spencer. Kenny brought to R.'s a copy of a letter from Trelawny, in which there is such a curious account of Lord Byron's conversation with him about his courage. Went to the Opera; sat in Mrs. A. Ellis's box, and Lady Jersey's. Lord W. Russell in the latter, who talked about Woolriche, and praised him. The opera, "Semiramide;" first time in England, and very imperfectly performed. Interesting to see Rossini himself presiding in the orchestra, and his anxious looks at the choruses, &c. &c.

16th. [Friday] Breakfasted at Holland House. Asked Lord Holland several questions about Burke, suggested to me by reading Prior's "Life of Burke" on my way to town.[1] Burke very anxious (Lord H. says) for the Coalition.[2] The fifty-four articles of Impeachment against Fox were written by Burke *before* the separation.[3] In his "History of the English Colonies," Burke suggested (Lord H. thinks) American taxation.[4] Burke always a jobber. Advised me, in giving Sheridan's character, to take into account the much looser notions of conduct that existed in his times; a strictness at the present day, of which they had not then any idea. The laxity of principle in the higher classes pervaded all Europe, and might be traced to the dissolute Court of the Regent. The consequence was, the people lost their respect for the higher classes in France. Acknowledged that in England, George III., by the decency of his private life, and Mr. Pitt ("though a drunkard") by his freedom from the more glaring irregularities of high life, kept up the tone of moral conduct, and that so far Pitt did more service to England than Mr. Fox (though so much more amiable) could ever have done, because the example of the latter rather tended in the other direction. Mr. Fox was never a member of the Friends of the People; never a Reformer, in the sense of those who think the people have a right to change the representation. When he was for Reform in 1797, "meant really Revolution," because he thought that a Revolution of another kind was coming on, and preferred, of the two, a *popular* one. His speeches at the time prove this. Has papers, which if well grounded, go to prove that the breach with Burke had such an effect on Mr. Fox, that but for party ties, he would at that time have left Parliament altogether; the breach, if not brought about, considerably widened and embittered, by Sheridan, Grey, &c. Sat with Lady

Holland some time in her own room. Joined by Lord H. and talked of Lord Byron. B. shocked by Lady H.'s calling her son Henry "hoppy-kicky," &c. His fancy and liking for persons who had this deformity; mentioned that Stanhope told me of his having taken into favour some Count in Greece who was thus deformed. Lord H. related the circumstances of his speaking to Byron about the attack upon Lord Carlisle. Byron's horror when he mentioned the personality of the line, &c. which had never occurred to him before; left him resolved to make an *amende* for it, and (as Lord Holland supposes) in the dedication of the "Corsair" to me, which he was just then about to write. But the very next day came out the attack upon Byron in the "Courier," which totally changed his conduct as he might be supposed (he feared) to have been bullied into the reparation of this abuse.[5] Lord Holland's remark on the singularity of all the best writers of Comedy having written their plays so early in life. This would prove that liveliness of fancy is more necessary for the task than knowledge of the world. Left them to meet Kenny by appointment. Lord Holland, by the by, having told me that when I came, in my "Life of Sheridan," to the period of the Whig Administration, he would (if I pleased) look over what I said on the subject, not for the purpose of communicating anything to me, which he could hardly do, but in order to prevent me from falling into error. Fixed with Kenny to meet Mrs. Shelley at breakfast with him to-morrow. Called upon Peter Moore, but ineffectually. Dined at Miss White's; company, Stratford Canning, Hallam, Captain Basil Hall, Lady C. Lindsay, Mrs. Tighe, and her sons; agreeable enough. A good deal of talk about Burke. Hallam mentioned *five* speeches of his, among which the choice was bewildered. Newton, Irving, and others in the evening. Sung to as ugly a group of old damsels (with the exception of Lady Listowel) as ever were brought together. Irving said that I ought always, on such occasions, cry "Send out for some girls, and I'll sing for you."

17th. [Saturday] With Kenny a little after ten. Mrs. Shelley very gentle and feminine. Spoke a good deal of Byron; his treatment of Leigh Hunt, by her account, not very good. Made some remarks upon him in a letter to Murray, which reached Hunt's ears, and produced an expostulation from him to Byron on the subject; B.'s answer aristocratical and evasive.[1] Asked her whom she thought this person could be, whom Sir Egerton Brydges had announced to the Longmans as about to bring out a sort of Boswell diary of Byron's Conversations, having lived much with him, and noted down all he had said. Supposed it must be a Mr. Barry, a partner in the bank at Genoa, with whom Byron used to sit up, drinking brandy and water, and tell him every thing; did not think it could be Captain Medwin.[2] The Guiccioli refused a settlement from him (ten thousand pounds, I think).[3] Spoke of the story of the girl in the Giaour. Founded (as B. has often told me) on the circumstance of a young girl, whom he knew himself in Greece, and whom he supposed to be a Greek, but who proved to be a Turk; and who underwent on his account the punishment mentioned in the poem; he met her body carried along in the sack. Must inquire of Lord Sligo about this, as B. once showed me a letter of his upon the subject.⁴ Sung to Mrs. Shelley and Miss Holcroft, who was with Kenny. All walked together to Newton's, where we found Irving. Had despatched in the morning a note to Edward Moore to know whether I might ask Irving, Newton, and Kenny to dine with him to-day; answer, to say I might. Walked about with Irving; called at Power's, &c. &c. Wrote to Mrs. Story to say we should all sup with her to-night. Dinner at Moore's (Fitzroy Stanhope making the sixth) very agreeable; the supper rather too much after it. Kenny to-day mentioned Charles Lamb's being once bored by a lady praising to him "such a charming man!" &c. &c. ending with "I know him, bless him!" on which Lamb said, "Well, I don't, but d——n him, at a hazard." Rogers yesterday, as an instance of broken metaphors, quoted a line of Croker's in his "Talavéra," "a column of the flower of France."⁵

18th. [Sunday] Breakfasted at the Athenaeum. Called upon Peter Moore, and found him at last. Told me a good deal about Sheridan, some of which I have noted in my memorandum books. Gave me the printed reports relative to Drury Lane, and told me that Burgess has all the deeds of that property from the beginning. Must apply to him. Mentioned the art with which S. got possession of his friend Ironmonger's house at Leatherhead, advising him to go to France, and he would take house, furniture, &c. &c. off his hands for five years. Ironmonger obliged to come home on account of Bonaparte's *sortie* from Elba, and had great difficulty in getting possession of his house again.¹ Sheridan, he says, raised £30,000 by new shares.² When S., after the theatre was in Whitbread's hands, went down to Stafford, they told him that if he could manage to raise £2500 it would secure his election; S. drew upon Whitbread for the sum, but it was refused.³ S. paid his way at Stafford most punctually, and I forget how much Moore said it had cost him; must ask again. Took a hackney coach and went off to Paddington, in consequence of a note from Miss R. Walked about the garden with her for an hour. Waited on Paddington Green for Mrs. Story, who had promised to meet me in her carriage there; and then walked into town. Called at Power's. Newton and Irving came to my lodgings between five and six; and all went off together to dine at Lord Listowel's; rather a dull party.

19th. [Monday] Off at a quarter before seven for home. Found all well on my return, and Mrs. Branigan still with Bessy, but Anastasia gone back to school. Forgot, by the by, to copy down from my pocket-book some things Rogers told me of Sheridan. S. said to him *twice* that every sentence in the "Stranger," as it is acted, was written by him. Can this be true?[1] R. saw Sheridan's pantomime of "Robinson Crusoe," the first act of which was very good; Grimaldi, as "Friday," excellent. Sheridan annoyed at school by being called a player boy and an actor. Said he never saw Garrick on the stage; never saw a play all through. Garrick played against the "Duenna," and some actor said, "The old woman will break the heart of the old man." Mr. Fox thought that Tom Sheridan ought to have accepted the Registrarship, but some of the violent of the party (Lady R. Spencer, R. thinks, among others) advised the rejection of it.[2] On some one asking S., after the Westminster Hall Speech, "Why he had mentioned the 'luminous page of Gibbon,'" he replied, with a wink, "I said *vo*luminous." Hobhouse, at Byron's funeral, told me that he looked at the corpse at Hanson's desire, who thought it necessary some one besides himself should see it, and that there was hardly a trace of identity left. Could hardly believe it was he; the mustachios, the puffy face, the shaggy eye-brows, &c. The brains weighed a third or fourth more than is usual.

20th to 26th. [Tuesday–Monday] Set to work at Sheridan. Lord Lansdowne called on me this week (the 22nd I believe), and I walked part of the way home with him. Told me that before he left town he had a long statement and a heap of papers from Wilmot Horton on the subject of the money, still insisting that I had no right to pay the money, and that I ought to receive it back again. "I am afraid you will be angry with me (said Lord Lansdowne), but I gave it as my opinion that you *ought* to receive the money." On inquiring the new points in their statements which decided him for this opinion, I found that they had dwelt a good deal upon Murray's protest against being paid the money, and that Lord L. in his answer told them he should have been a good deal embarrassed in coming to the conclusion he did if there had been anything like a *free* acceptance of the money on Murray's part, as that would have been, so far, an acknowledgment of the right of property in me, on the total absence of which they furnished their argument for my taking back the money from him. On my mentioning *now*, however, to Lord L. that Murray (after a no very strong protest) not only took the money himself, but ordered his clerk to bring the account of interest, &c. &c., and furnished me with the materials for drawing on Rogers for the amount; not only this, but that he sent the draft to Rogers the next morning, in due course, for payment, Lord L. acknowledged that these circumstances materially changed the ground on which he gave his opinion, and said that he should lose no time in writing an explanatory letter to say so. Asked me to dine next Tuesday to meet Dumont. Sent to

Power this week the poetry for two songs; one, "Array thee, love, array thee!" and the other, "As once a Grecian maiden wove."[1]

27th. [Tuesday] Dined at Bowood: company, Dumont, Lord and Lady King, Hickson and Mahony (both from Ireland). It was mentioned that the Bishop of Limerick, in his late tedious speech, had his notes written on cards, and the Chancellor said to Lord L., "I have always hated cards, but never saw a pack I took such an aversion to as that." They thought the Bishop never would have done, and when he *did* stop, Lord King cried out distinctly "bravo!"[1] Dumont, in talking of poetry, said, quoting from some one, *La difficulté, c'est la dixième Muse.* I mentioned some verses in which this is illustrated by the *jet-d'eau,* which is made stronger and higher by pressure. He remembered the verses, and repeated them. Came home at night.

28th to Aug. 2nd. [Wednesday–Monday] Working at Sheridan. Lady Lansdowne called one of these days, and asked us to dine next Tuesday to meet the Hollands, who came on Monday. Bessy had gone to Bowles's to hear some music from the Moravians. Had a letter from John Scully, informing me that the author of "Rock Detected"[1] is the Rev. Mr. Mortimer O'Sullivan, so that I guessed right. Expressed great admiration of "Captain Rock," which he says will do more for the fame of its author and the good of Ireland than any book that ever was published.

3rd. [Tuesday] Bessy and I dined at Bowood; she not a little alarmed at the encounter with Lady Holland, who, however, was all graciousness to her. Some ludicrous verses quoted at dinner; among others the following by Rogers on Theophilus:—

> When I'm drinking my tea
> I think of my *The*
> When I'm drinking my coffee
> I think of my Offee;
> So, whether I'm drinking my tea or my coffee,
> I'm always a thinking of thee, my Theoffy.

Lord H. mentioned some one being defied to find a rhyme for Carysfort; and writing—

> I'm writing a note to my uncle Carysfort,
> He has got the gout, and is gone to Paris for 't.

In talking of people who prepared their conversation, Lord Lansdowne mentioned a Frenchman who once dined at his father's, and who, taking him aside when they stood up from dinner, said, "There are one or two things which I had prepared to say to-day; but as there was not time or opportunity to bring them in, I will, if you will allow me, tell them now to you." In the evening talked with Lord Holland about Sheridan. Burke, though very magnanimous in forwarding Mr. Fox when he appeared in the arena of politics, did not feel the same to Sheridan, but regarded him with great jealousy. There are proofs, Lord H. says, that Burke, after leaving office upon Rockingham's death, was negotiating for a sinecure place with Lord J. Cavendish, who stayed in some time after him for the transaction of business; the proof of this is in the unpublished "Memoirs of Walpole," which Lord H. has in his possession.[1] Sheridan's strong wish to make his power felt in politics grew still stronger in his latter days from vanity and disappointment. Lord H. knows of no regular application from S. to see Mr. Fox when he was dying; never heard of his refusing to see him; though, at the same time, is sure that he would not have liked it. Thinks Sheridan was slow in argument; did not all at once see your drift. Looked over the new etchings to the story of "Fridolin" with Bessy, while Lady Holland explained the story. Came away before ten, promising to go to luncheon to-morrow.

4th. [Wednesday] Went to Bowood at two; met by Rogers halfway. Sat with Lady Holland, Rogers, and Allen in the garden talking. Offered Lady H. our little pony-chaise for to-morrow. Went with Lady Lansdowne and Mary Fox into the garden to eat strawberries. Lady H. and Rogers anxious that I should stay dinner, but, though having a general invitation, did not like to do so without a special one. Stayed till five o'clock, when Lady L. very kindly pressed me to stay, and ordered Rogers not to let me go; but I felt somehow as if I had forced the invitation from her by staying so late, and thought it better to come away. Found Bessy at Phipps's waiting for me, and the Phippses just sitting down to dinner. Joined them at it, and returned home early. Lady Holland, today, spoke highly of Bessy's beauty.

5th. [Thursday] Drove in the gig to breakfast at Bowood. Talked with Lord H. and R. afterwards about Sheridan. Question as to the things I might tell. Rogers mentioned that S.'s father said, "Talk of the merit of Dick's comedy! There's nothing in it. He had but to dip the pencil in his own heart, and he'd find there the characters of both Joseph and Charles."[1] Lord H. thought I might introduce this as an exemplification of the harsh feeling the father had towards him, which was such that "he even permitted himself to say," &c. &c. Must say something kind of Tom Sheridan; his case a hard one; brought up amid all the splendour attached to his father's name, and the extravagance of his mode of living; left without education or example, yet turning out so amiable. Lord H. mentioned a letter from the Prince to the King, after the first Regency question, exculpating himself; has a copy; does not think it has been printed.[2] At the time of Mr. Fox's assertion about the Prince's marriage with Mrs. F., the Prince wanted Grey to contradict it, but Grey refused; upon which the Prince said, "Then I must get Sheridan to say something." The Prince *did* authorize Mr. Fox to contradict the marriage, though he afterwards denied it.[3] Lord H. saw a letter from Monkton in answer to an appeal S. made to him, and saying, that so far was S. from being under any pecuniary obligation to him (Monkton), that if the balance was fairly struck, it would prove to be rather the other way.[4] His pride on being told by some physician that he had a very large heart. The Prince's reason for not going near Sheridan latterly was, that he feared his influence over him. The Prince, when the King last went mad, kept aloof from the Whigs, which Lord H. now thinks he was right in, though they all thought differently then. Never saw even S., though S. wished to have it supposed he did. S. latterly, though having his house in Saville Row, lived at an hotel, and used to chuckle at the idea of the bailiffs watching fruitlessly for him in Saville Row. "They talk (says S. one day to Lord H.) of avarice, lust, ambition, as great passions. It is a mistake; they are little passions. Vanity is the great commanding passion of all. It is this that produces the most grand and heroic deeds, or impels to the most dreadful crimes. Save me but from this passion, and I can defy the others. They are mere urchins, but this is a giant." Proposed to Lord Lansdowne to stay dinner, and he said he expected I would. When I told Lady Holland why I did not stay yesterday, she said, "I guessed it was so; England is the only country where such things could happen." Walked with Dumont and Rogers. D. mentioned Piron's reply to Voltaire, on his boasting that he did not hiss his tragedy, *Quand on baille, on ne siffle pas*. Rogers quoted Lord Chatham's saying, on some motion which he made and in which nobody seconded him, "My lords, I stand alone; my lords, I stand like our first parent, naked but not ashamed." Name of a novel, "Delia, by the author of Julia." It was at Osterley, the parish (?) where Child lived, and where Sheridan had a house, that he wrote the sermon for O'Beirne to preach; poor O'Beirne throwing his voice most pointedly into Child's pew. Child had been harsh in punishing some poor person for making free with a few vegetables; and the text (R. says, though this differs from O'Beirne's own account to me) was "it is easier for a camel," &c. &c. A storm coming on before dinner, Lady L. begged I would send home to say I should sleep at Bowood; I did so. Our pony chaise used to-day by Lady Holland in going over the pleasure-grounds; the set-out excellent; the poor pony led slowly along, with Allen walking on one side of the procession and Dumont on the other.

6th. [Friday] After breakfast had again some conversation with Lord H. about Sheridan. S.'s comparison of Lord Sidmouth's administration to Theseus, taken from a letter of Gilbert Wakefield to Mr. Fox. Looked for "Wakefield's Letters" in the library, and after a long search found it. The letter in which this was is evidently omitted, but Mr. Fox, in his answer, alludes to it; and Lord H. clearly recollects having seen it, and heard his uncle read it. Told me a good deal about Sheridan's conduct in the first negotiation of Lords Grey and Grenville for coming into power after the Regency; their remonstrance, and Sheridan's representations to the Regent upon it; all of which I have written down in one of my memorandum books. Also a whole account of Canning's early connection with Sheridan, which I have written down in the same book.[1] Lord H. mentioned a translation which he had just made of a Greek epigram, but did not recollect nor know where to find the original. It struck me I had quoted it in the notes on Anacreon, and that it was written by some poet whose name began with an A. Looked through the index of the Anthologia, but could not find it. Walked home at two, and Rogers accompanied me to the Cottage; looked over Bessy's books, kissed the children, and was very amiable.

7th. [Saturday] Interrupted by visitors all the morning; Bowles, with Archdeacon Nares, Nugent, &c. &c. What *am* I to do?

8th and 9th. [Sunday–Monday] Contrived to send off yesterday two songs to Power; one with music of my own, "When the Balaika;" and the other words for Bishop to set, "I come from a land in the sun-bright deep."[1]

10th. [Tuesday] Worked at Sheridan a little. Lords Holland, Lansdowne, and Belgrave, called near our dinner-time; was denied to them. Lord H. left word that he meant to leave Bowood to-morrow morning.

11th. [Wednesday] Drove over to Bowood at ten in the morning. Told Lord H. that the verses I meant were those by Ariphron, Ὑγίεια, πρεσβυτα μακαρων. Saw the Hollands off before twelve. Talked with Rogers and Lord John (who arrived on Sunday last); talked of Chatham. Rogers quoted what he said when commenting on a speech of the king's, which was known to be the joint composition of Lord Holland and Lord Mansfield;[1] "Here rolls the Rhone, black, turbid, and rapid; while here steals the Saône, whispering, with flowers on its banks." People used to repeat these beautiful things that Lord C. had said as they walked up Parliament Street. Pitt's style very unlike; more suited to business. Courtney said of Pitt's speeches, that "they were like Lycurgus's money that did not pass out of Sparta;" this very pretty, but not true, as Pitt's speeches *did* tell through the country. Lord John proposed to me to go to Longleat, when he and the Durazzos go there from Bowood; shall do so if I do not go to the Salisbury music meeting. Rogers sets off to-morrow for town.

12th. [Thursday] After writing a few sentences of Sheridan, set off to dine at Bowood, Bessy leaving me there, in her way to Buckhill. Company, Lord Belgrave and Lady Elizabeth, Lord John, and the Durazzos. Lord L. told me in the evening that old Sheridan once gave a very bad character of Richard Brinsley to his father Lord Shelburne; said he was a person not to be trusted. Lord S. met old Sheridan out riding when he had this conversation with him; and it happened on the very day of the dismissal of Lord North's administration; Lord S. finding on his return home, the message relative to the formation of a new one. Talked with him of the opinions of Fox on the Regency; Pitt's evident exultation when Fox committed himself in his first speech on that subject; slapped his thigh in triumph, and said to some near him (from whom Lord L., as well as I could understand, heard it), "I'll unwhig the gentleman for the rest of his life." Sung a good deal; tried over some Italian things with Madame Durazzo. Slept there.

13th. [Friday] At breakfast, Madame Durazzo, in talking of poor Miss Bathurst (who was drowned at Rome), mentioned that Talleyrand in reading an account of it (in which it was said that her uncle plunged in after her, and that M. Laval was in the greatest grief), said, "*M. de Laval aussi s'est plongé, mais dans la plus profonde douleur.*" Walked home, the Lansdownes having made it a point that I should return to dinner. Bowles came about our lodgings for Salisbury Music Meeting; but Bessy has given up her desire to go. Walked back in the rain to Bowood; the same party as yesterday. Singing in the evening. Slept there. Went after breakfast, with the ladies, on the roof of the house, to see the prospect; visited, too, all the bedrooms. Lady E. Belgrave having expressed a wish for a verse of "Oh, come to me, when daylight sets,"[1] written out by myself, did it for her. Lord John told me that Crabbe (who was here the beginning of the week, and whom I had but a glimpse of,) said that I was "a great poet when I *liked.*" My pony carriage arrived to take Lord John and me to the christening of our little Russell, which he had fixed for to-day; after the ceremony, Lord John lunched with us. Showed him some parts of my Sheridan work, which he seemed to like. Told me he had heard from Dudley North (one of the managers of Hastings' trial), that when the managers used to retire to take any doubtful point into consideration, Burke used to say, "Now let us defer to the superior wisdom of Mr. Fox." Drove Lord John back to Bowood, and returned to dinner. Mentioned what Brougham said lately, in allusion to the adoption by the Ministers of all the Whig measures, "The fact is, *we* are in power, and *they* are in place." Had some people, Hughes, Phipps, &c. to tea and supper; sung for them; a Miss Miller, too, sung some French songs very sweetly. The Lansdownes have invited Bessy to dine to-morrow, but she does not seem inclined to it; "Tell her," Lord L. said to-day, "we have nothing to offer her but a haunch of venison, and Lord John."

14th. [Saturday] Sent an excuse to Bowood. Worked at Sheridan.

15th. [Sunday] Lord John and the Durazzos called in their way to Longleat. Madame Durazzo full of amiable praises of every thing she saw; the children, library, &c. &c. Wanted to take me out with them, but I promised to join them on Thursday. Walked with Bessy in the evening.

16th. [Monday] Writing away. Luttrel and his sister, Mrs. Scott, called; had invited them and Nugent to come to dine to-morrow, but they go to Longleat. Received a very amusing letter from Washington Irving.

17th. [Tuesday] Writing a little. Began a song for Power on a subject from "Valerius Flaccus;" the transformation of Œa into an island.

19th. [Thursday] Set off in my pony carriage to go to Longleat; arrived at Warminster about three; lunched, and left that in a chaise for Longleat. Approach to the house by this road very magnificent. Found Crabbe just going out to walk, when I arrived; joined him; the gardens about the house beautiful. Company at dinner; the Durazzos, Lord John, Lady Clarendon, Luttrel, and Nugent, Miss Copley, Lascelles and Lady Louisa, and the Belgraves. Rather stiff and formal during dinner; the silence of the master of the house, and the largeness of the company naturally producing this effect. Crabbe told me of his visit to Walter Scott while the King was in Edinburgh; the King drinking a glass of wine with Scott to the health of the Ladies of Edinburgh, on being presented by him with some offering from them; Scott's begging of the King to allow him to have the glass as a memorial; and his letting it fall and break to pieces just as he reached his own door with it. Crabbe said this seemed to be a prognostic of the disfavour which he fell into with the King, who did not appear to like his pushing himself forward so officiously. Talking in the evening with Luttrel on some peculiar phrases of the Scotch; they say a man is married *upon* such a one. Sung, Lady Louisa joining me in some things; and so did Lord Belgrave. The first appearance of formality vanished, and all very agreeable. Lady Bath cried at "Oft in the stilly night,"[1] and was obliged to leave the room; told me afterwards it was because this song had been frequently sung to her by her sister, Mrs. Seymour, who is not expected to live long.

20th. [Friday] After breakfast walked through the grounds with Lord John and Madame Durazzo; she very agreeable. Lord J. mentioned what Voltaire said in his answer to an address presented to him by the College of some little town which called itself *fille de l'Université de Paris.* "I have no doubt of it," said Voltaire, "and certainly a *fille très sage, qui n'a fait jamais parler d'elle.*" Lord John reminded me of the circumstance mentioned by Lord Byron in his "Memoirs," of his receiving a letter from some young girl dying in a consumption, who said she could not go out of the world, without thanking him for all the pleasure his works had given her," &c. &c. Talking of mistakes made by private actors: "I wouldn't give *that* for you (snapping his fingers)," being all spoken, stage directions and all, in the same manner. The old Lord Lansdowne, in some private plays, always said, "I'll spoil your intrigue (aside);" pronouncing intrigue, too, as three syllables. I mentioned the actor who could never be got to say, "stand by, and let the coffin pass," but, instead of it, always said "stand by, and let the parson cough." Had music again in the evening; Lady Louisa sung "Dost thou remember,"[1] with me, very sweetly. Lady Bath mentioned the ridiculous anecdote Madame de Genlis tells of her losing her way between London and Dartford; and promised to look for the book it is in to show it to me. Looked over with Lord John Russell, to-day, some of the proof-sheets of his new work.[2]

21st. [Saturday] After breakfast prepared to set out with M. and Madame Durazzo to see Fonthill, and attend mass at Wardour to-morrow. Lord John stays in the meantime at Longleat, and will meet us in our way back to Bowood at Warminster, on Monday. Lady Bath produced Madame Genlis's book; and on my asking her for the loan of it, begged me to keep it entirely. It is evident, I think, from her account of her nocturnal wanderings, and the proceedings that followed, that it was all a concocted trick of Sheridan's to keep her some time longer in England.[1] Set off between one and two; arrived about four at Hindon. Despatched the letter we had from Lord Lansdowne to Lord Arundell, accompanied by one from myself, asking the hour of mass to-morrow. Set off for Fonthill; and to make sure of our admission there, drove first to Bennet's. No one at home but Anna, who represented her father's hospitality most worthily; asked me where we meant to sleep, and on my saying at Hindon (though she knew neither who nor how many were the party), exclaimed, "That is impossible; papa and mamma will be home from Salisbury in an hour or two, and you must all come here." Despatched a man and horse, bearing a note to Captain Philipps (the agent of Farquhar), in consequence of which he attended us, and showed us marked civility. Durazzo's astonishment at the oddity of Fonthill, exclaiming at every step, *Je ne conçois pas. Un homme doit avoir le diable au corps pour bâtir une maison comme ça.* Returned to the inn at seven; a good plain dinner. Durazzo went soon to bed, and left me with Madame, who was very agreeable. Gave me a whole account of the delirium which followed a typhus fever she had some years since; and which lasted so long after the fever, that it was thought her mind was gone. Her idea all the while was that angels were inviting and opening heaven to her; while the restraints under which she was kept prevented her from enjoying that happiness. Music the only thing that did her good; used to cry when she heard it; sung airs of her own during the time, to words of Metastasio and Shakspeare that she had in her memory. Notes from Lady Arundell, who had just returned from the music meeting, offering us accommodation at Wardour, and saying that mass would be at half-past ten in the morning.

22nd. [Sunday] Set off for Wardour after breakfast. Received very kindly by the Arundells. Bowles there, having come over from Salisbury; attended mass with us, which Durazzo could not understand. Bowles, himself, said to me, as we knelt together, "Only think of my being on my knees beside 'Captain Rock' at mass." The singing, to a fine organ, very good, Lady Arundell herself joining in it. Bowles remarked the effect of the light falling on her face as she sung. A most barbarous explication of the Gospel given by the priest; entering into particulars about the personal appearance and manners of Christ; almost said as much as that he was very gentlemanlike; and read the whole of the old spurious letter[1] to prove that, though some represented him as despicable in his appearance, he was very good looking. Went to see the old castle, and started at half-past two, Madame Durazzo in very beautiful alarm and despair at the idea of arriving so late at Bowood. Took up Lord John at Warminster, where he had been waiting long enough to read the whole "Dunciad" through. Wished me to go on to Bowood with them; but as I passed my own door, thought it better to stop there; found the Phippses, and dined off cold meat. Have written at intervals during these few days past three or four verses about Œa.

23rd. [Monday] Had a note from Lord Lansdowne, asking me to take a parting dinner with the Durazzos and Lord John to-morrow; promised to go. Luttrel and Nugent called in passing by, on their way from Longleat.

24th. [Tuesday] Sent Power the song I had written. Walked over to Bo-wood: company, the Hopes, Durazzos, &c. &c. Sung in the evening. Lady Lansdowne had ordered Asioli's duets, and made Mad. Durazzo and I try several of them over together. Sung also my own national duets, "Come to me when daylight sets," and "Dost thou remember?"[1] Intended to return home to-night, and William had come for me with the lantern; but they pressed me so much to stay and see Lord John off in the morning, that I could not refuse. William told me that the pony had kicked this evening with Mrs. Phipps, and broken the little carriage; so there is an end of poor Bessy's driving, as I cannot now in conscience ask her to venture again. Lord Lansdowne asked me to show him Irving's letter, Luttrel and Lord John having told him how clever and lively it was.

25th. [Wednesday] Lord John and the Durazzos off, after breakfast, to Middleton. Luttrel anxious for me to go to Lord Bathurst's next week, Seymour Bathurst having begged him, before he left Longleat, to try and persuade me to it. Should like to go, if it were only for the fun of the thing, *de m'y voir*, as the Doge said. Luttrel walked home with me. Called at Phipps's on our way to see the pony carriage, which was still there, Mrs. P. doubting whether I should wish to have the circumstance known to Bessy; thought it better, however, that she should be told. Sent off an invitation to Luttrel's sister, Mrs. Scott, and her husband, to meet L. and Nugent at dinner with us on Friday. William, our servant, ill, from the fright of the pony kicking last night. On my saying that I thought the strong beer at Bowood might have something to do with it, Luttrel said, "Yes, he's *aleing,* I suppose." Saw him back a good part of the way.

26th. [Thursday] Worked away a little at Sheridan.

27th. [Friday] Luttrel, Nugent, Mrs. Scott, and Luttrel's son came to din-ner; Mr. Scott, himself, being engaged. Luttrel had put his joke about "aleing" into verse:—

> Come, come, for trifles never stick,
>   Most servants have a failing:
> Yours, it is true, are sometimes sick,
>   But mine are *always aleing.*

Our dinner very ill drest, which was rather provoking, as Luttrel is particu-lar about the *cuisine;* it had no effect, however, either on his wit or good humour, for he was highly agreeable. . . . Remarked many unaccountable things in Ireland: plenty of plovers, but no plovers' eggs; chaises in abundance, but no return ones, &c. &c. The Lansdownes' carriage brought Luttrel and Nugent to dinner, but they walked home, with the assistance of my lantern

28th. [Saturday] Wrote before I got out of bed, a parody on Horace's *Sic te Diva potens Cypri,* addressed to the *lantern* that I lent Luttrel last night:—

> So may the Cyprian queen above,
> The mother of that link-boy Love;
> So may each star in Heaven's dome,—
>   Those *patent Smethursts* of astronomy,—
> That light poor rural diners home,
>   After a dose of bad gastronomy;
> So may each winter wind that blows
>   O'er down or upland, steep or level,
> And most particularly those
>   That blow round corners like the devil;
> Respect thee, oh! thou lantern bright,
>   By which for want of chaise and Houhwynmm,
> I trust my Luttrel home to-night[1],
>   With half a poet's larder in him.[2]
>
> That bard had brow of brass, I own[3],
>   Who first presumed, the hardened sinner,
> To ask fine gentlemen from town
>   To come and eat a d—d bad dinner;
> Who feared not leveret, black as soot[4],
>   Like roasted Afric, at the head set
> (And making tow'rds the duck at foot,
>   The veteran duck, a sort of dead set);
> Whose nose could stand such ancient fish
>   As that we at Devizes purvey—
> Than which I know no likelier dish[5]
>   To turn one's stomach topsy-turvy.
>
> Oh! dying of an indigestion,
> To him was *quite* out of the question[6],
> Who could behold unmoved, unbother'd,
> Shrimps in sour anchovy smother'd[7];
> Who, venturous wight, no terror had
> Of tart old pies, or puddings *sad;*
> Who could for eatables mistake,
>   Whate'er the cook had mess'd up blindly;
> And e'en, like famish'd Luttrel, take
>   To infamous Scotch collops[8] kindly.

---

[1] Navis, quæ tibi creditum
    Debes Virgilium—
[2] Et serves animæ dimidium meæ.
[3] Illi robur et æs triplex
    Circa pectus erat.

Sent off this to L.; and dined at the Phippses; company, Estcourts, Lockes, Fishers, &c. &c. Sung for them in the evening.

29th.[Sunday] A note early from Lord Lansdowne, to say that Capt. Basil Hall, who is at Bowood, wishes much to see me; and that if I cannot come over to-day to either luncheon or dinner, he will call upon me to-morrow. Answered that I would come to dinner to-day. Walked over at five. Went to Luttrel's room; and found he had written the following answer to my parody, with which he seemed pleased, particularly with the *serves animæ dimidium,* and *Quo non arbiter Adriæ:*—

> A fine feast is a farce and a fable,
>   As often, dear Moore, we have found it;
> Prithee, what is the farce on a table
>   To the Fair who sit sparkling around it?
>
> I see not what you'd be to blame for
>   Though your cook were no dab at her duty;
> In your cottage was all that we came for,
>   Wit, poetry, friendship, and beauty!
>
> And then, to increase our delight
>   To a fullness all boundaries scorning,
> We were cheer'd with your lantern at night,
>   And regaled with your rhymes the next morning.
>
>   H.L.

Company, only Capt. Basil Hall, Luttrel, and Nugent, and an *ad interim* tutor of Kerry's. Hall mentioned a good phrase of some American, to whom Sir A. Ball had been very civil at Malta, "most grateful for all the kindness shown to himself and his wife; and hoped some time or another to have an opportunity of *retaliating* upon Lady Ball." Luttrel mentioned some Irish member (Crosbie, I believe) who in speaking of some one in the House, said, "Sir, if I have any partiality for the Hon. Gentleman, it is *against* him." Hall gave me, before I came away, a journal written by his sister, Lady De Lancy, containing an account of the death of her husband at Waterloo, and her attendance upon him there, they having been but three months married. Walked home; took the narrative to bed with me to read a page or two, but found it so deeply interesting, that I read till near

---

[4]Nec timuit præcipitem Africum.
[5]Quo non arbiter Adriæ
    Major, tollere seu ponere vult freta.
[6]Quem mortis timuit gradum,—
[7]Qui fixis oculis monstra natantia.
[8]*Infames scopulos;* or as it ought evidently to be read, *collopos.*
N.B. Luttrel eat only of a dish of this kind at dinner. (Moore's notes)

two o'clock, and finished it; made myself quite miserable, and went to sleep, I believe, crying. Hall said he would call upon me to-morrow.

30th. [Monday] Had but an hour or two of study before Hall came; asked him to dine with us; said he had thought of reaching Badminton (the Duke of Beaufort's) to dinner, but would stay. The Scotts called, and wished me to fix a day, this week, to dine with them; but as I still thought of going to Lord Bathurst's, begged them to defer it. Hall said he had written every word in his last book (Account of Chili) seven times over.[1]

31st. [Tuesday] At work.

September 1st. [Wednesday] Dined at Locke's, Bessy and I; the weather flamingly hot. Company, the Phippses, M——, Edmonston, and the Frederick Bouveries. Sung in the evening, to the accompaniment of M——'s creaking shoes, and chatter, which never stops. This parson an amazing nuisance in society, though said to be an excellent man at home; ought to stay there. Bessy quite indignant at his rudeness during my singing; good girl for so being.

2nd, 3rd, &c. [Thursday, Friday] Nothing remarkable; hard at work. Sent Power two poems for Bishop to set for the Greek work. Lord Lansdowne called and arranged for our going together to the Book-Club dinner, on Wednesday next.

8th. [Wednesday] Walked over to Bowood to dress, and went with Lord L. to the Book-Club dinner at Chippenham. About fourteen or sixteen people. Made to follow Lord L. out of the room, and sat next him. Mentioned Sir B. Roche saying energetically in the House, "Mr. Speaker, I'll answer boldly in the affirmative, No." Joy (who was President) told us he was by at the memorable scene between Fox and Burke.[1] Said that there were a number of people in the House affected to tears. In proposing new books after the dinner, a member from the bottom of the table said, "There is a book called 'Rock Detected,' which I should like to propose;" upon which I said immediately, "Mr. President, I second that motion." I added, however, that they need not go to the expense of buying a copy, as I had one quite at their service.[2] Left between nine and ten. In talking of neatness of execution being the *sine quâ non* in epigrams, Lord L. mentioned one as rather happy in its structure. I forget the exact words, but it was something

(The hearer) "Perplexed
　'Twixt the two to determine;
　'Watch and pray,' says the text,
　'Go to sleep,' says the sermon."

Wished me to dine with him on Friday, but have a half engagement to Scott.

9th and 10th. [Thursday–Friday] Reading and writing.

11th. [Saturday] Dined with the Scotts, who changed their day. Was in Devizes early, and drew on the Longmans for £100 at three months. Company at Scott's; the Salmons, and Edmonston; rather agreeable. Wet, stormy night; meant to have walked all the way home, but on arriving at Devizes, found it too bad, and took a chaise.

12th. [Sunday] Walked over to Bowood to see the Lansdownes, who go tomorrow to the Isle of Wight. Told them of a long letter I had had from Fielding, who expects to be in England at Christmas. Lady L. said it was entirely Captain Hall's anxiety to see Bessy that made him persist in calling upon me on Monday.

13th. [Monday] At work.

14th. [Tuesday] Went to Bath with Bessy for commissions; took Tom and Russell; our dear Anastasia quite well. Home before seven. Had an invitation from the Arundells to go over there to-day, but sent an excuse.

15th. [Wednesday] Bowles called. Asked him to return to dinner with us, which he did. Is going pell-mell into controversy again; Roscoe has exposed a carelessness of his with regard to one of Pope's letters, which he is going to write a pamphlet to explain.[1] Mentioned an acquaintance of his, of the name of Lambert, who took a fancy to go to Egypt. When he came back, some one said to him, "Well, Lambert, what account of the Pyramids?" "The Pyramids! what are they? I never heard of them!" Was called, ever after, Pyramid Lambert. Fixed for us to come to him next Monday, to his Moravian Concert. Have received a pretty seal ring (a Lough Neagh pebble) from Ireland; the device an Irish harp, with my own words, "Dear harp of my country," round it.[2]

16th to 19th. [Thursday–Sunday] Working away at Sheridan. Sent Power two things for the Greek work, "Lonely Man of Athos," and "When thou art nigh," the latter my own music.[1] A flourishing speech of Shiel about me in the Irish papers. Says I am "The first poet of the day," and "join the beauty of the bird of paradise's plumes to the strength of the eagle's wing."

20th. [Monday] Had a chaise to go over to Bremhill. Stopped at Bowood on my way to get a volume of Burke's works. Found Bowles and his party fiddling away most industriously; besides the Moravians, who were six in number, there was Mr. Humphreys of Chippenham, and Mr. Fenwick, a parson. Had a card of the concert printed, in which I was set down both as composer and singer. The whole day highly amusing. Set to music again after dinner. Slept there.

21st. [Tuesday] Bowles showed me after breakfast the names in the "Tales of the Genii," that were transpositions of the author's (Ridley's) friends.[1] Ellor for Rolle, and Phesor Geneps for Joseph Spence. Lowth, another great friend of Spence's, who has inscribed to him his fine poem, "The choice of Hercules," in his work. Bowles took Bessy in the carriage as far as Buckhill, where she meant to pass the day; I walked about alone. Went to take a look at a pretty cottage there which I should like to have; then got the key of the pleasure grounds at Bowood, and sauntered about them in the sunshine, writing a few sentences of Sheridan till three o'clock, when I joined Bessy at dinner with Mrs. Hughes. The little ones came there to us in the evening, and all walked home together. Find that there is some pamphlet published (and mentioned in "John Bull,") which accuses me of having borrowed my translation of Anacreon from another translation.[2]

22d to 30th. [22 September: Wednesday, 30 September: Thursday] Rooting among Sheridan's papers, and scribbling. A letter from Corry, mentioning the accusation of plagiary against me in my Anacreon. The translation which I am accused of plundering is by Ogle, and it is odd enough if there should be (as Corry seems to intimate) any coincidences between us, as this is the first time I ever *heard* of such a translation.

Oct. 1st. [Friday] Saw Bessy and Tom in the evening at Buckhill, where she went to sleep, for the purpose of being able to see the cottage at Calne to-morrow. Called on Mrs. P. on my way back.

2nd. [Saturday] Set off to walk to Buckhill at half past ten. Arrived at the cottage at Calne, where I found Bessy and Hughes, at a quarter to twelve; good walking. The cottage very pretty, but the pleasure ground too extensive for our means, and every symptom of damp and smoking about the house. Dined at Hughes's, having walked to Bowood before dinner to look over some books. The last day I was there I gave half a sovereign to the wrong house-maid, and was therefore obliged to correct the erratum to-day, by giving ditto to the right one. Walked home with Bessy (for whom it was far too much) in the evening. Sent out some invitations for a dinner on Tuesday night.

3rd. [Sunday] Working at songs for Power.

4th. [Monday] Sent off two songs to Power. "When on the lip the sigh delays," and "Here take my heart;" the latter with music of my own to it.[1] The Phippses in the evening to tea and supper.

12th. [Tuesday] Received a letter from Corry to say he had arrived at Bristol on his way to me, and hoped to be with us to-day. Rather puzzled about our engagement to Locke and the ball, but wrote to Locke to say that if Corry came in time, we would take him with us. He arrived just as we were going, and most good humouredly consented to go with us. Dinner more agreeable than usual; having another Irishman to back me I made play, and we had a good deal of laughing. Danced a quadrille at the ball with a little *blonde,* who quite justified the name Mr. Barry Cornwall the poet gives to her sex in general, "White creatures!" Bessy danced all night and enjoyed herself exceedingly. Home at two. Corry and I had our beakers and to bed.

13th. [Wednesday] Corry gave us amusing accounts of my dear Mother's anxiety about me, and his making her laugh through her tears. Walked him over to Bowood; sorry the Lansdownes are not at home to receive him. In looking at the cascade, he mentioned what Plunkett said, when some one praising his waterfall, exclaimed, "Why, it's quite a cataract." "Oh, that's all my eye," said Plunkett. A delicious day. In the evening showed him Sheridan's MSS. of the "School for Scandal," which, being an enthusiast in the drama, he was delighted with.

14th. [Thursday] Off to Bath with Corry at half-past ten, thinking it as well to take advantage of the return of his chaise to bring home Anastasia, who is wanted for the celebration of Tom's birth-day. Told me that when Grattan was once asked his opinion about Sackville Hamilton (a well known man of office in Ireland), he answered, "Oh, red tape and sealing wax." Corry much pleased with my Anastasia's countenance, but sees, what I do myself, the loving and loveable nature of the dear child; and feels how ticklish will be the steerage of such a creature, when her affections are brought more strongly out. God protect her, and keep her innocent! Corry off in the mail at half-past three for Birmingham, and I home with Statia. Borrowed a volume of Wycherley from Upham.

15th and 16th. [Friday, Saturday] Finished the part relative to the School for Scandal.

17th. [Sunday] Worked for Power. Looked over the "Chants Populaires de la Grèce," by Fouriel, to find a subject for a song.[1]

18th. [Monday] Sent off to Power two songs, "There are two loves,"[1] and "Olympus late to Ossa said;" the latter taken from one of the songs of the Klepthes in Fauriel. Wrote to Rogers with respect to the injunction he laid on me not to apply to Byron's family on the subject of materials for his life till he gave me leave; said I thought, if they had any sense or feeling, they would rather have a hand upon whose delicacy they could rely, to gather decently together the fragments of Byron's memory, than have them scattered about for every scribbler to make his own little separate heap or tumulus of. Mentioned the misrepresentations in Medwin's book of my first acquaintance with Byron, but said, "I am glad they were no worse, as I expected mischief, and I am sure there *will* be some, in other quarters. To bring up a dead man thus to run a muck among the living is a formidable thing. In old times, superstitious thieves used to employ a dead man's hand in committing robberies, and they called it *la main de gloire*. I rather think the Captain of Dragoons (Medwin) is making use of a 'hand of glory' for not much better purposes."[2]

19th. [Tuesday] Walked over to Bowood. Not at home. Brought a book away with me. Note from Lord L. to ask me to dine there on Saturday.

20th. [Wednesday] Working.

21st. [Thursday] Celebration of Tom's birthday, kept to-day instead of the 24th, in order that "Statia" may return to school; plenty of children and noise. The Falkners and Phippses supped with us.

22nd. [Friday] Walked with Bessy and Anastatia to Buckhill, where Bessy slept preparatory to being taken by Bowles to Bath to-morrow. Met Lord L. on my return.

23rd. [Saturday] Dined at Bowood; company, Grossets and Clutterbucks; Mrs. Clutterbuck looking very pretty. Clutterbuck's story of the old lady (his aunt) excellent. Being very nervous, she told Sir W. Farquhar she thought Bath would do her good. "It's very odd," says Sir W., "but that's the very thing I was going to recommend to you. I will write the particulars of your case to a very clever man there, in whose hands you will be well taken care of." The lady, furnished with the letter, sets off, and on arriving at Newbury, feeling as usual, very nervous, she said to her confidant, "Long as Sir Walter has attended me, he has never explained to me what ails me. I have a great mind to open his letter and see what he has stated of my case to the Bath physician." In vain her friend represented to her the breach of confidence this would be. She opened the letter, and read, "Dear David, keep the old lady three weeks, and send her back again." Slept there.

24th. [Sunday] A good deal of talk at breakfast about the falsehoods and misrepresentations in Medwin's book about Byron. Told them the whole particulars of my first acquaintance with Byron, and the mis-statement about the "leadless bullet" that led to it.[1] Lord L. owned he himself had been always under the impression that the story was true, and that the pistols in my meeting with Jeffrey were really *not* loaded. A proof what a fast hold the world takes of any thing that disparages. He mentioned that the present Lords Hertford and Mansfield, when at the University, were mischievously set to fight in a room, by their seconds, and made to fire twice; the seconds not having loaded either pistol, and even having contrived a hole in the wainscot to make them think, after the first fire, that it was where the bullet went through. Walked to Buckhill to see Bessy, who slept there last night. Went with her some part of her way home, and then returned to Bowood. Dressed, and set off with Lord L. to dinner at Bowles'. Company, Bingham, Linley, Lord L, Phipps, and myself. Bowles mentioned that at some celebration at Reading school, when the patrons or governors of it (beer and brandy merchants) were to be welcomed with a Latin address, the boy appointed to the task thus bespoke them, "*Salvete, hospites celebeerimi,*" and then turning to the others, "*Salvete, hospites cele-*

brandi." A good deal of singing in the evening; Linley, Bingham, and I sung several of Calcott's glees, which went off particularly well; Bowles in raptures. Slept there (instead of returning with Lord L.) in order to look over the sheets of Bowles's new pamphlet to Roscoe,[2] in the morning.

25th. [Monday] At work for three hours after breakfast, trying to put Bowles's slipshod reasonings into some sort of order; but the task desperate. Left him between one and two. Called at Lord L.'s in the way, who asked me to dine on Friday next. Read the "Rehearsal"[1] (which I borrowed from Bowles) to Bessy in the evening.

26th. [Tuesday] Received Medwin's book and several others from town. Read Medwin through. A trumpery book, but on the whole gives an amiable impression of Lord B.; full of gross errors.

29th. [Friday] Walked to Bowood to dinner. Company, Lord and Lady Pembroke, Colonel Young, my old friend Sir Stamford Raffles, and the Bowleses. Lord L. mentioned a ship having been once cast away at Petersburgh, laden with the newest fashions from France, and all the fish that were caught for several days were dressed out in the different dresses, veils, caps, &c. &c. Raffles gave us an account of his misfortune (by the burning of the ship in which he left Bencoolen), very interestingly. Sung in evening with Lady Pembroke, who also gave us some very pretty Russian songs; did not seem to care much about my singing, except in my duets with her, which went very well; chiefly Asioli. Slept there.

30th. [Saturday] Wrote a verse or two of a song for Power, "The dying Warrior to his Sword." Walked home after breakfast, Lady Lansdowne having entreated me to stay over to-morrow, and to get Bessy to come over too. Lunched at home, and walked with Bessy; then back to Bowood to dinner. Sir S. Raffles gone. Had showed me in the morning, maps of his new settlement at Singapore. The India Company's servants much annoyed at his introduction of the principles of free trade so close to them. Lord L. mentioned that Cottu (the judge who wrote about England), after praising to him Scarlett and the other lawyers of the Northern Circuit, said, *Mais il faut avouer que leur cuisine est fade et bornée;* there was, it appeared to him, the same old goose at dinner everywhere he went. In talking of English architects, Lord P. said he would rank Chambers the highest of any; Lord L. said that Cockerell is of the same opinion. The Americans (I mentioned) call a cargo of fashionable goods, trinkets, &c. &c. being "laden with *notions*," and on being hailed by our ships, a fellow (without an idea, perhaps, in his head) will answer through a speaking-trumpet, that he is "laden with notions." Having some symptoms of a cold during my singing with Lady P. in the evening, Lady L. recommended me some sal-volatile in water; and her footman gave me a bottle of this stuff on my way to bed. Foolishly thinking it already mixed, I drank of a great dose of the pure sal-volatile, and was nearly suffocated; did not sleep all night with the uneasiness in my throat.

31st. [Sunday] Dreadfully wet to-day. Meant to have walked home to luncheon, but could not. Lord L. having recommended me to read Fielding's "Journey into the next World,"[1] did so, and was highly amused; few things so good as the first half of it. Went to chapel, and did not get out all day. In the evening, on my alluding to the story (told originally, I believe, of George II.) of George III. having once said upon being saved from falling, "Never touch a king," Lord Pembroke remarked, "No, no; he did not say that, I was with him at the time. Being very clumsy in his movements, in stepping over something he fell right on his nose, and Goldsworthy ran to help him up; upon which he said, rather testily, 'Don't you think I can get up myself?' and that was all." Could not sing a note this evening, on account of my throat; but Lady P. gave us again her pretty Russian airs, and a beautiful thing by Carafa,[2] *O Cara Memoria,* which I copied out. Slept there.

Nov. 1st. [Monday] Walked home before breakfast. Went to Lord L. to ask him to take the copy of Sheridan's Westminster Hall Speech to town for me; said, at the same time, that I had had half a mind to offer myself to him as a parcel. In answer, said that he had, by mere accident, as many live parcels already as his carriage could hold, but that if any occasion should take me up to town within the next ten days, he could easily bring me back.

2nd. [Tuesday] Sent the Speech over to Bowood.

3rd. [Wednesday] Sent to Power "The Dying Warrior to his Sword," and an air I have written to "When on the Lip the Sigh delays."[1] A couple of nice pine-apples from Bowood.

4th, 5th. [Thursday–Friday] At work at the "Duenna."[1]

6th. [Saturday] Dined at the Phippses to meet Amyot.

7th, 8th. [Sunday–Monday] A parcel from town, containing, among other things, "Murray's Notes on Captain Medwin," in form of a pamphlet,[1] sent by himself. The newspapers have all been giving extracts from the new number of "Irish Melodies," and praising them.[2]

9th. [Tuesday] Went to the Devizes ball; the Phippses took us. Walked about a good deal with Mrs. Fisher, and dined with Selina Locke, Bessy not looking at all well, but danced away the whole night, and suffered for it in violent cramps on her return home.

10th to 12th. [Wednesday–Friday] At work. The "Courier" I see has praised the "Melodies" very warmly.

15th, 16th. [Monday–Tuesday] Sent Power words to a ballet tune, "Tell her, oh, tell her!"[1] Have been endeavouring, but without success, to put words to Carafa's air.

17th. [Wednesday] Some anonymous person has sent me a framed drawing of our cottage ("Anacreon Cottage," as the writer calls it), with a very flattering letter; a woman's handwriting. We had observed a lady and a gentleman in a gig at the gate some weeks since sketching the house, and thought it must be for some magazine. Walked to Bowood to dinner; company, the A'Courts, Littleton (Lord Littleton's brother), Miss Napier, and Miss Talbot. Littleton more agreeable than he used to be when a young man; less of a rattle. Music in the evening. Mrs. A'Court sung to the Spanish guitar very prettily, and with me some of Asioli's duets. Lord L. told of Garat (I think) accompanying Chauvelin, when he came on his mission;[1] their bringing a large Amiens pie to eat on the road, which was fastened on the top of the chaise. Garat anxious to see the country got out and sat with the pie, and at the end of his journey said very innocently, that nothing could be more unjust than giving the English a character of gravity or *tristesse*, as he had seen nothing but *éclats de rire* all the way along. Slept there.

18th. [Thursday] Looked through the "Edinburgh Review" for articles on Commerce with France and the Sinking Fund. Talked with Lord L. upon

Mr. Fox's opposition to the commercial treaty in 1786; the very erroneous principles broached both by him and Burke on that occasion, &c.[1] Wanted me very much to stay over to-day; but, as I must come again on Sunday, to meet the Jerseys, thought it better to return home. The Falkeners to dinner with us. Worked in the evening.

19th. [Friday] Should have mentioned that I wrote to Doyle within these few days, begging him to communicate to Lady Byron and Mrs. Leigh, my intention to write a Life of Lord Byron; said it was always his own wish that I should, if I survived him, write something about him, and that I thought it must be equally now the wish of his own family that a hand, upon whose delicacy they could rely, should undertake the task, rather than have his memory at the mercy of scribblers, who dishonour alike the living and the dead.

20th. [Saturday] Received a note from Lady L. reminding me of to-morrow, and sending me the Russian airs that Lady Pembroke promised to copy out for me.

21st. [Sunday] Bessy by no means well; the same pains in her face and jaws that she had last winter. Walked over to Bowood; company, the Jerseys, Lord Carnarvon and his daughter, Charles Sheridan, and Lord and Lady James Stuart. Desired both by Lady Lansdowne and Lord Jersey to sit next Lady Jersey at dinner. In reading an extract from Dallas's book about Lord Byron before dinner, it occurred to me that by the "newly made friend," he mentions who turned Lord B. out of the path of courtiership into which Dallas thinks he was so laudably entering at one time, he must have meant *me,* and so Lord Jersey thought. But Lord L., at dinner, said it was quite as likely to be Lady Jersey; and so, upon reconsideration, I have no doubt it is. A good deal of laughing with her about this.[1] Sung in the evening. Slept there.

22nd. [Monday] Walked home after breakfast to see how Bessy was. Some talk with Lord L. before I came away on a point that has occupied my mind a good deal, namely, the project I have meditated of writing a Life of Lord Byron. Though the Longmans look earnestly and anxiously to it as the great source of my means of repaying them their money; and though it would be the shortest and easiest way I could effect that object; yet the subject begins to be so tarnished and so clogged with difficulties, that my *own* impression is that I *ought* not to undertake it. Mentioned this idea to

Lord Lansdowne, who quite agrees with me. Thinks that as to entering into the details of Lord Byron's life now, it is quite out of the question, and that all I could with any satisfaction to myself undertake, would be a critical examination of his works and genius, which after all, as I remarked, the public would not much thank me for. It is my intention, however, to leave both the Longmans and the public under the impression that I *do* mean to write the life. Found Bessy not much better. Got wet through in returning to Bowood. Received a letter from Elliston, asking me whether the G in Gheber was to be pronounced hard or soft, as he is bringing out a piece from "Lalla Rookh," and wishes to know. Lady Jersey this morning mentioned that Lord —— told her Croker was the author of "Rock Detected." Poor Croker's name is made as free with as the devil's is with the lawyers; everything is laid to him. Lord ——, she says, owned, at the same time, that it was very dull, and this it certainly would *not* be, if written by Croker.[1] An addition to the party to-day of Ponsonby and Lady Barbara, and the Puseys (Lord Carnarvon's daughter and son-in-law). Again ordered to sit next Lady Jersey. A dispute in the evening upon a passage in Cobbet's "Cottage Economy;" "It was, pigs of a different description that were," &c.; whether grammar or not. Lords Jersey and Lansdowne against, and Lord Carnarvon and I for; *i.e.* acknowledging it was awkward, but still grammar. As Lord C. said, only change it into "it was a different description of pigs," &c. and you will see that the fault is in the collocation of the words, not in the grammar." Sung again. Slept there. A tremendous storm in the night, actually shook Bowood. Trembled for the thatch of my little cottage. Charles Sheridan having read his father's speech, now agrees with me, that it would not be so desirable to have it all published.[2]

23rd. [Tuesday] Lady Lansdowne said, in coming down to breakfast, "It is an ill wind, &c.; you cannot go home to day." On my expressing my anxiety about Mrs. Moore, offered to send the carriage with me to see her, and then come back again. Could not, however, stay. On my mentioning what Sheridan said to Charles, when he was a boy, "Never do to-day what you can possibly put off till to-morrow," found that it was not Sheridan, but the old Lord Holland, who said it to Charles Fox, adding another maxim, "Nor ever do yourself what you can get any one else to do for you." Talked of Southey: the little reliance that is to be placed upon him as an historian; his base persecution of the memory of Sir J. Moore. Ponsonby mentioned a gross misrepresentation of his with respect to the request which he says Romana made to Moore to advance; said also, that the Duke of Wellington had spoken most warmly and liberally to Col. Napier (who is writing an account of the Peninsular War) on the subject of those calumnies against Moore. Lord Lansdowne mentioned at breakfast that Voltaire, in some historical work (?), had described the French as, immediately upon their taking possession of Munich, after a severe siege, collecting all the pretty girls of the town and dancing all night. The authors of the "Universal History," upon finding this anecdote, wrote to Voltaire to request he would inform them of his authority for it. Upon which Voltaire wrote back to say that he really forgot where he had met with it, but that it might be depended on, as *Les Français dansent toujours.* Talked of Jeremy Bentham; calls his walk after dinner his "paulo-post prandial vibration." Mills's article on Government, in the Supplement to the "Encyclopædia Britannica."[1] How quizzible this whole school is! Their method of analysis might be transferred so easily to some ludicrous question, and travestied, &c. &c. Came away before luncheon, and got pretty dry home.

24th and 25th. [Wednesday, Thursday] At work.

26th. [Friday] Bowles called. Walked over to Bowood to look at Fox's James II., and borrow a volume of the "Edinburgh Review;" found the Ponsonbys; lunched. Lord L. walked part of the way home with me. A good deal of conversation about politics. Asked us to dine to meet the Starkeys next Friday.

27th to 29th. [Saturday–Monday] At work. Wrote two things for Power, "Our home is on the sea, boy," and "Bring the bright garlands hither;" the latter to a pretty Russian air Lady Pembroke gave me.[1]

30th. [Tuesday] Writing away.

Dec. 3rd. [Friday] Dined at Bowood; the Phippses took us; company, the Starkeys and Holtons. The day rather different from Bowood days in general. Whatever it may be in politics, at a dinner, *men,* not *measures,* are to be considered.

4th. [Saturday] A wretched day: the Phippses dined with us. See (by extracts in the "Chronicle") that there is an article in the New "Edinburgh" on "Captain Rock:" evidently by Sydney Smith.[1] Sent an apology to Bowles, to whom I promised to go to-day; but the *nebulæ malusque Jupiter* prevent it.

12th. [Sunday] Walked over to Bowood; company there at present, Misses

Fox and Vernon, and Lord Seymour. Expect Lady Harrowby and the Ebringtons on Wednesday. Sorry to miss them, as I like the latter exceedingly. In talking of the French academy *éloges,* Lord L. mentioned one by the Duc de Levi, which he had heard. The defunct having written a play, which the Duke considered food for the royalist cause, he said it was "pity that the Théâtre Français had not been able to contain as many people at once as the Coliseum, for it had *la contre-revolution aurait été faite* by this play."

13th. [Monday] Set off in the York House coach for town. Lunched at Newbury. On my arrival in town did not dine, having to sup with Power. Called at Lady Donegal's; the house all silent and dark, supposed her out of town. Found Power full of kindness and satisfaction with me.

14th. [Tuesday] Called at Rogers's; not in town. Wrote a letter to Power, explaining what I wished him to do for me in the financial way. Met Charles Moore, who told me Lady D. was not only in town, but that he was to dine there to-day to go to see the "Freischütz;" just the thing I wished; wrote to her to invite myself. Called on the Hollands; Lady H. not very well. Found Woolriche with her; asked me to dine to-morrow, but engaged to the Longmans. Dined with Lady D., and went in the evening with Miss Godfrey, Barbara, and C. Moore to the Duke of York's box, at Drury Lane. Much struck with the "Freischütz." Thought the music sounds familiar, and full of passages to which one is inclined to take off one's hat as to old acquaintances.[1]

15th. [Wednesday] Called upon Charles Sheridan; has not yet given the speech to the Bishop of Rochester. Having written a song before I came up upon Pendeli (the modern Pentelicus) in which I made the second syllable short, every verse ending with it, *e.g.* "The marble caves of Pendeli;" but having some misgivings that the syllable was long, asked C. Sheridan. Could not tell me with certainty, but believed it was long. Called upon Hobhouse. Much talk with him about the various Byroniania since we last met. It was Sir F. Burdett advised him to withdraw his pamphlet in answer to Medwin, which he had printed and announced.[1] Showed me some proofs of old Dallas's manœuvring from Lord Byron's letters. Told him (what I feel), that all that has happened since the destruction of the Memoirs convinces me that he was right in advising their total suppression, as, if the remainder were published, much more mischief would be imagined to have existed in the suppressed part than there is even now. Begged of him to give me some time or other under his hand, for my own satisfaction, the assurance which had such weight with me in giving up the Memoirs, that Byron had expressed to him, when they last met, his regret at having put them out of his own power, and that it was only delicacy towards me that prevented him from recalling them; said that I might depend upon it that he would. Asked him about Pendeli, which is long, as I feared, and my song, accordingly, spiflicated. Called upon Woolriche. Saw the Duke of Bedford, who was all amiability, and very amusing; asked me to come to Woburn this Christmas; invited me also to dine to-day, and go to the play; but engaged. Walked with Woolriche, who pressed me to go to Woburn. There is to be a ballet got up, for young Lady Louisa, who dances, he says, beautifully. Called at Power's, who accedes most readily to my drawing upon him for six and eight months, but expressed regret that I should lose so much by discount. Sorry to find that the two works I am about now for him, will barely complete my annual tasks. Sad prospects before me; deep in arrears on all sides. Dined at Longmans'; had old Taylor of the "Sun" to meet me. Professed to tell me a great deal about Sheridan, but nothing in it, except boring, deadly boring; most of the company asleep. Brought me, however, a letter or two of S.'s, which may be of use; showed me also a curious original letter from Churchill to his bookseller, asking most anxiously for a guinea, for which he said he was "in pawn." Went to the Hollands; Brougham, Mackintosh, and Lord Sefton. Some talk with Mackintosh; said he believed Tooke had assisted Paine in his answer to Burke.[2] Mentioned, as like Tooke's manner, the passage about a king having a million a-year; his only duty being to receive the salary. I must see this passage, in which he objected to the word "nominal," as incumbering the point: asked him about Stone. Stone had got him (Mackintosh) made a French citizen at the time when he wrote the letter I have to Sheridan, taking merit to himself for preventing the same honour from being inflicted on him and Mr. Fox. Mentioned George Ellis's fright on account of the Rolliad,[3] when taken to dine with Pitt, the quotation of the latter, &c. &c. Thinks Richardson's the least good of the Rolliad papers.

16th. [Thursday] Breakfasted with Charles Sheridan. Looked over his translations from Fauriel's Greek songs, which he wishes to publish. Offered to speak to the Longmans about them. Called at the Duke of Bedford's for Woolriche; shown in by a stupid servant to the Duke and Duchess, who were in close conference for the purchase of trinkets; the Duke very kind. Walked with Woolriche; called on Shee, thence to the Donegals. Dressed at six, and drove to the Storys, to take my chance of a dinner with them. Found them at tea, and did not like to own my intention, but said I was engaged to the Hollands. Dined at the Athenæum, my first appearance there. Went to Covent Garden, where I joined Lincoln Stanhope, and saw part of the "Freischütz" and "Clari;"[1] cried at the latter as much as I used in Paris. Miss Tree, the only woman on the stage I would trust with a tender character.

19th. [Sunday] Breakfasted with Rogers. Conversation with respect to my undertaking "Byron's Life." Does not see that what has happened should alter my intention; thinks whatever of tarnish the subject may have lately received, will have passed away before I come to it, and that the falsehoods and nonsense which have been heaped upon his memory should rather make me consider the duty to do justice to it the greater. Dined at Lord Holland's: company, Sir J. Mackintosh, Dr. Holland, and Arguelles. The latter told Lord H. he remembered having met me eighteen years ago at Lady Heathcote's, when he came over as one of the deputies, and that I was less altered since then than any one he had met: I recollect well the evening he alludes to. He and Matarosa (now Torreno) were standing at the pianoforte while I was singing "Come tell me, says Rosa;"[1] and on the latter asking Lady Heathcote what was the subject of my song, she, with great quickness, replied, that "it was in honour of the Spanish Deputies," in consequence of which, whenever I came to Rosa, Matarosa bowed. Some talk with Lord Holland in the evening about Sheridan. Brougham and Lord Sefton came in. Went from thence to Mr. Story's, sung and supped. Before dinner to-day called upon Strangford, and found him in conference with Prince Esterhazy.

20th. [Monday] Breakfasted with Rogers. Showed me some prose essays he has written to intermix with the verses of his "Italy."[1] One "On Assassination," of which Mackintosh (to whom he sent it) wrote back, that "Hume could not improve the thoughts, nor Addison the language." Feel it would do one good to study such writing, if not as a model, yet as a chastener and simplifier of style, it being the very reverse of ambition or ornament. Objected to the phrase, "as if all hell had broke loose," and "nations worrying each other like curs." Talking of Fox's views in 1786, calling the French "natural enemies," &c., he said, "Fox's tone altered much as he got older and wiser, and that on his return from France he was even thought to lean too much the other way." Went to the Longmans on my money business. Drew upon Power for £400 at six and eight months, a hundred of which went to replace what I drew upon the Longmans for three months since, and eighty to Power for a similar purpose. Dined at Denman's, the party a most *Reginal* one; himself, Brougham, and Williams, with old Charles Butler to *dilute*. Very agreeable; talked of the Regency Question. The able article on the subject in the "Edinburgh Review" was written, Brougham says, by Allen. Brougham seemed to lay great stress upon the marriage with Mrs. Fitzherbert, and the forfeiture of the crown thereby; the nullity of the marriage having nothing to do with the forfeiture.[2] Mentioned a parallel case in law, where a man in consigning an estate might do what would forfeit his own claim to it, though it was null in the law and could not confer any title to it on another. On Charles Butler saying he wondered this was not thought of during the Queen's trial,[3] Brougham said that it *was* thought of; the only witness, however, to the marriage (I forget his name) was dead. Sung for the women in the evening; Brougham and Williams having gone off to a consultation. Agreed to go with Denman to-morrow to the trial of Miss Foote against Hayne.[4]

21st. [Tuesday] Up very early, and to breakfast with Denman at half-past eight. Mentioned Fox's famous reply to Grant on the Convention Bill. His side speeches to his friends, while working himself up to it; to Tierney and some one else, who were whispering behind, "Will you be quiet? it is no such easy speech to answer;" and of Michael A. Taylor, who was boring him with suggestions, he said aside to another, "Doesn't the —— think I have enough to do?" Staid in court till two, and was then obliged to attend an appointment with Bishop to correct some of our songs for the Greek work. Played me some things out of Weber's "Euryanthe;"[1] a beautiful cavatina and a yager song, not so simple or popular as that in the "Frei-schütz." Had a letter from Croker yesterday, asking me to dine with him on the 28th, and to fix Lord Strangford and Bushe for the same day. Called and left word with Rogers that I would dine with him to-day. Took my place for Thursday morning. Dined *tête-à-tête* with Rogers, and went to the play together to Lady Spencer's box: "As you like it," Miss Tree the Rosalind.

22nd. [Wednesday] All day performing commissions. Called at the Long-mans, and from thence went with Rees to the India House to try and see Dr. Wilkie, for the purpose of making inquiries about Halhed, Sheridan's early correspondent, who, it appears, is alive. This may make some differ-ence to me in the Life, as I doubt whether I can venture to give his letters, and they are among the most lively ingredients of the work; could not see Dr. Wilkie. After writing several notes, dined between seven and eight at Richardson's. Thence home to pack.

23rd. [Thursday] Off in the coach at quarter past six. Had for one of my companions a clergyman, brother of the Shearer who wrote "Recollections in the Peninsula," &c. &c. An odd and amusing person; quoted a neat remark of Lardner's on predestination, "if we were judged before we were born, then certainly we were never born to be judged." Found all pretty well at home, and my dearest Anastasia among the rest for her holidays. Shearer said the Longmans had told his brother that I had the most generous contempt for money of any man they ever met.

24th. [Friday] Surprised by an invitation to dinner from the Starkeys, they having from some unintelligible cause separated themselves from us for a long time. The return just as unintelligible as the breaking off. Upon consideration, however, resolved (as the most sensible and good-humoured plan) to accept the invitation.

25th. [Saturday] Eat my plum pudding at home. Dined at two on account of the servants, who were indulged with a dinner for their friends (about a dozen of them) and a large party in the evening. Very jolly and uproarious till twelve o'clock.

28th. [Tuesday] Received the account of my poor friend Richard Power's death.

29th. [Wednesday] Company at Bowood, Lord Auckland and the Misses Elden, Sir John Newport, Macdonald, Mr. Baring Wall, and Hallam. Mentioned Gilbert Wakefield's taking Pope's "Gently spread thy purple pinions" as serious, and saying that it was not in Mr. Pope's happiest style.[1] Sung in the evening. In talking of my own compositions, mentioned the tendency I had sometimes to run into consecutive fifths, and adding, some time after, that Bishop was the person who now revised my music, Lord Auckland said, "Other Bishops take care of the tithes, but he looks after the fifths." A good story of a man brimful of ill-temper, coming out of a room where he had lost all his money at play, and seeing a person (a perfect stranger to him) tying his shoe at the top of the stairs; "D—n you (says he), you're always tying your shoe," and kicked him down stairs. Slept there.

30th. [Thursday] After breakfast walked home to see Bessy, and returned to Bowood to-dinner. In talking at dinner of Lord Chatham's famous figure of the Saône and the Rhone, Lord L. and I maintained, against Hallam, that Fox and Lord Mansfield were the persons meant, and rather thought we had Lord Holland's authority for it. Hallam, however, insisted, upon the authority of Lord Orford's Correspondence, that it was the Duke of Newcastle and Fox. On referring to Lord Orford, found Hallam was right, and borne out by Lord Holland's note;[1] though in the text Lord O.

mentions four different persons (among whom was Lord Mansfield) to whom conjecture applied the passage. Had received to-day a modern Greek song upon Lord Byron's death (with the music), Ωδη προς τον Λορδ Βυρον. Hallam and I made out the words between us, but they are nothing remarkable. Slept there.

Notes to 1824 Entries

15 January

1. "Vocal Music," *Westminster Review* 1 (1824): 120–41. The article reviews, among other works, the fourth number of Moore's *National Airs* (1822).

20 January

1. In "Extract XVI" of Rhymes on the Road, Moore describes the reverence shown by visitors to Rousseau's home as "mean prostration before Fame." See *Works*, 7: 345 ff.

24 January

1. William Chillingworth, *The Religion of Protestants a Safe Way to Salvation. Or, an Answer to a booke . . . which pretends to prove the contrary* (1638).
2. William Prynne (1600–1669), a Puritan polemicist, was brought before the Star Chamber in 1632 for his attack on stage plays, *Histriomastix* (1632). He was imprisoned, fined, and mutilated, but according to several sources, Archbishop Laud remitted some of the terms of Prynne's harsh sentence. See H. R. Trevor-Roper, *Archbishop Laud* (London, 1940), pp. 159–66.
The histories to which Moore refers are: Daniel Neal, *The History of the Puritans or Protestant Non-conformists. . . ,* 4 vols. (1732–38); Bulstrode Whitelocke, *Memorial of the English affairs . . . from the beginning of the reign of King Charles the second, his happy restoration* (1732); John Rushworth, *Historical Collections of Private Passages of State. . . ,* 7 vols. (1659–1701).
3. *Mr. B. Whitlock's Account of his embassy to Sweden . . .* (1714).

28 January

1. Richard Laurence, Archbishop of Cashel, *A Charge, delivered at the primary triennial visitation of the Province of Munster . . .* (1823).

29, 30 January

1. Moore's *Fables for the Holy Alliance* was reviewed unfavorably in the *Westminster Review* 1 (1824): 18–27.

1 February

1. In the *Westminster* article on the *Fables* (see entry for 29, 30 January, 1824, and its n. 1),

the reviewer accused Moore of having spoken of Americans "with unbounded dislike and contempt." He described this sentiment as the insensitivity of a "god of drawing-room idolatry" to anything outside his own circle (p. 20). Moore's disclaimer was published in the *Times*, 4 February 1824, and also as the first footnote in the *Westminster's* review of Moore's *Captain Rock, Westminster Review* 1 (1824): 492.

28 February

1. A character in Scott's *Ivanhoe* (1820).
2. In 1823 George Colman, the newly appointed examiner of plays, rejected Sir Martin Shee's tragedy *Alasco* (published 1824). Shee appealed to James Graham, Duke of Montrose, the Lord Chamberlain, but the Duke refused to intervene. See Martin H. Shee, *The Life of Sir Martin Shee* (London, 1860), 1: 365–95.

29 February

1. See Marchand, *LJ*, 11: 84–85. The reference is to Moore's poem "The Legacy," *Works*, 3:244–45.

1 March

1. *Richard III*, 1: i.
2. The bill, named after its sponsor, Richard Martin (1754–1834), for the prevention of cruelty to animals was passed into law 22 July 1822.

5 March

1. Rossini, *Semiramide* (1823), first performed in England 15 July 1824.

7 March

1. Thomas Carte, *An History of James, Duke of Ormonde . . . To which is added . . . a very valuable collection of letters . . .* (1736).
2. Cromwell entered Dublin on 15 August 1649 as "Lord Lieutenant and General for the Parliament of England" and soon led his army in the seiges of Drogheda and Wexford in which thousands of soldiers and civilians were massacred. See Edmund Curtis, *A History of Ireland* (Norwich, 1936; reprinted , 1964), pp. 249–51.

8 March

1. *Criticisms on the Rolliad, Part The Second* (1790), no. 5, ends with the following lines on James, Marquis of Graham (later Duke of Montrose):

> With joy *Britannia* sees her fav'rite goose
> Fast bound and *pinion'd* in the nuptial noose;
> Presaging fondly from so fair a mate,
> A rood of goslings, cackling in debate.

13 March

1. William Hodge Mill (1792–1853), orientalist, principal of Bishop's College, Calcutta, and a frequent contributor to various periodicals.

14 March

1. *Captain Rock* was reviewed in the *New Monthly Magazine*, n.s. 11 (1824): 236–81.

16 March

1. The motion made on 8 April 1824 by John Bligh, Earl of Darnley (1767–1831) to appoint a select committee to investigate and improve internal affairs in Ireland failed 17 to 57. See *Parlia. Debates*, ser. 2, 11 (1824): 236–81.

22 March

1. "Poor Wounded Heart" and "Sing—Sing—Music Was Given," *Works*, 5: 146, and 4: 76–77.

23 March

1. Sir Cecil Wray (1734–1805) demanded a scrutiny of the Westminster election of 1784 in which he was defeated by Samuel, Viscount Hood (1724–1816) and Fox. Fox protested in his famous "scrutiny speech" (8 June 1784); however, scrutiny was granted. See Loren Reid, *Charles James Fox* (London, 1969), pp. 193–213, and *Parlia. Hist.*, 24 (1783–85): 884–928.
2. General Henry Edward Fox (1755–1811) was Charles James Fox's brother.

24 March

1. Bagenal Harvey (1762–98) and John Henry Colclough (1769–98) were tried, found guilty of treason, and executed by a courts-martial for participating in the Wexford uprisings of 1798. See Thomas Pakenham, *The Year of Liberty* (Englewood Cliffs, N.J., 1969), pp. 266–68. The "Scotch Judicature Bill" to which Moore refers finally failed in the House of Lords in 1825. See *Parlia. Debates*, ser. 2, 12 (1825): 127.

25 March

1. George King, Earl of Kingston (1771–1839), representing the parishioners of Bregaun, protested the Irish Tithe Composition Act (see entries for 2 August 1823, n. 2, and 5 August 1823, n. 1). Dudley Ryder, Earl of Harrowby (1762–1847) specifically questioned the propriety of Kingston's judgments on "the cruel Delaney" in the latter's absence. See *Parlia. Debates*, ser. 2, 10 (1824): 1385–93.

1 April

1. See entry for 12 February–15 March 1823 and its n. 2. Moore, of course, failed to regain possession of Byron's memoirs, and they were destroyed. See Doris Langley Moore, *The Late Lord Byron* (New York, 1961), pp. 12–45.

9 April

1. See entry for 16 March 1824 and its note.
2. A short but very favorable notice of *Captain Rock* appeared in the *Times*, 8 April 1824.

15 April

1. "One Dear Smile," *Works*, 5: 178.
2. "First-fruits" or "Annats" are the first year's income of a church living, which from the reign of Queen Anne were contributed to a fund for augmenting smaller livings and aiding poor clergymen. Bk 2, chap. 8 of *Captain Rock* discusses the abuses of the practice in Ireland.

24 April

1. *Works*, 4: 74–75 and 72–73, respectively. The correct title of the latter is "I Wish I Was by that Dim Lake."

3 May

1. *Westminster Review*, 1 (1824): 492–504.
2. See Marchand, *LJ*, 11: 125–26.

10 May

1. *Report of the Committee of the Hibernian Society . . . 1808–1822*, 15 pts., published by the "London Hibernian Society for establishing schools and circulating the Holy Scriptures in Ireland."
2. In his speech on 6 May 1824 Edward George Geoffrey Stanley (1799–1869) read several passages from a "recently published" pamphlet in order to illustrate the feelings of the Irish about the established church. The pamphlet is not identified in the report of the debate but was, apparently, Moore's *Captain Rock*. See *Parlia. Debates*, ser. 2, 11 (1824): 532–88.

12 May

1. A brief account of the meeting was given in the *Times*, 13 May 1824.

14 May

1. Byron died on 19 April 1824.
2. See Dowden, *Letters*, 2: 524, and the entry for 1 April 1824 and its n. 1.

18 May

1. *Works*, 1: 313, and 3: 244–45.
2. Ibid. 3: 344–45.

19 May

1. The London *Times* of 19 May 1824 stated that Moore had submitted the MS of Byron's memoirs to Augusta Leigh and allowed her to burn it in his presence. On 22 May the *Times* printed a correction of this account, stating that no one examined the MS before its destruction and that Murray had declined Moore's offer to pay for the MS and had insisted upon its destruction.

20 May

1. See, for example, Moore's satire on Edward Law, Lord Ellenborough, *Works*, 3:195–97.

21 May

1. See entry for 19 May 1824 and its n. 1.

22 May

1. Probably "Poor Broken Flower," *Works*, 5:149.

23 May

1. An article in *John Bull*, 24 May 1824, p. 172, reported that while Murray had acted honorably in the destruction of the memoirs, Moore had taken advantage of the situation to keep the money given him for the MS. On 31 May the paper printed Moore's letter of explanation but added that Augusta Leigh had forced Moore to surrender the MS and that, whatever Moore might say about his actions, "his regret at losing the two thousand pounds is not diminished." See Jones, *The Harp that Once—*, p. 349, n. 1. Apparently Moore saw an early issue of the *John Bull* dated 24 May.

24 May

1. The *Observer*, 23 May 1824, reprinted the inaccurate account of the burning of the memoirs that appeared in the *Times* on 19 May. See entry for 22 May and entry and note for 23 May 1824.
2. Wilmot Horton's account of the event, entitled "Narrative of the circumstances preceding the destruction of the Memoirs of Lord Byron . . ." was circulated but never published.

27 May

1. Moore's letter to the newspapers was dated 26 May and appeared on 27 May. It summarized his position as stated in the entries for 15 and 16 May, adding that he protested the total destruction of the Memoirs without perusal of them and consultation among the parties.

28 May

1. In Bk. 2, Chap. 12 of *Captain Rock* Moore quotes two passages from the speech by Sir Henry Brooke Parnell (1776–1842) on the Irish Insurrection Bill, in which Parnell moved that Commons appoint a committee to investigate the unrest in Ireland. The motion failed, and the House approved the second reading of the bill. See *Parlia. Debates*, ser. 2, 9 (1823): 1147–1203.

16 June

1. "The Ark: A Poem for Music," *The Poetical Works of William Lisle Bowles*, 2: 315–17.

17 June

1. Washington Irving, *Tales of a Traveller*, 2 vols. (1824). Irving adapted the story Moore told him into the "Adventure of the German Student" in Part 1 of *Tales*.

19–30 June

1. Walter King, Bishop of Rochester, was editing *The Works of . . . Edmund Burke*, 8 vols. (1792-1827), and 16 vols. (1803–27). Sheridan's speech was delivered 2 February 1780 at a meeting in Westminster Hall in support of universal suffrage and annual parliaments. See Moore, *Sheridan*, 1: 300–302 and Sichel, *Sheridan*, 2: 4.

2. For "Thou Lovest No More" see *Works*, 4: 231.

3. Moore's *Letters and Journals of Lord Byron . . .*, 2 vols., was published in 1830–31. Mme. Belloc's translation appeared in 1830.

4. Jacques Amyot (1513–93), whose translation of Plutarch's *Lives* into French served as the basis for other translations, especially that of Sir Thomas North (1579).

5. Mortimer O'Sullivan, *Captain Rock Detected . . .* (1824).

6. *Blackwood's* 15 (1824): 544–50; *London Magazine* 9 (1824): 583–98; *Westminster Review* 1 (1824): 492–504.

7. For Edward Stanley's reference to *Captain Rock* see entry for 10 May 1824 and its n. 2.

John Jebb, Bishop of Limerick, alluded to Moore's work in his long speech in support of the Irish Tithes Composition Amendment Bill, 10 June 1824. See *Parlia. Debates*, ser. 2, 11 (1824): 1104–65.

10 July

1. The short-lived *John Bull Magazine and Literary Recorder* (1 vol., 1824) published what purported to be an extract from Byron's Memoirs but in fact was written by Theodore Hook. Several paragraphs of this forgery are given in Doris Langley Moore's *The Late Lord Byron*, pp. 298–99.

14 July

1. See entry for 19 June 1824 and its n. 1.

16 July

1. Sir James Prior, *Memoir of the Life and Character of the Right Hon. Edmund Burke . . .* (1824).

2. The coalition ministry formed in 1783 with Fox as Foreign Secretary and Lord North as Home Secretary.

3. Burke resigned from the Whig Club in February 1793 as a result of his conflicts with Fox, primarily over the Fench Revolution, and then wrote a defense of his position, which was published in a garbled and unauthorized edition in 1797 as "Fifty-four Articles of Impeachment against Charles James Fox." See Sir Philip Magnus, *Edmund Burke* (London, 1939), pp. 242–46.

4. William Burke, *An Account of the European Settlements in America . . .*, rev. Edmund Burke, 2 vols., (1757).

5. Byron was infuriated by the refusal of his cousin Frederick Howard, Lord Carlisle (1748–1825) to introduce him into the House of Lords. He consequently included in *English Bards* a passage on Carlisle in which he referred to his "paralytic puling" (see Coleridge, *Byron's Poetry*, 1: 354–56). When Byron published *The Corsair* in 1814, the Tory reaction to the

tale was led by the *Courier,* which reminded its readers, among other things, of Byron's earlier attack on Carlisle. See Marchand, *Byron; A Biography,* 1: 168 and 434.

17 July

1. On 9 October 1822 Byron wrote to Murray admitting that his involvement in the *Liberal* was "a bad business" and implying that Hunt's family and financial difficulties forced Byron to continue in the venture. When Byron learned that Hunt knew of his statements, he wrote to Murray that he had intended for the letter to remain private, even though he had spoken only the truth. See Marchand *LJ,* 10: 12–13 and 67–70.

2. Thomas Medwin, *Journal of the Conversations of Lord Byron* . . . (1824). Medwin was a second cousin of Shelley.

3. In a letter to Douglas Kinnaird, Byron reported that the Countess Guiccioli had refused his offer of a £5000 legacy. See *Lord Byron's Correspondence,* ed. John Murray (London, 1922), 2: 284.

4. For an account of this incident, which served as the basis for *The Giaour,* see Marchand, *Byron; A Biography,* 2: 257–58, and notes. See also entry for 19 February 1828.

5. John Wilson Croker, *The Battles of Talavera* (1809).

18 July

1. See Price, *Sheridan's Letters,* 3: 214–15 and note.

2. A reference to the money Sheridan raised in 1794 to rebuild and disencumber Drury Lane Theatre. See Sichel, *Sheridan,* 1: 47, n. 3.

3. According to Sichel (2: 370 ff.), Sheridan in 1812 was offered the purchase of two seats, one by the Duke of Norfolk, the other by a Mr. Attersoll. To raise the necessary £3000 he first approached Samuel Whitbread, who owed Sheridan £2000. Whitbread refused to pay it unless Sheridan agreed to leave Parliament. Sheridan eventually received this sum, plus £3000 from the Prince, which Sheridan reportedly considered a loan. The actual amount of this money, and the circumstances surrounding the incident were to involve Moore in much controversy when he described it in his *Sheridan.* See entry for 14 January 1826 and note; and Dowden, *Letters,* 2: 547–48 and note.

19 July

1. See the entry for 26 November 1818 and its n. 4.

2. In 1803 Tom Sheridan was offered the position of Registrar of the Vice-Admiralty Court of Malta but declined the post. See Price, *Sheridan's Letters,* 2: 269.

20–26 July

1. *Works,* 4: 324–26, and 5: 47–49.

27 July

1. For the Bishop's speech see the entry for 19 June 1824 and its n. 7.

28 July–2 August

1. See entry for 19–30 June 1824 and its n. 5.

3 August

1. Charles Watson-Wentworth, Marquis of Rockingham (1730–82) became Prime Minister for the second time in 1782 and soon appointed Burke and members of his family to very lucrative posts. According to Walpole, Burke asked Lord Cavendish (1732–96), the Chancellor of the Exchequer, to appoint him clerk of the Pells before Cavendish resigned his position. See *The Last Journals of Horace Walpole*, ed. A. F. Steuart (London, 1910), 2: 452–54.

5 August

1. Joseph and Charles Surface in *The School for Scandal* (1780).
2. Moore printed Sheridan's rough draft of this letter, *Sheridan*, 2: 67–69. For the final version, dated 14 August 1789, see A. Aspinall, *The Correspondence of George, Prince of Wales*, (London, 1964), 2: 29–30.
3. See Loren Reid, *Charles James Fox*, pp. 225–29, and Sichel, *Sheridan*, 2: 104–19.
4. See Sichel, *Sheridan*, 1: 46 and n. 2.

6 August

1. For Sheridan's troubles with the ministry and Canning after the establishment of the Regency, see Gibbs, *Sheridan*, p. 217 and passim.

8–9 August

1. *Works*, 5: 18 and 252.

11 August

1. "More properly, I believe, Mr. Fox (afterwards Lord Holland) and the Duke of Newcastle." (Russell's note.)

13 August

1. *Works*, 4: 165.

19 August

1. Ibid., 4: 167.

20 August

1. Ibid., 4: 164.
2. *Memoirs of the Affairs of Europe from the Peace of Utrecht* (1824–29).

21 August

1. See Moore's *Life of Sheridan*, 2: 192–96, where Moore quotes a letter from Mme Genlis to Fox (who sent it to Sheridan). Moore conjectures that Sheridan contrived to have the post-

boys taking Mme Genlis from London to Dartford pretend to lose the way and eventually return to London, where Sheridan entertained her and her adopted daughter Pamela (to whom he was attracted) for another month, or until he could accompany them.

The reference to Mme Genlis's book here and in the entry for 20 August may be to her *Memoirs,* though they did not appear until 1825. Lady Bath may have obtained an advance copy. Moore quotes from the *Memoirs* in a footnote in his *Life of Sheridan,* 2: 196.

22 August

1. The "Epistle of Lentulus," a spurious medieval document written between the 13th and 15th centuries, purporting to be a contemporary description of Christ.

24 August

1. Two of the *National Airs, Works,* 4: 165–66 and 164 respectively.

30 August

1. Basil Hall, *Extracts of a Journal Written on the Coasts of Chili, Peru, and Mexico. . . ,* 2 vols. (1823).

8 September

1. A reference to the speeches by Burke and Fox on the occasion of Fox's "East India Bill" (1783), which would have transferred power of appointments to the East India Company from the Board of Directors to a court. The Bill passed the House of Commons but was defeated, through personal influence of the King, in the House of Lords. Burke and Fox delivered eloquent speeches on the occasion in Commons.

2. See entry for 28 July–2 August 1824 and its n. 1.

15 September

1. W. L. Bowles, *A Final Appeal to the Literary Public Relative to Pope* (1825); William Roscoe, "A Letter to . . . W. L. Bowles . . . in Reply to His *Final Appeal to the Literary Public Relative to Pope*" (1825). Bowles replied in *Lessons in Criticism to W. Roscoe . . .* (1826).

2. *Works,* 3: 354.

16 to 19 September

1. "When Thou Art Nigh," one of the *Ballads, Songs, Miscellaneous Poems, Works,* 5: 251.

21 September

1. James Ridley, *Tales of the Genii* (1764).

2. *John Bull,* 13 September 1824, p. 301, accused Moore of plagiarizing from the work of an anonymous translator of the *Odes of Anacreon.*

4 October

1. *Works,* 5: 142, 144.

17 October

1. Claude Charles Fouriel, *Les Chants populaires de la Grèce moderne* (1824).

18 October

1. "There Are Two Loves," *Works*, 5: 244.
2. Medwin's account of Moore's meeting with Byron (which is on the whole correct) is found in *Medwin's Conversations with Lord Byron*, ed. Ernest J. Lovell (Princeton, N.J., 1966), pp. 147–49.

24 October

1. See Dowden, *Letters*, 5: 161 ff.
2. See entry for 15 September and its n. 1.

25 October

1. The comedy attributed to George Villiers (1672).

31 October

1. Henry Fielding, *Journey from This World to the Next* (1743).
2. Michele Enrico Carafa (1787–1872) was mainly a composer of operas.

3 November

1. "Lay His Sword by His Side," *Works*, 4: 97; "When on the Lip the Sigh Delays," *Works*, 5: 142.

4, 5 November

1. Sheridan, *The Duenna* (1775).

7, 8 November

1. John Murray, "Murray on *Conversations of Lord Byron*," *Gentleman's Magazine* 136 (1824): 438–42.
2. The ninth number of the *Irish Melodies* (1824).

15, 16 November

1. *Works*, 5: 155.

17 November

1. François Bernard Chauvelin (1766–1832) was ambassador to England in 1792.

18 November

1. The treaty, signed in September 1786, was to be in force for twelve years. It provided for a much freer trade between France and England than had hitherto been carried on. Fox and Burke opposed the treaty, believing that commercially England stood to lose more than she gained. See W. E. H. Lecky, *History of England in the Eighteenth Century,* 7 vols. (London, 1913), 5: 307–14.

21 November

1. R. C. Dallas, *Recollections of the Life of Lord Byron* (1824), p. 235.

22 November

1. See entry for 19–30 June 1824, n. 5, where the work is attributed to the Rev. Mortimer O'Sullivan. See also entry for 28 July–2 August 1824.
2. Either the "Begum Speech" delivered on 7 February 1787 (see entry for 31 August 1818 and its n. 4) or that of 14 May 1794 in reply to the defense of the Begum charge (see entry for 18 October 1818 and Gibbs, *Sheridan*, pp. 142–43).

23 November

1. James Mill, *Essay on Government Jurisprudence* . . . written for the Supplement to the *Encyclopædia Britannica. CBEL* gives the date tentatively as 1825.

27 to 29 November

1. *Works*, 4: 335 and 228.

4 December

1. *Edinburgh Review* 41 (1824): 143–53.

14 December

1. One of several adaptations of Weber's *Der Freischütz* (1821). This version, adapted by G. Soane, was first produced at Drury Lane on 11 November 1824.

15 December

1. Hobhouse reviewed Dallas's *Recollections* and Medwin's *Conversations* in *Westminster Review* 3 (1825): 1–35.
2. *Rights of Man: Being an Answer to Mr. Burke's Attack on the French Revolution* (1791–92).
3. *Criticisms on the Rolliad* (1784), a collection of Whig satires against William Pitt and his followers. The satires purport to be reviews of an imaginary epic. John Rolle, from whose name the title was taken, was one of Pitt's supporters.

16 December

1. Sir Henry Bishop, *Clari, the Maid of Milan* (1823).

19 December

1. "The Catalogue," *Works*, 2: 86.

20 December

1. A collection of verse tales appearing between 1822 and 1828.
2. George IV (then Prince of Wales) married Mrs. Fitzherbert in 1785. The marriage was declared illegal under the Royal Marriage Act. There was an article on "The Speech of Mr. John Leach, Esq., M.P., upon . . . the Limitations of the Royal Authority in the Hands of the Regent," *Edinburgh Review* 18 (1811): 46–80. Since Moore does not indicate the date of the article, one can only surmise that he refers to this review.
3. The trial of Queen Caroline in 1820.
4. An action brought by the celebrated actress Miss Foote against a wealthy gentleman named Hayne for a breach of promise of marriage. A verdict was given in favor of the plaintiff and damages were set at £3,000. Because of the popularity of the actress, the court-room was crowded.

21 December

1. Weber, *Euryanthe* (1823).

29 December

1. Gilbert Wakefield, *The Works of Pope with Remarks and Illustrations* (1794), p. 326. The quotation is the first line of Pope's "Flutt'ring spread thy purple pinions."

30 December

1. On 13 November 1755 William Pitt (First Earl of Chatham) delivered a brilliant speech against subsidies for the proposed Hessian Treaty. In it he made the famous comparison between the coalition of Fox and Newcastle and the juncture of the Rhône and Saône, the one a placid river, the other a tempestuous one. See Horace Walpole, *Memoirs of . . . George II* (1846), 2: 58.

1825

January 1st. [Saturday] Received a note from Lady L. asking me to come and meet Sir James Mackintosh on Monday, and stay over Tuesday, saying also she hoped to persuade Bessy to come with the children to celebrate Twelfth-night; answered I should come, but could not stay over Tuesday.

2nd. [Sunday] Have written, for Power, words to a Spanish air composed by Mrs. Villamil, and to a German hunting song.

3rd. [Monday] Walked over to Bowood: company, Mackintosh and his daughter, Mr. and Mrs. Vernon Smith and Lewson Smith. Some good stories of old Lady Townsend after dinner. "Lord Anson round the world but never in it." A good deal of conversation about Burke in the evening. Mentioned his Address to the British Colonists in North America, "Armed as you are, we embrace you as our friends and as our brothers, by the best and dearest ties of relation." The tone of the other parts, however, is, I find, moderate enough. Burke was of opinion that Hume, if he had been alive, would have taken the side of the French Revolution. Dugald Stewart thinks the same. The grand part of Burke's life was between 1772 and the end of the American war; afterwards presumed upon his fame and let his imagination run away with him. Lord Charlemont said that Burke was a Whig upon Tory principles. Fox said it was lucky that Burke and Wyndham took the side against the French Revolution, as they would have got hanged on the other. Wyndham's speech on Curwen's motion for Reform an ingenious defence of parliamentary corruption, like the pleading of a sophist. Burke gave the substance of the India Bill, and Pigot drew it up. Slept there.

4th. [Tuesday] After breakfast talked of Lord John's last book. Lord L. approves highly of his defence of the Septennial Act: thinks it saved the country. A question, however, whether they had any right to extend it beyond the parliament then sitting, and whether they should not merely have recommended the principle for discussion to their successors.[1] Mackintosh thinks that if Anne and Louis XIV. had lived two or three years longer, the Pretender would have been restored. Looked over, with M., Bishop Berkeley's Querist,[2] in which there are remarkable instances of acuteness on subjects of political economy; also views with respect to Ireland and the Catholics, most liberal, considering the times in which he lived; all expressed clearly and ably. How much more truly patriotic than Swift, who put the great majority of the people wholly out of his account! Read over Burke, and made some extracts. After luncheon went with Lady Lansdowne and the two others to drive. Dressed at Phipps's, where Bessy and I dined, to go to the ball: company, Mrs. Houlton and her two daughters, and the Ashes. The ball very full and a number of pretty women; danced with Selina Locke. Home between two and three.

5th. [Wednesday] But ill fit for working after my late hours. Am labouring away at Sheridan.

6th [Thursday] The Lansdownes' carriage came for us, and Bessy, Anastasia, Tom, and I set off in it. Company at dinner, the Mackintoshes and Smiths, the Bowleses, and Mr. and Mrs. Hertford. Sung in the evening and played with the children; Anastasia drew Queen. Home between eleven and twelve. Found that the Starkeys had sent in alarm for Bessy, on account of Julia's illness. She insisted on going across the valley, and as soon as I could get on my boots I followed her. Found all in bed and returned.

7th to 9th. [Friday–Sunday] At work.

10th. [Monday] Walked over to Bowood. Found Mackintosh and Abercrombie. Showed M. some letters of Parr's and one of the King's, dated 1791, which he thinks alludes to something connected with the Duke of York's marriage.[1] Talked of Adair's mission to Russia. M. thought his letter to the Bishop of Winchester good, but A. did not consider it as quite satisfactory.[2] It seems the letter of Adair that was intercepted had been entrusted by him to some man at Petersburg in whom he had confidence, and at the man's own request. It contained a report of a conversation A. had had with some high person in office, and was laid before the council in England. Some were for proceeding on it, but Mackintosh had heard that

Mr. Pitt and Lord Grenville both said they would resign if any use was made of a document so obtained. Said I should perhaps come and offer myself for dinner to-morrow. Both pressed me to do so.

11th. [Tuesday] Walked over to Bowood, and wrote a verse of a song to Carafa's beautiful air in going. Met Lord L. and asked if I might dine with him; said he should be most happy. Went to the house and found Mackintosh. Read with him the Prince's letter in 1789, which he has always supposed to be Burke's.[1] Thinks the passage about "separating the Court from the State" and "disconnecting the authority," &c., much more in Burke's manner of thinking than Sheridan's. After reading this fine passage with great delight, he said comically, "who the devil would ever suppose that this was all about the power of creating lords of the bedchamber?" Turned to the protest of the Lords in 1778, against the plan of desolating America, which was written by Burke and (as Mackintosh heard from Lord Fitzwilliam) the Duke of Richmond conjointly.[2] A most magnificent piece of writing, and could hardly have had any other hand to it than Burke's. M. showed it to me for the purpose of comparing the style with that of the Prince's letter, and I confess I begin to think that Burke must have written some passages of that letter. The probability is that it was done by different hands. Abercrombie joined us; asked him about the Scotch boroughs. Gave me a general explanation of them; there is no popular election whatever in Scotland; it is as if the lords of the manor in England were to elect themselves; for it does not even depend upon property, but upon a sort of right, like that of the manorial right, which may be held independent of the property. Company at dinner, Dr. and Mrs. Fowler, the Mackintoshes, and Abercrombies. M. quoted from Churchill about Macpherson:—

> Ossian sublimest, simplest bard of all,
> Whom English infidels Macpherson call.

In Cesarotti's translation, Cachullin is made *Cucullino*.[3] Was expected to stay to sleep, but took an opportunity of running away, and walked home.

12th. [Wednesday] Am pestered with letters from all parts of the world. The other day received four, from New York, Frankfort, Paris, and Birmingham. That from Frankfort is an account of all that the writer (a Mr. Schonbart) has done for me in the German Gazettes, where I have been attacked, and he has defended me. The Birmingham letter is from a young gentleman who wants to be my amanuensis, and asks, "what remuneration I can give him for it." Last night I received a letter from a French gentleman about Miss Sophie——, who, he says, will die if she does not get a lock of Lord Byron's hair, and entreating me, in the name of her distracted family, to save her from the grave. Recollect some other things Mackintosh said. Wilberforce's good remark about the Catholics, that they were "like persons discharged from prison, but still wearing the prison dress." Mentioned an advertisement that appeared in 1792, "Wanted for a King of France, an easy good-tempered man, who can bear confinement, and has no followers." Wilberforce was made a citizen by the French Convention, and Courteney, who was in Paris at the time, said, "If you make Mr. W. a citizen, they will take you for an assemblage of negroes, for it is well known he never favoured the liberty of any white man in all his life." Dr. Thomson said of Godwin (who in the full pride of his theory of perfectibility, said he "could educate tigers,") "I should like to see him in a cage with two of his pupils." Pitt is known to have corrected but two of his speeches—that on the Union, and another on the Budget for the year 1792. Mr. Fox, but one; that about the Duke of Bedford. His Scrutiny speech (at least the greater part of it) was reported by Dennis O'Brien. To Dr. Lawrence, who was hideously ugly, Canning and Ellis used to apply

> "tetrior" alter
> Non fuit, excepto Laurentis corpore Turni.[1]

Lord Clifford has a copy of the secret treaty entered into by Charles II. with Louis XIV.,[2] which he is about to send to Mackintosh. Talked of the opinions of Eichorn, and other Germans, about the Gospels; that there was one original gospel, Matthew, from which the others have been compiled. Herbert Marsh pursues the same idea in his preface to Michaëlis.[3]

13th. [Thursday] Went into Devizes to dine with the Hugheses; Bessy and Mrs. Phipps had gone in the morning to attend the court, it being sessions time. Bingham of the party at Hughes's; some rather agreeable conversation. Singing in the evening by Bingham and me. In talking of Burke's paper upon evidence (on the trial of Hastings), Bingham said that the only fault to be found with Burke and Romilly in their notions of a reform in the law was, that they did not go far enough; while in Mackintosh's, still worse, everything he proposed was wrong. Had not an opportunity to ask him to explain this.

14th to 17th. [Friday–Monday] Sent Carafa's air, "O Memory,"[1] and another (of which I forget the words) to Power. Lord Lansdowne called on the 15th, and asked me to dine at Bowood, to meet the Morleys, on Tuesday 18th.

18th. [Tuesday] Walked to Bowood to dinner; none but the Morleys. Lady M. quoted some lines from a poem she said Delavigne had written lately on vaccination:—

> "Au fond de Glocester, ou les vastes campagnes
> Nourissent des *taureaux,* les fidelles compagnes."

Vache in poetry would be an abomination. In talking of the strange practice of foreign physicians, it was mentioned that at Lisbon they always order for inflammatory fevers, hen broth, and for low fevers cock broth. The Duc de Levi, in something he has written about England, is mightily pleased with a discovery he makes that *luncheon* is derived from *lounger.* Seeing the Bond Street loungers going into the cake shops so regularly, he traced the connection between them and the meal; thus *lounger, luncher, luncheon.* This Duc de Levi a ridiculous personage; had a picture once drawn of the Virgin Mary, and himself taking off his hat to her, the Virgin saying, as appears by a scroll out of her mouth, *Couvrez vous, mon cousin.* Quoted the line from Ariosto, *andava conbattendo ed era morto.* Sung, and slept there.

19th. [Wednesday] Lady L. proposed that they should take me to Col. Houlton's (where I have been asked to meet them) tomorrow. Col. H. himself had offered to drive over for me, but declined it.

20th. [Thursday] The Lansdownes called upon me at three. Company at the Houltons, their own family, Wilsons, Shirleys, &c. Elwin, and Lord James O'Brien. Sung in the evening, and Isabella Houlton delighted us with her figure and tones at the guitar; nothing can be prettier. I sung *Se fiato avete in corpo,* with John Houlton. Slept there. Elwin insisted upon my being his guest to-morrow night at Bath.

21st. [Friday] Lord Lansdowne at breakfast mentioned of Dutens, who wrote the "Mémoires d'un Voyageur que se repose,"[1] and was a great antiquarian, that on his describing once his good luck in having found (what he fancied to be) a tooth of Scipio's, in Italy, some one asked him what he had done with it, upon which he answered briskly, "What have I done with it? *le voici,*" pointing to his mouth, where he had made it supplemental to a lost one of his own. The Lansdownes off to Bath after breakfast, and I (after singing a little for the girls) followed them with Col. Houlton. The grand opening to-day of the Literary Institution at Bath. Attended the inaugural lecture by Sir G. Gibbs, at two. Walked about a little afterwards, and to dinner at six; Lord Lansdowne in the chair. Two Bishops present; and about 108 persons altogether. Bowles and Crabbe of the number. Lord L. alluded to us in his first speech, as among the literary ornaments, if not of Bath itself, of its precincts; and in describing our respective characteristics, said, beginning with me, "the one, a specimen of the most glowing, animated, and impassioned style," &c.; this word "impassioned" spoken out strongly in the very ear of the Bishop of Bath and Wells, who sat next him. On the healths of the three poets being given, though much called for, I did not rise, but motioned to Crabbe, who got up and said a few words. When it came to my turn to rise, such a burst of enthusiasm received me as I could not but feel proud of. Spoke for some time, and with much success. Concluded by some tributes to Crabbe and Bowles, and said of the latter, that "his poetry was the first fountain at which I had drunk the pure freshness of the English language, and learned (however little I might have profited by my learning) of what variety of sweetness the music of English verse is capable. From admiration of the poet, I had been at length promoted into friendship with the man, and I felt it particularly incumbent upon me, from some late allusions, to say, that I had found the life and the poetry of my friend to be but echoes to each other; the same sweetness and good feeling pervades and modulates both. Those who call my friend a wasp, would not, if they knew him better, make such a mistake in natural history. They would find that he is a *bee*, of the species called the *apes neatina,* and that, however he may have a sting ready on the defensive, when attacked, his native element is that garden of social life which he adorns, and the proper business and delight of his life are sunshine and flowers." In talking of the "springs of health with which nature had gifted the fair city of Bath," and of her physicians, I said, "it was not necessary to go back to the relationship between Apollo and Esculapius to show the close consanguinity that exists between literature and the healing art; between that art which purifies and strengthens the body, and those pursuits that refine and invigorate the intellect. Long," I added, "may they both continue to bless you with their beneficent effects! Long may health and the Muses walk your beautiful hills together, and mutually mingle their respective influences, till your springs themselves shall grow springs of inspiration, and it may be said,

> 'Flavus Apollo
> Pocula Castaliâ plena ministrat aquâ.'"

Quite overwhelmed with praises, I left the room. Elwyn and I, accompanied by Bayly, and a sensible Irishman, E. introduced me to (Ellis); went to the play together. Home to Elwyn's house, where I slept.

22nd. [Saturday] Bowles highly gratified with what I said of him. Asked by every one to give a correct copy of it for the newspapers, but shall not, for it would break the charm which all lies in manner, the occasion, &c. &c. Duncan of Oxford said to me, "I have had that sweet oratory ringing in my ears all night." Bowles gave me a copy of his "Roscoe pamphlet,"[1] with an inscription in it, *inter Poëtas suaves suavissimo*, &c. &c. Left Bath with Bowles, having bought some grapes for Bessy's patient, Miss Starkey. Bowles dropt me at Buckhill from which I walked home, carrying the basket of grapes. Found all pretty well.

23d to 25th. [Sunday–Tuesday] Received a Bath paper, giving an account of the dinner, and luckily rather describing than attempting to *give* my speech. Had a letter from Cruttwell asking me to send him a correct report of it, but too late to do so.

26th. [Wednesday] Took my dear Anastasia to school. Dined at Bayly's, in order to go to the Dramatic Ball in the evening: nothing could be more brilliantly got up than the latter. An amateur play first, and the fancy ball afterwards; an allusion to me in the epilogue spoken by Bayly, "Erin's matchless son," &c. which brought plaudits and stares on me. Introduced to quantities of people; came away with Elwyn before two, and supped and slept at his house.

27th. [Thursday] Mr. Duncan to breakfast, and some very agreeable conversation. Cruttwell has a pretended report of my speech, not one word of which I spoke. Left in the Devizes coach at half-past four. Had a chaise at Melksham, and home.

28th. [Friday] Walked to Bowood. Neither at home, but met Lord L. as I was coming back, and he dismounted and walked with me. Much conversation about the intentions of the Ministry about Ireland.

29th. [Saturday] Working at something for Power.

30th. [Sunday] Walked over to Bowood, and lunched with the Lansdownes, who start for London to-morrow.

31st. [Monday] Sent Power off "No, leave this heart to rest,"[1] and something else.

Feb. 1st to 8th. [Tuesday–Tuesday] Have kept no traces of these days except that they were all occupied with Sheridan. Bessy all this time attending upon Miss Starkey, and injuring her own health.

9th. [Wednesday] Took Bessy to Bath to see Liston. Had received an invitation from the Houltons to come over, Bessy and I, to them the following Saturday (12th), to stay till Monday, and go to the Subscription Ball at Bath; but the two frisks rather too much. The Phippses already at Bath. Dined at Elwyn's; company, Mr. and Miss Bayly, Miss Pinny and Tom Bayly. Went to the play afterwards, and laughed a good deal at Liston in "Solomon Grundy," and "Peter Finn."[1] Slept at Elwyn's. Had walked about in the morning with dear Anastasia; heard the "Infant Lyra" play, &c. &c.

10th. [Thursday] Duncan to breakfast. Suggested as a good topic for an Essay, "The choice of subjects for pictures." A man with a poetical head, and at the same time a connoisseur in painting, might make a great deal of this. Bowles in Bath, and offered to take us home, but we could not start time enough.

14th. [Monday] Sent Power a glee of my own, which I think rather pretty, "When o'er the silent seas alone."[1]

17th. [Thursday] The irritation between Phipps and the Starkeys has at last broken out into open war.

22nd. [Tuesday] Heard Phipps stirring at five; came down stairs soon afterwards, and found he had mounted his horse and rode off; Mrs. P. in a frightful state when she heard he was gone. Got her with great difficulty into the carriage to bring her to Sloperton. Advised Phipps, before he went away, to settle the matter at this side of the water, even at the risk of his £500.

23rd. [Wednesday] No intelligence to-day. Rumours of various kinds in the village, where all is known. Supposed that the parties had gone to fight on Lavington Down, and the country people collecting to see the combat. My attention all devoted to keeping Mrs. P. quiet, and dissuading her from her intention of going to Southampton, as much for Bessy's sake, who was to accompany her, as her own. Sent to Melksham this evening, but no tidings. Began to fear they must have crossed the water.

24th. [Thursday] Sent to Melksham at twelve, but no tidings. About four saw Mrs. Hughes (who had come over in the morning) running breathless and crying towards me. Feared something bad and ran to meet her, but found Phipps was returned and safe. In a short time his chaise appeared, and after a short scene with Mrs. P. learned the particulars. They had fought at Southampton; fired twice. His first shot went through John Starkey's hat, and Starkey's second, on the rebound, grazed his foot. He and Mrs. P. stayed to dinner and sleep.

25th to 28th. [Friday–Monday] Nothing particular; hard at work at Sheridan. Sent Power a glee of my own, "When o'er the silent seas alone."

March 1st to 12th. [1 March: Tuesday; 12 March: Saturday] One day exactly like another. Heard two or three times from Lord Landsowne; the Catholic Question making great progress. Received a new Magazine with a memoir of myself and portrait; answered the editor. Had a long letter from Shiel in answer to one I wrote to him containing advice as to the style of his oratory during his mission to England; recommended him to be as matter-of-fact, and as sparing of *flowers* as possible. Took my advice very amiably.

13th. [Sunday] Mary Dalby arrived to pass some time with us. Wrote for Power a ditty, "There's a song of the olden time."[1]

14th to 18th. [Monday–Friday] *Semper eadem.* Have done my Sheridan task as far as the year 1799, and shall now return to revise it from the very beginning.

24th. [Thursday] Dined at Money's to meet a Cambridge friend of his. Much talk about classics and public schools. M. remarked on the eloquence of Virgil. The speech of Dido to Æneas, beginning with scolding and ending with tenderness and tears, so like a woman. Sinon's speech, too, *Vos, eterni ignes, &c.* Some passages, too, from the Epistle of Laodamia to Protesilaus:

> "Aulide te fama est vento retinente morari;
> Ah, me cum fugeres, hic ubi ventus erat?"

And, further on, *Inter mille rates tua sit millessima puppis.* Story about *Academia.* Home early.

25th. [Friday] Our wedding day. A dish of salmon, as usual, with our friend Power. Fourteen years married to-day.

26th. [Saturday] Set off for Bath to take Anastasia to school, and forward the first batch of my Sheridan Life to the press. Dined with Crawford. Company, besides Elwyn and myself, the O'Briens, Lord and Lady St. Germans, and a beautiful girl, their niece. Sung in the evening. Slept at Elwyn's.

27th [Sunday] Read over, after breakfast, Ricardo's article on the Sinking Fund, in the Encyclopædia; and some passages of Tooke on the Bank Restriction.[1] Left Bath at three, and home at seven.

28th to 31st. [Monday–Thursday] Every day pretty nearly the same, working at Sheridan. Dined on the 30th at Hardman's, to meet Lord and Lady Ashtown, and Scott. The day very agreeable.

April 1st to 8th. [Friday–Friday] Still revising, and introducing new matter into the early part of the Life. Received the first proof. Under much anxiety about my dearest father, who is beginning at last, I fear, to yield to the weakness attendant upon years. My own mind prepared for the worst, but my poor mother will, I am afraid, be taken by surprise, and feel it dreadfully. Have written to insinuate, as gently as possible, into her heart those apprehensions with which my own is filled.

9th. [Saturday] Bessy and Mary Dalby (with little Tom of the party) set off to Bath, to pass a couple of days with Mrs. Branigan, who is just arrived there. Dined alone.

10th. [Sunday] Walked to Bremhill, to take my chance of finding Bowles. Dined with him. His illness much increased by his apprehensions; seemed to forget it all in the gaiety of conversation. Mentioned his anxiety, before he died, to write the Life of Bishop Ken, who voted for the exclusion of James, and yet afterwards sacrificed his bishopric rather than swear allegiance to king William. Was supported during the remainder of his days by Lord Weymouth, who gave him two hundred a-year, and had him to live with him at Longleat. Isaac Walton married Ken's sister, hence the name he gives her, "Kenna." Bowles has made a pretty glee of some very charming words from Cowley's Davideis,[1] "Awake, my Lyre." In talking of profane parodies, mentioned Swift's about Sir R. Walpole: "I believe in one infallible King," &c. &c., "one Minister,." &c. &c.

April 11th to May 11. [11 April: Monday; 11 May: Wednesday] For this whole month have been too closely occupied with my Sheridan task to write a word here, and must, therefore, only recollect what I can. Received a letter from some Mrs. F. (whom I never heard of before) in which she says, "Your talents and excellence have long been the idols of my heart. With thee were the dreams of my earliest love," &c. The object of the letter is to invite me to a dinner she is about to give to "a few select friends in *memory of* Lord Byron!" Her husband, she adds, is "a gentleman and a scholar;" I wish him joy of her. My dear father much recovered. Had a correspondence with Woolriche about Bessy's state of health; promised to leave the Duke of Bedford, on his way up from Devonshire, and come to see her. Did so on the 20th; does not think her liver affected, which is a relief; but is of opinion that, if the medicine he has ordered does not do her good, she must go to Cheltenham. Mrs. Branigan came to us from Bath on the 18th. Lady Campbell (Pamela) called with Mrs. Bowles. Dined one day at Brabant's, to meet the Nestor of Lewesden Hill; has got too deaf for conversation. The day rather agreeable. Bowles called upon me one day; has had a favourable answer from his friend Mr. Clark with respect to the application he made to him for our dear little Tom, whom he expects to get into Winchester for me. Wrote to Brougham (in consequence of a salutation on one of his franks, "Health and Fraternity") to ask him to give me the particulars of what he said with regard to the Prince's marriage with Mrs. F. when we met at Denman's; had an answer from him to say he would send me some curious matter on the subject. Wrote to Lord Holland too, about a paper which he promised to give me; had two letters from him; the second very lively. In writing to him mentioned that my occupation with the "Life of Sheridan," robbed me of all the gaiety that was going on in town, and that I might be said "*propter* vitam *vivendi perdere causas.*" Had a correspondence, too, with Dr. Bain on my intention to pay him a visit, which he has very hospitably pressed me to do. Sent up Power to more glees, "The Watchman," and "The Spirits."[1] Mrs. Branigan left us on the 9th of May. Mary Dalby still with us.

May 12th. [Thursday] A visit from Crofton Croker on his way from Ireland; says the whole feeling there is in favour of Emancipation. Hardly a dissenting voice on the subject.

15th. [Sunday] Received the 112th page of my printing. Wrote to Dr. Bain to say I should be with him on Tuesday next.

16th. [Monday] Copied out some parts of my revision, and prepared for my trip. Dined at half-past one; Bessy borrowed Farmer Gaby's donkey gig, and all set off for Buckhill. Drank tea there, and watched for the Bath coaches. Took the second and arrived in Bath at eight. Went to see my darling Anastasia; looked very well, but it struck me that her shoulder was a little more out than when I last saw her. Begged of Miss Furness to look carefully to it. Went for a short time to the play. Supped at the White Lion, and slept there.

17th. [Tuesday] Set off in the Poole coach at half-past nine. Went half the way outside from a mistake about the place. This contrary to my pact with Bessy, but shall not tell her of it. Arrived at Blandford a little after five. Took a chaise, and was at Dr. Bain's at a little after seven; received me very kindly. No one at dinner but himself and two daughters. A good deal of talk about Sheridan (the object of my visit) after dinner. Find Mrs. Canning's letter not quite correct about Mrs. Sheridan's last moments. Bain was sent for at midnight; Mrs. C. and S. in the room at the time. Mrs. S. begged them to go away for a moment, and bid Bain lock the door after them; then said, "You have never deceived me: tell me truly shall I live over this night?" B. felt her pulse; found she was dying, and said, "I recommend you to take some laudanum." She answered, "I understand you, then give it me." Said (in telling me this) that the laudanum, he knew, would prolong her life a little, and enable her better to go through the scene that was before her in taking leave of her family. S.'s kindness to her, quite the devotedness of a lover.

18th. [Wednesday] Walked around the grounds with Dr. Bain and his daughters; rather nice girls. Much talk with him about Sheridan, but got little more. Am very glad, however, I came, as I should have reproached myself for not having done so, and others would reproach me also. Vaughan told him that there were two hundred pounds placed at his disposal for Sheridan, but Bain never understood (as Croker and others assert) that there was more than that sum to come. Believes that Sheridan's dispositions were all good, and that his embarrassments alone were the cause of whatever was wrong in his conduct. Story of Sheridan's butler saying (when Bain was called in and found him in a high fever) that he had drunk nothing extraordinary the day before, "only two bottles of port." Sheridan's arm remarkably thin, though powerfully strong; contrary to the usual notion (Bain said) that an arm must be brawny and muscular to be strong. A most capacious chest; altogether a man of great strength; and but for his intemperance would have had a very long life. Talking to Bain, who had said that Pitt was a very extraordinary man, he answered, "He *is* an extraordinary man, and the more we press him the more he shines." Sung with the Misses Bain after dinner several duets of my own, and of Asioli's; also some old favourites of mine, out of the "Proserpina," *Ti veggo, t'abbraccio,* and *Mi lasci oh madre amata.*[1]

19th. [Thursday] Drove with the Doctor and his two girls to Wareham. Told me of Sheridan's having passed off a young country farmer at Crewe Hall as Richardson. Dined early in order that I might get to Blandford before dark; set off in a chaise, a little before seven; had tea at Blandford, and went to bed after mourning over the debate in the Lords on the Catholic Question. What wretched infatuation! A smug rector, in the morning, at Wareham, was waiting eagerly for the coming in of the post, and I left him chuckling over Lord Liverpool's anilities. These are the fellows to whom Ireland is sacrificed.[1]

20th. [Friday] Set off in the Poole coach at half-past eight: got to Bath at four: ran to see my sweet Anastasia. Had some cold meat at the York House, and took the Devizes coach as far as Melksham, from whence I walked, and got home about nine. Found all, thank God, pretty well.

21st. [Saturday] Sent to ask Dr. Starkey, and the new curate, to dine with us on Wednesday next.

22nd. [Sunday] Could not help (busy as I was) giving vent to some of my bile against the anti-Popery set, by writing a few lines for the "Morning Chronicle."

23rd. [Monday] Sent to Power a slight sketch of a glee, "Pretty Maid, pretty Maid." Not quite good enough, I fear, for the set of six I mean to do for him. Sent off, also, to the "Morning Chronicle," my squib against Lord Anglesey and the Bishops, beginning "A Bishop and a bold Dragoon."[1] Read it to Mary at breakfast, who, with all her High Church prejudices, enjoyed the fun of it.

24th. [Tuesday] Received a letter from some gentleman at Cork, telling me that he has been collecting Irish airs for me, and sending me some specimens. Must thank him.

25th. [Wednesday] Starkey, and four or five more, whom I had asked, being luckily engaged, my dinner consisted only of ——, ——, and ——. *Dullissimum.*

26th. [Thursday] Squib not in: must have been delayed by my enclosing it to Power. Went with Bessy, Mary, the children, and maids to the Bromham fair, and took them all to the show, where we made a great sensation among the clods. Rather a pretty girl one of the dancers.

27th. [Friday] "The Bishop and the bold Dragoon" inserted conspicuously. Walked to Devizes to draw upon Power. Dined late. Had a letter from Denman telling me that M. A. Taylor is anxious to give me some information about Sheridan. Mentioned, also, the "Bold Dragoon," as a proof that I was *in esse.*

28th. [Saturday] My birthday. What, again! well, the more the merrier; at least I hope so; and, as yet (with all my difficulties), have no reason to complain. An excellent, warm-hearted, lively wife, and dear, promising children. What more need I ask for? A little addition of health to the wife, and wealth to the husband, would make all perfect. Prepared for my trip to town to-morrow.

29th. [Sunday] Left for town. Dined with the Storys. Found a note from Lord Lansdowne asking me to dine with him to-morrow.

30th. [Monday] Called upon the Donegals, Lady Jersey, &c. Dined with Lord Lansdowne. Went to Lady Jersey's in the evening; Lady Belhaven wanted to take me off to the fancy ball on Lord B.'s ticket, but, having no dress, could not.

31st. [Tuesday] Dined with the Fieldings. Went to the Opera. Was to have taken Corry afterwards to Lady Lansdowne's assembly, but it was put off in consequence of the death of her niece, Lady C. Lemon's daughter. Sat some time in Lady Tankerville's box: thence to the Duke of Bedford's. Thanked the Duchess for the wish she had expressed through Woolriche to have me among the beautiful scenery of Endsleigh with them. Then to Lord Grey's box, where I sat for the rest of the night, talking with him and Lady L. Lambton. Went with Corry, and supped at Long's. Met there Sir Godfrey Webster; reminded by him of the night that Lord Byron and I found him in the same manner at Stevens's, and sat together till four in the morning. By the by, Charles Sheridan told me the other night at Lady Jersey's (to my great delight) that he had found a copy of his father's defence of his conduct in 1811.[1] This paper, which was addressed to Lord Holland, is of great consequence, and Lord Holland, who first told me of it, added that he did not feel himself authorised to give it me.

June 1st. [Wednesday] A letter from Bessy to say I may expect her to-morrow. Dined with Corry at the Piazza, and went to Almack's at night.

2nd. [Thursday] Dressed early (having to dine at Holland House), for the purpose of meeting Bessy at the coach. Mrs. Story took me, and after our waiting some time at Knightsbridge the Bath coach arrived with Bessy, Tom, and Mary Dalby. Deposited the two former at Mrs. Story's, and proceeded to Holland House. Sat next my Lady, who was very gracious, filled my glass amply with champagne, and descanted on the merits and prices of Rudesheim, Johannisberg, and Hockheim. Said to me during dinner, "This will be a dull book of yours, this 'Sheridan,' I fear." "On the contrary," I replied, "it will be a very lively, amusing book! not from my part in it, but" &c. &c. In the evening Lady Lansdowne came, looking so handsome and so good, that it was quite comfortable to see her. Told her of Bessy's arrival. "Then she'll come to me," she said, "on Saturday evening." "Bessy," I answered, "has brought no evening things, for the express pur-pose of *not* going anywhere." After a short pause she turned round, in her lively way, and said, "I'll tell you what: bring Mrs. Moore to see me to-morrow morning, and she shall have the choice of my wardrobe: I assure you it's a very convenient one, fits both fat and lean. I once dressed out four girls for a ball, and there were four gowns of mine dancing about the room all night." Lord John Russell drove me in his cabriolet. In talking of what Lady Holland said to me about my book, mentioned a sally of the same kind she made the other day upon Lord Porchester, who has a poem coming out. "I am sorry to hear you are going to publish a poem. Can't you suppress it?" Promised to dine at Holland House on Sunday. Called this morning upon Lucy Drew, who is just arrived.

3rd. [Friday] Breakfasted with Rogers. Went with me afterwards to the Arcade, to meet Bessy. Dined with the Longmans at Hampstead: company, Sir R. Ker Porter and his two sisters, the novellists. In the evening Joanna Baillie. Sang a good deal.

4th. [Saturday] Went out with Lucy and Bessy, in Lucy's *remise*. Bessy paid several visits to Lady Donegal, Lady E. Fielding, &c. Dined at Story's (Corry of the party): and all went to the Opera in the evening. Woolriche saw Bessy in the morning, and thinks she had better go to Cheltenham. Lady Donegal going there too, which will make it more comfortable. Went from the Opera, with Corry, to Lady Lansdowne's, where we heard "Pasta," &c. Found a note from Brougham on my return home; asking me to dine with him, if possible, to-morrow; as he is to have Creevy and M. A. Taylor, and "will make them talk Sheridan for me as long as I please."

5th. [Sunday] Lucy called for me. Much puzzled about my engagement to Holland House to-day. Resolved at last to throw myself on the good nature of Lady H., and tell her my reason for dining with Brougham instead. Drove to Brougham's, and despatched a note from thence to Holland House. Called on Lord John: told him I should bring Bessy to pay him a visit in the course of the day: did so. Called with her also at Miss White's, and Edward Moore's. Company at Brougham's: Creevy, M. A. Taylor and Mrs. T., Dr. Lushington, Lord Nugent, Lord and Lady Darlington, &c. &c. After dinner Creevy and Brougham got Taylor to tell his famous story about Sheridan's reply on Hastings' Trial, when Taylor was his assistant to hold his bag and read the minutes; but neither bag nor minutes were forthcoming. Shall make use of the story. Found them all adrift about dates; even Taylor, as to events in which himself was concerned, brought circumstances together that were in reality more than a year apart: have observed this invariably in all the men of that time. Went afterwards, for a short time, to Mrs. Story's.

6th. [Monday] Had the engraver and Charles Sheridan with me to consider the print of Sheridan, done for the work, which is very bad. Went out with Bessy and Lucy. Took them for half an hour to the Exhibition. Dined (Bessy, Tom, and I) at the Donegals'; and went in the evening to see Matthews. Bessy too tired to stay. Called with her this morning upon Lord and Lady Hastings, who were very kind to her. I had myself seen him a day or two before, and felt all my first sentiments of kindness towards him brought freshly back by the sweetness of his manner, as well as by a certain tone of melancholy, which looks as if he had at last found out what a mistake his life has been. The King, I understand, has completely dropped him.

7th. [Tuesday] Went about a little with Bessy. Dined at Story's: and having taken places for Bessy and Tom in to-morrow morning's coach, brought them to sleep at my lodgings for the greater convenience of getting off. Left them in bed, and went to Mrs. Bennet's ball for a short time.

8th. [Wednesday] Up at five; and saw my treasures safe in the coach. Returned, and went to sleep again for an hour and a half. Had Mr. Smythe (the professor) with me while I breakfasted. Told me a great deal about his connection with Sheridan; his first coming to town for Sheridan to look at him, and form his opinion: S. not coming to the dinner made for the purpose, but appointing Richardson and him to meet him at a tavern at supper: not coming there either. At last went to dine at Isleworth with him: no mention made of the business after dinner, but Sheridan wrote him a very handsome letter in a few days after: the salary, with apologies for not being able to give more, £300 a-year. At the end of the first year a groom came down to Wanstead with a letter to Smythe, enclosing a draft for 300 guineas: Smythe's anxiety in taking it to the bankers': his suspense while the men behind the counter conferred together, and his delight when asked "in what form would he take the money." Remembers Sheridan going down to Wanstead to prepare for his reply to the Counsel of Hastings: two or three days hard at work reading: complained that he had motes before his eyes with reading so much. Smythe heard his reply: his laceration of Law, powerful. Law had laid himself open by wrongfully accusing Sheridan of showing a wrong paper to Middleton to entrap him into the answer he wished; whereas it was Lord Camden that made this mistake, and Sheridan corrected it. Burke addressed S. in the box friendlily, and said he was sorry he meant to conclude in one day: also went up to him, and thanked him at the conclusion. Thinks that S. had no sordid ideas about money, and always *meant* rightly. Never forgave the Whigs for supporting the Duke of Northumberland's son against him at Westminster. The best man to advise *others* that could be found anywhere: no such man for a cabinet. Knew what would suit the public: his powers of winning over people, proved by his persuading the parson to bury Richardson over again for him. Smythe quoted as sublime S.'s phrase, "Let them go and hide their heads in their coronets;" also, the happy phrase applied to some of his own party at the time of the threatened invasion, "giving the left hand to the country." Smythe, one day, while looking over his table, while waiting to catch him coming out of his bedroom, saw several unopened letters, one with a coronet, and said to Wesley, "We are all treated alike." Upon which Wesley told him that he had once found amongst the un-opened heap a letter of his own to Sheridan, which he knew contained a ten pound [*sic*], sent by him to release S. from some inn where he was "money bound," and that he opened it, and took out the money. Wesley said, also, that the butler had assured him he found once the window-frames stuffed with papers to prevent them from rattling, and, on taking them out, saw they were bank notes, which S. had used for this purpose some stormy night and never missed them.

9th. [Thursday] Took Lucy and her pretty friend Clementina to Willis's in St. James's Street, to hear a Spaniard whom Sir William Carol had appointed to sing some of his national songs for me at one o'clock. The Spaniard sick in bed; but it being a drawing-room day, the sight from Willis's balcony was very gay, and we were regaled with luncheon, civilties, &c. &c. Went from thence with them to the Diorama. Dined at Lord Auckland's: company, Luttrel, Fielding, James Stuart, and young Greville. The latter sung a little in the evening, and so did I.

10th. [Friday] Breakfasted with M. A. Taylor by appoinment; beautiful house. Sat with him in his garden looking upon the Thames, and talked of Sheridan; mentioned his own share in the transaction of 1811.[1] Being sent for by the Prince at three in the morning, found him, Sheridan, and Adam together, the latter looking very black. The Prince produced Michael a rough draft of an answer to the Address of the Houses (which was to be given the next day), and said he must make two fair copies of it immediately, adding, "these d—— fellows (*i.e.* Lords and Commons) will be there in the morning." The draft was partly in the handwriting of the Prince, and partly in that of Sheridan. The Prince, by Michael's advice, went to bed, and Michael set to copying, while Sheridan and Adam were pacing up and down at opposite parts of the room. Presently Adam came to Michael's elbow and whispered him (looking at Sheridan), "that's the d——nedst rascal existing." A little after, Sheridan came and whispered Michael, "D—n them all!" (meaning Adam, Lords Grey, Grenville, &c.) Having performed his task, Taylor went home, and returned to Carlton House next morning, where he found the members of the Houses already arriving. The Prince, who was still in bed, sent for him, and said, "Are those fellows come?" "Yes, sir, some of them are arrived." "D—n them all," was the reply. He then told Michael that he must make fresh copies of the

Address, as there had been more alterations in it. Michael told me he saw very plainly, at this time, that there was mischief brewing against the Whigs. In the arrangements under the Regency, it was intended that Lord Moira should go to Ireland, and that Sheridan should be his secretary. Michael had been, I believe, first intended for this situation; but it was afterwards decided by the Prince that he should remain in England and be Judge Advocate. Lord Grey, who (as Michael expressed it), was "all upon stilts" at the prospect of coming into power, in talking to Taylor of his appointment, said he saw no objection to his having it, as the Prince desired; to which Taylor replied, that he thought it very doubtful whether *any of them* would come in, to the evident surprise and not a little pique of Lord Grey, who said, "How should you know anything about it?" The Prince a day or two after went to Windsor, where the Queen and the Duke of Cumberland settled the whole matter. Lucy Drew took me out to Holland House; found Lord and Lady Holland; and the latter gave me a little lecture on my transgression of Sunday last. Thence went and left my name at Canning's. Dined at Lord Jersey's: company, the Tankervilles, Lord Duncannon, Sydney Smith, Brougham, &c.

11th. [Saturday] A note from Lady Holland to ask me for two or three different days next week; sent her my list to show her how double, treble locked and bolted I am for dinners during my stay. Dined at Lord Lansdowne's with Corry: company, Lord Auckland, the Grahams, Murtado, and other Spanish Americans, and Lady Cochrane. Introduced to the last, who is pretty and odd; told me she would at any time have walked ten miles barefoot to see me. Some curious conversations after dinner, about Spanish America. Sung in the evening.

12th. [Sunday] Breakfasted with Rogers. Dined at Phipps's; company, Sydney Smith and his family, James Smith (of the "Rejected Addresses"),[1] Charles Moore, and Mrs. Siddons. Sung in the evening with the Miss Smiths. Lady Morgan's little niece sung very prettily with Madlle. Castelli; sung also myself, and went afterwards to Mrs. Fleming's music. Heard some things by Garcia, Caradori, &c. and then home.

13th. [Monday] Dined at Rees's in Paternoster Row with Corry. Tom Campbell of the party. The day not very agreeable. L.'s carriage called and took me to her at Mr. Barber's at the Charter house; a nice old man and nice old place. From thence to Lady Jersey's child's ball, the prettiest ball I have ever seen in London. Interesting, to trace the beautiful mothers in their daughters, Lady Cowper, Mrs. Littleton, Lady Grantham, &c. &c.

14th. [Tuesday] Dined at Lord Dacre's company, Lord and Lady Tavistock, Joanna Baillie, and Grattan. Rather agreeable.

15th. [Wednesday] Had a note from Lady Holland to ask me to join her to-night at the play. Miss Tree's last appearance. Said "I think you might *squeeze* in a day to dine with us." Dined at Lord King's: company, Sydney Smith, George Fortescue, Lord Fortescue, the Lansdownes, the Cowpers, &c. During Smith's visit to the Observatory, said to the man, "Mr——, it must be very interesting to observe the progress of comets." "No, indeed, sir," answered the astonomer, "comets are very foolish things, and give a vast deal of trouble." Went to the play to Lady Holland, who had Lord John with her. Was to have gone to music at Lord Ashtown's, but too late.

16th. [Thursday] Breakfasted at Rogers's: Sydney Smith and his family, Luttrel, Lord John, Sharpe, &c.; highly amusing. Story of Forth, who informed Mr. Pitt during the French war, that there were two persons on their way from the north of Europe to assassinate him. Measures were accordingly taken by the Ministers to track their progress; they were seized, I believe, at Brussels, and in prison there for some years. It afterwards turned out that these men, instead of being assassins, were creditors of Forth, who were coming over to arrest him for a large sum, and he took this method of getting rid of them. Talked of Sir Robert Wilson. After the battle of Leipsic, to the gaining of which he was instrumental, Lord Castlereagh, in sending over to Lord Stewart the public document containing the orders for thanks to Wilson, among others on the occasion, accompanied it with a private one desiring Lord Stewart to avoid the thanks to Wilson as much as he could, in order not to give a triumph to his party. Lord Stewart, by mistake, showed this letter instead of the public one, to Wilson, who has had the forbearance never to turn it against the Government since. Dined at Lord Listowel's: Corry and I and Latham went together. (By the by, C. has made me a present of a handsome dressing case.) Company, Spring Rice, the Bushes, the Knight of Kerry, &c. &c. Some agreeable conversation about Burke, Pitt, &c. after dinner. Thence to Lady Jersey's, having been ordered by Lady Holland to join her there, though not asked. Found the Duke of Bedford, Lord King, Lord John, and Tierney. Set off with Lord Jersey and Tierney to go to Prince Leopold's assembly. Stopped by the string of carriages at the top of St. James's Street. Lord J. got out to walk, and I stayed with Tierney, and had about half an hour's conversation. Seems utterly to despair of any change in politics; remarked the success of Peel in procuring popularity for himself by this new jury measure; his name associated with it at public dinners; the only reformer of the day.[1] On my saying that Canning might carry the Catholic Question by resigning and coalescing with the Whigs, he said, "Who the devil will coalesce with people that don't coalesce with themselves." The assembly very crowded; the Prince Leopold full of civility to me. Talked about his house being a curious old mansion, and that he meant to make an alteration in the doorways which are too small. I answered (not very courtier-like) that the rooms, too, were rather small. "Oh," he replied, "there's a good deal of space," and I tried to get out of the scrape by saying that I had as yet seen but few of them. Lord Hastings expressed a wish to have a minute's conversation with me, and on our reaching a retired part of the room said, that he heard I intended, in my forthcoming work, to bring forward proof of the King's marriage with Mrs. Fitzherbert. Instead of giving some uncertain answer which might have drawn from him an explanation of the object he had in this inquiry, I answered that I had no such intentions, nor, indeed, knew anything of the existence of such proofs, but merely meant to allude to the *constitutional* consequences that *would* have resulted from such a marriage had it taken place. It is evident, I think, that the Carlton House people have expressed some alarm on the subject, and that his lordship volunteered his mediation to prevent what they dreaded. But does not this look as if Lord Hastings was aware such proofs exist? I called upon him, by the by, the other morning, and after reminding him of what he had once told me (at a time when I little thought I should ever be the biographer of Sheridan), that, after Fox's death, he (Lord H.) and Sheridan were entirely slighted by the remaining ministry, asked him whether he had any objection to my alluding to this circumstance. He answered, "not the least;" and added, as another instance of their indisposition towards himself, that when the Prince afterwards associated him with Lords Grenville and Grey in drawing up an answer to the Address of the Houses, they refused to act with him.[2] Stayed but a short time, and after hearing one frightful squall from Veluti, came home.

17th. [Friday] Dined with Agar Ellis: company, Lord Clifton, the Ponsonbys, Brougham, the Berrys, William Bankes, &c. At night Lucy's carriage (which she lent me) called to take me to Paddington. Corry was to have gone with me, but could not, on account of some business connected with the Linen Trade Committee. Expected to meet there the celebrated poetess L. E. L.,[1] but was disappointed. Only two or three persons: among them a performer of the pianoforte, who sang some airs of his own to mine and Byron's words very prettily. Supped, and did not leave till between two and three. Left Miss Rennie and her sister at home, having kept L.'s carriage all night.

18th. [Saturday] Dined with the Spottiswoodes; a large family party.

19th. [Sunday] Walked with Corry in Kensington Gardens. Dined at the Barings': company, Lascelles, Wm. Bankes, &c. &c.

20th. [Monday] Dined at Lord Cawdor's: the Abercrombies, Ponsonbys, &c. Meant to have dined with Burgess first, but breakfasted with him this morning instead.

21st. [Tuesday] Busy in my arrangements for starting for Brighton to-morrow, where I am going to see a Mr. I——, who professes to be able to tell me much about Sheridan. Edward Moore has offered to take me in his carriage. Dined with him; only Corry besides. Bid my wine-merchant send some samples of port for me to try there.

I have set down here not one half of what occurred, as I was too busy all the time in town to make memorandums at the moment, but I shall here add a few more particulars. The day I dined with Brougham he gave me, in coming away, the observations he had promised me on the subject of the Prince's marriage with Mrs. Fitzherbert, filling about four sheets of note paper. How he can find time for every thing is quite miraculous: yesterday, besides his law business, he attended and spoke at two public meetings. A few mornings after I met Creevy at Brougham's, I called upon the former by appointment, and heard a good deal from him about Sheridan. Passed some time with S. in Northumberland (at Orde's I believe). S.'s gaiety: acted over the Battle of the Pyramids on Marston Moor, ordering "Captain Creevy to cut out that cow," pointing to a cow in a ditch. S.'s anxious efforts in 1805 to get the Prince to give the Receivership to Tom. Creevy has seen him cry while entreating the Prince on the subject. Sheridan one day told Creevy that having gone to Cox's (?), where he used to receive his money for the Receivership, and requested they would lend him ten pounds on account, the clerk said, "Haven't you received my letter, sir?" Sheridan answered in the negative, the truth being (Creevy said) that letters were very often not taken in at his house for want of assets to pay the postage. The clerk then told him, to his no small surprise and joy, that there were £1200 in their hands placed to his account, and arising from some *fine*, I think, connected with his office. S. instantly, on the strength of this, took a house at Barnes Terrace, set up a carriage, and spent the £1200 in a very few months. Sheridan very expert at dressing an Irish stew in a country party. Creevy was witness, in 1805, to the introduction of Sheridan for the first time to Hastings, by the Prince at the Pavilion. S. said something to this effect, "You are, I am sure, too much a man of the world not to feel that all I did on that occasion was merely in the spirit of politics," &c. &c. Hastings appeared much pleased by his declaration, and hinted that it would be no small gratification to him, before he died, to have these sentiments made known to the world. S. on this *backed out* as well as he could. C. says S. was *not* in the habit of borrowing: had Whitbread's authority also for this. Sheridan *twice,*he thinks, in a spunging house: Whitbread described his finding him there, speculating upon Westminster, Lord Cochrane having been just then disgraced.

The night of Lady Jersey's ball the Duke of Gloucester returned again to the subject of Captain Rock: said he had lent it to a great Tory, and it had converted him. On asking Burgess about Sheridan's debts, he said he had paid 150 per cent. upon them all The statement of his having drawn £330,000 from the theatre, he says, not true. His habit of carrying a bag of papers with him when he went to a coffee-house, to look over them there; took one day a bag of love letters by mistake, and getting drunk left them there: this was what Ward told me of. The sum asked by the person who got possession of them was one hundred guineas, but they were regained in the violent way I have mentioned.

22nd. [Wednesday] Set off between eleven and twelve, and arrived to a late dinner at Brighton. Mr. I——, as I heard before I left town, gone to London on a consultation till Friday, so I shall have to stay all over to-morrow. Walked about.

23rd. [Thursday] Sir Richard Phillips called, and bored me beyond measure. Heard that Lord John Townshend was in Brighton; went and sat some time with him; promised to drink tea with him and Lady John in the evening. Dined with Sir Richard (Moore and I); his daughter a fine woman, brought up entirely on vegetables, like himself, both telling well for this Pythagorean diet. Went to Lord John T.; had much talk with him about Sheridan.

24th. [Friday] Strolling about Brighton. Mr. —— was to arrive at four: conceived but little expectations from him; evidently a take in. Dined in a hurry at the inn, and then set off with Moore to ——'s, who had claret, fruit, and Sir Richard Phillips laid out for us. Just as I thought; a good, vulgar, jolly, ignorant gentleman, whom Sheridan laid hold of·in his latter days, and who was just as fit a recipient for his wit, as a hog trough would be for champagne. Got literally nothing out of him but a few glasses of wine, and escaped with Moore as soon as I could to a raffle at the Library. This is too bad; to come expressly too from London for such a bubble! If I had not met Lord John, I should have had just nothing for my pains. Lord John, by the by, told me that in Sheridan's song, "When 'tis night," it was originally, instead of "Some pretty girl and true" (which Lord J. suggested), "Who had his last adieu."[1]

25th. [Saturday] Set off for town between ten and eleven. Dined at Richmond, and while dinner was getting ready walked to look at Lord Lansdowne's beautiful villa. Got to town at seven. Saw L. Packed up.

26th. [Sunday] Started for Sloperton; Lucy's old friend, Mr. Barber, in the coach; rather an agreeable journey. The whole of this next month was devoted, with little interruption, to my Sheridan task, correcting proofs, and finishing what yet remained to be written. Found at home, on my arrival, an extract from Dr. Parr's will, sent me by his executors, in which he says, "I give a ring to Thomas Moore, of Sloperton, Wilts, who stands high in my estimation for original genius, for his exquisite sensibility, for his independent spirit, and incorruptible integrity." During the hot weather of this month, July (hotter than any remembered for many years), we were imprudent enough to have parties for the children on several of the most sultry evenings, at our own house, Prowse's (the curate, who has four or five little ones), and Phipps's: blindman's buff, and racing in such weather, was but ill likely to either old or young any good: none, however, suffered by it except Bessy, her leg not getting at all well. Towards the end of July the Lansdownes arrived. Bessy left home for Cheltenham on the 22nd, where Lady Donegal had provided lodgings for her, and Bowles took her and the two little ones (Tom and Russell) in his carriage. A few days before I had attended the funeral of Henry Joy's father, as pall-bearer, at Chippenham. Slept at Bowles's the night before. Long and amusing arguments with him, as usual, about the Church, the universities &c. &c. Looked at Milton's Latin sonnet to his tutor, Thomas Young. It was his zeal and affection for this tutor (B. said) that first led him into controversy. Young was one of the writers of "Smectymnuus" (which name was made up out of the initials of the different authors), and when the work was attacked, Milton stepped forward in its defence. Looked also over Wharton's beautiful passage in his Preface to Milton's Poems, expressing the regret that must be felt at his abandonment of poetry, &c., for the wrangling of politics. Nothing can be happier than his application of Milton's own passage, ending "What need a vermil-tinctured lip for this."[1] On the 28th my dearest Anastasia left me for school, having been my housekeeper since her mamma went. Dined with the Lansdownes three times, once at Phipps's, and once at Locke's.

August 4th. [Thursday] Set off for Cheltenham. Had a chaise to the Cross-Hands, where I took the coach. An Irish lady, who was not a little angry at my laughing at her country: told her who I was before we parted, and nothing could exceed her surprise and pleasure. Found darling Bessy in a snug little cottage, No. 10 Suffolk Parade; or rather found her at Lady Donegal's, whither she had gone to dinner. A little better, but the leg still continuing bad; not allowed to take exercise. The Donegals all kindness to her and her little ones; Tom calling Lady D. "Granny," and all like the same family. Proposed that Bessy and Barbara should go to the play. Did so: Young in Hamlet; the King and Ophelia laughable beyond anything. Little Tom much delighted.

5th. [Friday] Went out with Bessy; she in the chair, and I walking. Dined with the Donegals. In the evening, Lord and Lady Kenmare, and young Wilmot: sung a good deal to them.

6th. [Saturday] Went with Barbara and Miss Godfrey to see the humours of the Wells before breakfast. Drove about afterwards with Bessy and Barbara. Called and sat a little while with Lady Kenmare. After dinner went to the Walks (Sir A. and Lady Faulkner being of our party), and I had to stand the stare of the night.

7th. [Sunday] Started in the coach for town, with heart much lighter for having seen my dear girl and her urchins: arrived at eight. Slept for the night at Mrs. Soane's, but as she had none but the parlours vacant, resolved to change my quarters on the morrow.

8th. [Monday] Heaps of proofs from Longmans'. Corrected some. Moved to 19. Bury Street. Dined at the Athenæum, Lord Stowel and the Chief Baron dining at a table near me. Lord Blessington, whom I had called upon in the morning, came in; had been to my lodging; asked me to dinner to-morrow.

9th. [Tuesday] At work. Dined at Lord B.'s: company, Gen. d'Orsay and his aide-de-camp, who are travelling with Lord Blessington, and Powell (the Queen's); dull enough. In the evening the Speaker came. Talked of the mistakes of English people in French. The Speaker said that Lord W——'s French for "never mind" was "jamais esprit." Said also, that when he asked Lord Westmorland, in Paris, whether he meant to go on to Italy, Lord W.

said, "No, no, I have had enough of the sea already." This is too bad even for Lord W——.

11th. [Thursday] Got out at three. Called upon Burgess: told him of the scrape he was getting me into by giving me a copy of a letter as Brinsley Sheridan's that was written by his brother Charles; luckily it was so puzzling in its dates and circumstances, that it set me on inquiry before I ventured to make use of it. Promised to give me the answers of Lords Grey and Grenville to the address of the Houses in 1811.[1] Asked him to go with me and dine at the Longmans' to-morrow. Got down to the Charter House to dinner at a little after five. Only old Barber, L., and myself. Went to the Haymarket in the evening; dull enough. Read the papers at the Club, and in bed at one. Have got two letters from my darling Bessy since I came; she says she is better. Had taken greatly to the Kenmares, with whom she was going about a little.

12th. [Friday] Out for about an hour: went to see the Living Skeleton. Burgess called on me before six. Walked to Paternoster Row: company, Surgeon Thompson, Mr. Mills, Col. Hawker, &c. &c. A curious circumstance mentioned, that it was a Scotchman drew up the charter of the Bank of England, and introduced the rule that no Scotchman should be a director; knowing that if but one was admitted, all the rest would be Scotchmen too. Talked of sculpture. Singular that the ancients, with their imperfect knowledge of anatomy, should have represented the muscles in action so correctly, and even better than the moderns: seems as if this knowledge was unnecessary to a sculptor. The Apollo (Surgeon T. said) has no one part of him formed like a man, so that the artist gained his object of creating something quite unlike a human creature, yet producing the effect of most perfect and divine beauty. C. H. afterwards. Had a letter this morning from Walter Scott, in answer to one I wrote him before I left home, expressing my regret at not being in my own green land to welcome him, and saying how I envied those who would have the glory of showing him and Killarney to each other, there being no two of nature's productions so worthy of meeting.[1]

13th. [Saturday] Went out at three to call upon Burgess, who showed me some very curious papers indeed, particularly a letter, written for the Prince by Sheridan, after the dismission of the Whig ministry in 1806, explaining all the motives and feelings that then actuated him. The letter appears to have been written in consequence of some [left unfinished].[1]

Dined at Lord Blessington's: company, the Speaker, Comte d'Orsay, and his aide-de-camp. The Speaker gave us an account of the new commission established for examining and publishing the documents in the State Paper Office: it appears that there is a regular history from the time of Henry VIII.

14th. [Sunday] Called upon Burgess, who still keeps me in suspense as to giving those papers. Said he thought he might venture to let me have the letter of the Prince, but must consult a gentleman with whom he was to dine to-day: a sad shuffler. When I told him that I had no longer any interest about the work further than my anxiety for its fame went, having got all I was to get for it long ago, and spent it, he said he should stipulate with the Longmans that his contributions of these three papers should be repaid, in some shape, to me. Begged him to do no such thing, at least for me, as I had no right to claim anything more from them. Called upon one of my poetesses, Miss——, and Miss R. Dined alone at the Club, and went to sup with Power.

15th. [Monday] Called upon Burgess. His friend has advised him not to give me more than one of the letters: this is a sad disappointment to me. Dined at Holland House: company, Adair, Whishaw, Mr. Warburton, Mr. Hackett, Lord Affleck, &c. &c. Story of Lord W—— saying in one of his speeches, "I ask myself so and so," and repeating the words, "I ask myself." "Yes," said Lord Ellenborough, "and a damned foolish answer you'll get." Frere's beautiful saying, that, "Next to an old friend, the best thing is an old enemy." In the evening Warburton pointed out to me a remark in a work just published upon "Political Economy," that one thing cannot be said to have value without relation to some other thing, no more than one object can be said to have distance without reference to some other. This is the great mistake Smith, Malthus, &c. &c. have made in endeavouring to find something of *fixed* value, whereas no such thing exists. Some have taken *corn* for the standard, some *labour*, and some (by a strange sort of abstraction) a mean between labour and corn. Rogers arrived after dinner. In talking of Rose's Ariosto mentioned an odd phrase he uses of a lady "voiding a saddle," *voto*. In going to bed, Lord H. took me into his room to show me some passages we had been talking of before dinner, relative to the knowledge which the ancients had of hawking. His own remarks upon a passage in the "Odyssey," where a simile is used about the suitors, which he thinks *does* describe hawking. All depends, however, upon whether the word νεφεα in those lines may be taken, in Homeric language, to mean nets. A passage in Aristotle plainly describes hawking.

16th. [Tuesday] Lady H. had ordered the carriage to bring me into town early, but I walked, and Rogers with me, a part of the way. Mentioned Sheridan saying, when there was some proposal to lay a tax upon mile-stones, that it was unconstitutional, as they were a race that could not meet to remonstrate. Went down to Shoe Lane, thence to Paternoster Row, and made some money arrangements. Thence to the C. H.: stayed an hour. At my lodgings found a letter from dear Bessy, enclosing one from Miss Furness; by which it appears that the latter has had an execution put upon her house, and is obliged to dismiss all her pupils. Bessy has dispatched Hannah to bring our sweet Anastasia to her. Had a letter from the son of Theobald Wolfe Tone, who is about to publish his father's diaries, &c., and wants my assistance.[1] Went to Rogers's: looked over the notes he has from Sheridan. Walked out with him to Holland House: company, Lord and Lady Wm. Russell, Misses Fox and Vernon, Comte de Faux Guyon. A good deal of talk in the evening with Allen: praised Adam Smith's style in his "Theory of Moral Sentiments;"[2] cost him great labour. Hume's, on the contrary, written off easily; great part of his history without any erasure. Went with Lord Holland to his dressing-room, where he read me some remarks of his upon an unpublished pamphlet of Sir Charles Grey, which is meant to prove that Lord Orford (of all people) was the author of Junius. Forgot to mention that last night Lord H. read to me from a manuscript of his own, in several *cahiers*, what I rather suspect to be memoirs of his own times. The part he read to me related to Drury Lane and Lord Byron. There was also mention in it of the latter's verses on the Princess Charlotte, and my parody on the Prince's letter.[3] "Another poet," he said, "Mr. Moore, with more of Irish humour than of worldly prudence," &c. This is too bad, Lord Holland himself having been the person who first put it into my head to write that parody! Read me some epigrams and translations of his own, and others. Among the latter, the following on an indefatigable translator, Philemon Holland, publishing a version of Suetonius,—

> "Philemon with translations so doth fill us,
> He won't let Suetonius be Tranquillus."

Did not leave his room till near two.

17th. [Wednesday] Brought in, after breakfast, by Lord H., who was going to a dentist. Conversation chiefly upon teeth; has suffered from them since he was two or three and twenty, and his present false teeth (three or four in front) the only ones he has felt comfortable with. Has had a tooth fall out while speaking in the House of Lords, which he described as the most dreadful sensation possible. Large mouths, he said, favourable to good teeth, and remarked that that was one of the reasons of my having such "a deuced good set of teeth." Promised to dine again with them to-morrow, but found a note to say that Bishop had fixed to meet me at Power's. Received a letter from Lord Essex, "renewing his solicitations" for me to come to Cashiobury. Dined at the Club. Some talk with Lord Nugent. Met Bailey, and went to the Lyceum with him: the opera of "Tarare."[1] Went behind the scenes, and was introduced to Miss Paton. The Burghershes in the next box to us; went in, and had a good deal of conversation.

18th. [Thursday] Did not get out till near Power's dinner hour. Bishop mentioned a thing Poole told him of his travelling with a Yankee from Paris to Dover, who did not open his mouth the whole time, till, on their leaving Dover, he said, "What an extraordinary coincidence! I declare yonder's a 'Prospect Place,' and there's a 'Prospect Place' also at Philadelphy." In the evening went over the whole of the new number of "National Melodies" with Bishop, who thinks them the best of any yet. Sung also my own two glees with him, "Ship, ahoy!" and "The Watchman,"[1] which he likes very much. Met L. in Bury Street. Wrote to Lord Essex, to say I should come this day week.

19th. [Friday] In walking, to my great surprise, met Lord Lansdowne; he and she arrived last night in consequence of the illness of Lady Charlotte Lemon. Walked with him home. Dined at Paternoster Row; took Baily with me. Company, Merivale, Christie, Power, &c. &c. Afterwrads to the C. H.

20th. [Saturday] Went out early. Called on the Princess de Polignac. Thence to Shoe Lane to make some arrangements with the printers. Dined alone at the Club. Went for an hour to the Cobourg Theatre: wretched stuff.

21st. [Sunday] Met Lord Lansdowne, and walked a little with him: mentioned the *Retrospective Review* as latterly very well done; and was anxious I should find out for him who were the authors of it. Spoke of an article in it on the Catholic Mass, in which I am mentioned, he said, "in the way I deserved to be." They quoted my lines "From the Irish Peasant to his Mistress," to show with what charms persecution may invest even the worst superstition. "They take you," he said, "for a Catholic;" I answered they had but too much right to do so.[1] We then talked of the last stretch of fanaticism in Charles X., in putting all France under the protection of the Virgin, *Voué au blanc;* shops and all France dressed in white! Dined at Holland House. My Lady not very well; summoned me to sit next her.

Whishaw, Adair, &c. Told ghost stories in the evening. The lady haunted by the large *hat* always near her; had been faithless to her lover. They seemed to like very much my story of the young man climbing up to the window to look at his father dying: Lord H. said it would do for a poem. In talking at dinner of the disadvantage of people being brought up to wealth and rank, Lady H. said, "that if she were a fairy, wishing to inflict the greatest mischief upon a child, she would make him abundantly rich, very handsome, with high rank, and have all these advantages to encircle him from the very cradle;" this she pronounced to be an infallible recipe for producing perfect misery; and "in the mean time," she added, "I should have the gratitude of the child's relations for the precious gifts I had endowed him with." This produced discussion and dissent. Lord H. said it depended upon the natural disposition of the person. There were some that would be happy in all situations: "There's Moore," he said, "you couldn't make him miserable even by inflicting a dukedom on him." Lord and Lady Cowper came in the evening. Asked me to come to Panshanger to them. When all the rest went to bed, Lord H. kept me, reading Dryden's "Aurungzebe" [*sic*][2] to me. Magnificent passages in it; "And with myself keep all the world awake," applicable to Napoleon.

22nd. [Monday] Off in the morning to town before eight, having been led into this excess by the derangement of my watch. Breakfasted at Hatchett's, in Piccadilly. Called at the Lansdownes', and found that they were to bring me back from Holland House in the evening. Off to Shoe Lane, after working a little at home. Thence to L. Dined at Holland House: the Lansdownes, Dr. Holland, Adair, Lord Valletort, Lord Gower, &c. The Lansdownes brought me home.

23rd. [Tuesday] Worked a little. Called, according to promise, on the Burghershes. Veluti there; afterwards Braham, Hawes, Mercer, &c. Got up some things of Lord B.'s operas very beautifully. Braham's singing at sight remarkable. Veluti's look and manner particularly interesting, but his singing still disagreeable to me. Went afterwards with Sir Andrew——[1] (one of those many old friends of mine whose name I don't know) and Lord Burghersh to the Academy of Music, where Bochsa made the pupils play for me a fantasia of Beethoven's, where a chorus is introduced after a long instrumental symphony; all admirably executed. An Irish girl, Miss Chancellor, at the pianoforte; a remarkably fine player. Thence to Shoe Lane, with copy. Lord Nugent had called in the morning to beg I would meet him at the Athenæum at half past six; did so. Some talk about a publication of Spanish songs, which he meditates. Thence to dinner at Lady Westmoreland's: company, Lord Gower, Marquis and Marquise Palmella, &c. &c.

She, in her strange way, talked of "Captain Rock," which Palmella said he had read at Lisbon, and thought it the most original book he had ever met with. Lady W. said, "that never was there any thing to equal it, either in talent or mischief; that it was also the most *heartless* book ever written; and though those who knew me well said I had a great deal of heart, she would judge from this work I had none." All this half addressed to Palmella, and half to me. Sung in the evening. Walked on Waterloo Bridge.

24th. [Wednesday] Lord Lansdowne called on me, and left word he was going away to morrow. Found him at the Travellers' Club, and walked a little with him. Quoted the French proverb, *Si la jeunesse savait, ou si la vieillesse pouvait.* Went to meet Lord Nugent at the Athenæum. Brought in his words to Spanish songs; *rather* pretty. Amused me a little to think of "Lord George," the young man about town (vide "Twopenny Postbag")[1] consulting me friendlily on the subject of his poetry. Dined alone at the Athenæum, and thence to the C. H. Walked in the town till late. Had a note to-day from Lord Essex (in which he bids me use Cashiobury "as my villa" during my printing business) desiring I would persuade Barnes to come down with me to-morrow.

25th.]Thursday] Started for Cashiobury in the coach at two; got there at four. Found them driving about; Lady Davy and Young of the party, and joined them. A most lovely and enjoyable place. Some talk with Lord Essex in the evening about Sheridan.

26th [Friday] Drove with Lord E. and Lady Davy to call on Lady Elizabeth Whitbread, who was on a visit in the neighbourhood. On our return sung to Lady Davy. She talked much of the Guiccioli [*sic*] whom she knew intimately at Rome. Saw a note in a book of hers which she had lent Lord Byron, in which he said that it was his strong wish to believe that she would continue to love him, but there were three things against it, "she was nineteen, come out of a convent, and a woman." Lord E. asked me to take a drive with him through the grounds, which I most readily accepted; full of beauty. Showed me one or two cottages, and said he had many others to tempt me with, if I would come and live in his neighbourhood. Told me of his having taken Sheridan to Drury Lane, the first and only time he ever set foot in the new theatre, and (according to Lord E.'s account) the last time he ever was out of his house before his death. The actors drank his health in the green-room most flatteringly. Told the anecdote of the Prince pitching the Abbé St. Phar (half-brother to the Duke of Orleans) into the water at Newmarket. The Abbé had some method of making the fish lie still by tickling (or some such manœuvre), and proceeded to exhibit his skill, having first made the Prince and all the rest give their honours that they would not push him into the water. He then bent down to the river or pond, when the P., not being able to resist the temptation, pitched him head over heels into the middle of it. The Abbé was so enraged, that when he got out, he ran after the Prince, and but that the company favoured the escape of the latter, would have treated him rather roughly. The Prince once having applied, in speaking of Sumner (now member for Surrey), a cant phrase he was much in the habit of using, some one told Sumner, who, meeting Jack Payne afterwards in the street, said to him, showing a large stick he had in his hand, "Tell your master he had better keep out of my way, as, if I meet him, I shall fell him to the earth." When Fox questioned the Prince about the loan from the Duke of Orleans, and the bonds which the Prince had given for the purpose, the Prince denied most solemnly having ever given any bonds; upon which Fox produced them to him out of his pocket, thus convicting him of a lie to his very face. Errington was the person supposed to have been present at the marriage of the Prince and Mrs. Fitzherbert. When Lord Essex returned once from France, the Prince said to him, "I am told, but cannot believe it, that when at Paris you wear strings to your shoes." "It is very true, sir, and so do the Duke of Orleans &c., and so will your Royal Highness before six months are over." "No, no, I'll be damned if ever I do such an effeminate thing as that." Story of the P. Attempted once to shoot himself on account of Mrs. Fitzherbert; only fired at the top of the bed, and then punctured himself with a sword in the breast. Lord E. thinks the Queen of France was innocent; so thought Lord Whitworth. If she erred with any one, it was Fersen a Swede, he who assisted in her escape.

27th. [Saturday] Started at eight for town. Dined with Barnes (of the "Times"). A large party: Serjeant Rough and his two daughters, M. Comte (conductor of the "Minerve") and his wife, a daughter of Say, &c. &c.; rather agreeable. Talked of a variety of topics,—Burke, Dryden, Lord Thurlow. Dryden always gives you the idea of being capable of much more than he did. B. quoted a passage of Cicero, where, discussing different methods as more or less musical, of constructing a particular sentence, he decides for concluding it with the word *comprobavit*. Where is this?

28th. [Sunday] Dined at Holland House. Forgot, in going out there, to change my long morning coat for an evening one, and had to dine in the former costume, which was not a little disagreeable: company, Rogers and his sister, Rose, Stratford Canning, Palmella, Byng, Fazakerly, &c. Fazakerly mentioned that he had the other day met Lainé, the former Minister of the Interior in Paris, who told him that he had had a project of getting Captain Rock translated, and adding as an appendix to it, the late reports of the committee on Ireland, but he feared that the attacks on the principle of tithes would render the book obnoxious to the priests, and gave it up.

29th. [Monday] Walked into town in all the rain early; worked a little; went off to Shoe Lane and to Longmans' to get some money to send Bessy, who means to leave Cheltenham on Friday. Called at the C. H. Returned to Holland House to dinner: Lord Gower and Lady Stanhope of the party. Lord H. gave a good description of a Spanish bull-fight. The caciatero is a little fellow who comes and gives the bull the *coup de grace,* after the matador has conquered him; and in Spain, when they hear of an additional physician being called in to some one that is very ill, they call him the caciatero (?). The splendid thing for the matador is in making the homage of his victory to some fine lady present, to draw his bloody sword over the expensive dress he wears, so as to render it unfit for further use. Lady Stanhope asked me to dinner tomorrow, but engaged.

30th. [Tuesday] Started before breakfast. Rogers spied me from his window and joined me as far as the end of Kensington Gardens. Breakfasted at the Athenæum, and home to work. Dined at the Charter House; young Murray came in the evening.

31st. [Wednesday] Fixed to dine with Lord Strangford at the Athenæum, in consequence of a note he wrote me yesterday, saying, "Surely as none of your d——d Whig dukes are in town, you could contrive, once in a way, to *tête-à-tête* it with me at the Athenæum." Went to the printer with my proofs. Dinner with Lord S. at seven; a good deal of old fun between us. Told me of Canning's anger at him for not voting for the last Catholic Bill. Mentioned that on some one saying to Peel, about Lawrence's picture of Croker, "You can see the very quiver of his lips;" "Yes," said Peel, "and the arrow coming out of it." Croker himself was telling this to one of his countrymen, who answered, "He meant *Arrah,* coming out of it." Sat together till near ten.

Sept. 1st. [Thursday] Dined at Holland House: company, the Wm. Russells, Lady Davy, &c.; Lord H. not at all in good spirits. I mentioned after dinner Barnes's opinion of Lord Liverpool, as one of the cleverest men in the House of Lords, which brought on discussion. Lord H. mentioned as curious that political affairs had always prospered best under men who had changed their party: Godolphin, Lord Oxford, Mr. Pitt. I mentioned Mr. Fox, too, as an instance, which he tried not to admit; the short share that Mr. Fox took, when young, in Lord North's politics, not being on subjects that much committed his Whiggism. Sharpe mentioned to me the story of Sheridan and the milestones, and another. Sharpe was complaining of an ugly house built by D'Arblay just near them at Leatherhead, and Sheridan said, "Oh, you know we can easily get rid of that, we can pack it off out of the country under the Alien Act." Lady Holland very anxious for me to give her copies of the "Watchman" and "Ship ahoy!" to take to Paris to Lady Granville, but shall not. Lady Davy brought me home.

2nd. [Friday] Got out about three. Called upon Miss Furness, who wants her money, and though it is rather hard upon me (as Anastasia has not had much more than three months out of the half year) must, I suppose, pay her the whole sum, as she seems much distressed. Several letters from poets to answer; one, a Portuguese, who sends me a work of his from Havre, about Camoens, with a fine letter calling me the *ami* and *emule* of Byron. Bessy inclosed me a letter from a Bath schoolmistress, proposing to take Anastasia, and saying that "terms would be a very minor consideration indeed, with the daughter of such a man as Moore."

3rd. [Saturday] Strangford called and sat some time: read me part of a letter from Lady Strangford on his telling her of the day that he and I passed together; "Shall henceforth," she says, "love Moore as much as I have always admired him for having given you one day of happiness." Showed me the extracts he talked of the other night from a MS. book of George Villiers, Duke of Buckingham, which the old Lady Jersey had in her possession, and lent him many years ago at Cheltenham. Some very remarkable things in it, which I wrote down when he left me as well as I could recollect them.¹ Met Warrender while I was out, who invited me down to his place. Went and paid Miss Furness twenty pounds of her money. The printers have sent me nothing to-day, it being some annual festival with them. Went to Holland House: company, Rogers, Abercrombie, &c. The dinner very amusing from a contest maintained with great spirit and oddity by Lady Holland against Lord H. and Allen (the latter most comically personal and savage) on the subject of Gen. Washington, whom she, with her usual horror of the liberal side of things, depreciates and dislikes. The talent and good humour with which she fought us all highly amusing. In talking of the Game Laws, Rogers said, "If a partridge, on arriving in this country, were to ask what are the Game Laws? and somebody would tell him they are laws *for the protection* of game, 'What an excellent country to live in,' the partridge would say 'where there are so many laws for our protection.'"

4th. [Sunday] Lord H. told at breakfast of the old Lady Albemarle (I think) saying to some one, "You have heard that I have abused you, but it is not true, for I would not take the trouble of talking about you; but if I *had* said anything of you, it would have been that you look like a blackguard of week days, and on Sundays like an apothecary." Lord H. full of an epigram he had just written on Southey, which we all twisted and turned into various shapes, he as happy as a boy during the operation. It was thus at last:—

> "Omnibus hoc vitium est cantoribus."

> "Our Laureat Bob defrauds the king.
>   He takes his cash and does not sing:
>   Yet on he goes, I know not why,
>   Singing for us who do not buy."[1]

Walked to Brompton alone. Went to indulge myself with the sight of the house I lived in (in Queen's Elms) the first year I was married. Thence to Mrs. Montgomery's; to town, and back to Holland House to dinner: company, Adam and his two sons, Lord Gower, Adair, Lady Stanhope, &c. Lady S. said she had had a design upon me for the play last night, but that Strangford told her I was gone to Holland House. In the evening, to my great surprise and pleasure, Mrs. Leigh appeared. Could not help looking at her with deep interest; though she can hardly be said to be like Byron, yet she reminds one of him. Was still more pleased, when, evidently at her own request, Lady Stanhope introduced me to her: found her pleasing, though (as I had always heard) nothing above the ordinary run of women. She herself began first to talk of him, after some time, by asking me "whether I saw any likeness." I answered, I did; and she said it was with strong fears of being answered "No," that she had asked the question. Talked of different pictures of him. I felt it difficult to keep the tears out of my eyes as I spoke with her. Said she would show me the miniature she thought the best, if I would call upon her. Brought home by Lady Affleck. From this on't too busy to keep my diary regularly.

6th. [Tuesday] Dined alone at the Athenæum.

7th. [Wednesday] Went to Peel's Coffee-house and looked over the file of the "Morning Post" for 1816, in order to find D. O'Brien's article about

Sheridan.¹ Dined at Miss White's: party, Lady Charlotte Bury, Lady Davy, &c. Sung in the evening.

8th. [Thursday] Dined at Mrs. Montgomery's. An old acquaintance of mine (Miss Gore) of the party; likewise the two Montgomerys, Murray, and Lucy. Miss Gore mentioned a Frenchman saying to a party who were speaking English, *Pour l'amour de Dieu, parlez* Chrétien, meaning French. Saw Luttrel this morning. Walked about with him, but he was obliged to go home, not being well. Stayed with him a little while.

9th. [Friday] Went to Lady Maria Gore's in the evening; Mrs. Beauclerc and her daughters.

10th to 12th. [Saturday–Monday] Was to have gone down to Sir George Warrender's, but wrote to him on Friday to say I could not. Promised too to go from thence to Lady Stanhope at Lord Carrington's, but this, of course, frustrated too. Thought, however, I might be able to manage (as being nearer town) a trip to Farquhar's on the 12th, to Roehampton, but this likewise I was obliged to decline. Due also at Panshanger and at Lord Nugent's, but the printer's devils say "No." Dined with Rogers at his brother's at Highbury.

13th. [Tuesday] Returned home, after walking a little, at five, and worked away at copying out till past seven, when I walked down to Shoe Lane with what I had done, and returned to the Club, where I dined alone at about nine. Dr. Bain's card to-day informs me he is in town; must have some talk with him about Sheridan's last illness, which is the part I am just now correcting for the press: must keep back the sheet till I see him.

14th. [Wednesday] A note from Burgess asked me to meet Dr. Bain at dinner with him at five to-morrow. Am engaged to the Knight of Kerry, but as he will not dine till near eight, shall contrive to manage both.

15th. [Thursday] Wrote to Luttrel to Panshanger to make my apology to the Cowpers, having promised to go down there on Saturday, but find I cannot. Let off my dinner with the Knight of Kerry to-day, on account of the death of some friend of his. Felt so low (both from exhaustion of stomach and some melancholy thoughts suggested by my task) that I could not help crying a little. Went with L. and the Montgomerys to the painter's, where she is sitting for her picture: from thence to see the picture of Waterloo in the Park. They left me at Burgess's door, and Burgess having pressed Montgomery to stay for dinner, he did. A good deal of talk about Sheridan, but not many new lights on the subject. Went in the evening to Mrs. Montgomery's.

16th. [Friday] Did not get out till near four: met Abbot of Dublin: walked with me to Wardour Street, where I wanted to ascertain the name of Sheridan's pawnbroker: kept waiting a good while before I saw Mr. Harrison. Then home to dress, for an early dinner at Mrs. Montgomery's.

17th. [Saturday] Called at Power's on my way to Shoe Lane, and felt such a sinking in my stomach, that I stopped to dine with him.

18th. [Sunday] Called at Mrs. Purvis's: found she was in town, and left word I would dine with her. No one there but the Speaker, who told some amusing anecdotes about himself when a boy. His stopping to dine at Hatchett's on his way, alone, to school; begging of the waiter to dine with him, and offering to send out for a pineapple to bribe him to do so. Talked of fagging: the horror he has had ever since of the boy to whom he was fag: once bought a horse which he liked very much till he knew that it had last belonged to this man, and then took a dislike to it. Mrs. P. mentioned that, in the same way, there has been a deadly feud between Lord Blessington and his fagger all through life; lawsuits, &c. &c. The Speaker told also of the Duke of York's stupidity in reporting Bobus's joke about Vansittart and Hume, "penny wise and pound foolish;" "It was so good, you know," said the Duke, "calling Hume 'pound foolish,' and Van 'penny wise!'" Mentioned Canning's having met Lord Stowell one day on the road with a *turtle* beside him in the carriage which he was taking down to his country-house; Canning, a day or two after, said to him, "Wasn't that your *son* that was with you the other day?" I told in return a story of Jekyl's. Sir Ralph Payne begged of Jekyl to take him to see Philip Thicknesse's library, &c., which J., after cautioning him against saying anything to offend Thicknesse's *touchiness*, consented to do. Sir Ralph behaved very well, till, just as they were leaving the house, he saw on the library door the original sketch of the print that is prefixed to Thicknesse's Travels,[1] in which Thicknesse is represented in an odd sort of a travelling carriage, and his monkey with him. Sir Ralph having asked what it was, Thicknesse said it was a representation of the way in which he had travelled on the Continent. "Poor Master Thicknesse," exclaimed Sir R., "he must have been greatly fatigued with

the journey." This Sir Ralph, by the by, who was afterwards Lord Lavington, and governor of the Windward Islands, was the person of whom Jekyl
told that anecdote about consulting the Chief Justice, &c; "the guns will
be fired, the bells will be rung, the guards will all turn out," &c. &c. Called
on Bessy's mother this morning. Received from Burgess *one* of the letters I
was so anxious to get from him (that written by Sheridan to the Prince in
1812, about the exclusion of Lord Grey), which Dr. Bain, I find, persuaded
him to let me have: must see to-morrow how I can get it in.

19th. [Monday] Went pretty early to Shoe Lane, to see about getting Sheridan's letter in. Found the sheet was not printed off, and inserted part of it.[1]
Dined with Rogers at the Athenæum; the first time he ever dined at a club.
Went together in the evening to the English Opera, but could get no seats.
From thence to the Coburg, where we saw a strange thing: "The Last Days
of Napoleon:[2] where Bertrand and his wife were quietly listened to abusing
the perfidy and cruelty of the English towards Napoleon, who was represented throughout in the most amiable light. Left the Coburg soon, and
walked home by Waterloo Bridge; a beautiful moonlight night.

20th. [Tuesday] Left the last pages of my work at the printer's. Dined at
Longmans': company, Abbot, &c. Thence to Miss White's to meet Capt.
Lyon and his newly married wife. Sung a good deal, which they seemed to
like very much.

21st. [Wednesday] Was to have gone with Strangford to Sir George Warrender's to-day, but cannot spare the loss of to-morrow morning. He took
Lord Binning with him instead. Went with Abbot, Harry Harris, and
Beazeley to dine at Mathews's: company, Mrs. Purvis and her daughter, the
Speaker, a Mrs. Broderip, Price the American manager, &c. The day very
amusing. Mathews's imitation of Coleridge admirable; the "single-
moindedness," &c. &c. Sung a good deal. Mathews's Dramatic Gallery very
curious; his "Life of Garrick," illustrated, particularly so.[1] Has the first
playbill in which Garrick was announced to act, between the acts of a
concert, at Goodman's Fields. The French copy of the engravings of Sir J.
Reynolds's picture of Garrick between Tragedy and Comedy, is entitled
L'Homme entre le Vice et la Vertu.

22nd. [Thursday] Took my preface (which I wrote yesterday) to the
printer. Dined (I believe) at the Club.

23rd. [Friday] Felt myself free enough to sally out in the morning, and breakfasted at the Athenæum. Called on the Jerseys: found there Lord Bristol and Agar Ellis: Lord Jersey's face still wrapped up from the late abscess under his ear. Dined at the Speaker's, which *sounds* a greater honour than it *is:* company much the same as at Mathews's, and the day quite as amusing, with the addition of an admirable *cuisine* and cellar. Speaker very civil; had his levée-rooms and state dining-rooms lighted up in the evening, in order that I might see them. I mentioned having heard Lord Sidmouth say that the only time his gravity was ever tried in the Chair was once when Brook Watson getting up (on some subject connected with Nootka Sound) said, "Mr. Speaker, it is impossible, at this moment, to look at the north-east, without at the same time casting a glance to the south-west." The Speaker stood this pretty well; but hearing some one behind the Chair say, "By God, no one in the House but Wilkes could do that," he no longer could keep his countenance, but burst out into a most undignified laugh. My host, on this, mentioned an occasion, on which he too had not been able to refrain from laughter. The Opposition (as he described it) had been, to his no small amusement, squabbling with one another, and firing into their own ranks, when presently he perceived a large rat issue from under the Opposition benches and walk gravely over to the Treasury side of the House. This, he said, he could not resist. Felt my story to be rather awkward before I was half through it, as the Speaker squints a little. Had music and mummery all the evening, and did not leave this dignified mansion till just two.

24th. [Saturday] Was to have gone with Abbot to Hampton Court to-day, but made my excuse, as I wished to see the "Freischütz." Dined with Rees, and both went to Drury Lane.

25th. [Sunday] Went to Paternoster Row, for the purpose of packing up the Sheridan papers for Charles S. and the other persons who had entrusted them to me. Met Luttrel on my way, who asked me to dine with him at seven; did so. Mentioned to me a good rhyme of his:—

> "Of diamond, emerald, and topaz,
>   Such as the charming Mrs. Hope has."

Finished a bottle of côte rotie, of Champagne, and of claret with Luttrel, and went from thence to Power's to correct some music.

26th. [Monday] Corrected my last revises. Took a place in the coach for to-morrow morning, and transacted various little jobs. Dined at the Club. Came home and packed.

27th. [Tuesday] Started in the Emerald, and arrived at home at seven.

28th. [Wednesday] Dined at home.

29th. [Thursday] Dined at Bowood. The Agar Ellises, Fielding, and Talbot, Mrs. Collingwood, &c. Sung in the evening. Slept there.

30th. [Friday] Walked home after breakfast, to see Bessy, the boil coming to a head. Returned to Bowood to dinner; the Fazakerleys and Barings in addition to the party. Sung again in the evening. Slept there.

Oct. 1st. [Saturday] Bowles called at Bowood, while I was listening to Mrs. Fazakerley's singing to the guitar. Went down to him; wanted me to dine with him to-day, but told him that Bessy's illness made it impossible for me to stay longer away from her. After luncheon, Lady Lansdowne brought me home in the carriage with Lady G. Ellis and Mrs. Baring. Found Bessy better, and anxious that I should go to Bowles, on account of a nephew of his, who, he said, was to be with him, and could serve our little Tom at Winchester. Packed up fresh things, and set off to catch Lady L. on her return from Bromham. Met her at the corner of Sandy Lane, and went on to Bowood. Walked from thence to Bowles's: company, Mr. and Mrs. Fenwick, Young West, Linley, and a Miss Sotheby, but no nephew! Had a great many glees, duets, &c. in the evening; my singing much liked.

2nd. [Sunday] Looking over the sheets of Bowles's "More last Words" to Roscoe.[1] Having tried in vain to dissuade him from publishing it at all, did my best to get rid of some of the twaddle. Set off to walk home between eleven and twelve: called at Bowood in passing, and saw Lady E. Fielding, who arrived yesterday. Dined at home.

3rd. [Monday] Dined at Bowood: Fazakerleys, Fieldings, Bowleses, and Sir J. and Lady Campbell.

6th. [Thursday] The newspapers ("Times and Courier") at the breakfast table, full of extracts from the "Life." Fidgeted exceedingly by seeing people reading them, at which they were not a little amused. Entreated Lord Landsdowne to wait till he could read the book itself, which he promised me to do. Returned home. Dined at Money's to meet Linley, the Bowleses, and Campbells.

7th. [Friday] Did a song for Power to an air of Crescimbeni's, beginning "Fear not, that while around thee."[1] Received a letter from Charles Sheridan full of the warmest admiration and gratitude; a most seasonable relief to my mind, as I have been even more anxious about his opinion than that of the public.

8th. [Saturday] A triumphant letter from Longmans', congratulating me on the perfect success of the work, saying that, from the state of the sale, they must go to press with an octavo edition on Monday, and desiring me to send up the corrected copy by to-morrow night's mail. They also add that, from the extent to which I had carried the work, and its success, they felt called upon to place to my credit £300 more than the sum originally stipulated to be paid for it. A letter likewise from Lord John, in which he says he has read some of my book, and the extracts in the "Times," and thinks it "very much what it ought to be." Have made up my mind to take a run to Paris, Lord John having offered to take me there, and Lord Lansdowne having invited me to take up my quarters with him, while there. Looked over the Life, having time only for verbal corrections.

9th. [Sunday] Went to church with Bessy and Mrs. Branigan, who arrived here on Thursday. Sent off the corrected copy in the evening.

10th. [Monday] Walked over to Lord Lansdowne, who was much delighted with Longmans' and C. Sheridan's letters, which I had sent him. The Longmans had mentioned in theirs, that Henry Grattan had been with them, and seemed much disposed to put his materials for the Life of his father into my hands, but they said I must not do it till after the Life of Lord Byron. Lord Lansdowne much amused by the custom for Lives I was likely to have. I said I had better publish *nine* together in one volume, and call it "The Cat." Walked the greater part of the way home with me.

11th. [Tuesday] A letter from Lord John, saying he had read but little of my book when he wrote before, but that now he had got through two-thirds of it; and "I confess," he says, "I am all astonishment at the extent of your knowledge, the soundness of your political views, and the skill with which you contrive to keep clear of tiresomeness, when the subject seems to invite it." "Your wit and fancy," he adds, "we all knew before; and the latter is, as usual, perhaps a little in excess, but it is always so beautiful that we could not wish it to be other than it is." He says in a postscript, "I dined at Wimbledon yesterday, and all the Spensers sung chorus in praise of your book." This last circumstance gives me a good deal of pleasure, as I feared Lord Spenser would rather resent my remarks on him and the other Whig alarmists. Lord John had changed his mind about Paris, and will not go till Spring. Sent his letter to Lord L, and said that his change of mind would make no difference to my intentions.

12th. [Wednesday] A note from Lord Lansdowne, who starts with Lady L. on his way to Paris to-day.

13th. [Thursday] Receive every morning letters about the Life; one full of praise from Elwyn, another from Scott (of Devizes), and second from Lord John, relative to the remarks upon the funeral, which I foresaw would produce uneasiness in many quarters. Tells me the Duke had lent Sheridan £200 before his illness, and attended the funeral by Mrs. S.'s invitation; says this was probably the case with many.

14th. [Friday] Set off for Bath to dine at the mayor's great dinner; Mrs. Branigan and Mrs. Phipps went with me. Went with Elwyn to the dinner, and got well seated: 270 persons at the dinner, Lord Camden, Lord John Thynne, &c. &c. When my health was given from the Chair, I saw a speech was expected from me, and I had thought of some things to say, but as none of the great guns had gone beyond a simple return of thanks, I was resolved that neither would I; so merely said, that "after the brief manner the distinguished persons whose healths were already drunk had returned their thanks, it would ill become so humble an individual as myself to trespass further on their time and attention than merely to say that I felt very deeply," &c. &c. This was the best thing to do, but I saw it disappointed them. Left at ten, and went home with Elwyn. He mentioned a good Italian squib on the Neapolitan revolution, as follows,—

LETTER FROM A CORPORAL IN THE PATRIOTIC NEAPOLITAN ARMY,
AFTER ITS DEFEAT AND DISPERSION.
Pulcinello, mal contento
Disertor dal Regimento,

> Scrive a Mama a Benevento,
> Della Patria il triste evento.
> Movimento, Parlamento,
> Giuramento, Squarciamento,
> Gran Fermento, poco Argento,
> Armamento, e nel eimento,
> (Mene pento, mene pento)
> Fra spavento e tradimento
> Siam fuggiti come il vento
> Mama mia, Mama bella
> Prega Deo per Pulcinella.

Slept at Elwyn's.

15th. [Saturday] Bowles brought me back as far as Buckhill, where I eat a couple of cutlets, and walked home afterwards.

16th. [Sunday] A letter from the Longmans to say that they have sold every copy of the first 1,000, and that the octavo will not be ready for two or three weeks. Take for granted, therefore, that there is a second quarto edition. Much inclined to give up my Paris trip for various reasons; the expense, Bessy's health, the idleness, and one or two more things.

17th. [Monday] Bessy would not hear of my staying home: insisted that if I did not go to France, that I must go either to Scotland or Ireland, to amuse myself a little. Dear, generous girl, there never was anything like her for warm-heartedness and devotion. I shall certainly do no good at home, from the daily fidget I am kept in about my book. So perhaps an excursion somewhere, merely to change the current of my thoughts, would be of use.

18th. [Tuesday] Mean to set off to town on Thursday (as I had promised Power to meet Bishop there on musical business), and then afterwards, perhaps, to Derbyshire and Scotland!

19th. [Wednesday] More letters about the book. One from Barnes (of the *Times*) full of the most enthusiastic praise.

[*Transcription from Russell's edition ends with the entry for 19 October.*]

Thursday 20th. of October, 1825—Had a Chaise to Buckhill at seven in the morning—Bessy & Mrs. Branigan with me—The two first coaches full—got a seat in the Regulator—read my old French newpapers all the way—the following in them—"Since that time, as Scarron says *La Parque a diablement filé*"—Louis 14th said to Moliere on his producing the Bourgeois Gentilhomme "Je n'ai demandé qu'un Ballet et vous m'avez donné une bonne Comedie."—Got to Power's at nine—found that they had a friend staying with them, so would not sleep there, as I had promised, (tho they had every thing ready for me) but took up my quarters in Duke St.

21 [Friday]—Called on Lady Donegall—found her only at home—Talked of the Life—has not had it herself, but mentioned different opinions she had heard—& all praise. Told me an anecdote of the Prince when a very young man having gone disguised to Lord Donegall's house to leave £1000 for Lord Spencer Hamilton who was in fear of arrest for debt—said he had lately too sent £1000 to Edward Bouverie, when he was dying—called at Lord John's—he is at Woburn—Carpenter told me that he had heard nothing but praise of my book—but that he was told the Whigs were in a rage at it.—Wrote to Lord Lansdowne to Paris to tell him I had changed my mind, & could not come there—have almost resolved to go to Scotland to see Sr. Walter Scott. Dined at Power's—party Rees, Bishop, Millikin of Dublin—Rees all delight at the success of the Book—could have sold another edition of Quarto, if he had had them ready—Not a copy to be got for these several days past & the octavo will not be ready for a week—is negotiating with Charles Sheridan to buy him out of his stipulated share of the work—Latham this morning made me a present of a German Translation of Captain Rock.

22 [Saturday]—Went at eleven with Power to Bishop, in order to look over with him a couple of glees & a single song I have done—One of the glees Convivial having "Hip, hip, hurra" for the burden[1]—Bishop thought the melody too elegant for the purpose—so shall put other words to it—Called upon Donegalls—Dined at the Longmans—nearly the whole of the Second Edition is already disposed of & they are laying in the paper for a Third.—Decided to go to Scotland—despatched a messenger to have my place taken in the York Mail for Monday night.—Went to the Adelphi with Rees & Millikin.

23. [Sunday]—Tegart called & staid some time—praising my book—went out—called upon Denman—asked me had I heard of Lady Holland's triumph. There are some chambers of the Tuilleries which are never shown to strangers—accordingly Lady H. has long set her heart on seeing

them. During Louis 18th time, she was always told, in answer to her applications, that such a thing was "non nominandum"—now, however, it appears, on her returning to the charge, the answer has been that there was no door or gate of the Thuilleries that was not open to Lady Holland—Bought a copy of a low Sunday Paper, in which I had the pleasure of finding myself abused in all the flowers of Billingsgate—this "vile little fellow" this "filthy little fellow" &c. &c. {I should like to compare shirts with the fellow who wrote it.—} Called at the Knight of Kerry's—saw Mrs. Fitzgerald—Dined at Lady Donegall's, {with} only the Knight of Kerry—a very agreeable evening—Fitzgerald told some curious anecdotes of Grattan—called this morning at Mrs. Purvis's & sat some time with her and the Speaker.

24 [Monday]—Went to Power's—signed a renewed Deed between us, the other having expired this last year—went to Bishop's to look over the things that have been done for the Greek Work—After our singing together his glee "To Greece we give our shining blades," he turned exultingly to Power & said "That's worth one thousand pounds."—Presently we tried over my glee, "Here, while the moonlight dim,"[1] and he said "that's worth five hundred." Called upon Lady Donegall—walked with Barbara & Miss Godfrey—packed up & took my luggage to the Longmans, who sent it off immediately to the Mail Office—dined with them—nothing could exceed their attention—gave me letters of credit on York & Edinburgh—Green saw me to the mail—Kenny at dinner mentioned that Washington Irving, he thinks, is becoming independent of literature by the profits he derives from the Rouen steam-boat, in which he is a partner with his brother—started in the mail at eight. Two lively & (as far as the darkness would allow me to judge) good-looking girls my companions, who had just returned from a trip of four days to Calais with Pa (who was outside) and two or three more friends—as full of France as if they had been there for years—a good deal of laugh & talk, till all grew sleepy & at three in the morning we parted company.

25 [Tuesday]—Arrived at Stamford, where I breakfasted, between six & seven—got to York between eight & nine at night.

26 [Wednesday]—As soon as I was breakfasted &c called with my letter of introduction from the Longmans on Mr. Wilson, who attended me & an unknown acquaintance of mine that I picked up in the mail to the Mins-

ter.—Much as I had heard of this glorious piece of architecture, it went beyond my expectations—among the curiosities—the bowl given by Arch-bishop Scroope, with an inscription round it purporting that every one who drank out of it should have forty days' indulgence.—went to see the new Concert Room—walked on the walls—had also gone to the top of the Minster, which was no small trial to our legs. Before I started from town, I wrote a letter to Sidney Smith (as I did also to Sir Walter Scott) saying I should call on him in my way—on my arrival at Yorke last night, found he was at Mr. Yorke's (formerly Mr. Sheepsenks, who changed his name on marrying Lord Harewood's sister) & immediately despatched a letter to him by the Post, saying how I regretted he was not at home—fixed to dine with old Mr. Wilson at Fulford, two miles from York—on returning home found a letter from Sidney Smith, saying that Mr. & Lady Mary Yorke were most anxious I should come out there—But, though I should not mind any distance out of my way, to see him in his own house, it was not worth the time & expense to see him in another person's, so wrote an apology— Colonel Thornhill (of the 7th Hussars) who commands at York was the bearer of the note to me. Among the company at Fulford was Mrs. John Kemble. She mentioned an anecdote of Piozzi, who on calling once upon some old Lady of Quality was told by the servant "she was indifferent"—"Is she, indeed?" answered Piozzi huffishly—"then pray, tell her I can be as indifferent as she" & walked away—The day deplorably common-place— Found a letter from Col. Thornhill on my return home, begging me to make use of his horses, carriages &c. for my "locomotive adventures" dur-ing my stay at York.—Wrote him a letter of thanks—am not aware that I know Colonel Thornhill.

27 [Thursday]—Started in the Coach for Newcastle at a ¼ before nine—a young man in the Coach, who was an intimate of Lockhart's, (Scott's son-in-law) & told me a good deal about them—got a wretched bed at Newcastle— took my place in the Wellington for Kelso—

28 [Friday]—Up before five & started for Kelso—another young man in the Coach, who knew the Scotts—mentioned the application made in one of the Scotch Colleges of the motto of the City of Edinburgh, "Nisi Dominus, frustra"—"unless you are a Lord, you cannot get on here"— Arrived at Kelso at ¼ to five—The passengers, who had found me out, full of kindness at parting with me—Walked before I dined to the bridge, past the ruins of Kelso Abbey, and on, by the side of the Tweed to another

bridge opposite Sir John Douglas's gate—The evening delicious—slept at Kelso—an excellent inn.

29.[1] [Saturday] Set off between eleven & twelve in a chaise for Sir Walter Scott's—stopped on the way to see Dryburg Abbey on the grounds of Lord Buchan—the vault of Sir W. Scott's family is here—Lord Buchan's own tombstone ready placed, with a Latin inscription by himself on it, & a cast from his face let into the stone—Forded the Tweed below the chain-bridge, and passed through Melrose, having a peep at the Abbey on my way, but reserving my view of it till I could see it with Scott himself. Arrived at his house about two. His reception of me most hearty—we had met but once before so long ago as immediately after his publication of the Lay of the Last Minstrel[2]—after presenting me to Lady Scott & his daughter Anne (the Lockharts having, unluckily, just gone to Edinburgh)—he & I started for a walk—said how much he was delighted with Ireland—the fun of the common people—the postillion having run the pole against the corner of a wall, & broken it down, crying out "Well done, pole!—didn't the pole do it elegantly, your Honour?"—Pointing to the opposite bank of the river, said that it was believed still by some of the common people that the fairies danced in that spot; and as a proof it, mentioned a fellow having declared before him, in his judicial capacity, that having gone to pen his sheep about sun-rise in a field two or three miles farther down the river, he had seen little men & women under a hedge, beautifully dressed in green & gold— "the Duke of Buccleugh in full dress was nothing to them". "Did you by the virtue of your oath, believe them to be fairies?" "I dinna ken—they looked very like the gude people" (evidently believing them to be fairies)—The fact was, however, that the figures were puppets, belonging to an itinerant showman, which some weavers, in a drunken frolic, had taken a fancy to & robbed him of—but, fearing the consequences, when sober, had thrown them under a hedge where this fellow saw them—In talking of the commonness of poetical talent just now, he said we were like Captain Bobadil, who had taught the fellows to {beat us with our own weapons}[3]—When I remarked that every magazine now contained such poetry as would have made a reputation for a man some 20 or 30 years ago, he said (with much shrewd humour in his face) "Ecod, we were in the luck of it, to come before all this talent was at work".—agreed with me that it would be some time before a great literary reputation could be again called up—"unless (he added) something new could be struck out,—every thing that had succeeded lately owing its success, in a great degree, to its novelty."—Talked a good deal about Byron—thinks his last Cantos of Don Juan the most powerful things he ever wrote.—Talking of the report of Lady Byron being about to marry Cunningham, said he would not believe it—"no—no—she must never let another man bear the name of husband to her. {Being even a W—— would be better, perhaps, than that!"} In talking of my sacrifice of the Memoirs, said he was well aware of the honourable feelings that dictated it, but doubted whether he would himself have consented to it. On my representing, however, the strong circumstances of not only the sister of Lord Byron (whom he so much loved) requiring it but his two most intimate friends, Kinnaird & Hobhouse, also insisting earnestly upon the total destruction of the MS. & the latter assuring me that Lord Byron had expressed to him regret for having put such a work out of his own power & had said that he was only restrained by delicacy towards me from recalling it—when I mentioned these circumstances (and particularly the last) he seemed to feel I could not have done otherwise than I had done. Thought the family, however, bound to furnish me every assistance towards a Life of Lord B.—I spoke of the advantages of Scotland over Ireland in her national recollections, in which he agreed & remarked the good luck of Scotland in, at last, giving a King to England—In the spirit of this superiority he had himself insisted, in all the ceremonials attending the King's reception in Scotland, that England should yield the precedence—there had been some little tiffs about it, but the King himself had agreed readily to every thing proposed to him—In talking of Ireland said that he & Lockhart had gone there, rather hostilely disposed to the Catholic Emancipation, but that they had both returned converts to the necessity of conceding it—Dined at ½ past five—none but himself—a young clergyman, quite deaf, who is making a catalogue of his Library, Lady Scott & daughter, & a boy, the son of his lost friend, Sir —— Erskine. After dinner pledged him in some whiskey out of a *Quaigh*—that which I drank out of very curious & beautiful—produced several others—one that belonged to Prince Charles with a glass bottom—others of a larger size out of which he said his great grandfather drank—Very interesting tete-a-tete with him after dinner—said that the person who first set him upon trying his talent at poetry was Mat Lewis—he had passed the early part of his life with a set of clever, rattling, drinking fellows, whose thoughts & talents lay wholly out of the region of poetry—he therefore, had never been led to find out his turn for it, though always fond of the old Ballads. In the course of this conversation he, at last, (to my no small surprize & pleasure) mentioned the Novels without the least reserve as his own—"I then hit upon these Novels (he said) which have been a mine of wealth to me". Had begun Waverley long before, & then thrown it by—till, having occasion for some money (to help his brother, I think) he bethought himself of it, but could not find the MS.—nor was it till he came to Abbotsford that he at last stumbled upon it. By this he made 3000 pounds. The conjectures & mystification, at first amused him very much—wonders, himself, that the secret was so well kept, as about 20 persons knew it from the first—The story of Jeannie Deans founded upon an anonymous letter which he received—has never known from whom— the circumstance of the girl having refused the testimony in Court, & then taken the journey to obtain her sister's pardon is a fact[4]—Received some hints also from Lady Louisa Stuart (grand-daughter, I believe, to Lord Bute)—These, the only aids {with which he can remember} afforded to him.—his only critic was the Printer, who was in the secret, & who now & then started objections which he generally attended to—Had always been in the habit, (while wandering alone or shooting) of forming stories & following a train of adventures in his mind, and these fancies it was that formed the ground-works of most of his Novels. "I find I fail in them now, however—(he said)—I cannot make them as good as at first".—he is now near 57—Has no knowledge or feeling of music—knows nothing of Greek—indebted to Pope for even his knowledge of Homer—spoke of the scrape he got into by the false quantity in his Latin epitaph on his dog.[5]—I said that his letter on the subject was worth all the Prosody that ever existed—& so it is—nothing was ever in better or more manly taste—In the evening Miss Scott sung two old Scotch songs to the Harp—he spoke of Mrs. Lockhart (whom he seems thoroughly to love) as richer in this style of songs than Miss Scott.—I then sung several things, which he seemed to like—spoke of my happy power of adapting words to music, which, he said, he never could attain—nor could Byron either. Story of the beggar—"Give that man some half-pence & send him away"—"I never go away under six-pence"—Spoke of the powers of all Irishmen for oratory—The Scotch, on the contrary, cannot speak—no Scotch orator can be named—no Scotch actors. Told me Lockhart was about to undertake the Quarterly—has agreed for five years—salary £1200 a year, & if he writes a certain number of articles, it will be 1500 a year to him. Spoke of Wordsworths absurd vanity about his own poetry—the more remarkable as Wordsworth seems otherwise a manly fellow—Story told him by Wordsworth of Sir George Beaumont saying one day to Crabbe, at Murrays, on Crabbe putting an extinguisher on a tallow candle which had been imperfectly put out, & the smoke of which was (as Sir G. Beaumont said) curling up in graceful wreaths "—what you a Poet, & do that?"—This Wordsworth told Scott, as a set-off against the latter's praises of Crabbe, & as containing his own feeling on the subject as well as Sir G. Beaumont's—what wretched twaddle!—described Wordsworth's manly endurance of his poverty—Scott has dined with him at that time in his kitchen—but though a kitchen, all was neatness in it—spoke of Campbell—praised his Hohenlinden &c.,—considered his Pleasures of Hope as very inferior to these lesser pieces[6]—Talked of Holt, the Wicklow brigand, who held out so long in the mountains and who distinguished himself on many occasions by great generosity.[7] Once or twice gave up men who had been guilty of acts of cruelty—is still alive, keeping (I believe) a public-house, & in good repute for quietness. Sir Walter Scott had wished much to have some talk with him—but feared it might do the man harm, by giving him high notions of himself &c. &c. "I could have put (says he) a thousand pounds in his pocket, by getting him to tell simply the adventures in which he had been engaged & then dressing them up for him". In speaking of the circumstances in which my intimacy with Bryon began, & giving him an account of the message from Greville that followed, he spoke as if the thought had occurred to him at that time whether he ought not himself to have taken notice in the same manner of what Byron had said of him.[8]

30 [Sunday]—A very stormy day—Sir W. impatient to take me out to walk, though the ladies said we should be sure of a ducking—at last, a tolerably fair moment came, & we started—he would not take a great coat—Had explained to me after breakfast the drawings in the breakfast-room, done by an amateur at Edinburgh, W. Sharpe—and alluding to traditions of the Scotts of Harden, Sir Walter's ancestors—the subject of one of them was the circumstance of a young man of the family being taken prisoner in an incursion on the grounds of a neighbouring chief, who gave him his choice whether he should be hanged or marry his daughter, "muckle-mouthed Meg". The sketch represents the young man as hesitating—a priest advising him to the marriage & pointing to the gallows on a distant hill, while Meg herself is stretching her wide mouth in joyful anticipation of a decision in her favour.—The other sketch is founded on the old custom of giving a hint to the guests that the last of the beeves had been devoured by serving up nothing but a pair of spurs under one of the covers—the dismay of the party at the uncovering of the dish is cleverly expressed—our walk was to the cottage of W. Laidlaw, his bailiff, a man who had been reduced from better circumstances, & of whom Scott spoke with much respect, as a person every way estimable—his intention was, he said, to ask him to walk down & dine with us to-day—the cottage & the mistress of it very homely, but the man himself, with his broad Scotch dialect, showing the quiet self-possession of a man of good sense—The storm grew violent, & we sat some time—Scott said he could enumerate thirty places, famous in Scottish song, that could be pointed out from a hill in his neighbourhood—Yarrow, Etrick, Galla Water, Bush aboon Traquair, Selkirk ("Up with the souters of Selkirk") the "bonny Cowden-knows" &c. &c.—Mentioned {as one of the fine instances of amiability he knows of him} that the Duke of Wellington had once wept, in speaking to him about Waterloo, saying that "the next dreadful thing to a battle lost was a battle won".—Company to dinner, Sir Adam Ferguson (an old school-fellow & friend of Scott),[1] his lady, & Colonel Ferguson—Drew out Sir Adam (as he had promised me he would) to tell some of his military stories, which were very amusing—Talked of amateurs in battles, the Duke of Richmond at Waterloo &c. &c.—the little regard that is had of them—a story of one who had volunteered with a friend of his to the bombardment of Copenhagen; and after a severe cannonade, when a sergeant of Marines, came to report the loss, he said

(after mentioning Jack This & Tom That, who had been killed,) "oh, please your Honour, I forgot to say that the volunteer gentleman has had his head shot off".—Scott mentioned as a curious circumstance that, at the same moment, the Duke of Wellington should have been living in one of Bonaparte's palaces, & Bonaparte in the Duke's old lodgings at St. Helena—had heard the Duke say laughingly to some one who asked what commands he had to St. Helena "only tell Bony that I hope he finds my old lodgings at Longwood as comfortable as I find his in the Champs Elysée".—mentioned the story upon which the Scotch Song of "Dainty Davy" was founded[2]—{The Revd. David Williamson, a Covenanter, being hotly pursued, Lady Cherrytree, to *screen* him & trusting to his honour, put him to bed with one of her daughters—the soldiers searched all the rest of the house, but respected the bed of the young lady.—a little child, however, was the consequence, to the great scandal of the pious Covenanter—It forever procured Williamson's pardon from the King—who admired the energy of the Divine & said he himself could not have done the same thing in the Royal Oak for the life of him"—} Talking of ghosts, Sir Adam said that Scott & he had seen one—at least, while they were once drinking together, a very hideous fellow appeared suddenly between them, whom neither knew any thing about, but whom both saw—Scott did not deny it, but said they were both "fu'," and not very capable of judging whether it was a ghost or not—Scott said that the only two men, who had ever told him that they had actually seen a ghost, afterwards put an end to themselves.—one was Lord {Londonderry} [Castlereagh *interlined*],[3] who had himself mentioned to Scott his seeing the "radiant boy". It was one night when he was in barracks, & the face brightened gradually out of the fire-place & approached him—Lord Castlereagh stepped forward towards it & it receded again & faded into the same place—It is generally stated, to have been an apparition attached to the family, & coming occasionally to presage honours & prosperity to him before whom it appeared—but Lord Castlereagh gave no such account of it to Scott—It was the Duke of Wellington made Lord {Londonderry} tell the story to Sir Walter, & Lord L. told it without hesitation & as if believing in it implicitly—Told of the Provost of Edinburgh showing the curiosities of that city to the Persian Ambassador—the impatience of the latter & the stammering hesitation of the former—"Many pillar—wood pillar? stone pillar—eh?" "Ba-ba-ba-ba" (stammered the Provost)— "ah—you do not know—var well—Many book here—write book? print book, eh?" "Ba-ba-ba-ba-" "ah you not know—var well." A few days after on seeing the Provost pass his lodgings, threw up the window and cried "ah, how you do?" "Ba-ba-ba-" "ah-you not know—var well" & shut down the window—Account of the meeting between Adam Smith & Johnson as given by Smith—himself—Johnson began by attacking Hume—"I saw (said Smith) this was meant at me—so I merely put him right as to a matter of fact"—"Well, what did he say?" "He said it was a lie"— "and what

did you say to that?" "I told him he was a son of a b[itc]h."—Good this,
between two Sages—Boswell's father indignant at his son's attaching himself (as he said) to "a Dominie, who kippit a schule, and ca'd it an academy."
Some doubts, after dinner, whether we should have any singing, it being
Sunday—Miss Scott seemed to think the rule might be infringed in my
case—but Scott settled the matter, more decorously, by asking the Fergusons to come again to dinner next day, & to bring the Miss Fergusons.

31 [Monday]—Set off after breakfast, Scott, Miss Scott & I, to go to Melrose
Abbey—told him I had had a strong idea of coming on as far as Melrose
from Kelso on Friday night, in order to see the Abbey by the beautiful
moonlight we had then, but that I thought it still better to reserve myself
for the chance of seeing it with him, though I had heard he was not fond
now of showing it—he answered that, in general, he was not, but that I was,
of course, an exception—I think it was on this morning that he said, laying
his hand cordially on my breast, "Now, my dear Moore, we are friends for
life"—Forgot to mention that in the answer which he sent to me to Newcastle, & which was forwarded after me to Abbotsford, he offered, if I would
let him know when I should reach Kelso, to come for me there in his
carriage—nothing, indeed, could be more kind & cordial than the whole of
his reception of me—Explained to me all the parts of the Abbey, assisted by
the sexton, a shrewd, sturdy mannered fellow, who seemed to have studied
every thing relating to it *con amore*—Went up to a room in the Sexton's
house, which was filled with casts, done by himself, from the ornaments,
heads &c. of the Abbey—Scott, seeing a large niche empty, said "Johnny,
I'll give you the Virgin & Child to put there"—seldom have I seen a happier face than Johnny exhibited at this news—it was all over smiles. As we
went down stairs, Scott said to him "Johnny, if there's another Anti-Popish
rising, you'll have your house pulled about your ears." When we got into
the carriage, I said "you have made that man very happy"—"Ecod, (said Sir
Walter) then, there are two of us pleased, for I did not know what to do
with that Virgin & Child—Mamma (Lady Scott) will be particularly glad to
get rid of it"—A less natural man would have left me under the impression
that he had done really a very generous thing—Sir W. bought one of the
Books, giving a description of the Abbey (written every word of it by the
Sexton) & presented it to me. Went from thence to the Cottage of the
Lockharts, which is very retired & pretty, and then proceeded to pay a visit
to the Fergusons just near—Could not help thinking, during this quiet,
homely visit, how astonished some of those foreigners would be, to whom
the name of Sir Walter Scott is encircled with so much romance, to see the
plain, quiet neighbourly manner with which he took his seat among these
old maids, & the familiar ease with which they treated him in return—no
country squire, with but half an idea in his head, could have fallen into the

gossip of a hum-drum country visit more unassumingly.—This is charming—Left Miss Scott to proceed home in the carriage & he & I walked—
took me through a wild & pretty glen called "Thomas the Rhymer's
Glen."—Told me of his introduction to the Prince by Adam—their whole
talk about the Pretender—the Prince asked him would he have joined the
Jacobites—it would have been wretched taste of me (said Scott) to have said
"I would," and I merely answered that I should have at least wanted one
motive against doing so in not knowing his Royal Highness.—Adam said
afterwards, that the only difference, as to Jacobitism, between him & the
Prince during the conversation was that the Prince said always "The Pretender" & Scott said "Prince Charles"—Mentioned that when Buonaparte
expressed himself shocked at the murder of the Emperor Paul,[1] Fouché
said "Mais Sire, c'est une espece de destitution propre à ce pays-là."—on my
taking this opportunity of saying that I doubted whether I ought to allude
to a Work which it was supposed he was writing—the Life of Buonaparte—
he said that it was true, & that he had already finished, I think more than a
Volume of it,[2] but had now suspended his task, for the purpose of writing a
novel on the subject of the Civil Wars in which he expected to make something of the character of Cromwell, whose politics he certainly did not like,
but in whom there were some noble points which he should like to throw
light on.[3]—It gave me pleasure to find that some of the views he expressed
of the character of Napoleon were liberal—talked with scorn of the
wretched attempts to decry his courage—I said how well calculated the way
in which Scott had been brought up was to make a writer of poetry &
romance, as it combined all that knowledge of rural life & rural legends
which is to be gained by living among the peasantry & joining in their
sports with all the advantages which an aristocratic education gives—I said
that the want of this manly training showed itself in my poetry, which
would perhaps have had a far more vigorous character, if it hadn't been for
the sort of *boudoir* education I had received. (The only thing, indeed, that
conduced to brace & invigorate my mind was the strong political feelings
that were stirring around me when I was a boy, and in which I took a deep
& most ardent interest). Scott was good-natured enough to dissent from all
this—His grandfather, he told me, had been, when a young man, very
poor, and a Shepherd, who had lived with the family, came & offered him
the loan of (I believe all the money he had) 30 pounds, for the purpose of
stocking a farm with sheep—the grandfather accepted it, & went to the
fair, but instead of buying the sheep, he laid out the whole sum on a horse,
much to the horror of the poor shepherd—Having got the horse, however,
into good training & order, he appeared on him at a hunt, & showed him
off in such style, that he immediately found a purchaser for him at twice
the sum he cost him, and then, having paid the shepherd his £30 he laid
out the remainder in sheep, & prospered considerably.—Pointed out to me
the tower where himself was born—his father & uncle went off to join the

rebels in 1745, but were brought back—himself still a sort of Jacobite—has a feeling of horror at the very name of the Duke of Cumberland.— {Mentioned a scene he had with Lady Ancram,[4] (the divorced Lady Belmore) upon her oldest boy, who had been born before her marriage with Lord A. asking her why he was not Lord Newbottle—"Do you hear that?" she exclaimed wildly to Scott, & then, rushing to the Piano-forte played, in a sort of frenzy some hurried Irish airs, as if to drive away the bad thoughts that were in her mind.—It struck me that he spoke of this woman, as if there had been something more than mere friendship between him & her—described her as beautiful & full of character & before he told me the anecdote, said "now, never breathe what I am going to tell you to any human being," which, there being nothing in the story to require such an injunction seemed to imply a consciousness of something else altogether independent of it—} Came to a pretty lake, where he fed a large beautiful swan, that seemed an old favourite of his—The Fergusons to dinner maiden sisters & all—Showed me before dinner in a printed Song-book a very pretty ballad by his bailiff, Mr. Laidlaw, called "Lucy's Flitting"—In the evening I sung, and all seemed very much pleased—Sir Adam, too, & his brother the Colonel, sung—Scott confessed that he hardly knew high from low in music—told him Lord Byron knew nothing of music, but still had a strong feeling of some of those I had just sung—particularly "When he who adores thee"—that I have sometimes seen the tears come into his eyes at some of my songs—Another great favourite of his was "Though the last glimpse of Erin," from which he confessedly borrowed a thought for his Corsair,[5] & said to me "It was shabby of me, Tom, not to acknowledge that theft"—"I dare say" said Scott "Byron's feeling & mine about Music are pretty much the same." His true delight, however, was visible after supper, when Sir Adam sung some old Jacobite songs—Scott's eyes sparkled & his attempts to join in chorus showed much more of the will than the deed— "Hey, Tutti, taiti,"[6] was sung in the true orthodox manner, all of us standing round the table with hands crossed & joined, & chorusing every verse with all our might & main—he seemed to enjoy all this thoroughly—asked him this morning whether he was not a great admirer of Bruce the traveler—said he was his delight & I could have sworn so.

November 1. [Tuesday]—Proposed to take me to-day to the castle of Newark—a place of the Duke of Buccleugh's—sat with him some time in his study—saw a copy of the Moniteur there,[1] which he said he meant to give to the advocates library, when he was done with it. I said that what astonished foreigners most was the extent of his knowledge—"Ah, that sort of knowledge (he answered) is very superficial." I remarked that the manual labor alone of copying out his works seemed enough to have occupied all the time he had taken in producing them. "I write" he answered "very quick—that comes of being brought up under an attorney." Writes chiefly in the morning, from seven till breakfast-time—told me the number of pages he could generally produce in the day, but I do not accurately remember how much it was—mentioned to him that Lord Byron repeated me the first 120 lines of Lara[2] immediately after they were written, and said he had done them either that morning or the evening before, I forgot which—Went out at 12 in the open carriage, he & I & Miss Scott—the day very lowering—showed me where the Etrick & Yarrow {& the Galla water?} join—the Yarrow grows beautiful near the gate of the Duke, & the walk by it through the grounds is charming—lunched in a little summer-house beyond the bridge—showed me a deep part of the river into which he found Mungo Park once throwing stones—Park said it reminded him of what he used to do in Africa to try the depth of the rivers—after his first return from Africa he opened an apothecary shop in Selkirk, but the passion for wandering would not allow him to remain quiet—Day cleared up as we returned home—Saw the place where Montrose was defeated— 400 Irishmen shot near it after the battle[3]—In telling of his ignorance of music Scott said he had been employed in a case, where a purchaser of a fiddle had been imposed on as to its value—He found it necessary to prepare himself by reading all about fiddles in the Encyclopedia &c. & having got the names of Straduarius, Amati &c. glibly on his tongue, got swimmingly through his cause—not long after this, dining at the Duke of Hamilton's, he found himself left alone after dinner with the Duke, who had but two subjects he could talk of, hunting & music—having exhausted hunting, Scott thought he would bring forward his lately acquired learning in fiddles, upon which the Duke grew quite animated, & immediately whispered some orders to the butler; in consequence of which there soon entered {into} the room about half a dozen tall servants all in red, each bearing a fiddle case, and Scott found his knowledge brought to no less a test than that of telling by the tones of each fiddle, as the Duke played it, by what artist it was made—"by guessing & management" he said "I got on pretty well, till we were, to my great relief, summoned to Coffee."— Mentioned an anecdote which he had heard from Lady Swinton of her seeing when a child, a strange young lady in the room, whom she took for a spirit from her vanishing the moment she turned her head—it was a person whom her mother kept concealed, from some cause, within the pannel—This evidently suggested the circumstance in one of his novels—On our return home found that two gentlemen were waiting to see Sir Walter—proved to be young Demidoff son of the rich Russian, who has been sent to Edinburgh for his education, and, with his tutor was now come to pay a visit to Sir Walter—much talk with the young man, who is very intelligent about Russian Literature—I mentioned the Fables of Kriloff, of which I had seen a translation in French, & in one of which he talks of Voltaire being roasted in hell *à petit feu*.[4] This translation Demidoff said, was a very bad one—much pressed by Scott to defer my departure for a day or two.

2 [Wednesday]—While I was dressing Mr. Gordon (a Presbyterian clergy-man, whom I found at Abbotsford, & who is employed making a Catalogue of the Library) came into my room & requested as a great favour, a lock of my hair—told him to be careful how he cut it, as Mrs. Moore would be sure to detect the "Rape"—the carriage being ordered immediately after break-fast, to take me to the Coach & young Demidoff & his tutor to Melrose Abbey, I took leave of Scott, who seemed (as my companions afterwards remarked) to feel real regret at parting with me—finding a place in the Jedborough Coach, I set off for Edinburgh—some talk among the people in the Coach about Scott—said he was a "very peculiar man" & seemed all to agree that he had chosen a very bad situation for his house—Went outside for the last two or three stages, in order to see the country—but it was all dreary & barren—The entrance, however, into Edinburgh most striking—the deep ravine between the two towns, the picturesque sites of the buildings on the heights & in the depths, the grand openings to the sea—all is magnificent & unlike any thing else—By the bye, talking with the guard about Abbotsford, he told me Lady Scott had said that "it was quite a Hotel, in every thing but pay". Took a hackney Coach & drove to William Murray's (Husband to Bessy's sister), having received a letter from him at Abbotsford entreating me to take a bed at his house—found Anne not so much altered (though it is fourteen years since we last met) as Bessy led me to expect—a note while we were at dinner from Murray's sister, Mrs. Sid-dons, to ask me, if not too fatigued to drink tea there—We went—none but herself & daughters—sung a little, though very hoarse—one of the Miss Ss. Also sung—Had written to Jeffrey after dinner to say I was come & would be out with him at Craig Crook tomorrow—an answer from him to say "why not to-night?"

3 [Thursday]—Went out with Murray & a Mr. Bridges, to see the town—the day, though it looked dull, very clear, & favourable for seeing the distant hills—Went up to the Castle—thence through some of the old Town to Calton Hill—was quite enchanted with the views of the Forth—could see the Isle of May & the snow on Ben Lomond—had soup at a Restaurant on Calton Hill—returned home to meet Jeffrey, who came & proposed that I should call on him at his town-house in a Coach at ½ past four—did so—Craig Crook about 3 miles off—no one at dinner but Mrs. Jeffrey, a Mrs. Miller, & Cockburn, the celebrated barrister—Cockburn very reserved & silent, but full, as I understand, of excellent fun & mimicry when he chuses—a good deal of chat with Jeffrey before going to bed—

Cannot bear to stir without his wife & child—requires something living & breathing near him {in bed, something to touch—} & is miserable, when alone—{has often said to Mrs. J. when she hesitated to accompany him on a journey "well, then, my dear, pray get some nice good-humoured girl, that will go with me & lie by me, merely for company's sake—I promise solemnly there shall be no harm, but somebody I must have nearby, must have with me."} Slept in a curious bed-room, with two turrets for dressing rooms—The house was once a mad-house, & it was a common saying of any one that was flighty "He is only fit for Craig Crook—"

4 [Friday]—After breakfast, sitting with Jeffrey in his beautiful little Gothic study (from which he looks out on grounds sloping up to a highly wooded hill) he told me, at much length his opinion of my Life of Sheridan— Thinks it a work of great importance to my fame—people, inclined to deprecate my talents, have always said—"yes—Moore can, it is true, write pretty songs & launch a smart epigram, but there is nothing solid in him" even of Captain Rock they said—"a lively, flashy work—but the style not fit for the subject"[1]—"here, however, (added Jeffrey) is a convincing proof that you can think & reason solidly & manfully—& treat the gravest & most important subjects in a manner worthy of them.—I look upon the part of your book that relates to Sheridan himself as comparatively worthless—it is for the historical & political views that I value it, and am, indeed, of opinion that you have given us the only clear, fair & manly account of public transactions of the last fifty years that we possess."—Walked up to the wooded hill opposite the house to catch some beautiful views of the Forth & its islands as well as of Edinburgh—Went into town in a hackney coach with Jeffrey to Mrs. Miller—walked about with Jeffrey—called upon Lady Keith—Flahaut in Edinburgh, but not at home—promised she would make him come to dinner at Jeffrey's to-day, if he could—Called at Black's, the bookseller, at Constable's, at Sir Henry Moncrieff's—sat some time with this fine old man, who seems to be much looked up to—Returned to Craig-crook at ½ past 4, with Thompson (Mackintosh's friend) John Murray & Jeffrey—a large party to dinner—Lord Mackenzie (son to the Man of Feeling)[2] Mr. & Mrs. Kay, my old friend Shannon, &c. &c. Sung in the evening, Jeffrey having had a Piano-forte sent exclusively for the purpose—Have seldom seen people more pleased—Obliged to repeat the "Ship Ahoy"— the Watchman &c.[3]

5. [Saturday] After breakfast young Stoddard {(the son of "Dr. Slop"[1] &} grandson to Sir H. Moncrief) came out to beg I would fix a day to dine with Sir Henry—fixed for next Tuesday—Set off to walk to town, but near the House, met the Man of Feeling going out to call upon me—Jeffrey put me

into the carriage to him & he carried me into town—{a garrulous, Joc Millerish sort of old gentleman, and (as I was prepared to find) not at all like his writings—} told me that what put him upon writing Julia de Roubigny² was a wish expressed by Lord Kaimes for a novel without love in it—dosed me with old stories & civility, & having stopped his carriage half way down a hill in order to introduce me to his daughter who was coming up it, left me at last at Murray's house—Walked out with Murray & went to see Holyrood House—felt, as I looked at the wretched lodgings around it for the privileged, how much better I had been within the rules of the Allée des Veuves in 1820—Dined at Mrs. Siddons's with Murray & Anne— company the Lord Provost, Shannon, &c. &c. A party in the evening—Miss Gibson Craig, a pretty girl—two other nice girls, Miss Wilsons, very good musicians, rather a rare thing, it appears, in Scotland—sung with them some Italian Duetts & Trios—one of them sung my own "Say, what shall be our sport to-day?"³—the evening agreeable.

6 [Sunday]—Went off with Murray, in a hackney-coach, to see Roslyn Castle—the day clear & sunny, and considering the time of the year, very favourable, for the purpose—The colouring of the eaves, rocks & water brought out beautifully by the sunshine—did not go on to Hawthornden— the chapel very curious—Lunched at the inn well & cheaply—{Murray's story of the Devil in hell throwing dice for a soul in [*several words unrecovered*] "Ah! Here's the [*unrecovered*] does over those blessed miracles of his."}—company at dinner at Murray's—John Wilson, the Professor of Moral Philosophy (author of the novels,¹ Blackwood &c.) Ballantyne, the Printer (Scott's friend and as Scott told me, the only critic he had for his novels) and Shannon—Wilson, an odd, uncouth mannered person, but amusing—his imitation of Wordsworth's monologues excellent—Spoke of my Sheridan—thinks the bon-mots I have reported of his very poor; told him I agreed with him in this, but was obliged to put them in, both from the outcry there would have been had I not given anecdotes, and the value in which most of those I have given are held by Rogers, Lord Holland &c.— particularly the reply to Tarleton about the mule & the ass which I saw no great merit in myself, but which Lord H. & Rogers always quote with praise²—all agreed in thinking it not only poor, but hardly intelligible— Wilson praised my Book warmly & said that it was only so far unfair, that the biographer had in every page outshone his subject—seemed not to think very highly of Sheridan's genius, and in speaking of his great unreported speech said it appeared to him utterly impossible that, with such powers as his, he could ever have produced any thing deserving of such high praises.³—In comparing prose with poetry, remarked, in order to prove the inferiority of the former that there have been great Schools of Poetry, but no School of Prose—sat drinking till rather late, & sat again

with Wilson after supper till past one—not being able to dine with him any day before I go, fixed to sup at his house next Tuesday.

7 [Monday]—Walked about with John Murray—went with him to the Advocates' Library—rather too gay & ornamented—fitter for Ladies than Lawyers—called at Black's, the bookseller, who showed me a letter from the Longmans saying the Demand for the Life was "prodigious" & that they were bringing out the third Edition—called on Lady Keith—her children at dinner—lunched with them—fixed to dine with her on Wednesday—proved to me that I could perform all my visits to my Scotch friends in ten days—going to Lord Dunmore's on Monday—thence on Tuesday to her where I should be saved the trouble of going to the Gwydirs by seeing them with her—and so on she traced the route for me to Lord Belhaven's, the Dalrymple-Hamiltons' &c. &c.—should like it much, but too late in the season, I cannot, at all events spare the time.—Went to John Murray's at five to be taken out to Jeffrey's—MacCulloch the Political Economist went with us—Said he was very much pleased with the remarks I had made, in the Life relative to the Debates on the Commercial Treaty with France & the Irish Propositions[1]—Lord Lansdowne's speech on the latter measure one, he said, of considerable ability—a large party to dinner at Jeffrey's, Mr. & Mrs. Fullerton (she a fine woman) Mr. & Mrs. Rutherford (the latter, I found, an old acquaintance of mine in Ireland, Sophia Stewart), a Mr. Muir, a young man, {of} only 22, whom Jeffrey mentioned to me as having given great promise of talent, and as being the author of some late articles in the Review on Spanish Poetry,[2] {John Murray} &c. &c.—sung a good deal in the evening, & had no reason to complain of any want of enthusiasm in my audience—a Miss Young played two or three things with much feeling.

8 [Tuesday]—Company to breakfast Capt. Basil Hall & his wife, old Mackenzie &c. &c.—Sung for them after breakfast—have more than once seen Jeffrey (though he professes rather to dislike music) with tears in his eyes while I sang "There's a Song of the olden times"[1] one of those that make the most impression—John Murray having sent out his gig for me I took leave of Craigcook, leaving, I hope, as pleasant recollections of my visit as I brought away with me—Letters from Mrs. Dugald Stewart, and old Mr. Fletcher (a friend of Mackintosh's) full of the most flattering kindness—Mrs. Stewart says that her husband would have come expressly to Edinburgh to meet me, if it was not for the bad weather, & Mr. Fletcher, with many praises of my writings, expresses his regret that his infirmities would not allow him to do the same—both invite me to their houses—Took my place in the mail for Thursday morning—dined at Sir Henry Moncrieff's—

company Jeffrey, J. Murray, Dr. Thompson, young Stoddart & his sister and one or two more—Sung to a wretched piano-forte in the evening—went from thence to Miss Sinclair's {to (what she called) "a squeeze of beauties"—had but little leisure to look for them, being occupied the whole time with watching how to get away, as I saw there was a design to make me sing & the squeeze was by far too numerous for it—} With Mr. Murray's assistance escaped & he & I went to sup at Wilson's—an odd set collected there—among others the poet, Hogg²—{"take your Hog, and scrape him" well applied to this dirty fellow, who had just come from the Cattle Fair—owned to having drunk a bottle of whiskey before he came, & dispatched nearly another during supper—} we had also Williams, the master of the High School, the person to whom Lockhart addressed Peter's Letters³—said to be an able man—some ladies too—one of whom sung Duetts with an Italian singing-master. a fine contrast between this foreigner & Hogg, who yelled out savagely two or three Scotch Songs, and accompanied the burden of one of them by labouring away upon the bare shoulders of the ladies who sat on each side of him—He & I very cordial together—wanted me to let him drive me to his farm next day to see wife & bairns—I was much pressed to sing, but, there being no piano-forte, could not—at last, in order not to seem fine (the great difficulty one has to get over in such society) sung "the Boys of Kilkenny." {—Did not get home till late, & felt not at all well—the sour *Presbyterian* claret of Sir Henry disordered me.}

9. [Wednesday]—{Very ill—took some tincture of Rhubarb—} Called upon Constable, & sat some time with him—thence to Ballantyne's with Murray, & sung for Mrs. B. & a party there (among whom was G. Thompson, Editor of the Scotch Music)¹ though in violent pain—never, however, sung better & they all seemed much pleased—On coming home Murray insisted upon sending for Doctor Ross—went to dine at Lady Keith's—company only themselves, Jeffrey, John Murray & Stewart—Flahaut gave me 20 drops of laudanum before dinner—so ill I could not stay at table—Flahaut took me down to his bed-room, and attended me with all the kindness, that makes brave, warm-hearted soldiers like him such good nurses—lay in his bed some time, & then returned to the table—a good many people in the evening, whom I should like to have known something of—among others Cranstoun—but my head was turning round & I could enjoy nothing—{a flourishing Frenchman (Marquis de Salvo) bored me without mercy with his distinction between society "en masses" and society "en classes"—got away between 9 & 10—very sick again—} Murray all kindness—surrounded me with all possible comforts at night.

10 [Thursday]—Much better in the morning but determined to put off my

departure till Sunday (13th)—Staid at home all day—Flahaut called upon me & sat some time—

11 [Friday]—Went out in a hackney coach—called upon Lady Keith &c.— dined at home with the Murrays—Doctor Ross of our party—Murray full of talent & fun—{his imitation of his sister admirable—her horror, when he told her that he had given Dr. Abercrombie (a great Saint) an order for two to the boxes instead of a [*unrecovered*] tragedy start—"Good God, William—don't you know he's an Evangelist?"—} His story of "Jobson of Dundee"—ossification of the heart—bones turning to stones & blood to mortar— {her meeting Shannon afterwards—} His story of the fellow acting with Kemble in Coriolanus, and in the speech where he accuses Coriolanus

> "For that he has
> (As much as in him lies) from time to time
> Envied against the people seeking means
> To pluck away their power—"[1]

the fellow forgetting his part here, looked fiercely at Kemble, & added "and that he is always seen going about the streets, making every one uncomfortable". At the end of the play the unfortunate actor went to apologise for this awkwardness, but Kemble merely looked bitterly at him & said "Beast!"—Story of the little girl on being asked what kind of an animal man was—"he is a tripod"—Lord Sidmouth said that the great art of a Speaker of the House of Cs was "to know what to overlook"—applied by Murray to the {conduct of a} Manager of a Theatre—went with Murray & Ross in the evening to see the Theatre lighted up—it has been newly painted & is to open tomorrow night—The Courts also open tomorrow, so that it is lucky I stay.

12 [Saturday]—Went to the Courts after breakfast—found out Jeffrey & walked about with him to see every thing, being myself the greatest show of the place and followed by crowds from Court to Court. Had the pleasure of seeing Scott sitting, at his table, under a row of as dull-looking judges as need be—Jeffrey asked him to meet me & though I had already refused Jeffrey, (in order to dine with the Murrays) I could not resist this temptation.—begged of Jeffrey to dine pretty early in order that I might see the Theatre—met Scott afterwards, & told him this arrangement—"Very well" he said—"I'll order my carriage to come at eight o'clock, and I'll just step down to the play-house with you myself"—Company at Jeffrey's, Mr. & Mrs. Rutherford, Thomson &c.—Sir Walter, a different man from what he was at Abbotsford—a good deal more inert, & when he *did* come into play,

not near so engaging or amusing—When the carriage came, he & I & Thomson went to the Theatre, & I could see that Scott anticipated the sort of reception I met with—We went into the front boxes, and the moment we appeared, the whole Pit rose, turned towards us, & applauded vehemently—Scott said "It is you—it is you—you must rise & make your acknowledgment."—I hesitated for some time, but on hearing them shout out "Moore, Moore" I rose & bowed my best for two or three minutes—This scene was repeated after the two next acts & the Irish Melodies were played each time by the orchestra. Soon after my first reception Jeffrey and two of the ladies arrived & sat in the front before us, Scott & I being on the second row—He seemed highly pleased with the way I was received and said several times "This is quite right— I am glad my countrymen have returned the compliment for me." There was occasionally some discontent expressed by the galleries at our being placed where they could not see us, & Murray told me afterwards that he wondered they bore it so well—We had taken the precaution of ordering that we should be shown into one of the side boxes, but the proper box-keeper was out of the way when we came—At about ten o'clock we came away, I having first renewed my acquaintance with Mrs. Coutts, who was with the Duke of St. Alban's in a box near us. Home very tired with my glory, and had to pack for the morning—

13 [Sunday]—Up before six—Found that Murray in order to be ready for me had sat up reading all night—Got to the Mail-Coach office on time & was off at seven—A gentleman came into the coach in the middle of the day, who, after some time, guessed who I was, and asked my name—said he had been with some friends in Scotland, who were full of indignation at the People of Edinburgh for not giving me a Public Dinner—assured him that the People of Edinburgh were not in fault, as such a tribute had been proposed to me, but that the shortness of my stay rendered it impossible.

14 [Monday]—Got to Manchester in the morning—Had a letter of introduction from Constable to a gentleman of the town, but was too tired to deliver it. Resolved to give up my original intention of visiting Derbyshire & to get, as soon as possible, home—

15 [Tuesday]—Started in the Coach for Birmingham, where I arrived at night.—An odd fellow (an Irishman) in the traveller's room which was very full, recognized me & after various civilities, begging me to draw nearer to the fire &c. came up to me & said in a whisper "I know who you are,

whisht!—the last time I saw you, you were only seven years old, & I little thought what a great man you'd become—Do you remember Mrs. Molloy?" So he went on—got to bed, having taken my place in the Bath Coach for the morning[1]—

Dec. 11th [Sunday]—Received two letters (one of which I ought to have got yesterday) from my sister Ellen, telling me that my dearest father is dangerously ill—The event I had been but too well prepared for—God send he may not have pain or lingering—his long life has been one of almost uninterrupted health, and I have been able (thank Heaven!) to make his latter days tranquil & comfortable—It is my poor mother I have now most to feel for—Must start immediately for Ireland, but this being Sunday, can make no arrangements for money—The shock, at first, very great, notwithstanding the prepared state of my feelings—darling Bessy full of the sweetest sympathy & kindness about it—Wrote to Corry, to say I trusted in his friendship for every thing being done that ought to be done, and begging him to communicate to Ellen my intention to set off immediately—

12 [Monday]—Sent in to the Bank—have some fears lest the present panic may prevent them from cashing, as usual, my Bill on Power—walked to Bowood to see Lord Lansdowne, who returned from Paris on Saturday—took little Tom with me, my own thoughts not being such agreeable company as I am glad to say, they in general are—found Lord & Lady L.—soon got on the subject of Sheridan's Life—and his tone confirmed what his letter from Paris had pepared me for—namely that neither he nor any of my high Whig friends are quite pleased with my book—The fact is, what I stated to Agar Ellis, in my answer to the flattering letter he wrote me on the subject is but too true—"You are just of a standing that enables you to view the events, of which I treat, historically—but those who were themselves actors in the scene, will not I fear take so favourable a view of my impartiality"[1]—The points, which Lord Lansdowne mentioned as objectionable were—first—the censure upon those who attended the Funeral—secondly, what I have said, as to the surrender of principle by those Whigs who coalesced with Lord Grenville—and thirdly, the remark on the "overshadowing branches of the Whig Aristocracy" in my account of Canning's political debut—which he thought was going out of my way to throw a reflection on the Whigs[2]—In answer to this last objection told him {that} this whole paragraph is but the substance of Canning's own reasons for the line he took, as stated by him in a letter to Lord Holland at the time, and as mentioned more than once to me by Lord Holland—On the other points too I briefly defended myself, but have not time here to note down what I

said—He said also that, though I had not professedly drawn any parallel between the talents of Fox as a statesman, & those of Burke & Sheridan, yet he thought it might be deduced from my general sentiments that I was not inclined to place Fox so far above the other two as he (Lord L.) thought he deserved—To this I answered that neither had I in my book, nor would I venture now, to draw any parallel between Fox & Sheridan, with respect to political sagacity, but that I recollect Tierney once telling me that Pitt looked upon Sheridan as a much abler man than Fox. This surprized Lord Lansdowne, & I bid him ask Tierney whether I understood him rightly— Told him what Jeffrey had said with respect to the Life being useful to my reputation in a Department of intellect of which I had hitherto got but little credit—namely, sound political reasoning—Lord L. said he quite agreed in this. Expressed a strong wish that I should undertake the Life of Grattan— Talked much with him on the subject of Lord Byron's Life & mentioned Scott's advice that I should employ him (Lord L.) to negotiate between me & the family—This brought him to tell me (what he has hitherto, very much at my own desire, kept a secret from me) the nature of the negotiations which he had in that quarter this last summer.—It seems Wilmot Horton consulted Lord L. with respect to the question of paying me back the money & Lord L. gave it as his opinion that the obvious step for the family to take was (without any reference to me, who was decided upon refusing it) to settle it upon my family. This, Wilmot Horton said, was his own view of the matter exactly—On proposing it, however, to the family, they refused to pay the money otherwise than {(in the way, in fact, which they knew well, was impracticable)} making myself take it—{Accordingly, Wilmot Horton, in communicating this resolution of theirs to Lord Lansdowne, said that he would have nothing more to do with the business— evidently, Lord L. said, displeased with the manner in which the family had behaved. The only reason they appear to have given for not adopting his recommendation was, that it would look like a desertion of Murray!!—} From all this it appeared that Lord Lansdowne had no channel of communication (as I supposed) with the family—offered, however, most kindly to undertake any proposal to them I might wish— {Thinks Hobhouse indisposed towards my writing the Life. One of his reasons is that [*incomplete*]—had heard that he spoke slightingly of my Life of Sheridan, & thinks it possible that it was in contemplation of my Byron project he gave this opinion—as a sort of preparation for the line he meant to take on it—} Walked nearly home with me—All this conversation, added to the already deep sadness in my heart, threw me into a state of nervousness & depression on my return home, from which it required all the efforts of my natural cheerfulness to recover me—Bessy, too, did much for me by her own sweet, womanly fortitude—bless her!—Dined at three & set off at five in a chaise for Bath—Went on my arrival to see Anastasia—found the sweet child in the midst of gaity—it was the ball night, & she came out to me, "smiling, as if {the} earth contained no tomb." On my telling her of the sad mission I was going upon, she assumed that grave look which children think it right to put on at such news, though they cannot be expected—& indeed, *ought* not to feel it. She wore three or four orders of merit which she had gained—one, for general amiability of conduct (a lily of the valley) of which, she told me with much triumph, there had been but four given in the school—another (a rose) for her progress in music, and so on—Slept at the York House—got them to give me a letter to the Landlord of the Inn at Birmingham to secure me a comfortable bed—found in the coffee-room an old acquaintance (Birmingham, the clergyman) with two sons of Charles Butler, on their way to Ireland—

{13 [Tuesday] Journey to Birmingham—read on the way Hall's South America.}[1]

14 [Wednesday]—There being so many candidates for the Coach at the Albion, went to the Swan, to take my chance in the mail—got a place—my companions, a dull good-natured Scotchman and a young lady with a little girl under her care, who left us at Shrewsbury—Took in a gentleman as far as Oswestry, who proved to be a merchant of some kind at Liverpool— some interesting conversation in commercial matters—mentioned the great change that had taken place in late years from the manufacturers exporting for themselves without the intervention of merchants, as for- merly—the latter class, accordingly, quite extinct, and the business managed entirely between the manufacturers & the commercial agents abroad—All this done from greediness of profit, and their present suffer- ings (from bad remittances & the fall of cotton) little, he thought, to be pitied—Liverpool & Manchester have been wise enough to keep clear of local notes—many attempts made to introduce them, but all resisted—In one stage between Llangollen and Corwen, there came on the most dread- ful storm of thunder, lightning & hail that ever I witnessed—horses, though alarmed, behaved, luckily, very steadily—but the universal blazing of the sky & the pitch darkness that succeeded, the storm of hail blowing in the coachman's face, the horses in full career, & the guard crying out from behind, with evidently an alarmed voice, "Hold hard, hold hard", were altogether circumstances, by no means agreeable—Confess I felt a little frightened, and arranged myself on my seat in the safest attitude for an overset—Got safe, however, to Corwen—the Coachman owned he was once very nearly off the road—At Bangor (where we arrived between one & two) resolved, as it would be so miserably wet & dark in crossing the ferry, to stop at Jackson's, & pass the day of rest I meant to give myself

there, instead of Holyhead—Had to knock the people up & got to bed about three.

15 [Thursday]—After writing a letter to Bessy, walked to see the Menai Bridge, which is to be open for general passage next month. a grand achievement—dined at ½ past 3, in order to be ready to take the first chance of a place on that offered—Birmingham & the two boys arrived in a Chaise—told me there was but little hope of a place in either of the coaches & offered to take me on—willingly accepted & left my luggage to follow—Much talk about my Sheridan's Life, which Birmingham praised to the skies. Got to Holyhead between nine & ten, the wind blowing from the worst possible point, & with a fury that gave but a bad prospect for tomorrow—Had bid Corry write to me at Holyhead, but too late now to get a letter out of the Office.

16. [Friday] Up at five & aboard the Packet (Skinner's) at ½ past six—Got into my berth immediately, where I lay without moving for twelve long hours of our passage—by this means kept off actual sickness, but became even more deadly ill than if I had been sick. Overheard a man say to the Under Steward in the Cabbin, "Isn't Mr. Moore among the passengers?"—"I don't know indeed, Sir" was the answer. "His father (said the other) is _____" (I didn't hear the word)—"Is he, Sir?" said the Steward. This appeared to me conclusive that all was over; & it is a proof of the power of the mind over even sea-sickness that though I was just then on the point of being sick, the dread certainty which these words conveyed to me quite checked the impulse, and I remained for some time even without a qualm—Did not stir till all the passengers were gone off by the coach & then had a Chaise & drove to McDowell's, in order to get something to eat, not having tasted food for 28 hours. Found there Corry's two nephews—as they had only an open car to take them to Dublin, offered them seats in my chaise & put my luggage into their car—Drove to Corrys, & sent in for him—told me my Father was still alive, but that was all. Went with me to Bilton's Hotel, where he had a got a bed-room for me. Assured me that I need not agitate myself as I did, for that my father was closing his eyes on the world without any suffering, and that my mother had already brought her mind to as much composure as could possibly be expected—Undertook to go & consult my sister Ellen, as to whether it would be too much for my mother to see me to-night—returned to say that I must come to her by all means, as she was expecting me, and it would be (Ellen thought) of the greatest service to her. Was glad to find from him that it was their strong wish I should not ask to see my Father, as he was past the power of knowing

me, & it would only shock me unnecessarily—This, a great relief as I would not for worlds have the sweet impression he left upon my mind when I last saw him, changed for one which would haunt me, I know, dreadfully through the remainder of my life. It was Bessy's last wish that I should not arrive in time to see him alive, & her earnest request that I should not look on him afterwards. She knows how it would affect me. The meeting with my dearest mother, after the first burst, not so painful as I expected, & I soon found I could divert her mind to other subjects. My sister Kate had come up on the first alarm of his illness, & had taken her turn with Ellen in nursing & watching him ever since—. Left them for my Hotel between eleven & twelve & had a much better night than I should have had, if I had remained in ignorance of {the state of} my Mother's mind. At parting, Ellen bid me not come too early in the morning, & said she would write me a note.

17 [Saturday]—Took my time at breakfast, & waited for Ellen's note, but none came. Walked down to Abbey St, & found that all was over—my dear Father had died at seven in the morning.—Consulted about the funeral, which it was the wish of all to have as simple & private as possible— entrusted the management of it to Mr. Legh, the son of an old friend of my Mother's—dined at Abbot's, & returned to my mother in the evening.—our conversation deeply interesting—found that neither my Mother nor Kate were very anxious to press upon him the presence of a clergyman; but, on mentioning it to him at Corry's suggestion, he himself expressed a wish for it. The subject of religion was, indeed, the only one, it seems, upon which his mind was not gone. When the Priest was proceeding to take his con- fession, and put the necessary questions for that purpose to him, he called my mother & said "Auty, my dear, you can tell this gentleman all he requires to know quite as well as I"—This was very true—as she knew his every action & thought—and is a most touching trait of him. A few nights before he died, when Ellen was doing something for him, he said to her "You are a valuable little girl—it's a pity some good man does not know your value". The apothecary, who was standing by, said with a smile, "Oh, Sir, some good man will"—"Not an apothecary, though" answered my Father—which looked as if the playfulness, for which he was always so remarkable, had not even then deserted him.—Our conversation naturally turned upon religion, & my sister Kate, who, the last time I saw her, was more than half inclined to declare herself a Protestant, told me she had since taken my advice and remained quietly a Catholic—{Married as she is into a Catholic family, it would have been a most ill-judged, as well as unfeminine step, to branch off thus from the religion, both of parents & husband. So I told her at the time, and her own good sense, indeed, could not fail ultimately to have suggested it.} For myself, my having married a

Protestant wife gave me an opportunity of chusing a religion, at least, for my children, & if my marriage had no other advantage, I should think *this* quite sufficient to be grateful for—We then talked of the differences between the two faiths; & they who accuse all Catholics of being intolerantly attached to their own, would be either ashamed or surprised (according as they were sincere or not in the accusation) if they had heard the sentiments expressed both by my mother and sisters on the subject. Was glad to find I could divert my mother's mind from dwelling entirely on what had just happened—indeed, the natural buoyancy & excursiveness of her thoughts (which, luckily for myself, I have inherited) affords a better chance of escape from grief than all the philosophy in the world. Left them late, after fixing every thing for Monday.

18 [Sunday]—Staid within till dinner—dined with my mother at Mrs. Legh's, an old friend of hers, to whose house we persuaded her to go out of the way of the sad preparations for tomorrow—saw my sisters Ellen & Kate at night & found them both much shocked & agitated by the scene they had gone through with the undertakers.—wished to spare me the operation of the mass in the morning, and advised me not to come till after the service was over—but thought it better for every reason to attend.—Felt my heart full of sadness when I got to my bed-room but was relieved by a burst both of tears & prayer, & by a sort of *confidence* that the Great & Pure Spirit above us could not be otherwise than pleased with what he saw passing within my mind—This, perhaps, not Christian humility, but let it be what it will, I felt consoled & elevated by it.

19 [Monday]—Awake at a little after four—got up at half past five & was in Abbey St. at half past six. The Priest not yet come—at seven he arrived & we had mass in the room with the Coffin.—There had been very few invited; but others came of themselves, & after a long delay of the Hearse (which had been promised at 7, but did not come till half-past eight) we set off for St. Kevin's Church—The Mourning Coach was a relief to me, for the delay had been dreadful—There were mourners with me, Corry, Abbot & young Legh, and in the coach after us were, Philip Crampton, Mr. Mara, Grierson, Lyne & two more. The weather was wretched, and—altogether the scene shocked & afflicted me beyond anything—The vulgar apparatus of the ceremony seems such a profanation!—went to breakfast with Abbot—thence to my mother at Mrs. Legh's, and afterwards to Ellen & Kate—dined at Corry's—doubted whether I ought or not—but any thing to escape from such thoughts. The company, Grierson, Abbot, & his family. {The conversation rather amusing which did me good & Corry's story of Grattan describing Daly (a great saint) with Lady March "a man of much

piety & very broad shoulders—Lady M. on the sofa—Daly standing beside her when his &c. what becomes of his piety?"—Lord Norbury saying of a man who had snatched a writ from a Bailiff that was pursuing him, & swallowed—"I hope that writ is not returnable in this Court."} Abbot brought me home.—Forgot to say that the night before last I received a letter from Crampton, enclosing one from Shaw (the Lord Lieutenant's secretary) the purport of which was that the Lord Lieutenant meant to continue my Father's half-pay in the shape of a pension to my sister—Resolved, of course, to decline this favour, but wrote a letter full of thankfulness to Crampton—Find since that this was done at Crampton's suggestion—that Lord Wellesley spoke of the difficulty there was in the way, from the feelings the King must naturally entertain towards me, & from himself being the personal friend of the King, but that on further consideration he saw he could do it without any reference to the other side of the Channel & out of the Pension Fund placed at his disposal as Lord Lieutenant—All this very kind & Liberal of Lord Wellesley; and God knows how useful such an aid would be to me; as God alone knows how I am to support all the burdens now heaped upon me—but I could not accept such a favour—it would be like that *Lasso* with which they catch wild animals in South America; the noose would be only upon the *tip* of the horn, it is true, but it would do—Find that Crampton & Corry, though the chief movers of the act, highly approve of my refusal. Had a kind letter from Bryan to-day, begging me to take my mother & sisters down to Jenkinstown—answered him that I would come down myself as soon as possible—

20. [Tuesday] Had some talk with my sister Kate as to what is to be done for my mother—{having found from the latter that what I counted upon as the most economical & comfortable plan, namely, her living with Kate, is out of the question from this impossibility of my mother & John ever agreeing—Learned now from Kate that it is equally out of the question to expect any pecuniary assistance from John—In the true Irish way, he muddles away all his money upon outward show, & has not a disposeable sixpence even for his daughter's education—Kate very anxious to make me feel it is not her fault, and I believe her—He has completely mastered her, and though she confesses herself much happier than she was during the struggle of their tempers, it has left her without a will or power of her own. But it is really not a little hard to think that here are they, with but one child, not able (or rather, in his case, not willing) to lighten by a single guinea the burden that lies upon me, and yet keeping a fine house, & five servants and giving balls, dinners &c. to the tag, rag & bobtail of Tipperary—it is too bad— &} there was my admirable Bessy, before I left home, planning how *we* might continue to do with but one servant, in order that I might be the better able to assist my mother—Dined at Abbots—no one but Dr. Litton.—

Abbot said (in talking of the necessity of a man's *ruining* himself in Ireland in order to get the character of being any thing of a good fellow) that he who had a Pipe of Port coming down to him *with a Custodiam on it* was thought the only true & proper {sort of} gentleman—Went to Mrs. Legh's afterwards, and from thence with Ellen to Abbey St., where I found John (who had arrived to day) & supped—

21 [Wednesday]—Sent Crampton my letter, in answer to Lord Wellesley's offer—had a note from him back, in which he said "It is (like every thing that comes from you) as perfect in expression as it is noble in thought."— Can get no place in any of the Coaches for Bryan's, it being Christmas time—Dined with my mother, who returned to Abbey St. this morning— John Scully of the party—{He & Kate complaining of their cook being so capricious in changing her kitchen around!}

22 [Thursday]—Resolved to give up going to Bryan's till Monday, and to dine with my Mother on Christmas Day.—Receive letters from my dearest Bessy every day which is a great delight to me—Corry told me from Crampton that Lord Wellesley was highly pleased with my letter—said it was very creditable to me—that he hoped I was not too sanguine in taking so much upon my own shoulders, but that if I should see reason to change my opinion, I should find him equally disposed to serve me. Dined with my mother.—Sent Dr. Mills a copy of Sheridan's Life as a mark of gratitude for his attendance on my father.

23 [Friday]—Corry & I called at Philip Cramptons to leave word we should dine with him—Gervais Bushe sat some time with me in the morning, and spoke with great praise of Sheridan's Life—told me some fine tenets of Grattan—In the year 1778, when from the Tenants in most places having neglected to renew their Leases, the Leases had lapsed, Grattan who was very poor, & might have had a great accession to his little property by taking advantage of this circumstance, was himself the person to bring a Bill into the House making it imperative on the Landlords to renew the Leases on the old terms.—Another circumstance was—when Fox in 82 wrote to the Whig Party in Ireland to announce the coming of the D. of Portland, & expressed a wish for their support, Grattan & Lord Charlemont met together on the subject at Grattan's lodgings, & the latter said, "You, Lord C. are the poorest Peer in Ireland & I am the poorest Commoner—what I propose is that neither of us shall accept any thing from the new Government, but try to serve the Country." In 1806, he likewise de-

clined taking office & said "Let us be consulted but not considered."—[By the bye, on my mentioning at Abbots the other evening what I had heard of Grattan's having provided in his Will for 12 natural children, they both said that his gallantries among the cottagers in his neighbourhood were notorious, & that he was any thing but fastidious in the objects of his amours—] Dined with Crampton—none but he & I & Corry—Crampton very lively & amusing—[enquired about the vinaigrette in the shape of an Irish Harp which he sent to Sir W. Scott's daughter with some verses.—did not tell him that Miss Scott said "it is very odd that a man of Mr. Crampton's good senses should send one verses"—] Went to sup with my Mother—Paid to-day fifteen guineas to Mr. Donough the tailor—half of it for a suit of clothes which my poor father had last year—paid also for the expenses of the Funeral 17 guineas—Should have mentioned that, before I left home, I wrote to the Longmans to know whether I might (for the expenses I was about to encounter) draw on them whatever little balance might, by their late goodness, be coming to me on the Sheridan account—That I had no right to draw it, as every thing ought to go into that chasm of debt that was open between us, but that I could not help it—Received a kind letter from them since my arrival, to beg that I would draw upon them for whatever I wanted "without any reference to the amount"—

24 [Saturday]—Drove with Crampton in his gig to the Park to leave my name with Lord Wellesley—went from thence with him to Goulburn's, and while he was paying his visits, wrote out for him in Goulburn's study, my verses "A bishop & a bold Dragoon"[1] which he had never seen,—told me that Mrs. Goulburn had expressed a wish to know me & that I should dine with them—gave me some very pretty verses of his own to Miss Edgeworth, with Sir Walter Scott's pen—showed me also some verses of hers to himself—strongly laudatory, but very bad—Dined with Corry—company, North, Henry Grattan, Gervais Bushe, Wallace—North, slow & sententious, and apparently not much above the level of ordinary official talent—said before dinner that he had discovered in an old act of Parliament an illustration of the phrase "gouts of blood" in Shakespeare—in speaking of the *sewers* of Dublin the Acts called them "gouts."—This, however, I remarked, has a more direct origin in the French word égouts which means *sewers*, while the "gout" of Shakespeare is, as directly & evidently from the French word "goutte."—Like a man, accustomed to lay down the law, he did not appear willing to give up his own view of the matter.—A variety of subjects brought into play after dinner, upon most of which Wallace struck me as by far the most sensible man of the party— [Grattan, a mere flash in the pan.] In the evening there were two nice girls, the Miss Hens, who sung Italian with very good taste—I sung also a good deal—In singing "There's a song of the Olden Time" the feelings which I had been so long suppress-

ing, broke out—I was obliged to leave the room and continued sobbing hysterically on the stairs for several minutes—

25 [Sunday]—Dined with my dear Mother & sisters, & were all as happy as the circumstances would admit of.

26 [Monday]—Set off in a Coach from Duke St. for Kilkenny—six inside—some rather intelligent men—{Story of the sandy-haired children in the village—"Pray, is the Priest of this Parish sandy-haired—?"—"No, Sir, but his Coadjutor is"—} one of them said in talking of Conolly, the rich merchant "he is a safe man to ride behind on the back of a seven-shilling stamp."—Mentioned Sir Boyle Roches dream—his head being cut off & placed upon a table—"Quis separabit?" says the head—"Naboclish" says I, in the same language.—Arrived at Kilkenny, at eight—a servant at the Inn waiting to tell me that Bryan & Mrs. B. had come in to meet me & were waiting dinner for me at Rice's Hotel.—a very thoughtful & welcome attention—Drove to Jenkinstown in Bryan's Coach & four, after dinner.—slept in one of the large cold state bed-rooms, and might have sung "Can nothing, nothing warm me?"

27–28 [Tuesday–Wednesday]—No Company—walked about a little with Bryan, and dined late—told me that he had not found any satisfactory way of vesting Anastasia's thousand pounds, & had therefore left it to her in his will, bearing interest from the date of the will.—{His anecdote of a lady of a certain description at Nancy, whose name was Laloi—"Que voulez-vous? notre General même se met au dessous de la Loi." Story of the Chevalier of St. Louis that undertook to get all the girls of the opera for five guineas a piece—"I know, ladies (he said to them in the foyer) you are all too rich for me to think of being of much service to you—but the richest may sometimes want assistance & if any of you, in any emergency, should happen to want five guineas, you will always be sure to find it with me". This emergency happened to all in their turn, & he gained his point cheaply.}

29 [Thursday]—Dined rather early, & set off at eight for Kilkenny where I had ordered a bed for the purpose of starting next morning for Dublin.

30 [Friday]—Left Kilkenny at seven—Two Dublin tradesmen (Catholics) my companions in the Coach—sensible & rather cultivated men—one of them had some numbers of Cobbet's History of the Reformation, which I

read on the way.¹—In speaking of Cromwell, one of my companions said he thought the character of the Emir in my Fire-Worshippers had many points of resemblance to that of Cromwell—The other asked me whether by the Parson near Roscrea, whom I mentioned in Captain Rock, I meant the Revd W. Hamilton?—told him not. Arrived in Dublin at four, went to Crampton's, with whom I had promised to fix my residence on my return.—Set off to see my Mother before dinner—found she had not been so well during my absence—In consequence of the distance of Crampton's house from Abbey St., resolved to return to my old quarters at Bilson's—Company at Dinner at Cramptons—Sir C. & Lady Morgan, John Doherty, the Corrys, Col. Shawe &c.—Crampton told me that he had shown my lines about "the Bishop & the Bold Dragoon" to Lord Wellesley & on the lines "To whom no harlot comes amiss, save Her of Babylon" Lord W. said—"Well, I make no exception to the general rule—for *she* does not come amiss to me *either*"—Additional company in the evening—Mrs. Sewell & her daughter—Mrs. Bowles & her sister, Miss Montague—Miss Caton, Mrs. Ponsonby &c. &c.—Sang a good deal, & happened, in spite of cold & my morning journey, to be in good voice.

31 [Saturday]—Went (after breakfast at Crampton's) to call on Henry Grattan, accompanied by Corry, who had fixed the meeting for the purpose of talking with Grattan about his father's Life, & his intentions with respect to transferring the materials for it to me.—Found him as shilly-shally as ever—[no sequence whatever in this man's mind]—will evidently neither perform the task himself nor (though professedly inclined to do so) ever bring himself to relinquish it to another.—Showed me several volumes of memoranda & sketches on the subject, but unfortunately almost all in his own hand-writing—very little of the father's—even the conversations of the Father come all darkened & diluted through the medium of the son's memory & taste—this will never do. Said ultimately that he must write to England to consult his family on the subject.—Dined at Wallace's (Corry & I) out of town. Company, North & his wife, Mr. & Mrs. Jos. Crampton, Mr. & Miss——, Gervais Bushe &c. &c.—The day rather dull.—North, in talking of language (evidently a favourite subject of his) said, that certain words "in the course of time sunk in the scale of gentility, & passed like houses, into the hands of humbler occupants."—By the bye, Crampton reminded me this morning of my having once said to him of the Spenser stanza, that when (as often occurs in Lord Byron) the sense is continued without any stop from one stanza to another, it is like going on another stage with tired horses.—In the evening a gentleman played Sonatas on the Piano-forte & I sung—with (apparently) but little echo in the hearts of my audience.—Got back with Corry to Crampton's at twelve, & eat oysters & drunk brandy & water till two—slept at Crampton's.

Notes to 1825 Entries

4 January

1. *Memoirs of the Affairs of Europe* (1824–29). The "Septennial act" refers to the Septennial Bill of 1761, which would limit the duration of the Irish Parliament to seven years.
2. *The Querist, Containing Several Queries Proposed to the Consideration of the Public* (1735–37).

10 January

1. The Duke of York married Frederica, daughter of Frederick Wilhelm II, King of Prussia, in 1791. The couple soon separated.
2. Sir Robert Adair (1763–1855) was in St. Petersburg at the outbreak of the French Revolution. Political opponents thought he was sent by Fox to thwart the policy of Pitt, an accusation reproduced in the Bishop of Winchester's *Memoir of Pitt* (1821). This pamphlet resulted in an angry correspondence in print between the Bishop and Adair.

11 January

1. The reply of the Prince of Wales to Pitt's letter announcing to him the intended plan for the Regency. The composition of the letter, a cogent argument against the Regency Bill, was entrusted to Burke. See Lecky, *History of England*, 5: 438. See also the entry for 22 June 1823.
2. Probably a reference to the speech, given on 6 February 1778, supporting Burke's motion against the use of Indians in the war with America.
3. Melchiorre Cesarotti translated Macpherson's *Ossian* into Italian in 1763.

12 January

1.   "———pulchrior alter
       non fuit &c."
              Aen. VII. 650. (Russell's note.)
2. In 1661 Charles II accepted a large subsidy from Louis XIV to attack Spain. Later he accepted other subsidies to favor the French queen's claims to the Spanish succession and to support French designs on the Netherlands.
3. Johann Gottfried Eichorn (1752–1827), Protestant theologian and orientalist. In 1793 Bishop Herbert Marshall translated and annotated Johann David Michaelis, *Introduction to the New Testament* (1750).

14–17 January

1. One of the songs in *Evenings in Greece*, *Works*, 5: 29.

21 January

1. Louis Dutens's *Mémoires* appeared in 1806.

22 January

1. *Lessons in Criticism to William Roscoe* (1826), one of the pamphlets in the Pope controversy.

31 January

1. One of the *National Airs, Works,* 4: 223.

9 February

1. Moore obviously refers to Solomon Gundy, a character in George Colman's *Who Wants a Guinea* (1805); Richard Jones, *Peter Finn, or, a New Road to Brighton* (1822).

14 February

1. "The Meeting of the Ships," 5: 129.

13 March

1. *Works,* 5: 201.

27 March

1. David Ricardo (1772–1823) and Thomas Tooke (1774–1858), economists, published articles and books on current economic problems. For Ricardo's opposition to the Government's use of the Sinking Fund see Halévy, *History,* 2: 39–40; for a discussion of Tooke's theories see *ibid.,* 2: 116, 121–22.

10 April

1. Abraham Cowley. *Davideis* (1656), Book III.

11 April–11 May

1. "The Watchman," one of *A Set of Glees, Works,* 5: 134. By "The Spirits" Moore apparently refers to the Glee "Hush, Hush," *Works,* 5: 132.

18 May

1. Lully's *Prosperpine* (1680).

19 May

1. The debate in the House of Lords was touched off on 27 April by the Duke of York, who spoke against Catholic Emancipation and in favor of the position that the King was bound by his oath to defend the Established Church. The bill passed the House of Commons but was defeated by the Lords. See Halévy, *History,* 2: 224–25.

23 May

1. *Works*, 9: 203.

31 May

1. Sheridan objected to the subject matter and wording of the address on the Regency question prepared by Lords Grey and Grenville to be given by the Prince to both Houses. His objection gave rise to a bitter controversy which he attempted to put in proper perspective in his letter to Lord Holland of 15 January 1811. See Gibbs, *Sheridan*, p. 242 ff. and Moore, *Sheridan*, 2: 394–406, where the letter is reprinted.

10 June

1. See entry for 31 May 1825 and its note.

12 June

1. Horace and James Smith, *Rejected Addresses* (1812).

16 June

1. During his tenure as Home Secretary (1821–27), Peel brought about sweeping humanizing reforms in the criminal law, including a measure dealing with the law of juries.
2. See entry for 31 May 1825 and its note.

17 June

1. Letitia Elizabeth Landon (1802–38), who wrote under the initials L. E. L.

24 June

1. "When 'Tis Night and the Mid-Watch Is Come," in Rhodes, *Plays and Poems of Sheridan*, 3: 238. The line reads "some pretty girl and true."

26 June

1. *Smectymnuus* was the name adopted by Stephen Marshal, Edward Calmy, Thomas Young, Mathew Newcomen, and William Spurstow in their pamphlet attacking episcopacy. Milton defended the pamphlet in his *Animadversions . . .* (1641) and again in *Apology against a Pamphlet . . .* (1642). For Milton's Latin sonnet to Young ("Elegia Quarta, Anno Aetatis 18, ad Thomam Qunium") and a translation see *Paradise Regained, The Minor Poems, and Samson Agonistes*, ed. Merrit Y. Hughes (New York, 1937), pp. 82 and 83. Moore refers to the "Preface" in *Poems upon several Occasions . . . with Notes Critical and Explanatory . . .* by Thomas Warton (1785). The passage quoted is from *Comus*, 1. 752.

11 August

1. See entry for 31 May 1825 and its note.

12 August

1. See Dowden, *Letters,* 2: 537.

13 August

1. Russell's brackets.

16 August

1. In 1826 William Theobald Wolfe Tone edited and published *The Life of . . . Tone;* the following year he brought out his edition of Tone's *Memoirs.*
2. *The Theory of Moral Sentiments* first appeared in 1759.
3. "Lines to a Lady Weeping," Coleridge, *Byron's Poetry,* 3: 45, and Moore, "Parody of a Celebrated Letter," *Works,* 3: 160 (on the letter of 13 February 1812 addressed to the Duke of York by the Prince Regent, explaining why he chose to retain the Tory ministry).

17 August

1. Antonio Saliéri, *Tarare* (1787).

18 August

1. *Works,* 5: 129, 134.

21 August

1. *Ibid.,* 3: 276, "Missale Romanum," *Retrospective Review* 12 (1825): 96. Moore notes that by "mistress" he means, "allegorically, the ancient Church of Ireland," and the author of the article on the mass concludes by quoting the second stanza beginning "The rival was honour'd, while thou wert wrong'd and scorn'd." He notes that "there are few . . . who cannot sympathize . . . with the filial expressions of the poet—more beautiful than any hymn of his church."
2. Dryden's tragedy *Aureng-Zebe* appeared in 1676.

23 August

1. "*Barnard* was afterwards inserted." (Russell's note.)

24 August

1. In "Letter V, from the Countess Dowager of C-rk to Lady ____," *Works,* 5: 119–21.

3 September

1. Russell placed the following quotations in a note to this passage; they were probably originally part of the MS text: "I can as little live upon past kindness as the air can be warmed with the sunbeams of yesterday." "A woman, whose mouth is like an old comb, with a few broken teeth, and a great deal of hair and dust about it." "Kisses are like grains of gold or silver, found upon the ground, of no value themselves, but precious, as showing that a mine is near." "That man has not only a long face, but a tedious one." "One can no more judge of the

true value of a man by the impression he makes on the public, than we can tell whether the seal was of gold or brass by which the stamp was made." "Men's fame is like their hair, which grows after they are dead, and with just as little use to them." "A sort of anti-blackamoor, every part of her white but her teeth." "A woman, whose face was created without the preamble of 'Let there be light!'" "How few, like Danaë, have God and gold together."

4 September

1. Russell placed the following in a note to this passage:

> *Aliter,*
> "And yet for us, who will not buy,
> Goes singing on eternally."

7 September

1. When Sheridan lay ill and was threatened by the bailiffs, Denis O'Brien published an article in the *Morning Post* that called the attention of the public to the true state of his case. See Sichel, *Sheridan,* 2: 380 and Moore, *Sheridan,* 2:459.

18 September

1. Philip Thicknesse published several books on continental travel between 1766 and 1784.

19 September

1. See Moore, *Sheridan,* 2: 429.
2. On 20 September the *Times* advertised a "Grand historical melodrama and novel and military spectacle called *The Last Days of Napoleon Buonaparte*" at the Royal Coburg Theatre.

21 September

1. A reference to a collection of "Theatrical Portraits" noted in the *Catalogue of the Miscellaneous and Dramatic Library, Engraved Theatrical Portraits . . . of Charles Mathews* (1835).

2 October

1. See entry for 22 January 1825 and its note.

7 October

1. One of the *National Airs, Works,* 4: 240.

22 October

1. One of *A Set of Glees, Works,* 5: 130.

24 October

1. *Evenings in Greece, Works,* 5: 36.

29 October

1. The National Library of Scotland owns a transcript in Moore's hand of that part of the Journal covering the visit to Scott. Moore sent this copy to John Gibson Lockhart, who was writing his *Life of Scott*. It differs only in minor details from the original. See Dowden, *Letters*, 2:809.

2. Scott, *The Lay of the Last Minstrel* (1805).

3. *Every Man in His Humour*, 4. vii. 91. The part of the sentence in ornamental brackets is taken from the National Library of Scotland MS. Moore left this blank in the original.

4. In *The Heart of Midlothian* (1818). *Waverly* appeared in 1814.

5. Scott's epitaph on the monument of his dog Maida reads as follows: "Maidae Marmorea dormis sub imagine Maid,/Ad januam domini sit tibi terra levis." The Epitaph, in what Scott describes as "Teviotdale Latin," was sent in a letter to his son Charles at "Brazen-nose College," Oxford. Lockhart, *Life of Scott*, 4: 186.

6. Thomas Campbell, *The Pleasures of Hope, with Other Poems* (1799). "Hohenlinden" was first published with "Lochiel's Warning" in *Poems* (1803).

7. Joseph Holt (1756–1826), an Irish rebel, who was transported for rebellious activities in 1797–8 to Botany Bay. He returned to Ireland after being pardoned (ca. 1814) and lived for the remainder of his life in Dublin and Kingstown.

8. For an account of Moore's first acquaintance with Byron see his *Life of Byron* (1834), 2: 79–92. See also Dowden, *Letters*, 1: 161–68. The "message from Greville" refers to a letter written in 1812 from Colonel Greville and delivered to Byron by Mr. Leckie, in which the Colonel asked reparations for allusions in *English Bards*, ll. 620–88, to his activities as manager of the Argyle Institution. Byron gave the letter to Moore and asked him to manage "whatever proceedings it might render necessary." The affair was settled amicably after Greville rewrote the letter, deleting certain angry passages to which Byron objected. See Moore, *Life of Byron*, 2: 139–41. For Byron's lines on Scott see *English Bards*, ll. 147–82.

30 October

1. Sir Adam Ferguson (1771–1855), son of Professor Adam Ferguson, lived with his sisters in the mansion-house of Toftfield, which was owned by Scott. Through Scott's influence he was appointed "Keeper of the Regalia of Scotland."

2. An old Scottish song included in Playford's *Dancing-Master* (1657).

3. Robert Stewart (1769–1822), who was the second Marquis of Londonderry, was better known by the title Viscount Castlereagh, which was bestowed upon him when his father became an earl in 1796.

31 October

1. Emperor Paul I of Russia was assassinated in 1801.

2. Scott's *Life of Napoleon* was published in nine volumes in 1827.

3. *Woodstock* (1826).

4. Lady Ancram was Henrietta, eldest daughter and co-heir of John, second Duke of Buckinghamshire. She married the first Earl of Belmore on 2 March 1780. The marriage was dissolved by an act of Parliament in 1793. On 14 April 1793 she married William, the 6th Marquess of Lothian, Earl of Ancram.

5. "When He Who . . . ," *Works*, 3: 228, "Though the last . . . ," *Works*, 3: 234. Byron's *Corsair* appeared in 1814. See the opening lines.

6. An old Scottish song, the more ancient title of which is "Hey, Now the Day Daws." Burns used the melody for "Scots Wha Hae wi' Wallace Bled."

1 November

1. *Gazette Nationale, ou Le Moniteur Universel* (1789–1865). After January 1811 called *Le Moniteur Universel*.

2. Byron's *Lara, a Tale* was published with Rogers's *Jacqueline* in 1814.

3. James Graham (1612–50), the fifth Earl and first Marquis of Montrose, was defeated by David Leslie at Philiphaugh on 13 September 1645.

4. Ivan Andreevich Kruilov's Fables appeared in translation as *Fables russes tirées du recueil de M. Kriloff et imitées en vers français et italiens par divers auteurs . . .* (1825).

4 November

1. Moore's *Life of Sheridan* was published in 1825; the *Memoirs of Captain Rock* appeared in 1824.

2. Henry Mackenzie's *Man of Feeling* was published in 1771.

3. "Ship Ahoy: The Meeting of Ships," *Works*, 5: 129; "The Watchman," *Works*, 5: 134.

5 November

1. The name of Sterne's uncouth doctor in *Tristram Shandy* was applied to Sir John Stoddart during his editorship of the *New Times*.

2. Published 1777.

3. "Say What Shall Be Our Sport," *Works*, 4:190.

6 November

1. John Wilson, *Lights and Shadows of Scottish Life* (1822); *Trials of Margaret Lindsay* (1823); *The Foresters* (1825).

2. Moore, *Sheridan*, 2: 467–68.

3. Moore may refer here to Sheridan's speech on the Coalition in 1783. In *The Life of Sheridan*, 1: 388, he notes that "the reporter of the speech . . . continued to turn all the brilliancy of his wit into dull and opake verbage."

7 November

1. *Sheridan*, 1: 463–68 and 424–35.

2. "Early Narrative and Lyrical Poetry of Spain," *Edinburgh Review*, 39 (1824), 393–432.

8 November

1. *Works*, 5:201.

2. James Hogg (1770–1835), known as the Ettrick Shepherd Scottish poet; friend of Scott, Byron, Wordsworth, and Southey.

3. The Reverend David Williams (1785?–1825), to whom Lockhart addressed "Peter's Letters."

9 November

1. George Thomson collected English, Welsh, and Irish as well as Scottish airs, for which Burns wrote lyrics.

11 November

1. *Coriolanus*, 3. iii. 94–97.

15 November

1. Two-thirds of the MS page following the entry for 15 November is blank, and no entries were made between that date and 11 December. Moore gave no explanation for the hiatus.

12 December

1. See Dowden, *Letters*, 2: 543.
2. See Moore, *Sheridan,* 2: 461–62, where Moore lists the mourners at Sheridan's funeral and then censures them by asking where they were when life remained in Sheridan; by intervening on his behalf only a few weeks earlier, they could have prevented his heart from breaking.

For the "surrender of the Whig principles" see *Sheridan,* 2: 387. The passage in question refers to the less-than-satisfactory letter sent by the Whig leaders to the Prince on the question of the Regency.

The reference to Canning occurs in 2: 243–44: "Whether this and other friendships, formed by Mr. Canning at the University had any share in alienating him from a political creed . . . perhaps, adopted rather from habit and authority than choice . . . or whether . . . he saw the difficulties which even genius like his would experience, in rising to the full growth of its ambition, under the shadowing branches of the Whig Aristocracy . . . none, perhaps, but himself can fully determine."

13 December

1. The passage in square brackets was placed at the end of the MS page with asterisks indicating its proper location. Moore probably refers to Basil Hall, *Extracts from Journals Written on the Coasts of Chile, Peru, and Mexico, 1820–22,* 2 vols. (1824).

24 December

1. "A Recent Dialogue," *Works,* 9: 203.

30 December

1. William Cobbett, *A History of the Protestant "Reformation" in England and Ireland* (1824).

Index

This index includes only names of people closely associated with Moore or prominent during the period covered in this volume. A comprehensive index will appear in Volume 6.